Collections for a
History of
Staffordshire

FOURTH SERIES, VOLUME TWENTY-FOUR

The Staffordshire Record Society was founded, as the William Salt Archaeological Society, in 1879, and it published the first volume of its Collections for a History of Staffordshire in 1880. The Society took its present name in 1936. Its Collections have been generally, although not exclusively, devoted to the publication of historical records of all kinds relating to the history of the county.

Collections for a History of Staffordshire

FOURTH SERIES, VOLUME TWENTY-FOUR

CRIMINAL CASES ON THE CROWN SIDE OF
KING'S BENCH: STAFFORDSHIRE, 1740–1800

Edited by Douglas Hay

STAFFORDSHIRE RECORD SOCIETY
2010

The Staffordshire Record Society gratefully acknowledges the continued financial support of Staffordshire County Council.

ISSN 1469–5480
ISBN 978 0 901719 52 2
Printed by 4word Ltd, Bristol for the
Staffordshire Record Society©

Contents

Preface

I first looked at a roll of the court of King's Bench in 1969, when my dissertation supervisor, the late E. P. Thompson, drove me to Ashridge, a country house near Berkamstead. Many of the documents had been stored there since the beginning of the second world war.[1] Thompson was making soundings in King's Bench for his own research, but it was not until the late 1970s that I began systematic work on the crown side records of the court to find criminal cases that would complement my doctoral work on Staffordshire assize and quarter sessions records.[2] It was immediately apparent that it would be a very different kind of task. The bulk and complexity of the immense surviving archives of the courts of Westminster Hall is staggering. The rolls of King's Bench run in almost continuous series from Trinity term 1234. By the eighteenth century the crown and controlment rolls are about 23 cm wide, 75 cm or so long, each containing dozens of membranes written on both sides in widely varying hands; there are also hundreds of volumes of draft and final order books, docket books, and other registers, and many thousands of affidavits for the period covered by this book.[3] None are indexed by county.

In completing this volume 40 years later I have thought of Arthur Agarde. He was a deputy chamberlain of the Exchequer from 1570 to 1615, and in the late sixteenth and early seventeenth centuries he compiled 56 volumes of accurate indices to the cases in the rolls for 1272 to 1422. In his notebook Agarde eventually wrote of himself: 'Here at last, after thirty-four years spent in reading through these records and other

[1] KB series 1 to 7, 10 to 15, 28, 30 to 32, 101, 119, 122, 139, 144 (letter from J. Walford, 21 Nov 1969). The King's Bench material was moved from Ashridge in 1980, when that repository was closed. Most of it is now at Kew, although KB 28 (and perhaps other series) are currently stored off-site in a disused salt mine near Northwich in Cheshire. A large body of pre-restoration court of common pleas files is also there, still unlisted. (Information from David Crook, formerly of The National Archives.)

[2] Douglas Hay, 'Crime, Authority and the Criminal Law: Staffordshire 1740–1800' (2 vols., Warwick University, 1975). Much of this research has been published, more is forthcoming.

[3] See the General Introduction. There were 549 affidavits found for the 129 Staffordshire cases in this volume, covering 61 years in one out-county, perhaps 2% of the total business of the court in that period.

registers and after great weariness and injury to health had resulted from the assiduous reading of them, he has decided to put an end to his labours, having been taught by experience that, in accordance with the judgement of Solomon, to the making of many books there is no end.' His words were quoted by G. O. Sayles, whose exemplary transcription of all the documents for King's Bench cases for the years 1272 to 1422, published between 1936 and 1971, compels enormous respect. Each page of a full transcription of the original Latin is matched with a facing page in English, to produce a 'faithful text'.[4] The task took him 48 years to complete.[5]

For records dating from 1422 to 1688, the listing and cataloguing undertaken intermittently over the centuries (especially in the early 1600s, the 1660s, 1830s, 1840s, and 1930s) was useful in making more records known, while introducing mistakes and leaving large quantities of paper and parchment from much of the period in confusion and inaccessible. A huge step forward was the listing and sorting done by C. A. F. Meekings from 1966.[6] The eighteenth-century records of the court, all in English, were described in detail in TNA lists and an article by David Crook between 1990 and 1994. The National Archives now also maintains an on-line Research Guide for 'King's Bench (Crown Side) 1675–1875' and introductions to each of the series of records generated by the court.[7]

I am grateful for the expert assistance of TNA archivists and staff over many years, for early advice, supplying photographic reproductions, and checking some details before publication.

---

[4] *Select Cases in the Court of King's Bench* (7 vols., London: B.Quaritch, 1936–1971), published as volumes lv (1936), lvii (1938), lviii (1939), lxxiv (1955), lxxvi (1958), lxxxii (1961), and lxxxviii (1971) of the Selden Society series. The quotation of Agarde appears in vol. lviii, p. xc. Sayles's editorial principles are set out in vol. lv, p. cxxvii. For those used here, see below, Editorial Notes.

[5] On Sayles, see the review by F. B. Wiener, 'Tracing the Origins of the Court of King's Bench', *American Bar Association Journal*, lix (July 1973), 753–8.

[6] See Meekings's account, edited by John Baker, of excavations (sometimes, literally so) of the records of King's Bench to 1688, of earlier attempts at organizing and listing, and of the work carried out from 1966 at Hayes: C. A. F. Meekings, 'King's Bench Files', in *Legal Records and the Historian*, ed. J. H. Baker (London: Royal Historical Society, 1978), 97–132.

[7] David Crook, 'Recent Work on Lists of Common Law Records in the Public Record Office', *The Journal of Legal History*, xv (1994),163–174. The class lists in the hard-copy catalogue at Kew contain information not always found in the online TNA Catalogue.

The internal workings of the court in the eighteenth century are still not much explored, although its proceedings received prominent coverage in the press of the period, and not only in the case of state trials. There is no full historical account of the crown side of the court for any period after 1490, and historians of the eighteenth and later centuries are only beginning to exploit its records.[8] In part this is due to the fact that the archive is voluminous, and to reconstruct the process

---

[8] The principal secondary works are medieval or Tudor and Stuart in coverage, and do not focus primarily on the criminal side of the court. See Marjorie Blatcher, *The Court of King's Bench 1450–1550: A Study in Self-Help* (University of London: Athlone Press, 1978); E. Powell, 'The King's Bench in Shropshire and Staffordshire in 1414', in E. W. Ives and A. H. Manchester, eds., *Law, Litigants and the Legal Profession* (London: Royal Historical Society, 1983); Edith G. Henderson, *Foundations of English Administrative Law: Certiorari and Mandamus in the Seventeenth Century* (Cambridge: Harvard University Press, 1963). There is of course a large legal literature on the law developed by the court, some of it cited in this volume in connection with particular cases. In recent years historians have begun using the records of the crown side for later periods. Ruth Paley's ongoing research on the London and Middlesex records of the court from the Restoration to the early nineteenth century is the most important; a first taste is 'After Somerset: Mansfield, Slavery and the Law in England, 1772–1830', in Norma Landau, ed., *Law, Crime and English Society 1660–1840* (Cambridge, 2002). My own publications dealing with aspects of the court and its judges include 'The State and the Market: Lord Kenyon and Mr Waddington', *Past & Present* , no. 162 (February 1999), 101–162; 'The Last Years of Staffordshire Jacobitism [The Earl Lecture, Keele University]', *Staffordshire Studies*, vol. 14 (2002), 53–88; and 'Dread of the Crown Office: the English magistracy and King's Bench, 1740–1800', in Landau, ed., *Law, Crime and English Society*, 19–45. See also Elizabeth Foyster, 'At the Limits of Liberty: Married Women and Confinement in Eighteenth-Century England', *Continuity and Change*, xvii (1) (2002), 39–62; Foyster, *Marital Violence: An English Family History 1660–1857* (Cambridge, 2005); Paul D. Halliday, *Habeas Corpus : From England to Empire* (Cambridge, Mass. and London, 2010); and Greg Smith on the violence evidenced in King's Bench affidavits (forthcoming). James Oldham, *The Mansfield Manuscripts and the Growth of English Law in the Eighteenth Century* (Chapel Hill and London: University of North Carolina Press, 1992), particularly i, ch. 2, describes the court under its most famous chief justice, emphasising case law. An examination of some of the procedures of the crown office in the nineteenth century is A. S. Diamond, 'The Queen's Bench Master', *Law Quarterly Review*, lxxvi (October 1960), 504.

and outcome in any given case, material from many different record series must be brought together. Surviving contemporary indices, while useful, are misleading because they are incomplete. And, as explained in the Introduction, the process of the court was kept obscure, even to legal practitioners, by the group of clerks (or their deputies) who created its documents and took the fees charged for them. The summaries of cases published in this volume illustrate a wide variety of the stages of process that either had to be used, or could be exploited, by litigants. Proceedings in King's Bench were usually far more complicated than criminal prosecutions on indictment at quarter sessions or assizes, and this complexity also has deterred historians from making much use of the court's records.

This calendar has been in preparation, competing with my other projects, since 1983, when Michael Greenslade and Douglas Johnson, then General Editor and Secretary of the Record Society, first expressed interest in having it as a volume in this series. I am deeply grateful for their constant encouragement and assistance over so many years, and I greatly regret that Michael Greenslade did not see the book completed before his death in 2005. I can only hope that it meets his exacting standards, and that he would have found it a useful contribution to the history of Staffordshire, for which he himself did so much. The patience of both editors was remarkable, their advice always helpful. They read much of the manuscript at several stages and caught many errors; I am responsible for those they did not. The final stages of copyediting and arrangements for publication by the Society were cheerfully undertaken by the current General Editor, Nigel Tringham, and Matthew Blake, Secretary of the Society.

My largest scholarly debt is to Ruth Paley, who shared with me the very large task of a complete examination of the affidavits series (KB 1) for the years covered by this volume, and many years of the rule books (KB 21), as well as checks in other series; she made it possible to continue the work at times when I was unable to be in England. I have benefited greatly from our many conversations over the years, and she commented on the drafts of the introductions. Her own account of the role of the court in Middlesex will be an essential complement to the calendar presented in this volume: the quantity, nature, and significance of Middlesex prosecutions in King's Bench differed greatly from those in the 'out-counties', as the clerks termed all other parts of England and Wales.

Over such a long period of time I have accumulated many other debts: it is a pleasure to thank those who helped most. At the Public Record Office (now The National Archives) Roy Hunnisett advised on calendaring decisions at an early stage, and David Crook at a later;

Mandy Banton caught errors in citation, and Amanda Bevan and Liz Hore helped in checking specific references. John Beattie, Jim Phillips, and the other members of the Toronto Legal History Seminar prompted questions and encouraged me to try out ideas that helped shape this project and will appear in other publications. The work could not have been completed without secretarial and research assistance at Osgoode Hall Law School at York University in Toronto by Elaine Glossop, Deanna Jubas, Felicia Holder, Miriam Spevack, Hazel Pollack, Jeff Bookbinder, Reid Rusonik, Jamie Trimble, Earl Stuart, Carey Nieuhoff, Jane Burton, Eva Sommer, Alice Mrozek, Sarah Jackson, Siobhan McClelland, Claire Mummée, Lisa Lui, Bevan Brooksbank, Aleksandra Lipski, and Leila Mehkeri. Professor Emeritus Balfour Halévy, the former Librarian of Osgoode Hall Law School, offered his generous support and great bibliographic expertise from the beginning, and arranged for a reprint to be made of the main contemporary guide to the court. His successor Louis Mirando, and the library staff, have supported the project throughout. Valerie Church and Anna Hay shared with me the tedium of reading the voluminous rule books, and Louise Tsang and Louise Wilkinson assisted with many checks in other series.

I am grateful to the Canada Council, the Social Science Research Council of Canada, and Osgoode Hall Law School and York University, for funding research and editorial costs over many years. Without their generous support the volume could not have been completed. Nor would it have seen the light of day had I not been able to set it aside from time to time while other projects took over. The editors and secretaries of the Society were unfailingly understanding. To Jeanette Neeson and our daughter Anna, who have lived with this project off and on for three decades, my gratitude has no bounds.

By publishing a calendar of the Staffordshire cases I hope to make the work of King's Bench and the nature of its records clearer to all those working on the history of English criminal law, and to provide complete coverage of all Staffordshire persons and places found in the records between 1740 and 1800. As explained in the General Introduction, one kind of document, the sworn affidavits, were very lightly calendared, in the end most of them coming close to a full transcription, with only redundancies removed. They provide detailed, if often contested, evidence on many aspects of the social, political, and family histories of Staffordshire, as well as revealing the way in which lower and higher courts could be used, and abused. A brief survey of the cases is presented in the General Introduction and the introductions to the sections of the book, and I give more detailed accounts of many of them in forthcoming publications. Errors and unresolved obscurities doubtless remain; I hope there are not too many. Other students, with different questions in mind, will explore the records of the court and in doing so provide more exact knowledge of its procedures, customs, and personnel. I hope this volume assists and encourages such research.

Douglas Hay
Toronto and Oxford, 2009

Editorial Notes

DATES AND TERMS IN KING'S BENCH

The rule books (KB 21), rolls (KB 28, KB 29) and other series express almost all dates of process in terms of feast days and regnal years. All such dates have been changed to calendar dates, new style or old as appropriate, and are enclosed in square brackets in the text. For dates before 1752 both years are given when the date falls before 25 March.

The history of the terms held in the common law courts at Westminster is complex, and since practice varied over the centuries it is necessary to examine the records carefully to establish the conventions used by the clerks, in addition to taking into account legislative changes.[1] For the period of this book, Hilary term began 23 January and ended 12 February, except when either of those days fell on a Sunday, in which case it was the day following.[2] Easter began 17 days after Easter and ended the Monday next before Whit Sunday. Trinity term began the Friday after Trinity Sunday and ended the Wednesday next after two weeks (that is, on the Wednesday after Trinity 3). Michaelmas term, in the years before 1752, began 23 October if it was not a Sunday, in which case it began the day following; it ended the 28 November, if not a Sunday, in which case the day following. In 1752 and later years, legislation provided that the interruptions caused to that term by the many saints' days should be remedied by changing the start to the Morrow of All Souls (i.e., 3 November), or, if a Sunday, the day following.[3]

The dates given for process are sometimes the day on which a motion or rule was actually made; they had to be made on specific days in the term, called 'return days' (see below). Because a term was a single day in the eyes of the law, some stages of process were conventionally

---

[1] See *A Handbook of Dates for Students of British History*, ed. C.R. Cheney, revd. Michael Jones (Cambridge University Press, 2000) (Royal Historical Society Guides and Handbooks No. 4), 96–111 for an outline of the history and assumptions of legal chronology, and 112–144 for the beginning and end dates of the law terms in each year.

[2] Jacob, i, 149. Conventionally, the terms were thought of as running from Michaelmas to Trinity.

[3] 24 Geo II, c.48; *Handbook of Dates*, 103.

recorded as the first or last day of term, even though they might have occurred weeks later or earlier.[4]

Non-juridical days and return days
The following were not days in court: all Sundays; Purification of the Blessed Virgin Mary (2 Feb) in Hilary term; Ascension Day in Easter term; St John the Baptist's Day (24 June) when it fell in Trinity term; All Saints' Day (1 Nov) and All Souls' Day (2 Nov) in Michaelmas term.[5] The length of the terms was determined, in fact, by the number and dates of return days, those days on which writs and process were made returnable, 'i.e., are by a clause in the same directed to be brought into court, when executed by the sheriff, etc.'[6] In King's Bench they were four in Hilary (octave and quindene of Hilary (20, 27 January), morrow and octave of the Purification (3, 10 February)); five in Easter (quindene of Easter, Easter three weeks, one month, five weeks, and morrow of the Ascension); four in Trinity (morrow, octave, quindene of Trinity and Trinity three weeks); and (before 1752) six in Michaelmas term (Michaelmas three weeks and one month, Saturday next after morrow of All Souls, and morrow, octave and quindene of Martin). From 1752, because the term now began on the morrow of All Souls, Michaelmas had only four returns. The length of a term could be crucial to litigants, because in some circumstances process could not be carried from term to term. Return days determined the pace of cases through the court: most proceedings in the court conventionally could occur only on those days.

Dating days of process
A typical entry in the King's Bench records is 'Saturday next after fifteen days of the Holy Trinity, in the eighth year of King George III'. This is 18 June 1768.[7] In this case, as in others, dating depends first on the regnal year and then on whether or not a moveable feast is involved, as it is in this case. In the period covered, the regnal years may cause con-

---

[4]   An example is the dating of posteas. See General Introduction. In cases F.12 to F.15, the posteas were received 14 and 28 Nov 1772, but the rule for judgment (which followed receipt of the posteas) is dated the first day of term, 6 Nov 1772. See also the introductions to Sections A and F, on the dating of informations and writs of certiorari.
[5]   Jacob, i, 153; *Handbook of Dates*, 99.
[6]   Jacob, i, 148.
[7]   A date in the proceedings in a well-known case, *R v Wilkes* (1768), 4 Burr. 2574–5.

fusion (because the boundary between two regnal years occurs in the term) only in Trinity in the reign of George II and Michaelmas in the reign of George III. Once the appropriate calendar year is ascertained, Cheney or another perpetual calendar can be used to establish the principal moveable feasts used in dates in King's Bench at this period: Easter, Ascension, and Trinity are the most commonly encountered. Dating in other parts of the year is from certain fixed saints' days, notably Hilary (13 January), Purification of the Blessed Virgin Mary (2 February), St. Michael's (29 September), All Souls Day (2 November), and St. Martin's (11 November).

Dating from these days was made by reference to an octave (one week after the feast day), or a quindene (two weeks after the feast day), or months (four weeks after the feast day). An octave is expressed in the records of the court as 'after eight days', a quindene as 'after fifteen days', although the meaning is 'after seven days' and 'after fourteen days' respectively.[8] Thus, when the date falls after a quindene, the date is expressed 'Saturday' (or whatever) 'next after fifteen days of Holy Trinity' (or another day). Using the example above, since Trinity Sunday fell on May 29 in 1768, the quindene ('fifteen days', actually fourteen) was June 12, and the next Saturday therefore was June 18. And to take another, 'Saturday next after eight days of Hilary' in 1748 (old style), similarly, is the Saturday that fell next after the seventh day after 13 January.[9] Since Hilary (13 January) falls on a Wednesday in 1748, the Saturday concerned is 23 January.[10]

PRESENTATION OF THE CASES

The entry for each case begins with the name and other information about the defendant or (in habeas corpus cases) the prisoner. It is followed by the charge given in the information (Sections A,B,C, D) or shown by the writ of certiorari and returned conviction or indictment (Sections E, F); for habeas corpus (Section G) the writ and return give the answer of the person alleged to detain the prisoner; in Section H, the writ of attachment and return are given. The progress of the case as gathered from all the sources used is then summarized by date under the heading 'Rules and process'. The affidavits for the parties are then

---

[8] A literal translation of the Latin form used before 1731.

[9] For leap years it is important to use the appropriate correction (in *Handbook of Dates*, the first two columns of the tables in Chap. 8.)

[10] Case C.4, first rule to plead. This was also the first appearance day of Hilary term (see above, 'Non-juridical days and return days'). On rules to plead, see the introduction to Section A.

presented separately, for prosecution and defence, arranged in the sequence in which they were filed with the court, by term. Those filed within each term are usually but not always arranged chronologically; in some cases the evidence is more clearly presented in a different sequence. Where the affidavits were given sequence numbers by the solicitors or clerks (as in case A.3, affts [7] to [16]), these have been added. A note on the sources used to reconstruct the case concludes each entry.

Editorial conventions
Square brackets [ ] are used in the text for a) supplied dates, usually a conversion from regnal year and feast day; b) separate counts in indictments and informations; c) numbering affidavits; d) italicized explanatory matter inserted by the editor.

Parentheses ( ), when they occur in the process notes, surround the surname of the barrister or clerk making a motion for a rule. Full names where known are given in the index.

Place names have been modernized, with the original also given in doubtful cases.

Where several versions of a given or family name appear in the records, that used by the person (if they have signed an affidavit) is used throughout.

Approach to calendaring
The extent of detail preserved has been governed by the original aims of the research into criminal law in Staffordshire out of which this calendar, and my other publications on the court of King's Bench, emerged. The cases were first collected to assess the numbers, kinds, and outcomes of criminal cases from Staffordshire that originated or ended in King's Bench. For this purpose it was usually sufficient to summarize process, using the contemporary aids of the clerks, notably the Great Docket Books (IND 1/6669 ff) to the Crown Rolls (KB 28) and the Controlment Rolls (KB 29), as well as the Rule Books (KB 21); no attempt was made to verify the existence and content of every writ necessary for a particular stage of process, as outlined in Gude, Hands, or Corner.[11] After the decision was taken to prepare a calendar, most effort went into ensuring that the main series of sources were exhausted (see General Introduction, 'Sources used'); when soundings indicated that other series, notably the Crown Rolls (KB 28) and Draft Minute Books (KB 36), were unlikely to add further important information, they were

---

[11]   A. B. Corner, *Forms of Writs and Other Proceedings on the Crown Side of the Court of Queen's Bench, with Practical Directions* (London, 1844).

not further explored. The approach means that some personal names in the sources have not been preserved. All names appearing in affidavits, indictments, and informations do appear in the text, and the names of prosecutors, defendants, and persons making a return when they appear in writs; all clerks in court and counsel named in the Rule Books (KB 21) also appear. However, names that are a formal part of the form of a writ or the documents returned (e.g. the list of jurymen in the caption, and the obligatory reference to the lord chancellor or chief justice in the *teste*) are not preserved, nor are the names of possible or actual jurors, sheriffs, or justices of the peace that commonly appear in a *venire facias juratores* and similar writs, and the crown rolls.[12] Nor has the formal wording of writs, rules, and orders been preserved. These are usually verbose, always fixed in form, and the Glossary provides references to Hands and Gude, where the standard wording is given in full, allowing the reader to expand the greatly abbreviated versions used in the 'Rules and process' section of each case.

The affidavits have been calendared to preserve details of interest to social, economic, and legal historians, including all names of persons and places. A more abbreviated calendaring would have concealed much of the evidence on which these cases turned. Most of the material deleted is repetitive and formal phrasing, a consequence of the fact that affidavits were drawn by clerks and commissioners, then read to the deponents, who signed. The general approach has been light calendaring. The bulk of the affidavits has been reduced to between a third and a quarter of the original, although in a work of this length, prepared over many years, and including many different kinds of cases, the amount of detail preserved undoubtedly varies between cases. In two circumstances a different policy has been followed. Where affidavits have annexed to them other original documents not prepared by legal officers (e.g. letters, printed handbills), they have been transcribed fully; in the case of manuscript material, the original spelling and use of upper case has been preserved in most cases.[13] In case H.1 a full transcription has been given of interrogatories and answers to them [5], [6], the only example in the volume, and one which illustrates the redundancies found in most documents filed with the court. A few other examples of standard documents are given in full transcription.[14] In a

---

[12] In a few cases where procedure is unusual (e.g. F.19, in which talesmen were called) names of jurors have been given.

[13] Except for copies of writs, rules, notices and other process in King's Bench, where the shortened forms are used.

[14] Writ of mandamus (case B.4 affdt [4]); warrant of committal (case G.5 affdt [1]).

few cases, where a great many affidavits were filed that reiterate evidence given by other deponents, the detail has not been fully reproduced but a cross-reference supplied.

A similar approach was taken to lengthy informations and some other formal documents, where the redundancy is even greater than in affidavits. As with an indictment, exactitude in wording a criminal information was crucial, and both informations and indictments for misdemeanours were often much longer than the average felony indictment. In this book the wording of each count of an information is distinguished (the number of the count being given in square brackets) but greatly abbreviated. Thus the information in case B.12 is summarized in four lines; Hands reproduces it in six pages of his treatise.

Abbreviations and References

affdt	affidavit
defdt	defendant
Ea	Easter term or sessions
edn.	edition
Ep	Epiphany sessions
ER	*The English Reports* (see below, 'Cites to cases')
FDT	first day of term
FNT	first day of next term
Hil	Hilary term
ITKB	In the King's Bench
LDT	last day of term
Mich	Michaelmas term or sessions
n.d.	no date
NT	next term
PRO	(*see* TNA)
prosn	prosecution
prosr	prosecutor
prosx	prosecutrix
RO	Record Office
s.d.	same date
SRO	Staffordshire Record Office
ST	same term
TNA	The National Archives (Kew), formerly the Public Record Office
Trans	Translation sessions
Trin	Trinity term
WSL	William Salt Library, Stafford

CITES TO CASES

References to reported cases, the record of the common law, are given to both the nominative reports published in the period, and also to the consolidated reprint published in the early twentieth century and known to lawyers as *The English Reports* (178 vols., London, 1900–1932). Both are cited in legal style. For example, in case B.4, the reported case of *R v Corbett and Coulson* (1756), establishing that an information may be filed against justices of the peace for disobedience to a mandamus, is cited to both Sayer 267 (the original nominative report), and to 96 ER

875, the *English Reports* reprint, where it appears in volume 96 at page 875. Where the name of a case is not italicized, it is 'unreported', found in other sources, including this volume.

REFERENCES ABBREVIATED IN THE NOTES

ABG	*Aris's Birmingham Gazette*
Bacon	Matthew Bacon, *A New Abridgement of the Law* (7th ed., 8 vols., London, 1832)
Blackstone	William Blackstone, *Commentaries on the Laws of England* (12th ed., 4 vols., London, 1793–5)
Chitty	Joseph Chitty, *A Practical Treatise on the Criminal Law* (4 vols., London, 1816; repr. New York, 1978)
Gude	Richard Gude, *The Practice of the Crown Side of the Court of King's Bench* (2 vols., London, 1828; repr. 1990)
Hands	William Hands, *The Solicitor's Practice on the Crown Side of the Court of King's Bench* (London, 1803)
Holdsworth	William Holdsworth, *A History of English Law* (revd edn., 17 vols., London, 1903–1972)
Jacob	Giles Jacob, *The Compleat Attorney's Practice in English, in the Courts of King's Bench and Common-Pleas at Westminster* (2 vols., 2nd edn., [1740?]).
ODNB	*Oxford Dictionary of National Biography*
VCH Staffs	*Victoria County History: Staffordshire*

Illustrations

1 Westminster Hall, c.1755
John Boydell, *A view of New Palace Yard, Westminster*, c.1755.

2 Westminster Hall, 1805
Joshua Bryant, *Buildings on the South Side of New Palace Yard*,1805.

3 The Courts and Booksellers in Westminster Hall, c.1730: King's Bench left of stairs
Charles Mosley after Hubert Gravelot, *The First Day of Term, Westminster Hall*.

4 King's Bench, 1804, enclosed within walls erected in 1755
Edward Pugh, *Court of King's Bench Westminster*, 1804.

5 Westminster Hall, 1801
George Hawkins, *Internal view of Westminter Hall*,1801.

6 Westminster Hall, c.1809
J. Bluck after Pugin and Rowlandson, *Westminster Hall*, c.1809.

7 One of Justice Gough's libels on Justice Lane, 1800
Case A.24.

General Introduction

The court of King's Bench was one of the central royal courts of the common law (Common Pleas and Exchequer being the others), and by the eighteenth century the most important of the three. In part its salience arose from the attraction of its 'plea side' for civil litigation. That success was the outcome of a centuries-long battle among the common law courts of Westminster Hall and between them and the court of Chancery, which also sat there, for doctrinal dominance and for the fees that litigation generated for lawyers, clerks, and judges.[1] But the social, political, and legal significance of King's Bench arose also from its exclusive criminal jurisdiction, exercised on its 'crown side'. Although all twelve common law judges heard criminal cases tried on indictment at assizes in the counties, and sat in rotation at the Old Bailey with the recorder and magistrates, it was the four justices in King's Bench, headed by the lord chief justice of England, who most often made criminal law as well as enforced it.[2] They sat in the south-east corner of Westminster Hall, next to the court of Chancery, as their predecessors had done for centuries. This book illustrates the role of the crown side

---

[1] Chancery's rulings ('equity') provided remedies not obtainable in the common law courts. The court of Exchequer had both a common law and an equity side. Common Pleas and King's Bench were solely common law courts, and only King's Bench had a criminal jurisdiction.

[2] All twelve common law judges occasionally gave their opinions on points of law in cases reserved at trial for their consideration: see David R. Bentley, ed., *Select Cases from the Twelve Judges' Notebooks* (London: J. Rees, 1997). Contemporary legal theory only admitted that the judges found, and clarified, the common law and the meaning of statutes. Atiyah points out that the 'fairy tale' that judges do not change the law has been abandoned only very recently: Patrick Atiyah, 'Common Law and Statute law', *The Modern Law Review*, xlviii/1 (Jan 1985), 1. The role of the King's Bench judges in making law as well as enforcing it, their significance for politics and the ideologies of law, and the daily work of the court, will be dealt with in Hay, *The Judges and the People: King's Bench and the Criminal Law in English Politics and Society, 1750–1820*; the place of the court in the administration of the criminal law in Staffordshire, including an analysis of cases in the present volume, is the subject of Hay, *Crime, War and Justice in Industrial England 1740–1820* (forthcoming).

of King's Bench by reproducing the cases of one county from 1740 to 1800.

Most recent writing on the criminal law of this period concentrates on the county courts of quarter sessions, where a bench of magistrates tried crimes on indictment with juries; on the activities of those magistrates sitting alone or in pairs to hear minor cases summarily; and on trials on indictment at assizes, when twice a year the twelve common law judges of Westminster Hall went on six routes or circuits throughout England during the vacations between the law terms, to clear the gaols and hear and determine at trial ('oyer et terminer') the most serious criminal cases, including capital felonies.[3] Cases brought in King's Bench itself were of a different kind from all these, arising from the supreme jurisdiction the court had over all inferior criminal courts, and also from a form of prosecution, the criminal information, to be had only there.[4]

Although few in number (a little more than two percent of all Staffordshire cases at quarter sessions, assizes, and King's Bench), cases in King's Bench had unusual importance for both the nation and the county. They could change the common law, and they often involved prominent members of county society, both as litigants and as jurors. For reasons explained below, there were very few felonies before the court, but the serious misdemeanours it dealt with were immensely varied, and its role as a court of review brought many lesser cases before it also. The 129 cases presented here illustrate, often in great detail, some of the most contentious political and social issues in the county, and a wide range of personal and family conflicts.

Politics, religion, and sedition had close ties in Staffordshire, particularly in the earlier part of the century, when a significant proportion of the gentry were believed to hold Jacobite sympathies, and to encourage a highly destructive mob. Two cases arose from election contests in

---

[3] Lent (spring) assizes took place between Hilary and Easter terms; summer assizes between Trinity and Michaelmas. See Editorial Notes. For an analysis of the differing attitudes of some of the King's Bench judges to capital punishment in this period, see D. Hay, 'Hanging and the English Judges: The Judicial Politics of Retention and Abolition', in David Garland, Randall McGowen, and Paul Merantz, eds., *America's Death Penalty: Between Past and Present* (New York: New York University Press, 2010).

[4] It was possible but rare to proceed by information in lower courts, usually by an information qui tam (see section D for their use in King's Bench). But informations in the name of the master of the crown office (the cases in sections A and B), and informations ex officio by the attorney general (section C), took place only in King's Bench.

Lichfield in 1742 and Tamworth in 1761, the first an accusation of libel and the latter a very expensive attempt to prove electoral corruption.[5] The county's central importance for Jacobite and high Tory politics emerges most clearly in the determined prosecutions carried on by the government law officers after riotous assaults on Whig leaders, supporters, and their property in 1747 at Stafford, Handsworth and Whittington Heaths, and Burton, and again in Walsall and Lichfield in 1750.[6] The eighteen defendants convicted in 1747 of attacking the house of William Chetwynd MP of Stafford were dealt with leniently, but the nine men and women convicted in the Walsall riot (in which an effigy of George II was shot at, burned, and hanged) were sentenced to imprisonment in London; four of the men also were exposed there in the pillory on several successive dates. Sedition during the French revolutionary wars at the end of the century, in contrast, did not appear in King's Bench, since most prosecutions took place at quarter sessions and assizes.[7] Juries then were willing to convict Jacobins and democrats, whereas earlier in the century Jacobite grand juries blocked indictments, leading the government to use ex officio informations, described in section C. Religious disputes centred on Wesleyan Methodists and on dissenting congregations, sometimes arising in conflicts within such religious groups, and at times closely tied to Jacobite and anti-Jacobite politics: seven such cases, including violent attacks on meeting houses and their occupants, were brought before the court between 1744 and 1754, all from the Black Country.[8] Two attacks in the 1760s were probably due to conflicts over doctrine, and the personal authority of a preacher and a schoolmaster.[9]

Fights over rights to game and the use of commons centred on Cannock Chase and Needwood, provoking violent affrays between keepers and deerkillers, and the quarrels of gentlemen and magistrates involved in controversies over hare-coursing.[10] Two prosecutions for fishing were brought before the court, but the single most common kind of case was an information for poaching, 35 of which were begun in these years.[11] It is likely that a prosecution in 1792 for maiming a

---

5 Cases A.1, A.16.
6 Cases C.1 to C.13, A.8. For an examination of these cases in context, see D. Hay, 'The Last Years of Staffordshire Jacobitism', *Staffordshire Studies*, xiv (2002), 53–88.
7 A.22, and possibly B.13 mention Jacobin issues.
8 Cases A.2 to A.5, A.9, A.11, F.1.
9 Cases A.19, F.9.
10 Cases A.6, A.7, A.12, F.10, F.22; and A.20 and B.6.
11 Cases E.8, F.4, and D.1 to D.35.

horse belonging to the Earl of Uxbridge, by shooting it in the stable, also arose out of disputes on the Chase over game, common right, and the suppression of a popular custom of horse-racing.[12]

Many personal quarrels led to litigation on the crown side. For a few assaults, the origins are unclear.[13] Other cases arose from a wide variety of circumstances: an assault by a short-tempered solicitor, an ejected tenant who prosecuted for riot when the house was torn down around him, a challenge to duel from a 17-year-old who felt his mother was not being offered a large enough settlement by her gentleman lover (who had married another), a prosecution for being libelled in the *Gentleman's Magazine* by a competitor for church briefs, a riotous rescue of horses distrained for rent, and two quarrels between justices of the peace. The first apparently began with a mistake, when Fettiplace Nott of Lichfield mistakenly caused a horse (taken for breach of the turnpike laws described below) to be forfeited, although John Landor's servants had settled the case.[14] The second dispute between justices was a veritable feud. The Reverend Thomas Lane and John Gough, a wealthy landowner in Perry Barr, had quarrelled about church pews and tithes in the 1770s, and an escalating dislike led to Lane prosecuting Gough in 1790 for encroaching on the highway with his new park wall. Then from 1794 Gough conducted a spectacular campaign of public libels against Lane, who finally retaliated with a King's Bench prosecution in 1800, but died before it came to trial.[15]

The intimate enmities and shocks of family life also came before the court. Several fathers, including a prominent Lichfield musician, attempted to recover eloping or seduced daughters through the use of habeas corpus, and an accusation of attempted rape of a wife by a neighbour was also begun.[16] A bitter quarrel over inheritance led to the prosecution of a justice of the peace involved in the case, and the refusal of the Reverend Robert Robinson of Waterfall to provide for the children of a son he had disinherited caused the poor law officers to

---

[12] Case G.5. The following year the park stable housing all the farm horses was set on fire: see D. Hay, 'Poaching and the game laws on Cannock Chase' in D. Hay, P. Linebaugh, and E .P. Thompson, eds., *Albion's Fatal Tree: Crime and Society in Eighteenth-Century England* (Harmondsworth, Mddx, and New York, 1975), 253.

[13] Cases F.3, F.20, F.24.

[14] Cases F.19, F.17, A.23, A.13, F.12 to F.15, B.7.

[15] Cases A.24, F.23. See D. Hay, 'Dread of the Crown Office: the English magistracy and King's Bench, 1740–1800', in Norma Landau, ed., *Law, Crime and English Society 1660–1830* (Cambridge, 2002), 34–41 for details of the feud.

[16] Cases A.17, G.1, A.18.

Figure 1   **Westminster Hall, c.1755**
John Boydell, *A view of New Palace Yard, Westminster,* c.1755.

prosecute him.[17] But three cases in particular illustrate in great detail the pathologies of domestic relations that could lead to such high-level litigation. One, the prosecution of a wealthy uncle by the supporters of his orphaned and abused niece who suffered beatings and degradation as a household servant, resulted in more affidavits in evidence than any other case.[18] Another, a widely reported prosecution of Sir William Wolseley for conspiracy to force marriage on Ann Whitby, began with her allegations of a drugged, midnight ceremony, and evidence for the defence that she was already secretly married to the MP for Stafford, John Robins. The case was litigated both in King's Bench and in the ecclesiastical courts, in a war for public opinion that was also fought through pamphlets.[19] Similarly criminal accusations (and a pamphlet

[17]   Cases B.5, F.5.
[18]   Case F.11.
[19]   Case A.10.

rejecting them) arose in the unsuccessful attempt of Viscountess Valentia to deny custody of their child to her estranged husband, on the grounds that he had habitually shared 'indecent familiarities' with his male servants.[20] (His father, a notorious libertine, had also used King's Bench, prosecuting several citizens of Arley Over who assaulted him when he was acting as a magistrate.)[21]

Viscount Valentia used the writ of habeas corpus to recover his son; most of the other successful applicants for the writ were professional criminals, accused of horsetheft and lesser larcenies, or counterfeiting.[22] Four cases (a criminal information, habeas corpus application, and two proceedings for contempt) all involved a criminal gang centred on a butcher of Rowley Regis and his brother, a farmer who occupied Wednesbury Hall. They had close connections with horsethieves and with a crooked London solicitor (who was struck from the roll and himself imprisoned), using perjured false bailsmen and a good understanding of the complexities of legal procedure to protect themselves from retribution. The court also dealt with another case of conspiracy to acquit through perjury.[23] At the other extreme, a conviction by a justice of the peace for the theft of potatoes and turnips was removed into the court by the defendants, presumably in order to quash it, although the outcome is unknown.[24]

A few cases illustrate other issues of legal practice, including fees, the role of solicitors in King's Bench practice, and the way litigation could involve several of the high courts.[25] All the remaining cases arose from the role of justices of the peace and borough magistrates in the administration of justice and local government. Proceedings against magistrates for their decisions in law enforcement (particularly criminal committals), or contesting their summary convictions, were two distinct classes of proceedings in King's Bench.[26] Some of these cases, and a few others involving magistrates, reflect their other important duties in local government: overseeing the poor law,[27] ensuring that highway and other regulations were enforced,[28] and hearing summarily cases involving economic issues like the licensing of tradesmen, fraudulent

---

[20] Case G.8.
[21] Case F.18; *ODNB*, 'Grace Eliot'.
[22] Cases G.2, G.3, G.4, G.6, G.7.
[23] Case F.16.
[24] Case E.6.
[25] Cases F.19, H.1, H.2.
[26] The cases in sections B and E.
[27] Cases A.15, B.1, B.2, B.4, F.5, and F.21.
[28] Cases A.14, E.1, E.2, E.5, F.18, and F.23.

transactions, exercising a trade without having served an apprentice-ship, and enforcing the excise laws. These cases, a tiny proportion of the total number heard by Staffordshire magistrates, came before King's Bench when litigants invoked the high court's general supervisory jurisdiction over all lesser criminal courts.

PROCEEDINGS ON THE CROWN SIDE

None of these cases were simple trials on indictments, the mode of pro-ceeding at quarter sessions and assizes. King's Bench was a court of first instance for trials on indictment, but only in Middlesex, and in this it was simply one (if the most impressive) of the great many courts that litigious inhabitants of the capital could use to seek justice or harass their opponents.[29] More visible to the nation at large, and the subject of this book, were other kinds of criminal proceedings that began or ended in Westminster Hall, although they had their origins elsewhere in the country. Cases arising outside London and Middlesex, in what the clerks of the court called the 'out-counties', led to pleas in Westminster Hall, and manoeuvres and remedies there under a variety of rulings and writs, but the trials themselves were almost always held in the county where the litigation began: for these cases, at Stafford assizes. Final judgments and sentences were then pronounced in Westminster Hall. Punishments were usually carried out in the county where a case arose, but could be inflicted in the metropolis, as was the case with the 1750 Walsall rioters.

The most notorious criminal proceedings in King's Bench were pros-ecutions on criminal informations. They were of two kinds: those exhib-ited by the master of the crown office on behalf of private prosecutors, and informations ex officio exhibited by the law officers of the crown on behalf of the government.[30] Both could be brought only for serious mis-demeanours. Compared to prosecution on indictment, prosecution by criminal information was speedy, expensive, and held some significant opportunities and dangers for both parties, if the proceeding was between private persons.[31] When the state was the prosecutor, the

[29] This aspect of the court is being explored in work by Dr Ruth Paley.
[30] See the introductions to Sections A, B, and C.
[31] A third species of proceeding, possible in murder cases, was the appeal of felony, a private prosecution akin to a civil suit. The last such case, *Ashford v Thornton* (1818), involved a Staffordshire man; none occurred in the county in the period covered by this volume. See Hay, *the Judges and the People*.

Figure 2   **Westminster Hall, 1805**
Joshua Bryant, *Buildings on the South Side of New Palace Yard*, 1805.

advantages were heavily on its side. The court was the only venue for such cases, which came to it from throughout England and Wales.

King's Bench was also the supreme court of criminal review for England and Wales. Summary convictions before justices of the peace, and proceedings on indictment before quarter sessions and even assize judges in certain circumstances, could be removed into King's Bench on writ of certiorari.[32] Verdicts in the lower courts could sometimes be overturned on writs of error or motions for new trials. In these ways the court was held to have a general supervisory power over all inferior criminal jurisdictions, a power also manifested in other remedies, not all of them exclusively criminal in nature, that were nonetheless exercised on the 'crown side' rather than 'plea side' of the court. The

[32]   See the introductions to Sections E and F.

most important were writs of habeas corpus,[33] prohibition, and mandamus. Challenges to the right to hold office could be tested by informations in the nature of a quo warranto. It was also in King's Bench that the final proceedings in contumacious or impotent prosecutions took place, in the form of attachments and interrogatories for contempts,[34] and the punishments for flight or noncompliance: outlawry (arising from proceedings in the state's courts, both criminal and civil),[35] and excommunication (on proceedings in church courts).[36]

Although relatively few criminal cases came from any single county other than Middlesex, when they did so and particularly when they resulted in trials, they attracted attention both in the county and in London, particularly later in the century, when the press more consistently reported cases in Westminster Hall.[37] Decided at the highest level of the criminal law, argued by leading barristers, and often incurring great expense, they were widely discussed in county society. The threat of a King's Bench prosecution commanded respect and indeed fear. According to Daines Barrington (1727–1800), vulgar errors about the law included the notion 'that any one may be put into the Crown-office, for no cause whatsoever, or the most trifling injury.'[38] That belief may have arisen from the fact that the crown side of the court dealt with cases ranging from minor poaching offences to the most serious seditious libel and riot; many examples of both appear in this volume, together with a wide range of other kinds of prosecutions. The fear arose from the expense of such prosecutions. The complexity of the procedure, the need to pay clerks, attorneys and counsel at every stage of process, swiftly generated great expense. Although it was a general principle of English law that the crown neither received nor paid costs, legislation changed that rule for litigants in King's Bench, who in effect were only borrowing the name of the king. Misdemeanours always savoured somewhat of civil litigation, unlike felonies, and as a consequence procedural rules were more complex, and the opportunity to

[33] See the introduction to Section G.

[34] See the introduction to Section H.

[35] See the introduction to Section F.

[36] References to these and other courts occur in a number of cases in this volume: for an example see A.10 for the ecclesiastical Court of Arches.

[37] For an estimate of the number of criminal cases in Staffordshire see D. Hay, 'Legislation, Magistrates, and Judges: High Law and Low Law in England and the Empire,' in David Lemmings, ed., *The British and Their Laws in the Eighteenth Century* (London: Boydell and Brewer, 2005), 63.

[38] Daines Barrington, *Observations on the More Ancient Statutes* (4th ed., London, 1775), 474 note [z].

exhaust an opponent with costs that much greater. Litigants were well aware of the fact.[39]

The clerks of the crown side worked in the crown office and managed all its criminal litigation. What could be prosecuted, however, depended on the views of the judges, and the doctrines of the common law. Most of the cases that came before the court, from London and Middlesex and from the rest of the country, were misdemeanours, a category of crime ranging from serious offences, like seditious libel and riot and attempted rape, to private libels and assaults; minor statutory offences decided by lay magistrates also came before the court on review.[40] Very little material on felonies appears in this volume, and only then because felony indictments might sometimes come into the court on certiorari or outlawry proceedings, or lead to bail hearings on habeas corpus.[41] The process in misdemeanour was very different from that in felony, one of the differences being that the accused in felony had to appear in person in court. Ellenborough, the lord chief justice, commented in parliamentary debate in 1808 that 'in ninety-nine cases of misdemeanour out of a hundred, in the court of king's bench, the defendants were not present at their trials.'[42]

THE VARIETIES OF CASES

The cases presented here are all, or nearly all, the criminal cases on the crown side of the court arising in Staffordshire between 1740 and 1800.[43] 'Crime' is not a term of legal art; I have used it here to include proceedings that could result in imprisonment, or a fine that went at least in

---

[39] E.g. case A.9 affdt [1], case A.12 affdt [3]. See the introductions to each section for details on costs.

[40] See Section C, and cases A.18, A.1, A.2, and Section E.

[41] See case F.22, in which certiorari was used to effect outlawry, and some of the habeas corpus cases in Section G.

[42] *Cobbett's Parliamentary Debates*, ser. 1, xi, col. 417 (19 May 1808); see also Gude, i, 101 on the possible disadvantage of being present, if convicted, and the affidavits in case C.13 for the difficulties imposed on defendants by personal appearance. Other important differences in the procedure governing misdemeanours are outlined below. On passing of sentence the defendant had to be present unless the court ruled otherwise: see the introduction to Section A.

[43] Cases for which the first dated occurrence, given in the heading for each case (see Editorial Notes), fell between 1 Jan 1740 and 31 Dec 1800.

part to the crown, for felonies and misdemeanours.[44] Misdemeanour proceedings could also be used to force private pecuniary settlements of disputes, sometimes arbitrated by the master of the crown office, after the formality of a judgment and small fine, or by an agreed local arbitrator or panel of arbitrators; related civil litigation might also be dealt with in this way.[45] Habeas corpus and contempt proceedings have also been included where they arose out of criminal proceedings, or could have led to them.

Each of the eight sections of this book presents one type of case:

A) criminal informations for serious misdemeanours, brought by prosecutors other than the attorney general, usually members of the public (24 cases);

B) the specific subset of such criminal informations that were brought against magistrates, entailing slightly different procedures and greater difficulties of proof (13 cases);

C) ex officio informations, which could be brought only by the attorney general and solicitor general, the law officers of the crown (15 cases);

D) informations qui tam in King's Bench, so-called 'penal actions', in which the 'common informer', who could be anyone, was entitled to a share of the penalty for a conviction (35 cases);

E) writs of certiorari to remove summary convictions by magistrates, mainly qui tams heard before them, into King's Bench (8 cases);

F) writs of certiorari to remove indictments or informations from quarter sessions or assizes (24 cases);

G) proceedings on writs of habeas corpus (8 cases);

---

[44] Treason, felony, and misdemeanour were the three main categories of crimes at common law, each with its own procedural distinctions; the assignment of a particular offence to one of these categories was the outcome of a long historical process. Treason trials, for which King's Bench was frequently the venue, were tried *en banc* (that is, in Westminster Hall) or on special assize commissions, and none appear in this volume. As noted above, almost all those reproduced here are misdemeanour cases.

[45] See cases A.14, A.20, B.1, B.4, F.1, F.5, F.11, F.14. Such compromises and arbitrations probably lie behind many cases in which a prosecution simply stops. Hands, 391 gives the example of a failure by the prosecutor to join in demurrer: 'The indictment was compromised, and this judgment was entered by consent.'

H) writs of attachment for contempt (2 cases).[46]

Process related to attachments and interrogatories for contempts also appears in other cases (B.4, F.1, F.5), as does that for several outlawries (F.10, F.22).

A variety of proceedings recorded in the crown side records are omitted from this book, although some of them were nominally criminal in nature. Many involved the poor law and other aspects of local government, such as the maintenance of roads. In the eighteenth century a great part of local government, and its querying by central government as well as aggrieved citizens, took place in the courts, including the crown side of King's Bench as well as in criminal prosecutions at quarter sessions and assizes in the counties.[47] Including material of this kind would have made this a much longer volume, and shifted the focus from what we now think of as criminal law. In all, eight categories of proceedings have not been reproduced. Informations in the nature of a quo warranto by the eighteenth century had largely replaced the use of the writ quo warranto. Like the writ, the information was used to try rights to offices and franchises, and many in King's Bench arose in the course of trying to influence the results of general elections by questioning the rights to office of aldermen or others who controlled votes. William Blackstone commented that it was 'properly a criminal prosecution, in order to fine the defendant for his usurpation, as well as to oust him from his office; yet usually considered at present as merely a civil proceeding.'[48] Writs of prohibition would have been included if they had involved criminal cases, but none were found; this is true also

---

[46] The total given of 129 cases is somewhat arbitrary: for clarity and economy, a 'case' may involve multiple defendants to the same charge but named in separate writs (E.5), combine several different types of proceedings involving the same defendant(s) (A.17, B.4, G.7), or combine several related applications for informations and other remedies (A.16, B.4). In other cases closely related litigation involving the same defendant (F.6, F.7) or several different writs or procedures (A.21, G.2, H.1, H.2) are presented as several cases, sometimes distributed in different chapters, with cross references. These choices were made with a view to making the course of litigation clear.

[47] Holdsworth, x, 243ff. See cases B.1, B.2, B.4 and B.8 for the use of criminal prosecutions in poor law proceedings, included in this volume because they were informations brought against magistrates.

[48] Blackstone, iv, 312; Christian's footnote in the 12th edn. notes that therefore King's Bench would grant a new trial on an information quo warranto even after an acquittal.

of writs of mandamus, by which justices or other authorities were required to act when they had not done so.[49] Writs of certiorari to remove vagrant passes or orders of courts of quarter sessions, common in poor law cases of sharp interest to local ratepayers, have not been included,[50] nor those arising from criminal prosecutions to enforce repair or maintenance of highways and bridges.[51] Attachments for contempts and resulting interrogatories have been identified for a few Staffordshire cases concerning felony or misdemeanour and are included in Section H; many others arose out of the enforcement of judgments in civil proceedings and are not reproduced here.[52] Articles of the peace were not found for Staffordshire, although that may be a consequence of how they were recorded.[53] Excommunications to enforce the decisions of the church courts have not been included.

The chronological sequence of cases within each section is determined by the date of the first record of the case in King's Bench: either the date

---

[49] However, some appear in connection with other proceedings: see case B.4 affdt [4] for a writ of mandamus reproduced in full.

[50] But see the certioraris on indictments brought by poor law officials of Waterfall in 1757 and 1784 for failure to maintain grandchildren (case F.5) and against them for conspiracy (F.21). An instance of the use of certiorari for poor law documents such as passes and orders of sessions can be seen in B.1, in which the order is quashed. The role of magistrates in the poor law also appears in cases A.15, B.1, B.2, and B.4.

[51] But see cases F.23 (certiorari of indictment for the nuisance of obstructing highway) and A.14 (criminal information against supervisors of the highways for Wolverhampton). The former was part of John Gough's litigation war with the rector Thomas Lane (see A.24); the latter contained allegations of malice similarly arising out of previous disputes. See also the other cases cited in note 28 above.

[52] But see case H.2. Some habeas corpus proceedings dealing with criminal matters may have been missed, because attachments for contempts and applications for writs of habeas corpus are sometimes titled only 'In the King's Bench. England. The King against A.B.' in KB 1 (affidavits) and in KB 21 (rule or order books) and other registers, without the addition of the county in the margin or as an endorsement. Finding all of them for a given county would entail opening and reading every affidavit in KB 1 and every writ in KB 16; see Gude, i, 256. Complete examination of substantial parts of both series (KB 1/7 to KB 1/32, all bundles marked 'Staffordshire'), KB 16/13 to KB 16/21, and also of KB 32/19 to KB 32/21 (interrogatories) turned up some of those reproduced in Section G.

[53] As with habeas corpus, county names often are not associated with entries for articles of the peace (see preceding note).

of the first affidavit, or in the absence of affidivits (as is usually the case with ex officio informations, for example) by the earliest date on the writ, the information, or other records of the court. In virtually all the sources other than affidavits, dates were expressed in terms of saints' days and regnal years, and legal convention determined that some stages of process were always recorded as happening on the first or last day of the current term, regardless of the actual date (see Editorial Notes). In several cases the same facts gave rise to more than one kind of proceeding, such as a writ of habeas corpus and a criminal information (A.17), or habeas corpus and certiorari (G.7), or habeas corpus to bring before the court a defendant to an ex officio information (C.6). In some instances these are presented together in one section, with a cross-reference; in some more complicated cases different but closely related proceedings appear in different sections, again with cross references (see A.21, G.2, H.1, H.2, all arising out of the same circumstances).

Each section of the book is prefaced by an introduction explaining the process and records of the court particularly important for the type of case in that section, and an overview of the kinds of crimes that arose in Staffordshire and came before the court. Since many details of procedure are common to more than one kind of proceeding, the fullest accounts are given in the introductions to Section A on criminal informations, and in Section F on certioraris to remove indictments.

AN OUTLINE OF CRIMINAL PROCEDURE ON THE CROWN SIDE

The procedural details for each case are set out under headings for the relevant writs or informations, with rules of the court and stages of process summarized under the heading 'Rules and process'; the most common ones are explained in the introductions to each section, and defined briefly in the Glossary. Innovations in practice undoubtedly took place continuously, in small ways, and occasionally in larger ones.[54] A list of general rules and orders of the court includes 72 made

---

[54] William Samuel Jones, the master of the crown office, noted in 1844 that on an indictment being found (in the Middlesex practice of the court), a venire had formerly issued, but that that had been discontinued 'for the last thirty or forty years.': *Parliamentary Papers* 1845 [656], xiv, Eighth Report of the Commissioners on Criminal Law, Appendix (B), 344, q 47. The law changed too, for example in the willingness of the judges to grant rules for criminal informations: see D. Hay, 'Dread of the Crown Office: the English Magistracy and King's Bench, 1740–1800', in Norma Landau, ed., *Law, Crime and English Society 1660–1840* (Cambridge, 2002), 19–45 and D. Hay, *The Judges and the People*.

Figure 3 **The Courts and Booksellers in Westminster Hall, c.1730: King's Bench left of stairs**
Charles Mosley after Hubert Gravelot, *The First Day of Term, Westminster Hall.*

between 1740 and 1800, the period covered by this calendar.[55] A number of statutes, and some case law, also affected practice in the court in the period between the first of the cases published here and 1800. Some changes have been remarked in footnotes and the introductions to sections, but there are undoubtedly other minor ones that either do not appear in the records used, or are of marginal significance in understanding the history and outcome of a given case.

All cases on the crown side began in Westminster Hall, and the following account is an outline of proceedings described in more detail

<hr />

[55] Gude, i, 367–93.

in the introductions to each section of the book. Many cases, but not all, began with the filing of affidavits for the prosecution; 549 were found for the 129 cases in this volume. In qui tam prosecutions (Section D) an affidavit was filed only as the basis of the information, and for informations brought ex officio by the attorney general or solicitor general (Section C) even that preliminary was omitted, although affidavits were used by the clerks in drawing the information once the law officers had decided to prosecute.[56] But in all other criminal informations (Sections A, B), counsel for the prosecution moved the court for a rule nisi, which was a rule for the defendant to show cause why the court should not grant the information (or, to use the court's terms, allow it to be exhibited.) The motion was supported by affidavits filed in the crown office, where the clerks of the crown side of the court kept its records; the defence case, if it was made at this point, was similarly supported.[57] Affidavits were filed by term bundle; if dated in vacation time, they were filed with the affidavits of the preceding term, not the term in which they were in fact used.[58] Many cases proceeded no farther than argument for and against a rule nisi. A prosecution might be abandoned, or a settlement reached; more rarely, a stay of proceedings, also called a nolle prosequi, was granted by the attorney general at the request of one of the parties, at this or later stages.[59]

The preliminaries in cases of indictments removed by certiorari (Section F) were broadly similar, although the procedure generated far fewer surviving affidavits. The writ was obtained, either by motion in court or (in the vacations between the law terms) by fiat from a judge in chambers. If sought by an agent of the crown, either for the prosecution or (infrequently) the defence, it was granted as of right; if by a private

---

[56] See the introduction to Section C.

[57] Gude, ii, 1 noted in 1828 that it was 'formerly the practice to file affidavits before they could be read or made use of in Court' (citing rules of court of 1735 and 1777) 'but the practise has long been discontinued, on account of the inconvenience and delay attending it, except in cases where a rule to show cause is enlarged; and if affidavits are not filed within the time specified on an enlarged rule, the Court will not allow them to be read.' (Compare Hands, 5.) Thus affidavits were sometimes filed after oral argument, although they would of course be before the judges, and subsequently filed. For an example of the requirement under an enlarged rule, see case A.2, rule of 19 Nov 1744.

[58] See case F.11, note 82.

[59] See above.

[60] See the introductions to Sections E, F.

prosecutor, again the court would grant it on request, although the defendant could contest its issue. A defendant could only obtain it by showing a reason through affidavits.[60] In the case of criminal informations (ordinary and ex officio) and certioraris on indictments, if a rule absolute resulted, or the fiat was granted, and the party or parties chose to proceed, in almost all cases from out-counties a notice of trial was entered for the case to be tried at the next assizes in the county in which it arose.

Motions made on affidavits gave the judges discretion to grant rules or orders, but for many of the less important stages of process 'side bar rules' could be obtained on simple application. The side bar was literally that, a bar at the side of the court. As William Hone, who had an intimate knowledge of King's Bench as a defendant, explained in 1825, 'the Side Bar in Westminster hall stood, till very lately, within a short space of the wall ... Formerly, attorneys stood within this bar every morning during term, and moved the judges for the common rules, called side-bar rules, as they passed to their courts ... These motions have long been discontinued; the rules are applied for and obtained at the rule-office as rules of course; but each rule still expresses that it has been granted upon a "side-bar" motion.'[61]

When cases went to trial, either on information or on indictment removed by certiorari, the trials were held at Stafford assizes. The twelve common law judges went on circuit twice a year, in the vacations between the law terms, to hear cases at Lent and summer assizes; Staffordshire was on what was called the Oxford circuit, as it included that county. There were two assize courts: the crown court, where most felonies and misdemeanours were tried, on bills of indictment found by a Staffordshire grand jury, and the nisi prius court, where all civil trials took place. Misdemeanour cases in which process began in King's Bench (including those in this volume) were also heard in the nisi prius court, unlike all other felonies and misdemeanours. In general, the nisi prius court at Stafford was held before the more senior of the two assize judges on the circuit, and was the one in which counsel found most work, the most remunerative cases, and the greatest opportunity to raise points of law.[62] Because prosecutions on information or certioraris on indictment also frequently involved gentlemen, as prosecutors and defendants and jurymen, such occasional criminal proceedings on the

---

[61] William Hone, *The Every-day Book* (London, 1825), 156–7.

[62] TNA, ASSI 10/1, printed table, 'Oxford Circuit: Account of the Right Honorable and Honorable the Judges Who Went This Circuit', footnote.

nisi prius side of assizes also attracted the attention of county society.[63]

The jury in a trial of a civil cause at nisi prius, like a jury in King's Bench itself, could be a 'special' jury, but so too could the jury in the criminal trial of a misdemeanour 'depending in the court of King's Bench', whether tried at Westminster or at nisi prius in the county. In Staffordshire, as in other counties, a special jury was an elevated one indeed. Even an ordinary jury was recruited from the wealthiest quarter of the adult male population, but a special jury consisted of gentlemen, wealthy merchants, magistrates, and other notables, probably all of them from the top 3% of the social order.[64] Misdemeanours prosecuted in King's Bench were in fact the only criminal cases in Staffordshire or any other county that could be tried by such a jury. Ordinary felons and misdemeanants in the crown court at assizes and at quarter sessions could have only an ordinary jury.[65] It was part of ordinary criminal process to issue the writ *venire facias juratores*[66] (noted under the heading 'Rules and process'), but at nisi prius either party in a misdemeanour prosecution could call for a special jury, on paying the

---

[63] The terminology may confuse: cases on the 'crown' side of King's Bench, if not tried before the court itself in Westminster Hall ('at bar'), were sent for trial to the 'nisi prius' court, rather than the 'crown' court, at assizes in the county.

[64] D. Hay, 'The Class Composition of the Palladium of Liberty: Trial Jurors in the Eighteenth Century', in James S. Cockburn and Thomas A. Green (eds.), *Twelve Good Men and True: The Criminal Trial Jury in England 1200–1800* (Princeton University Press, 1988), 305–57.

[65] Chitty, i, 372, 522–25; Blackstone, iii, 358 (and note 5 in the 12th edition). On special juries in general see three articles by James Oldham: 'Origins of the Special Jury', *University of Chicago Law Review*, l (1), 137–213; 'Special Juries in England: Nineteenth Century Usage and Reform' (September 1987), *The Journal of Legal History*, viii (2) (Sept 1987), 148–166; 'Jury Research in the English Reports in CD-ROM,' in John W. Cairns and Grant McLeod, eds., *The Dearest Birth Right of the People of England: The Jury in the History of the Common Law* (Oxford: Hart, 2002), 131–154. The rules respecting juries in treason cases were again distinctive, regulated by the Treason Act, 7 & 8 Will III, c.3 (1695).

[66] Gude, i, 687 and passim refers to the writ for a jury as a venire facias juratorum; apparently the only other contemporary instance of this usage occurs in an appendix, copied from a document of the deputy clerk of the peace for the North Riding of Yorkshire, reprinted in J. Minchin and A. Herbert, *The Crown Circuit Companion, in Which is Incorporated the Crown Circuit Assistant* (9th ed., London, 1820), 619. All other sources call it a venire facias juratores.

costs incurred.[67] In short, a trial of a criminal information or case removed by certiorari usually involved the highest levels of county society, often as litigants, almost always as jurors. In most of the cases in this volume that reached the stage of a jury being called, there was a rule granted to one party or the other for a special jury.[68] However, in some cases not all special jurors called by the sheriff chose to attend, perhaps because they did not want to be involved in quarrels among their peers. In such a case the under sheriff was obliged to fill out the jury with talesmen, bystanders in court.[69]

After a verdict at nisi prius at Stafford, process returned to King's Bench, formally in the form of a 'postea', a very large parchment record of the case endorsed with the verdict. At this point the defendant might make a motion in arrest of judgment. If successful, no judgment or sentence was pronounced (see case F.1, where it led to an arbitration). Otherwise, final judgment and sentence were pronounced in Westminster Hall. In most of the cases in this volume the defendant did not have to be personally present, except for final judgment and sentence, and sometimes that too was excused. In a few successful prosecutions, notably those involving sedition, the Staffordshire defendants were not only present in Westminster Hall for sentencing, but suffered their sentences in the streets of the capital, exposed to the humours of the mob.[70]

Although they superficially resemble other informations, informations qui tam were an anomaly. All of them in this collection (Section D) are poaching cases, brought before King's Bench simply in order to increase the penalty exacted from the defendant, and hence provide a far more crushing punishment (when costs were included) than the simple summary conviction before a magistrate otherwise provided by the statute law. They too began with affidavits (no longer preserved) but their subsequent route was through exchequer, the process used to

---

[67] 3 Geo II, c.25 s.15 (1729); 24 Geo II, c.18 (1750). The latter put all costs on the party asking for the special jury, to deter 'many applications for special juries on very trivial occasions' brought about by a decision reported in 1737, *Wilks* v *Eames* 2 Strange 1080, 93 ER 1044, that had held that all costs except the striking were to be paid by the losing party. Chitty, i, 522–23. On the procedure for striking a special jury, see the introduction to Section A.

[68] At the instance of the defendant: A.2 (four times), B.12, C.1, C.7, C.10, C.11, C.12, F.9, F.16, F.17, F.19, F.23. Of the prosecutor: A.16, C.14, C.15, F.10, F.12, F.13.

[69] See case F.19.

[70] Case C.13. See also the introduction to Section A. On posteas, see also p. xiv and below, note 109.

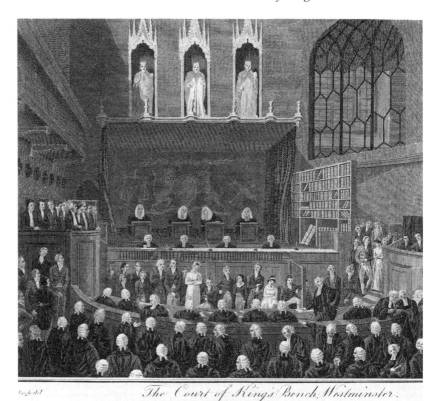

Figure 4   **King's Bench, 1804, enclosed within walls erected in 1755**
Edward Pugh, *Court of King's Bench Westminster*, 1804.

exact the penalty in the final instance. Other qui tams also came before the court from outside, for review: most of the summary convictions before magistrates took this form, and the court exercised a general jurisdiction over all inferior tribunals through the removal of such cases into it by certiorari. All the cases in Section E are attempts to have the court quash a summary conviction before a magistrate. The judges made this decision after hearing arguments by counsel.

Section G contains cases of writs of habeas corpus (usually connected with bail hearings), and Section H deals with attachments for contempts, two of the main powers exercised by the judges of King's Bench in a wide variety of cases through their inherent powers under the prerogative writs and ancient common law.[71]

---

[71]   See the introductions to Sections G and H.

THE USES OF AFFIDAVITS

Many motions for rules by the court had to be supported by affidavits for the prosecution or for the defence, and frequently both survive; to some of them are attached original letters as evidence, or copies of rules of court or other documents. Affidavits, 549 of which form the bulk of this volume, are less common survivals in the records of quarter sessions or assize, since criminal procedure there was dominated by oral testimony and the informations sworn at committal proceedings were often brief.[72] We are thus able in many King's Bench cases to reconstruct more of the evidence than is typically possible for eighteenth-century criminal trials outside London (where the Old Bailey cases, now available on-line, provide printed summaries, more or less detailed, of evidence for many thousands of felony cases in London and Middlesex.) The King's Bench affidavits give a great deal of information about litigants, localities, other citizens, and the social context in which the cases arose. Because we sometimes have evidence on behalf of both parties, we can make some assessment of how the judges viewed particular litigants. In this respect the affidavits are usually more revealing for the general historian (although often contradictory in their content) than the reports of arguments and judgments in the Law Reports, the authoritive sources for the common law, which deal only with specific points of law. Affidavits are also far more numerous: only four of the Staffordshire cases reproduced in this volume (B.4, D.9, E.3, E.4) raised points of criminal law important enough for them to be reported, although related litigation in one case (A.10) generated reports on ecclesiastical law.

Affidavits were sworn before commissioners in the counties, or before the court itself, or sometimes before a judge in his chambers. They are folded, and usually endorsed (*verso* in this calendar, given near the beginning of the text of the affidavit) with the number of the bundle in that term (if the outermost affidavit), the name of the case and/or the deponent, and sometimes instructions to the barrister in court, his name and his fee, the sums of recognizances entered into, the rule granted, and the number of folios (a folio was nominally 72 words)

---

[72] On the other hand, the lack of affidavits in King's Bench for most certioraris can sometimes be supplied from quarter sessions or assize records: e.g. case F.19. Note that the 'informations and examinations' found in the records of these courts are the counterparts of affidavits in King's Bench, not of the entirely different 'criminal informations' in King's Bench. The latter are equivalent to indictments at quarter sessions and assizes.

charged by the clerks. Usually the name of the instructing attorney appears at the bottom.[73]

These names of barristers, attorneys, and commissioners remind us of the significant shortcomings of these documents. Affidavits were a particular kind of sworn evidence, a fact reflected in the ways in which they were treated in the case law. An affidavit was a sworn statement made by one party, or his or her witnesses, before a commissioner or judge; before whom, when and where was embodied in the jurat at the end of the affidavit, and had to be in proper form; if sworn only before an attorney they were not accepted.[74] In this calendar the jurat is summarized at the beginning of the affidavit. Affidavits had to be headed 'In the King's Bench' (abbreviated in this calendar as ITKB); the name of the cause before the court ('The King against [defendant's name]') appeared on affidavits only after both parties had appeared by counsel, except when they had done so on showing cause against a rule nisi.[75] Affidavits were not sworn in the presence of the other party, nor subject like oral testimony to cross-examination. Unlike depositions (although the word was sometimes used loosely for affidavits also), they were not made in response to interrogatories[76] administered by an officer of the court; hence they were often called 'voluntary affidavits.' For all these reasons the common law courts had complex rules on how affidavits could be used as evidence. Where witnesses refused to make affidavit, and appeared to be under the control of the party accused, the court sometimes permitted secondary evidence of what they had previously asserted.[77] To support motions affidavits were often required; counsel referred to them in argument; if they were used in mitigation or aggravation in proceedings before the master of the crown office, they might be voluminous (see case F.11). But for many cases they were filed for only one party, or not at all.[78] If a case made it to trial at nisi prius,

[73] Hands, 344, 350 gives examples 'only inserted here to shew the young practitioner the manner of indorsing common motion papers.'
[74] Gude, ii, 1. For the form see ibid., ii, 380.
[75] Ibid., i, 116–7 and ii, 1–2; Chitty, 853. E.g. case A.16 (beginning at affdt [19]), B.4 (affdts [9] and [17]). In a few cases in this volume this information is not provided.
[76] For an example of interrogatories on an attachment for contempt, see case H.1.
[77] Chitty, 852–3. See case F.11, affdts [52] and [62].
[78] See Chitty, 691ff. See below on how the text of affidavits is treated in this volume.

the court privileged *viva voce* evidence by witnesses appearing before it, and oral argument by counsel.

Legally charged accounts of the ordinary doings of women and men are, as is well known, highly problematic documents. We want to read them as expressions of unmediated fact or belief, but we know that to do so is most unwise. King's Bench affidavits testify to fragments of events; even within one affidavit, separate deponents speak to different elements of the 'history of the offence.' Sequences are inverted; corroborative evidence betrays its legal purposes by being cast in exactly identical phraseology issuing from different witnesses.[79] But of course it does not issue from the witnesses except through the dictation of the lawyers. Affidavits are usually carefully constructed legal documents, and their often stilted and redundant wording, careful choice of words, and uniform if turgid literacy, mark them as the product of law offices rather than of the deponents. The calendared versions in this book are on average a little more than a quarter the length of the originals, deleting the redundancy while seeking to preserve all relevant legal detail, social interest, and the names of all persons and places. Wording is generally close to the original, and exactly so when an unmediated utterance shines out at us, apparently the authentic voice of the deponent, for affidavits vary considerably in the degree to which an attorney modified the words of the deponent. But we can never forget that affidavits are documents that have been very carefully considered, and often rewritten, by lawyers, not by the men and women who signed or put their marks to them. Many affidavits in this volume have other documents attached to them, however, and when they are not the product of law clerks, they are reproduced in full.[80]

The affidavits, although large in bulk, constitute only a portion of the surviving records of the crown side of the court: the rest are the registers, plea rolls, and many other series kept by the clerks to record process in the court. Those used for this book are described below (see the next section, and also that on 'Sources used', below) and in the introductions to Sections A to H.

The records of the court do not give any account of oral argument. Sometimes, judging from pamphlet or press accounts, this appears to have been no more than a reading, or elaboration, of the material in the

---

[79] For example, those for the prosecution in case A.9 copy most passages word for word.

[80] The redundancies eliminated from the calendared affidavits are preserved however in the interrogatories and answers for contempt in case H.1 [5] and [6], which are reproduced in full.

Figure 5 **Westminster Hall, 1801**
George Hawkins, *Internal view of Westminster Hall*, 1801.

affidavits.[81] When we can compare the two, we sometimes find counsel giving particular emphases to the material in the affidavits, but the lawyers could not, without fatally harming a case, depart materially

---

[81] See for example the published report of case G.8, and case A.10 note to affdt [14].

from it.[82] For cross-examination of witnesses at trial (of which there were few) we are dependent on other sources, including the press and, where they survive, the manuscript notes of the judge as he sat on the bench, or briefs for one or other of the parties. A very few of these sources have been found for the cases in this volume. In one case (E.4) a manuscript note made at the time by a law student, Lloyd Kenyon (later in the century chief justice of King's Bench) records the arguments of counsel on an argument to quash a conviction. On the other hand, the reasons for judgment, particularly if they turned on points of law as well as the evidence heard by the judges, do not appear in the manuscript records of the courts. They have been supplied, where possible, from newspaper accounts and the very few law reports of these cases, and for one case, the defence brief (F.10).

COUNSEL, ATTORNEYS, THE CLERKS AND PROCEDURE

King's Bench was the highest forum for any man active at the criminal bar, and the names of some of the most famous barristers and attorneys general, including men later judges in Westminster Hall, are to be found in the records of the Staffordshire cases: William Henry Ashhurst, John Dunning, Thomas Erskine, William Garrow, Vicary Gibbs, Lloyd Kenyon, George Nares, Dudley Ryder, John Willes, Joseph Yates and many others. Sometimes counsel for a litigant was the attorney general or solicitor general, who often maintained their private practice at the bar while in office. For reasons already noted, virtually nothing of the eloquence of these advocates is found in the records of the court (but see the notes to case G.8). Two other groups of professionals were also crucial to its work. The role of beginning litigation, preparing affidavits, filing process, and retaining counsel was the work of the attorneys, whose names appear endorsed at the bottom of the *versos* of the affidavits. A very large part of their responsibilities was dealing with the clerks of the crown office.

The clerks ran the bureaucracy and, in many respects, the court. The direction, timing of process, and duration of a litigant's case to a large

---

[82] In a Staffordshire case in 1802, the prosecutor admitted in his sworn affidavit to giving his 15-year-old servant 'a smartish flogging' with a waggoner's whip. His counsel, the famous barrister Thomas Erskine (lord chancellor from 1806), rephrased this in argument as 'a slight blow over his smock frock – no very severe discipline.' See Hay, 'Dread of the Crown Office', 39–40. Erskine had been a midshipman in the navy and an officer in the army, which perhaps coloured his views on corporal punishment.

extent was determined by the rules for filing affidavits and recording writs, motions, and process in the many record series kept by the clerks. They worked in the crown office, which at the end of the eighteenth century was located at no. 2, King's Bench Walks, Temple, and was open in both the law terms and vacations from 10am to 2pm, and from 5pm to 8pm.[83] The office was headed by the 'king's attorney and coroner', usually called simply the 'master of the crown office', and different clerks were responsible for keeping particular sets of records. The clerks were also crucial to the actual conduct of a case, for many of the daily and routine proceedings in the court were carried out by the parties' 'clerks in court', rather than by counsel.[84]

Throughout the eighteenth century, and for much of the nineteenth, the details of the procedure followed on the crown side of King's Bench was very much the procedure of the clerks, rather than that of the lawyers or even the judges. Lord Mansfield, chief justice from 1756 to 1788, was alluding to this point (albeit with respect to proceedings in chambers rather than open court) in a famous case in 1770:

> Matters of practice are not to be known from books. What passes at a Judge's chambers is matter of tradition: it rests in memory. In cases of this kind, Judges must inquire of their officers. This is done in Court, every day, when the practice is disputed or doubted. It is, in its nature, official. The officers are better acquainted with it, than the Judges.[85]

His successor Lord Kenyon made a similar comment while hearing a case, in which he referred to an earlier one, 'which he read from a MS. note of the late Mr Masterman of the Crown Office.' In the same case counsel referred in argument to 'the constant practice of the Crown office ...'[86]

Thus, although the judges made many general rules or orders that affected the operation of the court (some are cited below), exactly how a prosecution would proceed, the steps and fees that had to be followed and paid by a litigant's attorney, were authoritatively known only to the clerks on the crown side, of whom there were about a dozen, some of them taking more than one office, at the end of the century: the mas-

---

[83]   Hands, [iii].

[84]   I describe the bureaucracy of the court in *The Judges and the People*.

[85]   Mansfield explaining why he felt free to amend John Wilkes's information for seditious libel: *R v Wilkes*, (1770) 4 Burr 2527 at 2566.

[86]   *R v Battams et al.* (1801),102 ER 118; 1 East 305. See also *R v Horner* (1783), cited in the introduction to Section G.

ter; the secondary; the clerk of the rules; the clerk of the affidavits; the examiner, calendar keeper and clerk of the grand juries; seven clerks in court; and the clerk in court for the crown.[87] The clerks in court made many of the motions for litigants, and divided the work up geographically: the clerks for cases arising on the Oxford assize circuit (which included Staffordshire) over this period were J. Wace, Samuel Midgley, Francis Barlow, Henry Dealtry, and Henry Barlow.[88]

As a case proceeded, whether on information, certiorari, habeas corpus, or contempt, progress and process was inscribed in crown rolls and controlment rolls, affidavit files and recognizance registers, docket books and minute books, and rolls of returned writs and informations.[89] The clerks considered this their domain and guarded it jealously, a fact that became clear during the preparation of this volume when a search was made for practitioners' guides to the crown side of the court.

Two treatises have been used extensively in reconstructing the procedures followed by the clerks in King's Bench, and in identifying stages of process. William Hands was a solicitor who published *The Solicitor's Practice on the Crown Side of the Court of King's Bench* (London: Butterworth, 1803), a work of some 500 pages, of which all but 100 were forms.[90] Jeremy Bentham, investigating government packing of special juries in King's Bench a few years later, discovered that Hands's work was the only published guide to the workings of the crown side of the court.[91] Although useful (especially so in the absence of anything else) it was clearly far from exhaustive, and sometimes in error. A much fuller treatise, in two volumes, was subsequently published by Richard Gude, *The Practice of the Crown Side of the Court of King's Bench* (London: Pheney, Sweet, Maxwell, Stevens, 1828; repr. 1990). In addition to describing stages of process, and giving forms and precedents, it reprinted the general rules of the court from the time of James I, and tables of fees and costs — over 1300 pages in all.

---

[87] Hands, iii; Gude, i, 21ff.

[88] Based on the cases in this volume, and references in KB 15/50; KB 16/17; and the treatises discussed below.

[89] See below, 'Sources used', for those examined in the preparation of this volume.

[90] He also published *Selection of Rules in the Prosecution and Defense of Personal Actions in the Court of King's Bench* (1795), *Practical Treatise on Fines and Recoveries in the Court of Common Pleas* (1st ed., 1800), *Law and Practice of Patents for Inventions* (1808), *Solicitor's Assistant in the Court of Chancery* (1809), and *Proceedings on Election Petitions* (1812).

[91] Jeremy Bentham, *The Elements of the Art of Packing, as Applied to Special Juries* (London, 1821), 38.

Moreover, Gude had been 'upwards of thirty-three years in the
Crown Office', as he advertised on his title page, and was therefore
conversant with many of the details of the daily practice of the clerks.
Entering the office in 1789, he was articled in 1811, serving the usual
five years under one of the them, Mr Gabriel Lepipre, and then waited
for an opening to be appointed a clerk himself. By his own account
he was a principal assistant to the master, received all the fines, acted
as the coroner of the King's Bench prison, and confidently expected an
appointment at the first vacancy. It was refused, apparently at the
request of some of the clerks. Denied his expectations of 'a considerable
share of the business' handled by the clerks, and the status of attorney,
which went with a clerkship, he resigned in disgust, refusing to serve
under men he considered his juniors and inferiors.[92]

His guide to practice, which he published after his retirement, was
undoubtedly written in the hope of financial gain based on his long
experience. He may also have hoped to take revenge on his former col-
leagues. For the lack of adequate reference works on the court put the
clerks in an enviable position: practioners were obliged, as Gude put it,
to ask for information

> upon almost every occasion, from the Clerks in Court — not only an
> inconvenience, but an expensive evil: — and as this body derive the
> fees and emoluments of their office from the knowledge of their prac-
> tice, they have no interest to render familiar the various forms and
> proceedings with which they alone are conversant.[93]

A practitioner armed with Gude was undoubtedly better informed,
although whether he was thereby able to circumvent the clerks to any
great degree may be doubted. And Gude's account of the common and
statute law was quite general, and sometimes in error.

Some further light was cast on the interests of the clerks by the testimony in 1844 of the then master of the crown office, William Samuel
Jones.[94] He had been a clerk in court at the time Hands wrote his book,
and was a contemporary of Gude when he was still a clerk in court.
Jones had been in the crown office for over half a century. Asked by the
Commissioners on Criminal Law whether the rules of the court were
'published in any authentic form', apart from some that appeared in

[92] Gude, i, Preface.
[93] Ibid.
[94] *Parliamentary Papers* 1845 [656], xiv, 'Eighth Report of the Commissioners on
      Criminal Law', Appendix (B), 344.

1843, he denied that they were. There were manuscript records of practice in the hands of a number of people in the office, himself included, but 'not in any condensed or corrected form.' They were private documents. When the commissioners asked if there were any manuscripts of the general rules of the court to which they could have access, Jones replied 'Certainly not.' Any points of practice would have to be 'orally communicated to the Commissioners upon our general practical knowledge, arising from the notes we have taken of cases which have occurred.'[95]

The exploitation of the clerks' monopoly of practical knowledge, deplored by Gude, was clearly still cherished in the office. The master and clerks were also jealous of their control of the records of the court, and the fees they received for maintaining them. Later in his testimony Jones remarked in annoyance that formerly there had been a roll for the entry of venires, 'which has been taken away from us.'[96] Jones was asked about Hands's and Gude's treatises, and he dismissed them as of little or no authority. Hands's work, he said, had been given him to correct,

> but he would not agree in the principles which I laid down; he would have it his own way, and made it incorrect from the beginning. The other is Mr Gude's Crown Practice, which, as far as a common clerk, having practical knowledge, can give information, is more correct than the other, but is still incorrect in many particulars. Those are the only two works upon the Crown Office practice.[97]

Some further information about how the master and the clerks viewed Hands's book in particular can be gleaned from the very large number of manuscript corrections and interlineations made in a copy of the volume kept in the crown office.[98] As far as they can be dated from content, the manuscript additions appear to have been made between publication in 1803 and the 1820s. Comparisons suggest that the additions are

---

[95] Ibid., qq 1 to 9. These are likely those now found in class KB 15.

[96] Ibid., q 43. Remnants of this may be in KB 17/1, among a miscellany of papers.

[97] Ibid., q 4.

[98] This copy, which I purchased from Wildy's some years ago, is bound in brown buckram, the spine stamped in gold: 'Practice on the Crown Side. Hands. Supreme Court Library R[oyal].C[ourts of].J[ustice].' On the inner fly leaf is stamped in upper case in ink 'master of the crown office.' I shall publish a digitized version with a link on the website of the library of Osgoode Hall Law School, York University, Toronto.

either by, or copied from, Gude, or that Gude copied in part from this annotated version of Hands.[99]

I have also used a number of contemporary manuscript collections of rules, orders, and procedural points kept by the clerks, and now preserved in KB 15; some other details have been supplied from later treatises, or those dealing primarily with the plea side of the court: among the most useful were Matthew Bacon, *A New Abridgement of the Law* (5th edn., 1798; 7th ed., 8 vols., London, 1832); Joseph Chitty, *A Practical Treatise on the Criminal* Law (4 vols., London, 1816; repr. in 5 vols., New York, 1978); W. R. Cole, *The Law and Practice Relating to Criminal Informations, and Informations in the Nature of Quo Warranto* (London: Sweet, Stevens & Norton, 1843); Giles Jacob, *The Compleat Attorney's Practice in English, in the Courts of King's Bench and Common-Pleas at Westminster* (2 vols., 2nd ed., [1740?]); and William Paley, *The Law and Practice of Summary Convictions on Penal Statutes by Justices of the Peace* (London, 1814).

The records of the crown side of the court

The documentation for the crown side of King's Bench is vast, and a full account of the cases heard from any given county for any length of time involves collation of very scattered references in many different series, none of them indexed by county.[100] Some series give information that is redundant, in that it is also found in another, but the clerks were not consistent. Not all the main documentary series have been exhaustively used for the cases presented in this volume. Some details of process were repeated in different series; for details of process in each type of case, and brief explanations, see the introductions to Sections A to H, and the Glossary. What follows here is an overview of some of the

---

[99]   For example, interlineated manuscript additions to pages 35 and 36 appear word for word in Gude, i, 222–23. See also the introduction to Section E. It is clear that Hands was in error on central matters. The first page of ch.VI, dealing with the removal of indictments by certiorari, completely garbles the distinction between rights of prosecutors and defendants to the writ; the correct statement of the law is given in the manuscript corrections. See the introduction to Section F.

[100] An important loss brought to my attention by David Crook appears to be the brevia regis files (KB 37), which do not survive after 1692: see the introduction to the series list. The description of series given below should be supplemented by the detailed descriptions prepared by Dr Crook as introductory notes to the various series, in the on-line TNA Catalogue, and (sometimes with more detail) in the hard-copy catalogue at Kew.

main series, and a list of those used in preparing this volume. After 4 Geo II, c.26 (1731) proceedings were recorded in English, and in an ordinary, rather than court, hand, and abbreviations disappear. The names only of the original Latin writs continued to be used.

The original informations and writs of certiorari are to be found in KB 11: out-counties indictments files. Here are found the original informations qui tam, informations exhibited by the master of the crown office at the suit of a private prosecutor, and informations ex officio by the attorney general. Here too are the returned writs of certiorari; most have pinned to them the original indictments, records of conviction, or records of orders of the lower courts to which the writs were addressed and from which the returns came, and the 'schedules' from the returning officials. The cases are sequentially numbered on the file. There is a contemporary index to KB 11, the 'pye books', extant from 1766 only (IND 1/6681, 6 George III to 25 George III; IND 1/6682, 25 George III to 48 George III). They are indexed alphabetically by the name of the accused in each case. Counties are not given, and hence they are useless for a regional study unless names are already known.

Usefully associated with the indictment rolls is the series KB 29, the controlment rolls, one for each year, beginning Michaelmas term. The master of the crown office used them to follow the progress of cases in which process issued. The rolls give short statements of the point reached in process, and have marginal references to give the locations in KB 11, by session, regnal year, and number of document in the file. Certain writs and stages of process had to be entered on these rolls, and marginal references are given to the crown rolls (KB 28).[101] The first part of a controlment roll, called the bag roll, enumerates informations, certioraris, and other proceedings under the initial process.[102] The

---

[101] Gude, i, 23; ii, 158; also KB 15/50 fol.5 for 'what things' were and were not to be controlled: to be controlled were appearances, pleas of not guilty, disclaimer, and acts of indemnity; special pleas; replications to pleas; rejoinders to replications; and some others. See also *Parliamentary Papers* 1818 (292) 'Report of the Commissioners for examining into the Duties, Salaries, and Emoluments, of the Officers, Clerks and Ministers, of the several Courts of Justice, in England, Wales, and Berwick-upon-Tweed' (5 January 1818; ordered by the House of Commons to be printed, 14 May 1818), 40 on duties of clerks with respect to 'controlling'. Some types of cases, such as proceedings on habeas corpus, are not noted on the rolls.

[102] Those for all out-counties are grouped together, as are those for London and Middlesex. In KB 29/410 Hil 24 Geo II they appear in that order; KB 29/461 Trin and Easter 42 Geo III begin with London and Middlesex. See also the introduction to series KB 29 in hardcopy at TNA.

process entries for certioraris on indictment (Section F) record the initial summons by writ of venire facias: 'Cause to come [*defendant's name*] to answer for [*offence*] whereof he is indicted'. Informations (Sections A, B, and C) conclude instead with the words 'whereof he is impeached'. However, initial process on a game information qui tam (Section D) was an attachment rather than a venire, and since the penalty was divided between the crown and the informer, the full form for a game information qui tam is (in case D.1) 'Attach ... to answer as well to our Lord the King as to Samuel Law for a certain trespass and contempt whereof he is impeached.'[103] The bag roll indicates certioraris on convictions (Section E) with the words, 'record of conviction'. Later stages of process for all cases appear in later sections of the roll.

The fact that a case appears in KB 29 or in KB 11 shows that it was actually moved into King's Bench on writ of certiorari, or that an information was in fact exhibited. But informations and certioraris were often moved for but not allowed by the court, or occasionally allowed but not exhibited or issued. Evidence of an attempt for an information will exist in the form of entries in the rule books, KB 21, if a motion was made (even unsuccessfully), but only for some certioraris, as judges' fiats for applications in vacations have not been preserved. But in some cases affidavits were filed as the preliminary to a motion that was never, in the end, made. The affidavits in KB 1 therefore contain much material about cases that went no further. On the other hand, other cases that resulted in process, and even a verdict, conviction, and punishment, have left few or no affidavits either because they were not preserved (this seems to be true of qui tams) or because they were unnecessary. Thus the attorney general exhibited ex officio informations without filing any affidavits with the court (see Section C); in the case of certioraris, only affidavits on the application for the writ by defendants, and then only in term time, or in mitigation or other later parts of process such as attachments for contempt, were necessary (see above, and the introductions to Sections E, F). The very voluminous affidavits series is therefore a rich but very incomplete description of cases before the court.

The affidavits are packaged by term, in more than one part in terms with large numbers of affidavits; as noted above, affidavits taken in vacation before the start of a term usually are filed with the affidavits of

---

[103] Or, as in D.20, reflecting the terms of the statute, 'Attach ... to answer as well to the poor of the parish as to one William Tinling who etc ... for the like offences whereof they are impeached.' Given as 'attached' in this volume.

the preceding term.[104] A series of contemporary indices exists (KB 39/3–10, formerly IND 1/6690–7) but there is a gap from 1756 to 1759 inclusive. Moreover, this index series is incomplete throughout. The contemporary title of KB 39/4 is 'Affidavits copied from Trin 27 Geo 2 1753 – Hil 28 Geo 2 1755'. The phrasing suggests that the book was in fact kept by the clerks as a record of their earnings in issuing office copies of affidavits on file. Thus many affidavits found by a complete examination of KB 1 for the period of this study are not listed in KB 39, and some affidavits are noted there more than once.[105]

The rule books, KB 21, record the motions of counsel for rules, side bar rules, the respiting and continuation of recognizances, and the decisions of the court. They also give the 'general rules of court' promulgated from time to time by the judges (and collected, as noted above, by Gude). Associated with the rule books are the draft rule books, KB 36, which are small parchment-bound paper books, one per term. For the most part these give, in draft form, the orders more formally inscribed in KB 21, but sometimes they are more complete, perhaps because the clerks were not assiduous in copying every stage of process into the rule books.[106] In some years the draft rule books also give the numbers of the filed affidavits associated with a case and/or the number of entries made by the clerks, and the sums owed them for doing so.

Probably the largest volume of records is comprised in the crown rolls, KB 28. Confronted with their bulk one wonders how any parchment manufacturer, even the unimpressive father of Dr Johnson, could have failed in the trade. (KB 11, KB 16, KB 20, and KB 29 are also on parchment.) The contemporary guide to the crown rolls, the great docket books (IND 1/6659 to 1/6664) give pleas, imparlances, judgments, verdicts, outlawries, excommunications, affirmations or dismissions of convictions, and other information about the outcome of cases. Without a much fuller examination than has been possible for this book, it is difficult to tell how complete and consistent either rolls or docket books are. In some cases it is clear that the clerks have given very abbreviated forms of informations on the rolls (e.g. case C.13), and my impression is that in many cases the later stages were not copied there.

---

[104] After most of the affidavits had been photocopied and calendared for this book, the KB1 series was reboxed and hence renumbered. The National Archives guide to the series contains a conversion table, and references are easily found by terms and years. All KB1 references in this volume have been converted to the new numbering.

[105] For example there are three entries in KB 39/4 for affidavits [1] and [2] of case A.10, probably 'office copies' required by clerks or counsel.

[106] The discharge of the rule in case A.8 is an example.

Figure 6   **Westminster Hall, c.1809**
J. Bluck after Pugin and Rowlandson, *Westminster Hall*, c.1809.

The controlment rolls (KB 29, already mentioned) give, in the later sections of each roll, roll numbers in KB 28 for informations and certioraris, allowing process recorded there to be located. The principal writs and details of process (venire, capias, etc) are usually recorded also in KB 29.[107] The first section of a KB 29 roll (called the bag roll) gives the number and term of the filed information or writ in KB 11. Finally, the KB 28 entries of process give the same number for KB 11, allowing process to be tied to particular informations or certioraris.

The appearance books (KB 15/2–5) record the imparlances and pleas of defendants.[108] The notice of trial books (KB 15/14–17) record the motions of counsel for the case to go to trial at the next assizes in the county in which the case arose.

The series of posteas (KB 20/1–8, large formal records of the case, endorsed with the verdict and with the jury panel attached) appears to be a deposit of only a proportion of those returned from assizes. The postea books (ASSI 4/4–8) kept by the clerk of assize record many Staffordshire cases returned to Westminster after a verdict (although those for 1736 to 1763 and summer 1777 to summer 1779 do not survive). In each case there is a record of the names of counsel and the signatures of the solicitors who in each case 'received this postea.' The reason that no posteas have been found in KB 20 for Staffordshire appears to be that they were usually collected by the solicitors for further use by the clerks in court; the clerk of assize or clerk of the rules presumably filed only those not so collected.[109]

Cases stayed by a nolle prosequi granted by the attorney general to either prosecutor or defendant, which ended the prosecution, may now be impossible to identify. Nolle prosequi fiats survive in KB 35, but only

---

[107] But see note 101 above for 'what is to be controlled'. Returned writs are found in KB 16. See case F.10 for an example in outlawry.

[108] Also in the Great Docket Books (IND 1/6658ff). The application for leave to imparl, 'prays a day to answer', is recorded in KB 29.

[109] 'The solicitor for the prosecutor must apply to the Associate [if a Middlesex case] or Clerk of Assize [for Staffordshire or other 'out-counties'] for the postea, and deliver it to the Clerk in Court, and the Clerk of the Rules will enter a rule for judgment as of the first day of the Term, which rule expires on the fifth day, when judgment may be signed.' Gude, i, 102, 152, 305. No Staffordshire posteas were found in KB 20 for the terms Trin 1749 to Trin 1782, Mich 1787 to Mich 1795, Mich 1798 to Mich 1802. For evidence that the solicitors collected them see the notes to case F.12. See also p. xiv.

for the years 1802–1840, and 1887–1906.[110] In one of the cases presented here (A.6) we know from another source that a stay was entered. A summary of rules used by the clerks gives the form of a petition for a nolle prosequi, and of an entry of cesset processus, the entry made on the record.[111] A stay did not preclude a future prosecution.

Returned writs are found in KB 16, a voluminous series filed in no consistent order. The questions and answers in interrogatories (such as on attachments for contempt as in case H.1) are filed, following a rule of court made in 1704, and are now found in KB 32.[112]

SOURCES USED

The following series were completely checked through the entire period for references to Staffordshire cases: KB 1 (out-county affidavits[113]), KB 15 (appearance books and notice of trial books), KB 21 (rule or order books), KB 29 (controlment rolls), KB 32 (interrogatories), KB 39 (indexes to affidavits), ASSI 4 (postea books), and the great docket books (IND 1/6659–6664) to the crown rolls (KB 28). References to all cases found were then used to find the relevant certioraris and informations in KB 11 (out-county indictments), and writs of habeas corpus and other returned writs in KB 16. Many years of KB 11, KB16 (1747–1764, 1770–1791), KB 20 (1749–1782, 1787–1802), and KB 32 were examined completely to gauge the coverage of the indexes and references in the rolls; similar although more limited soundings were made in the voluminous but often very incomplete entries in the crown rolls (KB 28) and in the rough minute books (KB 36), which were consulted when expected process or outcomes of cases were not found in the other series.

---

[110] TNA, catalogue description of KB 35. The fiats were among the records proposed for destruction in 1907: *Reprint of Statutes, Rules and Schedules Governing the Disposal of Public Records by Destruction or Otherwise 1877–1913* (London: HMSO, 1914), 109. Entries of some stays appear on the controlment rolls, e.g. KB 29/457 Trin 38 Geo III, for the inhabitants of Burton extra, but none have been found for the cases in this volume, in any of the series examined.

[111] KB 15/65; the volume also contains an account of the law of pardons.

[112] Gude, ii, 353.

[113] Some Staffordshire affadavits respecting habeas corpus may have been missed: see above, note 52.

Section A

CRIMINAL INFORMATIONS AGAINST PERSONS OTHER THAN MAGISTRATES

Ordinary criminal informations were abolished by the *Administration of Justice (Miscellaneous Provisions) Act* of 1938.[1] For over two centuries before that date they were exhibited in the name of the master of the crown office (the coroner and king's attorney) at the request of private persons, after the judges granted a rule. They were the equivalent of an indictment, but without the need to be found by a grand jury. They could be used to prosecute only misdemeanour, not felony or treason. In the eighteenth and nineteenth centuries criminal informations were a highly visible part of the criminal law, occupying much of the time of King's Bench and often widely reported in the press, although relatively few in number.[2] Informations often came before the court in earlier centuries, but after 1692 an information could be exhibited only by order of the court, and after the prosecutor had entered into a recognizance.[3] What misdemeanours could be so prosecuted therefore depended on the decisions of the judges. In the eighteenth century a wide variety of misdemeanours aroused their sympathy, and their decisions, which could make law, enlarged and contracted the scope of offences for which they would grant a rule. The offence, however, usually had to be a grave one.[4] In applying for an information, the weight given the evidence of the parties, as set out in their affidavits, was crucial. Not least was the requirement that to be successful a prosecutor had to come with clean hands: the principle, originating in equity, that there could be no taint of fraud in the request for an information. Any failure to meet these standards led to the court telling a complainant to

---

[1]   1 & 2 Geo VI, c.63 (1938), s.12; J. Ll. J. Edwards, *The Law Officers of the Crown* (London, 1964), 266. The act preserved informations ex officio (see Section C).

[2]   Those initated in London, or against magistrates (see Section B), were most likely to be reported.

[3]   The act applied only to informations exhibited in the name of the master of the crown office: that is, ex officio and qui tam informations were unaffected. The act also provided that the demise of the monarch no longer required a defendant to plead afresh. 4 & 5 Wm & Mary, c.18 (1692) ss.2, 5, 6.

[4]   See Hay, *The Judges and the People* (in preparation) for an account of the case law, origins, and political and social significance of criminal informations, including discussion of some of the cases calendared in this section.

prosecute 'in the ordinary way', that is, on indictment at assizes or quarter sessions.

From the affidavits filed by prosecutors to support their applications we can sometimes infer the reasons for the response of the judges, or for a settlement. No rules were granted in five cases, perhaps because the prosecutor did not proceed after a settlement, the evidence was thin, or the offence deemed not serious enough: a criminal libel circulated only locally, three assaults, and an attempted rape. Rules nisi were granted in 19 cases, but in only seven of those in which the prosecution continued did the judges see fit to make a rule absolute. They were an assault and affray instigated by a clergyman, a mob attack on a man and his family in his house, a brutal assault by a gamekeeper on a man standing in his own field, a libel in the *Gentleman's Magazine*, a conspiracy by parish officers to force a pregnant pauper to marry a poor man with a settlement in another parish, electoral corruption in Tamworth, and repeated and highly public libels of one justice of the peace by another. In only four of those cases was an information actually exhibited. Three cases in this section generated more and lengthier affidavits than the others: A.8, for assaults and abuse of the law toward a whig gentleman by the Jacobite corporation of Lichfield (30 affidavits); A.10, an accusation of conspiracy against Sir William Wolseley for forcing marriage on Ann the wife of the Stafford MP, John Robins (22 affidavits); and A.16, the Tamworth election case (90 affidavits).

Obtaining a rule for an information
Very few Staffordshire attempts to prosecute on a criminal information proceeded very far, in part because of the reluctance of the judges to grant a rule nisi or a rule absolute, in part because the complexity and expense of the procedure encouraged negotiated outcomes. Possibly none of the 24 attempted prosecutions came to trial; most were abandoned or settled as costs mounted, as is the case with modern litigation. Sometimes the fact of a settlement is recorded in other sources (see case A.6).

When the defendant was a private individual, there was no need to give notice that the court would be asked for an information.[5] The prosecutor's attorney prepared the whole case in prosecution affidavits (found in KB 1 for all cases in this section; for **A.1, A.7, A.18, A.19** they are the only evidence of an attempt at prosecution). (The case numbers in bold show the latest stage reached by each case.) Supplementary affidavits were not allowed without leave of the court. The attorney also

---

[5]   See Section B, 'Criminal Informations against Magistrates', below, for the different procedure required in such cases.

prepared a brief[6] for counsel, who made a motion for a rule nisi (19 are recorded for these 24 cases in the order books, KB 21), which was a rule for the defendant to show cause why an information should not be granted.[7] Only counsel (barristers) were allowed to make motions for criminal informations, as Henry Hunt discovered when he tried to move for an information against the magistrates of Manchester after Peterloo.[8] If the motion was successful (for **A.9, A.17, A.21, A.22, A.23** this is the last stage reached), a copy of the rule nisi, drawn up by the clerk of the rules in the crown office, was served on the defendant by the prosecutor's solicitor. On an affidavit of service (now found in KB 1), the solicitor then redelivered the briefs to counsel to move the court to make the rule absolute (KB 21).

The defendant might or might not show cause against the rule. Hands remarks in 1803 that formerly it was common for the defendant to allow the rule to be made absolute, rather than expose his defence before trial, but that by the time he wrote it had become more usual for the defendant to prepare defence affidavits (KB 1) to show cause against the rule.[9] They did not have to be filed before the motion for a rule absolute was made, unless the defendant decided to ask for an enlarged rule nisi on grounds that she or he had insufficient time to prepare. A motion for an enlarged rule nisi, made either on affidavit or by counsel (KB 21) was obtained by the defendant in 12 cases, in one case over five terms, and for three cases (**A.3, A.8, A.14**) this was the final stage reached. If granted by the court, the enlarged rule bound the defence to file the affidavits before the day of showing cause (usually a week before). This allowed the prosecutor's solicitor to obtain copies of them from the clerk of the rules.[10] In all, defence affidavits were filed in

---

[6]   Briefs are not filed with the court records, but sometimes found in government or attorneys' papers. Instructions to named counsel for motions frequently appear endorsed, with the fee and name of the attorney, on affidavits.

[7]   The following account, unless otherwise indicated, is from Hands, 3ff, and Gude, i, 116ff. References to the full form of rules, writs, and other formal entries in the records of the court are given in the Glossary. References to manuscript additions to Hands are to the interlineations in the crown office copy I own, described in the General Introduction at note 98.

[8]   Gude, i, 113. In legal practice (and sources like Hands and Gude) it was increasingly common to refer to attorneys as solicitors, a term which properly applied only to those who attended the court of Chancery. Both terms are used in this book without distinction.

[9]   Hands, 4.

[10]   Gude, i, 117.

10 of the 24 cases, either immediately or on an enlarged rule. Once a rule absolute had been granted, the defendant had to 'appear' (although not in person), and plead, within four days of the filing of the information. If he did not, the prosecutor had judgment by default. A prosecutor's solicitor too could move for an enlarged rule, as a matter of course, if he could not, or did not, serve notice of the rule in the original time.

Rules absolute and rules discharged

The court, on hearing counsel (defendant's counsel spoke first, although none of the court records preserved such arguments) either discharged the rule nisi if the defendant showed sufficient cause (seven cases, **A.3, A.4, A.8, A.10, A.12, A.16, A.20**)[11] or made it absolute (seven cases).[12] The court might advise an unsuccessful complainant to proceed in civil litigation, or 'in the ordinary way', that is, on indictment. If the court made the rule absolute, the case might end there nonetheless, probably either because of a private settlement or because of expense (**A.5, A.13, A.24**). To continue the prosecution required other preliminaries. In the late seventeenth century concerns that criminal informations were being used for malicious prosecutions prompted some statutory changes in the procedure, requiring a £20 recognizance on the part of the prosecutor, and providing that the judges could award costs to the defendant if the prosecutor did not proceed within a year, or the defendant got a verdict, unless the judges certified that the prosecution had reasonable cause. If costs awarded to a defendant were not paid, the defendant benefited from the recognizance.[13] The recognizance was prepared by the prosecutor's clerk in court, acknowledged before the master of the crown office or a magistrate in the county where the cause arose, and was put on the file of 'bails in court' by the master, who also entered it upon record.[14] The prosecutor's solicitor then settled the wording of the information, usually with the advice of counsel,[15]and delivered it to the clerk in court, to be engrossed

[11] In A.16, comprising several related prosecutions and counter-prosecutions, some rules were discharged, some made absolute.

[12] On costs, see below.

[13] 4 & 5 Wm & Mary, c.18 (1692) s.2; Blackstone, iv, 311. The act also reformed some aspects of outlawry (see the introduction to Section F). For the form of the recognizance see Gude, ii, 626 no.2.

[14] The filed recognizances for 1743 to 1791, and probably other years, appear to have been destroyed: *Reprint of Statutes, Rules and Schedules Governing the Disposal of Public Records by Destruction or Otherwise* (London, 1914), 108.

[15] Exactitude in wording was necessary, as with indictments, to prevent an acquittal at nisi prius, or a later motion in arrest of judgment: Hands, 8.

accurately on parchment, and signed by the master on payment of a fee (8*s* 8*d* in Gude's time). The information was filed (KB 11).

Process could not issue until both recognizance and information were filed. Only four cases (A.2, A.6, A.15, A.16) of the 24 in this section resulted in an information being exhibited: in the others, the prosecutor did not proceed because of a settlement not found in the court records, or because of expense or the unlikeliness of winning, or because the judges refused to grant a rule absolute, or (perhaps A.24) because the defendant died.

An ordinary criminal information in KB 11 can be distinguished from an ex officio information or qui tam information, which it superficially resembles, by the words with which it commences: 'Be it remembered, that [*name of master of the crown office*], coroner and attorney of our sovereign lord the now king, in the court of our said lord the king, before the king himself, who for our said lord the king in this behalf prosecutes, in his own proper person comes here into the court ... and ... gives the court here to understand and be informed ...'[16] It is signed by the master of the crown office, at the foot; there is no endorsement. The act of exibiting an information (presenting it to the court) was the equivalent of a bill of indictment being found a true bill. The date given in the information is the first day of term, regardless of when the judges made the rule absolute to grant it.[17]

Costs on discharge of a rule

If the rule nisi was discharged, rather than made absolute, the court decided whether, and in favour of which party, to order costs.[18] If the judges thought the prosecution frivolous, vexatious, or based on misrepresentation, the rule was discharged with costs (KB 21) in favour of the defendant (A.10, A.12, A.20). The defendant's solicitor then obtained a copy of the rule from the clerk of the rules and made an appointment with the master to tax the costs (**A.10, A.12**).[19] The solicitors and their clerks in court attended the taxation. Payment of costs was enforced, if necessary, by an attachment for contempt (KB 16 and

---

[16] Hands, 132.

[17] Thus in A.16, the information is dated 22 May 1761, the first day of Trinity term, although the rule absolute was made 3 June.

[18] Gude, i, 115. In the eyes of the court, the prosecutors of an information against a magistrate or a private person (that it, presumably, other than qui tam and ex officio informations), were the 'persons who make the affidavits upon which the rule nisi was granted': interlineation in my crown office copy of Hands, 7.

[19] In case A.20 costs were settled.

KB 21 for the writ and the rule; KB 32 for interrogatories and answers on an attachment.)[20] Costs were also awarded against a prosecutor who had given notice of trial, but then neither proceeded to trial nor countermanded notice (A.2).

Process on an information
If the court made the rule absolute, and an information was exhibited, process on an information began with a subpoena to the defendant, who had four court days from the return[21] (exclusive of Sundays) within which to appear to it (although appearance in person was not required). If the defendant was not in custody, there was the right to imparl: the procedure was for the defendant to 'pray a day to answer', which meant to defer pleading until the next term for out-county cases, or anytime within the present term for Middlesex cases (Appearance books, KB 15/2 to 6, great docket books IND 1/6659 to 6664)(**A.11**).[22] In four cases the defendant was given leave to imparl, and/or did so. However, the defendant might already be under terms to appear as a result of an enlarged rule nisi (above). If the defendant was already in custody, the prosecutor obtained a writ of habeas corpus to bring the defendant into court, to be asked how he or she would plead. If the defendant asked for and was granted time, and remanded to the King's Bench prison, a side bar rule for the marshal to bring the defendant into

---

[20] See case H.2.

[21] For return days, see Editorial Notes.

[22] Sir John Comyns, *A Digest of the Laws of England* (4th ed., 6 vols., 1800), iv, 403; but if on a capias or attachment, the defendant had to plead *instanter*. 'Imparlance is taken for a petition in Court of a Day [i.e., a term] to consider or advise what answer the Defendant shall make to the Action of the Plaintiff; being a continuance of the Cause 'till another Day, or a longer Time given by the Court.' (Jacob, i, 402. See also Chitty, i, 867–8.) Imparlance was abolished, except in cases of informations quo warranto or for non-repair of bridge or highways, by 60 Geo III & 1 Geo IV, c.4 (1819). The Latin form for leave to imparl was *licentia loquendi*, abbreviated by the clerks to *li lo*. The petition is entered on the rolls as 'prays a day to answer.' Rules of court of Mich 1654 provided that for cases other than those in London and Middlesex, on appearances before *crastinum Martini* (12 Nov) or *mensum Paschae* (a month or *quindena* of Easter), there could be 'no imparlance without consent or special rule; but if upon or after those returns, an imparlance of course.' Gude, i, 320, 354 (citing a rule of Ea 1706). Imparlances or leaves to imparl in Section A are recorded only for cases A.2, A.6, A.11 and A.16. They are much more common in other proceedings (see for example Section F).

court (KB 21) was followed by a motion to compel her or him to plead.[23] When the defendant was in custody and under terms to appear (above), the prosecutor could enter an appearance for the defendant, in order to be able to file rules to plead (see below) immediately, enabling the prosecutor to force a trial at the ensuing assizes, rather than have to wait another term.[24]

The defendant's clerk in court usually entered an appearance in the crown rolls and great docket books (KB 28 and IND 1/6658 to 6664 for this period), delivering to the solicitor a copy of the information. If the defendant failed to enter an appearance, the prosecutor's solicitor, on filing an affidavit of the service of the subpoena (KB 1), could get an attachment against the defendant for non-appearance. To be discharged from custody the defendant then had to enter an appearance, on which his or her clerk in court could issue a supersedeas.[25]

If the defendant had not pleaded, the prosecutor's clerk entered two successive four-day rules to plead, and on their expiry the prosecutor's solicitor moved for a peremptory rule to plead (all recorded in KB 21), which was drawn up and served by the prosecutor's clerk on the defendant's clerk, who gave notice of it to the solicitor. In London and Middlesex the cumulative time of the three rules to plead was 12 days, but 18 for the out-counties.[26] The full sequence occurred in only one case in this section (A.2; see also **A.6**). Within that time the defendant's clerk usually entered the plea (recorded in the appearance book KB 15/2 to 5, the crown rolls KB 28, the great docket books IND 1/6659 to 6664, and the controlment rolls KB 29), for if no plea was entered, the defendant suffered judgment by default. In only two cases in this section is a plea recorded (A.15, A.16). In some cases, however, a defendant with little hope might deliberately default, both to save the expense of a trial and to be able later to argue, on the motion for judgment (below), extenuating circumstances.[27]

---

[23]   Gude, i, 121, 143–4.

[24]   Gude, i, 121.

[25]   Gude, i, 121.

[26]   Gude, i, 87 note a. Ruth Paley suggests that this difference may account for the separate record series for out-county cases and London and Middlesex cases. A greater proportion of cases on ex officio informations and on certiorari reached trial, and hence saw the full sequence of rules to plead: see Sections C, F.

[27]   Hands, 9. A manuscript addition in my copy adds, 'And when a defendant proposes to suffer judgment by default, a judge on summons will stay execution until the next term.'

The prosecutor's clerk gave notice of trial (notice of trial books, KB 15/14 to 17), that the case would be heard at the next assizes in the county (**A.16**), and both clerks made copies for the solicitors. Notice of trial had to be given again if the case continued from one term to another.[28] One of the parties at this point usually requested a special jury (KB 21), and the clerk of the rules gave such a rule without any motion in court: in this section there was one by the defence (A.2) and one by the prosecution (A.16).[29] The solicitors and clerks in court, and the sheriff's agent, then met with the master's clerk at an 'appointment to nominate', who extracted forty-eight names from the sheriff's list of eligible special jurors. At a second meeting (the 'appointment to reduce')[30] the solicitors and clerks in court for each party reduced the list to twenty-four by striking out twelve each alternately, and the sheriff summoned the remaining twenty-four, from whom were chosen the twelve sworn on the jury.[31]

The prosecutor's clerk in court prepared the record, the jury process, and subpoenas for witnesses, and the solicitor entered the cause for trial, subpoened the witnesses, prepared the brief for counsel, and attended the trial. If the defendant had called for the special jury, his clerk in court could prepare the process for it.[32] If the prosecutor did not proceed to trial, the defendant could get costs, unless given sufficient warning, or other cause shown (**A.2**).[33] The prosecution might countermand notice of trial (**A.15**), perhaps because a settlement had been reached; proceedings in cases might also cease with the death of a defendant or prosecutor, unpaid fees, or other reasons.

---

[28] Gude, i, 98, citing practice on trials on indictments. See case A.2, where notice of trial is given three times.

[29] Hands, 9.

[30] Gude, i, 99.

[31] On this form of the special jury, and such juries in general, see the General Introduction. Before 1825 there is no mention of the special jury as such in the record. The procedure of striking a special jury was changed by the Jury Act of that year, 6 Geo IV, c.50. See Chitty, i, 522 and Gude, ii, 654.

[32] Manuscript addition, my copy of Hands, 11. The venire facias juratores for an ordinary jury was also entered in all cases on the controlment roll, KB 29. The writs themselves appear to have been destroyed: *Reprint of Statutes, Rules and Schedules*, 109. For an instance of an error in summoning a special jury see case A.2.

[33] Gude, i, 321 (rule of Mich 1654) and i, 376 (rule of Ea 1790, that in country cases short notice of trial must be at least four days before commission day). See case A.2.

Trial

By this stage, 23 of the 24 cases in this section had come to an end. The only case that might have gone on to trial was a prosecution against Thomas Hinckes, one of the defendants in A.16, a case that when it began involved prosecutions against a great many defendants. This was an information for attempting to corrupt a Tamworth voter in the parliamentary elections of 1761, one of a mass of accusations and counter-accusations, detailed in 90 affidavits, in which no expense was spared. It appears however that not even this case resulted in a trial.[34]

Since the ensuing steps of process are common to proceedings in other sections of this volume (B, C, D, F), some of which did go to trial and verdict and sentence, they are set out below.

Cases that went to trial did so before an assize judge on circuit in the county in which the case had arisen, on the nisi prius (civil) side of assizes.[35] The verdict was therefore given by a jury of the county (in this case Staffordshire), but that verdict had to be returned into King's Bench, and judgment and sentence pronounced there. For accounts of the trial itself we are dependent on newspaper or other non-legal sources, but the verdict, sentence, and any further proceedings appear in the court records.

Conviction

On a conviction, the prosecutor's clerk in court by affidavit could seek bail for the defendant's appearance for sentencing, or to increase the amount of an existing recognizance.[36] The prosecutor's solicitor obtained a rule for judgment (KB 21) from the clerk in court, and entered the conviction (Crown rolls KB 28, great docket books IND 1/6659 to 6664). But until the rule for judgment expired (they were rules nisi until the fifth day of term), the defendant's counsel could make a motion for a new trial, and if the court thought there were grounds, they granted a rule nisi for a new trial (KB 21), ultimately made absolute or discharged. The defendant's counsel might also make a motion in arrest of judgment (KB 21), at any time before sentence was pronounced, on which the court would make a rule nisi. The defendant had to be personally present for either motion. If in King's Bench prison, the

---

[34] No record of a verdict has been found in either KB 28 or KB 29; unfortunately the postea book (ASSI 4) for 1736 to 1763 has not survived.

[35] See the affidavits in case A.2 for some of the expenses, and complications, that might ensue.

[36] Gude, i, 101–2.

defendant was brought up by a rule; if in another prison, by habeas corpus.[37]

On a conviction where neither a new trial nor arrest of judgment were obtained, or in cases where the defendant suffered judgment by default, the prosecutor's solicitor gave the defendant's clerk in court and solicitor notice of motion for the judgment of the court (KB 21); the defendant's solicitor also could give the notice. On the motion, affidavits in aggravation or mitigation, on the prosecutor's and defendant's behalf respectively, could be brought before the court. Hands comments that 'the judgment of the court commonly depends much on the contents of these affidavits, and they are therefore of such material consequence to both prosecutor and defendant, that it is prudent to have the best assistance which can be procured in preparing them previous to their production to the court.'[38] On a conviction the affidavits of the defendant were read first, followed by those for the prosecution; defendant's counsel was heard next, and finally counsel for the prosecution. After a judgment by default, the order of readings and argument was the opposite, with those for the defendant heard last. When no affidavits in aggravation or mitigation were produced, counsel for the prosecution was heard last.

On the passing of sentence, the defendant usually had to be personally present.[39] If the court decided to take time to consider the sentence, the defendant (if imprisoned) was ordered to stand committed to a future day, unless the prosecutor consented to his or her remaining out on bail.[40] Judgments were entered on the controlment rolls (KB 29) by the master of the crown office.[41]

However, the court might recommend the defendant to avoid judgment by a reference of the matter to the master of the crown office (KB 21). An appointment with the solicitors ensued, at which the master

---

[37] An instance of such an habeas corpus under an ex officio information is case C.6. If the motion was made afterwards, it was discretionary in the court whether to grant the rule or not. There was a prescribed sequence to the two motions. Hands, 12–13, 15.

[38] Hands, 14, who also describes the sequence in which the affidavits were read, and in which counsel presented their arguments.

[39] Manuscript addition in my copy of Hands, 15: 'unless his personal appearance has been dispensed with by rule of court.'

[40] For an example, see *Waddington's Case*: Douglas Hay, 'The State and the Market: Lord Kenyon and Mr Waddington', *Past & Present*, no. 162 (Feb 1999), 148.

[41] Gude, i, 23.

considered the affidavits in aggravation and mitigation, and then gave his opinion on the proper course to be taken by the parties. The defendant usually complied, according to Hands, to escape sentence by the court.[42] (The same procedure, albeit less formally, existed at quarter sessions and assizes in misdemeanour cases, where the defendant 'spoke with' the prosecutor, and pleaded guilty, with a nominal sentence, in order to compose the difference for a consideration.) The master frequently directed the defendant to pay the costs, and make an apology or other compensation. In case of costs, the master taxed them at a subsequent appointment.

If the court did not recommend a reference, but instead passed sentence in the form of a fine, the prosecutor was entitled to a third of it towards his or her costs. To do so entailed taxation by the master, and a certificate from him; then a fiat from two of the judges. If the costs were larger than a third of the fine, the crown sometimes allowed more of the fine.[43]

No conviction
On an acquittal at trial, or in cases in which the prosecutor did not proceed to trial within a year, or entered a nolle prosequi, the court awarded the defendant costs, with one exception. If an acquittal was followed by the trial judge certifying on the record that there was reasonable cause for exhibiting the information, the prosecutor was not liable. However, a prosecutor was not in fact liable to the full amount of costs in many cases. If she or he did not pay, the defendant was entitled to the £20 of the recognizance, or the prosecutor could be discharged the recognizance for the same sum. But the costs might amount to much more than that. The consequence, as Hands pointed out, was that the defendant was then out of pocket for all the remainder of the costs owed that exceeded £20.[44]

---

[42] Hands, 16. None of the cases in this section ended this way, but see case F.11, after confession by defendants to an indictment removed on certiorari.
[43] Hands, 17.
[44] Hands, 18. See also John Hullock, *Law of Costs* (London, 1792), 575–6.

CASES

A.1 Information applied for (19 May 1742)

Defendant: Joseph Simpson, son of Stephen Simpson, attorney of Lichfield.

Accusation:
Libel in accusing Theophilus Levett of Lichfield of corrupt practices in Lichfield elections.

Rules and process:
[*None found*.]

Affidavit for prosecution:

Ea 15 Geo II 1742

[1] Affdt of John Heath gentleman of Leek sworn before W. Wills at Leek 19 May 1742.[45] ITKB [*Verso*]: 'Staffords. Afft of Heath for Infn agt Joseph Simpson'.
    That the deponent was in Lichfield 14 Sept 1741 at Slaughter's, the sign of the Three Crowns. He was conversing with Joseph Simpson, the son of Stephen Simpson attorney of Lichfield, when the deponent mentioned the name of Theophilus Levett, another attorney of Lichfield. Simpson recounted some differences between Levett and his father and gave to the deponent a printed paper relating to Levett's management of the elections for the city of Lichfield [*annexed*], and asked him to read it and tell his thoughts about it. The next morning the deponent gave Swinfen Jervis, another attorney and intimate acquaintance of Levett, the paper to read, telling Jervis what had passed between Simpson and himself. Jervis asked Heath to get a few more copies of the paper and the deponent did get a few more copies from Simpson the same day.

[*Printed broadsheet annexed*]:

[*Verso*]: 'To Mr Theo Levett in Lichfield.' [*Postmarked STONE*.]
[*Another hand*]: 'Had this from Mr Heath. S.J.'

---

[45] Wills describes himself as 'a Master Extraordinary of the High Court of Chancery'; these words are struck out, and replaced by 'a Commissioner appointed to take affidts in the said Court [*i.e., King's Bench*] and County.'

[*page 1*]

'Copy of Mr Levett's account of money received and paid by him in the management of elections; and a challenge to all mankind to disprove him: given under his own hand the 19th of May, 1741: in order to clear himself of some imputations of self-interest laid to his charge.

'Dec. 6 1735 Sir Rowland Hill's agent (Mr Everett) settled accounts with Theophilus Levett; and after all the election bills were discharged, there remained in the hands of

Theophilus Levett	£37 13s 10d
Out of which Theo. Levett paid to Mr Everett, and by his order, before he left town	16 16 00
Feb. 25 1736 Paid Mr Smallwood upon account of the clock and chimes	15 15 00
Sept. 15 1737 Paid Mr Everett upon account	10 10 00
Afterwards I paid to the churchwardens of St Mary, to make up the fifteen guineas paid Mr Smallwood, £50 for a clock and chimes	34 05 00
	77 06 00
Deduct the money received as above	37 13 10
Sir Rowland would remain debtor	39 12 02

'But Sir Rowland hath paid rent to some of the Walsh [*sic*] and Shropshire gentlemen, who purchased votes here; and I have received their rents here; which are unaccounted, but upon the whole I am some small matter in Sir Rowland's debt.

'This is the state of the account between Sir Rowland and me since the last election: And I never received one penny from him, or by his order, or from any other person whatsoever; to support an interest in Lichfield: Save only that Sir Lister Holt left a small sum in my hands, when he was last in town, to pay his bills and give to the poor. This is fact, and I challenge my enemies and all mankind to disprove me.

Lichfield, May 19, 1741.

Theo. Levett'

[*page 2*]

'An impartial account of Mr L-v-tt's conduct in the management of elections for the city of Lichfield, with regard to his private interest; occasioned by his challenge in writing, published the 19th of May, 1741.

'In the year 1727, when Mr L-v-tt professed himself strongly in the country-interest; he not only sacrificed his own principles, but drew in his well-meaning brethren of the corpor—n to suffer their honour to be tainted in the choice of two representatives, one of whom was a place-man or pensioner; in order to gain himself the lucrative post of town-clerk of the city: in which he hath acquitted himself so well, that whilst he had the pleasure of governing others; they were so wise as to think they governed him.

'At the same memorable time, he compounded for the city, and made a venal bargain with the Rep—t—ves for £800 one half whereof was paid to St Mary's parish, the other half he hath kept to himself ever since; without so much as paying the interest of it (which amounts to £280) to the two other parishes, for whose benefit the same was intended: And to skreen [*sic*] such practice from censure, he gives out, that the sole disposal of the last £400 was lodged in the C—p—n; and that he had made a purchase with the money in their names, (though they knew nothing of it) and had put out some apprentices; but when or where is not yet discovered.

'*Note*, It is now given out, that Mr L-v-tt is making up an account how some part of the interest-money hath been applied; and that since his conduct is disliked by the town, he will transfer this trust to his friend in the north and two other of his creatures, if they will lay out the money in support of his workhouse at Greenhill.

'The practice of buying of houses and lands, and selling them again to make votes to the C-nd-tes and their friends against Mr V-rn-n's first election, and his second election in conjunction with Sir R-l-d H-ll at extravagant rates, is another way of Mr L-v-tt's amassing great heaps of wealth to his own private use; he having by common consent of the city the sole privilege of monopolizing this trade to himself, in regard it was his own scheme, and which he managed with so much art and dexterity, that the gentlemen who purchased of him, thought it absolutely necessary so to do, to support an interest, which at the same time met with no opposition from any quarter.

'By Mr L-v-tt's own declaration, it appears that he is the receiver of rents for the Walsh and Shropshire gentlemen, who purchased such votes of him, and that such rents are unaccounted for by him; from which small fund some profit must certainly arise in a course of years, or he will discover that he does not know the use of money so well as the world imagines.

'Sir R-l-d H-ll and Mr V-rn-n gave £100 towards buying a clock and chimes for St Mary's church, £50 whereof only appears to be brought to account by Mr L-v-tt. Quere, What is become of the other £50.

'Mr L-v-tt mentions an account that he had made up with Sir R-d H-ll's agent: Why does he not produce the account, instead of only saying [*page 3*] that a Ballance of £37 13s 10d remained in his hands? which nobody questions from the long experience the town hath had of his frugality and good management in the disposal of publick [*sic*] money, and since it is well known that a penny saved from others is a penny got to himself. And the publishing of such an account would have this use in it, that the world might judge whether the expence of an uncontested election be not a sufficient motive to deter any wise man from offering himself a candidate a second time.

'If Mr L-v-tt had no view to private interest or a show of power, how came he to pretend that he and his C-p-n were able to bring in two members? By which means, most of the tradesmen and substantial inhabitants (who were not of the body) were neglected, and deprived of the honour of ever seeing the new candidate till the day of election.

'If Mr L-v-tt had no view to gain, how came he to influence the C-p-n so much, that they would chuse [sic] no citizen to be sheriff, that would not promise to name him under-sheriff? which is an office not only inconsistent with that of town-clerk, (particularly in the trial of criminals) but is also a place below a man of his great fortune to accept of, if he had not a sordid way of thinking, and a mean heart that can suffer nothing to go by him. Indeed were publick favours heaped thus upon him from his own superior merit, it would be some excuse to his avarice: But alas, merit is not the source from whence these favours flow! Fawning and condescension, even to the lowest shift of begging business by himself and friends, are the methods by which he hath attained his present grandeur; and art so mean, that whilst he advanced himself by it, he robbed others of that bread, which they were justly intitled to, and which modesty alone deprived them of enjoying.

'Mr L-v-tt says, that he never received one penny, save only that Sir L-st-r H-lt left a small sum in his hands when he was last in town (which was late in April) to pay his bills and give to the poor. Now I appeal to Mr L-v-tt's own conscience, whether this is not false? and whether he had not £40 left in his hands so long ago as last Christmas? and whether he did not withold the same from the poor till the month of May, notwithstanding the hardships they sustained during that time? And it is much questioned whether the money had ever been applied to its proper use at all, had not Sir L-st-r given positive directions about the payment of it at the election. Therefore quere, What that small sum was that was so lately left in his hands?

'The voters have been told of great favours that would be bestowed upon the city, the case they sat tamely down to Mr L-v-tt's election of two members without opposition; and they have accordingly done so: Yet are afraid (though they do not question the honour of their members) that ways and means will be found out for the body politick to ingross more than an equal share with their fellow-citizens.

'As the majority of voters were no ways chargeable to the members, (except by the billets which were forced upon them) it is hoped when the trifling expence of the election is certainly known, including proper qualifications and gratuities, it will be made publick; that the managers may have the thanks of the city at least, if they have no other reward for their indefatigable labours.

'Some friends of Mr L-v-tt alledge, that he had so much gratitude to Mr. Ch-tw-nd for procuring him the confirmation of town-clerk, that he [*page 4*] promised him his vote and interest at the second succeeding election. But Mr. V-r-n happening to come and offer himself a candidate, he deserted his colours, broke his promise, and gave up his old friend and brother, as not being able to do him any more service.

'The last attempt of Mr L-v-tt (had it succeeded) would indeed have been a masterly performance (i.e.) the getting of the poor of the three parishes into his work-house at Greenhill, at a reserved rent of eight pounds a year from each parish; (which house used to be set at four pounds a year) and then selling it to the candidates at twenty-five year's [*sic*] purchase; under pretence that such a present would be acceptable to the people, and infallibly procure them a return without opposition. This would have brought £600 into his own pocket against the last election; but he unfortunately left the great design to be executed by the body, (being sure of success, as he had ever been in former undertakings of the like sort) and neglected the independent citizens; by which means his interest was tried, and his friends out-polled at a publick vestry-meeting of the parishioners: And he lost the fine booty, that he had set his heart upon, and which he had been contriving to lay hold of, for some months before the experiment was made.

'That such private mercenary views may always be opposed and frustrated, and a publick spirit be revived amongst us, is heartily to be wished by the disinterested and uncorrupted citizens of Lichfield.'

Sources: KB 1/7 Ea 15 Geo II. KB 39/2 Ea 15 Geo II.

A.2 Information exhibited (27 July 1744)

Defendants: John Oakes, clerk; Robert Rhodes and Peter Darlington, labourers; all of Handsworth.

Information:
Hil 18 Geo II [1744/5] [Exhibited 23 Jan 1744/5; FDT][46]

---

[46]   The date here is that on which the informant 'gave the court to understand', i.e. the date on which the information was said to be 'exhibited'. It was by convention the first day of term; for the date on which the rule absolute for the information was actually made, see below under *Rules and process*.

[1] Assault and affray, violently and maliciously, on Charles Hodgetts, at the parish of Handsworth, 5 June [1744], after calling him out of a parish meeting at the house of Richard Fidian, to the interruption of the public business of the parish; [2] assault and affray, violently and maliciously.[47]

Rules and process:
Mich 1744: affdts [1] to [5] filed. ST [6 Nov 1744]: on reading affdts [1] to [5], rule nisi for an information to [21 Nov 1744] against Oakes, Rhodes, and Darlington (Serjeant Birch for prosr). ST [19 Nov 1744]: enlarged rule nisi for an information to FNT, on condition that if an information is granted, they take notice of trial for next assizes and file affdts one week before term (Legge for defdt). Hil [7 Feb 1744/5]: rule absolute for an information. ST [12 Feb 1744/5]: rule for a special jury, instance of defdts (Wilson). Ea [1745] pray a day to answer; leave to imparl; imparl. Trin [14 June 1745]: first rule to plead (to Monday next, 17 June). ST [18 June 1745]: second rule to plead (to Friday next, 21 June). ST [25 June 1745]: peremptory rule to plead in a fortnight (Harvey). ST [3 July 1745]: rule for a special jury, instance of defdts (Yate). ST venire facias juratores. Trin Vac 9 July 1745: notice of trial for the King (H. Walrond). ST 7 Aug 1745: notice of trial countermanded for the King (H. Walrond). Hil [12 Feb 1745/6]: rule for a special jury, instance of defdts (Wilson). Hil Vac 27 Feb 1745/6: notice of trial for the King (H. Walrond). Ea 24 May 1746: notice of trial for the King (H. Walrond). Trin 1746: affdts [6] to [9] filed. ST [14 June 1746]: [rule for taxation.] ST [18 June 1746]: rule for a special jury, instance of defdts (Holden); venire facias juratores. ST [same day]: on reading affdts [7] to [9] and the writ of distringas issued in this cause, rule nisi to FNT for discharge of the rule for taxation of costs to be paid by prosr for not proceeding to trial at last Stafford assizes (Sir John Strange).[48]

---

[47] The numbers supplied in square brackets distinguish separate counts. The use of the word 'violently' in an indictment or information made the charge one of 'special assault'. W. Stubbs and G. Talmash, *The Crown Circuit Companion* (London, 1799), 94 adds that the clerk of indictments at assizes therefore charged 3s 4d instead of 2s. 'But as this is a *very dear word*, it may safely be omitted in all cases of common assault.'

[48] The rule for taxation in this case has not been found, but was supplied from the affidavits. The rule in the text is the result of a motion to discharge such a rule: 'Should the prosecutor or defendant in any case, after having given notice of trial, not countermand the notice of trial in due time, or neglect to try under such notice, upon an affidavit ... of the facts, the Court will in the

Affidavits for prosecution:

Mich 18 Geo II 1744

[1] Affdt of William Winsor labourer of Handsworth, sworn before Richard Simcoe at Birmingham (Warws) 18 Oct 1744. ITKB [*Signed with a mark*.]

That the deponent was leaving Richard Fidian's alehouse 5 June 1744 when he heard an angry argument and saw the Reverend Oakes, minister of the parish, tell his servant Robert Rhodes to beat Charles Hodgetts, overseer of the highway. Rhodes beat Hodgetts violently in the presence of Peter Darlington, Richard Tompson and Thomas Cullwick. When Cullwick tried to part them, he was beaten by Darlington. While the four men were on the ground, Oakes struck some of them with a stick. The deponent pulled Oakes away, but he ran back and struck more blows until the deponent stopped him once more.

[2] Affdt of William Hodgetts yeoman of Handsworth, sworn before Richard Simcoe at Birmingham (Warws) 21 Aug 1744. ITKB

That the deponent was at Mr Walker's farm near Fidian's alehouse 5 June 1744. He saw the Reverend John Oakes angrily pacing before the house. With Oakes were Rhodes (stripped to his waistcoat), Darlington (stripped to his shirt) and Tompson, who were generally employed in Oakes's husbandry. The deponent heard Oakes tell Rhodes to fetch out and beat Hodgetts, which Rhodes did. [*Substantiates affdt [3]*.] Darlington struck Cullwick several times. Fidian, the parish constable, ordered them to keep the peace, but Oakes ignored him and told Rhodes to hit Hodgetts again. The deponent tried but failed to prevent him from doing so.

There was a parish meeting about poor relief to be held that afternoon at Fidian's. The deponent heard several people say that Oakes brought his servants to beat those attending the meeting.

[3] Affdt of Thomas Cullwick yeoman of Handsworth, sworn before Richard Simcoe at Birmingham (Warws) 27 Aug 1744. ITKB [*Signed with a mark*.]

That the deponent attended the parish meeting on poor relief at Fidian's alehouse 5 June 1744. He approached Oakes, Rhodes and Darlington, a labourer in husbandry employed by Oakes, and overheard Oakes apparently encouraging a quarrel. The deponent told

first instance, on application, make a rule absolute, and refer the costs to the Master to be taxed, for not proceeding to trial under such notice.' Gude, i, 96, and see cases at 97ff.

Oakes it would be better to keep the peace than to foment disputes but Oakes sneered at him, and called out 'beat him', upon which Rhodes knocked Hodgetts down. Since Hodgetts appeared to have been hurt, the deponent tried to separate the two but Darlington beat the deponent almost senseless, and he spat blood for several days afterwards.

[4] Affdt of Charles Hodgetts yeoman and one of the overseers of the highway at Handsworth, sworn before Richard Simcoe at Birmingham (Warws) 10 Aug 1744. ITKB [*Signed with a mark.*]

That Oakes had refused to do his duty on the highway for the past year. On 5 June the deponent and John Hollings, the other overseer of the highways, went to Oakes's house to summon him to duty for the current year. In a rage, Oakes called the deponent several reproachable names and directed Rhodes to lead him out of his house by the collar, which Rhodes did. The deponent then went to Fidian's for the parish meeting on poor relief. Two hours later Oakes, Rhodes, Darlington and Tompson arrived. The deponent heard Oakes tell Rhodes to fetch the deponent out of the alehouse. While Rhodes was pulling him along by the collar, Oakes called out to Rhodes to beat this deponent, and 'knock his head off his shoulders'. Rhodes beat the deponent almost senseless. He believes Oakes came to the alehouse with the intent of abusing some of those attending.

[5] Affdt of John Dutton yeoman of Handsworth, sworn before Richard Simcoe at Birmingham (Warws) 27 July 1744. ITKB

That after working on the highways 5 June 1744 he went with William Winsor and other labourers to drink at Fidian's. Rhodes told the deponent that Oakes wanted to speak with him outside. Oakes railed at him for allegedly having struck Rhodes earlier and said he had a mind to have Rhodes 'thresh' him. Then Oakes ordered Rhodes to drag Hodgetts outside. Fidian as constable charged Rhodes and Oakes to keep the peace, but Oakes ordered Rhodes to beat Hodgetts, which he did. Oakes was involved throughout the ensuing fight.

Affidavit for defence:

Trin 19 & 20 Geo II 1746

[6] Affdt of Robert Rhodes yeoman, defendant, of Handsworth and Edward Hickman clerk to Richard Rann, attorney for the defendants, of Birmingham (Warws), sworn before A. Mainwaring at Birmingham 4 June 1746. ITKB 'The King agt John Oakes and others.' [*Verso*]: 'Staffordshire. The King agt Oakes & others. Affidt for costs for not going to tryal.'

[Robert Rhodes]: That, pursuant to notice of trial given for the last assizes at Stafford, Hickman, Joseph Horner, Richard Tompson, John Hollins, John Robins, Ralph Trickett, and himself, all material witnesses, attended at the assizes, 16 miles from their homes. The prosecutors did not proceed to trial nor did the defendants receive a direct or indirect countermand. The deponent, witnesses and Hickman were away from home some two days, and the deponent has paid for horse-hire and other expenses and for lost time the sum of £1 12s 6d to attend trial.

[Edward Hickman]: That he paid £19 5s 6d for counsel and clerk fees and his own expenses.

Further affidavits for prosecution:

Trin 19 & 20 Geo II 1746

[7] Affdt of John Rogers gentleman of Birmingham (Warws), sworn before Richard Simcoe at Birmingham 5 May 1746. ITKB 'The King agt Oakes and others.' [*Verso*]: 'Easter 19 George 2d. The King agt Oakes & al. Affdt Rogers.'

That the deponent, attorney for the prosecutor, attended the last Stafford assizes on the commission day with the record. The prosecution witnesses attended early the next morning, and the deponent delivered briefs to counsel. The cause was to have been tried by a special jury of gentlemen, according to information from Mr Richard Banister, the deponent's agent. Before the court sat, the deponent, on applying to the undersheriff for a return of the writ of distringas [juratores], learned that neither he nor his predecessor had returned a writ of venire [facias juratores]. Therefore they had not summoned any jurors.

The deponent had no notice of these facts until he came to the assizes. He proposed that the undersheriff send for one or two of the gentlemen returned on the panel in order to have the deficiency of the rest of the jury supplied by a tales. Although he told the undersheriff that he had a warrant to do so, the latter refused to do more than return a tarde on the back of the writ of distringas. The deponent was therefore incapable of bringing the cause to trial at the last assizes for want of a jury.

[8] Affdt of Richard Banister, agent for the prosecutor, of Fetter Lane (London), sworn in court 16 June 1746. ITKB 'The King agt Oakes and others upon an information for certain trespasses and assaults.' [*Verso*]: 'The King agt Oakes & ors. Mr Banister's Affidt.'

That at the instance of the defendants, a rule for a special jury was granted and a jury struck by James Burrow [master of the crown office] and returned to a venire facias issued for that purpose by the late undersheriff of Staffs. Notice of trial was given and the record and distringas sent down against the last assizes. On 14 June the deponent served Mr Wakelin's clerk in the Inner Temple with a copy of a written notice that the court would be moved the Monday then next or as soon after counsel could be heard, that the rule made on [14 June 1746] to refer it to the master of the crown office to tax the costs to be paid by the prosecutor for not going to trial, be discharged. Wakelin is agent for the defendants.

[9] Affdt of Edmund Antrobus gentleman of Eccleshall, sworn in court 16 June 1746. ITKB 'The King against Oakes and others.' [*Verso*]: 'Staffordshire. The King agt. Oakes. Affdts Rogers Banister and Antrobus to disch Rule for Costs. The King agst Oakes and others. Mr. Antrobus's Affidt.'

That 4 March 1746 the deponent was appointed undersheriff to Charles Bosvile, high sheriff of Staffordshire. The deponent never received any panel of a special jury in this case from Harris, the late undersheriff, or anyone else. Nor did the deponent receive notice of any venire facias being returned with a special jury, nor was he served with any rule or notice thereof. The deponent has recently been informed that Harris or his agent attended the master of the crown office and struck a special jury for the trying of the case at the last assizes and returned the venire facias for that purpose, but neither notice of this, nor the panel, was ever delivered to this deponent.

Sources: IND 1/6659 Ea 18 Geo II. KB 1/8 Mich 18 Geo II no.1. KB 1/9 Trin 19 & 20 Geo II. KB 11/36/12 Hil 18 Geo II [1744/5] #15. KB 15/2 b58v. KB 15/14 Trin Vac, Hil Vac, Ea 19 Geo II. KB 21/35, pp. 772, 784, 814, 832. KB 21/36 pp. 3, 7, 14, 29, 87, 132, 134. KB 29/404 Hil 18 Geo II, Ea, Trin. KB 36/114.

A.3 Information applied for (12 Nov 1744)

Defendants: Alexander Barr, dissenting minister; James Brett, bucklemaker; John Adams, toymaker; John Lort, swivelmaker; William Worton, labourer; all of Wolverhampton.[49]

Accusation:
Violently assaulting Joseph Turton the elder ironmonger of Wolverhampton and James Maullin yeoman of Sedgley, 26 Sept 1744.

[49] Occupations supplied from affidavits. See the related case F.1.

Rules and process:
12 Nov 1744: affdts [1] to [5] taken. Mich [17 Nov 1744]: on reading
affdts [1,] [2] and one other, rule nisi to FNT for an information (Sir John
Strange). Hil [12 Feb 1744/5]: enlarged rule nisi, to FNT, on the undertaking of Mr Hughes that defdts will immediately appear if information
granted, and all their affdts to be filed a week before term (Gundry). Ea
[3 May 1745]: enlarged rule nisi to [13 May], same condition (Ford). ST
[21 May 1745]: rule discharged.[50]

Affidavits for prosecution:

Mich 18 Geo II 1744

[1] Affdt of Joseph Turton the elder ironmonger of Wolverhampton,
sworn before W. Perks at Wolverhampton 12 Nov 1744. ITKB [*Verso*]:
'Staffordshire Affidts Maullin Turton Harper Marshall & al Green &
Bedhouse for Infn against Barr & al. fo: 78.'
    That Alexander Barr, minister of the protestant dissenting congrega-
tion (Presbyterian) of Wolverhampton, had been dismissed by a letter
from the great majority of its members. Barr had refused to leave until
money owed to him was paid. The congregation sent the deponent to
tender all the money owing. He took James Maullin (who had delivered
the letter) as a witness on 26 Sept 1744. James Brett was also present. In
the kitchen of Barr's house, Barr refused the money without his attorney being present, locked the door, and taking up a hammer threatened
to knock their brains out as they were a couple of rogues and swore that
they should never leave the place alive. He blamed Maullin for bringing the letter and the deponent for trying to take away his good name.
James Brett, who was with Barr, seized Maullin by the hair as he tried
to flee. Barr left and returned with Thomas Price, John Lort and William
Worton; he again locked the door. Brett again pulled Maullin's hair and
struck him. When John Adams, toymaker, was let in he took the hammer from Barr, who then let in Thomas Hill, John Clemson, and two
others. Barr told the group that the deponent and Maullin had tried to
evict him by force. The deponent insisted he came with no such intent.
When he attempted to escape, believing his life was in danger, he was
dragged back, his hat and wig were pulled off, his clothes torn and his
arms bruised. He appealed to Thomas Brett, a passerby, and he and
Maullin were released, having been detained for about three quarters of
an hour. They believe that Barr, James Brett, Adams, Lort, Worton and

---

[50] Marginal note in KB 36/113: [?] 'Deb[itum] P[ro] Ult [*or* Litt] Reg[is]'.

Price intended either to have murdered or beaten them very near to death; Barr said that if they escaped with their lives they should 'think it the greatest mercy that ever befell them'. The deponent had no other design than to deliver the money.

[2] Affdt of James Maullin yeoman of Sedgley, sworn before W. Perks at Wolverhampton 12 Nov 1744. ITKB
That Alexander Barr, having offended his congregation with his indecent behaviour, was given a letter 26 Aug 1744 declaring that they no longer wanted him as their pastor and requesting him to withdraw peaceably. The deponent went to Barr's house with the letter on 22 Sept 1744; Barr refused to receive him but the deponent left the letter. Barr refused to give up the congregation and pretended that there was money owing to him. Joseph Turton was then appointed by the congregation to tender the interest to Barr and asked the deponent to go with him to tender the monies. [*The remainder of the affidavit is substantially similar to [1].*]

[3] Affdt of William Harper nailer of Sedgley, sworn before W. Perks at Wolverhampton on 12 Nov 1744. ITKB [*Signed with a mark.*]
That the deponent was at the house of John Mansell 26 Sept at 3pm and while there saw Joseph Turton and James Maullin go into Alexander Barr's house. The deponent then heard some disturbance and went closer to have a better look. Barr let Price, Lort and Worton, then Adams and later Clemson into the house. After Adams, Clemson and Thomas Hill victualler arrived the deponent heard Maullin cry out murder and Barr then threatened to knock Turton down. Adams warned Barr to restrain himself and Turton was pulled back by Adams and Barr as he tried to escape. When Turton and Maullin appeared in the street, Turton's clothes were torn and Maullin appeared beaten.

[4] Affdt of John Marshall linendraper and John Mansell ironmonger, both of Wolverhampton, sworn before W. Perks at Wolverhampton 12 Nov 1744. ITKB
[Both]: That on 26 Sept 1744, Turton and Maullin went to Barr's house in John's Lane to tender money to Barr. After a short while Barr had let in John Lort, William Worton and Thomas Price. Hearing a disturbance, the deponent Marshall went closer to the house. John Adams then knocked on the door, was let in and removed the hammer from Barr's hands. They heard Barr threaten to 'knock anyone down' and when Turton and Maullin came out, Maullin appeared to be very much beaten and abused.

[5] Affdt of Joseph Green baker of Wolverhampton, sworn before W. Perks at Wolverhampton 12 Nov 1744. ITKB

That on 26 Sept 1774 at 4pm, the deponent was walking along the street where Barr lived and met Thomas Hill. Hill stopped the deponent and told him that the Devil had been at Barr's house and said had it not been for him, Turton and Maullin would have been murdered. Hill told the deponent that Barr had a hammer in his hand, that several fellows abused Maullin, and that they would do Maullin mischief again.

[6] Affdt of Joel Bedhouse yeoman of Wolverhampton, sworn before W. Perks at Wolverhampton 12 Nov 1744. ITKB

That on 28 Sept 1744 at 3pm, the deponent met Thomas Hill who told him that two days earlier he had been at Barr's house where he saw Turton and Maullin. Hill told the deponent that had he not gone to Barr's house when he did, Maullin and Turton would have been murdered. When Hill arrived at Barr's house, several people there were beating Maullin on the ground. Hill said that Barr had intended to get a mob to drag them 'up John's Lane by the head and down by the heels as long as they had life'.

Affidavits for defence:

Hil 18 Geo II 1744/5

[*The following ten affidavits are numbered 1) to 10) in the bundle.*]

[7] 1) Affdt of Alexander Barr clerk and minister of the protestant dissenting congregation of Wolverhampton, sworn before F. Stuart at Wolverhampton 19 Jan 1744/5. ITKB

That the deponent had received several letters of invitation, signed by Joseph Turton, James Marshall, John Marshall, Richard Fowler and about 79 others of the sect of protestants called dissenters or Presbyterians in Oct 1739 and had accepted the office of their minister.

The deponent was assaulted by Turton 4 and 11 March last and brought an action against him for which he recovered £5 damages 25 July. One night last June he was in the house with Jane Bird and Isaac Cardale. John Clemson came in at about 10pm and advised Barr to be on guard as 20 to 30 people were about his house.

While sitting with James Brett 26 Sept 1744, the deponent saw John Marshall, John Mansell and William Harper outside his door, and later James Maullin and Joseph Turton entered the deponent's house without knocking, claiming to pay Barr money owed to him. The deponent told Turton that he would not accept any money without his attorney,

Walter Asteley, present. The deponent believed and had heard there was a plot afoot to throw him out of his house. He left to get witnesses and was pushed by John Marshall when outside. The deponent returned with Thomas Price, John Lort, and William Worton. Turton repeated that he had come to pay money owed. The deponent, seeing no money, asked William Bellamy in the street to summon his attorney.The deponent picked up a hammer to protect himself. About 20 minutes later, John Adams knocked and entered, and took the hammer from him. Shortly after, Turton and Maullin quietly left the house. The deponent claims that during the time Turton and Maullin were in the house, neither he nor the others attacked them. Turton and Maullin were in the house about 15 or 20 minutes.

[8] 2) Affdt of James Brett bucklemaker of Wolverhampton, sworn before F. Stuart at Wolverhampton 16 Jan 1744/5. 'King's Bench.'

That the deponent had been visiting Barr at his home to sing an anthem for him when Barr noticed several of his enemies outside the window. Turton and Maullin then entered the kitchen and Turton said that he had come to pay Barr money but produced none. Barr told Turton to pay his attorney, Asteley, because he would have nothing to do with him and asked that both he and Maullin leave. When they did not do so, Barr left the house. Brett, Turton and Maullin began to exchange harsh words and the deponent seized Maullin by the hair in defence. Barr returned with Thomas Price and John Lort, and took up a hammer to protect himself. At no time did Worton, Adams, Lort, Price or Barr strike Maullin or Turton.

[9] 3) Affdt of John Adams toymaker of Wolverhampton, sworn before F. Stuart at Wolverhampton 19 Jan 1744/5. ITKB

That as the deponent was walking to his house he saw a crowd gather in front of Barr's house including John Marshall, Joseph Swain, and William Harper, some of Barr's reputed enemies. Marshall told the deponent that Turton was inside. The deponent was admitted into the house, took the hammer that Barr was using to protect himself and cast it under the table. Turton told the deponent that he had come to pay Barr some money, but the deponent believed that Turton intended to injure Barr. The two exchanged angry words. He then heard Turton offer to go to the attorney's with Barr, but Barr said that Asteley had already been sent for. Although the deponent asked them to stay, both Turton and Maullin left freely. He had heard that James Brett had pulled Maullin by the hair. While the deponent was present neither he nor anyone else assaulted the two. Turton and Maullin were in the house about ten minutes.

[10] 4) Affdt by John Lort swivelmaker and William Worton labourer, both of Wolverhampton, sworn before F. Stuart at Wolverhampton 19 Jan 1744/5. ITKB [*Worton signed with a mark.*]

[John Lort]: That he, Worton, and Thomas Price were asked by Barr to be witnesses to the events at his house. They saw a crowd gathering outside Barr's house, including some of his enemies, among them John Marshall, Joseph Swain, William Harper, Thomas Brett and others. On entering the house the deponents saw Turton and Maullin. Barr had asked Turton if he had brought the money and he replied that he had not but could send for it. Barr refused to receive any money without his attorney present and the two exchanged angry words. Barr picked up a hammer and accused Turton of taking his good name, but he did not use the hammer. Barr asked Turton and Maullin to stay and pay his attorney when he arrived.

[William Worton]: [*Substantiates Lort's account.*]

[11] 5) Affdt of Isaac Cardale baker and Jane Bird widow both of Wolverhampton, sworn before F. Stuart at Wolverhampton 18 Jan 1744/5. ITKB

[Isaac Cardale]: That for a long time before 26 Sept 1744 Joseph Turton, John Marshall, John Mansell, Joseph Green and other reputed enemies of Barr's were planning forcibly to evict him from his house. Barr had often asked the deponent to accompany him when he went out, fearing he would be assaulted.

[Jane Bird]: [*Substantiates Cardale's account thus far.*] That Barr removed his books, writings, and other valuables and left them in the care of the deponent. She was also present last June when John Clemson the elder came to warn Barr that there were 20 or so of his enemies around his house. Barr had asked the deponent to stay the night with him, but she refused, fearing for her own safety.

[12] 6) Affdt of Thomas Hill victualler of Wolverhampton, sworn before F. Stuart at Wolverhampton 19 Jan 1744/5. ITKB

That on 26 Sept 1744 the deponent was told by John Clemson the elder that Turton, Marshall, Mansell and a group of Barr's enemies were going to murder Barr, or drag him out of his house and beat him. As he was leaving Barr's house, the deponent met Joseph Green, one of Barr's enemies, and asked Green why he was not with the crowd. Green said he knew nothing of it, and the deponent told him that it was a good thing he was there to stop Maullin and Turton from being further drubbed. The deponent has not spoken with nor is an acquaintance of Joel Bedhouse. After he arrived at Barr's house, no blows were struck against anyone.

[13] 7) Affdt of John Clemson[51] the younger whitesmith of Wolverhampton, sworn before F. Stuart at Wolverhampton 18 Jan 1744/5. ITKB

That on 26 Sept 1744 the deponent saw William Harper, Joseph Swain, John Marshall, John Mansell, and John Adams amongst a group of Barr's enemies at Barr's house, and heard Barr ask William Bellamy to get his attorney, Asteley. The deponent was threatened after asking Harper why he was Barr's enemy. Thomas Brett, a wicked fellow, stood by the door and offered to break it down. When the deponent expressed dismay that Barr was being disturbed, Harper threatened to throw him out of the shop where he stood. The deponent believes the crowd was assembled to turn Barr out of his own house.

[14] 8) Affdt of William Bellamy cordwainer of Wolverhampton, sworn before F. Stuart at Wolverhampton 18 Jan 1744/5. ITKB [*Signed with a mark.*]

That on 26 Sept 1744, the deponent saw Joseph Swain, John Marshall and William Harper on the steps of Barr's house and looked for John Adams at his home to warn him of this disturbance. Finding Adams later at Barr's house, the deponent saw Marshall attempt to force his way into Barr's house. Seeing the deponent, Barr summoned him to get his attorney, Asteley. Asteley had instructed the deponent to get a constable, but instead he returned to Barr's house where he heard Harper threaten Clemson the younger.

[15] 9) Affdt of John Clemson the elder whitesmith of Wolverhampton, sworn before F. Stuart at Wolverhampton 19 Jan 1744/5. ITKB

That the deponent was warned by his daughter, Martha Davies, that a crowd of Barr's enemies were about to abuse him. When the deponent went to Barr's house, after stopping to get Thomas Hill, he saw a crowd of people by the door, including John Marshall, Joseph Swain and Thomas Brett. Both the deponent and Hill were let into the house but he saw no disturbance at the house, no assault on Turton or Maullin, nor any money being passed. It was the common report that Barr's enemies intended to throw him out of the house and Clemson had told him this more than once.

[16] 10) Affdt of Thomas Price victualler of Wolverhampton, sworn before F. Stuart at Wolverhampton 21 Jan 1744/5. ITKB

---

[51] Both the son and the father sign 'Clemson' (affidavits [13] and [15]), but the affidavits give 'Clempson' throughout.

That on 26 Sept 1744 Alexander Barr requested the deponent and John Lort to be witnesses to a disturbance at his home. There, James Maullin and Joseph Turton claimed to have come to pay money owing to Barr on instructions from his attorney. The deponent believed this to be a lie as Turton had no money. Neither Turton nor Maullin was struck with the hammer that Barr used to protect himself.

Sources: KB 1/8 Mich 18 Geo II no.2, Hil 18 Geo II no.2; KB 21/35 pp. 782, 831, 839. KB 36/113.

A.4 Information refused (23 Jan 1744/5)

Defendants: John Butler, William Spittle, Benjamin Spittle, Samuel Haldright,[52] all of Wednesbury, locksmiths .

Accusation:
Attacking the household of John Bird, carpenter, at Wednesbury 5 Nov 1744.[53]

Rules and process:
Hil 1745: affdt [1] filed. ST [4 Feb 1744/45]: on reading affdt [1], rule nisi to FNT for an information (Sir John Strange). Ea 1745: affdt [2] filed. ST [1 May 1745]: rule nisi enlarged to FNT, on condition they shall plead and take notice at next assizes (Ford). Trin 1745: affdts [3] to [5] filed. ST [15 June 1745]: rule nisi discharged (Gundry).[54]

---

[52] Also given as 'Hallwright' or 'Holdwright'.

[53] The carpenter John Bird and his family, with many other Methodists of Wednesbury, were attacked in June 1743 and Feb 1744 (the 'Shrovetide riots') by mobs of colliers and others at Wednesbury and Darlaston. In April 1744 Bird applied without success to the magistrates Walter Gough, John Dolphin, and William Pershouse for a warrant; the last told him that all the justices in the neighbourhood had agreed to grant no warrant to them against the rioters. *Modern Christianity Exemplified at Wednesbury and Other Adjacent Places in Staffordshire* (1745), reprinted in John Wesley, *Works*, ed. T. Jackman (repr. 3rd ed, London, 1872), xiii, 169ff, at 174, 180, 189. See also cases A.5, A.9.

[54] The entry in KB 36/114 has a marginal note, 'Bach 3'. Bach was a clerk in court.

Affidavits for prosecution:

Hil 18 Geo II 1744/5

[1] Affdt of John Bird carpenter; his wife, Ellen; his daughter, Mary; Jane Fielding[55] widow; and Elizabeth Hall wife of George Hall locksmith; all of Wednesbury, sworn before Thomas Fisher at Birmingham (Warws) 23 Jan 1744/5. ITKB [*Ellen Bird, Elizabeth Hall and Jane Fielding signed with a mark.*] [*Verso*]: 'The King agt Spittle & others Affidts. R. Banister. fo: 23. Staffords Afft of Bird & al for Infn agt Spittle & al.'

[Ellen and Mary Bird]: That on the night of 5 Nov 1744 at about 11pm, the moon being bright, they were sitting in Bird's house after he had gone to bed and heard a noise of stones against the window shutters and door. When they opened the door the noise stopped, then began again when they went inside.

[Mary Bird]: That she went upstairs and from the casement window saw Benjamin Spittle and others throwing stones and brick ends at the house; he encouraged them, calling 'Well done lads, break the door and window and Damn my soul if we won't have the house down before morning and kill that old rogue old Bird.' She then said in a loud voice, 'Benjamin Spittle I know thee.'

[Ellen and Mary Bird]: That they went out of the house and saw Benjamin Spittle with William Spittle, Robert Spittle and Samuel Haldright and asked them to stop. Instead they threw more brick ends, breaking the windows. They fled back into the house; soon after the door was broken open.

[Ellen]: as she was making fast the door a brick hit her right knee as she and Mary fled into the house. They cried out murder. William and Benjamin Spittle came near the door and said, 'Damn you we will have the house down before morning and let that old rogue Bird come out and we will sacrifice him, we will murder him.'

[Jane Fielding]: A neighbour of the Birds, she saw the disturbance, walked to the house and asked Benjamin Spittle, John Butler and the others if they were not ashamed of their behaviour. William Spittle said 'Damn you for an old bitch, what is that to you', and pushed her away. She returned home, fearing for her safety.

[Ellen Bird and Elizabeth Hall]: That they saw John Butler break down the door with a piece of timber, and it was fastened again..

[John and Mary Bird]: After the door was fastened they saw through a casement window Butler break it open again.

---

[55] Jane Fielding swore separately on the same day.

[Mary Bird]: Butler broke the window shuts open, then broke the windows, and a great many stones coming into the house, she and Ellen and Elizabeth ran upstairs, crying out 'for Christ's sake don't murder us.' When the fright was a little over she went down stairs and found John Butler outside the door with one of John Bird's chairs on his shoulders; she asked him to return it and he went back into the house with William Spittle.

[Ellen and Mary Bird and Elizabeth Hall]: That Butler took a chair in his hand, said he would break all the goods in the house, and broke the chair.

[Mary Bird]: When she tried to stop him, Butler seized her by the throat and swore to kill her if she tried, but the deponents stopped him.

[John Bird]: For fear of being killed he kept upstairs until John Butler and William Spittle left, between 3am and 4am. He estimates the damage at about 20s and upwards. A few days later he and Mary Bird went to see Walter Gough and William Pershouse, the nearest justices to Wednesbury (save John Lane, who was then very ill), at their respective houses, to get a warrant against John Butler, William Spittle and Samuel Haldright. Pershouse declared he would have nothing to do with it nor grant any warrant; Gough did so also. Hearing that another attack on his house was planned, he went again to Pershouse 15 Jan, who again refused a warrant; 17 Jan he applied again to Gough, who also refused.

Ea 18 Geo II 1745

[2] Affdt of William Devey yeoman of Dudley (Worcs), sworn before George Holyoake at Wolverhampton 22 April 1745. ITKB [*Verso*]: 'Staffordshire. The King agt Butler and others. Affidt of Service of Rule. R. Banister fo:5.'

That 18 Feb he served true copies of the rule nisi [*annexed*] on the defendants by leaving a copy with Hannah Spittle, mistress of Butler; with Eleanor, wife of John Grove with whom William Spittle lived; with Anne wife of Benjamin Spittle; and with Samuel Haldright; in each case showing them and acquainting them with the contents.

Affidavits for defence:

Trin 18 & 19 Geo II 1745

[3] Affdt of John Butler locksmith of Wednesbury, sworn before Theo. Levett at Lichfield 30 April 1745. ITKB [*Signed with a mark.*]

That the deponent was not in the company of William Spittle, Benjamin Spittle, Samuel Haldright, or any of them on the night of 5

Nov 1744, nor see them damage John Bird's property, or utter threatening words; nor was he drinking in a public house with them. He admits that he was at Brown's public house in Wednesbury from 8pm until 1am or 2am, and being a little flushed with liquor and being very intimately acquainted with Bird's daughter, Mary, stopped by Bird's house and found Ellen and her two daughters. Mary was more shy than usual, and he was a little noisy, but denies that he broke open the door with a piece of timber or broke the windows and shutts with stones and brickends, or broke a chair. Ellen Bird asked William Spittle, who was passing by the house, to take Butler home. The deponent went home with him and is certain that Spittle did not then damage the Birds' property, nor did the deponent. He agreed at the time to make satisfaction for windows broken that night and is still willing to do so but he is only a poor apprentice to a locksmith and hath nothing but what his master pleases to give him. He would not have gone to the house had it not been for the familiarity that had been between him and Mary Bird, and the freedoms he had been permitted to take when he was there.

[4] Affdt of Benjamin Spittle and his wife Anne, William Spittle, Robert Spittle, John Haldright, and Samuel Haldright, all locksmiths of Wednesbury, sworn before Theo. Levett at Lichfield 30 April 1745. ITKB [*All the deponents signed with a mark.*] [*Verso*]: 'Staffordshire. Affts of Benjn Spittle & al Walter Gough Esqr & al & John Butler to shew cause agt Infn. fo 34.'

[All]: That they have heard affidavit [1] read.

[Benjamin, William, and Robert Spittle, and John and Samuel Haldright]: That they were on their way home from bell ringing at the parish church 5 Nov 1744, and about 8pm stopped for a drink at a public house with the 10s allowed by the parish for ringing on that day. As they left to go home and were passing the house of John Bird about 11pm, Ellen or Mary Bird said 'Benjamin Spittle I know thee', and accused him of breaking their windows and doors with barrel staves and bricks. The deponents denied that any of them did such a thing and went peaceably home; they deny all the accusations in the affidavit.

[Robert Spittle, John and Samuel Haldright, Anne Spittle]: That they were with William and Benjamin Spittle from the time they left the public house to the time they passed Bird's house and swear that they heard no threat nor saw either man damage the house. They remember Benjamin Spittle telling the Birds they were 'sorry scandalous people and kept a bad house'. They then left for home.

[William Spittle]: That he continued to another public house in Wednesbury and when he was returning home near 2am he heard a noise coming from Bird's house. He found John Butler inside, pretty full of liquor and very noisy, but no damage had been done. He escorted Butler home at Ellen Bird's request. He did not throw bricks or stones, or break the door, or see Butler do so; some windows had already been broken. He was not in Butler's company earlier that night, nor present during the conversation at 11pm.

[All]: That Butler had not been in their company earlier that evening. Bird, formerly a carpenter, is now a bailiff's follower, and keeps a reputed bawdy house; his daughter is reputed a lewd and wanton woman. They encourage young fellows to come to her, and his house is often stoned by unlucky boys from Wednesbury; it is rare to see all their windows whole. Elizabeth Hall and Jane Fielding are women of ill repute.

[5] Affdt of Walter Gough of Perry Barr and William Pershouse of Reynolds Hall in the parish of Walsall, JPs for Staffs, sworn before Theo. Levett at Stonnall in Shenstone parish 29 May 1745. ITKB

[Walter Gough]: That he remembers that John Bird, who is of very bad character, came to his house making a complaint against some people of Wednesbury whose names he does not know. He told Bird that as there had been great disturbances and disorders in the parish by the people called Methodists (and the deponent understands Bird encourages such people), he advised him to go home and live in peace with his neighbours, or to come to the next justices' meeting for a warrant. The deponent did all in his power to suppress the late disturbances and is certain that had Bird come to him in the manner described in his affidavit, the deponent would not have refused a warrant.

[William Pershouse]: That he remembers Bird having applied for a warrant, and the deponent having before granted a general warrant to the constable to seize riotous persons at the time the sect of Methodists imposed upon the vulgar there and created great disorder, he told Bird he could apply to the constable, who would bring any person guilty of disorder before him or some other justice, and that they would see justice done them. Bird, who he has known for many years to be a person of a very vile character, left the room, clapping his hand on his backside in an insolent manner.

Sources: KB 1/8 Hil 18 Geo II no. 1, Ea 18 Geo II, Trin 18 & 19 Geo II. KB 21/35 pp. 817, 838; KB 21/36 p.5.

A.5 Information applied for, granted against some but not exhibited (22 May 1745)

Defendants[56]: Richard Hobnett+; Richard Colbourn*; Benjamin Bate +; Stephen Bradford*; John Argill*; James Devereux*; Joseph Hodgkins; Richard Yardley; Henry Timmins +; John Shaw +; Joseph Davis*; Joseph Clerk*; Benjamin Jevon*; George Webb*; John Jackson+ .

Accusation:
Attacking John Darby's house, Sedgley, 23 April 1745.[57]

Rules and process:
Ea 1745: affdt [1] filed. ST [25 May 1745]: on reading affdt [1], rule nisi for an information to FNT (Serjt Birch). Trin [26 June 1745]: rule absolute for an information against defdts*, and enlarged rule nisi to FNT for defdts+ (Birch).[58]

Affidavits for prosecution:

Ea 18 Geo II 1745

[1] Affdt of John Darby nailer of Sedgley, Anne Darby, his wife, and Anne Darby spinster, his daughter, sworn before Thomas Haden at Haden Hill (Staffs) 22 May 1745. ITKB [*All signed with a mark.*]
[John Darby]: That he is the proprietor of a messuage, barn, shop, garden and parcel of land. Richard Hobnett, Richard Colbourn, Benjamin Bate, Stephen Bradford, John Argill, James Devereux, Joseph Hodgkins, Richard Yardley, Henry Timmins, Elizabeth wife of Charles Douty, John Shaw, Joseph Davis, Joseph Clerk, Benjamin Jevon, George Webb, John Jackson, and a great number of unknown persons assembled at the deponent's house 23 April 1745 about 10pm. Yardley, Hobnett and Bradford threw coals against the door of the house, then

---

[56] See *Rules and process* for *, +.
[57] The house of John Darby 'of Brerely' was attacked during the anti-Methodist riots of Jan–Feb 1744, when the mob broke down the door, destroyed household goods and five stalls of bees, and threw the hay out of his barn. *Modern Christianity Exemplified*, 178–9.
[58] No information or further process has been found; there may have been a settlement, or the prosecutor may have used the rule absolute as a threat, without proceeding further. Occupations of the accused are not given in the affidavits.

broke it down; some coal hit this deponent's right arm and hip, so that he was unable to work for nine days, nor can he yet turn himself in his bed without pain and great difficulty. Hobnett and Yardley demanded guineas a piece [*sic*] from the deponent, threatening to pull his house down. When he refused, saying he had nothing to give, the mob forced their way in and took two chanks of pork, one spare rib, two linen aprons, one pair of woollen stockings, one hone, one razor, half a dozen pewter spoons, bread and butter, and (out of the garden) three stalls[59] of bees, in all worth £2 and upwards. They broke his brass kettle, a large brewing tub, two glass windows, one window case, one casement, a parcel of earthenware, two shelves, the ceiling and tiling of the house, his stable door, shop door, paling about his fold yard, and garden stuff, to his loss and damage £2 12*s* and upwards. They did not go away until about 12 midnight.

His wife, daughter and five other children were so affrighted and for fear of murder that they ran into the fields and left him alone in the house, which is about a quarter mile from any other.

[Anne Darby, wife and Anne Darby, daughter]: That that night as they sat in the house they heard a dreadful noise of blowing of horns, and a crying or calling of 'John Darby God damn you come out of your house or else God damn them if they did not pull the house down on his head.' That they ran from the house to hide in the fields, under the hedges, for fear murder should be committed. [*Confirm account of the damage and losses.*]

Trin 18 & 19 Geo II 1745

[2] Affdt of James Shaw gentleman of Dudley (Worcs), sworn before J. M. Wheeler at Birmingham (Warws) 12 June 1745. ITKB 'The King agt [*names of the defdts*].' [*Verso*]: 'Staffordshire. Afft of Shaw of service of rule for infn agt Hobnet et al. In the King's Bench. The King agt Hobnet et al.: affidavit of service of rule to show cause. R Banister.'

That the deponent served notice 10 June 1745 of the annexed rule nisi for an information to the defendants Richard Colbourne (by leaving a true copy with his mother Rebecca with whom he lived); Stephen Bradford (by leaving a copy with Mary the wife of Joseph Burrows, with whom Bradford lived); John Argill; James Devereux and Joseph Clerk (by leaving a copy with Anne the wife of John Birch, with whom they lived); Joseph Hodgkins, Richard Yardley, Joseph Davis, Benjamin

---

59 Spelled 'stauls' in the original. 'Stall, n.4. A hive of bees; a 'stock' of bees in or for a hive; also, a bee-hive'. *Oxford English Dictionary Online*.

Jevon, and George Webb. He served notice 12 June 1745 to Richard Hobnett.

Sources: KB 1/8 Ea 18 Geo II, Trin 18 & 19 Geo II. KB 21/35 p. 856; KB 21/36 p.15.

A.6 Information exhibited (23 Nov 1748)

Defendant: John Cooper, yeoman and gamekeeper of Rugeley.

Information:
Ea 22 Geo II 1749 [Exhibited 12 April 1749; FDT]
[1] Intending to murder John Trigg the younger, 29 Oct [1748], in a piece of land called the Cow Pasture in the occupation of Trigg, assault and affray with a gun on the defenceless Trigg and violent assault; Cooper cocked the gun, pushed it against Trigg's right eye so that blood gushed out, and gave Trigg dangerous blows on the face, cheek, breast, and belly, so that Trigg languished of his wounds for three weeks in fear of losing his life; [2] intending to injure Trigg, armed with a gun, violent assault etc. [*as in the first count*]; [3] violent assault only.

Rules and process:
23 Nov 1748: affdts [1] and [2] taken. Hil [24 Jan 1748/9]: on reading affdts [1] and [2], rule nisi for an information to [10 Feb] (Sir Richard Lloyd). ST [13 Feb 1748/9, LDT]: enlarged rule nisi to FNT, all affdts to be filed a week before[60] (Leigh). Ea [13 April 1749]: rule absolute for an information (Sir Richard Lloyd). ST: prays a day to answer; has leave to imparl; imparles. Trin [26 May 1749]: first rule to plead.[61]

Affidavits for prosecution:

Hil 22 Geo II 1748/9

[1] Affdt of Alexander Godwin ironplatemaker of Rugeley, sworn

---

[60] [*In margin of the KB 36/128 entry*]: 'Def: Deb & Cops Req'.
[61] Robinson, an attorney of Rugeley (presumably the Michael Robinson who took the affidavits), related in 1759 that he had prosecuted in this case. He said that Cooper threatened to blow Trigg's brains out, and forced the muzzle of his gun into Trigg's eye. According to Robinson, the prosecution was stayed after the rule absolute on Cooper making his submission to Trigg. SRO, D603 Ridgway to Lord Uxbridge, 3 March 1759. For the context, see the introduction to Section F, 'The expense of certiorari'.

before Michael Robinson at Rugeley 23 Nov 1748. ITKB [*Verso:*] 'Staffs Affidts Trigg & al & Godwin for Infn agt Cooper fo: 16.'

That hearing voices of men quarrelling about 3pm 29 Oct, the deponent ran into a stable of John Trigg the younger, feltmaker of Rugeley, which stands in a field rented from Walter Chetwynd esquire. He looked through the dunghole and saw Trigg and Cooper in the land adjoining the stable. Cooper several times presented a gun towards Trigg and as oft swore 'God damn him if he [Trigg] offered to come towards him, he [Cooper] would blow Trigg's heart out.' That evening in Rugeley the deponent met Cooper and asked him how he could be so barbarous as to offer to shoot a man on his own land, to which Cooper replied that if Trigg had stepped one foot towards him he would have shot him dead.

[2] Affdt of John Trigg the younger, felt maker, and John Burden, husbandman, both of Rugeley, sworn before Michael Robinson at Rugeley 23 Nov 1748. ITKB

[John Trigg]: That as he was with his team drawing dung on a piece of land called the cowpasture which he rents from Walter Chetwynd esquire, he met John Cooper walking with a gun through the deponent's land. He asked Cooper why he had shot his dog, saying he was sure neither he nor his very young dog had ever offended him. Cooper making no reply, the deponent called him a pitiful fellow, and said he deserved to have his arse kicked. Cooper then without any other provocation cocked his gun, advanced with it cocked and presented it to the deponent's body; he pushed the muzzle aside, on which Cooper pushed the muzzle into his right eye. He was so stunned by the blow that it was some time before he could recover to go to have his wounds cared for. His eye and cheek immediately gushed with blood, there was swelling in the other eye, and for three weeks he had difficulty seeing enough to walk, even under the care of an eminent surgeon. After the assault Cooper kept the gun pointed at him from a distance of five or six yards, and warned him not to step closer or he would blow his heart out.

[John Burden]: [*Confirms Trigg's account of the conversation with Cooper.*] That he was with his master Trigg spreading dung on his land, Trigg using a spade to do so. He saw Cooper punch Trigg in the belly with the muzzle two or three times, and then in his right eye, which gushed with blood. Cooper swore he would blow Trigg's heart out if he stirred one foot toward him. There was no provocation apart from the words recounted by Trigg.

Sources: IND 1/6659 Ea 22 Geo II. KB 1/9/1 Hil 22 Geo II 1748/9. KB 11/39 Ea 22 Geo II #5. KB 15/2 b71v Ea 22 Geo II. KB 21/36 pp. 405, 423, 430, 455. KB 29/408 Ea 22 Geo II. KB 36/128, /129.

A.7 Information applied for (20 April 1750)

Defendant: John Cooper, yeoman and keeper of Rugeley.

Accusation:
Assaulting John Berresford, husbandman, 26 Feb 1749/50.

Rules and process:
[*None.*][62]

Affidavits for prosecution:

Ea 23 Geo II 1750

[1] Affdt of John Berresford husbandman and James Berresford, father of John, both of Cannock Wood in the parish of Cannock, sworn before Richard Hinckley at Rugeley 28 April 1750. ITKB [*John Berresford signed with a mark.*]
  [John Berresford]: That he was sent to get five or six holly sticks for his master on 26 Feb 1749/50 while in the employ of John Cope, farmer and tenant of the Earl of Uxbridge. To find the holly he went to his father's grounds at Beaudesert Park. John Cooper confronted him while on his father's land, asked him why he cut the berries and then asked for his hook, but he refused. Cooper threatened to strike him with the butt end of his gun. Cooper then put down the gun, kicked him, and took the hook, then pushed him into a ditch. The deponent asked Cooper to help him out as he had broken his arm. Cooper refused and left. The deponent struggled back to his master's house where he noticed that his elbow was dislocated and his arm swollen and blackened from his shoulder to his finger.
  Simon Weston, surgeon, set his elbow. For a fortnight he suffered intolerable pain and sleep was impossible without medicine. The arm was useless for a month and is still weak.
  [James Berresford]: That the holly tree from which the sticks were cut were cut on his lands which are held in lease for himself and his two sons. He has used holly from the tree in question for 50 years as of right.

[2] Affdt of Simon Weston surgeon of Rugeley, sworn before Richard Hinckley at Lichfield 30 May 1750. ITKB [*Verso*]: 'Affdts Berresford & al & Weston for Infn agst Cooper. Barlow fo 10'.

[62] See also case A.6. This second prosecution of Cooper apparently did not proceed farther than filing the affidavits: no motions are recorded in Easter term 23 Geo II (KB 21/36).

That the deponent was sent for 26 Feb 1749/50 to see John Berresford, then servant to John Cope, warrener and farmer of Rugeley. Berresford's left arm was much bruised and blackened and his elbow dislocated. Two or three days later it was very swelled from his elbow to wrist, with many black blisters. Within a week the danger of mortification disappeared, and he reduced the arm, but for a month or more it was useless to Berresford.

Sources: KB 1/10 Ea 23 Geo II.

A.8 Information refused (18 June 1750)

Defendants: William Kent, journeyman housepainter and late disbanded soldier; Henry Foster the younger, alias Bromsgrove, journeyman joiner; Thomas Harvey, writing clerk to the clerk of the city of Lichfield; Henry Edwards, writing clerk; Thomas Statham, butcher; Samuel Buckley[63] the younger, journeyman shoemaker; George Betts, labourer; Thomas Mallett, husbandman; William Bailye, apothecary; John Wright, gentleman and justice of the peace of Lichfield; Thomas Cleaver, apothecary; Thomas Foster, alias Bromsgrove, joiner[64]; all of Lichfield.

Accusation:
Certain 'trespasses, contempts, riots, unlawful assemblies, assaults and misdemeanors' in riotously seizing Edward Bronsdon 26 May 1750, and committing him to gaol.[65]

Rules and process:
Trin 1750: prosecution affdts [1] to [14] taken, filed. ST [27 Oct 1750]: rule nisi to [9 Nov 1750], based on affdts [1], [5] to [9], [11], [13], [14] (Ford). 6 Nov 1750: affdt [15] taken, filed Mich. Hil 1750/1: defence affdts [16] to [27] taken, filed Hil; prosn affdt [28] to [29] taken, filed Hil. Hil [11 Feb 1750/1]: enlarged rule nisi to FNT (Ford). 24 April 1751: additional prosn affdt [30] taken, filed Ea. Ea [10 May 1751]: rule discharged.

---

[63] Spelled Buckeley in some of the affidavits.
[64] Occupations supplied from affidavits.
[65] For an account of this case see D. Hay, 'The Last Years of Staffordshire Jacobitism', *Staffordshire Studies*, xiv (2002), 75.

Affidavits for prosecution:

Trin 24 Geo II 1750

[1] Affdt of John Topping gentleman of Lichfield, sworn before Richard Hinckley at Lichfield 18 June 1750. ITKB

That Edward Bronsdon, a gentleman of considerable fortune, who had lately come to live in Lichfield in the Cathedral Close, fled 26 May into the shop in Topping's house; the door was bolted against a great mob that gathered outside. A rabble of more than a hundred besieged the house for three hours. Kent, and Foster alias Bromsgrove, encouraged by Harvey and Edwards, partly shattered the shop door with poleaxes, and then burst in the back door. The defendants named were among the rioters; Buckley had a hatchet, Betts a drawn hanger. The intruders rushed up to the room where the deponent's wife lay ill (endangering her life) and forced his daughter in law, also ill, to flee. They broke open the door to the cellar, where Bronsdon was hiding. The deponent did not open his doors because the rioters were generally reputed to be persons of bad character and of turbulent and riotous dispositions, in low circumstances, unable to make reparation for any damage to the shop or goods in it. They neither showed nor mentioned any warrant, nor does he know that the two constables of the city were present. He knows of no crime committed by Bronsdon to justify such actions. Bronsdon was seized and imprisoned for two days under pretence of some breach of the peace. Had Bronsdon resisted, he would have been murdered.

[2] Affdt of Edward Bronsdon esquire of the Cathedral Close, Lichfield, sworn before Richard Hinckley at Lichfield 23 June 1750. ITKB

That the deponent came to reside in Lichfield from London 3 April, helped by Topping. He met some gentlemen at the Swan 16 April to commemorate Culloden with a bonfire, and pealing bells. A set of mobbish fellows intruded, kicked the bonfire, and challenged the celebrants. He helped drive the rioters away, but was warned not to pursue them further because of danger of an ambush headed by Thomas Harvey, writing clerk to Joseph Adey, town clerk.

The next day he was insulted in the street by Charles, a brother of John Wright, butcher and chief magistrate, and by William Deakin, the son of a magistrate, and others. They and Edward Bird, a common soldier, pursued him into Topping's shop, for no other reason than that he had commemorated Culloden.

From that time he was often insulted in the streets. On coming from church he was accosted by Jonathan Mallett the younger, apprentice to

Charles Hassells apothecary; on giving him gentle correction he was assaulted by Thomas Statham butcher, and had the peace sworn against him.

Bailye and others refused to act for him, and the mobbish tribe were left at full liberty to insult him with impunity. He therefore went armed. When Mallett's father threatened him he in turn threatened to blow out his brains, but only in terrorem; Mallett swore the peace against him. When he was further insulted in the streets he complained to Bailye, but was refused help: 'the laws took no hold of words'. The deponent then said, 'You may kiss my backside', and was ordered seized. He drew his sword. He had his attorney, Stephen Simpson, wait upon the justices to offer reasonable bail for his appearance and good behaviour. They said they would decide bail, but instead Bailye led an attack on him in the street. He fled to Topping's shop where he was seized and arrested, and taken before Adey and Robinson.

He did not present a pistol at Bailye, nor assault him. The bailiffs and town clerk refused to allow Simpson, his attorney, to read or hear any of the informations. Bail was set at £1,000 to answer Wright's complaint, £200 for Mallett's complaint, and £300 for Bailye's complaint. Fettiplace Nott encouraged his being gaoled for want of sureties, an imprisonment that lasted a day longer than necessary because none of the justices could be found to take his bail. When Simpson asked William Thrapp the gaoler for copies of the several warrants, Thrapp said he had only one; but the following day two more were produced (copies annexed).

The deponent is worth more than £15,000, but was obliged to deposit securities worth more than £10,000 for the indemnity of his sureties, being a stranger in Lichfield.

[*Annexed copies*]:

Warrant signed by Joseph Robinson, 26 May, to William Thrapp, keeper of Lichfield gaol, on information of William Bailye that Bronsdon pointed his pistol at him (bail of £300).

Warrant signed by Bailye 25 May, on complaint of Jonathan Mallett the younger that Bronsdon cocked and pointed a pistol at him on 21 May (£200).

Warrant signed by Bailye on complaint of John Wright gentleman, senior bailiff, justice of the peace and quorum, that Bronsdon insulted and drew his sword, Wright being in the execution of his office (bail of £1,000).

[3] Affdt of John Chunall clogmaker of Lichfield, sworn before Richard Hinckley at Lichfield 19 June 1750. ITKB

That Bronsdon and some other gentlemen celebrated Culloden at the Swan inn 16 April with a bonfire in the street and loyal toasts. Betts,

Grundy, Buckley and three others challenged Chunall and others present to fight, and when Bronsdon came out to inquire about the dispute, Betts said 'Damn you who are you' and struck him a violent blow in the face. Bronsdon returned the blow, and he and his friends drove the intruders away from the bonfire but did not pursue them, thereby preventing a possible riot. Since that date, Bronsdon has been continually affronted in the streets of Lichfield, and has frequently complained to the magistrates, although without redress. He has been obliged either to bear perpetual insults or to carry arms, but has not, the deponent believes, done anyone the least injury by doing so.

[4] Affdt of Joseph Hincks shoemaker of Lichfield, sworn before Richard Hinckley at Lichfield 19 June 1750. ITKB

That Charles Wright brother of John Wright, butcher and senior bailiff of the City, called out to Bronsdon 17 April in the morning, 'Oh you poor Snubb! What you pawned your coat last night to treat your company with?' To which Bronsdon calmly replied, 'I suppose you belong to the Corporation' and passed by. Further on he was insulted by William the son of Nicholas Deakin, baker and a magistrate. At the house of Henry Bird, currier, he was chased by Edward Bird, late a common soldier, to the house of Topping, where Bird called Bronsdon snubb and scoundrel and challenged him to come out. The deponent asked Edward 4 June why he had done so; he confessed on his knees 'and wished his hands might rot off' if he lied, that his brother offered him a guinea to do so. The deponent believes that Bronsdon has given no other cause of offence than celebrating Culloden at the Swan.

[5] Affdt of John Shaw turner of Lichfield, sworn before Richard Hinckley at Lichfield 19 June 1750. ITKB

That the Culloden celebration was interrupted by Joseph Grundy, journeyman or servant to his brother John Grundy baker and sheriff of the city, John Betts bricklayer, George Betts labourer, and Edward Buckley late of Manchester, journeyman cabinet maker late of Manchester. They cried out 'Prince Charles for ever and down with the Rump' [*describes the skirmish as before*], which was appeased by some gentlemen coming out of the Swan. Betts, Grundy and others returned with large sticks and attempted to beat off the deponent and others, but were repulsed. Bronsdon has become the object of their resentment. On 26 May in the evening the deponent heard that Topping's house was beset by a mob seeking Bronsdon, and he saw William Bailye, a bailiff of the city, standing in a back garden near the house, tell others, 'Stand to him lads for he'll run at the sight of a stick and let the first man that sees him knock him down.' Henry Foster the younger alias Bromsgrove, Thomas Foster alias Bromsgrove, Thomas Statham butcher, John Hill and Samuel Buckley the younger were all armed; one young man had a fork.

[6] Affdt of Thomas Slaughter innholder of Lichfield, sworn before Richard Hinckley at Lichfield 20 June 1750. ITKB

That a mob of 40 or more besieged Topping's house, and that the door was attacked by or with the encouragement of William Kent housepainter, Henry Foster the younger, alias Bromsgrove, journeyman joiner, William Bailye apothecary (who had a thick stick), Charles Hassells apothecary, Ezekiel Betteridge journeyman watchmaker, Martin Foster the elder alias Bromsgrove joiner, Charles Wright butcher, James Wright shoemaker and Thomas Harvey writing clerk to Joseph Adey. The deponent remonstrated with Bailye, junior bailiff of the City, who expressed his determination to get in. No warrant was shown or mentioned. Bailye later produced a copy of the *Riot Act*,[66] which he gave to John Grundy, baker and sheriff, ordering him to read the *Act* if the mob did not disperse. But Bailye changed his mind, in spite of the deponent's entreaties, on the grounds that many present were neighbours.

[7] Affdt of Richard Eardley gentleman of Lichfield, sworn before Richard Hinckley at Lichfield 19 June 1750. ITKB

That the deponent entered the house when it was first surrounded by the mob and found Ann Topping and Elizabeth James, her daughter, both very ill and in the greatest terror of the mob breaking into the house, where Ann Topping keeps a shop stocked with fine laces, silks, linens and other goods of great value. He conducted Elizabeth James safely out of the house, then returned and stayed. Later in the evening a large mob broke in [*as described*]. The deponent saw Kent, Henry Foster, Thomas Statham and Samuel Buckley the younger among those who entered Ann Topping's chamber and almost terrified her into fits. When they came downstairs the deponent saw Thomas Foster, alias Bromsgrove, and Samuel Green, late a sailor who had lately come out of Lichfield gaol after a whipping for some criminal offence. Once Bronsdon was found he was hurried away to the gaol or the town hall within its limits, without chance to get bail. Bronsdon carries arms but never uses them, causing William Bailye to declare him a coward. But once Bronsdon was committed Bailye swore the peace against him

---

[66] 1 Geo I st.2, c.5 (1714).

in order to make it more difficult for Bronsdon, who was almost a stranger in the place, to get bail.

[8] Affdt of Peter Sedgwick wine merchant, servant to Peter Garrick of Lichfield, wine merchant, sworn before Richard Hinckley at Lichfield 23 June 1750. ITKB

That he saw Thomas Harvey lead Kent and Henry Foster the younger round to the back of Topping's house and, after the door was broken in, saw them and Thomas Foster, Thomas Cleaver apprentice to William Bailye, and others in the house. Cleaver was armed with a common axe; others had halberds and various offensive weapons inside the house. The deponent saw Henry Foster break open the cellar door.

[9] Affdt of Thomas Kennedy yeoman of Lichfield, sworn before Richard Hinckley at Lichfield 19 June 1750. ITKB

That the deponent saw 26 May a riotous mob of upwards of 100 people including Thomas Statham butcher, Henry Foster the younger alias Bromsgrove journeyman joiner, and William Kent journeyman house-painter (which two last are the most notorious, turbulent and mobbish fellows within the city) surrounding Topping's house. Foster and Kent carried poleaxes and barrel staves and tried to break down the door of the shop. The mob did substantial damage to the door, then broke down the back door of the house. The mob was encouraged by Thomas Harvey, writing clerk to Joseph Adey. Henry Edwards mercer, John Grundy baker, Charles Hassalls apothecary, and Samuel Green late a sailor and convicted felon, were among the rioters who encouraged them. The deponent further believes that the mob had no warrant or authority to enter the house.

[10] Affdt of Anne Bailye wife of Thomas baker of Lichfield, sworn before Richard Hinckley at Lichfield 19 June 1750. ITKB

That Bronsdon had been frequently abused in the streets by Martin Foster the younger, alias Bromsgrove. She saw John Wright, senior bailiff, in conversation 21 May with Bronsdon, who said 'You may kiss my backside.' Wright ordered John Grundy, baker, who was not a constable, to seize Bronsdon; the latter drew his sword to defend himself, but made no other belligerent moves, and quickly left. Wright and others present treated it as a joke. The deponent further believes that Wright, although he had not been acting as a justice at the time, later had his brother justices commit Bronsdon to the common gaol until he could pay £1,000 bail for his good behaviour.

[11] Affdt of Solomon Edly mason of Lichfield, sworn before Richard Hinckley at Lichfield 20 June 1750. ITKB

That the mob around Topping's house increased from about 20 to over 100 in the course of several hours. Thomas Harvey, writing clerk and leader of the mob, encouraged William Kent, housepainter and late a common soldier, Henry Foster alias Bromsgrove journeyman joiner, and John Wright labourer, three bold and desperate fellows, to break down the door or pull down the house. The deponent later saw Kent, Henry Foster, Thomas Foster alias Bromsgrove, Thomas Statham butcher, Samuel Buckley journeyman shoemaker, persons of little or no property, and Samuel Green a common felon, enter the house. Also in the crowd were William Webb baker, John Onyon butcher, Jonathan Mallett the younger apprenticed apothecary, Thomas Mallett husbandman, John Thornton blacksmith, Richard Barford innkeeper, and Humphrey Bond shoemaker. Bronsdon was roughly handled, and taken to the gaol and confined from Saturday to Monday when he gave bail. The rioters did not so much as mention a warrant, nor did they charge Bronsdon with any crime to justify these outrageous proceedings.

[12] Affdt of John Eardley apprentice to Carey Butt, apothecary of Lichfield, sworn before Richard Hinckley at Lichfield 20 June 1750. ITKB

That he saw Jonathan Mallett the younger, maltster, presenting a very heavy stick at Edward Bronsdon 21 May, and cursing loudly. Bronsdon drew out his pistol, saying 'You dog if you strike me I'll blow your brains out', and left. The pistol was not cocked and the deponent believes that Bronsdon did not intend to shoot Mallett or do him any harm. The deponent met William Bailye junior bailiff 26 May, running up Market Street; he said that Bronsdon had run away 'like a cowardly dog' but was now in Topping's and they were sure of him.

[13] Affdt of Carey Butt apothecary of Lichfield, sworn before Richard Hinckley at Lichfield 20 June 1750. ITKB

That the deponent was treating Ann Topping, wife of Sir [*sic*] John Topping, and their daughter. The daughter was so ill 26 May that she was under the care of Dr Wickham. When the mob broke in, Ann Topping relapsed into illness and is under Dr Wickham's care again.

[14] Affdt of the Reverend John White of Lichfield, sworn before Richard Hinckley at Lichfield 20 June 1750. ITKB [*Verso*]: 'Lichfield Staffordshire. Affts of Bronsdon Esqr, Kennedy, Shaw, Hincks, Sedgewick, Rd Eardley, Chunall, Topping, Baylye, Slaughter, Edly, Jn.

Eardley, Butt, & White for Infn agt. Mr White's affidt. 1 Copy 14 Affidts fo: 185 fo: 11.'

That the deponent was told by a terrified guest, Mrs Pratt, of the crowd mobbing Topping's house; she retired from the parlour for some drops and to take the air. The deponent went to help the family, all of whom were in ill health, and was in the house when the mob broke in. Neither of the city constables was present when the house was entered nor did anyone have or pretend to have a warrant. The deponent recognized only Edwards, Harvey, and Mallett. They must be a set of very low and abandoned wretches that could be prompted to do so rash and cruel an act to a man that bears so good a character as Mr Topping.

Further affidavit for prosecution:

Mich 24 Geo II 1750

[15] Affdt of John Clifford writing master of Lichfield, sworn before Uppingham Bourne at Lichfield 6 Nov 1750. ITKB

That the deponent served notice of the rule to Kent, Harvey, Edwards, Statham, Buckley the younger, and Cleaver 30 Oct; to Henry Foster, Mallett, Bailye, and Wright 1 Nov; to Thomas Foster 5 Nov. The deponent has taken two journeys to Birmingham and one to Wednesbury to serve Betts, without success.

[*Annexed*: rule of court of 27 Oct 1750.]

Affidavits for defence:

Hil 24 Geo II 1750/1

[16] Affdt of Thomas Statham butcher, George Betts labourer, Thomas Bromsgrove joiner, John Wright labourer, Thomas Cleaver apothecary, Samuel Buckley the younger shoemaker, and Thomas Mallet yeoman, all of Lichfield, sworn before Richard Hinckley at Lichfield 10 Jan 1750/1. ITKB

[Thomas Statham, George Betts and Thomas Bromsgrove]: That William Bailye junior bailiff and JP of the City informed them on 25 May that he had granted warrants against Bronsdon for several breaches of the peace against John Wright, senior bailiff and JP, and Jonathan Mallett the younger, maltster. William Emery a high constable had been afraid to execute them for fear of being murdered by Bronsdon or his servant; William Brooks the other high constable was ill. Deponents consented to accept two warrants (copies annexed to affdt [26]) to try to arrest Bronsdon, who was armed with sword and pistols and threatened death to anyone who tried to arrest him; they were to be aided by Kent, Henry Bromsgrove, William Pershouse, Richard Darlaston and the constables and dozeners of the city. At Bailye's request they attended at Topping's house on the 26th to arrest Bronsdon under the warrants.

[John Wright]: That as one of the sworn dozeners or petty constables he attended at the arrest.

[Thomas Cleaver, Samuel Buckley the younger, and Thomas Mallet]: That their assistance was requested by the bailiff and constables. The deponent Cleaver denies that he was in the house or had a poleaxe or halberd as Peter Sedgwick swears; nor was he near the back door.

[Samuel Buckley the younger and Thomas Mallet]: That they did not help Kent and Henry Bromsgrove break open the door, but that they did assist in the arrest.

[All]: That they deny all charges of riot.

[17] Affdt of Mary Bailye spinster of Lichfield, sworn before Richard Hinckley at Lichfield 12 Jan 1750/1. ITKB

That Elizabeth James, daughter in law to Topping, and William Bailye (deponent's nephew and junior bailiff of the city) came to her house on the evening of 26 May. James asked Bailye to send word to ask Topping to give up Bronsdon, but Bailye thought it improper to do so. The deponent advised James to ask one Mr Bailye a tanner, and intimate acquaintance of Topping, to do so; James left for his house. She appeared to be greatly afraid that Bronsdon, not the peace officers, would do some harm or mischief.

[18] Affdt of Joseph Adey gentleman, town clerk, and clerk of the peace of Lichfield, sworn before John Hickin at Stafford 16 Jan 1750/1. ITKB

That on 24 April Jonathan Mallett the youngest,[67] apprentice to Charles Hassells apothecary, laid an information before William Bailye, junior bailiff and JP, against Bronsdon for assault and battery with a great stick. Being informed that he appeared a gentleman, rather than grant a warrant, the deponent met Bronsdon on 2 May to request a settlement with Mallett. Bronsdon acknowledged the battery, said Mallett had winked at him, and showed the deponent a loaded pistol: he said that he would blow out the brains of any person affronting him with words, looks, laughter, or any dumb show. The deponent remon-

---

[67] The depositions name both a Jonathan Mallett the younger, maltster, and a Jonathan Mallet the youngest, apprentice apothecary, as well as Jonathan Mallett the elder.

strated; Bronsdon replied that he had killed one man already, and 'that he had money enough and great friends that would save him from being hanged'. Since then Bronsdon has insulted and threatened the deponent, and has committed many outrageous breaches of the peace. The deponent believed that there was a real necessity to break open Topping's door to arrest Bronsdon. After the arrest he often heard him say he was worth nearly £20,000 'and that he would spend £500 with all his heart to put the justices and corporation to £100 expense or less [*sic*], and would prosecute them in all shapes that could be found out in law'. This prosecution is carried on for that purpose.

At the [Lichfield] quarter sessions of 12 July, three bills of indictment against Bronsdon were unanimously found true bills [*copies annexed*].[68] When they were found, the deponent advised the court to insist upon sureties and recognizances for Bronsdon to appear and traverse at the next sessions. Joseph Simpson esquire counsellor at law, and Stephen Simpson gentleman, opposed this advice, arguing that it was illegal or impractical, and that instead the clerk should make out a certificate of the bills being found, so that the justices might issue a warrant of arrest, upon which Bronsdon would find sureties. The Simpsons otherwise threatened the justices with prosecution. The justices were intimidated; soon after Bronsdon left Lichfield, it was said for Scotland, but the deponent is informed that he is in London.

[*Annexed*]: Copies of three indictments, city and county of Lichfield, against Edward Bronsdon late of the parish of St Mary, '16 January 1750 Annexed at the time of swearing before me [*signed*] John Hicken':

Assaulted, and 'did greatly degrade, vilify, menace and insult' John Wright gentleman, justice of the city, in execution of his office, 'then and there telling him ... that he might kiss his ... arse, that the said John Wright was a Jacobite justice and that he could have no Justice there', upon which Wright commanded the arrest of Bronsdon, who thereupon drew his sword and threatened justice and constable in the execution of their offices, so that he avoided apprehension; and for violent assault with swords, pistols, sticks and whips, threatening Wright with a drawn sword. John Wright, prosecutor and witness; Charles Wright, witness.

---

[68] The finding of the indictments as true bills is briefly noted in Lichfield Record Office, manuscript 68, 'Lichfield Quarter Sessions Book 1726–1758', Quarter Sessions of 12 July 1750, held before John Wright (whose name is struck out) and William Bailye, gentlemen bailiffs of the City, and Joseph Parker and Joseph Robinson, gentlemen justices, and Gaol Delivery of 31 Aug 1750.

Common assault 24 April on Jonathan Mallett the youngest, prosecutor and witness; Thomas Statham, witness. Jonathan Mallett the youngest, prosecutor, sworn; Thomas Statham, sworn.

Violent assault with swords, pistols, sticks and whips, on Jonathan Mallett the younger of Lichfield, maltster on 21 May 1750; and for violent assault, by pointing a cocked pistol at Mallett and threatening to kill him. Prosecutor, Mallett.

[19] Affdt of Charles Hassell apothecary, John Grundy baker, Richard Barford innholder, and Thomas Adey innholder, all of Lichfield, sworn before Richard Hinckley at Lichfield 9 Jan 1750/1. ITKB

[All]: That Henry Edwards, Thomas Harvey, William Kent and Henry Bromsgrove (the last two holding constables' staves or poleaxes) stood at Topping's shop door, that Edwards and Harvey told him they had a warrant for Bronsdon's arrest for breaches of the peace, and that if necessary they would break down the door to take him. Harvey then produced a great book from which he read aloud to show that they were entitled to do so. Topping put on his spectacles to read it also, but was interrupted by Uppingham Bourne, attorney of Lichfield, who advised Topping not to admit them. Topping ordered everyone off his premises and shut his shop doors. The deponents did not see the Reverend John White nor do they believe he was present.

[Richard Barford and Thomas Adey]: That they were sworn dozeners or petty constables at the time.

[Charles Hassell]: That some considerable time after Bronsdon entered the house, John White came out of Topping's shop and went to the house of Thomas Slaughter, the Three Crowns, evidently to fetch Bourne.

[All]: That no riot was committed.

[20] Affdt of William Emery breeches maker, one of the head constables of the city of Lichfield, sworn before Richard Hinckley at Lichfield 9 Jan 1750/1. ITKB

That he and William Brooks innholder, the other chief constable, on 23 May received warrants signed by William Bailye for the arrest of Bronsdon. On the 25th Bronsdon stood outside Brooks's house with a brace of pistols, and said 'Let Mr Brooks turn out his three serjeants to take me, and I will send three balls through the first man.' That afternoon the deponent saw Bronsdon's servant riding with a drawn pistol, and Bronsdon with a sword in one hand and a pistol in the other. The deponent laid an information before Bailye, and desired that special constables might assist him in arresting Bronsdon. Brooks was ill; the deponent spent the 26th at a fair at Rugeley.

[21] Affdt of Charles Wright butcher of Lichfield, sworn before Richard Hinckley at Lichfield 11 Jan 1750/1. ITKB

That Bronsdon and his servant came to the door of John Wright, senior bailiff and JP, where Bronsdon said 'Where is the bailiff, damn him, I am come to give him bail', and cursing and swearing, said that he would give bail by blowing out the brains of the first man that should meddle with him.

[22] Affdt of William Bailye apothecary and JP of Lichfield, sworn before Richard Hinckley at Lichfield on 9 Jan 1750/1. ITKB

That on 3 May Bronsdon was brought before him on a warrant issued on the information of Mallett the youngest, when Bronsdon entered into a recognizance to keep the peace and to appear at the next quarter sessions. On 21 May Mallett the younger and John Wright JP laid informations against Bronsdon [*for the acts later indicted: see indictments 1) and 3) in [18] above*]. On 21 and 23 May several more informations were laid on the oaths of Joseph Wheatly the younger, Henry Edwards, Thomas Wakelin, Ralph Spenser the younger, and Joseph Adey against Bronsdon for going armed and threatening murder if even slightly offended. The deponent issued warrants for Bronsdon's arrest. On 25 May William Emery laid an information [*see [20] above*]. The deponent called in the warrants of 23 May and altered them for the 25th, entering also the names of Kent, Pershouse, Statham, Betts, Henry and Thomas Bromsgrove, and Richard Tarleton as special constables. Later that day the deponent saw Bronsdon near the deponent's house, with drawn pistol and sword; the deponent ordered him seized, at which Bronsdon presented his pistol, and then fled into Topping's house.

The deponent took a copy of the Riot Act to Topping's house, fearful that a riot might prevent the arrest of Bronsdon. He gave it to John Grundy, sheriff, and asked him to read it; but as those present appearing to be neighbours and the curious, the *Act* was not read.

[23] Affdt of John Wright gentleman and JP of Lichfield, sworn before Richard Hinckley at Lichfield 12 Jan 1750/1. ITKB

That Bronsdon insulted and threatened the deponent in his office on 21 May [*as in indictment 1), above*]. [*Then corroborates affidavits of Emery and Charles Wright.*] The special constables were all young men of honest and good character, stout resolute young men. On 25 May the deponent received the letter annexed. He cannot remember in the last forty years in Lichfield such disorder and breaches of the peace caused by one man.

[*Annexed*]: Gilb. Walmesley to Mr Bailiff Wright, Friday, 25 May 1750. That he is informed there is a scheme to take Mr Bronsdon this evening, on his return from Sir Richard Wrottesley's, on Wright's warrant. Walmesley believes that such extremities will end in murder.

[24] Affdt of Henry Edwards mercer, and Thomas Harvey gentleman, both of Lichfield, sworn before Richard Hinckley at Lichfield 9 Jan 1750/1. ITKB

[Henry Edwards]: That on 26 May he was summoned to the Old Crown, where he met William Bailye, Fettiplace Nott, Joseph Adey, and Thomas Harvey and others, and was told of Bailye's warrants and the special constables [*named*], and of Bronsdon's flight to Topping's wife's shop. Kent and Bromsgrove and Thomas Adey had the warrants read to them, and the deponents were asked to go to Topping's and inform him of those warrants and that they would be justified in breaking down his door if he did not admit them. The deponents were to take Hawkins's *Pleas of the Crown* in order to show Topping the first three sections of chapter 14.[69]

At Topping's they asked the Reverend John White to ask Topping to speak with them. When he did so, within the hearing of Kent, Bromsgrove, Adey, Hassell, Grundy, and Barford, but not of White, they told Topping that Kent and the others were come to arrest Bronsdon on Bailye's warrants, and read to Topping from Hawkins. Topping was rereading the passage himself when Uppingham Bourne, attorney, told them they could not justify breaking in, and Topping warned them off his premises and shut up his doors. The deponents returned to the Old Crown for instructions.

[Thomas Harvey]: That Bailye then gave instructions that the back door should be entered, and that when he told Kent and Bromsgrove, who had begun to break open the front door, they went around to the back door, broke in and arrested Bronsdon.

[Both]: That they deny involvement in any riot, or activities other than those set out here.

[25] Affdt of Richard Chamberlain barber and peruke maker of Lichfield, sworn before Richard Hinckley at Lichfield 12 Jan 1750/1. ITKB [*Verso*]: 'Affdts of Kent & al, Statham & al, Mary Bailye, Adey, Hassell & al, Emery, Cha: Wright, Wm Bailye, John Wright, Edwards & al & Chamberlain & to show cause agt Infn. 13 Jany 1750 13 Sta fo [*torn*]. 2 Copy 11 affts fo: 233 Each copy 13 [*illegible*] Each copy in the whole 466. fo:5'.

---

[69] William Hawkins, *A Treatise of the Pleas of the Crown* (London, 1716), the most authoritative general treatise on criminal law at the time.

That the deponent lives near Topping and after Bronsdon had taken shelter there, the Reverend John White of the Cathedral Close went from Topping's to Thomas Slaughter's house, the Three Crowns. Topping did not accompany him. Bourne shortly thereafter went from Slaughter's house to where Edwards and Harvey stood at Topping's door, Harvey having a great book in his hand.

[26] Affdt of William Kent joiner and housepainter, and Henry Bromsgrove joiner, both of Lichfield, sworn before Richard Hinckley at Lichfield 1 Jan 1750/1. ITKB

[Both]: That on 25 May they agreed to Bailye's request that they and others, under proper warrants [*copies annexed*], attempt to arrest Bronsdon.

[William Kent]: That on the 26th he and Bailye chased Bronsdon, drawn sword and pistol in hand, into Topping's house. He and Bromsgrove went at 6pm to the Old Crown kept by Richard Barford, where Bailye and Adey provided them with warrants [*copies annexed*] which were read over to them. They were also provided with staves or poleaxes to identify them as peace officers. [*Confirm matter in other defence affidavits.*] Bromsgrove pulled his warrant out of his pocket, showed it to Topping, and told him what it was.

[Both]: That they began breaking down the front door, but desisted because it was strong and because less damage would be done to Topping's house if they entered by the back. Topping denied to them that Bronsdon was in his house, and on his refusal to admit them at the back door they broke in. During the search of the house they never used any indecent words or did a rude action to any one. In the cellars, where they found Bronsdon, they reassured him that 'A hair of your head shall not be hurt'; he surrendered his primed pistols and sword, and then himself. Bronsdon read the warrants and consented to go with them. Samuel Buckley the younger, Thomas Cleaver, and Thomas Mallett were charged to assist the deponents; Thomas Statham, Thomas Bromsgrove, George Betts and Richard Darlaston were four of the special constables in the original warrants [*copies annexed*]. No riot was committed.

[*Annexed*]: Warrant of William Bailye, on the complaint of Jonathan Mallet the younger, maltster, to the constables and dozeners of Lichfield, [*insert*: and also to William Kent, William Pershouse, Thomas Statham, George Betts, Henry Bromsgrove, Thomas Bromsgrove, and Richard Darlaston, appointed hereby as special constables] and the gaoler, William Thrapp, to bring Bronsdon before Bailye to enter a recognizance with two sureties amounting to £1,000 in all to appear at the next quarter sessions and to keep the peace; if Bronsdon refuses, to commit him to gaol. Dated 23 May and 25 May. [*Signed twice*].

[*Another warrant, same terms, same dates, on the complaint of John Wright, gentleman, senior bailiff, and JP.*]

[27] Affdt of John Wright JP of Lichfield and Joseph Adey gentleman, town clerk and clerk of the peace, sworn before Richard Hinckley at Lichfield 28 Jan 1750/1. ITKB

[John Wright]: That he was not present at the Lichfield quarter sessions of 12 July last, which were held before William Bailye, Joseph Parker, and Joseph Robinson. He appeared only as a witness on a bill he preferred against Edward Bronsdon esquire, which was found a true bill by the grand jury. Nor was he involved in the proceedings as a magistrate, or in discharge of Bronsdon's recognizances on 12 July, as is untruly sworn by James Hubbard and Francis Cobb.

He will prosecute further when he can compel Bronsdon's appearance.

[Joseph Adey]: That the discharge of Bronsdon's recognizances was due to the fact that the justices were menaced by Joseph Simpson esquire and his father Stephen, although Adey advised the justices first to require Bronsdon to enter recognizances to appear to the indictments.

Further affidavits for prosecution:

Hil 24 Geo II 1750/1

[28] Affdt of James Hubbard cider merchant and Francis Cobb mercer, sworn before Richard Hinckley at Lichfield 21 Jan 1750/1. ITKB

That Bronsdon's recognizances and sureties were for £1,540, the charges were frivolous, and the bailiffs Wright and Bailye were both judges and parties.

[29] Affdt of the Reverend John White of the Close of the Cathedral Church in Lichfield, sworn before Uppingham Bourne at Lichfield 26 Jan 1750/1. ITKB [*Verso*]: 'Staffordshire. Addl afft of White to discharge rule for infn agt Kent et al.[70] Mr White's supplemental affidavit.'

That the deponent has been informed that in order to invalidate his former affidavit [14], some of the persons charged with breaking into John Topping's house pretend that he was at the Three Crowns in Lichfield for a quarter of an hour while they were endeavoring to break into the house, and that a warrant might have been produced to which

---

[70] Incorrectly endorsed by the clerk as a defence affidavit.

he was not privy. His former affidavit is true. To have left Topping's house would have permitted the mob to enter; he did not go to the Three Crowns until they broke in the door.

Additional affidavit for prosecution:

Ea 24 Geo II 1751

[30] Affdt of John Topping gentleman of Lichfield, sworn before Uppingham Bourne at Lichfield 20 April 1751. ITKB [*Verso*]: 'Lichfield Staffords Additional affdt Topping for Infn agt Kent & al.'
    That he neither knew nor was informed that any warrant had been granted for the arrest of Bronsdon until after his house was broken into, contrary to the affidavits of William Kent and Henry Foster alias Bromsgrove. If they had produced or mentioned a warrant, others in the street would have heard them do so; no one but Kent and Bromsgrove make the claim.

Sources: KB 1/10 Hil 24 Geo II No. 2, Ea 24 Geo II, Trin 24 Geo II, Mich 24 Geo II. KB 21/36 pp.594, 649. KB 36/137.

A.9 Information applied for (30 April 1752)

Defendants: Richard Edge, locksmith, and Henry Wood, mercer and chandler, both of Wednesbury, churchwardens.

Accusation:
Violently assaulting and forcibly detaining the Reverend Henry Saunders of Wednesbury for three hours, 29 Jan 1752.

Rules and process:
Ea 1752: affdts [1] to [3] filed. Trin [8 May 1752]: on reading affdts [1] to [3], rule nisi to FNT for an information (Sir Richard Lloyd).

Affidavits for prosecution:

Ea 25 Geo II 1752

[1] Affdt of Henry Saunders clerk of Wednesbury, sworn before Thomas Howard at Birmingham (Warw) 2 May 1752. ITKB
    That the deponent was sent for 29 Jan 1752 to the house of George Ashbey, clothier and victualler, of Wednesbury, by James Corbett, linendraper and chapman of Bridgnorth (Salop), who invited him to

smoke a pipe with him. Henry Wood, mercer and chandler, Richard Edge, locksmith, John Bird, carpenter, all of Wednesbury, and several others were there.[71] They asked him to play cards, and when he refused, Edge invited him to accompany him in a sociable pipe.

Edge immediately asked with a sneer why the deponent might not have a calf's head for dinner on the morrow[72] rather than on the 29th or 31st. The deponent said that it was his own choice, but that it was unnecessary for Edge to distinguish himself so remarkably as he was a churchwarden. Edge replied that he thought he had seen Tom Aldright walking on the Church Hill like a madman, but that when he got closer, he saw it was the deponent. Edge argued that the Church of England was not orthodox, and that the Kirk of Scotland was. The deponent replied that it was very improper to dispute such things in a public house, but that he would do so at a more convenient place if it pleased Edge. Encouraged by Wood, the other churchwarden, Edge damned the deponent as a fool who could not dispute. The deponent was willing to discuss the matter quietly and if Edge agreed to define terms, to be intelligible to the company. Edge agreed. When Edge used the word 'Kirk', the deponent asked him the meaning of the word. Edge threw his pipe bowl in the deponent's face, and when the deponent asked him why he did so, Edge threw pipes and tobacco, forced a candle several times into[73] his mouth, seized the deponent by the chin and called him an illiterate dog.

Later, in other conversation, Edge repeatedly used the word 'orthodox'. When the deponent asked the meaning of the word 'orthodox', Edge struck him a backhand blow[74] in the face and threw a candlestick with the snuff still burning below his left eye, causing swelling and bleeding afterwards. Edge then struck the deponent several blows, one of which on the temple caused him to stagger and fall against a chair and then[75] into a cradle; Edge and Wood declared the deponent had a soft place in his head which was now made softer. Wood then damned

---

[71] Henry Wood, grocer, and Richard Edge, gunlocksmith, both of Wednesbury, were accused in 1752 of picking the pocket of Joseph Perry, toymaker, of Bilston, for his account book. Recognizances were entered by all three, but no prosecution ensued. SRO, Q/SPr2 Ea 1752, and Q/SBe20 Mich 1752. For John Bird, see case A.4.

[72] i.e., on 30 Jan, the anniversary of the execution of Charles I, a fast day for non-jurors.

[73] Affdt [2] says 'into or near'.

[74] Affdt [3] adds 'but as to that fact can't be very certain'.

[75] Affdt [2] 'believes'.

the deponent for a dumb dog and said the deponent had not yet received a blow, even though the deponent pointed out he was bleeding. Edge asked for a whip to whip this[76] deponent as a scandalous dog. Edge and Wood called him a scrub dog, a scoundrel, a scandalous dog unfit to keep them company, and said that the deponent's whole family was not worth a guinea and the deponent himself was not worth two guineas. The deponent said 'God's will be done' and told Edge he would have to answer for this ill usage, to which Edge retorted 'Damn thee and the law too.' He further threatened to spend £100 pounds on the case. The deponent replied that if he would not take it ill he would put him in a way to spend £500.

Both Edge and Wood seized the deponent on two different occasions, swearing that as churchwardens they would put him in the crib. Some of the others and John Bird unsuccessfully tried to hold back Edge, but Edge seized the deponent by the throat to choke him, and hauled him so that the deponent's shirt collar was torn in two. Wood, mentioning a Miss Butler, said that had the deponent so spoken to his sister, he would have run his sword through him for a scrub dog. Edge and Wood threatened him again, saying that wherever he was on whatever business, even if it were 11 o'clock at night, they would fetch him and put him in the crib. Told that it was locked, they damned themselves if they would not force it off.

In all, the deponent was forcibly detained upwards of three hours,[77] and his face was black from the strokes and bruises, all without the least provocation. He now goes about his work with such trepidation that he is unable to perform his parish duties as he ought and otherwise should do.

[2] Affdt of John Bird carpenter of Wednesbury, sworn before Thomas Howard at Birmingham (Warw) 2 May 1752. ITKB
   [*Repeats affdt [1] almost verbatim; see the notes to that affdt.*]

[3] Affdt of James Corbett, linendraper and chapman, of Bridgnorth (Salop), sworn before George Calley at Bridgnorth 30 April 1752. ITKB
[*Verso*]: 'The King agt Edge & others affdts. R. Banister. fo:12'.
   [*Repeats affdt [1] almost verbatim, with the exception of Saunders's threat to go to law, the reference to Miss Butler, and the threats to seize Saunders at any time to put him in the crib.*]

Sources: KB 1/11 Ea 25 Geo II. KB 21/36 p. 824.

[76] Affdt [2] uses identical language, evidently copied (incorrectly) verbatim, like most of the rest of the text.
[77] Affdts [2] and [3]: 'several hours'.

A.10 Information refused (23 Jan 1753)

Defendants: Sir William Wolseley, baronet; John Clements, clerk; and his wife Mary Clements.

Accusation:
Conspiring to force Ann Robins (late Mrs Ann Whitby) to solemnize a marriage with Sir William Wolseley against her will.

Rules and process:
Hil [5 Feb 1753] on reading affdts [1] to [8], rule nisi to FNT (Bathurst). Ea [28 May 1753]: rule discharged; prosecution to pay costs to be taxed by James Burrow, master of the crown office[78] (Sir Richard Lloyd).

Affidavits[79] for prosecution:

Hil 26 Geo II 1753

[1] Affdt of Ann Robins wife of John Robins esq of Stafford, lately the wife of John Whitby esq of Whitby Wood deceased, and daughter of William Northey esq late of Compton Basset (Wilts), sworn before T.

---

[78] 'Coroner and attorney of the court', the formal designation of the master of the crown office.

[79] Some of the affidavits in this case were reproduced nearly verbatim, with names partially deleted, and pungent editorial comments, in [Benjamin Victor], *The Widow of the Wood* (London: for C. Corbett, 1755) (208pp); citations below are to this edition. Others are *The Widow of the Wood: Being an Authentic Narrative of a late Remarkable Transaction in Staffordshire* (Dublin: S. Powell, 1755 108pp; Glasgow, 1769 164pp). The calendared affidavits given here include some further detail. There was related litigation in the church courts; some of the proceedings in the court of arches were reported as *Robins* v *Wolseley* in 1 Lee 616, 161 ER 225 (25 June 1754); 2 Lee 34, 161 ER 254 (9 Dec 1754); 2 Lee 149, 161 ER 294 (9 May 1755); 2 Lee 421, 161 ER 391 (1 Dec 1757). This attempt by Wolseley to sue Ann for adultery failed (without costs) on the grounds that her marriage to John Robins did take place 16 June 1752 and that Wolseley's witnesses were perjured; Victor refused to answer when questioned if he was the author of the pamphlet. The issue of the marriage was also raised in *Robins* v *Crutchley* (1760), 2 Wilson KB 118, 95 ER 718; 2 Wilson KB 122, 95 ER 721; 2 Wilson KB 127, 95 ER 724. One account of the case is S. A. H. Burne, *The Widow of the* Wood [privately printed pamphlet; Stafford, 1964]; I shall publish another.

Denison at Serjeants' Inn 29 Jan 1753. ITKB [*The mark of Mary Nutt, deponent in affdt [2], appears next to Ann Robins's signature, with the remark, 'referred to in her afft'.*]

That Sir William Wolseley baronet, of Wolseley in Colwich, John Clements clerk of Colwich, his wife Mary, and Richard Wolseley, a relation of Sir William commonly called Captain Wolseley, entered into a conspiracy to force her to solemnize a marriage to Sir William against her will. The deponent was then the wife of John Robins but the marriage at that time was not publicly known. Sir William, John Clements, Mary Clements, and Richard Wolseley also conspired to charge Ann with being actually married to Sir William.

Sir William visited the deponent in June through August of 1752 in a neighbourly manner. Clements and his wife, also neighbours, often visited and told the deponent that Sir William had a great regard for her, but she took no notice given the great disparity in their ages. In July 1752, Sir William asked her to marry him, adding that her refusal would make him 'the most wretched man upon earth'. He offered her a jointure independent of him, and whatever additional income she thought proper after his death, for his estate was unsettled. She refused his generous offer but desired he would speak no more of it, and said she would never entertain any thoughts of him. A few days later Sir William returned to repeat the request, but she insisted he never mention the subject, and agreed to see him on the same grounds as the rest of the neighbourhood. During several visits between that time and 26 Aug 1752 no other mention of courtship was made. Clements and his wife continued to visit the deponent to tell her of how dearly Sir William loved her, of which she took no notice, not suspecting a confederacy.

The deponent was informed 26 Aug 1752 that Sir William had sent for her servant, Richard Derry. When Derry returned from Sir William's house, about a half mile distant, he appeared in a strange confusion and said that Sir William's servants had accused him to Sir William of speaking disrespectfully of the deponent. Derry protested his innocence and told her that Clements would be able to inform her more fully of the affair as he was also at Sir William's house. She went the same day to see Clements who informed her that it was a damned odd infamous affair. Derry had spoken very slightingly of her to Sir William's servants and disrespectfully of Sir William; they had told their master, and it was also insinuated in his family that Derry had intimated that he and she were too familiar. When Sir William heard of this he sent for all the servants in order to clear the deponent's character. It was wrong to make such a bustle about the nonsense of servants, added Clements, but Sir William loved her dearly.

The deponent replied that she did not know by what authority Sir William took it upon himself either to asperse her character or to clear it, which she thanked God was never in question. Derry, who had lived with her many years, had always behaved himself extremely well. Clements replied that Sir William did not believe the least ill of her, but warned that it would make a rumour in the parish, and advised the deponent to marry Sir William. Clements then reaffirmed Sir William's love for the deponent, to which she said she 'would not have him if the whole world depended upon it' (being then married to Robins, although secretly, for particular reasons.)

After being pressed by Clements and his wife, she agreed to stay and dine with them, Mary Clements saying that she would send for the deponent's clothes, being then in her morning dress. After dinner Mary Clements brought her a glass of wine while she was dressing, as the room was cold, and ten or fifteen minutes later, in the parlour, she fell violently ill. She complained to Mary Clements, left the room to buy cloth from a scotsman in the hall; the deponent vomited in a most violent manner out the parlour window. She saw Sir William come into the room, but became insensible and recalls nothing.

When she came to herself, Sir William, John and Mary Clements were standing about her, John Clements with a book in his hand. She again vomited violently. Clements asked her how she could fall into such a fit as it was her wish as well as Sir William's to marry. Alarmed and astonished, she told Clements that he must be mad, for she never would have married Sir William. She said she would call in all the people in the house to know what happened while she was out of her senses. Clements said that making such a noise did not signify, as Sir William was determined take her to his house that night unless she signed a paper; Sir William swore by all that was sacred that he would do so. Being fearful and ill, she signed without knowing its contents. Clements called for cards and one Mr Arms[80] and Clements's children came into the room. The deponent was urged to stay at Clements's house, and Sir William offered his coach, but she refused and called her own coach. After supper she found herself extremely ill again. Sir William rode home with her without her consent but stayed only three minutes at her house. The deponent's servant Mary Nutt undressed her and put her to bed. She vomitted again in the night, fainted two or three times, and for three days after was sick after eating anything.

The next morning Sir William came to see her. When Mary told her, she responded 'good God Mary I never can bear the sight of that base wretch more.' She met him downstairs nonetheless in order to discover

---

[80]   Thus in original; this must be Alms (see affdt [18]).

the contents of the paper she signed the night before, in hopes of having it delivered up to her, and to hear what he had to say in excuse for his behaviour. She told him how ill she had been and added 'Til I drank that cursed glass of liquor I was very well.' Sir William hoped that in her illness she remembered that they were married the last night. In a violent passion, she replied 'Sir I now begin to see through all your plots and suppose you and your base friend Clements gave me that dose that you might afterwards face me out of my reason but I in my senses was never married to you in my life.' Sir William replied, 'married you was to me', that the Clements would be his witnesses, and that 'if any advantage was taken it proceeded from the love I had for you and without you I could live not', and that he would do all in his power to make her happy if she would go with him publicly to a church to be married. If she did not, he would give her a few days to think about it and then send his coach to fetch her to his house. She replied 'I believe there never was so base a plot upon the face of the earth'.

Later the same day John and Mary Clements came to her house, and when he asked if she had seen Sir William, she replied 'Mr Clements can you be so ungrateful to me as to join with Sir William in so vile an aspersion as saying you married me to him', on which Clements swore to her that he had performed the marriage, and that if she did not consent to be publicly married Sir William would come in a few days to take her to his house, for he and Sir William would bring witnesses enough to swear to the marriage, and that he had married the deponent with a licence and therefore was afraid of nobody. He wondered she could object to a person of Sir William's great fashion, and be not pleased with being the top of the parish. Mrs Clements said she was ready to swear that her husband had married the deponent to Sir William. The deponent told her she did not in the least doubt that she would do or swear anything considering she had brought the liquor which so much disordered her, and *hoped God Almighty would punish such crimes* and declared that 'she would be torn in a thousand pieces before she would marry Sir William.'[81] After 26 Aug John Clements persisted in visiting and saying that she was married to Sir William.

After this the deponent behaved civilly to the conspirators in hopes of obtaining the paper they had compelled her to sign. A few days before 23 Sept, Sir William said he had to leave the country as he could not bear to see her if she would not have him. He apologized for her uneasiness, and said he hoped she did not have too bad an opinion of him. She said she was glad that he had some remorse, and that she

---

[81] The italicized words appear so in *Widow of the Wood*, 71, but are not emphasised in the original.

would try to forget her injury, but insisted she must see the paper she had signed. Clements and Sir William said that she might see it at her convenience. On 23 Sept she went to Clements's house to do so. He said she might see it after dinner. Mrs Clements said she expected Miss Sneyd to come for tea in the afternoon or that she might go to see Mrs Copes, another neighbour, to play cards. Sir William was also expected that afternoon. The deponent stayed after dinner and spent time with Mrs Clements while Clements disappeared to get the paper. She later found Clements, Sir William and Captain Wolseley in the parlour. Clements whispered to her that he had the paper in his pocket and that she would get it once Sir William and his nephew left. Frustrated, the deponent went to get into her coach when Sir William approached and asked her to carry him and his nephew to Wolseley Bridge. The deponent consented and before she left Clements assured her that he would bring her the paper.

The morning of 24 Sept Mary Nutt told her that Richard Derry had told Mary that the deponent was seen last night and she had married Sir William at Colwich Church. The deponent sent for Clements. When he arrived, Derry and the deponent went into the room with him and she ordered Derry to relate the whole story he had heard and ordered Clements to declare whether it was true or false. Clements called it a 'damned lie' and swore he married no one last night. The deponent left for Colwich Church and met Sir William there. She asked him to come to her house and that she was resolved to know the author of this report. Sir William asserted he had no idea how such a scandalous lie could be spread, but she insisted he do his utmost to find out who did. Sir William returned in the afternoon with Clements. Sir William said that a woman named Coleman started the lie, but when questioned said she was only relaying what Draper, a tailor, had told her. Sir William sent for Draper but he was not at home. The next morning, 25 Sept, Clements came to the deponent's house and pretended to be in a great fright and told her that everyone believed he had married her to Sir William. If the bishop heard this, Clements feared his 'gown would be stripped over his ears'. He begged the deponent to marry Sir William to cover his mistake from the bishop. She asked how he could take her for such a fool, telling him that he was a liar. That night Sir William informed her he had spoken to Draper who, under oath, said he never saw the two married but rather heard they were from Clements's servant. The next day Clements returned and admitted to the deponent that he, Sir William and his nephew had been in the church on 23 Sept looking at his family monument. The deponent accused them of scheming to cause the report of marriage themselves, and told him his previous oaths were a sham and mockery. Clements then said that she had better come to church to be married and that he would swear anything to serve Sir William as he had indemnified him. At this point the deponent left the room and got Mary Nutt to listen at the door. When she returned Clements said no one would believe her story. Sir William came later that night and did not deny he indemnified Clements to swear they were married. He insisted there were others besides Clements who would swear to the marriage. If she would not marry him in public he and Clements would continue to spread the story.

In order to avoid their company, the deponent confined herself to her chamber for days and was ill. Mr Robins returned and heard the rumour. The deponent sent Nutt to tell Robins of the terrible situation. In the meantime, Sir William continued to visit her and now threatened to take her away by force. Later, Clements came into her room without her consent and started to drag her out of bed to church. She had Nutt and Derry outside the door. She screamed and Nutt burst into the room. Clements left at that point. Sir William returned again and threatened to take her by force to the church. Clements and Sir William came another day and Nutt (who was always called to the deponent's side when either Clements or Sir William came, to act as a witness) told them she was determined to send for the deponent's brother William Northey esq. Nutt left, and Clements said he would turn Northey and all her friends against her. Mrs Clements came another day and said she should marry Sir William first because he was old and would not live long, and then she could marry Mr Robins. Clements and Sir William came another day and the deponent asked to see the paper she signed on 26 Aug. They refused because she was 'so damned obstinate' and said they would make use of it if they thought proper.

The deponent believes the paper she signed was a marriage contract, and that the liquor she was given contained laudanum or some other opium extract. The deponent believes Clements has made an entry in the Colwich register of her marriage to Sir William on 23 Sept last, but believes the entry was not made until November. She never married nor agreed to marry Sir William. The deponent believes that Captain Wolseley has sworn to the marriage and to having given her away.[82]

[82] See *Widow of the Wood*, 52–97, where the transcribed affidavit is followed by the comment: 'The Reader, I am of Opinion, is very glad to see the End of this *famous Affidavit* of A-N THE WIFE OF J-N R—-NS, ESQ;—Copies of which, I am well informed, were industriously sent to most of the Counties in *England!* The next read in Court was the long Affidavit of M—Y N—T, the Lady's Chamber-maid; which I will not tire my Reader by inserting, since it only *corroborates* and *confirms* every Article where she is mentioned in the foregoing tedious, tautological Affidavit.'

[2] Affdt of Mary Nutt servant to John Robins esq of Stafford, sworn before T. Denison at Serjeants' Inn 29 Jan 1753. ITKB [*Signed with a mark.*]

That her mistress Ann Robins left the house 26 Aug 1752 before dinner in perfect health. She returned before 11 pm with Sir William Wolseley who did not stay three minutes. With great difficulty deponent got her upstairs, undressed her, and put her to bed; she was sick and ill and for three hours she was quite stupid and had no sense left in her. She vomited extremely. She was ill and for two or three days was sick after she had eat anything. When the sickness was a little over her mistress shed tears and said, 'Oh Mary it was something Mrs Clements gave me at Mr Clements's they told me it was wine but I think it will kill me for I was taken just as bad at Mr Clements's in a few minutes after I had drank it.' She fainted two or three times, wept violently in her agony, and said 'ill usage I have met with at Mr Clements's hath shocked my very soul.'

When Sir William came the following morning Robins said, 'Good God Mary I never can bear the sight of that base wretch more' before going down to meet Sir William; the deponent followed and hearkened at the door. She said she thought the cursed glass of liquor would have killed her. Sir William said he hoped that in her illness she had not forgotten that he and Robins had been married last night. Robins asked how he could state so infamous a falsity, and said 'Sir I begin now to see through all your plot and suppose you and your base friend Clements took care to give me a does that you might after that face me out of my reason'. She went to her room and fell into a sad passion of weeping. She then recounted to the deponent all the events that transpired the night before. [*Substantiates affdt [1].*][83] The next day Wolseley called to say that as he could not have her he could not bear to see her, that once he had settled his affairs he would leave the country[84] and see Wolseley no more.

Robins went to see Clements 23 Sept 1752 between 1pm and 2pm and returned that night. The next day the deponent with some hesitation told Robins that Derry had told her that Robins and Sir William had been seen married at Colwich Church that night, 23 Sept, at the

---

'The Third produced, was the copious Affidavit of R——-D D——Y, the Lady's chief Man-servant; which corresponds, in every Circumstance, with the former Two; which the Reader, I doubt not, will give Credit for—but the Fourth [*see [4]*], read in Court, must not be omitted.' Thus Derry's important affdt [3] is omitted from *Widow of the Wood*.

[83] Mary Nutt's signature also appears on [1], to show that Nutt had read it.

[84] In the common eighteenth-century sense of 'county'.

communion table, and that they designed ringing the bells, which would shock her and make Mr Robins uneasy. His mistress had Derry fetch Clements immediately, who went with Derry and Robins into a room. He came again the next day, pretending to be in a great fright; the deponent was at the door listening. He said Draper would swear that he married them, and that if the bishop heard of it he would strip his gown over his ears and he therefore begged Robins to marry Sir William the very next day. A day or two later Clements came back and the deponent was ordered to stay at the door to hear the conversation. Robins said she would tell of all the base usage and threats she had suf-fered from him, to which Clements answered no one would believe her for she would be the only witness on her side. Clements said he would swear whatever Sir William wanted him to. Her mistress said their gang could swear what they wished until they died but she would never marry Sir William.

Mr Robins had been from home, and on his return to his house at Stafford sent to know the reason of this report of marriage. Her mistress sent her to him to tell him the terrible situation: Sir William repeatedly coming by to take her to church to be married, threatening to do so by force, and saying he had friends who would swear they were married anyway.

Clements coming most days, her mistress ordered Derry or this deponent to be at the doors. One day Clements asked the deponent what she thought was the matter with her mistress, and said 'surely your mistress is not uneasy at the talk which is in the neighbourhood ... that people were pleased to say she was married to Sir William.' The deponent said, that never can be, and he said 'No by the Heavens she was not by his soul he would take his sacrament oath she was not mar-ried to Sir William.' He asked if she could be uneasy about Mr Robins, and the deponent said she could not have any cause to be. He asked her to tell him how her mistress spent the night; she reported to him next day that she had spent a bad night, had two fits, and had cried out 'Hold me Mary and keep me from those black dogs for I will never see them more Oh I will be torn to pieces before I will see those black devils more.' When she came to herself she begged the deponent to give her some opium that she might sleep and never wake more. The depon-ent asked her what she could mean by such a request; she replied the villains would 'drive her distracted for she could not bear to live and have such infamy laid to her charge which she knew herself innocent of.' Clements said he believed her mistress was not ill and he would go up and take her with him to Colwich to divert her and then he thought much would not ail her. Clements went up, and then she and Derry ran up and listened at the chamber door. Clements said to Robins, you are not ill but must come with me to be married at Colwich church to Sir William. She ordered him out of her room, then screamed, and the deponent ran in and found Clements dragging her mistress out of the bed by the arms; she cried out 'Lord Mary help me', and fainted. Clements left without one word more.

Sir William came a day or two after and this deponent heard him threaten that he would bring his coach the next morning and take her away by force, for he had people enough that would swear he had married her 23 Sept. She refused absolutely to marry him. On another day when Clements and Sir William came, the deponent said she would send for Mr Northey, her mistress' brother, as she was so miserable and no friend with her. She left the room, listened at the door, and heard Clements complain of this deponent's great impertinence, and to take care as they would set Mr Northey and all her own friends against her, and she would never be believed. He swore on his soul that they would take care to make her ashamed to show her face amongst any of her friends. Her mistress replied that so long as she knew her own innocency, she should never fear such villains as them.

Having heard that Richard Wolseley has declared he saw them married, she believes he was in confederacy with Sir William Wolseley and the Clements.

[3] Affdt of Richard Derry servant to John Robins esq of Stafford, sworn before T. Denison at Serjeants' Inn 29 Jan 1753. ITKB [Verso]: 'Richard Derry's Affidavit. Richard Derry's Affidavit. fo: 46.'

That the deponent was called to Sir William's house 26 Aug 1752 by his servant George Everill. Benjamin Victor was there, and told the deponent in the presence of Sir William that his servants charged the deponent of speaking disrespectfully of his mistress; he denied it, and he did not know any ill of her. After a great many threats Victor produced a paper acknowledging his guilt and begging his mistress's pardon, and insisted he sign it. Sir William and Victor pressed him to sign, saying it signified nothing, but that he had better sign or it would be all over the neighbourhood and county, and worse might come of it. Clements, who was also present, kept winking at the deponent telling him to sign because it meant nothing. He absolutely refused for the best part of an hour. When Sir William threatened to call the deponent to account, he signed it. When Clements and the deponent rode away together, Clements told him he was a 'damned fool' to sign the paper. He replied that he would not have signed it had it not been for Clements's hints. Clements said nothing and rode away.

When the deponent reached home he explained to his mistress Ann Robins what had happened; she immediately took her hat and went to see Clements. She came home in a stupor in her coach at 11pm with Sir William, who stayed only three minutes; apart from the coachman, Mary Nutt, and himself, all the servants had gone to bed. [*Substantiates the account of the illness given in affdt [2] and the overheard conversation with the Clements reported in affdt [1].*]

On 23 Sept accompanied his mistress to Clements's house, she came home that night. Meanwhile the deponent went to Stafford came round by Great Haywood, where he heard a report that his mistress had been married to Sir William that night, by night with two candles on the communion table of Colwich church; that Draper would swear to it; and that they planned to ring the bells. He related this to Mary Nut, who told her mistress. She had him fetch Clements the next morning, when he told him what he had heard. Clements said it was a damned lie; he never knew such a parish for raising damned lies. She asked for assurance, and he said 'upon his soul and as God was his judge and wished he might be damned if he had married any soul that night.' He left; his mistress told the deponent to tell the ringers that she would resent it extremely if they rang the bells.

One day standing at the door (as his mistress had ordered Mary Nutt and himself to do whenever Clements or Wolseley visited), he heard Clements tell Robins that she and Sir William should be married at the church for Sir William had given him £1000 security to indemnify him and he would swear anything to serve Sir William; she had better make the marriage her own act rather than risk being exposed to her friends and all the world.

[*Substantiates account in affdt [2] of bringing Clements to Mary Nutt, and her account of Clements conversation with Robins, and bursting into the room when she screamed.*] Mary Nutt and himself were the only servants his mistress thought proper to trust in this affair, as she hoped by keeping it secret they would drop their designs against her.

John Robins had been away on a journey but sent a letter back through his servant William Thompson saying that he was surprised and uneasy because he heard his wife had married Sir William. Thompson was told Robins's own servant would inform him, as she was too ill to write. The deponent and Mary Nutt went to John Robins and told him all they knew; he said that he was too ill to come immediately but would ride over in a day or two. In the meantime he ordered the servants to repell with their own force every insult offered to his wife, and that he would justify them. The deponent has heard Captain Richard Wolseley say several times that he gave Robins away at the wedding, and therefore believes him to be in confederacy with Sir William and John and Mary Clements.

[4] Affdt of John Robins esquire of Stafford, sworn before T. Denison at Serjeants' Inn 29 Jan 1753. ITKB

That in June 1752 the deponent and Ann Whitby, widow of John Whitby, were married. At her request he agreed to keep the marriage secret for 12 months. He allowed his wife to live in her own house at Whitby Wood and go by her widow name. After a journey into Derbyshire where he stayed for ten days in September and October, the deponent returned home to hear to his great surprise that his wife Ann Whitby (so called because their marriage was not publicly known) had been married to Sir William. He sent to her to know the reason, and Mary Nutt immediately afterwards in person informed him of the treatment his wife had had at the hands of Sir William and the Clements and their plot or conspiracy to forcibly marry her to Sir William without her consent, as set out in her affidavit, which the deponent has heard read over and carefully attended. It corresponds in all material circumstances to the account she gave him. To prevent further ill treatment he determined to publish his marriage to his wife, and soon after caused his wife to be brought home to him *with whom he was ever since since cohabitated!* A few minutes after she entered his house she fell into violent fits, fainting or swooning away, and when she recovered raving, calling for the deponent when he was in her presence, crying out 'those rogues will swear my life' and other frantic and disordered expressions, which he believes resulted from the ill-treatment she received from Sir William and John and Mary Clements.[85]

[5] Affdt of John Hickin gentleman of Stafford, sworn before John Dearle at Bishton[86] in the parish of Colwich on 23 Jan 1753. ITKB

'John Robins Esq & Ann Whitbey were married — 16 June 1752.'

That the preceding entry is a true copy of the register book of the parish of Castle Church. There is a report being spread in the neighbourhood that Ann Robins was married to Sir William by John Clements September last. On 12 Oct 1752 the deponent checked the marriage register from 12 Oct 1751, the date on which Sir William's former wife was still alive, to the 25 Sept 1752, the date of the last entry then in the book, for the baptism of Jeremiah the son of Joseph Price. There was no entry for the marriage of Sir William to Ann Robins. On 12 Oct Clements and his wife, and their maid, swore upon their souls that Ann Robins and Sir William were not married by John Clements

---

[85]   Printed in *Widow of the Wood*, 98–101, with emphasis as shown (although not in the original).

[86]   Bishton Hall. This and the following three affidavits are cited but not printed in *Widow of the Wood*, 101.

nor are they married at all. Clements told the deponent that a mis-
understanding arose when Clements and Sir William went to the
church to take an inscription of a family monument where Sir William's
ancestors are buried. A neighbour saw Clements and Sir William come
out of the church; Ann Robins was at Clements's house at this time, and
the neighbour started the rumour about a marriage. Clements and the
deponent went through the registry together to satisfy the deponent
there was no marriage.

The deponent has since heard that the entry for Robins's and Sir
William's marriage of 23 Sept was not made until 29 or 30 Nov 1752. He
and others were told 2 Jan by George Whiston, parish clerk and schoolmaster, that Clements had him make an entry in the register that Robins
and Sir William were married; Whiston said he had not been a witness
to the marriage. About 16 Dec 1752, Whiston was sent for by Clements.
He found Clements in company with Edward Whitby, esq, and they
made a true copy of the entry of Robins's marriage to Sir William from
the register. On the instructions of Whitby, Whiston swore an affdavit
before John Dearle 16 Dec saying that the copy of the entry was a true
copy.

The deponent has seen two modus receipts dated 13 Nov 1752 signed
by Clements to John Robins which he believes to be true. One was for
6s 8d for Whitby Wood and the other for 10s for upper Prentice Hays
both occupied by Ann Robins before her marriage to John Robins. On
13 Oct 1752 the deponent visited Sir William and told him of the entry
of marriage for John and Ann Robins of June last, and that they were
married at Castle Church by the Reverend Corne, curate. Sir William
desired the deponent to give his compliments to Mr and Mrs Robins
and wished the couple happiness. He did not intimate that he was married to Ann but rather said that he had such expectations of doing so
that he had sent away to London last Saturday to order new liveries for
his servants.

[6] Affdt of William Brookes gentleman of Stafford and William Atkins
yeoman of Bishton in Colwich parish, sworn before John Dearle at
Stafford and Bishton respectively 23 Jan 1753. ITKB

[William Brookes]: That 'John Robins Esq & Ann Whitby were married 16 June 1752' is a true copy of an entry in the registry of the parish
of Castle Church. On 22 Jan 1753 the deponent was going to church to
look for an entry of the marriage of Robins and Sir William in the register when he met Clements who said he would not let the deponent see
it and was advised not to let anyone see it. He asked a second time that
day but Clements refused. If any entry was made of the marriage it was
not made until the 29 or 30 Nov 1752 and it stated that Ann and William

were married on 23 Sept 1752. He believes this because George Whiston, who is parish clerk, schoolmaster, and clerk to Sir William, who is an acting justice of the peace, told him and others 2 Jan that Clements sent for him to make an entry of the marriage, which he did. Whiston said there was no entry of the marriage in the register before that time, nor was he present at the marriage. Whiston said he was also sent for 16 Dec 1752, when he found Clements and Edward Whitby examining the entry concerning the marriage of Sir William and Ann Robins. He made a copy which was certified a true copy by Clements. At the request of Whitby he went to Stafford and swore before Dearle that it was a true copy and confirmed Clements's signature.

[William Atkins]: That he was present when Whiston made his statement, and confirms Brookes's evidence in this affidavit. Sometime in Nov 1752, after Ann and John Robins made their marriage public and began cohabitating, he asked Clements if he had married Sir William and Robins, and he said no. He heard Clements refuse 22 Jan to let Brookes examine the register book.

[7] Affdt of Walter Cartwright barber of Little Haywood in the parish of Stowe [*sic*],[87] sworn before John Dearle at Little Haywood 23 Jan 1753. ITKB

That Clements sent for the deponent on 12 Nov 1752 and told him to go to Stafford the next morning to bring back two modus from John Robins which were due to Clements as vicar of the parish from Ann's estate. Clements gave the deponent two receipts dated 13 Nov 1752. Clements also instructed the deponent to ask for the marriage fees due to Clements because Ann was a parishioner. John Robins gave the deponent the money for the two modus, one for 6*s* 8*d* and the other 10*s*, and 5*d* for the money due on the marriage fees and he gave Robins a receipt. He gave Clements all the money owing to him. The signature on the receipts is the true handwriting of John Clements.

[8] Affdt of William Draper tailor of Colwich, sworn before John Dearle at Bishton on 23 Jan 1753. ITKB [*Verso*]: 'Stafford. Affts of Robins Nutt Derry J Robins Hickin Brooke and one other Cartwright and Draper for Infn agt Wolseley Bart & al. Vaughan 2 Gns fo: 296 10:11:0 Rec'd H A fo: 7 fo: 52.'

That the deponent was at the Clements's house 23 Sept 1752 when John Aston, Clements's servant, informed the deponent that Ann Whitby had married Sir William just a half hour before although he

---

[87] Little Haywood is in the parish of Colwich.

himself had not seen them married, if they were married at all. The deponent told Alice Coleman, wife of William Coleman, innkeeper, of the marriage, and a report immediately spread. The deponent was not present, nor does he known on his own knowledge of a marriage. On 25 Sept Clements asked the deponent how dare he spread news of the wedding and denied that he had ever married them, but said he thought they soon would be married and told the deponent to go with him to Sir William's house. Sir William had him swear an oath on a prayer book or testament to tell the truth. The deponent told him he had never seen a marriage but heard of it in the manner deposed above.

Affidavits for the defence:

Ea 26 Geo II 1753

[9] Affdt of Sir William Wolseley bart of Wolseley, sworn in court 9 May 1753. ITKB[88] [*Verso of bundle*]: 'Stafford. Affdits of Sir W. Wolsely, the Revd J. Clements, Victor, Wolseley, Alms, Walker et al, E. Clements et al, Asston, Whiston & Spilsby to show cause agt Informatn for Sr Wm Wolseley et al. Easter Term 1753 fo 417'.

   That the deponent did not conspire with Clements or his wife or Richard Wolseley to compel Ann Whitby to marry him. The marriage took place lawfully 23 Sept last. The acquaintance and intimacy between the two did not start as Ann Whitby alleges. The acquaintance was begun by the friendship of his sons and hers when they met on 6 June last on the deponent's land, with her encouragement, and she invited his sons to stay supper with her. He took tea with her the following day. He was surprised, as for many years there had been great shyness between the two families. He met Mrs Whitby at her invitation on a number of occasions, including visits with Mr and Mrs Chetwynd and Sir Richard Wolseley, bart, the deponent's brother, who with his lady stayed with him 18 June on their way to Ireland from London. Mrs Whitby sent her compliments and visited. In July and August he frequently visited, dined, and stayed alone with her in the evenings, and met her also at Mr Clement's house in Colwich. His intimate friend Mr Victor accompanied him to Mrs Whitby's 7 Aug, where they met Mrs Eld wife of Master Eld, who asked all of them to dine at Seighford, where they stayed until about 11, coming back with Mrs Whitby in her coach, to which she made no objection.

---

[88]   Printed in *Widow of the Wood*, 104–150. The italicized passage is not reproduced there.

Her friendly behaviour toward him led the deponent to believe that his addresses to her by way of marriage would not be disagreeable to her. The deponent's proposal in mid-August was accepted, but Mrs Whitby enjoined secrecy, fearing her brother Northey would prevent the wedding and fearing opposition from the Whitby family of Haywood. The deponent opposed the secrecy and repeatedly insisted she write to her brother, asking for his consent and approbation, and even dictated a letter to that effect. Although she said she had written Northey, she did not. The deponent continued to visit her nearly every day. It was known to the whole neighbourhood that a marriage would take place.

At this time, Robins lived close by, about five or six miles from the deponent's house and at Ann Whitby's house, at Stafford or at Beaudesert. John Robins knew of the deponent's addresses to Mrs Whitby and was told by several persons in September of the reports of her marriage to the deponent. The deponent was not told about a marriage between John Robins and Ann Whitby until Hickin told him 20 Oct.

The deponent consented to the private marriage and on 19 Aug Benjamin Victor, confidant to both parties, became bound with the deponent and bond and licence were executed at Clements's house in the presence of Mrs Whitby, when she was in her perfect senses and understanding. On 17 or 18 Aug Victor went to her house to fix the date of the wedding and 25 August, the first day of Lichfield races, was agreed upon, as her servants would be there and the secret better kept. On 22 Aug the deponent gave Victor a writing to be executed before the marriage, a release of dower if he died first. Before Victor could so so she desired to see the deponent, who then produced the writing. She seemed to disliked it, said she would consider, and the marriage was postponed. The deponent then declared he could not marry on any other terms for fear of prejudice to his present children.

On 27 Aug the deponent examined Richard Derry for speaking disrespectfully of Mr Whitby, having said 'He could, or would, bring his ... mistress on her knees for her former sins.' The deponent believes he spoke this way to prejudice the deponent against Mrs Whitby and prevent the marriage, since Derry would probably lose his place after the marriage. He reprimanded Derry, and proposed that he beg his lady's pardon and sign the following paper drawn up by Victor:

'Whereas I Richard Derry livery servant to Mrs Ann Whitby, widow of Whitby Wood, in the county of Stafford, do hereby declare, in the presence of the Rev. Mr Clements, curate of the parish of Colwich, in said county, and Benjamin Victor, of the city of Dublin, gent. That I have spoke some base and injurious expression of my lady, the said Mrs Whitby, before some of Sir William Wolseley's servants at Wolseley Hall: Now I do hereby declare, that my said expressions, then and there uttered, were false and scandalous, and that I know nothing bad or criminal ever done or transacted by the said Lady. And do heeby most humbly ask her Pardon for the said injurious expressions. Witness my hand the 21st day of August 1752.' It was witnessed by Clements and Victor. Some time later at her house, Mrs Whitby was very uneasy and exclaimed vehemently about the examination but the deponent assured her that he trusted her honour and on the terms proposed would marry her the next day publicly.

Later, it might be 26 Aug, Clements came and took him to see Mrs Whitby at his house. She was very distressed about Derry, cried, and fell into a fainting fit. Water and hartshorn was brought, and held to her nose, and given her to drink. She then fell into an hysteric fit for three quarters of an hour while he held her head on his arm, crying out 'That villain Victor has done this to break the match', 'I will never injure Sir William or his children', 'Mrs Clements where is Sir William, I love him, send Mr Clements for him, pray you Mrs Clements send for him'. The deponent commented to Mrs Clements that he had never known someone speak so rationally during a fit. Clements, who was also present, had no book in his hand then, or at any time that evening or night. On recovering, Mrs Whitby drank tea, played at cards, and seemed perfectly well and very merry. The deponent left her at her home. He did not tell Mrs Whitby that she was married to him then, or at any time before 23 Sept. Nor did he use any threats or arguments to induce her to sign any paper as set forth in her affidavit. She never vomited, nor declared in his hearing that wine given her by Mrs Clements had caused the fit or illness. He continued to visit her almost daily, and she still freely consented to marry him.

On 29 Aug Victor left for Ireland, having written to Mrs Whitby without the deponent's knowledge or privity, expostulating with her to sign the release of dower on the Wolseley estates, as she already had an affluent fortune for life which would revert to her children by Mr Whitby, and telling her that this deponent's relations could not possibly ever visit her on any other terms as she would have it in her power to injure the children of this deponent's family; the deponent read a sealed copy left for him by Victor. On the afternoon of 29 Aug the deponent received a letter from Mrs Whitby in her own hand, proposing a meeting that evening, and mentioning the letter from Victor, who she was sorry had judged 'so horridly of one who in spite of him, and all the world, will ever be a sincere Well wisher to yourself and family.'[89] From that day until 23 Sept the deponent visited her almost every day at her house or Clements's, and they often discoursed about the

---

[89]   The original is attached to affdt [10].

application of her jointure, she insisting that this deponent not receive the whole for his own use. At last it was agreed that the deponent should have only £300 a year of her former jointure of £400 a year, and that the residue together with £160 a year, which she was otherwise entitled to, she should have to her separate use, and that the deponent should provide for any children he might have by her in the same manner as his present younger children. A paper writing to this effect was prepared by the deponent and Clements.

Mrs Clements invited the deponent and his nephew Lieutenant Richard Wolseley to her house 20 or 21 Sept, and found Mrs Whitby there; they stayed late and just before leaving she asked them to come to her house at Whitby Wood 23 Sept to drink tea and play at cards. That day Clements came after dinner in a great hurry and said Mrs Whitby asked them to come directly to his house, that something had prevented the afternoon meeting. Mrs Clements met them and said Mrs Whitby had a mind to be married that afternoon. The deponent said it was short warning but that he would be married with all his heart. Clements said Mrs Whitby would execute the release of dower, and the deponent and his nephew walked to Colwich church. Before the marriage the respective writings were signed sealed and delivered by him and Mrs Whitby at the church; they were witnessed by Lieutenant Wolseley and Clements.

As the deponent had no ring, Ann took the ring from her finger and he used that. Lieutenant Wolseley gave her away to the deponent in Colwich church, and they were married between the hours of 5pm and 6pm according to the rites and ceremonies of the Church of England. The company returned to Clements's house, where the company toasted the health of the new Lady Wolseley. Mrs Whitby insisted that Clements swear an oath on the Bible that he would keep the marriage secret. They parted that night, the deponent remarking that it was unprecedented for a bride and groom to be parted on the wedding night, but the marriage was afterwards consummated by her free will and consent. They were often together both at the deponent's house and in her own bedchamber.

Before the settlement as executed was reduced into the form it now is, he received from Clements a draught, which he said he had written at her dictation; after making some alterations the deponent returned it to Clements. The agreement executed before the marriage is to the following effect:

'Articles of agreement made and concluded on the 23d day of September, 1752, as follows:

'Whereas a marriage is intended to be solemnized between Sir William Wolseley, in the county of Stafford, baronet, of the one part, and Ann Whitby, widow and relict of John Whitby of Whitby Wood, in the said county, esq., deceased, of the other part. Now it is hereby agreed and consented to, on the part of said William Wolseley, that as soon as the said intended marriage takes effect, that he, in consideration of the annual sum of three hundred pounds to be paid him by the said Ann Whitby, clear of all deductions whatsoever, by half-yearly payments—the first payment of one hundred and fifty pounds to begin and to be made within six calendar months from the date hereof: That the said Sir William Wolseley does hereby quit all right, claim, or pretence whatsoever, to all and every part of the rest of her jointure, rent-charge, or annuity, which the said Ann is now in the actual possession of; and that she shall receive the whole, and every part thereof, entirely to her own use, provided the said annual sum of three hundred pounts is duly paid to the said Sir William Wolseley by the said Ann Whitby, and not otherwise: And he the said Sir William Wolseley does also promise and agree to make the same provision for, and give the same portion to any child, or children, which he shall happen to have by the said Ann Whitby, as is made, or he shall give to any younger child, or children which he had by his former wife Dame A— W—y [*sic*].' Signed, sealed, and witnessed by Richard Wolseley and John Clements.

Transcribed onto stamped paper, the agreement was sent to Mrs Whitby, who has it unless she has destroyed it. Her signed agreement, on stamped paper, is in the words following:

'Articles of agreement made and concluded on this 22nd day of September in the year of our Lord 1752 between Sir William Wolseley ... and Ann Whitby widow and relict of John Whitby esquire ...

'Whereas a marriage is intended to be had and solemnized between the said Sir William Wolseley and the said Ann Whitby, it is hereby agreed and consented to, on the part of the said Ann Whitby, that in case she shall happen to survive the said Sir William Wolseley, and become his widow, that then she consents and agrees to be satisfied and contented with her present jointure, dower, or thirds, charged on, and payable out of the estate and lands of the said John Whitby, her late husband; and shall, nor will, not lay any title, right or claim to any jointure, dower, or thirds, from , or out of the estate or estates, lands or tenements of the said Sir William Wolseley: But does, for herself, for ever quit claim to, and discharge the said estate, or estates, lands and tenements, from any payment, sum or summs of money to her whatsoever.' Signed, sealed and delivered in the presence of Richard Wolseley and John Clements.

This renunciation of dower was dated 22 Aug when it was intended to be executed, but before execution the word August was erased by the deponent and the word September inserted instead, but without altering the day of the month, which is why it is dated 22 Sept instead of 23 Sept, when it was executed. His nephew and witness did not come into Staffordshire till the week deponent was married; no agreement was made on 22 Aug as Mrs Whitby alleges. No other paper writing given her to sign.

Soon after the marriage Mrs Whitby asked him to part with his London house, as she wanted to stay in the country and the proceeds could be used for any children they might have. She would let him go to London for two or three months but she would stay in the country. He said he would take her next spring and afterwards he would do as she wanted.

On 26 Sept Mrs Whitby took head of his table as Lady Wolseley and afterwards remained alone with him for two hours. On 27 Sept she asked him to go away for a few days or a week to avoid suspicion of marriage. As he prepared to leave she fell into tears, he imagined it arose on his going from home. He said he would stay, she replied he must go. He returned 1 Oct and found her ill in bed, although he had left her in perfect health, and in tears. Then and often since she has said they must be remarried publicly. On 5 or 6 Oct Mrs Whitby asked him to visit her late husband's mother, brother and sister at Haywood to ask if she could have guardianship of her sons (precluded under her husband's will). If she could not, he was to ask whether he could have the care of them and of her. He went and obtained a very satisfactory answer. On 12 Oct the deponent went to see Mrs Whitby and asked the maid Mary Nutt at the door how his lady was. Nutt said she was comical, explaining that her mistress got up before 11am and dressed herself but having little sleep in the night felt faint from dressing and sat down. He found her ill in bed.

That same day he received a message from Hickin, an attorney at Stafford, at the house of John Dunn, Wolseley Bridge, asking to see him. The deponent visited him on his way to Mrs Whitby's. Hickin told him that Mrs Whitby was married to John Robins. They had lain together at Robins's house, at Mrs Whitby's, and at Beaudesert. Her illness was feigned. The deponent had no idea of a marriage to Robins and insisted on knowing details. On 13 Oct, Hickin told him that John Robins and Mrs Whitby were married at Castle Church, Stafford, by Corne in June last. The deponent did not think it proper to reveal his own marriage. During the period 1 to 12 Oct when Mrs Whitby was feigning illness, she refused to send for an apothecary or physician although the deponent often asked her to do so. He denies the conversation of 27 Aug, or liquor, or paper writings, or pretended marriage, as falsely alleged by Mrs Whitby, Derry and Nutt. He denies the conversation of 23 Sept about the discouragement of his advances or his proposing to leave

Wolseley. On the contrary, in all conversations about their intended marriage after he had proposed, she expressed great regard and affection for the deponent. After morning service at Colwich 24 Sept, the day after the marriage, he handed her into her coach; after evening service she told him that Mary Nutt knew or suspected the marriage and seemed uneasy about public talk. But he denies any conversation relating to the reports and inquiry and examinations charged in Mrs Whitby's affidavit. *The deponent being informed that William Draper had said that Sir William and Mrs Whitby were married in the night by candlelight at Colwich church (a false report), Draper came voluntarily to the deponent who admits examining him; Draper said he did not see them married, of which this deponent acquainted Mrs Whitby.* The deponent denies the allegations that he and Mrs Whitby discoursed about indemnifying Clements, about swearing to the marriage, or about forcing her to be publicly married or to go and live with this deponent, or about any rudeness Clements had showed her or about sending for her brother Mr Northey. The deponent knew nothing of these allegations until reading the affidavit. Nor did he use threats to induce her to marry, or threaten to take her away by force in his coach, or ask her for any such paper as is alleged. Since she began cohabiting with Robins, the deponent has often tried to get a proper affidavit from Corne of the time and manner of her marriage to Robins but has been unable to do so. The deponent does not know if he is legally married or not but is very much afraid the late Mrs Whitby is his wife.

[10] Affdt of Sir William Wolseley baronet of Wolseley, sworn by the court 21 May 1753. ITKB [*Copy.*] [*Verso*]: 'Staffords. Office copy of Sir William Wolseley's affidt. Filed in Easter Term 1753 26 Geo. 2d.'

That the annexed letter was written by Mrs Whitby 29 Aug 1752 and was received by the deponent as stated in his previous affdt of 9 May 1753. He recognizes the handwriting as Mrs Whitby's.

[*Annexed*]: 'I am obliged to go out this afternoon, but shall return Home, between seven and eight o'clock, if you are not ingaged at that time, shall be extremely glad to see you, I was this morning favoured with a letter from Mr Victor, I am only sorry, he should judge so hardly of one, who in spite of him, and all the world, will ever be a sincere well wisher to yourself, and family. Saturday 4 o'clock.'

[11] Affdt of Ann Walker spinster, Abraham Lakin groom,[90] and Thomas Greatholders coachman, all of Wolseley, sworn before Richard

---

[90] Lukin in the ecclesiastical court case.

Hinckley at Wolseley 24 April 1753. ITKB [*Thomas Greatholders signed with a mark.*]

[Ann Walker]: That intimacy between her master Sir William and Mrs Whitby grew from June last, after his sons visited her son at Whitby Wood [*and gives details of other visits*]. The families had been estranged for some four years. After Sir William returned from London, there were daily visits, cards, and messages between him and Mrs Whitby. Richard Derry was often at the house, inquiring to speak to her master or to Mr Victor.

[Abraham Lakin]: That Richard Derry was servant to Ann Whitby, and now appears to serve John Robins. In mid-August Derry told the deponent that Mrs Whitby had promised to take care of him if she married Sir William.

[Thomas Greatholders]: That in mid-August Derry told him that he had asked Mrs Whitby 'what she could think of by marrying an old man ... in about two or three years time she would nock him up.' Derry also said she promised to take care of him and her other servants.

[Abraham Lakin and Thomas Greatholders]: That Derry said he would bring Mrs Whitby to repentence for her former crimes. They repeated this and it came to Sir William's notice, who called them into a room with Mr Clements and Mr Victor, and examined Derry in their presence, when he confessed it. A third witness to Derry's remarks was John Hodgkin, gardener, since dead.

[12] Affdt of Elizabeth Clements age 16 spinster, eldest daughter of John Clements, Mary Goodwin spinster of Colwich, Alice Coleman wife of William Coleman of Colwich, innkeeper, and John Goodwin shoe-maker of Little Haywood, parish of Colwich, sworn before Richard Hinckley at Colwich 24 April 1753. ITKB [*Mary Goodwin and Alice Coleman signed with a mark.*]

[Elizabeth Clements]: That she recalls that her mother and father were engaged in the afternoon of 23 Sept to have tea at Mrs Whitby's house, but Ann Whitby came unexpectedly alone and on foot to dine. She went to the church with her mother. When they returned, Sir William Wolseley and Richard Wolseley arrived soon after and joined them in the parlour, where Richard Wolseley toasted Mrs Whitby as Lady Wolseley.

[Mary Goodwin]: [*Confirms that the women went into the church 23 Sept.*]

[Alice Coleman]: That she saw Sir William and his nephew in the churchyard, saw Mary Clements and Mrs Whitby walk to the other side, and saw John Clements coming to the church. Later that evening William Draper told her that Sir William and Mrs Whitby had been married and the bells would ring for them that night or the next morning.

[John Goodwin]: That he heard William Draper, tailor, say on 24 Sept that the marriage had taken place the previous day, and that he had seen the ceremony.

[13] Affdt of John Asson,[91] now servant to William Welch esq of Lichfield, sworn before Richard Hinckley at Rugeley 24 April 1753. ITKB

That the deponent was servant to John Clements until last November. Mrs Whitby visited, or the Clements visited her, almost every day from midAugust throughout September except for a week when the Clements were away from home. On 25 or 26 Aug he was sent to fetch Mrs Whitby's clothes. She dressed in them, and Sir William visited. He heard that she had fainted, and water and hartshorn were given to her. She was well at supper and left about 11pm with Sir William.

On 23 Sept Mrs Whitby arrived at the house unexpectedly. Very little wine was drunk at dinner. Later he saw Mrs Whitby and Mary Clements leaving the church, and then Sir William and Richard Wolseley leave the church and cross the churchyard. They went into the parlour, where Richard drank a toast to Lady Wolseley. Draper told him and the entire neighbourhood that Sir William and Mrs Whitby had been married.

[14] Affdt of George Whiston, parish clerk of Colwich, sworn before Richard Hinckley at Colwich 24 April 1753. ITKB[92]

That 23 Sept on his return from Rugeley he heard that Sir William and Mrs Whitby had been married at the parish church. He was not told by John Clements, and therefore made an entry of the baptism of Joseph Price on the following Monday. Clements was much displeased, and told him that a different entry should have been made first, and that a separate record of all christenings, marriages, and burials should be kept on a loose sheet of paper and that Clements would see to the regular entries himself. No entry was made until 10 Nov, when Clements gave him the licence for the marriage of Sir William Wolseley, and ordered him to enter the marriage in the register, from a memorandum at the bottom of the licence. The deponent did not tell Hickin that he made the entry 29 or 30 Nov. Clements would not allow an alteration

---

91   *Widow of the Wood*, 184, gives 'J—N A—P.'
92   This and the following are referred to in *Widow of the Wood*, 101 as prosecution affidavits; the prosecution did file affdt [20], also by Whiston.

or erasure, but ordered him to number the entries 1 for the marriage and 2 for the baptism, to show how they ought to have been inserted as to priority afterwards.

The entry is in his handwriting, and reads '1752 September 23. Married was Sir William Wolseley at Wolseley Bridge to Ann Whitby widow of Whitby Wood both of this parish by licence.' On the evening of 13 Nov Walter Cartwright asked the deponent to go to Whitby Wood, where Derry gave him a crown for Mr Robins's marriage fee and told him that if Clements had not sent over to Stafford for his fee that his master or mistress would have sent Mr Clements a guinea. He told Clements, who said he wanted only his usual fee.[93]

[15] Affdt of William Spilsbury clerk of Stafford, sworn before Thomas Gant[?] at Stafford 1 May 1753. ITKB

That the deponent resided at Stafford all last summer, and heard a rumour of Sir William paying addresses to Ann Whitby. She now calls herself Mrs John Robins. She went to live with Robins about 12 Oct. He saw Robins at Stafford several times, including during the time the marriage to Sir William was being widely reported.

[16] Affdt of Benjamin Victor gentleman of Dublin, sworn before H. Winshaw at Chester 20 April 1753. ITKB

That the deponent visited Sir William last July. [*Substantiates Sir William's account of the courtship.*] He was confidant to both parties in negotiations for the marriage. Mrs Whitby set 25 Aug for the ceremony, *the first day of Lichfield races, when Clements could send all his family and she could send her servant Derry, to keep the marriage secret. She enjoined this deponent to secrecy, of which he attempted to dissuade her. She gave as reasons that her brother and aunt, of whom she had expectations, would be violently opposed, and her brother would set the country in an uproar. The deponent then told her that the one remaining thing necessary was that she sign a deed renouncing all claims of dower on the Wolseley estates, as she had a jointure of £600 a year, which would revert to her two sons by her former marriage at her death. As there might be a new race of children out of the intended marriage, and since Sir William had four children already, she ought to put it out of her power to hurt those children. She denied any such intention, and on 19 Aug Clements filled up a marriage license at the request of the parties and in their presence. The usual bond was given, binding the deponent and Sir William.*

---

[93] The emphasised passage does not appear in *Widow of the Wood* version of the affidavit, 188-90, which concludes 'And thus end these tedious Affidavits; many of which I have omitted; and the Whole employed the Court three long Days.'

On 22 Aug the deponent transcribed for Sir William a document for Mrs Whitby, renouncing all claim to dower, and intended to give it to her that evening, when she sent word to see Sir William, not the deponent, who said, 'The lady thinks she can deal better with you than with me.' Sir William took the paper, and on his return said that she disliked it, but he added that if she did not sign it there would be no marriage.

Accordingly the marriage was postponed. *Richard Derry, her servant, had spoken disparagingly of his mistress in the hearing of several people, and Sir William examined him on the advice of the deponent, in the presence of Clements. Derry utterly denied speaking the words, but Sir William's servants confirmed that he had, and Derry admitted it. He signed a paper prepared by the deponent, agreeing that the words were false and scandalous, and begging her pardon.* The deponent left Wolseley 29 Aug to go to Ireland, but wrote and sent a letter to Mrs Whitby that day, arguing the reasonableness of the release. It was the only letter he wrote her; he left a copy with Sir William.[94]

[17] Affdt of Lieutenant Richard Wolseley in General Bland's regiment of dragoon guards now quartered in Scotland, sworn before William Jeffreys at Berwick upon Tweed 10 April 1753. ITKB

That the deponent visited his uncle Sir William from 21 Sept, and accompanied him to Clements's house where he met Mrs Whitby. He heard that they were courting, a rumour confirmed by their behaviour. [*Confirms Clements's and Sir William's account of events of 23 Sept.*] Later that evening they were joined by Alms, a naval lieutenant.

To prevent suspicion, Mrs Whitby and Mrs Clements agreed to enter the church through another door. The deponent and Sir William arrived between 5pm and 6pm, and the deponent and Mr Clements witnessed the agreements signed, sealed and executed by Sir William and Mrs Whitby before the ceremony. It was performed according to the rites of the Church of England. Mrs Whitby provided the ring off her finger, as Sir William did not have one. The company returned to Clements's house, where the usual wishes of joy were made; the deponent drank to the new bride as Lady Wolseley and she did not seem displeased; they parted at 11pm. The deponent and Sir William went into Mrs Whitby's coach, but she let them alight and they retired to their separate houses.

A day or two after the marriage, while on a walk with deponent, Sir William professed his surpise at Mrs Whitby's conduct in being so very forward in bringing about her intimacy, and explained how her

---

[94] The emphasised passages do not appear in *Widow of the Wood*.

invitation to his sons had led to the intimacy and then a proposal of marriage. On 26 Sept Mrs Whitby took head of the table at Sir William's house as Lady Wolseley. Soon after the marriage, the deponent had written to his father and brother telling them of the marriage. He rejoined his regiment at Manchester, where he was told Mrs Whitby had gone to live with John Robins, Member of Parliament for Stafford, at which story he expressed great indignation as he had been at her marriage to Sir William Wolseley, and had given her away.

[18] Affdt of James Alms gentleman of Gosport (Hants), sworn before William Hollis at Gosport 23 Feb 1753. ITKB

That the deponent visited the Clements from the end of July until October, during which time there were frequent visits from Mrs Whitby. On 23 Sept she came unexpectedly about 11am. He went out shooting, and when he returned, Sir William and Richard, commonly called Captain Wolseley, were there. That evening, he heard Captain Wolseley toast Mrs Whitby as Lady Wolseley. He understood and believed that a marriage had taken place. He never heard that she was compelled to go to the church, and never saw John Clements compel or press her to drink. She was not intoxicated but calm, serene, composed sedate and sober all that day.

[19] Affdt of John Clements rector of Long Whatton (Leics), and vicar of Colwich, of Colwich, and Mary Clements wife of John Clements, sworn before Richard Hinckley at Colwich 24 April 1753. ITKB

[Both]:That neither entered into a conspiracy with Sir William Wolseley and Richard Wolseley or with any other person to force the late Mrs Whitby, widow, now calling herself the wife of John Robins esq, to solemnize marriage with Sir William Wolseley against her will. Nor did they conspire to charge her with being actually married to him otherwise than as after mentioned. They frequently visited Mrs Whitby as neighbours for three or four years past during the life of her husband John Whitby, esquire, and since his decease. They were on civil and friendly terms and continued such visits during June, July, and August last. At the end of July they heard a common report that Sir William paid his addresses to Mrs Whitby but did not know it for certain and did not see Sir William at her house until 7 Aug when they were invited by Mrs Whitby to her house at Whitby Wood, and saw Sir William already there. He invited them and Mrs Whitby to dine at Wolseley the Monday following. There they saw for the first time marks of Sir William's complaisance toward Mrs Whitby; they had never mentioned him to her before, there having been a great coolness between the families for some years.[95]

[95] The emphasised paragraph is not printed in *Widow of the Wood*.

[John Clements]: That a day or two before 21 Aug Victor, visiting Sir William, told him that Sir William wanted to speak with him. The deponent went with Victor to Wolseley Hall. Sir William said he wanted to consult him as a clergyman and a gentleman about his marriage and that Mrs Whitby had consented to marry him on 25 Aug. Victor asked if he had a licence and the deponent said he had a blank one. Sir William enjoined him to secrecy, saying Mrs Whitby wanted it kept secret. The next day the deponent breakfasted at Mrs Whitby's and she told him she was to marry Sir William and gave him instructions about how it could be done secretly: she could go in the church by the chancel door and not be seen by her servants from her house. She would wear one of Mistress Clements's gowns. That afternoon she walked to the deponent's house, spoke of avoiding the suspicion of her servants, saying she would send some of them out of the way. She was joined by Sir William and Victor. Victor asked the deponent to get a bond and licence.

[Both]: *The bond and licence were brought and filled up for and executed in the presence and with the consent of Mrs Whitby, the bond executed by Sir William and Victor, and the licence filled up and prepared for the marriage by Clements. Mrs Whitby stayed to supper and played cards.*[96] On Sunday 23 Aug, the deponents dined at Mrs Whitby's, went to church with her and Mr Nichols of Stafford, and returned to her house.

[John Clements]: Sir William arrived and offered, in John Clements' presence, a paper for Mrs Whitby's signature, a renunciation (in case of marriage to Sir William, should she survive him) of her thirds and rights of dower, which the deponent had been told was Sir William's intention, and had acquainted Mrs Whitby thereof. She looked at it, folded it up, and put it between her gown and stays and said she would consider it. Later she told the deponent it was an ungenerous act and said it was put in Sir William's mind by *'that vile rascal'* Victor.[97] Mrs Whitby said that she and Sir William understood each other very well: he was entitled to her jointure and she to her thirds, and there was no need for any writing between them. The deponent believes she refused to sign the paper, and the marriage, which was to have been on the 25th, was postponed. Soon afterward the deponent expostulated with Mrs Whitby about the disproportion in years between herself and Sir William, and advised her to consult her brother, Northey. She was pleased to answer, 'You know, Mr Clements, that we are entirely independent, he (meaning, this deponent believes, her brother) has

---

[96]   The emphasised material does not appear in *Widow of the Wood*.
[97]   The emphasised words are omitted in *Widow of the Wood*, 156.

pleased himself, and I see no reason why I may not do the same.' She asked the deponent's advice and he advised her not to sign the paper, and that she might obtain better terms. Between 20 and 27 Aug, on the day Derry was examined, Mrs Whitby came to the deponent's house, said there had been 'fine work at Wolseley Hall that morning', and enquired about Derry's examination. 'This is Victor's doings, who is an enemy to me, and will do everything in his power to obstruct the match.' The deponent told her that Derry had told Sir William's servants that[98] 'he would bring his mistress upon her knees for her former sins or crimes.' Sir William examined him about this and Derry denied it, but Sir William's servants confirmed it.

[Both]: Mrs Whitby seemed very much affected and uneasy at the said report, but the deponent told her that he did not believe Sir William credited any such idle report and still retained a great affection for her.[99]

[John Clements]: *He denies that he winked or gave any kind of signal to Derry during the examination or had a conversation on the road as Derry alleges. He was present at the examination and saw Derry sign a confession, which he witnessed.*

[Both]: *They deny that the deponent Clements used any indecent expressions or arguments to convince Mrs Whitby to marry Sir William, as are alleged in her affidavit.*

[John Clements]: *After this conversation, Mrs Whitby came to the deponent's house in morning dress, invited herself to dinner, and asked Mary Clements to send for some clothes. Mary accordingly sent her servant to get them from Mrs Whitby's housekeeper. After dinner Mrs Whitby asked the deponent to get Sir William, which he did.*

[Mary Clements]: *Mrs Whitby went upstairs to dress, complained of the cold, and asked for a glass of wine. It was the same white wine as had been drunk at dinner, out of the same bottle, and had no laudanum or other preparation. Mary Clements denies that Mrs Whitby said she wished she had not drunk the wine or that she had been invited to stay the night.*

[John Clements]: *About 4pm Sir William came. Mrs Whitby seemed a good deal confused about Derry's report and examination. She said to Sir William, 'you have treated me cruelly', and fainted, her head falling on Sir William's breast. She continued in the fit for about three-quarters of an hour.*

[Both]: *She cried out frequently, 'Mr. Clements, fetch Sir William, tell him I love him dearly. I won't injure his children, that damn'd rascale Victor is done*

---

98 The words 'this his Mistress must take Care of him, for' are inserted at this point in *Widow of the Wood*, 156–7; they do not appear in the affidavit.

99 The following emphasised passages are omitted in *Widow of the Wood*.

this to break the match.' Sir William held her head upon his breast the whole time. Pure spring water with hartshorn drops was administered to her. These deponents believe the faint was feigned or owing to her anxiety over Derry's examination. When she recovered, Sir William assured her of his belief in her honour and innocence and said he would marry her whenever she pleased, and that what was done that morning was only to give a check to the impertinence of servants and to free her character from the foul aspersion. Mrs Whitby grew more composed, she drank tea, played cards, supped and stayed until 10pm when she left with Sir William in her coach. She did not vomit during the fit or at any other time that day, nor asked the deponent John Clements to take her to the window. No marriage was solemnized or intended. No marriage was attempted. There was no book in the deponent John Clement's hand, no paper signed or attempt to obtain one, and no conversation about marriage or paper, either on the day she had the fit, 26 Aug, or any time later, as alleged in the affidavits of Mrs Whitby and her servants Richard Derry and Mary Nutt.

After the time of her alleged ill-treatment, and forced marriage, she continued to visit and be visited by these deponents in that free and easy manner used amongst them. On the evening of Sunday 30 Aug they went after an evening service with her in her coach to [Thomas] Anson's at Shugborough where they found Lord Chetwynd, Sir Walter Bagot, Sir William and others. On the way back to her house Mrs Whitby told the deponent John Clements that 'her children were in a great measure dependent upon her, that the estate was greatly incumbered with 3 jointures.' She had an allowance of £90 per annum for her children but had never received it. He advised her to make a reserve of a considerable part of her jointure for the sake of her children, in regard to the memory of *his friend* Mr Whitby. Mrs Whitby seemed well pleased and intreated the deponent to make a representation to Sir William. That evening in the presence of Mrs Whitby the deponent asked Sir William to make better terms for her. Sir William agreed to consider doing so.

[John Clements]: That he did not see Mrs Whitby until sometime between 16 and 18 Sept, when she told him that some 'busy impertinent person' had informed her brother Northey of Sir William's courtship. Her brother wrote 'that he had rather follow her to her grave than that she should be married to Sir William Wolseley.' The deponent advised that if her friends were so adverse to the match she should let the matter drop. Mrs Whitby replied, 'No, I shall either run distracted or die if I have him not.' She offered the deponent £500 to marry them secretly in his house, and to induce him to do so, said that she was married to her former husband in a room and that she would get Sir William to indemnify him, but the deponent refused, as he would never be concerned with such a thing without property authority.

The deponent was with Mrs Whitby and Sir William every day from 17 or 18 Sept to 23 Sept endeavouring to settle an agreement. Such agreement was reached by 23 Sept; Mrs Whitby dictated the agreement, which is in his custody, *in the following words:*

'*It is this day agreed between Sir William Wolseley of Wolseley Hall in the county of Stafford Baronet on the one part; and Ann Whitby of Whitby Wood in the said county, widow, on the other part; That if the intended marriage between the said parties take effect, — First that Sir William Wolseley does hereby quit all right, claim, or pretence whatsoever to all and every part of her jointure rent and charge or annuity which she the said Ann Whitby is in present possession of; and that she receive the whole and every part thereof entirely to her own use and that her receipt shall be a proper and plenary discharge for the same; Only subject to this exception: That she allow to Sir William Wolseley the sum of three hundred pounds per annum for her maintenance and the support of his table, and that this sum free from all encumbrances and deductions of any kind whatever be paid to the said Sir William Wolseley by half yearly payments; the first to commence six months after the date hereof. Secondly, the said Sir William Wolseley does hereby covenant and agree to make the same provision for and give the same portion to each child or children which he the said Sir William shall beget on the body of the said Ann Whitby as is made, or he shall give to any younger child or children, which he had by his former lady Dame Ann Wolseley. Thirdly, in consideration of such provision made for any child or children begetted by Sir William Wolseley on the body of the said Ann Whitby, she does hereby promise covenant and agree to exonerate renounce and quit all pretence, right and claim to the thirds of Sir William Wolseley's estate and to all and every part of his estate both real and personal. Agreeably hereto the parties above mentioned have interchangeably set their hands and seals the day and year above mentioned.*'

The deponent was very unwilling to write the agreement, and pressed Mrs Whitby to employ a lawyer to draw it, which she refused to do as it would jeopardize her secret, and said it would not be valid unless on stamped paper. The deponent delivered the paper to Sir William who made some alterations (in form but not substance) and asked the deponent to transcribe it onto stamped paper, which he did. [100]

[Both]: On 23 Sept Mrs Whitby came to their house, to their surprise, as they were engaged to go to her home that evening with Sir William and Lieutenant Wolseley, his nephew. Mrs Whitby said she came to keep out of the way as [William] Chetwynd of Brocton had sent a

---

[100] The evidence and agreement as quoted here with emphasis does not appear in *Widow of the Wood*, 161; nor do the other passages italicized in this affidavit.

message that he was coming to drink tea with her and she said she was engaged. She did not want him to see Sir William at her house.

[Mary Clements]: That after dinner 23 Sept Mrs Whitby asked her to take a walk in the garden, which adjoined her own house. Mrs Whitby said that she had sent Richard Derry to Stafford and that with no one about 'now was the time to be married.' Mrs Whitby asked her to send for Sir William and his nephew; John Clements did so.

[John Clements]: On his return home Mrs Whitby asked for the transcribed articles of agreement, now on stamped paper. She read them over several times, said it was in every respect agreeable, and did not ask for any other paper. After Sir William arrived with his nephew Sir William and Mrs Whitby pressed the deponent to marry them, and when he scrupled to do so, both said they would come to Colwich Church in three or four weeks' time and be married in a public manner, which induced him to marry them.

[Both]: They executed the agreement and were married by him in Colwich church about 5pm or 6pm using Mrs Whitby's own ring; throughout she spoke distinctly with an audible voice. Richard Wolseley gave her away in marriage. Sir William and Mrs Whitby pressed the deponent John Clements not to make an entry in the parish register until the intended remarriage but the deponent entered a memorandum of the marriage at the foot of the licence. Both enjoined him to secrecy. Mrs Whitby wanted her mother-in-law's consent for fear of losing guardianship of her children, which would break her heart. She also wanted to soften her brother's opposition. *The evening was spent very cheerfully at the deponent's house, Mrs Whitby's health was drunk as Lady Worselely, and Sir William, Richard Wolseley and Mrs Whitby left in her coach.*

[John Clements]: *On 24 Sept 1752 Mrs Whitby said her servants had told her they had heard that the bells were to be rung to celebrate her marriage. She asked that it not be done, as the marriage was to be kept secret, and upbraided him for not keeping the marriage more private. William Draper of Colwich had talked of the marriage, and she apprehended he must have peeped through the church window. She insisted that the deponent must use all his endeavour to silence Draper, if necessary with the assistance of Sir William and his nephew. Neither Derry nor any other person was present during this conversation as reported in the affidavits of Derry and Mrs Whitby.*

[Both]: *After church that day Sir William and Richard Wolseley took tea and supper at Mrs Whitby's with the deponents. Mrs Whitby, she appeared cheerful and highly pleased with her honour, again asked the deponent, in the presence of the others, to speak to William Draper 'to silence that fellow' and that 'the marriage would then rest snug and private' and made the same request to Sir William. The next day at Great Haywood, having baptized the child of*

Jeremiah and Mary Price, and hearing Draper was working there, the depon-
ent told him that reports of the marriage were spreading in the parish. Draper
told the deponent that the ceremony was at night and by candlelight, a fact the
deponent knew was not true, and denied. The deponent does not remember that
he told Draper that he would make oath that he did not marry them, that they
were not married. But he might tell [sic] Draper that he thought they soon
would be married. The deponent thought he could not have seen the ceremony,
and took Draper before Sir William where he confirmed that he had not seen the
marriage and was reproved. There was no conversation on 25 Sept with Mrs
Whitby or Sir William as alleged in affidavits by Mrs Whitby and Mary Nutt
except that he told Mrs Whitby of Sir William's meeting with Draper, with
which she seemed very well satisfied, and that it was generally believed that he
had married her 23 Sept and that Draper had declared it to him and others. On
the 26th he told her that everyone at Shugborough wakes believed she was mar-
ried to Sir William.

The deponent denies the conversation of 26 Sept as reported in affidavits of
Whitby and Nutt except that then and at several other times he tried to per-
suade her to be publicly remarried. He denies that he or Sir William ever
used threats or menaces to induce her to marry or remarry. He never
intruded into her company without her consent or was guilty of rudeness or incivility. He never went into her bedchamber or tried to drag
her out of bed and force her to be married, nor talked about Mr
Northey, as was untruly sworn by Mrs Whitby, Mary Nutt, and
Richard Derry.

On 1 Oct Derry came to the deponent saying his mistress was dangerously
ill. The deponent went after church and Mary Nutt suggested sending for
Northey to which the depondent agreed, and he advised sending for Dr Wilks.
Mrs Whitby was in bed in her clothes covered by a quilt, coughed much, and
complained of a pain in her side. She never asked to see the paper signed
26 Aug, as it did not exist. The deponent did have custody of the paper
signed 23 Sept before the marriage. Immediately before he performed
the ceremony, Sir William and Mrs Whitby each executed a separate
paper writing, and he kept the copy signed by Sir William for her.
About three or four days before 12 Oct *(when Mrs Whitby went to cohabit*
with John Robins esq) she sent for the deponent to bring the paper, which
he did. As Sir William and Mrs Whitby said they would be remarried,
he did not make an entry of the marriage until 10 Nov last, when he
directed the parish clerk George Whiston to do so. It does appear that
the baptism of the child of Price on 25 Sept appears in the register before
that of the marriage, which took place earlier, because Whiston without
his knowledge entered the baptism, and was not present at the marriage. The deponent has made and certified a copy of the entry on or
about 16 Dec for Edward Whitby esq as mentioned in William

Brookes's affidavit. The deponent denies any conversation with Mary Nutt, as she alleges, about Mrs Whitby and John Robins.

John Hickin of Stafford came 10 Oct to search the register for the burial of Abraham Jordan of Little Haywood, but he never pretended he came to check the marriage entry. There was at that time no entry of the marriage. Hickin copied something out of the register which he apprehends from his affidavit to be the baptism of Jeremiah Price. Hickin told him that he had heard of the marriage at 11 o'clock by candlelight while at the Royal Oak Inn at Eccleshall, but had contradicted the rumours. The deponent told him the report was false. Hicken told him he was glad to hear it and that he would satisfy the bishop of Lichfield and Coventry about it, where he was to dine.

He wrote out a declaration that the deponent had not married the parties, but the deponent refused to sign, in spite of Hickin's entreaties. Asked to stay for dinner, Hickin said he was dining at Sir Walter Bagot's, but instead, these deponents are informed, he went directly to Mrs Whitby's and carried her on horseback to the house of John Robins in Stafford. The deponent admits he has denied marrying them but did so because he was enjoined to secrecy by both parties. His denials were meant to be of the particular circumstances and not of the marriage itself.

[Both]: That to keep the marriage secret they said they had gone into the church to copy the inscription on the Wolselely monument. They thought Hickin was asking idle questions, having no idea that he intended to turn their remarks into a criminal accusation; they had no intention to ensnare, they thought public remarriage was imminent, and Hickin gave not the least hint or intimation of a marriage between Mrs Whitby and John Robins.

[John Clements]: That after he had been informed that Mrs Whitby and Robins married in June and that Mr Corne, who is represented to have married them, would attest to it, the deponent considered the marriage to Wolseley was invalid; he received moduses and the fee for the marriage with Robins, and gave receipts as mentioned in Hickin's affidavit [5] and Walter Cartwright's affidavit [7]. On 22 Jan last, William Brookes of Stafford asked to search the register for the Wolseley marriage and the deponent refused. The deponent cannot recall a conversation with William Atkins denying the marriage as mentioned in Atkin's affidavit [6]. On 30 Jan a Mr Sudall, a proctor from Lichfield, came for a copy of the register of the Wolseley marriage and was shown it and the memorandum on the licence.

[Mary Clements]: That she denies trying to induce Mrs Whitby to stay on 23 Sept by saying that he expected the Miss Sneyds, and denies conversations about Sir William and John Robins. Nor did she ever tell her she could marry Sir William first and John Robins after. However, a few days after Derry's examination, Mrs Whitby said that rumours were circulating that she would marry John Robins, but that he never asked the question. After the wedding, Mrs Whitby showed every fondness for Sir William and despite enjoining secrecy she took the head of the table at his house. The deponent saw Mrs Whitby leaning on Sir William's bosom with her arm about his neck. Mrs Whitby told the deponent in her bed chamber when she was supposed to be sick that she had denied the marriage to Mr Chetwynd, as she had to others at other times, and that she had clapped her hand to her side and said that her illness was all counterfeited. On another occasion she told deponent that she had given £300 of her jointure to Sir William, that she loved him, and that he was welcome to it, and that she would endeavour to live on the remainder but would not go to Wolseley.

[Both]: *That they have to the best of their belief given a full just and true account of all the conversations and transactions, and the statements of the prosecution witnesses are false.*

Further affidavits for the prosecution:

Ea 26 Geo II 1753

[20] Affdt of George Whiston schoolmaster and parish clerk of Colwich, sworn before John Dearle at Stafford 17 March 1753. ITKB [*Verso*]: 'Addl affdts of Sudall and Whiston for infn agt Sir William Wolseley Bart Filed 19th April 1753 fo 15'.

That John Clements sent for the deponent in November last and ordered him to make an entry of the Wolseley marriage, at which time Mrs Whitby had publicly cohabited for six weeks with John Robins esq MP as his wife. He did so. The deponent was not present at, nor does he know of his own knowledge that such marriage was solemnized. He entered the Wolseley marriage and dated it 23 Sept; there was no entry for the marriage before he did so.

Clements sent for him about 16 Dec. Edward Whitby and John Clements were together and told him they wanted to examine the register for the Wolseley marriage. They took a copy of the entry and Clements certified it was a true copy. On 16 Dec the deponent went to Stafford on the order of Edward Whitby and made oath before John Dearle, a master extraordinary of the court of chancery, in the petition of Thomas and William Whitby infants for a guardian (whose petition was depending in the court of chancery), that the copy of the entry was a true one and was signed by John Clements.

[21] Affdt of Edward Burslem Sudall gentleman of the Cathedral Close of Lichfield, sworn before Thomas Harvey at Lichfield 11 April 1753. ITKB

That on 30 Jan last, by order of John Hickin gentleman, the deponent examined the parish register of Colwich to see if there was an entry of the Wolseley marriage. The entry followed that of a baptism of Jeremiah Price on 25 Sept and was therefore not regularly and duly entered. John Clements was very uneasy and several times refused, and then held the book half open and said he might see the entries but then shut the book before he could read them. He eventually allowed the deponent to make copies, and certified them as true.

Removal of affidavit for use in the ecclesiastical court:

[22] 'In the matter of Sir William Wolseley Bart.' Order 1 May 1756 by Sir Dudley Ryder, chief justice, for Francis Barlow esq, clerk of the rules on the crown side, to deliver to Nathaniel Bishop the original of the affdt dated 21 May 1753 of Sir William Wolseley and the attached letter signed A. Whitby, for use at the trial in the Court of Arches in Doctor's Commons. Nathaniel Bishop to leave with Barlow a true copy and paper writing, and return the original immediately after trial. [*Receipt of the original is acknowledged by Bishop 3 May 1756.*] [*Verso*]: 'Staffords. Chief Justice's Order.'[101]

Sources: KB 1/11 Hil, Ea 26 Geo II. KB 21/37 pp.20, 61.

A.11 Information applied for (30 April 1754)

Defendants: Richard Cooper, boxmaker; Robert Silvester, boxpainter; Thomas Watson, boxpainter; William Cooper, bucklemaker; all of Bilston; Richard Curtis, labourer of Walsall; and William Hipwood, chapefiler of Bilston.

Accusation:
Making a riotous attack on a dissenting meeting house at Bilston, 8 April 1754.

Rules and process:
Ea 1754: affdts [1] and [2] filed. Ea [11 May 1754]: on reading affdts [1] and [2], rule nisi to [24 May 1754] (Aston). Trin [1754]: pray a day to answer; leave to imparl.[102]

---

[101] This order is filed with affdt [10], in Ea 26 Geo II.
[102] And perhaps imparlance: the Great Docket Book (IND 1/6659) omits 27 Geo II.

Affidavits for prosecution:

Ea 27 Geo II 1754:

[*Wrapper*]: 'Staffords. Affidts Taylor et al & Hurp for Infn agt Cooper et al. fo:22.'

[1] Affdt of Edward Taylor tailor, Samuel Perry boxmaker, and John Mills bucklemaker, all of Bilston in the parish of Wolverhampton, sworn before J. W. Sm. Stevens at Wolverhampton 30 April 1754. ITKB
[Taylor]: That they were at the licensed dissenting meeting house in Bilston 8 April listening to the preaching of Reverend William Dyer, when they observed a large number of people including the Coopers, Silvester, Watson, and Curtis, approach the meeting house in a riotous and tumultuous manner, shouting, hallowing, and clapping their hands, terrifying the congregation for one hour. Richard Cooper called to Dyer, 'By God you are drunk and damn your soul I should like to see you stript.' Dyer replied that both he and the house were licensed for preaching the gospel; Cooper said 'the gospel of the devil'. Watson damned Dyer and the rioters threw muck, stones and boards through the windows of the meeting house to the great danger of the congregation, and would not stop when asked.
[Perry]: [*Confirms the preceding account.*] Richard Cooper then came into the meeting house shouting that his pocket was picked. The congregation was kept shut in by the mob for half an hour after Dyer was done preaching.
[Mills]: That he was knocked down three times on his way home from the meeting house.

[2] Affdt of Edward Hurp chapefiler of Bilston, sworn before J. Stevens at Wolverhampton 30 April 1754. ITKB [*Signed with a mark.*]
That the deponent saw Hipwood and Richard Cooper and several others gather in a riotous and tumultuous manner at the dissenting meeting house in Bilston. He saw Hipwood throw a brickend through one of the windows; other rioters broke windows while the minister and his congregation were inside.

Sources: KB 1/11 Ea 27 Geo II 1754. KB 15/3 a12, Trin 27 Geo II. KB 21/37 p. 198. KB 29/413 Trin 27 Geo II.

A.12 Information refused (25 April 1755)

Defendants: Isaac Mousley, farmer and maltster; John Boon, farmer; Richard Hunt, butcher; John Hingley, farmer; Samuel Sparkes, nailer; James Muse, tailor; William Rea, blacksmith; Robert Hardy, jersey-comber; and Thomas Hardy, whittawer; all of Barton under Needwood.

Accusation:
Riot, and burning gorse and furze, in Needwood Forest, 1 Feb 1755.

Rules and process:
25 April 1755: prosn affdt [1] taken. Ea [29 April 1755]: on reading affdt [1], rule nisi to [31 May 1755] (Serjt Willes). 20 to 23 May 1755: defence affdts [3] to [5] taken (filed Trin). ST [28 May 1755]: enlarged rule nisi to FNT. Trin [18 June 1755]: enlarged rule nisi to second day next term (Gilbert). 31 Oct 1755: prosn affdt [5] taken; filed Mich. Hil [10 Feb 1756]: enlarged rule nisi to FNT (Serjt Willes). Ea [28 May 1756]: enlarged rule nisi to FNT (Serjt Willes). Trin [5 July 1756]: enlarged rule nisi to FNT (Perrot for defdts). Mich [20 Nov 1756]: previous rule discharged, prosr to pay costs, to be taxed by James Burrow [master of the crown office] (Perrot).

Affidavit for prosecution:

Ea 28 Geo II 1755

[1] Affdt of Thomas Turner deputy keeper of Barton under Needwood, called the Forest of Needwood in His Majesty's Duchy of Lancaster, and Thomas Keble assistant to Thomas Turner, sworn before Richard Hinckley at Lichfield 25 April 1755. ITKB [*Verso*]: 'Staffordshire. Affidt of Thomas Turner & ano:r for Inform ag:t Mousley & al for Riot &c. Fo: 19.'
   [Both]: That on 1 Feb they came upon 40 or 50 people including the defendants, riotously assembled, burning the gorse and furze on Dunstall Banks on the Chase of Needwood. The deponent Turner told Mousley that the group was trespassing and warned them against further burning or trespass. John Boon replied for all of them that they had come with the purpose of burning the gorse. The deponents also burned the shrubs and small trees necessary for the shelter and food for the deer that frequented and delighted to be in that part of the Chase. In past years (and on 2 and 3 Feb of this) great quantities of gorse, furze, hollies, whitethorn and other underwood have been clandestinely

burnt, and all seedlings under them necessarily also destroyed, in this and other wards, to the destruction of the timber and deer.

On this occasion, threats and persuasion failed, and the deponents were insulted by huzzas as they left. They believe the crowd had been gathered by the tolling of Barton church bell.

Trin 29 Geo II 1755

[2] [*An office copy of [1]. Verso*]: 'Staffordshire. Needwood Forest. Office Copy of Prosecutors Afft: Turner & Keble's. 8 May 1755. Copy sent per post to Mr Fenton per JP. Trin: 1755 fo: 19 & 1 Sta: 13s. 8d.' [*Copy of rule nisi attached.*][103]

Affidavits for defence:

Trin 29 Geo II 1755

[3] Affdt of Isaac Mousley farmer and maltster, John Boone farmer, Richard Hunt butcher, John Hingley farmer, Samuel Sparkes nailer, James Muse tailor, William Rea blacksmith, and Robert Hardy jersey-comber, all of Barton under Needwood, sworn before J. Fenton at Barton under Needwood 23 May 1755. ITKB [*Verso*]: 'Staffordshire. Afft of Mousley et al. agt Information. Perrott. fo 23.' [*James Muse signed with a mark.*]

[All]: That these deponents and others were burning gorse and furze on Mosey Meere Bank as had been usually practised for many years in the belief that it was customary and lawful for the members of the townships bordering the Chase to do so. Turner did not ask them to desist, nor did they abuse them, nor burn gorse on Dunstall Banks nor burn any shrubbery or small trees. The deponents believe that it was proper for them to burn the gorse, not only because it was their customary right, but because John Turton JP, lieutenant of the Chase, notified the constable of Barton 30 March 1754 that furze could not be burned between 2 Feb and 24 June. The deponents are not responsible for the burning on 2 and 3 Feb; they burned only the low running gorse, and they burned no underwood nor seedlings. As inferior freeholders and farmers at a rack rent who enjoy common right (valued at a quarter of their rent) to use the forest pastures, they have the right to burn off the gorse to make better pasturage for both their cattle and the deer, and to preserve the value of their common. The Chase is now overrun

---

[103] This and affdts [3] to [5] are now found with those of Michaelmas.

with gorse, and they have heard from their fathers and other ancient people who are now dead that it has been always been their usual and constant practise to burn the gorse in the Forest or Chase of Needwood whenever it has been thought requisite by the jury at the woodmote or any of them so to do.

[John Hingley]: That he was asked by the former keeper, father of Thomas Turner the present keeper, to burn the gorse and was assisted by him.

[All]: That most of the crowd were children and boys, and they are persons of inferior rank who cannot well bear any extraordinary expense. They think it a hardship to be called before King's Bench for such an inadvertent trespass (if it be one) as such trespasses have always been laid formerly before the woodmote jury. They believe that much prime timber has been taken out of the forest by the forest officers for their own use.

[4] Affdt of Egerton Alcock age 65 [a former keeper], and Henry Hadderton age 52, gentlemen of Newborough, sworn before H. Hawkins at Barton under Needwood 20 May 1755. ITKB [*Verso*]: 'Afft of Mr Alcock & anr. Perrott fo 11.'

[Both]: That they have always lived near the Chase of Needwood and have for some decades served on the jury of the woodmote courts. It has been usual and generally esteemed lawful for the inhabitants of the 20 or so townships or villages with a right of common on the Chase to burn off the gorse or furze. A juryman must be present to observe that there is no damage done by the burning, and that sufficient people are present to prevent the burning from spreading beyond low growing gorse. Burning is permitted because to cut it by hand would be too slow, and not allowing it to be burned would destroy the pasturage and throw the poor onto the parish. There is ample shelter and shade left for the deer.

[5] Affdt of Henry Lee age 60 and upward, yeoman of Dunstall, sworn before J. Fenton at Dunstall 23 May 1755. ITKB [*Verso*]: 'Lee's Affidavit. Perrott fo 9.'

That the deponent knows the Chase of Needwood and has served on the jury at the woodmote courts. There is a common right to the Chase of Needwood. It is the responsibility of the jurymen of the woodmote courts to ensure that the burning of the gorse is done properly, and the juries have often made orders and given directions to jurymen of the several townships to see the gorse burnt. As a boy he had been sent out by his father to do so. The deponent remembers Philip Turner, former keeper and father of Thomas Turner, encouraging the burning of the gorse to improve the pasturage for cattle and deer. This deponent believes that no undue damage was done other than to gorse, and that far less was burnt this year than in the past.

Further affidavit for prosecution:

Mich 29 Geo II 1755

[6] Affdt of Thomas Turner of Sherholt Lodge, deputy keeper of the Chase of Needwood, sworn before Richard Hinckley at Lichfield on 31 Oct 1755. ITKB [*Verso*]: 'Kings Bench. Staffordshire. Tho: Turners Affidt: The King v Moseley et al: Additional. Filed in Michas Term 1755. fo 6.'

That he has lived on the Chase all his life and that he has heard or knows personally of cases within the last 20 years in which several persons, namely William Oliver, John Sutton, William Merry, Richard Holley, John Sherratt, Thomas Moore, Joseph Levett and John Cleeves have been committed to prison or have fled arrest for setting fire to or burning gorse in the said Chase.

Sources: KB 1/12 Ea 28 Geo II, Mich 29 Geo II no. 2; KB 21/37 pp. 352, 404, 467, 505, 538, 563. KB 36/157.

A.13 Information granted but not exhibited (22 Nov 1755)

Defendant: Robert Hodgson gentleman of Stafford.

Accusation:
Libelling John Hall gentleman of Stafford in the *Gentleman's Magazine*, 1754.[104]

Rules and process:
Mich [25 Nov 1755]: rule nisi to FNT (Morton). Hil [27 Jan 1756]: rule absolute for an information (Morton).[105]

Affidavits for prosecution:

Mich 29 Geo II 1755

---

[104] For the affair see W. A. Bewes, *Church Briefs* (London, 1896), 50–4, which reprints Hodgson's letter but does not mention Hall's libel action against him.

[105] No information appears to have been exhibited.

[1] Affdt of John Byrd gentleman of Stafford, sworn before John Dearle at Stafford 22 Nov 1755. ITKB [*Verso*]: 'The Affdt of John Byrd. Salop March 5th 1757 [*sic*]. The King agt Hodgson. Read for the Prosecutor R.P. Fo: 11.'

That Hodgson distributed 26 Aug 1754 copies of a printed paper (annexed) and declared that John Hall was the author of the article and that the article was indicative of Hall's true character.

[*Annexed*]: 'Annexed at the time of swearing.'

'Whereas proposals have been dispersed through the kingdom for laying and collecting of briefs, at a more easy expence to the sufferers, as also in a more expeditious manner, than is at present; I take the liberty of making it public, by sending a true copy of the scheme taken from the 425th page of the Gentleman's Magazine for September 1754, and is as follows.

'Mr Urban.

'After having trifled away above sixty years of life, and mightily diverted myself and others with female foot-races, sky-rockets, and paper lanthorns, I begin to think of the *utile dulci*, and from a manager of shows and entertainments, I am now become an undertaker of briefs.

'This undertaking I shall transact in the same method, and as cheap as the present undertaker; and though I know nothing at all of the people employed under me, I would have every body believe, that I shall conduct the brief business with the same expedition and fidelity.

'I shall pay my collectors not according to the number of briefs brought in to account, but shall give them a settled annual salary. This, I know, will make them not so solicitous in collecting as in laying their briefs. But what then? Suppose they only bring into account five thousand briefs out of ten thousand, so much the better. I shall have my full salary, and the trustees for the sufferer will have but half the trouble in passing the account with me.

'If I fail of success in this arduous and uncertain undertaking, I shall have this comfortable reflection, that I am not the first that has failed in the same attempt, and may not be the last; and therefore give me but a single set of briefs to go out with, and I'll venture. If I find it too expensive to my pocket, to fetch them in again, I flatter my self, that when the present undertaker's collectors consider the great loss that must otherwise inevitably happen to those that employ me, they will be so friendly as to collect my papers for me.

'But why should I think of not succeeding? The clergy, who are always consulted in every application for a brief, are, or at least ought to be, my particular friends, and will most assuredly be for me. For though I often take some liberties, in the modern tast [*sic*], with these reverend gentlemen, yet I think my self entitled to their good wishes and encouragement. I do assure you, from the sincerity of my heart, there is not a man in the kingdom that has given them les [*sic*] trouble than I have done. I never frequent any place of publick [*sic*] worship, never enquire the road of these spiritual guides, and have no notion at all either of revelation or morality. And, to shew that I am not a projector for myself only, I have been thinking of a most noble scheme, for the ease and emolument of the clergy. If I succeed, I know my success must be owing to them; and therefore when they have established me in the brief business, I will, from the gratefulness of an overflowing heart, communicate to the world this scheme of mine, which, if it takes, will render the pastoral care more easy, will turn every living in the kingdom into a fine cure, and every church into a heathen temple, for the worship of the idol *Mammon*. Yours, etc. PHILO CLERICO. *N.B.* I am to be heard of at my house in *Crab-tree Lane*, or seen at my office under the *Conjuror's Cap*, in the Market-place, *Stafford, Staffordshire*.'

[2] Affdt of John Hall gentleman of Stafford, sworn before John Dearle at Stafford 24 Nov 1755. ITKB

That the deponent, John Byrd and John Stevenson entered into a partnership in July 1754 to attempt the carrying on the business of undertakers or collectors of charities on briefs. Robert Hodgson was the only other one in the business, and expressed uneasiness about the new partnership. The deponent heard about a month later from a person well acquainted with Hodgson that something would appear in print. A libelous letter later appeared in the *Gentleman's Magazine* of Sept 1754, at p. 425, designed to appear to be written by the deponent, who lives in Crabbery Lane, Stafford. Hodgson took great pains to have it believed that the deponent wrote the letter. Hodgson showed the magazine to many in Stafford long before the bookseller there had copies. After the magazine appeared an advertisement was pasted up in public places in Stafford, in which Hodgson reflected on the deponent and his partners and made reference to the *Gentleman's Magazine*. As if the publication in this magazine were not sufficiently odious, Hodgson distributed copies so published at Hindon (Wilts) and Ruthin (Denbighs), where the partnership had secured briefs. Hodgson did so in the hope that the inhabitants would give the undertaking to him instead of to the deponent and his partners.

Shortly before the chancellor's order was published in the *London Gazette* 5 Aug 1754 relating the method of obtaining an undertaking of briefs appointment, the deponent and his partners obtained a certificate of appointment from the petitioners of Stoke upon Tern (Salop) to be undertakers for rebuilding the parish church of Stoke. In order to obtain a new permit agreeable to the lord chancellor and to consider further about the brief, a vestry was held there 26 Aug 1754, when the deponent applied to get a fresh appointment and Hodgson attended to apply also. At the meeting, Hodgson distributed many copies of the magazine. The ministers and inhabitants of the parish selected Hodgson for the undertaking. The deponent's character has suffered greatly from these false, malicious, and scandalous aspersions where he is not well known.

[3] Affdt of Thomas Dicken gentleman of Drayton in Hales (Salop), sworn before Henry Wase at Norton (Salop) 24 Nov 1755. ITKB

That a vestry meeting was held 26 Aug 1754 at the parish church of Stoke upon Tern (Salop) for parishioners to consider a proper person to be undertaker for collecting charities upon briefs for rebuilding their parish church. At the meeting John Byrd applied on behalf of himself, John Stevenson and John Hall, gentleman. Hodgson, who also applied, spoke ill of Hall and distributed several printed papers, including the paper annexed [*this second copy was annexed to affdt [1]*], claiming that they were written by Hall and that they revealed his true character.

[4] Affdt of Joseph Loxdale gentleman and William Brookes gentleman both of Stafford, sworn before John Dearle at Stafford 24 Nov 1755. ITKB [*Verso*]: 'Staffordshire. The affidt of Joseph Loxdale & Wm. Brookes for information agt Hodgson. Filed Michas Term 1755 29th Geo 2d. 4 affdts. Fo: 39.'

[Both]: That they believe the copy of the magazine article annexed to the affidavit of Byrd was written by Hodgson or a person under his direction and that it was published with intent to prejudice and defame Hall and hurt his business.

Hil 29 Geo II 1756

[5] Affdt of John Dearle of Stafford of service of rule nisi to Robert Hodgson, sworn before Richard Drakeford at Stafford 22 Dec 1755.

Sources: KB 1/12 Mich 29 Geo II no. 1, Hil 29 Geo II. KB 21/37 pp. 434, 451.

A.14 Information applied for (22 Nov 1755)

Defendants: William Savage innholder and John Spicer bricklayer, supervisors of the highway in Wolverhampton.

Accusation:
Threats against James Darbyshire whitesmith of Wolverhampton, and
malicious damage to his property.[106]

Rules and process:
Hil [26 Jan 1756]: on reading affdts [1] to [4], rule nisi to [11 Feb 1756]
for an information (Nares). ST [12 Feb 1756]: enlarged rule nisi to FNT.

Affidavits for prosecution:

Hil 29 Geo II 1756

[1] Affdt of William Brumfield pavior[107] of Wolverhampton, sworn
before Thomas Holyoake at Wolverhampton 22 Nov 1755. ITKB
    That on or about May last the deponent was employed by William
Savage, John Spicer, John Langley and Andrew Wall, supervisors of the
highways for Wolverhampton, to pave Hollow Lane which was out of
repair. Before taking up the old pavement, which was about 120 yards
in length from the top of the lane, the deponent took a level of the
ground according to the scheme laid by the supervisors for the new
paving. The fall was one yard and three quarters. He believes that a
gradual fall of one yard would have been sufficient and informed the
supervisors that the lane might be repaired as well and at much less
expense without it being taken up but Savage insisted on having it
taken up according to the supervisors' orders. The old pavement was
taken up, and in laying down the new pavement the street was raised
close and higher to the buildings of James Darbyshire than before: six
to 18 inches against the cellar windows, doors, a lane entry, water-
courses, and stable doors. As a result the buildings are greatly damaged
and the deponent believes that the doors of some of the buildings have
been blocked. On 27 May last Darbyshire forbade the workmen to continue paving and threatened to bring actions. Savage told the workmen
to continue in the same manner as planned. James Smith and Matthew
Davis, two paviors with their labourers, followed Savage's order. The
deponent left work the next day because he foresaw the prejudice the
work would be to Darbyshire. The work could have been done for £10
without prejudice to Darbyshire instead of upwards of £30.

---

[106] Although ordinary proceedings on highways for non-repair have not been
    included in this volume, this prosecution is included because it alleges mal-
    ice in the prosecutor.
[107] 'Paver' in the original.

[2] Affdt of Ann Moss wife of Francis Moss chandler of Hollow Lane in Wolverhampton, sworn before Thomas Holyoake at Wolverhampton 22 Nov 1755. ITKB

That William Savage innholder, John Langley currier, Andrew Wall tailor, and John Spicer bricklayer, all of Wolverhampton, were appointed as supervisors of the highways in Wolverhampton. Some of the supervisors caused the lane to be taken up and laid by Matthew Davis, James Smith and William Brumfield paviors, together with labourers employed for the job. The pavement was laid against the buildings of James Darbyshire in Hollow Lane opposite the dwelling of the deponent's husband Francis Moss. [*Substantiates account in affdt [1] of damage to Darbyshire and Darbyshire's order to stop.*] The deponent heard Savage call Darbyshire a 'damned rogue and beggarly rascal and said if he took one stone he would make him as good as eat it and bid him come out of his house for a poor dog and he would ring [*sic*] his nose of [*sic*] his face.' 'I have made a rod for you and it's now soaking you dam'd rogue.' The pavement had been raised against Darbyshire's building and the tenement of the deponent's husband 18 inches in some places. Her husband was forced to raise the floor of the tenement seven inches because of water running in from the blocked watercourse. James Smith and Matthew Davis were the chief workmen on the job.

[3] Affdt of Charles Walter and John Ansell labourers, both of Wolverhampton, sworn before Thomas Holyoake at Wolverhampton 22 Nov 1755. ITKB [*Both signed with a mark.*]

[Both]: That in May last they were employed as labourers by William Savage, John Langley, Andrew Wall and John Spicer supervisors of highways to take up the pavement in Hollow Lane. The supervisors directed the pavement to be taken up and laid down so that the pavement was raised against the buildings of James Darbyshire. On 27 May Darbyshire told the workmen to stop work to prevent damage to his buildings, and told them that he would bring an action if they persisted.

[Charles Walter]: That he informed Savage of Darbyshire's statements, but Savage told him to continue with the business 'for it shall be done if it be only for spite'.

[Both]: That Savage and Spicer came to the work and Savage told the workmen that he would not pay them for the work they had done if the job were not completed, and that if any offered to hinder them to take up a stone and knock them down. Darbyshire was looking out the window of his house and Savage called him a 'damned rogue and beggarly rascal' and bid him come out of his house and he would 'ring his nose off his face'. By this time the pavement had been laid according to the scheme. James Smith and Matthew Davis paviors were employed in finishing the work which Darbyshire had told them not to finish, and which some other workmen had chosen not to finish. [*Substantiates damage to Darbyshire and to Moss's buildings in affdt [2].*] They believe the lane could have been sufficiently repaired without the pavement against Darbyshire's building.

[4] Affdt of James Darbyshire whitesmith of the Hollow Lane, Wolverhampton, sworn before Thomas Holyoake at Wolverhampton 22 Nov 1755. ITKB [*Verso*]: 'Mr Nares will move tomorrow for an Infn.'

That the deponent is possessed of an ancient freehold messuage or tenement and several outbuildings and now also a tenement and stable in the possession of Thomas Davis. The said Lane leads from the bottom of Cork Street into Dudley Street. Until a few years past the Lane was only a common lane, so narrow that two carriages could not pass one another. In 1750 the deponent was appointed one of the supervisors of highways for Wolverhampton. The owners of several buildings in Hollow Lane proposed that the lane be filled up and turned into a street, and £70 was raised by voluntary contributions of several of the principal inhabitants of Wolverhampton for this purpose. The deponent and other supervisors called a public meeting to take opinions. Many principal inhabitants appeared and agreed. The lane was paved and the expense exceeded the money contributed by about £21. With the deponent's consent the ground adjoining his buildings was raised several inches.

In 1755 William Savage, Andrew Wall, John Langley, and John Spicer were appointed supervisors of the highways of Wolverhampton. Some of the pavement in the lane was broken and could be repaired for about £10. Instead of repairing the lane the supervisors raised the pavement in the lane against the front of the deponent's buildings. Several windows and doors were blocked, including the front door, as well as the watercourse from the deponent's yard and the yards of Elizabeth Poutney and Jeremiah Eginton. The work renders the deponent's buildings almost useless, and the front door of his dwelling house is now no more than four feet five inches high. William Brumfield master pavior informed the deponent that one yard of fall would have been quite sufficient. Savage directed the work in a manner to prejudice the deponent because of previous disputes between the deponent and Savage. The deponent 27 May forbade James Smith, William Brumfield, Thomas Gardener, Charles Walters and John Ansill to stop work and threatened actions against them; Brumfield and Gardener did stop work.

[*Substantiates the account of threats in affdt [2].*] Savage and Spicer ordered the workmen to complete the pavement in the manner which they originally directed. The pavement was raised at a cost of upwards of £30.

Affidavit for defence:

Ea 29 Geo II 1756

[5] Affdt of William Savage innholder of Wolverhampton, sworn before W. Perks at Wolverhampton 1 May 1756. ITKB [*Verso*]: 'Staffordshire. The King agt Savage & Spicer. Deft's affidts. Fo 12 Baynes.'
     That at the end of January last the deponent was served with a copy of a rule of this court ordering him and John Spicer to show cause why an information should not be exhibited against them for certain misde-meanors; the rule was enlarged to the next term. On 12 April last James Darbyshire whitesmith of Wolverhampton (the person applying for the information), Spicer and the deponent respectively became bound each to the other in the penal sum of £50 with conditions written to stand to and obey the award of George Holyoake and John Jesson gentlemen and arbitrators of Wolverhampton. The award was to be delivered on or before 26 April last. The parties agreed to stand to the umpirage of William Archer surgeon of Wolverhampton if the arbitrators did not make their award by that time. The umpire should make his award in writing on or before 24 May. Holyoake and Jesson met to compose the differences between the parties, but could not agree to make any award. The deponent has great hopes that Archer will make an award as he heard Archer declare that he would take upon himself the business of the award. If Archer does not make any award, the affidavits on the part of the deponent and Spicer against the rule nisi will be long and many. A material witness for the deponent and Spicer is a person of no settled place of abode. It may be difficult to find the person but the deponent will make immediate inquiries. He humbly hopes this court will take the circumstances of this case into consideration and give the deponent and Spicer such further time to show cause.

Sources: KB 1/12/4 Hil, Ea 29 Geo III. KB 21/37 pp. 448, 476.

A.15 Information exhibited (27 Oct 1759)

Defendants: Thomas Bradshaw, yeoman and overseer of the poor; Thomas Wright, yeoman; Roger Fowke, gentleman; Robert Reynolds, gentleman; John Whittingham, gentleman, clerk, curate of the parish; all of the parish of Gnosall.

Information:
Hil 33 Geo II 1760 [23 Jan 1760; FDT]

[1] Conspiracy to cause and procure Thomas Pooler a poor person under 21 years of age who is legally settled in Chetwynd (Salop), to marry another pauper, Mary Chettoe, singlewoman, 19 years old and legally settled in Gnosall, who is pregnant with a child which is likely to be a bastard, to enable the parish of Gnosall to impose its obligations on the parish of Chetwynd, by bringing Pooler into the dwelling of Whittingham and threatening him that he would be sent to gaol or for a soldier if he failed to marry her. Chettoe was removed 6 Feb [1759] to the parish of Chetwynd; [2] [*same, but no mention of the threat*]; [3] [*same, but no mention of the threat or taking to the house*]; [4] conspiracy through an attempt to solicit and persuade Pooler to marry Chettoe; [5] conspiracy to contravene the Act for the Better Preventing of Clandestine Marriages;[108] [6] conspiracy to bring about a marriage of persons under-age, with neither banns nor father's consent.

Rules and process:
Mich [7 Nov 1759]: on reading the affdts of Thomas Pooler and others and of Mary Chettoe alias Pooler, rule nisi to [23 Nov] (Morton). ST [23 Nov]: enlarged rule nisi to FNT, on undertaking of Mr Barlow that defdts shall appear to any information and shall plead so as to take notice of trial, and all defence affdts to be filed a fortnight before next term (Hall). Hil [1 Feb 1760]: enlarged rule nisi to [8 Feb 1760] (Hall). ST [8 Feb 1760]: rule absolute for an information (Morton). ST: appearance entered, plead not guilty; venire facias juratores. Hil Vac, 28 Feb 1760: notice of trial for the King (Barlow); countermanded 6 March 1760 (Francis Barlow).

Affidavits for prosecution:

Mich 33 Geo II 1759

[1] Affdt of Thomas Pooler miller of Leegomery (Salop), son of John Pooler miller of Chetwynd Heath (Salop); the said John Pooler and his wife Sarah; and John Pooler the younger miller of Hales Heath (Staffs),

---

[108] 26 Geo II, c.33 (1753), also known as Hardwicke's Marriage Act. It required either public banns or a licence, and a clergyman solemnizing a marriage without one of these was liable to 14 years transportation; parties of whom either was under the age of 21 marrying by license required parental consent; the marriage was to be entered immediately in the parish register. Making any alteration or false entry in a register was made punishable by death.

sworn before John Leeke at Newport (Salop) 27 Oct 1759. ITKB [*John Pooler the elder and Sarah Pooler signed with their marks.*] [*Verso*]: 'RR Squire & Baxter.'

[Thomas Pooler]: That he was taken into custody 2 Feb 1759 at Hales Heath by Thomas Bradshaw and Thomas Wright, both of Gnosall, who informed him they had a warrant issued on the plea of Mary Chettoe charging him with being the father of the bastard child she was then big with. Bradshaw and Wright took him to Chatcull[109] detaining him until the following morning when his brother John Pooler the younger arrived.

[Thomas Pooler and John Pooler the younger]: That the following morning Wright and Bradshaw took the deponent Thomas Pooler with his brother the deponent John Pooler the younger to Gnosall. Wright and Bradshaw told Thomas that he must marry Chettoe, go to gaol, or go for a soldier, to which both deponents repeatedly replied that Thomas was not of age, about 18. When they arrived in Gnosall, Wright went for Roger Fowke and Robert Reynolds, heads of the parish. Reynolds and Fowke took the deponents and Chettoe to the house of John Whittingham, curate of Gnosall, who asked Thomas Pooler and Chettoe their ages. Whittingham refused to marry them without a bond, as they were 18 and 19 respectively. Reynolds refused to give bond, but Fowke agreed, 'as they and their parents were all poor folks, there would not be any disturbance made.' The deponent John the younger offered to give bond to Fowke, certain his father would refuse to consent to marriage to a girl of such infamous character. Fowke refused to take bond, saying Thomas Pooler should either marry, go to gaol, or for a soldier. Bradshaw and Wright added that if the deponent Thomas married her, he might overrun her as soon as they left the church. Terrified that this was the only way to obtain his liberty, the deponent Thomas agreed to marry Chettoe. Fowke then executed a bond to Whittingham and the court, which they believed was to indemnify Whittingham and the court from any damage which might result from issuing a licence. A licence was made out and they were married in Gnossal parish church. As soon as the deponent Thomas Pooler emerged from the church, Bradshaw and Wright under Fowke's orders took him into custody, saying he must not go until he had sworn his settlement.

[Thomas Pooler]: That he was forceably detained by Bradshaw, Wright and Edward Thomas until the morning of 5 Feb 1759. He was taken to Stafford where Ralph Sneyd and Brooke Boothby, both JPs for

---

[109] 'Chattall' in original.

Stafford, examined him and made an order for removing him and Chettoe from the parish of Gnosall to the parish of Chetwynd. Bradshaw and Thomas took them there 6 Feb and delivered them to William Taylor, overseer of the parish. It was impossible for him to ask for his father's consent or Chettoe to ask for her father's consent to be married because they were married immediately after they agreed to wed and their fathers lived three and six miles distant.

[John Pooler the younger]: That he went to the house of John and Dorothy Chettoe, parents of Mary, and informed them that their daughter had been married to his brother. They were greatly surprised and had heard nothing of it before. They said they felt sorry for Thomas Pooler since their daughter was so vile a girl and so great a thief; John said he dared not let her lie in his house or come near it. On 4 Feb the deponent told his father who was surprised and concerned. About 15 June 1759 the deponent went to Whittingham and told him to search the register to determine Chettoe's age. The search yielded nothing. He went to Chettoe's parents' house and asked Dorothy her daughter's age. She replied about 20. She gave him a book which showed a birthday of 19 April 1739.

[John Pooler the elder, his wife Sarah, Thomas Pooler and John Pooler the younger]: That together with Chettoe they attended Stafford sessions 24 April on trial of an appeal to an order for the removal of Thomas Pooler and Chettoe from Gnosall to Chetwynd. The deponent Thomas Pooler was examined at trial on behalf of Gnossal about his being settled in Chetwynd but the court would not permit him to answer questions relating to whether his father consented to his marrying Chettoe, and objected to her being examined with respect to her father's consent. The court also objected to the deponents John Pooler and wife Sarah being examined on that trial because John Pooler rented a cottage at Chetwynd for 5s a year.

[John Pooler the younger]: That notwithstanding his proving at the trial that his brother and Mary were married without either of their fathers' consent, and that his brother was not 21, the order was confirmed against the parish of Chetwynd. Chettoe had been a great expense to the parish of Chetwynd having given birth to a son.

[Thomas Pooler]: That he has never cohabited with nor known Chettoe since their marriage.

[John Pooler the elder and his wife Sarah]: That Thomas was born in late Oct or early Nov 1738 and he is not 21.

[John Pooler the elder]: That he was never asked nor gave consent to his son's marriage nor did he know anything about it until two days after the marriage when John Pooler the younger informed him.

[2] Affdt of Mary Chettoe otherwise Pooler[110] of Chetwynd (Salop), sworn before John Leeke at Newport (Salop) 27 Oct 1759. ITKB [*Signed with a mark.*] [*Verso*]: 'Staffordshire. BR The King agt Bradshaw & al. Affidts for Information. Michas 1759 Squire & Baxter 32 5 37.'

That 3 Feb 1759 the deponent went to the house of the Reverend John Whittingham curate of Gnossal together with Bradshaw, Wright, Fowke, Reynolds, Thomas Pooler and John Pooler the younger. The deponent did not know why she was taken there. Whittingham asked the deponent how old she was and she said 19. Whittingham asked Thomas how old he was and John replied his brother was about 18. Whittingham then read the Marriage Act and asked who would give bond to indemnify him and the court for his marrying them. Roger Fowke said he would and signed a paper writing. She and Thomas Pooler were married. She is certain she never asked her father for consent nor did anyone else, and she had no thought of marrying Thomas right until an hour before the marriage. She was not 20 years of age at the time of the marriage.

Affidavits for defence:

Hil 33 Geo II 1760

[3] Affdt of Thomas Wright yeoman, Thomas Bradshaw yeoman, Roger Fowke gentleman, Robert Reynolds gentleman, and John Whittingham clerk curate, all of the parish of Gnosall, sworn before John Dearle at Alston in the parish of Gnosall 1 Jan 1760 (Thomas Wright) and at Stafford 31 Dec 1759 (the other deponents). ITKB 'The King agt Bradshaw and others.' [*Verso*]: 'In the King's Bench Staffordshire. The King agt Bradshaw & al to show cause for defts. Filed Jany 8th 1760 fo: 38'.

[Thomas Wright]: That 30 Jan 1759 he was informed that Chettoe was pregnant with of child with a bastard and likely to be chargeable to the parish. On the same day he took Chettoe to see Bradshaw, overseer of the poor. He asked Chettoe if she would go with him before a JP to father her child to which she freely consented. On 1 Feb 1759 Bradshaw told him that Chettoe had fathered the child on Thomas Pooler of Blimhill labourer (but now late of Leegomery, miller). Bradshaw had a warrant from Sir William Wolseley baronet to apprehend Pooler. He, Bradshaw and John York apprehended Thomas at Chatcull[111] 2 Feb 1759. He, Bradshaw, and Thomas Pooler went to Bradshaw's house

---

[110] No occupation is given.
[111] 'Chatwell' in the original.

the following day; Chettoe was there. Several persons present asked Chettoe if she would have Thomas Pooler for her husband. She said she would and Thomas Pooler said 'I will have thee' and kissed her. 'I hope thou wilt make me a good wife', and she answered she would do her very best.

[Thomas Bradshaw]: That when Wright and Chettoe came to his house 30 Jan 1759 he asked her if she was willing to father her child. She said yes, and he and Chettoe went 1 Feb to Sir William Wolseley and she voluntarily and freely fathered her child and declared herself on oath to be with child. She said the child was likely to be a bastard and that Thomas Pooler was the father. Wolseley granted a warrant the same day which called for the immediate apprehension of Thomas Pooler to find security to indemnify the parish and to find security for Thomas's appearance at the next quarter sessions all of which is in pursuance of an Act Concerning Bastards.[112] He, Bradshaw and York apprehended Thomas 2 Feb 1759 at Chatcull.[113] He and Thomas Pooler went to his house 3 Feb; Chettoe was there. On the way there Thomas asked what they would do with him; deponent said if he had no person to be bound for him they might send him for a soldier, but that he would do the best he could to save him from any hurt. Pooler said he had had carnal knowledge of Chettoe and that he would marry her. Fowke and Reynolds arrived. [*Substantiates Wright's account of Thomas Pooler asking Chettoe to marry him and identifies Fowke as the one who prompted the question.*]

[Thomas Wright and Thomas Bradshaw]: That neither they nor anyone they knew terrified Thomas Pooler with threats of sending him to gaol or for a soldier or with any other punishment if he did not marry Chettoe. They were married by mutual consent not under threat, and went voluntarily to Whittingham's house to be married.

[Roger Fowke]: That he went to Bradshaw's house 3 Feb 1759 where he met Thomas Pooler and Chettoe and was informed that Thomas Pooler fathered Chettoe's child. He knew neither of them. He asked them if they would marry. He denies threatening Thomas Pooler with gaol, or sending him for a soldier, or that Thomas told him that he was under 21.

[Robert Reynolds]: That Fowke asked the pair whether they would marry.

[Roger Fowke]: That he told Thomas Pooler that if he was not willing to marry Chettoe he should not be forced without his own free consent.

---

[112] 18 Eliz., c. 3 (1575).
[113] 'Chatwell' in the original.

He joined with Thomas in a bond to the surrogate but denies saying that they were all poor folk and that no disturbance would be made.

[Robert Reynolds]: That he was never asked to give bond to marry Thomas Pooler and Chettoe and that he never refused to enter into a bond.

[Roger Fowke and Robert Reynolds]: That neither threatened Thomas Pooler with gaol or soldiering and that Thomas Pooler and Chettoe were married of their own free will. The deponents were very willing to take a bond to indemnify the parish from the bastard or for Thomas Pooler's appearance at next sessions, and deny a bond was offered and then refused.

[Roger Fowke]: That he believes John Chettoe consented to the marriage, and he has since told him so. John Leeke gentleman before whom the prosecution affidavits are sworn is attorney for the prosecutors.

[John Whittingham]: That on 3 Feb between 10am and noon Fowke, Reynolds and Bradshaw came to him and informed him that they had a couple who desired to be married. He said he would marry them if Fowke would be bound as usual to the surrogate since the marriage was not by banns but by licence, and Fowke answered that some person should. He asked Thomas Pooler and Chettoe if they desired to be married and both answered yes. Neither were in any terror of mind as if forced or affrighted and the marriage appeared to be by their own agreement and assent. He denies Thomas or John Pooler claimed that Thomas was under 21. Thomas Pooler swore he knew of no impediment to lawful marriage. Thomas Pooler and Fowke entered the usual bond to indemnify the court and the deponent made out a licence and married the two.

[All]: That they deny that they heard John Pooler the younger say that his father would never consent to his son's marrying a girl or so infamous a character and that he would rather give bond for him.

[4] Affdt of John Whittingham curate and Roger Fowke gentleman both of the parish of Gnosall, sworn before John Dearle at Stafford 5 Feb 1760. ITKB

[Both]: That Thomas Pooler and the deponent Fowke, before the marriage, entered into a penal bond for £100 to the Reverend Richard Smallbroke, doctor of laws, vicar general of the Diocese of Lichfield and Coventry: 'The condition of this obligation is such that if hereafter there shall not appear any lawful let or impediment by reason of any pre-contract entered into before the 25th day of March 1754, consanguinity affinity or any other lawful means whatsoever but that the above bound Thomas Pooler and Mary Chettoe of the parish of Gnosall may lawfully solemnize marriage together and in the same afterwards lawfully remain and continue for man and wife according the laws in that behalf provided And morever if there be not at this present time any action suit plaint quarrel or demand moved or depending before any judge ecclesiastical or temporal for or concerning any such lawful impediment between the said parties nor that either of them be of any other parish or of better estate or degree than to the judge at granting of the license is suggested and by him sworn to before the said John Whittingham And lastly if the same marriage shall be openly solemnized in the church or chapel in the license specified between the hours appointed in the constitutions ecclesiastical confirmed and according the the form of the Book of Common Prayer now by law established And if the above bounden Thomas Pooler and Roger Fowke do save harmless the said Richard Smallbrooke his surrogates and other his officers whatsoever by reason of the premises Then this obligation to be void or else to remain in full force and virtue.' No other bond was entered into by the parties pertaining to this marriage.

[John Wittingham]: That about Nov 1759 he entered the bond in the register of the peculiar collegiate and exempt jurisdiction of Gnosall, it being customary of surrogates to return bonds into the proper register upon granting licences.[114] He cannot more particularly describe the bond because it is not in his possession, but can recite it because it was a common printed bond used in such cases. Thomas Pooler made oath viva voce before the marriage that he knew of no lawful impediment to the marriage between himself and Chettoe.

Affidavit for prosecution:

Hil 33 Geo II 1760

[5] Affdt of John Leake gentleman of Newport (Salop), sworn before Charles Finch at Sutton 18 Jan 1760. ITKB 'The King against Thomas Bradshaw and others.'

That the deponent is attorney for the prosecutor, and that John Leeke before whom the prosecution affidavits were taken resides at Wellington (Salop) and is a different person from the deponent.

Sources: IND 1/6659 Hil 33 Geo II. KB 1/14 Mich 33 Geo II no. 3, Hil 33 Geo II no. 1. KB 11/44 Hil 33 Geo II #11. KB 15/3 a38v Hil 33 Geo II. KB

114 Until the nineteenth century Gnosall was one of the peculiar jurisdictions in Staffordshire, exempt from the jurisdiction of the bishop's court and granting its own licenses for marriage.

15/14 Hil Vac 33 Geo II. KB 21/38 pp. 275, 288, 326. KB 29/419 Hil 33 Geo II.

A.16 Information exhibited against one defendant; others applied for by the defendants against witnesses for the prosecution
(11 April 1761)[115]

Defendant: Thomas Hinckes*, clothier, late of the borough of Tamworth.[116]

Information:
Trin 1 Geo III 1761 [22 May 1761; FDT]
[1] Corruptly attempting to persuade and procure Boaz Reynoldson, scot and lot householder, to give his vote for George Bussy Villiers in parliamentary elections held 31 March 1761 in the borough of

---

[115] Several attempted prosecutions for bribery, and a parliamentary petition by Simon Luttrell, arose out of the Tamworth election of 31 March 1761, when Sir Robert Burdett and George Bussy Viscount Villiers (later Earl of Jersey) defeated Luttrell (later Earl of Carhampton) and William Abney. See *Collections for a History of Staffordshire ... 1920* (Staffordshire Record Society, 1920), 280, and L. Namier and J. Brooke, eds., *The House of Commons, 1754–1790, History of Parliament* (3 vols, 1964), i, 376–7, 518; iii, 68–9 for the election. Of the many charges laid in the affidavits against many defendants on both sides, only one, against Thomas Hinckes, resulted in a Staffordshire information.

[116] The process and affidavits arising from the prosecution brought by Luttrell against Hinckes, Sir Robert Burdett and many other defendants, and simultaneous attempts at counter prosecutions, generated a great many affidavits, and since Tamworth fell in both Warwickshire and Staffordshire, process issued in the names of both. Clearly counsel and the clerks had some difficulty keeping straight which affidavits related to which prosecutions (see the comment on the *verso* of affidavit [16] of Joseph Wilkins, 15 April 1761: 'Who is this affidavit against'.) For the most part the process is headed Warwickshire, sometimes both counties are mentioned, but the information exhibited against Hinckes is styled Staffordshire. The rules and process relating to Hinckes alone are identified here with an asterisk. One other information was exhibited, against William Norton (KB 11/44 Trin 1 Geo III #5), styled Warwickshire, and therefore not included in this volume. The rule absolute against Morley Jenkinson led to an information in Trinity 1 Geo III, to which he made imparlance in Easter term (IND 1/6660 fol. 29v, Ea 2 Geo III).

Tamworth (Staffs), by promising to pay him £3 10*s* to put his son out as an apprentice, to be paid out of the charitable benefaction of Lord Viscount Weymouth for the apprenticing of four children annually, or out of Hinckes's own pocket, if the steward of Lord Weymouth should not pay it; [2] [*preamble much abbreviated, no mention of the charity*]; [3] [*preamble much abbreviated, both money and the charity mentioned*]; [4] [*describes it as a gift of money amounting to £3 10s*]; [5] [*describes it as money to place as an apprentice, no sum mentioned.*][117]

Rules and process:[118]
Ea [15 April 1761]: on affdts [8-9], [12], [16], rule nisi for an information to [27 April] against **Sir Robert Burdett baronet, Joseph Hughes, William Norton, Joseph England, John Kendall, Humphrey Milner, Edward Russ, John Watterson, William Wallis** (Norton); on affdt [1] same rule against **William Greaves, Edward Wolferstan the younger** (Whately); on affdt [2] same rule against **Edward Russ and Thomas Hinckes*** (Webb); on affdt [4] same rule against **Nathaniel Crosland** (Morton); on affdt [7] same rule against **Thomas Butler** (D'Oyly); on affdt [10] same rule against **Thomas Hinckes*** (Skynner); on affdt [11] same rule against **Joseph Tetley** (Blencowe); on affdt [5] same rule against **Samuel Crosland** (Wheler); on affdt [6] same rule against **John Haywood** (Clayton); on affdt [3] same rule against **Daniel Astle** (Aston). ST [22 April]: on affdt [25], rules nisi for an information to [1 May] against *George Ball* (Winn), *John Wilcox* (Gascoyne), *Edward Phillpotts* (Green). ST [24 April]: on affdt [18] rule nisi for an information to FNT against **Edward Wolferstan and Edward Russ** (Morton); on affdt [17] same rule against **Edward Wolferstan the younger, Edward Russ, William Norton,** and **John Watterson**; on affdts [13–14], [15], [22], same rule against **Morley Jenkinson and Edward Wolferstan the younger**. ST [28 April]: enlarged rule nisi for an information to FNT to **Sir Robert Burdett, Joseph Hughes, William Norton, Joseph England, John Kendall, Humphrey Milner, Edward Russ, John Watterson, William Wallis,** on the undertaking of William Hughes that if an information is granted the defendants will appear immediately and plead so that notice of trial may be given for the next assizes, all affdts to be filed 4 days before next term (Gascoyne). The same rule for **William Greaves and Edward Wolferstan the younger** (Yates), **Thomas Hinckes*** (Price), **Edward Russ and Thomas Hinckes** (Lawson), **Nathaniel**

---

[117] The information is unusually long and carefully drawn, including details of the electoral writ.
[118] Defendants associated with Sir Francis Burdett are in bold; those associated with Simon Luttrell are in italics.

Crosland (Serjeant Nares), **Thomas Butler** (Gould), **Samuel Crosland** (Winn), **Daniel Astle** (Ashhurst), **John Haywood** (Caldecott), **Joseph Tetley** (Lucas). ST [2 May 1761]: on affdt [34] rule nisi for an information to FNT for *James Dawes* (Munday); on affdts [25], [26–7], [29], [32], same rule for *Simon Lutrell esq* (Winn); on affdts [27–29], same rule for *William Abney esq* (Gascoyne); on affdts [26], [33], same rule for *William Robinson* (Burland). ST [4 May]: enlarged rule nisi to FNT for *John Wilcox*,[119] *Edward Phillpotts, George Ball*, on the undertaking of Mr Barlow that if an information is granted defdts will immediately appear and plead that notice of trial may be given for the next assizes, all affdts to be filed four days before term. Trin [28 May 1761]: rule nisi discharged for *George Ball, John Wilcox, Edward Philpott* (Serjeant Hewitt); *William Abney* (Morton); *James Dawes* (Harvey); *William Robinson* (Clayton). Rule nisi discharged for *Simon Lutrell esq*, with costs to be paid by the prosr and to be taxed by the master of the crown office (Norton). Rule nisi discharged for **Sir Robert Burdett, Joseph Hughes, Joseph England, John Kendall, Humphrey Milner, Edward Russ, John Watterson and William Wallis**, costs to Burdett, to be taxed by the master (Serjeant Nares). Rule absolute for an information against **William Norton**.[120] Rules discharged against **Daniel Astle** (Gould), **Joseph Tetley** (Serjeant Nares), **John Haywood** (Gould), **Samuel Crosland** (White), and **William Greaves** and **Edward Wolferstan** (Gascoyne). ST [3 June 1761]: rule absolute for an information against **Thomas Hinckes*, Morley Jenkinson** (Mr Harvey). Rules discharged against **Thomas Butler** (White), **Edward Russ** and **Thomas Hinckes*** (Winn), and **Nathaniel Crosland** (Gould). ST [10 June]: rule for a special jury in the prosn of **Hinckes***, instance of the prosr (Yates); venire facias juratores; imparls, pleads not guilty. ST 4 July 1761: notice of trial for the King (Hughes).[121]

Affidavits[122] *for Luttrell and Abney:*

Ea 1 Geo III 1761

[1] Affdt of John Barber grocer of Birmingham (Warws), sworn before Edward Palmer at Coleshill (Warw) 10 April 1761. [*Signed with a mark.*]

---

[119] Altered from 'Wilton'.
[120] KB 11/44 Trin 1761 #5 (Warws).
[121] No record of a trial has been found in either the records of the court or in *Aris's Birmingham Gazette*.
[122] Because both sides sought informations, and were also defendants, the use of the terms 'prosecution' and 'defence' would be unclear.

[*Verso*]: 'Affidt of John Barber. Gn. Whately fo: 10. Wm Greaves Edw. Wolferstan.'

That John Wallis gardener of Tamworth took the deponent to the Castle Inn in Tamworth, Burdett's headquarters, around noon on 30 March. He was introduced to William Greaves of Foremark (Derbs), gentleman, the steward to Sir Robert Burdett and his agent, as the son of William Barber, the weaver. Greaves asked whether the deponent wanted something for his father's vote. The deponent asked Greaves to cash a bond (which the deponent believes is not worth sixpence), and Edward Wolferstan the younger, gentleman, town clerk of Tamworth, JP for Tamworth, and agent for Villiers and Burdett, asked him to fetch it. Wolferstan said the bond would not do unless it was assigned, offering instead to pay £10, the equivalent of the deponent's travelling expenses. The deponent was promised the money after the election was over.

[2] Affdt of John Onion shoemaker of Tamworth (Staffs), sworn before Edward Palmer at Tamworth 11 April 1761. [*Verso*]: 'Affdt of John Onion. Gn Edwd Russ & Thos Hinckes Fo 5.'

That a week before the election, Edward Russ, agent for Villiers and Burdett, and Thomas Hinckes, clothier and also an agent, offered the deponent £3 10s to set one of his sons apprentice in exchange for a vote. Russ told the deponent 27 March 1761 that Wolferstan would give him the money owed at 9am Saturday morning.

[3] Affdt of Richard Hollis gardener of Tamworth (Staffs), sworn before Edward Palmer at Tamworth 11 April 1761. [*Verso*]: 'Affdt of Richard Hollis. Gr. Mr. Morton. Danl Astle fo:3.'

That on election day 31 March 1761 Daniel Astle of Needwood Forest, keeper, who was there to aid George Buckston, steward to the Right Honourable George Townshend esquire, to make interest on behalf of Villiers and Burdett, offered the deponent 15 guineas not to vote for Luttrell.

[4] Affdt of Joseph Bolton mason of Tamworth (Staffs), sworn before Edward Palmer at Tamworth 11 April 1761. [*Signed with a mark.*] [*Verso*]: ' Affidt of Joseph Bolton. Mr Morton. Nath Crosland. fo: 4.'

That Nathaniel Crosland, assessor and collector of land tax for Tamworth (Staffs) and agent for Villiers and Burdett, told the deponent 24 March 1761 that he would assess a little tenement of the deponent's to the land tax. On election day, Crosland said his lands would not be rated or assessed to land tax for seven years if he agreed to vote for Burdett.

[5] Affdt of Samuel Dones wool scribbler of Tamworth (Staffs), sworn before Edward Palmer at Tamworth 11 April 1761. [*Verso*]: 'Affidavit of Saml Dones. Franc. Wheler. Gn. Wheler. fo: 3. S. Crosland.'

That Samuel Crosland of Tamworth, woolstapler and surgeon, agent for Villiers and Burdett, several times requested the deponent's vote particularly for Burdett if not them both. In return, Crosland promised to do all in his power to procure him an apartment in the almshouse at Tamworth founded by Thomas Guy esquire, of which Crosland was a trustee, and promised to be his friend in the trust money belonging to the almshouse.

[6] Affdt of William Brittan maltster of Tamworth (Staffs), sworn before Edward Palmer at Tamworth 11 April 1761. [*Signed with a mark.*] [*Verso*]: 'Affidavit of William Brittan. Gn Clayton. Jno Heywood. fo: 2.'

That in Dec 1760 John Haywood tailor of Seckington (Warws) asked the deponent to vote for Burdett; when he refused, Haywood offered him three guineas, which he held in his hand.

[7] Affdt of Boaz Reynoldson gardener of Tamworth (Staffs), sworn before Edward Palmer at Tamworth 11 April 1761. [*Verso*]: 'Affidt of Boaz Reynoldson. Gn D'Oyly. Thos Butler fo: 2.'

That a week before the election, Thomas Butler whitesmith of Tamworth (Staffs), an agent for Villiers and Burdett, asked the deponent to vote for Burdett in exchange for £3 10s or more in a fortnight's time.

[8] Affdt of Thomas Dones sawyer of Tamworth (Warws), sworn before Edward Palmer at Tamworth 11 April 1761. [*Signed with a mark.*] [*Verso*]: 'Affidt of Thos. Dones. fo: 12. Mr Norton. Edw. Russ. Edw. Wolferstan Wm Norton Humphrey Wilson John Watterson and Wm Wallis.'

That 25 Nov 1760 Russ, Wolferstan and William Norton pressed the deponent to drink with them at the Sign of the Castle where they urged him to vote for Villiers and Burdett. Russ and later Norton in particular promised that the fine of £5 that the deponent paid for killing a hare five years ago would be refunded and other 'services' provided. Humphrey Milner of Seckington (Warws), a tenant of Burdett who has been busy making interest for him, said that Burdett had promised him the same. Thomas Wilkins the younger came to him 21 March 1761 when he was sawing in the yard of John Kendall and told him that his father, Thomas Wilkins, and his uncle William Wallis wanted to see the deponent at Wilkins the elder's house, called the Angel. Watterson and all the others pressed the deponent to vote for Burdett. They offered him money for his vote, leaving £6 30s and three guineas in a plum tree.

[9] Affdt of Richard Phillpotts shoemaker of Tamworth (Warws), sworn before Edward Palmer at Tamworth 11 April 1761. [*Verso*]: 'Affidt of Rich Phillpotts. Easter 1761. Mr. Norton. Wm Norton. fo:3.'

That in late Nov 1760, William Norton chandler solicited the deponent to vote for Villiers and Burdett, saying 'if you will vote for Sir Robert Burdett I will make your wife a present of five pieces. And what do you think of ten pieces to vote for Lord Villiers and Sir Robert Burdett.'

[10] Affdt of Boaz Reynoldson gardener of Tamworth (Staffs), sworn before Edward Palmer at Tamworth 11 April 1761. [*Verso*]: 'Affidt of Boaz Reynoldson. Gn Skinner. Thos. Hinckes. fo: 3.'

That a week before the election, Thomas Hinckes (agent or manager for Villiers and Burdett) asked the deponent to vote for Villiers in exchange for £3 10s to set his boy out apprentice. The money was to be paid at mid-summer, and Hinckes said that if he could not get it of Lord Weymouth's steward, he would pay it himself.

[11] Affdt of James Reynoldson weaver of Tamworth (Staffs), sworn before Edward Palmer at Tamworth 11 April 1761. [*Verso*]: 'Affidt of Jas. Reynoldson. Agt Joseph Tetley. J. Blencowe. Gn Blencowe. Jos Tetley fo: 3.'

That Joseph Tetley potter of Ticknell (Derb), landlord and owner of a house held by the deponent in Tamworth, came to the deponent 30 March 1761 and offered him a house rent-free and an abatement of rent then due in exchange for his vote for Sir Robert Burdett.

[12] Affdt of Elias Willcox millwright of Tamworth (Warws), sworn before R. Hinckley at Lichfield 11 April 1761. [*Verso*]: 'Tamworth Staffordshire Elias Wilcox's Affidt. 13 Affts 13 Sts fo: 70. Ld Weymouth Sr Robt Burdett Jos Hughes Wm Norton Joseph England John Kendall Humphrey Milner Allen England. Fo: 16.'

That 28 March 1761 Joseph Hughes ropemaker of Walsall offered the deponent 10 or 20 guineas to vote for Burdett, which he would not do for the world. The deponent and Hughes went to the Castle inn and drank there. Daniel Astle (a keeper of Needwood) and George Buckston (steward to the Right Honourable George Townshend esquire, who was making interest for Viscount Villiers) arrived, followed by Joseph Jones of Tamworth, carrier, and Burdett. Burdett told Jones that if he voted for him he would get the carting contract of Mr Pratt of Ashby and offered Hughes a bond of £100 as surety for this promise. William Norton of Tamworth, who acted as an agent for Lord Villiers and Sir Robert Burdett, then came into the bar and promised Joseph Jones all his carriage also, and another bond as surety, to vote for

Burdett. Joseph Hughes also promised Joseph Jones his carriage and a bond to vote for Burdett.

That the deponent was with Joseph England of Alder Mills (Staffs) and John Kendall carpenter of Tamworth (tenants of Lord Weymouth), and Humphrey Milner of Seckington (a tenant of Burdett) at William Brown's inn, the King's Arms 30 March 1761. England, Kendall and Milner pressed the deponent to work for Burdett. He said that he had not worked for Lord Weymouth and felt no obligation to him or to those who worked for him. They then offered him the opportunity to do all Lord Weymouth's work in the future if he voted for Burdett. The deponent wanted to see a statement from Lord Weymouth confirming this. On election day, the deponent met England, Milner and Allen England of Alder Mills at the King's Arms, when they gave him a letter signed 'Weymouth', offering to place all his future work with the deponent should he oblige him. The deponent returned the letter and answered that he would not serve any of them.

[13] Affdt of Elizabeth Bellfield[123] wife of Joseph Bellfield yeoman of Tamworth (Staffs), sworn before Edward Palmer at Tamworth 15 April 1761. [*Verso*]: 'Staffordshire. Affidt of Elizth Bellfield. Jenkinson fo: 9.'

That the deponent was at the house of her sister Hannah, wife of John Dickinson, where Morley Jenkinson asked the women to get their husbands to vote for Sir Robert Burdett. Jenkinson promised to have Edward Wolferstan the younger, a JP and agent of Villiers, deliver up to them two notes of £5 each, given by the father of the deponent, which the sisters and their husbands were liable to pay. Jenkinson also offered to deliver up the deeds to two family houses to the women without charge. Other land gifts were offered as well, involving the properties of Edward Allport of Bitterscote and Lord Weymouth's estate.

[14] Affdt of Hannah Dickinson wife of John Dickinson tailor of Tamworth Staffs, sworn before Edward Palmer at Tamworth 15 April 1761. [*Verso*]: 'Affidt of Hannah Dickinson. Jenkinson. Fo: 9.'
[*Substantiates affdt [13].*]

[15] Affdt of John Dickinson tailor of Tamworth (Staffs), sworn before Edward Palmer at Tamworth 15 April 1761. [*Verso*]: 'Affidt of John Dickinson. Mr Aston fo: 7. Jenkinson and Wolferstan.'

That Morley Jenkinson, an election manager of Burdett and Lord Viscount Villiers, asked the deponent to vote for Burdett. Any out of

---

[123] She signs 'Belfield'; in affdt [23] her husband signs 'Bellfield'.

pocket expenses, and other favours or services, were offered in exchange for his vote. [*Substantiates offers of bribery made to the deponent's wife in affdt [13].*]

[16] Affdt of Joseph Wilkins the younger, yeoman of Saint George, Hanover Square (Middx), sworn in court 15 April 1761. [*Verso*]: 'Warwickshire. Joseph Wilkin's Affdt.' [*Another hand*]: 'Who is this affidt against fo: 4.'

That the deponent was born and lived in Tamworth until about a fortnight ago and knows very well what entitles a person to vote there. He knows Richard Phillpotts shoemaker, Elias Wilcox millwright, William Barber weaver, William Brittan maltster, Richard Hollis gardener, Samuel Dones wool scribbler, Boaz Reynoldson gardener, James Reynolds weaver, Joseph Bolton mason, John Onion shoemaker, Thomas Dones sawyer, and Joseph Jones carrier, all of Tamworth. He has heard and believes that they all voted in the last election for Tamworth and were entitled to do so.

[17] Affdt of Thomas Moore maltster of Tamworth (Staffs), sworn before Edward Palmer at Tamworth 15 April 1761. [*Signed with a mark.*] [*Verso*]: 'Affidt of Thomas Moore. Mr. Clayton. Wolferstan. Russ Wolferstan Norton Watterson. fo: 8.'

That the deponent was heavily canvassed 31 March 1761 by Edward Russ of Drayton Bassett, steward to Lord Weymouth and agent for Villiers and Burdett, and by Edward Wolferstan the younger, town clerk and JP of Tamworth and agent for the same candidates. Also present were John Watterson currier of Tamworth and William Norton chandler of Tamworth, also agents for Villiers and Burdett. Russ promised the deponent land at old or easy rents or rent free on Lord Weymouth's estate for a vote. Wolferstan prepared an agreement to this effect, giving him title to land at High Bridge now held by Mrs Beardsley, effective at her death. Russ and Norton signed their names to the agreement and it was delivered to the deponent. Before he voted, the deponent delivered the agreement to Norton, not feeling he should vote under such conditions. Watterson then offered the deponent, immediately or on or after 5 April, more land in the parish of Tamworth. Lord Weymouth and Russ promised the deponent tenancy under Weymouth with rent at £2 5s a year.

[18] Affdt of Joseph Vincent butcher of Tamworth (Warws), sworn before Edward Palmer at Tamworth 15 April 1761. [*Verso*]: 'Tamworth. Affidt of Joseph Vincent S.C. Mr. Morton of Easter Term. Wolferstan & Russ. fo:6.'

That Edward Wolferstan the younger told the deponent several times between 20 Nov 1760 and 31 March 1761 to vote for Villiers and Burdett. In return, the deponent would receive title to his father's farm on the estate of Lord Weymouth, something he could arrange with Weymouth's steward, Edward Russ. Russ, who had previously denied the deponent's requests for his father's estate, visited him in November to confirm his cooperation in return for the farm and Dunstall Close after the death of Russ's father.

[19] Affdt of John Willington gentleman and Joseph Jones yeoman, both of Tamworth (Warws), sworn before Edward Palmer at Tamworth 18 April 1761. ITKB [*Verso*]: 'Warwickshire In the King's Bench Tamworth. The King agt Sr Robt Burdett Bart and eight others. Affidt of service of rule nisi for an Information or Informations. fo:12.'
  That the rule nisi of [15 April 1761] was served on Robert Burdett (through his servant Achan Potterton), Humphrey Milner, William Norton, John Kendall, William Wallis, John Watterson, Joseph Hughes and Joseph England (through his nephew Allen England). The deponent served Edward Russ by laying a copy of the rule on the porch after Mrs Russ and Russ's servant Thomas Montgomery had said that Russ was not at home.
  [*Annexed*]: first rule nisi of [15 April 1761].

[20] Affdt of John Willington gentleman of Tamworth (Staffs) and Joseph Jones yeoman of Tamworth (Warws), sworn before Edward Palmer at Tamworth 18 April 1761. ITKB [*Verso*]: 'In the King's Bench. The King agt Wm Greaves and another. Affidt of service of rule nisi for an Information or Informations.'
  That the deponent served notice to William Greaves through his servant Thomas Norwood and Edward Wolferstan through his servant Elizabeth Phillpotts.
  [*Annexed*]: second rule nisi of [15 April 1761].

[21] Affdt of Joseph Jones yeoman of Tamworth (Staffs), sworn before Edward Palmer at Tamworth 18 April 1761. ITBK [*Verso*]: 'In the King's Bench. The King agst Edward Russ and Thos. Hinckes. Affidt of Service of Rule nisi and information or informations. Rules enlarged till next term to appear and plead and file affidts. 4 days. fo: 6.'
  That the deponent served notice to Thomas Hinckes on 17 April 1761 and went to the house of Edward Russ at Drayton Bassett on 18 April 1761 where he met Thomas Montgomery, his servant, who directed him to Mrs Russ. She refused to take the rule of court and told Montgomery

not to do so. The deponent told her he would put it in the porch, and did so.

[*Annexed*]: third rule nisi of [15 April 1761].

[22] Affdt of Joseph Wilkins the younger yeoman of Saint George, Hanover Square (Middx), sworn in court by the court 20 April 1761. ITKB [*Verso*]: 'Affdt of Wilkins Junior. fo:3.'

That the deponent has lived in Tamworth (Staffs) until recently and knows Thomas Moore, Joseph Vincent, Joseph Bellfield, John Dickinson, and Seth Smith dyer, all of Tamworth (Staffs), and believes each voted in the last election and was legally entitled to do so.

[23] Affdt of Boaz Reynoldson gardener, Joseph Bellfield yeoman, John Dickinson tailor, Richard Hollis gardener, William Britain maltster, Thomas Moore maltster, John Onion shoemaker, Samuel Dones wool scribbler, James Reynoldson weaver, all of Tamworth (Staffs), and Richard Phillpotts shoemaker, Joseph Vincent butcher, William Barber weaver, and Thomas Dones sawyer, all of Tamworth (Warws), sworn before Edward Palmer at Tamworth (Staffs) 22 April 1761. [*Moore, Barber and Dones signed with a mark.*] [*Verso*]: 'In the King's Bench Warwicks Affidt of Boaz Reynoldson & others of their right to vote for Members to serve in Parliament for the Borough of Tamworth. fo:4.'

[All]: That they all had the right to vote in Tamworth. Joseph Bolton of Tamworth (Staffs), Elias Wilcox and Seth Smith dyer of Tamworth were also eligible to vote.

[24] Affdt of Thomas Olivant gentleman of the Inner Temple (London), sworn by the court before the court 4 May 1761. [*Verso*]: 'Mr Olivant's Affidavit.'

That it was impossible, given the usual course of the post, to receive the affdts from Tamworth by 1 May 1761, the day for showing cause according to the two rules made on 22 April against John Wilcox and Edward Phillpotts of Tamworth. The deponent knows this fact from his observations on letters he has received from his client John Willington at Tamworth.

Affidavits for Burdett and Villiers:

Ea 1 Geo III 1761

[25] Affdt of William Gough tailor of Saint Bartholomew the Great (London), sworn before E. Wilmot at Serjeants' Inn 21 April 1761.

[*Signed with a mark.*] [*Verso*]: 'Warwickshire. King's Bench Affidt of Wm Gough. fo:5. Cox Gray's Inn Solr Mr. Hughes Clk.'

That the deponent was in Tamworth for four or five days before the election. Three days prior to the vote, John Wilcox labourer and an agent for Luttrell, told the deponent that if he persuaded his father to vote for Luttrell, Wilcox would pay his father £4 a year for life. Edward Phillpotts and George Ball offered to pay him 20 guineas if he persuaded his father to vote for Luttrell. The deponent communicated both offers to the father and was induced by such offers to attempt to persuade his father to vote for Luttrell contrary to his father's choice, inclination, and promises to vote for Villiers and Burdett.

[26] Affdt of John Gough weaver of Tamworth (Staffs and Warws), sworn before R. Hinckley at Tamworth (Staffs) 25 April 1761. ITKB [*Signed with a mark.*] [*Verso*]: 'John Gough Mr Winn agt. Simon Luttrell Esqr fo: 10.'

That the deponent lived in the borough for upwards of 40 years and paid scot and lot. George Ball, servant to Luttrell, and William Robinson, wool scribbler, visited him 21 March 1761 at John Mace's house. They took him by force to Joseph Robinson's Star alehouse where he met Luttrell and William Abney of Tamworth. When he refused Luttrell's request for his vote, Luttrell offered him £5 a year for life to persuade his son to vote for Luttrell. On the Friday before the election the deponent's only son William Gough of Long Lane near Smithfield, tailor and broker, insisted that the deponent, who was in bed, accompany him to the Swan alehouse, where he tried to persuade him to vote for Luttrell. The deponent refused and went home. His son caught up with him within the hour and offered him 20 guineas to vote for Luttrell.

[27] Affdt of James Keeling bricklayer of Tamworth (Staffs and Warws), sworn before R. Hinckley at Tamworth (Staffs) 25 April 1761. ITKB [*Verso*]: 'James Keeling. Simon Luttrell Esq. Agt Abney only. fo: 9.'

That the deponent paid scot and lot for 16 years and can vote. He was with Edward Ashford and Christopher Shemmonds at John Wallis's house 26 Nov 1760. Luttrell and William Abney, both candidates in the election, and John Willington arrived, and Luttrell tried repeatedly to get the deponent to vote for him but he refused. Lutrell then asked Ashford, who said he could not vote for Luttrell because his landlady, Mrs Knight, would turn him out. Abney promised Ashford a rent-free house if this occurred. Ashford still refused. The deponent said that he had voted for Villiers at the last election.

[28] Affdt of John Woodcock innkeeper of Tamworth (Warws and Staffs), sworn before R. Hinckley at Tamworth 25 April 1761. ITKB [*Verso*]: 'Tamworth. John Woodcock. Wm. Abney Esq fo:9.'

That the deponent has been an inhabitant of Tamworth for more than 40 years, a householder paying scot and lot, and is now a chief constable for the hundred of Hemlingford (Warws) and deputy postmaster of the borough. In Nov 1760 Abney and others came to his house and asked him to vote for Luttrell but he had already pledged to Villiers and Burdett and would not go from his word for ever a man living. Abney said that he could summon several justices, including Palmer, Worley and Wolferstan, to deprive the deponent of his chief constableship. The deponent replied that he would not change his mind. Abney then told the deponent that Luttrell would be of service to him at the post office, meaning that the deponent would lose his position as deputy postmaster. The deponent voted at the last election.

[29] Affdt of Edward Ashford nailer of Tamworth (Staffs and Warws), sworn before R. Hinckley at Tamworth 25 April 1761. ITKB [*Verso*]: 'Tamworth. Edward Ashford. Simon Luttrell Wm Abney Esq. fo: 6.'

That for five years he has paid scot and lot in Tamworth and has never received alms and therefore can vote. On 26 Nov at the house of John Wallis he was pressed by Simon Luttrell and William Abney to vote for Luttrell. The deponent refused for fear that he might by turned out of his house by his landlord Mrs Knight. In front of all the neighbours Abney promised him a free house if Mrs Knight (his present landlady) turned him out for doing so. He refused. He voted for Villiers at the last election.

[30] Affdt of James Lindford collar maker of Tamworth (Staffs and Warws), sworn before R. Hinckley at Tamworth (Staffs) 25 April 1761. ITKB [*Verso*]: 'Tamworth James Lindford Joseph Robinson Denied E. 1761 Cox fo 5.'

That he has been an inhabitant for the last 15 years and is otherwise qualified as a voter. While at the Star alehouse 6 March with Joseph Robinson and William Moggs (both voters), Robinson asked if he would vote for Luttrell. When he said he would not, Robinson offered him a house rent-free, a pail full of ale every week, and small beer whenever he would, and a side of a pig every Christmas, two cowhides and five or six horsehides to begin with. Robinson also asked the deponent to send for Wolferstan or Willington (both attorneys in the borough) and that he would article with the deponent for life.

[31] Affdt of Edward Dickenson gentleman of Tamworth (Staffs), sworn before R. Hinckley at Tamworth 25 April 1761. ITKB [*Verso*]: 'Tamworth B. Gascoyne Mr Morton Enlarged sine terms'.

That the deponent served notice to John Wilcox on 24 April of the annexed rule.

[*Annexed*]: rule of [22 April] that on reading the affdt of William Gough, John Wilcox be given until [1 May] to show cause why an information should not be exhibited (Gascoyne).

[32] Affdt of Robert Smith clothworker of Tamworth (Staffs and Warws), sworn before John Clay Hallen at Tamworth 27 April 1761. ITKB [*Signed with a mark.*] [*Verso*]: 'Robt Smith Luttrell fo:6.'

That the deponent, a voter who paid scot and lot for upwards of 40 years, was called in January into Joseph Vincent's house and asked to vote for Luttrell. Luttrell and the deponent talked and Luttrell promised him work in exchange for one or two votes, meaning a single vote for Luttrell or a vote for Luttrell and another vote for another candidate. After this Luttrell went to John Lattimer, a bailiff and master clothier to find the deponent work. The deponent went to confirm this with Lattimer,who damned him and said he would not be tied to him for seven years. The deponent voted for Villiers and Burdett.

[33] Affdt of John Jones mason of Tamworth (Staffs and Warws), sworn before John Clay Hallen at Tamworth 27 April 1761. ITKB [*Verso*]: 'John Jones Wm Robinson fo:5.'

That the deponent kept company with William Robinson who told him he was at the bedside of John Gough and offered to pay Gough £7 or £10 for his father's vote for Luttrell, which the deponent took to mean that Robinson had attempted to bribe Gough. The deponent and Robinson were both in the interest of Luttrell, and had many conversations about how to promote his interest. Both Robinson and Gough voted at the election.

[34] Affdt of Joseph Marlor jerseycomber of Tamworth (Staffs and Warws), sworn before John Clay Hallen at Tamworth 27 April 1761. ITKB [*Verso*]: 'Marlor Mr Munday agt James Dawes.'

That at the beginning of last November the deponent, who lived in the borough upwards of 30 years, paid scot and lot, and did not receive alms, was at Lawrence Spooners's Horseshoe alehouse where James Dawes, a supporter of Luttrell, pressed the deponent to vote for Luttrell. The deponent stated his intent to vote for Villiers and Burdett. Dawes then offered to pay him any money if he would vote for Luttrell, which he refused, saying that he had promised to vote for the two old members (Villiers and Burdett) and that nothing should prevail on him to do otherwise. He had voted for them at the last election.

[35] Affdt of John Gough weaver of Tamworth (Staffs and Warws), sworn before John Clay Hallen at Tamworth 27 April 1761. ITKB [*Signed with a mark.*] [*Verso*]: 'Tamworth. John Gough. Wm. Robinson. S.C. Mr. Burland fo:5.'

That the deponent, who has lived in the borough upwards of 40 years and has paid scot and lot, was woken out of bed by William Robinson of the said borough, scribbler, who offered him £7 10s or more; he understood it was to vote for Luttrell. He voted for Villiers and Burdett.

[36] Affdt of John Steadman gentleman of St Andrew Holborn parish (London), sworn in court before the court 2 May 1761. [*Verso*]: 'W Norton. Enl[arge]d on the usual Terms'.

That the deponent served the annexed notice to George Ball 22 April.

[*Annexed*]: rule of [22 April], on reading affdt of William Gough, rule nisi to 1 May for an information against George Ball.

Affidavits for Luttrell and Abney:

Trin 1 Geo III 1761[124]

[37] Affdt of William Willcox tailor of Tamworth (Staffs), sworn before Edward Palmer at Tamworth 27 April 1761. [*Verso*]: '3. Affdt of Wm Wilcox. fo: 5.'

That William Gough of the parish of St Bartholomew the Great London, tailor and salesman, approached the deponent 30 March 1761 at the Woolpack alehouse, and this deponent asked him how his father John Gough would vote. William answered 'I cannot tell yet for Lord Weymouth Lord Villiers and Sir Robert Burdett have promised to be friends to me in my business in case my father votes for Lord Villiers and Sir Robert'; he swore he would have it done in black and white before he polled for anybody.

That when Luttrell came to Tamworth in November to offer himself as a candidate, the deponent took John Gough at his request to the gates of the house of William Abney in Tamworth, where Luttrell was.

---

[124] Defence and prosecution affidavits in Trinity 1761 appear to have been disturbed from their original arrangement, but the following groups occur in sequence: [37], [47], [49] to [51], [56] to [66], [68], [70], [72] to [81], [83]; [38] to [46], [48], [52] to [55]; [84] to [90]; and [67], [69], [71], [82].

Because of the great number of people there Gough said he would see Luttrell but meet him at Gough's house when Luttrell canvassed; he said he liked Luttrell who was a good neighbour. About three weeks later the deponent met Gough and said 'I hear you have promised the two old members', Villiers and Burdett, to which Gough answered he had not and that he must have money to vote for who he would. The deponent replied, 'You will not vote for Mr Luttrell for he will not give you a penny.'

[38] Affdt of John Willington gentleman of Tamworth (Staffs), sworn before Edward Palmer at Tamworth 16 May 1761. ITKB [*Verso*]: 'Luttrell & Jno Gough 18. Mr Willington's affidt. fo: 6.'

That the deponent was with Luttrell and Abney at the Star alehouse 11 or 12 March, when William Robinson and George Ball came in with John Gough. Gough and Lutrell sat at opposite sides of the room. The deponent stood close to Gough and Luttrell all night and never heard Luttrell offer £5 a year for life, or services for Gough's vote. Lutrell was not in Tamworth December to Feb; he came 10 March at 9:30pm, left 13 March, and did not return until 30 March.

[39] Affdt of William Robinson wool scribbler of Tamworth (Warws), sworn before Edward Palmer at Tamworth (Staffs) 16 May 1761. ITKB [*Verso*]: 'Self. J. Gough. 17. Wm Robinson's affidt. fo: 13.'

That the deponent never offered John Gough £7 10s. Since the election the deponent has heard Gough say he has never been offered any money by Lutrell or friends. On 27 April 1761, in the hearing of John Willington, Edward Wolferstan the younger summoned Gough and asked him to swear that Luttrell offered him money. Gough refused. Wolferstan was furious, saying that John Jones had sworn an affidavit. Gough refused to swear an affidavit denying that he was bribed (when asked to do so by Willington), but offered to testify on Luttrell's behalf in court.

Wolferstan again attempted to get him to swear an affidavit 5 May 1761. Gough refused. The deponent could not have given Gough £7 10s for his vote because he did not have that much money and was unauthorized to do so. Luttrell has frequently instructed him not to make any bribes. The deponent and George Ball did not go to the house of John Mace at any time before the election, nor take Gough by force to Joseph Robinson's alehouse. Lutrell was not in Tamworth between 13 and 30 March. The deponent and George Ball met Gough 11 or 12 March 1761 on Market Street and asked Gough to go to Joseph Robinson's Star alehouse. Neither the deponent nor Ball introduced Gough to Luttrell. Gough sat on one side of the room and Luttrell on the other.

[40] Affdt of William Abney esquire of Tamworth (Staffs), sworn before Edward Palmer at Tamworth 16 May 1761. ITKB [*Verso*]: 'Self. Ashford. 12. Mr. Abney's Affidt. C. fo: 7.'

That the deponent went with Luttrell to John Wallis's house 26 Nov 1760, where he met Edward Ashford the younger nailer, James Keeling bricklayer and Christopher Shemmends weaver, all of Tamworth. Luttrell asked these three for their vote. Ashford said that if he voted for Luttrell he would be turned out of his house. Upon hearing that Ashford's landlady was Mrs Knight the midwife and the deponent's butcher's mother, he said he would give Ashford a house free if things were not patched up with Mrs Knight, since she had attended his wife in many lyings-in, and he bought almost all his meat from her son. He had no doubt he could prevail upon her not to turn Ashford out. The deponent had no intention to become a candidate on 26 Nov, or until the poll had commenced, when one or two voters voted for him without application.

[41] Affdt of Benjamin Lakin clothier and Joseph Jones yeoman, both of Tamworth (Warws), sworn before Edward Palmer at Tamworth (Staffs) 16 May 1761. ITKB [*Verso*]: 'Marlor Dawes. 11. Affidt of Lakin and Jones. fo:2.'

[Both]: That they heard Joseph Marlor of Tamworth say 24 April that he was never offered any money or reward to vote for Luttrell.

[42] Affdt of James Dawes mercer of Tamworth (Warws), sworn before Edward Palmer at Tamworth (Staffs) 16 May 1761. ITKB [*Verso*]: 'Marlor. Self Luttrell. 10. Jms Dawe's Affidt. fo: 10.'

That the deponent was never with Joseph Marlor jerseycomber at the Three Shoe or Three Horseshoe alehouse in November. Lutrell did not appear as a candidate until after 23 Nov. In Dec 1760 or Jan 1761 the deponent asked Marlor to vote for Luttrell. Marlor said he could not because Edward Wolferstan the younger had a mortgage on his house for £70 or £80 and unless he could discharge the mortgage he would have to vote for Villiers and Burdett. The deponent never offered Marlor money or services for his vote. He heard Wolferstan say December last in the kitchen of the White Hart alehouse that if he could not win by fair means, he would win by foul means.

Marlor has declared he never offered any money to Robert Birch, cooper, William Hunter, butcher, Benjamin Lakin clothier or Joseph Jones yeoman. Birch will not make an affidavit declaring this for fear of Wolferstan and Russ. Hunter will not for fear of Russ. Marlor congratulated the deponent 24 April that the court of King's Bench had not been moved against him.

[43] Affdt of Joseph Jones yeoman and Francis Thickbroom both of Tamworth (Warws), Charles Knight shoemaker and Edward Phillpotts shoemaker both of Tamworth (Staffs), sworn before Edward Palmer at Tamworth (Staffs) 16 May 1761. ITKB [*Verso*]: 'W. Robinson J. Gough. 8. Affidt of Jones, Thickbroom, Knight, and Phillpotts. fo: 2.'

[All]: That they have heard John Gough declare that he was never offered any money by Luttrell or his agents or friends.

[44] Affdt of Samuel Adams baker of Tamworth (Warws), sworn before Edward Palmer at Tamworth (Staffs) 16 May 1761. ITKB [*Verso*]: 'W. Robinson J. Gough. 9. Saml Adams' Affidt. fo: 2.'

That at 9am on 27 April 1761 the deponent heard John Jones ask John Gough to swear that he had £7 10s offered to him; Gough replied that it had never been offered.

[45] Affdt of John Willington gentleman of Tamworth (Staffs), sworn before Edward Palmer at Tamworth 16 May 1761. ITKB [*Verso*]: 'J. Gough W. Robinson. 7. Mr. Willington's Affidt. fo: 5.'

That the deponent heard John Gough tell William Robinson 27 April that Edward Wolferstan the younger, who was landlord to Gough, had called for him and asked him to swear that Robinson had offered him money in return for voting for Luttrell. Wolferstan was angry when Gough refused to do so, and said that John Jones had sworn that Robinson had offered him, Gough, money. Gough said he would not take such an oath now he was near his end for the world. The deponent asked Gough to swear that Robinson had never offered him money. He refused but said he would testify on behalf of Robinson in court.

[46] Affdt of John Wilcox labourer of Tamworth (Warws), sworn before Edward Palmer at Tamworth (Staffs) 16 May 1761. ITKB [*Verso*]: 'Tamworth. W. Gough. 5. Affidt of John Willcox. 14 Affidts. Filed on Motion of Mr. Oliphant. fo: 8.'

That John Gough and his son William were drinking together 28 March 1761 at the Woolpack alehouse, his son attempting to persuade John to vote for Luttrell. John Gough asked the deponent to convince his son to give him £5 a year for life, and if he did, he would vote for Luttrell. The deponent told William Gough about this, and William said 'If Mr Luttrell will insure me that I shall cloath the troop, then I will engage that my father shall oblige him.' If Luttrell could not, he would take up Burdett and Villiers's previous handsome offer of money. The deponent replied he was suggesting the payment out of good nature to the father, for a son ought to care for his ageing parent. The deponent never offered William £4 a year or any other sum for his father's vote, nor could he, having often heard Willington, Lutrell's chief agent, say no money could be offered for votes. The deponent is not an agent for Lutrell; he often before the election heard John Gough wish he could vote for Luttrell.

[47] Affdt of William Robinson clothworker of Tamworth (Warws), sworn before Edward Palmer at Tamworth (Staffs) 16 May 1761. ITKB [*Verso*]: '2. Affidt of Wm Robinson. fo: 4.'

That the deponent has heard William Gough say that he the deponent was present and heard Phillpotts and Ball offer 20 guineas to sway his father's vote for Luttrell. But Phillpotts and Ball have never, to the deponent's knowledge, offered money or any promise to Gough. John Gough has said he will vote for Luttrell anyway. William Gough told the deponent 30 March that Villiers and Burdett promised him business worth £60 a year for his father's vote.

[48] Affdt of George Ball servant to Simon Luttrell of Four Oaks (Warws), sworn in court by the court 17 May 1761. ITKB [*Verso*]: 'In the King's bench. Smith. 23. Affidt of George Ball. fo: 6.'

That Luttrell was not in Tamworth between Dec 1760 and 10 March 1761 and then stayed only until 13 March, not returning until 30 Mar. The deponent asked Robert Smith clothesworker to vote for Luttrell. Smith said his master, John Lattimer, had refused to employ him because he knew Smith intended to vote for Luttrell. Lattimer said he did not hire Smith because he was not as good a worker as others. The deponent at no time asked Lattimer to employ Smith.

[49] Affdt of Edward Phillpotts shoemaker of Tamworth (Warws), sworn before Edward Palmer at Tamworth (Staffs) 16 May 1761. ITKB [*Verso*]: 'Tamworth. Affidt of Edwd. Phillpotts. Filed May 18 1761 by Mr. Olephant. 5 Affidts. fo: 27.'

That neither the deponent nor George Ball, Luttrell's butler, has ever offered William Gough 20 guineas or any other sum to sway his father's vote. Deponent has heard John Gough frequently wish he could vote for Luttrell.

[50] Affdt of John Barlow tailor and salesman of St Bartholemew the Great parish (London), sworn before Lord Mansfield at the Guildhall (London) 16 May 1761. ITKB [*Verso*]: '5. Affidt of John Barlow. fo: 7.'

That the deponent and William Gough, the deponent's brother-in-law, went to Tamworth to work for Luttrell arriving on 25 March 1761. Gough declared that if Luttrell won, their horse should have cockades on the side of its head. George Ball never promised Gough 20 guineas to persuade his father to vote for Luttrell.

[51] Affdt of George Ball servant to Simon Luttrell esquire of St George, Hanover Square parish, (Midd), sworn before Lord Mansfield at the Guildhall (London) 18 May 1761. ITKB [*Verso*]: '4. Affidt of George Ball. fo: 8.'

That the deponent asked William Gough to persuade his father, John Gough, to vote for Luttrell but denies having offered Gough 20 guineas for this. He asked townspeople to vote for Luttrell but not for money. Upon receiving a rule of the court made on the affidavit of William Gough, Ball confronted him asking how he could possibly make such an accusation. Gough insisted that this deponent and Phillpotts did make him such a promise if he persuaded his father to vote for Luttrell, and that William Robinson clothworker was present and heard the same offered.

[52] Affdt of William Abney esquire of Tamworth (Staffs and Warws), sworn before the court in court 27 May 1761. ITKB [*Verso*]: 'In the King's Bench. 24. Mr. Abney's affidt. fo: 5.'

That the deponent was with Luttrell, John Willington, John Gough and others at Joseph Robinson's Star alehouse on 11 or 12 March 1761. Although he left the room momentarily to escape the heat, he never heard Luttrell tell Gough that he would give him £5 a year. Luttrell was not in Tamworth in Nov or Dec, only from 10 to 13 March 1761.

[53] Affdt of Simon Luttrell esquire of Four Oaks (Warws), sworn by the court 27 May 1761. ITKB [*Verso*]: 'In the King's Bench. Smith. 22 . Affidavit of S. Luttrell Esq. fo: 7.'

That the deponent was not in Tamworth between Dec 1761 and Feb 1761, but was there from 10 to 13 March and 30 March 1761. He was never in private company with Robert Smith and did not attempt to have Lattimer re-employ Smith. On 30 March the deponent did send Ball to speak to Lattimer to see if the sole reason for Smith's discharge was his intention to vote for Luttrell. Lattimer said the reason was that Smith was not as good a worker as the others.

[54] Affdt of George Ball servant to Simon Luttrell of Four Oaks (Warws), sworn before the court in court 27 May 1761. ITKB [*Verso*]: 'In the King's Bench. 21. The Affidavit of George Ball. fo: 8.'

That neither he nor William Robinson went to Thomas Mace's house, nor seized John Gough to take him to the Star alehouse about ten days before the election, nor did they force him into a room where Abney and others were. Luttrell was not in Tamworth in January, February, or the second half of March, and returned 30 March. On 11 or 12 March 1761 the deponent and Robinson met Gough on Market Street and asked him to go to the Star alehouse to meet Luttrell, to which Gough readily agreed. He never heard Luttrell offer Gough £5 a year or any other financial service or bribe.

[55] Affdt of Simon Luttrell esquire of Four Oaks (Warws), sworn by the court in court 27 May 1761. ITKB [*Verso*]: 'In the King's Bench. J. G. 20 The Affidt of S. Luttrell Esq. fo: 8.'
 That the deponent was with William Abney and others at the Star alehouse 11 or 12 March 1761 when John Gough came in; John Willington introduced Gough and the deponent asked him for his vote. He never offered Gough £5 a year for life. He did not even know that Gough had a son and could not have told Gough that the son would give him the money in exchange for his vote. He does not know of the conversation between Abney and Ashford mentioned in James Keeling's and Edward Ashford's affidavits.

Affidavits for Villiers and Burdett:

Trin 1 Geo III 1761

[56] Affdt of Samuel Crosland woolstapler of Tamworth (Staffs), sworn before Robert Nevill at Tamworth 14 May 1761. ITKB [*Verso*]: 'Saml Crosland sworn. 20. Saml Dones. fo 7.'
 That the deponent is a trustee of a charity established by the will of Thomas Guy, being an almshouse and an annual stipend for aged people of Tamworth. There is often a surplus to be distributed by the trustees. Thomas Dones is kindred to Guy and a proper subject for the charity; before the election he had wanted the benefit. The deponent promised him an apartment in the almshouse and to be friends in the trust money, while encouraging Dones to vote for whom he pleased. Dones voted only for Luttrell; the deponent always told him to vote for whom he would.

[57] Affdt of Daniel Astle one of the keepers of Needwood Forest, sworn before Robert Nevill at Tamworth 15 May 1761. ITKB [*Verso*]: 'Daniel Astle. Hollis. fo:7.'
 That 31 March 1761 the deponent accidentally met Richard Hollis, gardener, a voter. Someone who knew Hollis well told the deponent that Hollis's vote could easily be bought. The deponent asked Hollis if 5 guineas would buy his vote. Hollis replied that he had been offered

fifteen guineas to vote for Luttrell. Hollis said he would switch his vote for 20 guineas or more. The deponent denies actually ever offering Hollis the money and he was not ever employed by a candidate. Hollis voted for Luttrell.

[58] Affdt of Nathaniel Crosland clothier of Tamsworth (Staffs), sworn before Robert Nevill at Tamworth (Staffs) 15 May 1761. ITKB [*Verso*]: 'Nath Crosland. Bolton. fo: 8.'

That the deponent is an assessor and collector of land taxes for Tamworth (Staffs). The deponent was at the town hall for most of the election. Joseph Bolton of Tamworth, mason, told him on election day that he had been told that part of his tenement would be rated to the land tax. The deponent told Bolton that this would not happen as his tenement was too small, under 20s, and that he never knew of a tenement of so small a value being rated. He asked Bolton to vote for Burdett, but did not attach any conditions or threats related to the tenement being rated. The deponent is not an agent of Villiers, and Bolton voted for Luttrell.

[59] Affdt of John Haywood tailor of Seckington (Warws), sworn before Robert Nevill at Tamworth (Staffs) 15 May 1761. ITKB [*Verso*]: 'Jn Heywood. 9. Brittan. fo: 5.'

That in Dec 1760 the deponent was with William Brittan and asked him to vote for Burdett. Brittan replied he would not. The deponent denies that he offered Brittan three guineas or anything else for his vote. The deponent was never requested by Villiers or Burdett to procure votes.

[60] Affdt of Thomas Hinckes clothier of Tamworth (Staffs), sworn before Robert Nevill at Tamworth 15 May 1761. ITKB [*Verso*]: 'Mr. Hinckes. 12. Jno. Onion. fo: 6.'

That John Onion of Tamworth, shoemaker, complained that Russ promised to put his sons on the list of Lord Weymouth's charity two or three years ago for the £3 10s. Hinckes agreed to speak to Russ, who said that Onion was on the list and that it would be his turn at or soon after Easter. Russ said he might offer Onion the chance to be on the list a week before the election and might ask Onion to vote for Villiers. But the deponent denies that he or Russ ever tied the offer to the vote, or meant to bribe or compel Onion or unduly or unfairly influence his vote.

[61] Affdt of William Greaves gentleman steward to Sir Robert Burdett of Ingleby (Derbs), sworn before Robert Nevill at Tamworth 15 May 1761. ITKB [*Verso*]: 'Wm Greaves 13. Barber. fo: 11.'

That the deponent is Burdett's steward but not his agent, nor does he know personally John Wallis. John Barber of Birmingham (Warws) came to the Castle Inn 30 March 1761 to influence the vote of his father, William Barber, who had already promised to vote for Luttrell. Edward Wolferstan the younger came in and John Barber told him that he had £30 due him on a bond. Wolferstan said it appeared the bond was not payable to Barber and would have nothing to do with it. The deponent denies that Wolferstan ever offered to pay Barber's travelling expenses to influence his father's vote, or that he offered £10 to Barber for the same purpose or that the £10 would be given to John Wallis. The deponent was never in the company of Barber a second time. Barber's father voted for Luttrell.

[62] Affdt of John Wallis gardener of Tamworth (Staffs), sworn before Robert Nevill at Tamworth 15 May 1761. ITKB [*Verso*]: 'John Wallis. 14. Barber. fo: 11.'

That the deponent knows John Barber. Barber came to the deponent's house at 8am 30 March 1761 and asked him what he thought of Barber's father, William, voting for Burdett. Barber said that his trip was expensive and that he needed to raise some money. He said he would get the money from someone before his father voted, meaning he was looking for a bribe. They went to the Castle Inn at 9am and saw no one but Joseph Heath. After this, the deponent left. He never saw William Greaves, nor knew of him until that day. The deponent believes Barber voted for Luttrell.

[63] Affdt of Edward Russ gentleman steward to the Right Honourable Thomas Lord Viscount Weymouth of Drayton Bassett, sworn before Robert Nevill at Tamworth 15 May 1761. ITKB [*Verso*]: 'Edwd Russ. 15. Vincent. fo: 5.'

That the deponent did not refuse to lease Joseph Vincent part of the farm now held by his father after his father's death. The deponent was always willing to lease it. In Nov 1760 he told Vincent he could have his father's farm and Dunstall Close at the rent his father paid if he looked after his ageing mother. The deponent does not remember or believe that Vincent was promised the farm or a lower rent for his vote. Vincent voted for Luttrell.

[64] Affdt of Edward Wolferstan the younger gentleman of Tamworth (Staffs and Warws), sworn before Robert Nevill at Tamworth (Staffs) 15 May 1761. ITKB [*Verso*]: 'Edwd Wolferstan. 16. Vincent. fo: 5.'

That the deponent has frequently asked Joseph Vincent to vote for Villiers and Burdett, but never in connection with assuming the tenancy of the farm his father now holds. The deponent believes he may have told Vincent that Russ intended him to have the farm, or the greatest part of it, but no promises were made contingent on Vincent's vote.

[65] Affdt of Edward Russ gentleman, steward to the Right Honourable Thomas Lord Viscount Weymouth of Drayton Bassett, sworn before Robert Nevill at Tamworth 15 May 1761. ITKB [*Verso*]: 'Edwd Russ. 17. T. Dones. fo 5.'

That the deponent does not remember himself, Wolferstan, or William Norton pressing Thomas Dones to drink with them at the Castle in Tamworth 25 Nov 1760 or to vote for Villiers and Burdett. He denies promising the return of a fine for Dones's killing a hare. He was told by Villiers not to buy votes and Burdett never hired him as an agent or manager of his campaign. The deponent was on bad terms with Dones, never entertained the least hope of getting his vote, and had been cautioned by Villiers not to try to get votes by any pecuniary or undue means. The deponent was not an agent of Burdett.

[66] Affdt of Edward Russ gentleman steward to the Right Honourable Thomas Lord Viscount Weymouth of Drayton Bassett, sworn before Robert Nevill at Tamworth 15 May 1761. ITKB [*Verso*]: 'Edward Russ. 11. John Onion. fo: 12.'

That it has been customary for Lord Weymouth to commit £14 yearly to put poor children out as apprentices, at the rate of £3 10s each, every Easter. The deponent has given out these sums for the last nine years, keeping a list of the charity applicants. He promised John Onion that his children would be put out not realizing that other children were already on the list. Still he gave Onion an award, not realizing that Onion had pledged his vote to Villiers. Neither the deponent nor Hinckes told Onion to vote this way in exchange for charity.

[67] Affdt of Thomas Hinckes clothier of Tamworth (Staffs), sworn before Robert Nevill at Tamworth 15 May 1761. ITKB [*Verso*]: 'Thos. Hinckes. 25. Boaz Reynoldson. fo: 8.'

That it is customary for four poor children to be put out apprentices at £3 10s each at Easter at Lord Weymouth's expense. Two apprentices work under the Tamworth bailiffs and the other two under Lord Weymouth. Boaz Reynoldson wanted his son to receive this charity, but by March 1761 his turn had not come. The deponent applied to receive charity on behalf of Reynoldson and Russ informed him it would be available next Easter, a week before the election. The deponent told Reynoldson that Russ would pay the money, and believes he might ask [*sic*] Reynoldson to give a vote a vote for Villiers, but denies that he did then promise that he would help him to any money other than and except the charity money promised by Russ.

[68] Affdt of Edward Dickenson gentleman of Tamworth (Staffs), sworn before Robert Nevill at Tamworth 15 May 1761. ITKB [*Verso*]: 'Edwd Dickinson. 24. Moore. fo: 11.'

That Thomas Moore of Tamworth maltster came to Wolferstan's house at 8am 31 March 1761 with William Norton. The deponent and Russ were there as was Watterson and William Norton. No person strongly solicited Moore's vote for Villiers or Burdett, nor did Russ promise he would have land from Lord Weymouth at old or easy rents. Nor does the deponent believe that they tried to solicit anyone else's vote. But Moore did importunately press for the lands at High Bridge which Mrs Beardsley now occupies. Wolferstan proposed an agreement, signed by Russ, for Moore to get Beardsley's land after she left it for £3 a year, 10s more than the current rent. This transaction was not conditional on Moore's vote. Watterson did not offer to let land he held in Tamworth from Lord Weymouth by 5 April if Moore gave his vote, nor did Russ add that this land could be had for £2 5s a year.

[69] Affdt of William Norton chandler of Tamworth (Warws), sworn before Robert Nevill at Tamworth (Staffs) 16 May 1761. ITKB [*Verso*]: 'Wm Norton. 22. T. Moore. fo: 12.'

That the deponent was with Thomas Moore at Edward Wolferstan the younger's house with Russ and Edward Dickenson. Moore said that he was going to vote for Villiers and Burdett. Russ and Wolferstan thanked him. Moore then said that he needed land near the High Bridge. Russ and Moore agreed that Moore would get the land when Mrs Beardsley quit it for £3 10s, more than now paid. The land was not promised in return for a vote. John Watterson arrived after the others had been talking and offered land then held by him to Moore for £2 5s, but this was not done in exchange for a vote.

[70] Affdt of Edward Russ gentleman steward to the Right Honourable Lord Viscount Weymouth of Drayton Bassett, sworn before Robert Nevill at Tamworth (Staffs) 15 May 1761. ITKB [*Verso*]: 'Edwd Russ. 21. T. Moore. fo: 9.'

[*Subtantiates Edward Dickenson's account of Russ's dealings with Thomas Moore in the preceding affidavit.*] The agreement was signed by deponent and witnessed by William Norton. The land was promised to Moore a month before the election for 10s more than the old rent. The deponent, Wolferstan, John Watterson and William Norton never solicited votes from Moore, Moore was not promised land held by Watterson in exchange for his vote, and Moore voted for Luttrell.

[71] Affdt of John Watterson currier of Tamworth (Warws), sworn before Robt Nevill at Tamworth (Staffs) 15 May 1761. ITKB [*Verso*]: 'John Watterson. 23. Moore. fo:9.'

That the deponent went to the house of Edward Wolferstan the younger 31 March at 8am and found Russ, Norton, and Johnson. The deponent denies that he urged Moore to vote for Villiers and Burdett. [*Substantiates affdts [69-70].*]

[72] Affdt of Daniel Astle one of the keepers of the Forest of Needwood (Staffs), sworn before Robert Nevill at Tamworth 15 May 1761. ITKB

That about 28 March 1761 at the Castle inn, the deponent was in company with Joseph Jones, Elias Wilcox, William Norton, and Joseph Hughes when Burdett arrived. Someone other than Burdett asked Jones to vote for him. Someone said Burdett should speak to Mr Pratt of Ashby about Jones having Pratt's carriage business. Burdett said he would speak to Pratt, but he did not then or ever say to Jones 'If you will promise me a vote I will engage you shall have all the carriage of Mr Pratt of Ashby and that if you are afraid of his not performing my promise I will give you a bond for a hundred pounds to insure it you.' Nor did any other person present make such a promise. Deponent was in the bar the whole time, and had such words been spoken he would have heard them.

[73] Affdt of William Norton chandler of Tamworth (Staffs and Warws), sworn before Robert Nevill at Tamworth (Staffs) 15 May 1761. ITKB [*Verso:*] 'William Norton. fo: 7.'

That 28 March he was in company with Sir Robert Burdett bart, Elias Wilcox millwright of Tamworth, Joseph Hughes ropemaker of Walsall, Daniel Astle one of the keepers of Needwood Forest, and Joseph Jones carrier of Tamworth, when someone present told Burdett that he might serve Jones by speaking to Mr Pratt of Ashby to let Jones have Pratt's carriage. Burdett said he would but did not tell Jones that he would have all Pratt's carriage 'if you will promise me a vote', nor offer to give a bond of £100 as insurance for the promise. Nor did this deponent promise all his carriage to Jones, with a bond to insure it to him, if he would vote for Burdett. This deponent had constantly employed Jones since he first set up in business as a carrier. This deponent was never employed by Lord Villiers and Sir Robert or either of them as an agent or manager at the election.

[74] Affdt of Joseph Hughes ropemaker of Walsall, sworn before Robert Nevill at Tamworth (Staffs) 15 May 1761. ITKB [*Verso*]: 'Tamworth. Joseph Hughes. Wilcox. filed May 18th 1761 by Mr Cox. fo: 11.'

That the deponent went to Tamworth 28 March 1761 to go to the market and for no purpose connected with the election, as he was unable to vote. He never spoke to any of the candidates, and was not personally acquainted with them. Having heard about Villiers and Burdett he said to Elias Wilcox that he would be pleased if Burdett won, but never said 'If you will vote for Sir Robert Burdett you shall have ten guineas or twenty or will five more do' or any similar words. [*Substantiates account of Castle Inn exchange re Jones and Pratt in affdt [73].*]

[75] Affdt of Humphrey Milner gentleman of Seckington (Warws), sworn before Robert Nevill at Tamworth (Staffs) 15 May 1761. ITKB [*Verso*]: 'Humphrey Milner. 2. Wilcox. fo: 10.'

That the deponent was at the King's Arms 30 March 1761 with Joseph England miller of Alder Mills, John Kendall carpenter, Elias Wilcox millwright, and Edward Wolferstan the younger, all of Tamworth. England asked Wilcox to vote for Villiers and Burdett, and if not both, then Burdett. Wilcox replied he had been ill used by Lord Weymouth's steward and injured £10 by being turned out of his work, and a tenant of General Townsend being employed in his stead. England said someone should be asked to speak to Weymouth. No one said Wilcox would have all Weymouth's work for voting for Burdett. The following day at the King's Arms Allen England of Alder Mills came in, and Joseph England produced a letter from Lord Weymouth expressing regret that he had been ill treated and stating that he should be employed again if he worked well. No other letter to Wilcox was produced or read at the King's Arms. The deponent has no vote, is not an agent, and did not solicit votes for either candidate.

[76] Affdt of John Kendall carpenter of Tamworth (Staffs and Warws), sworn before Robert Nevill at Tamworth (Staffs) 15 May 1761. ITKB [*Verso*]: 'John Kendall. 3. Wilcox. fo: 8.'

[*Substantiates affdt [75].*]

[77] Affdt of Edward Wolferstan the younger, town clerk and one of the justices of the peace for Tamworth (Staffs and Warws), sworn before Robert Nevill at Tamworth (Staffs) 15 May 1761. ITKB [*Verso*]: 'Edward Wolferstan fo: 12.'

That 30 March he went to the Boot and King's Arms inn where he met Elias Wilcox tenant to Lord Weymouth and John Kendall both of Tamworth, and Joseph England of Alder Mills miller. They told him

Wilcox had been ill used because a tenant of General Townshend was employed in Lord Weymouth's works in prejudice to him. Wilcox asked the deponent to speak to Weymouth, but deponent advised him to do so himself. Wilcox said a line or two from the deponent would do him more service. The deponent called for ink and paper and took the following words from Wilcox's mouth, 'Elias Wilcox who has been a tenant of Lord Weymouth's for upwards of four years complains that he has been ill used with regard to the engine work at the colliery in Wilnecote Field. That he was at first employed there about the work and was afterwards turned off and another person employed and that whatever other work is done in the millwright's way is done by another person except at Alder Mills where he is employed altogether by his Lordship's tenants Mr Englands.' The deponent then went into another room and transcribed the words verbatim, and wrote a covering letter to Weymouth. Weymouth replied [as in affdt [75]]. No person present promised Wilcox Lord Weymouth's work for his vote; Wilcox voted for Luttrell.

[78] Affdt of William Sharp husbandman of Daniel Heys Repton[125] parish (Derbs), sworn before Robert Nevill at Tamworth 16 May 1761. ITKB [Verso]: 'William Sharp. 28 32 29. Reynoldson. fo: 4.'

That the deponent was at Tamworth 30 March with James Reynoldson weaver of Tamworth, Joseph Tetley potter of Heath End in the parish of Ashby de la Zouch (Leics) and Achan Potterton labourer of Caulke (Derbs). Tetley did not promise Reynoldson a house rent free or a full abatement of rent now due in exchange for his vote for Burdett.

[79] Affdt of Achan Potterton labourer of Calke (Derbs), sworn before Robert Nevill at Tamworth 16 May 1761. ITKB [Verso]: 'Achan Potterton. 33 26. Reynoldson. fo: 4.'

[Substantiates affdt [78].]

[80] Affdt of Humphrey Milner gentleman of Seckington (Warws), sworn before Robert Nevill at Tamworth (Staffs) 16 May 1761. ITKB [Verso]: 'Humy Milner. 19. T. Dones. fo: 3.'

That the deponent never promised Thomas Dones repayment of a £5 fine Dones had paid some years ago, for killing a hare, in return for a vote for Burdett. He believes Dones voted for Luttrell.

[81] Affdt of Thomas Butler whitesmith of Tamworth (Staffs and Warws), sworn before Robert Nevill at Tamworth (Staffs) 16 May 1761. ITKB [Verso]: 'Thos Butler 10. Boaz Reynoldson. fo: 7.'

---

[125] Probably Daniel Hay farm, which is in Smisby, not Repton, parish.

That several times before the election the deponent asked Boaz Reynoldson to vote for Villiers and Burdett. The deponent never offered Reynoldson £3 10s for his vote. Reynoldson complained to the deponent that years earlier Russ had promised him £3 10s for putting out his son as apprentice and asked the deponent to speak to Russ about this. He did, and Russ said that he would give Reynoldson the money for this next Easter. He never tied the promised repayment to Reynoldson's vote. Reynoldson voted for Luttrell. The deponent was not employed or desired to act as an agent by either Villiers or Burdett.

[82] Affdt of Joseph Tetley potter of Heath End, Ashby de la Zouch parish (Leics), sworn before Robert Nevill at Tamworth 16 May 1761. ITKB [*Verso*]: 'Joseph Tetley. 27. Reynoldson. 28 Affidts. fo: 5.'

That the deponent was with James Reynoldson, William Sharp and Achan Potterton 30 March 1761. He asked Reynoldson to vote for Burdett, but he never offered him a house rent-free and a cancelling of other rent due. Reynoldson voted for Luttrell.

[83] Affdt of William Norton chandler of Tamworth (Staffs and Warws), sworn before Robert Nevill at Tamworth (Staffs) 16 May 1761. ITKB [*Verso*]: 'Wm Norton. 18. Thos. Dones. fo: 5.'

That the deponent is not an agent of Villiers or Burdett, but on 25 Nov 1760 he may have asked Thomas Dones to drink with him, Russ, and Wolferstan at the Castle inn. He may have asked Dones to vote for Villiers and Burdett but no one ever promised that they would refund the fine levied for killing a hare. Dones voted for Luttrell.

[84] Affdt of Edward Wolferstan the younger gentleman of Tamworth (Staffs), sworn before Lord Mansfield at his house at Kenwood (Middx) 18 May 1761. ITKB [*Verso*]: 'E Wolferstan. 35.'

That Morley Jenkinson never promised to tell John Dickinson that if Dickinson voted for Burdett, Jenkinson would have the deponent deliver a note of Dickinson's father in law for £5. About a month before the election Dickinson came to consult with the deponent concerning two houses which had descended to Hannah his wife and Elizabeth the wife of Joseph Bellfield of Tamworth, labourer, as their father's only heirs. Dickinson, who had no issue with his wife, asked if he could enjoy a moiety or any share of the houses if his wife died in his lifetime. Deponent told him it would require a fine of £6 or £7 but he might be able to make it less. When Dickinson expressed great uneasiness the deponent having then a kindness and respect for Dickinson told him that he would pass him a fine of the estate, and not charge him anything. The deponent absolutely denies that this or any other promise was made on condition that Dickinson vote for Sir Robert Burdett. Dickinson voted for Luttrell and Abney and Bellfield voted for Luttrell only.

[85] Affdt of Morley Jenkinson watchmaker of Tamworth (Warws), sworn before Lord Mansfield at his house at Kenwood (Middx) 18 May 1761. ITKB [*Verso*]: 'Tamworth. Mr Jenkinson. Filed 18 May 1761. Trinity. fo: 22.'

The deponent several times asked John Dickinson to vote for Burdett, but denies the allegation about the £5 note; Dickinson indicated he wanted to oblige Wolferstan for his generous offer [*see preceding affdt*]. Wolferstan replied he could best oblige him by voting for Burdett, but that irrespective of his vote the promise would be performed. The deponent met Hannah Dickinson and Elizabeth Bellfield at Christmas at Hannah's request to try to persuade both their husbands to vote for Burdett. He never linked this discussion to any promise and denies offering them land of Edward Allport of Bitterscote. He also denies telling them that they could have one of Lord Weymouth's charity schools [*Substantiates affdt [84].*] Dickenson voted for Abney and Luttrell while Bellfield voted for Luttrell only.

[86] Affdt of Sir Robert Burdett baronet of Foremark (Derbs), sworn before Lord Mansfield at Mansfield's house at Kenwood (Middx) 18 May 1761. [*The affidavit is not headed ITKB.*] [*Verso*]: 'Sr Robt. Burdett. fo: 6.'

That the deponent went into the bar of the Castle Inn 28 March 1761 where he met Elias Wilcox, Joseph Hughes, Daniel Astle, Joseph Jones and others. While talking with Jones, others said that the deponent might be of service to Jones by speaking to W. Pratt to let Jones have his carriage. The deponent flatly denies linking this to Jones's vote or offering a £100 bond as a surety. Not feeling bound to aid Jones, he let the matter drop when he learned Pratt was engaged to Mrs Rice.

[87] Affdt of Edward Wolferstan the younger gentleman of Tamworth (Staffs), sworn before Lord Mansfield at Mansfield's house at Kenwood (Middx) 18 May 1761. [*The affidavit is not headed ITKB.*] [*Verso*]: 'E. Wolferstan. 34. fo: 12.'

That at 8am on 31 March 1761 Thomas Moore and William Norton came to the deponent's house and were introduced by Edward Dickenson while Russ was present. Moore declared that he came from Wishaw (Warws) where he has been at work, to vote for Villiers and Burdett. The deponent and Russ thanked him, and he stayed to eat and drink. [*Substantiates affdt [69] respecting Moore's request for a tenancy near the high bridge, his reply, and Watterson's offer.*]

[88] Affdt of Edward Wolferstan the younger, gentleman of Tamworth (Staffs), sworn before Lord Mansfield at his house at Kenwood (Middx) 18 May 1761. [*The affidavit is not headed ITKB.*] [*Verso*]: 'E. Wolferstan. 32. fo: 23.'

That the deponent recalls being at the Castle inn on the morning of 30 March 1761 where he met William Greaves and John Barber. Barber said that his father was going to vote for Luttrell but that he wanted him to vote for Burdett. Barber said that he would like Greaves or the deponent to pay and assume a bond due to him from a person in Wales. Barber's wife was the legal representative of the surety. There was a problem with improper assignment of the bond to the obligee, and Wolferstan said it was not worth 6*d*. Barber then asked for his travel expenses to be paid. The deponent walked away and is positive he never insinuated payment of £10 to Barber to defray travel expenses in exchange for Barber's father voting for Burdett. The deponent does not believe that Greaves or anyone sent for Barber to come to the Inn. Barber's father voted for Luttrell.

[89] Affdt of Joseph England miller, one of the people commonly called Quakers, of Alder Mills, affirmed before Lord Mansfield at his house at Kenwood (Middx) 18 May 1761. [*The affidavit is not headed ITKB.*] [*Verso*]: 'Jos. England. 31. fo: 11.'

That the deponent was with Humphrey Milner, John Kendall and Elias Wilcox 31 March 1761. He told Wilcox that if he voted for Villiers or Burdett he would be very much obliged to him. The deponent did not promise Wilcox that he and Milner would do all Wilcox's future work for Lord Weymouth. Wilcox complained that he had been put out of work and that Wolferstan returned 30 March with a letter from Weymouth to Wolferstan stating his regret that Wilcox had been ill treated and offering work for Wilcox for as long as Wilcox worked well.

[90] Affdt of Edward Wolferstan the younger gentleman of Tamworth (Staffs), sworn before Lord Mansfield at Mansfield's house at Kenwood (Middx) 28 May 1761. [*The affidavit is not headed ITKB.*] [*Verso*]: 'E. Wolferstan. 33. Infr & ex Dones. fo: 9.'

That the deponent did not press Thomas Dones to drink with him, Edward Russ, and William Norton at the Castle 25 March 1761. Russ did not promise to return the £5 penalty to Thomas Dones which Dones had paid for killing a hare some years before, nor did the deponent. Dones has expressed great resentment and malice against Russ, and the deponent and Watterson heard both Dones and his wife say at Mary Hayn's house in Dec 1760 or Jan 1761 that he would never vote for a friend of Lord Weymouth's as long as Russ was his steward. They said that they hoped 'the sturdy beggars', meaning some friends of Luttrell's who called themselves that, would be able to turn Russ out of his stewardship.

Sources: KB 1/14 Ea 1 Geo III no.1 and no. 2, Trin 1 Geo III. KB 11/44 Trin 1 Geo III 1761 #4. KB 15/15 Trin 1 Geo III. KB 21/38 pp. 473, 480, 483, 487, 495, 497, 507, 513. KB 28/238 roll 20. KB 29/420 Trin l Geo III.

A.17 Information applied for, and writ of habeas corpus ordered
(29 Oct 1762)

Defendant: Mary Ward, widow of Lichfield, with habeas corpus to Mary Ward to produce Elizabeth Vernon, a spinster under the age of majority.

Accusation:
Refusing to restore Elizabeth to the custody of her father, and assault.

Rules and process:
Mich [6 Nov 1762, FDT]: on reading affdt of Richard Vernon gentleman and others, ordered that a writ of habeas corpus issue[126] directed to Mary Ward widow to bring into this court the body of Elizabeth Vernon spinster (solicitor general; by the court); on reading affdt of Vernon, rule nisi for an information to [23 Nov 1762] (solicitor general; by the court).

Affidavit for prosecution:

Mich 3 Geo III 1762

[1] Affdt of Richard Vernon gentleman and William Connley yeoman, both of Astley (Worcs), and John Lester husbandman of Yoxall; Vernon and Lester sworn before George Norris at Droitwich (Worcs) 29 Oct 1762, Conley sworn before Thomas Parker 30 Oct 1762 [*no place given*]. ITKB [*Verso*]: 'Nov 1762, B R Litchfield. The King & Ward for Information and Ha Cor. Mr Solr Gen. Ha Cor. Gr. Mary Ward. Wido she to show c. why Inform. not be granted. fo:16. Litchfield. Affidt of Rd Vernon & al for Ha Cor. & Inform. agt Mary Ward wido fo:16.'
   [Richard Vernon]: That his daughter Elizabeth Vernon spinster, an infant under the age of 21, has been for some time at the house of Mary Ward, his mother-in-law, in Lichfield. He wanted his daughter back

---

[126] No returned writ is filed in KB 16/15/5–8.

and wrote to her, then went to Lichfield 30 Sept. Elizabeth told him that she could not then come into Worcs but would do so shortly. He went again with his servant William Connley to Mary Ward's house 16 Oct; she told him that Elizabeth should not go out of her house. He believes Elizabeth was in agitation of going to Scotland to marry an officer with whom she kept company, without the deponent's consent. The match would be injurious to her, being entitled to a very genteel fortune. He gently laid his hands on Elizabeth to take her out of the house when Ward's servant Anne Benton, and William Page of Burton upon Trent, seized him and by force and violence rescued his daughter from him. Ward knew he had an undoubted right to take his underage daughter, but she said that she would send Elizabeth far enough that he could have nothing to do with her.

[William Connley]: [*Substantiates Vernon's evidence.*]

[Richard Vernon]: That he believes Ward sent Elizabeth away since 17 Oct 1762, or otherwise concealed her as in spite of diligent inquiries he can't hear anything of her.

[William Connley]: That he was at Ward's house 22 Oct 1762 and could not see Elizabeth there, or hear where she was. He believes Ward sent her off.

[John Lester]: That he well knows Elizabeth Vernon as Richard Vernon was his landlord, and by his order for some time he paid his rent to Elizabeth Vernon. He believes Elizabeth is in agitation to go to Scotland to marry an officer. The deponent could not see her at Ward's home 22 Oct. Ward would not give him any information about her whereabouts, and he believes she has sent her off or concealed her.

Sources: KB 1/15 Mich 3 Geo III. KB 21/39 p.1.

A.18 Information not pursued (4 May 1763)

Defendant: Justinian Snow, yeoman of Stafford.

Accusation:
Attempted rape of Mary Lucas Milward, wife of Thomas Milward hoopshaver of Stafford.

Rules and process:
[*None found.*]

Affidavit for prosecution:

Ea 3 Geo III 1763

[1] Affdt of Mary Lucas Milward wife of Thomas Milward hoopshaver of Stafford, sworn before Samuel Harding[127] at Drayton in Hales (Salop) 4 May 1763. ITKB

That Justinian Snow yeoman of Stafford entered the deponent's house 23 April 1763, shut the door and laid violent hands on her with intent to rape her, and said he would debauch her. He was extremely rude and indecent with her, and had she not cried loudly to Snow's wife, who lived in the adjoining house, and struggled and cried out, and told him there was a person in the parlour, she believes Snow would have raped her, by his violence, tearing of her clothes, using her in the most indecent, rude, and cruel manner, at the same time declaring he would have carnal knowledge of her body.

Sources: KB 1/15 Ea 3 Geo III.

A.19 Information not pursued (22 Nov 1768)

Defendants: John Groome, John Devey, John Sheldon, Samuel Peach, trustees of the charity school in Trysull, and Joseph York, constable; all of Trysull.

Accusation:
Assault on Anbrook Stringer, schoolmaster of Trysull, and expelling him from the school.

Rules and process:
[*None found.*]

Affidavit for prosecution:

Mich 9 Geo III 1768

[1] Affdt of Anbrook Stringer gentleman of Trysull, sworn before John Winnall at Stourbridge (Worcs) 22 Nov 1768. ITKB [*Verso*]: '54 Staffordshire In the King's Bench. Affidt of Mr Anbrook Stringer for Infn agt John Groome and others. fo: 9. R. and S.S. Baxter Furnivals Inn.'

That the deponent has been a schoolmaster at a charity or free school in Trysull for near six years, teaching eleven or twelve boys and girls of the parish reading, writing and arithmetic without further compensation than the yearly stipend. He was ready to have taught more

---

[127] Possibly the gentleman and attorney Samuel Harding, of Audlem (Ches): Shropshire Archives, Lady Curteis' Collection, 741/52 (26 Sept 1781).

children had they offered. During this time John Groome, John Devey, John Sheldon, Benjamin Stokes, Thomas Devey and Samuel Peach, all gentlemen of Trysull, acted as trustees of the school and paid the deponent a yearly salary of £9 10s. half yearly. He believes the trustees approved of his conduct and behaviour throughout.

On 4 Aug 1768 Groome, John Devey, Sheldon, Peach and Joseph York, constable of Trysull and several others broke the door into the school at 4pm, seized the deponent's books, papers and accounts relating to the school and to the deponent's private affairs. The deponent went to the school and found the door broke open, the lock taken off, several children in the school and a padlock put on the door. He desired the children to walk out, put the padlock in his pocket, and went into his school. Groome, Devey, Peach, Sheldon and York came to the school and asked him to get out, which he refused to do. The other men present ordered York the constable to lay hands on the deponent, and turn him out. York at first refused, saying he thought he could not justify it. They insisted, and York held him while they took the padlock. Groome struck and kicked him and beat his head against the wall and held him by the throat until he was almost dead. He was badly bruised, then put out of possession of his school, which they locked up. The next day the above named trustees gave possession of the school to Billinge, a former Jesuit, and who has kept the deponent out of the school.[128] He consulted a physician and surgeon who informed him that he thought the deponent was in great danger of his life for a considerable time.

Source: KB 1/17 Mich 9 Geo III no.1.

---

[128] Charles Billinge (1735–1805) entered the Society of Jesus in 1753 and was Prefect at their college of St Omer in 1761. He subsequently became missioner at Moseley Old Hall, near Wolverhampton, where he neglected his duties, fell in love, and abandoned the Roman Catholic church for marriage and Anglican orders. He preached a recantation sermon in Lichfield cathedral in 1767 and thereafter supported himself and his family by teaching French at Wolverhampton and by doing occasional duties in nearby parishes: [John Kirk], 'Catholic Chapels in Staffordshire', *Catholic Magazine and Review*, vol. 5 (1834), pp. 393–4 (facsimile reprint in *Staffs Catholic History*, vol. 14 (1974)); Henry Foley, *Records of the English Province of the Society of Jesus*, vol. 7 (London, 1882), p. 58; F. W. Hackwood, *Sedgley Researches* (Dudley, 1898), p. 51

A.20 Information applied for, followed by settlement
(20 Jan 1782)

Defendant: Francis Newdigate esquire of Wootton Hall.

Accusation:
Threatening John Port esquire of Ilam with a gun and challenging him to a duel.

Rules and process:
17 to 22 Jan 1782: affdts [1] to [3] taken. Hil [7 Feb 1782]: by consent of counsel on both sides, enlarged rule nisi to second day of NT, and that all affdts for defdt be filed ten days before NT (Bower for prosr, Davenport for defdt). 7, 8 Feb 1782: affdts [4] and [5] taken. Ea 1782: rule discharged with costs settled.[129]

Affidavits for prosecution:

Hil 22 Geo III 1782

[1] Affdt of John Port esquire of Ilam, sworn before E. Willes at his house in Lincoln's Inn 19 Jan 1782, and of Matthew Bloxam esquire of Tissington (Derbs), sworn in court by the court 28 Jan 1782. ITKB
[John Port]: That he was on horseback coursing hares 20 Dec 1781 in part of an estate belonging to the Reverend John Dewes, his brother-in-law, on a piece of land called the Red Hall occupied by William Poyser, a tenant farmer. Newdigate approached him and asked him to stop killing hares and to keep off the property. He replied that he had his brother-in-law's permission during his absence at Bath, and that there-fore he should take no notice of Newdigate, who said the deponent was 'no gentleman.' Deponent replied 'I return the same to you.' Newdigate: 'You are an impertinent man.' Deponent: 'I return the same to you.' Newdigate levelled his gun at the deponent from a distance of three yards, and said 'God-damn you , I'll fetch you off your horse.' The deponent replied, 'You think yourself a man of consequence but you are of no more weight than the boy who holds my dogs.'
    Later that day the deponent received a letter [*annexed*] from Newdigate, challenging him to a duel. He replied by letter that he

---

[129] The rough minute book for Hil 22 Geo III (KB 36/256) lists, inside the back cover, 'motions appointed to come on peremptorily in Easter term 1782', and the list for the second day includes this case, with a later marginal note, 'discharged with costs settled.' There is no note of this outcome in KB 21.

ought to receive an apology from Newdigate because he had witnesses to attest that Newdigate had molested him, and offered to refer the matter to his brother-in-law or to any other person Newdigate chose to have in the neighbourhood. On 22 Dec he informed Bloxam, who lived three miles away, of these events. Later that day at Ilam the deponent's servant told him that Newdigate had been by earlier and would return on the morrow. The deponent asked Bloxam to be a witness on 23 Dec to this exchange, but Newdigate never called. The deponent did not intend to duel with Newdigate.

[Matthew Bloxam:] That he was with Port on 22 Dec to witness a conversation. He believes that Port did not intend to duel.

[*Annexed*]: 'The Language you made use of to me this morning demands an explanation and an apology which I shall insist upon, or that you will meet me as a gentleman, the place, time and weapons I shall leave to your determination. Francis Newdigate. P.S. I shall be from home from tomorrow ten o'clock till Sunday morn.'

[2] Affdt of William Poyser yeoman of Ellastone, and Anthony Oakden servant to John Port esquire of Ilam, sworn before John Child at Ellastone 22 Jan 1782. ITKB
   [*Substantiates affdt [1].*]

[3] Affdt of John Child gentleman of Cheadle, sworn before Francis Brookes at Stafford 17 Jan 1782. ITKB 'The King against Francis Newdigate Esquire.'
   That the deponent served notice 14 Jan 1782 to Francis Newdigate.
   [*Annexed*]: That the court will be moved Wednesday 23 Jan instant, the first day of next Hilary term to file an information against Newdigate for a misdemeanor in sending a challenge to John Port esquire to fight a duel. Basil and William Herne, attorneys for John Port.

Affidavits for defence:

Ea 22 Geo III 1782

[4] Affdt of Francis Newdigate esquire of Wootton, sworn before William Fallows at Derby (Derbs) 7 Feb 1782. ITKB 'The King agst Francis Newdigate Esquire.' [*Verso*]: 'The King agt. Newdigate Esq: Afft. Parker fo: 11.'
   That for about two years the deponent's gamekeeper Benjamin Finney has had the deputation as gamekeeper for the manors of Wootton, Ellastone, Ramshorn, Stanton and Northwood from Davies Davenport esquire and William Davenport esquire, the lords thereof.

The deponent resides within the manor of Wootton. For several months before 20 Dec 1781 John Port coursed and sported for hares in the manors of Wootton and Northwood very frequently with a number of unqualified persons with him for the purpose of killing hares. The deponent and his gamekeeper, Benjamin Finney, met Port and several other unqualified persons coursing hares within a short distance of the deponent's manor house. The deponent asked Port civilly to stop coursing hares so near his house, as he was trying to preserve a few, to which Port responded that he would course 'when I please, how I please and where I please.' The deponent replied, 'I am sorry to hear you say so as I have not molested you in any other parts of the manors I am deputed to here', to which Port repeated his former words. The deponent asked whether he thought that was the behaviour of a gentleman, to which Port insultingly answered 'If it is not it is like your behaviour, you are come into this country to kill all the game yourself and give yourself airs of great consequence whereas you are of no more consequence than this boy', or words equally taunting and to that effect which insolent assertion provoked this deponent to reply that if he thought he had one particle of a gentleman in him he would knock him off his horse. To which Port replied 'I should like to see you do it'. Whereupon this deponent left. During this whole conversation and meeting he did not to his knowledge level his gun at Port neither did he positively menace him with personal injury.

In the evening of 20 Dec he received a letter from Port asking that the dispute be referred to the Reverend John Dewes and to any other person this deponent should appoint. On receipt of the letter he was and always since has been ready to submit the difference to Mr Dewes and any other gentleman of known character but Dewes being from home and out of Staffordshire, and being himself indisposed with a cold the day after the meeting with Port, he could not go from home but did so 22 Dec and wishing an accommodation went to the house of the Reverend William Beresford to have him come with him to Port in order to make an apology and to receive an apology from Port but Beresford was from home. He then went to Port's house to settle the matter but Port was not at home. Since 22 Dec he has been very often from home and regarded the dispute at an end and nothing further to be done but making the reference proposed by Port, until to his great surprise he received notice of the motion in King's Bench.

[5] Affdt of Benjamin Finney, gamekeeper to Francis Newdigate esquire, of Wootton, sworn before Charles Upton at Derby (Derb) 8 Feb 1782. ITKB 'The King against Francis Newdigate Esquire.' [*Verso*]: 'The King agt. Newdigate Esq: Afft Parker. 2 fo 7.'

That for about six months before 20 Dec 1781, Port had sported and coursed for hares on the property of Francis Newdigate. [*Substantiates affidavit [4].*]

Sources: KB 1/22 Hil 22 Geo III, bdl 17; Ea 22 Geo III no. 1. KB 21/43 Hil 22 Geo III [*volume unpaginated*]. KB 36/256 Hil 22 Geo III.

A.21 Information applied for (13 June 1787)

Defendant: Littleton Scott, keeper of Stafford gaol.

Accusation:
Altering and making a false return to a writ of habeas corpus.

Rules and process:
Trin [26 June 1787]: on reading affdts [1] and [2], and affdt [3] and a paper writing annexed, rule nisi to Littleton Scott to FNT for an information against him for certain misdemeanours, on notice of this rule to be given to him in the mean time (Leycester, by the court).

Affidavits for prosecution:

Trin 27 Geo III

[1] Affdt of William Keen gentleman and deputy undersheriff to Thomas Whieldon sheriff of Stafford, sworn before Henry Smith at Stafford 23 June 1787. ITKB [*Verso*]: '44 Trin 87 Staff. Affts for Infn v Littleton Scott. 26 June R. Nisi. Price Cursitor J. W. fo: 9.'

That in April last James Mason was a prisoner in Stafford gaol under a writ of capias ad satisfaciendum issued out of the court of exchequer at Westminster returnable [23 April 1787] to satisfy Thomas Parker of £42 4s 1d. Parker recovered this amount in the court of exchequer for costs and charges adjudged to him by the court under the statute by reason of the unjust vexation Parker suffered in a plea of trespass on the case by Mason against Parker, whereof he was convicted.[130] Later a writ of habeas corpus out of King's Bench for the removal of Mason and the cause of his detention by the sheriff was brought to this deponent's office. The writ with the return that Mason was held under the capias was sent to Scott for the purpose of removing Mason to King's Bench in obedience to the writ.

Deponent has heard and believed that Scott procured the return to the writ of habeas corpus to be altered or a fresh return made, thereby

---

[130] On this litigation see case H.2 affdt [3]. Other related cases are G.2 and H.1.

falsely returning that James Mason was also detained under another writ of capias ad satisfaciendum from King's Bench to satisfy John Stanley for a debt of £20, and damages of 63s. Scott sent this return to King's Bench as the return of the county sheriff.

No writ of capias ad satisfaciendum had been delivered to the sheriff's office until after the return was made to the writ of habeas corpus nor until after Scott returned from London. The alteration in the return was made without the knowledge or consent of the deponent or Thomas Whieldon or any other authorized person.

[2] Affdt of Henry Smith gentleman of Wolverhampton, sworn in court by the court 26 June 1787. ITKB [*Verso*]: 'To move for an information. H. Leycester fo: 3.'

That on 23 June 1787 Littleton Scott acknowledged to the deponent that he had procured the alteration of the return of Thomas Whieldon esq sheriff of Staffordshire to the writ of habeas corpus [*as described in affdt [1]*] and said he would not attempt to deny it if called upon to answer for so doing.

[3] Affdt of Phillip Seckerson writing clerk of Stafford, sworn before W. Keen [*no place* given] 13 June 1787. ITKB

That the deponent served Littleton Scott, keeper of Stafford gaol, with the annexed notice13 June 1787.

[*Annexed*]: 'Take notice that the court of King's Bench at Westminster will be moved on Monday next or as soon after as counsel can be heard for leave to exhibit an information against you for certain contempts offences and misdemeanours in procuring the return to a writ of habeas corpus issued out of the same court for the removal of James Mason to be altered stating that the said James Mason was in the custody of the sheriff of Staffordshire under a writ issuing out of the said court of King's Bench when in truth no writ issuing out of the said court of King's Bench against the said James Mason had been delivered to the sheriff of Staffordshire or to his undersheriff or deputy undersheriff nor did the sheriff of Staffordshire or his undersheriff of deputy know any thing of such alteration till after you had procured such return to be made and the said James Mason turned over to the King's Bench.

Dated 11th June 1787

Hen: Smith by Ben: Price Attorney for the Prosecutor.

To Mr Littleton Scott

Stafford.'

Sources: KB 1/25 Trin 27 Geo III no.1 bdl 44. KB 21/44 p.378.

A.22 Information applied for (26 June 1794)

Defendant: Daniel Seddon, lieutenant and esquire, 22nd Regiment Light Dragoons, stationed at Lichfield.

Accusation:
Assaulting Thomas Walton, constable of Lichfield, June 1794.

Rules and process:
Trin [2 July 1794]: on reading affdt [1], rule nisi to 8 July (Bower).

Affidavit for prosecution:

Trin 34 Geo III 1794

[1] Affdt of Thomas Walton druggist, grocer, and constable of Lichfield, sworn before William Gill the younger at Lichfield 26 June 1794. ITKB [*Verso*]: '48 June 94 Litchfield In the Kings Bench Afft for Infns Daniel Seddon Esq. The King agt Danl Seddon: Affts 2 July R nisi Kinderley & Long fo:11.'
   That 16 June the deponent received a warrant of William Wooley and Samuel Barker, JPs of Lichfield, to arrest Richard Leech on a complaint of John Howell, shoemaker of Birmingham (Warws). Richard Leech was a private in the 22nd Regiment of the Light Dragoons, which were quartered in Lichfield. The deponent first met Major Richard Lister, who demanded to see the warrant. He complied with the request. When he asked of Leech's whereabouts the major damned the deponent for his impertinence and told him to look around. Soon the deponent found Leech and brought him before Justice Wooley. At 4pm the regimental sergeant major requested and received from the deponent a receipt for the body. At 6pm the deponent received a message from the major requesting his attendance at the parade in Boar Street to exchange Leech's discharge for a receipt. The deponent approached the major on parade who, in return, held his whip to the deponent's chest and said 'Damn you Mr Constable walk back we want no constables here don't interrupt us in the parade.' The major then said that if he had anything to say he must first remove his hat, which the deponent respectfully declined to do. Then lieutenant Daniel Seddon esquire said, 'Damn you for a democrat I don't love to strike constables' and he struck the deponent a violent blow on the side of the head. Afraid of further personal injury, he immediately went away.

Sources: KB 1/28 Trin 34 Geo III 1794. KB 21/46 p. 255.

A.23 Information applied for (25 Nov 1796)

Defendant: Francis Macworth Trefusis, esquire.

Accusation:
Challenging John Heyliger Burt, esquire of Colton to a duel, May 1796.

Rules and process:
25 Nov 1796: affdt [1] taken. Mich [26 Nov 1796]: on reading affdt [1], rule nisi to FNT (Gibbs). [*Rules nisi related to this case were obtained the same day against Ann and Charlotte Slater, Thomas Walton and Thomas Turner, and against George Thomas Smith esq; in both cases the rules were captioned Leics*].[131]

Affidavit for prosecution:

Mich 37 Geo III 1796

[1] Affdt of John Heyliger Burt esquire of Colton, sworn before John Armishaw at Hill Ridware 25 Nov 1796. ITKB 'The King against Francis Mackworth Trefusis Esquire.' [*Verso*]: '30 Mic 96. Staff Affdt for Infn v Fras Mackworth Trefusis Esq. The King v Trefusis Esq. Affidavit of John Heyliger Burt Esq 26 Nov Rule nisi Grahams fo: 24.'
   That the deponent was riding in a carriage with his sister from Colton to Lichfield on 27 May when the defendant Trefusis rode alongside in a post chaise, demanding a private conversation concerning the settlement which the deponent intended to make on Maria Anna Trefusis, otherwise called Maria Anna Tuite, the defendant's mother, with whom the deponent had lately cohabited but from whom he was then separated. The deponent answered the questions but Trefusis followed the deponent all the way to the Swan inn in Lichfield where the conversation was continued. The deponent then proceeded to the house of Judith Okeover (then a widow, now the wife of the deponent) in Sheepy (Leics) where the deponent spent the night. He was aroused at 4am when one of his servants from Colton gave notice that Trefusis had made a great scene in his house around midnight, demanding to see the deponent. While returning home in the morning the deponent was again accosted on the road by Trefusis, who delivered a note: 'Sir – Agitated in mind! miserable, harassed, well assured that the Settlement you have made on my Mother cannot be secure unless you become

---

[131] In the Leicestershire prosecution five affidavits were filed: KB 1/29 Mich 37 Geo II, bdls 78, 79.

personally responsible which you directly refuse, I now demand from you as the only means left me of doing justice to my Mother's honour and my own feelings. Gentlemanlike satisfaction – it was my intention to have expressed myself to you as I do now yesterday Evening had not the presence of your sister restrained me. However I now call on you as a Man of honor to give me this meeting. I beg leave to remind you that your own words "that I knew you was not afraid to meet me on any ground in England" induce me to expect to [*sic*] it. Francis Trefusis Saturday Morning. I request an answer as to the time and what ground you think proper to meet me on.' Trefusis requested a reply to the George Inn, Lichfield.

The deponent replied, taking no notice of the challenge, writing 'Sir, In answer to your note can only say if your Mother is satisfied with the settlement well and good you will please to observe I shall never take the least notice of any of your letters to that purport. I am Sir John Heyliger Burt.' At 11pm his servants informed him that Trefusis was in the breakfast parlour. The deponent, accompanied by two servants whom he refused to send away, told Trefusis that he would not have a private conversation with him, and that in spite of his threats to pursue the deponent everywhere in order to call him to strict account, he would not risk the blame of duelling with a boy of seventeen. Trefusis was very angry at the word 'boy', and replied that although he was in Burt's eyes a boy, 'the time was not far remote when he ... might call for satisfaction as a man.' Quintin Dick esquire arrived and persuaded him to leave. The deponent believes that Trefusis still intends unlawfully to provoke a duel and that he still bears much ill will against the deponent.

Sources: KB 1/29/2 Mich 37 Geo III 1796 bdl 90. KB 21/46 p. 594.

A.24 Information granted but not exhibited (25 Oct 1800)

Defendant: John Gough esquire and JP, of Perry Hall, Perry Barr.[132]

Accusation:
Libelling the Reverend Thomas Lane, JP, 1800.

Rules and process:
29 Oct to 20 Nov 1800: affdts [*below*] taken. Mich [20 Nov 1800]: on read-

---

[132] This case is discussed in D. Hay, 'Dread of the Crown Office', 37–39. See also case F.23.

ing affdts [1] to [5], rule nisi to 27 Nov (Erskine).[133] ST [27 Nov 1800]: on hearing counsel both sides, enlarged peremptory rule nisi to 4th day NT (Erksine for prosr, Miller for defdt). Hil [27 Jan 1801]: no cause being shown, rule absolute (Erskine).[134]

Affidavits for prosecution:

Mich 41 Geo III 1800

[1] Affdt of the Reverend Thomas Lane rector of the parish of Handsworth and acting JP for Staffordshire, sworn before Roger Williams Gem at Handsworth 29 Oct 1800. ITKB [*Verso*]: 'Staff. Affidt of the Revd Thos Lane sw. 29 Oct 1800. Bolton Savage & Spike fo: 31.'

That while on his way to the quarter sessions at Stafford on 17 July, the deponent saw a large picture displayed opposite the Blue Pig inn in the parish of Aldridge. It showed several men, among them a clergyman and his clerk (representing the deponent and his clerk), attended by the devil, tearing down a house with the inhabitants still inside. On 26 Aug Joseph Size, blacksmith, told him that the sign had been brought by Christopher Newly, a labourer employed by Gough, and later removed by John Vickers, Gough's coachman. On 19 Aug when the deponent met Gough in his carriage, Gough shouted and threw defamatory handbills, and had his footman deliver one to this deponent [*annexed*]. On 20 Aug the deponent removed from the wall of a house belonging to Gough a handbill advertising the painting: 'The Infernal Monster with Old Nick at this back, and Clerk Solomon and other monsters assisting him to pull down houses of great value, over the heads of several distressed families, with their helpless infants crying for mercy, attended by his Father in Law a fiddler, and his own mother a kitchen maid.' On the same day he found and took away a board covered with libellous and indecent songs and handbills [including the annexed Job Chance, Anticipation, and The Bulliad] against the house of another of Gough's tenants, James Harlow. Also on the same day he saw on an unoccupied house owned by Gough, two effigies, one dressed as a clergyman, each holding a pickaxe, with signs identifying himself and his clerk as men who unlawfully untiled and undermined the houses in 1788, afterward rebuilt by Gough, on Perry Warren.

[133] *The Times*, 21 Nov 1800, reported the rule nisi.
[134] No information appears to have been exhibited (KB 11), and there is no entry in KB 29 for Hil 1801 or later terms. Lane died 12 Oct 1802: *Staffordshire Advertiser*, 16 Oct 1802.

The painting, handbills, or signs asking 'How can such rancor dwell in an holy breast', were shown at the houses of Joseph Size, James Harlow, Charles Lebon, Thomas Boughey, John Hewey, William Howell and Isaac Horton, all tenants of Gough's. Each man told the deponent that they were told by Gough to exhibit the signs and handbills in clear places or be evicted. When the deponent took the sign from the house of James Harlow, Harlow's wife pleaded for it back because Gough now threatened eviction. The deponent sent his clerk, Arthur Rowley, to Gough's home at his invitation to get copies of the handbills.

[*Annexed*]:[135]

[*At top of page*]: 'Tuesday Aug. 19th, 1800 delivered by J. Gough to T.L.'[136] [*Verso*]: '[*illegible*]ber 29th 1800. This handbill was produced and shewn to me by the Reverend Thomas Lane Clerk and is the same mentioned and referred to in his affidavit hereunto annexed this day sworn before me Roger William Gem.'

[*Printed broadsheet*]:

'When spite and malice, rancour and revenge, can be proved the incentives of human action; when a series, or system of acts, can fairly be traced to such mean sources; and when the individual actuated by such base motives, is under the strongest obligations from his professional duty, (and for which he is amply and liberally paid) to pursue a contrary line of conduct: surely the depravity of such actions can not be sufficiently exposed to public hatred and contempt.

'How far these charges will apply to a certain Rev. Personage, not forty miles from Handsworth, let the following facts (which exhibit some of his actions and amusements) testify, as they had no tendancy [*sic*] to redress any injury, or render any service to himself or society; they can be traced to no other source, or motive, than what are above named; some of the charges against him are as follows.

[*In margin*]: 'Tried and cast in 1789.'

'I. Pulling down houses belonging to a neighbouring gentleman (one of his parishioners) over the heads of several poor families, merely out of spite or revenge to the owner; or as he himself has expressed it, to bring him to; for this (upon trial) a verdict was given against him, with costs.

[*In margin*]: 'Tried and cast in 1790.'

'II. Pulling down several yards of park walling, belong to the same gentleman, under pretence of an encroachment, though the road and the public were no ways injured.

[135] For earlier versions of this handbill, from December 1794, see WSL, broadsheets 3.

[136] This and the marginal notes below are handwritten.

'III. Indicting the same gentleman for four hundred yards of park walling, that had been built by his father 50 years before; and for stopping a pretended road, that had never existed; and endeavouring to support such indictment by the perjury of infamous witnesses, who had been previously in gaol for other charges than debt; the iniquity of which was seen through by the court, and the indictments quashed, with a proper reprimand.

'IV. Prosecuting the same gentleman for money that had been tendered him.

'V. Putting the same gentleman into Lichfield court for tythes overcharged, and afterwards taking half the sum.

'VI. Laying a malicious information against the same gentleman's two servants, for taking one brace of partridges, though their master was out at the same time, and had a proper certificate.

[*In margin*]: 'Tried and cast in 1797.'

'VII. Causing a distress to be taken against the same gentleman, for five shillings that was assessed to himself. At the next sessions the court ——med the assessment.

'VIII. Endeavouring twice to indict the same gentleman and others for hanging a wooden figure, called the Devil, Tom the Fiddler's Son, &c. &c.

'IX. Turning off one poor tenant and raising the rent of another, because they would not swear against their consciences in support of his indictments.

'X. Using his utmost influence to prevent a public house being licenced, (merely out of revenge to the owner of such house, as can be proved from expressions from his own mouth) although it had been a very ancient public house, and in as proper a situation, and as regular rules observed by the occupier, as in any public house in the country; and in which by falsehood and misrepresentations to persons in power, he had temporary success; the consequence of which was, throwing a man, his wife, and several small children out of the means of getting their bread, and greatly injuring their circumstances.

'XI. Procuring himself to be made a magistrate, and employing acquisition of power in the same way; insomuch that the poor man above named, having no other way of supporting his numerous family, had been encouraged to continue selling ale, (though without defrauding the revenue, the Excise Officer having regular information thereof, and calling as usual,) to be revenged, the worthy Rev. Personage above alluded to, has twice committed him to goal, and thus deprived his family of their father and protector, and means of subsistance; and twice levied a penalty upon him, to the great injury and almost ruin of himself, his numerous and helpless family.

'The writer of this would be much obliged to any one, who can rec-
oncile such actions and practices, to the laws and principles of benevo-
lence and christian [*sic*]charity, or even of common honesty: as for his
own part, he can think the mildest of them consistent only with the
character of a person actuated by malice, revenge, and an implacability
of disposition; and some of the most inveterate can be referred to nothing but the malevolent turpitude of an unfeeling, unprincipled hard-
hearted villain. May 30, 1799. JOB CHANCE, Esq.'

[2] Affdt of Joseph Storer farmer of Perry Barr parish of Handsworth,
sworn before Roger Williams Gem at Birmingham (Warws) 29 Oct
1800. ITKB
   That in 1796 the deponent, a tenant of Gough's, was required by one
Webb a servant of Gough's to display against his house during the day
(and to take in at night) a picture of several persons pulling down a
house. One of the figures was intended to represent the Reverend
Thomas Lane, rector of the parish of Handsworth. This spring the
deponent saw the same picture displayed at the house of Joseph Size,
another of Gough's tenants, situated on the turnpike road between
Birmingham and Walsall, opposite the Blue Pig inn.

[3] Affdt of Arthur Rowley bailiff to the Reverend Thomas Lane, rector
of Handsworth, sworn before Roger Williams Gem at Handsworth 29
Oct 1800. ITKB
   That he went 27 Aug 1800 by his master's order to Perry Hall, where
Gough asked him if he was sent for some papers. Gough said he would
send Lane as many as he would like, and told him that thousands had
been distributed in and around Birmingham; Charles Lebon also
had many copies. He also heard George Webb tell Gough that the sign
had been taken down from the Blue Pig, Gough's public house, because
it was cracked and warped. Gough showed him a picture, the same
as one he had seen opposite the Blue Pig. The figure of the cleric is
intended to represent his master, Thomas Lane.

[4] Affdt of Thomas Gem the younger gentleman of Birmingham
(Warws), sworn before Roger Williams Gem at Birmingham 20 Nov
1800.[137] ITKB
   That between 25 Oct and 15 Nov he spoke to Size, Boughey, Newly,
Howell, and Horton [*confirming Lane's affidavit of 29 Oct*]. He also spoke to
Gough's labourer, Christopher Newey, who placed the sign at the home
of Size. All were asked to swear affidavits against Gough but refused.

---

[137] A copy of this affidavit is found in Birmingham City Archives, Gough 246/5.

[5] Affdt of the Reverend Thomas Lane, sworn before Roger Williams Gem at Handsworth 17 Nov 1800.[138] ITKB [*Verso*]: 'Staff. Revd Tho Lane sw: 17 Nov: 1800. Bolton Savage & Spike fo: 19.'

That in answer to the eleven charges made by Gough in a handbill [*annexed to the deponent's affidavit of 26 Oct*] which was distributed throughout the county:

1. The deponent did not pull down any houses on the heads of any poor inhabitants. The deponent pulled them down after the tenants had been properly evicted, because the houses encroached upon the waste, and because those evicted had apparently been placed there solely to make them parishioners of Handsworth. The deponent believes that Gough had actually turned out many of his own cottagers and inhabitants of small houses, tenanting them with poor strangers to some of whom he parcelled out parts of his own farm to make their tenements of £10 annual value, which lands he caused to be made leys of, and the monies paid for the ley of cattle thereon to be paid to his own agent, thereby to secure the rents; and others he swore in either constables or headboroughs.
2. The deponent did pull down several yards of a park wall belonging to Gough because it encroached upon the public highway in contravention of statute; Gough was fined 40s for the encroachment.
3. The deponent was not involved in any perjury; the accused was convicted on the indictment, which was not quashed.
4. The deponent loaned 12 guineas to Gough and refused a conditional repayment; he sued for the whole sum and recovered it and costs.
5. The deponent recovered, in Lichfield Ecclesiastical Court, tithes which Gough refused to pay, the libel in such cases stating a larger quantity than was really demanded.
6. The deponent successfully prosecuted Gough's two servants, who netted partridges that the deponent was hunting on land not belonging to Gough; Gough did not appear, nor justify their conduct.
7. The deponent granted the warrant to distrain Gough for a rate that he was obliged to pay, and did so according to this deponent's best judgment as a magistrate.
8. The deponent admits this charge to be true.
9. The deponent believes this charge to be untrue, as he does not understand to what it alludes.

---

[138] Lane's exculpatory affidavit; a copy is also found in Birmingham City Archives, Gough 246/5.

10. The deponent did not use any undue influence on the magistrates; they exercised their discretion in deciding to refuse to license the house in question until the libellous signs depicting this deponent were removed.

11. The deponent convicted the person alluded to, without the least malice and according to his duty as a magistrate, for selling ale without a license. It was on the information of a total stranger, and the defendant refused to pay the penalty on the orders of Gough, whereupon he was sent to prison.

[*Annexed printed handbill (see Figure 7)*]: [*Verso*]: 'This handbill was produced and shewn to me by the Reverend Thomas Lane Clerk and is the

Figure 7 **One of Justice Gough's libels on Justice Lane, 1800**
Case A.24 (detail).

same mentioned and referred to in his affidavit sworn before me this 17th day of Novr 1800 and hereunto annexed. Roger William Gem]

'ANTICIPATION OF THE Death-bed Confession of a NOTORIOUS SINNER.

'My Father was a celebrated cocker, my mother the daughter of a fiddler, and previous to her marriage had employed her charms to some advantage. By these laudible means my parents were possessed of some wealth: no expence was spared to give me an education, and the accomplishment of a gentleman; but alas, my steril nature was never able to abide the first rudiments of a scholar, and all my attempts at gentility only served to make me ridiculous.

'How I have fulfilled the duties of the cloth, my charity towards the poor cottagers will evince, and having obtained the rank of a magistrate, I unblushingly first exercised my authority in convicting and sending to prison a poor honest man, the father of a large family, for selling ale without a licence; though all my neighbours knew it was through my influence alone that a licence had been refused him; I was induced to commit this act of meanness and wanton cruelty, only because he was the tenant of a respectable gentleman, richer and more respectable than myself, whom I hated for obliging me strictly to observe the pious duties I had undertaken, and was amply paid for, but had no inclination to perform.

'Manifold have been my sins, and at the awful moment of dissolution their horrid deformity presents itself to my disturbed mind. I humbly ask forgiveness of the numbers I have oppressed, and hope these my last words may be published as a warning to those of mean extraction, who, like me, may become possessed of some little power, and employ it to the injury of their fellow-creatures.

'A Penitent SINNER.'

Affidavit for defence (to enlarge rule nisi):

Mich 41 Geo III 1800

[6] Affdt of John Gough esquire of Perry Hall, sworn before Thomas Welch at Birmingham (Warws) 25 Nov 1800. ITKB 'The King against John Gough Esquire.' [*Verso*]: '74 Mic 1800 Staff. Afft to enlarge Ni for Infn ag John Gough Esq 27 Nov. Enlarged to next Term. Swain & Stevens. fo: 3.'

That a copy of the rule founded on the affidavits of Thomas Lane clerk and a paper thereunto annexed and of Thomas Gem the younger, Arthur Rowley, and Joseph Storer, which ordered that Thursday next be given to the deponent to show cause why an information should not be exhibited against him for misdemeanours, was not delivered to the deponent until 3pm on 24 Nov 1800. Because of the lack of notice, the deponent cannot be prepared to show cause having not yet seen the affidavits upon which the rule is based.

Sources: KB 1/30 Mich 41 Geo III, pt 1, and KB 1/31 Mich 41 Geo III pt 2 bdl 74; KB 21/47, pp. 428, 439, 450.

Section B

In most respects prosecutions on information brought against magistrates, both justices in the county commission of the peace and borough magistrates, followed the same rules as those against private citizens (Section A). There were, however, a few significant differences in both law and practice that were intended to protect magistrates from harassment and punishment. The purpose was to ensure that the unpaid magistracy, on whom so much of the work of the criminal law and local government fell, were not discouraged from serving; there was also the felt need to preserve their authority in the case of even egregious error on their part, or indeed malice. Troublesome defendants with lawyers might prosecute them for errors in committal proceedings (cases B.3, B.8, B.9, B.10), or on their summary convictions (B.5, B.6, B.7, B.11). Magistrates also carried out many of the tasks of local and national government which exposed them to prosecution, including the poor law (cases B.1, B.2, B.4, B.8), licensing alehouses (B.12), and enlisting soldiers (B.13).

The role of the judges

Probably the most important protection for magistrates was the attitude of the judges of King's Bench. Lord Mansfield, chief justice from 1756 to 1788, declared that a criminal information against a magistrate was 'extraordinary assistance' to a prosecutor, which the court 'ought to dispense with caution and discretion'; mere irregularities would never suffice.[1] The implicit contrast was to an 'ordinary' prosecution on indictment at assizes (or perhaps quarter sessions), open to anyone aggrieved by a magistrate's behaviour in office. But such prosecutions virtually never took place against county justices, probably because a grand jury would first have had to find a true bill, and at Stafford assizes most of the grand jurors were fellow justices of the peace. The judges of King's Bench refused to grant informations in most of the few Staffordshire cases that came before them, because the most common test, as Mansfield established it, was whether the magistrate had acted corruptly, in the sense of having a personal pecuniary interest in the prosecution. Such an interest was extremely unlikely, and justices who merely acted in an ignorant, vindictive, oppressive, or negligent

---

[1] *R v Fielding* (1759) 2 Burrow 719, 97 ER 531.

way, were therefore almost entirely safe from prosecution on criminal information, particularly if they were country gentlemen in the commission of the peace. [2] Only six such men in Staffordshire had prosecutions begun against them. However, twelve aldermen, bailiffs, or other officers of boroughs, who were magistrates as a function of their office, did have to defend themselves in King's Bench. Two of the three Staffordshire magistrates who actually suffered the exhibition of an information were such tradesmen, a maltster and a tanner (case B.6). In contrast, the irascible John Gough of Perry Hall, a wealthy country gentleman justice of the peace, against whom there were more attempts to bring a criminal information than any other Staffordshire magistrate, never bore the stigma of a rule absolute being granted against him (B.8, B.9, B.10).

Notice and costs
There were also procedural requirements that differed from those for ordinary criminal informations. One was the requirement of notice, proved by affidavit. Before the plaintiff could move the court for a rule to show cause, the justice had to receive reasonable notice in writing, either in person or left at his home, of the intention to do so. What was reasonable notice was not defined as a set number days.[3] In an attempted prosecution of a Staffordshire magistrate for his conduct in Easter term 1753, not included in this book because no affidavits were ever filed, delays in instructing the local solicitor to serve notice were caused by letters not arriving. When notice was finally served on 26 June in Trinity term, the prosecutor's solicitor was aware that the court might object that one week's notice, only eight days before the end of term, was probably insufficient. The prosecution was deferred until the next term, Michaelmas, to allow time for fresh notice to be given, but if notice was served, no motion was made in court. It is possible that counsel now advised the prosecutor of the second procedural

---

[2]   For a fuller development of this argument, based on these cases and also on an analysis of the case law, see D. Hay, 'Dread of the Crown Office: the English magistracy and King=s Bench, 1740–1800', in Norma Landau, ed., *Law, Crime and English Society 1660–1840* (Cambridge University Press, 2002), 19–45, which also describes civil litigation against one of the magistrates in this section. See also cases A.24, F.23.

[3]   Hands, 2–3; Gude, i, 115. Gude at 111 note (a) cites *R v Richard Carpenter Smith* (1796) 7 Term Reports 80, 101 ER 865, in which the court agreed that notice late in the term was possible only when the alleged offence took place during that term. The number of days notice required was set at six in *Ex parte Fentiman* (1834), 2 Adolphus and Ellis 127, 111 ER 49, borrowing from a statutory requirement for certiorari.

protection enjoyed by magistrates: that King's Bench would not usually grant an information against a justice if too long a time had elapsed since the offence. In this case more than two terms had passed.[4]

The consequences of an unsuccessful complaint against a justice were serious. Costs (in what was a very expensive form of litigation) were awarded by the court against the prosecutor if the judges thought the magistrate had not acted illegally or corruptly, nor with what Gude called 'any bad view or ill intention'. Since all the persons who made affidavits against the justice were considered to be prosecutors, it could be very difficult to find witnesses.[5]

A magistrate who received notice of an intention to move for a criminal information against him could oppose the application for the rule nisi, but the usual course of the defence was to wait for the rule nisi, then show cause against it, usually in the next term. In this way it was possible for the magistrate to see the prosecution's affidavits before his lawyers prepared and filed the defence affidavits (cases B.1, B.4, B.5, B.6, B.10, B.11, B.12, B.13).[6] Two cases ended after the filing of prosecution affidavits (**B.2, B.3.**)[7] Most rules nisi were discharged (**B.1, B.5, B.7, B.8, B.9, B.10, B.11, B.13.**) Of three cases in which a rule absolute was granted, informations were actually exhibited in only two (**B.6**, B.12).[8] Such an event was so rare that it must have carried some stigma. Notice of trial was given in the prosecution of a single magistrate (**B.12**), but there is no record of a trial taking place.

Prosecutions could be collusive, an agreement between the parties to test a right or obligation, a device used during eight years of litigation involving the Walsall magistrates concerning the administration of the poor laws in the borough and foreign (B.4). But their continuing recalcitrance after three and a half years of proceedings convinced the chief justice that their conduct was 'so extremely perverse and obstinate, that it must have proceeded from a partial or corrupt motive.'

---

[4]   R v Nott, discussed in Hay, 'Dread of the Crown Office', 27–28 and 41–2. (See also B.7 for another case against Nott.) Gude, i, 111 note (a) cites an unreported case, R v Sir William Rea (1793) in which the judges declared that two whole terms was too late. In 1811 the court ruled that a prosecution had to be begun in the second term after commission of the offence complained of, there being no intervening assize, and sufficiently early to allow the magistrate to show cause during the same term. *R v Harries and Peters*, 13 East 270, 104 ER 374; *R v Marshall and Grantham*, 13 East 322, 104 ER 394.

[5]   Gude, i, 119.

[6]   Hands, 3; Gude, 115.

[7]   Cases given in bold terminated at that point.

[8]   In B.4 a rule absolute was subsequently discharged.

CASES

B.1 Information against a justice, settled with damages and costs (26 Feb 1740)

Defendant: Samuel Corbett, mayor and justice of the borough and foreign of Walsall.

Accusation:
Misdemeanour in removing a vagrant, Mary Lander, and her child from Walsall to Romsey (Hants).

Rules and process: Ea [17 Apr 1741]: on reading affdts [2] to [4], rule nisi for an information to [4 May 1741] (Henley). ST [9 May 1741]: ordered that Samuel Corbett justice of the peace of Stafford return the writ of certiorari for a pass he made for conveying Mary Lander and her child from Walsall foreign and borough to Romsey parish (Hants) within ten days (side bar; by the court).[9] Trin [11 June 1741]: ordered that the writ (in Walsall v inhabitants Romsey) and return be filed. ST [16 June 1741]: by consent of counsel both sides, ordered that the pass made by Samuel Corbett mayor and justice 10 Nov 1740 for conveying Mary Lander and Mary her child from Walsall to Romsey be quashed, and by the like consent further ordered that they be conveyed by a pass from the parish of Romsey Extra to Walsall the place of their legal settlement; no appeal to be made to such pass; Corbett to pay Romsey £5 charges maintenance and damages also the costs of removing into this court the pass and a certain other pass made previously by Henry Knollys esquire justice of the peace of Hampshire for removing Mary Lander to Walsall. Corbett to pay likewise the costs of the application for and the prosn of the rule nisi for an information against him. James Burrow, master of the crown office, to tax the costs and by like consent further ordered that on payment of such damages and costs by Corbett the said rule made against him be discharged. (Motion and consent of Matthew Henley for Romsey Extra and Ford for Samuel Corbett).

Affidavits for prosecution:

Ea 14 Geo II 1741

---

[9]   Certiorari was granted to remove the pass, after Corbett was served notice on 6 April 1741. KB 1/7/1, affdt of Jonathan Egginton 11 April 1741.

[1] Affdt of Brome Blackbourn gentleman of the city of Lichfield, sworn before Theophilus Levett at Lichfield 4 March 1740. ITKB [*Verso*]: 'Stafford. Affidt Notice motion for Infn agt. Corbet.'

[*Verso*]: 'Staffordshire Affidt Lanndor Nowell and Withers for Infn agt Corbet.'

That this deponent served Samuel Corbett mayor of Walsall 2 March 1740 with a true copy of the notice hereunto annexed.

[*Annexed*]: Notice from Jonathan Godfrey to Samuel Corbett 26 Feb 1740 that the court will be moved for an attachment against Corbett for a misdemeanour in sending Mary Lander and her child by a pass from Walsall to Romsey.

[2] Affdt of John Nowell wheelwright and overseer of the poor of the parish of Romsey Extra (Hants), sworn before Thomas Penkridge at Romsey 24 Nov 1740. ITKB

That Mary Lander was brought by the deputy of the keeper of the house of correction at Winchester and delivered to this deponent 22 Nov 1740 with a pass, a true copy of which is annexed, said to be granted by Samuel Corbett. The pass was addressed to the constable of the county of Stafford and also to the master of the house of correction at Stafford and others. Mary Lander was in Romsey 15 August, and was sent there by a pass granted by Henry Knollys esquire justice of the peace for Hampshire, against which no appeal was ever made.

[*Annexed*]: That Mary Lander and her child Mary, age one month, have been apprehended in the borough of Walsall as rogues and vagabonds. Mary Lander was born in the parish of Romsey[10] (Hants) and has not gained a settlement elsewhere. The constable is to convey them to the first house of correction or to the parish of Romsey, to the overseer of the poor or churchwardens. Sealed 10 Nov 1740. Samuel Corbett Mayor.

[3] Affdt of Mary Lander wife of James Lander of Walsall tailor, now a grenadier in Colonel Wolfe's Regiment of Marines, sworn before Thomas Penkridge at Romsey (Hants) 24 Nov 1740. ITKB

That she was married to her husband in the parish church of St Martins in Salisbury in September 1739 and lived with him till the end of last July, when he went from the Isle of Wight where he had been encamped and boarded a transport in the harbour. She was not permitted to accompany him as she was with child; she went to Romsey and was apprehended by the constable who heard her ask for relief. She was

---

[10] 'Rumsey' in the affidavit.

under the pass of Henry Knollys esquire and was conveyed to the house of correction at Winchester and then to the house of correction at Walsall. The master of the house sent her to the overseer of the poor, who sent her to a workhouse. Her husband had a settlement at Walsall as he served an apprenticeship there for Mr Thomas Cox, tailor; when she arrived with her pass she was acknowledged as a parishioner. She was released from the workhouse and went to visit her husband's mother, where she was entertained as her daughter-in-law. She later found lodgings in town and worked and maintained herself until 13 October when she delivered her daughter. From this time she received 6*d* a day for a fortnight and then 4*d* a day, and then 3*d* a day. She applied for more relief before Corbett, who advised her to beg, but she refused, insisting she was a parishioner. On 10 November Corbett caused her to sign and swear to an examination touching the place of her birth; he then caused her to be conveyed by a pass to the house of correction at Romsey, her place of birth. None of the officers of the parish of Walsall ever made any appeal against the said first mentioned pass to the knowledge or belief of this deponent. She believes their main pretence of sending her away to Romsey was that she did not bring a marriage certificate with her.

[4] Affdt of Richard Withers gentleman, sworn before Thomas Penkridge at Romsey (Hants) 24 Nov 1740. ITKB

Mary Lander, having been apprehended as a rogue and vagabond, was sent from the parish of Romsey (Hants) to Walsall 15 Aug 1740 on a pass from Henry Knollys esquire justice of the peace. The deponent has examined the duplicate of the pass, annexed, and swears that it is a true copy. Mary Lander was sent back to Romsey and was brought there by virtue of another pass.

[*Annexed*]: 'To the constable headborough tythingman and other officers of the peace, and to the governor or master of the house of correction of Winchester and to any other governors or masters of all houses of correction, and to the churchwardens and chapelwardens or overseers of the poor of the parish of Walsall to receive and obey. Mary Lander wife of James Lander a soldier was apprehended in the parish of Romsey as a rogue and vagabond and brought before me. Her last legal settlement was at Walsall. You the said constable are required to remove Mary Lander to the house of correction at Winchester and you the said governor to receive her into your custody and to convey her to the first house of correction in the next county on the way to the parish of Walsall, until she reaches the parish of Walsall. Sealed 15 Aug 1740. Henry Knollys.'

[5] Affdt of John Egginton gentleman of the city of Lichfield, sworn before Theophilus Levett at Lichfield 22 April 1741. ITKB [*Verso*]: 'Affdt service rule for infn agt Corbet. Staffordshire.'

That he personally served Corbett, mayor, with the rule of court annexed on 21 April by delivering to him a true copy and at the same time showing him said annexed original rule.

[*Annexed*]: Rule nisi of [17 April 1741].

Affidavit for defence:

Trin 14 and 15 Geo II 1741

[6] Affdt of Samuel Corbett baker and maltster of Walsall, sworn at Lichfield before Robert Dorset 22 May 1741. ITKB

That the deponent was not in any public office in Walsall from 24 June 1740 until 29 Sept 1740, other than being one of the assessors of the land tax, and a capital burgess. He was elected mayor 29 Sept 1740 and since then has been a justice of the peace. Mary Lander was brought before him as a vagabond 10 Nov 1740. She declared that she was the daughter of Matthew Ivey and Susanna his wife and was born in the parish of Romsey (Hants), that she married James Lander and had one child by him, and that she had heard her husband had a settlement in Walsall and that she wanted some relief. This deponent, not knowing of any former pass removing Mary from Romsey to Walsall, directed a pass to convey her as a vagabond from Walsall to Romsey as the place of her birth. It did not appear to this deponent that James Lander was really settled in Walsall, nor did it appear that James Lander had served Cox, a tailor, as his apprentice, nor that James Lander lived with Cox as an apprentice. The examination of Mary Lander was taken by Thomas Hinchsliffe who then acted as a clerk or writer to Richard Nevill the town clerk, who was away and who generally transacted all business. Thomas Hinchsliffe also prepared the pass which removed Mary Lander from Walsall. Neither Thomas Hinchsliffe nor the deponent claim to know much of the law in these cases, but the deponent, having the latest act of Parliament concerning vagabonds, thought he might justify making such a pass without any further advice. If the pass is irregular or illegal it is merely an error in judgment. The deponent denies that he ever advised Mary Landor to beg, or that she swore that she would not as she was a parishioner. The deponent denies that he knew that Mary had been sent by pass from Romsey or that he pretended that the reason she was sent back to Romsey was that she did not have a marriage certificate. On her examination Mary seemed pleased to be able to return to Romsey as her own parish and place of birth. Corbett did not know of Mary receiving any relief in the said borough of Walsall.

Sources: KB 1/7 Ea 14 Geo II no.1, no. 2, Trin 14 & 15 Geo II no.1. KB 21/35 Hil 14 Geo II pp. 281, 304, 332, 344. KB 39/2 Ea and Ea Vac 1741.

B.2 Information against a justice and others, not pursued (11 Oct 1748)

Defendants: Richard Kilby, late a justice for the city of Lichfield; William Cotton, late junior bailiff of the City; Thomas Heawood and Thomas Smith, late overseers of the poor of the parish of St Chad, Lichfield.

Accusation:
Misdemeanours relating to the levying of a poor rate, and distraining the goods of Harvey Robinson, March 1748.

Rules and process:
[*None found.*]

Affidavits for prosecution:

Mich 22 Geo II 1748

[1] Affdt of Harvey Robinson yeoman and churchwarden of the parish of St Chad, otherwise known as Stowe in the county of Lichfield, John Hartwell stuffmaker of the Elms of the parish of St Chad, William Horton weaver, William Mainwaring gardener, John Worrall turner, John Stanley wheelwright, Thomas Slater yeoman, James Smith weaver, Joseph Smith yeoman, John Acton tailor, William Grow weaver, Henry Walton mason, Richard Walton tailor, John Price mason, Thomas Bird yeoman, Benjamin Hodson tailor, John Green weaver, Henry Summers yeoman, Samuel Allen carpenter, Simon Twiford barber, Nathaniel Starkie the younger gardener, all of the parish of St Chad; at the Close of the Cathedral Church of Lichfield; sworn before John Simpson in the county[11] of Lichfield 11 Oct 1748. ITKB [*Verso*]: 'In the King's Bench. Affidt of Harvey Robinson & others.' [*Harvey Robinson, Samuel Allen, John Worrall, Joseph Smith, William Grow, John Price, Thomas Bird, Benjamin Hodson, John Green and Henry Summers signed with a mark.*]

---

[11] Lichfield City was a county corporate, with exclusive jurisdiction in its quarter sessions and gaol delivery. See also cases F.6, F.7.

[All]: That the parish of Stowe extends into two counties: Lichfield and Staffordshire. From time immemorial there have been two church-wardens elected annually, one by the curate, the other by parishioners. All parishioners, whether in Lichfield or in Staffordshire are chargeable to the church rates of the parish of St Chad. When the town church-warden is absent, the country churchwarden has always helped in levy-ing the rates and in doing other acts which require the concurrence of the majority of overseers.

Since 43 Elizabeth[12] it has been a general practice in the parish of Stowe to give a list of six substantial householders to the bailiffs of Lichfield who appoint two persons to act with the churchwardens and the overseers of the poor. The deponents attended at the vestry meeting held Sunday 6 March 1748 where Fettiplace Nott esquire and parishioner, and John Fletcher gentleman and landowner, proposed to lay four levies totalling £4 11s 3d for poor relief and were supported by Thomas Heawood and Thomas Smith, overseers of the parish, and by Richard Deakin, John Hartwell weaver, John Whittaker, Timothy Alton and Joseph Cook, all parishioners. The levy was opposed by Harvey Robinson churchwarden, all the other deponents, and all parishioners present, who numbered over 30. They believed the over-seers wanted the levy not for the relief of the poor but to get money into their hands for some private purpose. With the consent of all the other deponents, Robinson and Hartwell proposed to the overseers that they would also consent to the proposed levy if the overseers would give an account of the monies already collected and levied, which totalled £63 17s 6d. Robinson would then consent to laying one levy of £4 11s 3d to carry them through their office which would end in five weeks. The overseers refused. To prevent injustice, Robinson, with the consent of the other deponents, offered to care for all the poor as churchwarden and to pay for this himself. Without the consent of Robinson or the 30 parishioners present, Heawood and Smith, with the aid of Nott, Fletcher, Deakin, Hartwell, Whittaker, Alton and Cook, unilaterally laid four levies for the relief of the poor, claiming they had the right to do so.

[Harvey Robinson and John Hartwell]: That with the consent of the other deponents, they immediately applied to Nicholas Deakin and William Cotton, bailiffs of Lichfield, giving them notice of the manner in which the levies were laid. The deponents asked them to suspend the overseers' allowance until a full public hearing of all parties had been conducted. Despite the irregularities, the bailiffs signed their approba-tion of the four levies.

[12] 43 Eliz. I, c.2 (1601), Relief of the Poor.

[Harvey Robinson]: That he was summoned to appear before the bailiffs at Lichfield town hall on 31 March to show cause why they did not pay for the levies. He brought witnesses. Cotton and Richard Kilby justice of the peace asked him whether he would pay for the four levies. The deponent refused, arguing the levies were illegal. Without allowing him to show cause, Kilby and Cotton signed a warrant of distress, produced by Joseph Adey town clerk already sealed, and delivered it to Heawood and Smith with orders to execute it against the deponent. To avoid the inconvenience of a vexatious prosecution the deponent immediately told the overseers that he, as churchwarden, would look after the poor himself or would furnish them with money until the overseers laid out their accounts to the parishioners to show need for more money, if they would waive the execution of the warrant.

Notwithstanding this offer, Heawood and Smith went to the deponent's house 9 April 1748, opened the door without consent and took six pewter dishes allegedly to pay for the 16s owed for the four levies. At the time the deponent was out of pocket at least 30s for poor relief. He went with two bondsmen and located Jonathan Mallett the younger, then high sheriff of Lichfield, within half an hour of the taking of the dishes, and asked him to grant a replevin. The deponent also looked for Caesar Arden Colclough, undersheriff of Lichfield, but he was out of town. Mallett told him that the dishes had been sold to Kilby, a brazier and justice for Lichfield. The deponent's repeated requests for a replevin were denied; his offers of the requisite security, and of payment of the 30s in fees because the dishes had been sold, were also refused. The sheriff offered to see if the dishes had been sold and on arrival asked Kilby if he had bought them. Kilby said he had bought them from Heawood and Smith. The deponent believes a scheme had been previously laid between Kilby, Mallett, Heawood, Smith and others to deprive the deponent of his right to a replevin or of an appeal to the quarter sessions to be held at Lichfield 24 April 1749. He believes Fletcher was instrumental in causing the dishes to be taken and sold because Fletcher had told the deponent in a sneering manner soon after the goods were sold that he had prevented Mallett from granting a replevin. He did this by reaching Mallett's wife and uncle who lobbied on Fletcher's behalf to refuse to grant the replevin.

[All]: That Heawood and Smith had no need to relieve the poor with extra levies and were only pretending to need the funds for that reason. When they finally accounted to the parish on 11 May 1748, three weeks after the time accounting was customarily done — after several voluntary payments pretended to be made by them for advice on how to recover the levies — they had £8 8s ½d remaining in their hands. To prevent being harassed with a vexatious distress, several parishioners have already paid their share of £18 5*s* (the amount of the four levies). Some deponents have been threatened by Fletcher, whom Cotton and Kilby have appointed overseer for the current year, contrary to custom and practice. Kilby will distrain the parishioners' goods and chattels for the four levies if they are not soon paid.

[Harvey Robinson]: That Lichfield is a county to which the judges have not come for over 60 years. Actions against bailiffs, justices, and overseers of the poor are local and to be tried where they arise.

[2] Affdt of John Green weaver of the parish of St Chad Lichfield, sworn before John Simpson at Lichfield 18 Oct 1748. ITKB [*Signed with a mark.*] [*Verso*]: 'John Green's further afft.[13] Mr Rile Lyons Jun rec'd 1: 1: 0. Litchfield Staffordshire. Affts of Harrison [*sic*] & others, and Green for Infn agt Kilby & al.'

That on 2 May 1748 the deponent went to see Kilby for some pewter. Kilby offered him four pewter dishes for nine pence a pound and said they were the best in his shop. The deponent bought two and paid 9*s* 2*d*. Kilby told him these dishes were Robinson's and were taken as a distress by Smith and Heawood for the four levies. It was clear to the deponent that the dishes were seized under Kilby's warrant. The deponent also saw the other two pewter dishes which made up the half dozen seized from Robinson. Had all dishes been taken to the town hall, as distresses usually are, they would have fetched some nine pence a pound at least, whereas Kilby bought them privately at his own shop for seven pence a pound and no more.

[3] Affdt of John Willington gentleman of Lichfield, sworn before Uppingham Bourne at Lichfield 12 Nov 1748. ITKB

That 11 Nov 1748 the deponent delivered written notice to William Cotton, late junior bailiff of the city, and to Heawood and Smith, overseers of the poor for St Chad otherwise Stowe, that the court of the King's Bench would be moved against them 15 Nov 1748, or as soon after as counsel could be heard, for certain misdemeanours. He notified Richard Kilby, late a justice of the peace, in writing 12 Nov 1748 that the court would be moved at the same time for an attachment or information against him for certain misdemeanours committed by him relating to the said rate.

Sources: KB 1/9/5 Mich 22 Geo II.

---

[13] No other affidavits have been found; perhaps this is a reference to an earlier version of Green's affidavit that was not filed.

B.3 Information against a justice, not pursued (23 Nov 1751)

Defendant: Thomas Unett, deputy mayor and justice of Stafford .

Accusation:
Forcibly and maliciously imprisoning and detaining Margaret Hammersley, widow and miller of Stafford, and illegally obliging her to enter into a recognizance with sureties to appear at Manchester quarter sessions.

Rules and process:
[*None found.*]

Affidavits for prosecution:

Hil 25 Geo II 1751

[1] Affdt of Thomas Lawton gentleman of Stafford, sworn before John Dearle at Stafford 23 Nov 1751. 'In the court of King's Bench at Westminster.'
   That Unett requested the deponent 1 May 1752 to take an information or complaint made by John Oldham chapman of Bolton near Manchester, that James Shaw had stolen jeans or fustians out of Oldham's whitening yard and sold some to Margaret Hammersley and others in Stafford. The deponent also wrote a search warrant on this information at Unett's direction to all constables of Stafford borough to search all houses they had reason to suspect. Edward Mackerness constable searched the houses of Hammersley, Thomas Harvey and Samuel Peake, finding one woman's petticoat in the first, a man's waistcoat lined in fustian in the second, and a child's fustian petticoat in the third. Without allowing her to call witnesses to prove that she had bought the cloth, and without either confession or accusation on oath by Oldham, Unett detained Hammersley for two hours and threatened to commit her to prison if she did not find bail for her appearance at Manchester quarter sessions. Detained, she sent out for Thomas Lees skinner and Samuel Peake baker who became sureties for her at £20 each, and she entered into a recognizance of £40 for her appearance at Manchester.
   The deponent privately warned Unett before the recognizances were taken that the proceedings were erroneous or illegal; the justice refused to listen and said that Hammersley was 'a sorry woman and he knew her to be such, and that he had a power to proceed in such manner as he thought.' In spite of the deponent's advice to treat all the accused

equally, Unett let Harvey go, taking him by the shoulder or arm in a friendly manner, saying that the goods in his house were of so small value that Oldham and his companions would take no notice and that no harm would come to him. The deponent engrossed and delivered the recognizances to Oldham, who he believes took them to the clerk of the peace for Lancaster, for Unett in June asked the deponent to write to the clerk in order to retrieve them because he feared prosecution by Hammersley. Lees, Peake and Hammersley attended the next general quarter sessions held at Manchester for Lancashire, where Oldham's prosecution against Hammersley was found no true bill.

He has known Hammersley for ten years during which she has worked as a miller, renting mills under the Earl of Stafford and doing a very considerable trade; she is an honest and fair trader.

[2] Affdt of Margaret Hammersley miller of Stafford, sworn before John Dearle at Stafford 23 Nov 1751. 'In the court of King's Bench at Westminster.' [*Signed with a mark.*]

That for the past 18 years the deponent has been a miller keeping her and her family in credit. For many years she has rented a set of corn mills from the Earl of Stafford at the rent of £46 a year besides taxes. She purchases great quantities of wheat and corn from Staffordshire farmers and from those outside the county. Until the last 7 months she carried on her business with good name and credit. [*Describes search of her house; dates it 2 May.*] Mackerness carried away a fustian petticoat she had bought honestly from a hawking Scotsman, and took her before Unett. She offered to produce Elizabeth Babb, the wife of Thomas Babb, Ann Parker, the wife of William Parker, and Elizabeth Fallows, the wife of John Fallows, all of Stafford borough, as witnesses. Unett absolutely refused and demanded immediate sureties on threat of gaol; he kept her in custody for two hours without either confession or a sworn accusation from Oldham that the fustian was his, and without allowing her to leave to find sureties. She sent for Thomas Lee and Samuel Peake to become bound in the sum of £20 apiece as sureties for her appearance. The recognizances were to answer a charge of having bought cotton goods, the property of Oldham, at an undervalue from James Shaw, his having stolen them from Oldham and his copartners. Oldham also entered a recognizance of £40 to prosecute. To avoid the penalties in the recognizances, she travelled 50 miles to the quarter sessions for Lancashire at Manchester 25 July last, where the charge of receiving five yards of white fustian was found no true bill.

She has spent a considerable sum in expenses and payments, is greatly hurt in her good name and character, has lost much business and credit with farmers, by reason of the malicious prosecution contrived and executed by Unett. She delayed moving this court because, until ten days ago, Unett promised to recompense her.

[3] Affdt of William Nicholls the younger, clerk to William Nicholls the elder gentleman of Stafford, sworn before John Dearle at Stafford 23 Nov 1751. ITKB

That on 23 Nov 1751 the deponent served Thomas Unett with a true copy of the annexed notice.

[*Annexed*]: Notice 23 Nov 1751 by William Nicholls, attorney for Hammersley, to Unett that court would be moved Tuesday next for an information for forcibly and maliciously imprisoning and detaining Hammersley, illegally obliging her to enter into a recognizance and to find sureties to attend the quarter sessions for Lancashire at Manchester 23 July last, where she was indicted for receiving stolen goods knowing them to be stolen.

Sources: KB 1/10 Hil 25 Geo II.

B.4 Informations against justices: 1) applied for but dropped in favour of a feigned action; 2) ordered but not exhibited because rule discharged; 3) applied for (4 Nov 1752 to 22 Nov 1760)

Defendants: Samuel Corbett, Martin Pashley, John Coulson, Thomas Nicholls, and Samuel Short, justices of Walsall.

Accusations:
1) Corbett, Pashley, Coulson and Nicholls for making a false return to a writ of mandamus;
2) Corbett and Coulson for refusing to appoint overseers for Walsall foreign after a verdict and peremptory mandamus;
3) Short and Corbett for refusing pauper removals from Walsall foreign.

Rules and process: Trin [17 June 1752]: on reading affdts [1] and [2], rule nisi for a writ of mandamus commanding the justices of Walsall to nominate and appoint two substantial householders of the foreign to be overseers of the poor for the foreign for this year (Bathurst).[14] Mich [7 Nov 1752]: enlarged rule nisi to 14 Nov (Lloyd). ST [22 Nov 1752]: order for a mandamus to appoint the overseers (Mason). Hil [9 Feb 1753]: side

---

14   Affidavits are filed as 'Staffordshire' but much of the process is entered as 'Borough and foreign of Walsall in the county of Stafford.' The writ of mandamus is given in full as an annex to affdt [4] below.

bar rule to order the justices to return the writ of mandamus within the next month, showing that two or more of them, one of the quorum as required by the statute, have appointed two or more overseers. Ea [12 May 1753]: on reading affdt [5], rule nisi to [28 May 1753] for an attachment for contempt against Pashley, Coulson, and Nicholls (Beard). Mich [24 Nov 1753]: on reading affdt [6], rule nisi for an information against Corbett, Pashley, Coulson and Nicholls for a false return to a mandamus (Mason).[15] Hil [29 Jan 1754]: enlarged rule nisi to FDT Mich next for an information against Corbett, Pashley, Coulson and Nicholls; with consent of counsel on both sides, to be tried in a feigned action at assizes after Trin term, in which John Stubbs, Nicholas Parker and Thomas Cox shall be plaintiffs, and Thomas Nicholls, Samuel Corbett, and John Coulson defdts, the question on trial to be whether from time immemorial there has been a division called the foreign, and whether the farmers and householders there inhabiting have maintained the poor, and have had and ought to have overseers; costs to be paid according to outcome of the trial (Sir Richard Lloyd for defdts, consent of Hume for prosr). Trin [28 June 1754]: rule nisi to [1 July 1754] for Nicholls et al, to refer the issues to James Burrow master of the crown office to settle the issues to be joined between the parties in the feigned action upon the return to the mandamus in this cause, on notice of this rule to be given to them in the meantime (Gilbert). ST [2 July 1754]: order that the issues be referred to Burrows. Trin [1755]: rule nisi for prosecutor's costs to be taxed in Nicholls et al. ST [7 June 1755]: on reading affdt [10], rule nisi to [17 June 1755] for an information against Corbett and Coulson for certain misdemeanours (Hume). ST [12 June 1755]: previous rule nisi for taxation of costs against Nicholls et al discharged (solicitor general). ST [18 June 1755]: enlarged rule nisi to FNT for Corbett and Coulson (Hall). Hil [29 Jan 1756]: information ordered exhibited against Corbett and Coulson for certain misdemeanours (Pratt).[16] ST [9 Feb 1756]: ordered that the rule against Corbett and

---

[15] Offence supplied from affdts [6], [7], [10]; the rule book entry in KB 21 is 'for certain misdemeanours.'

[16] This and the following order are reported in *R v Corbett and Coulson* (1756), Sayer 267, 96 ER 875: on 'a rule to show cause, why an information should not be filed against the defendants, it appeared; that the defendants, who were justices of the peace for Walsall Borough, had refused to appoint overseers of the poor for the division of Walsall foreign; and that they had refused to do this, after it had been found by a verdict, upon a signed issue ordered by this court with consent, that Walsall Foreign is a distinct division in the parish of Walsall; and after peremptory mandamus had, in consequence of the verdict, been awarded, for appointing separate overseers for the division of Walsall Foreign.

Coulson be discharged on payment of costs and also upon the undertaking of the said defendants in this cause that overseers of the poor of and for the foreign of Walsall shall be duly appointed at Easter next for the year then next ensuing by the justices of the peace of and for the said borough and foreign of Walsall. And that the rates and assessments to be made by such overseers shall be duly signed and allowed and (if necessary) warrants of distress shall be granted thereon by the said justices. Referred to James Burrow master of the crown office to tax the said costs (solicitor general). Ea [13 May 1760]: on reading affdt [15], rule nisi for an information against Samuel Short and Samuel Corbett (Aston). Trin [6 June 1760]: enlarged rule nisi to [20 June 1760] for Shortt and Corbett, all affdts on behalf of defdt to be filed two days before (Gilbert). ST [23 June 1760]: further enlarged rule nisi to FNT for Shortt and Corbett (Norton).[17]

Affidavits for prosecution:

Trin 25 & 26 Geo II 1752

[1] Affdt of Thomas Tranter yeoman of Bescot in the parish of Walsall, sworn before Thomas Smyth at Bescot 10 June 1752. ITKB [*Wrapper*]: 'Staffords. Affidts Tranter & Hodgetts for Mands in Walsall. Trin 25 & 26 Geo II 1752. Wd fo:8.' [*Verso*]: 'Staff. Trin 25 & 26 Geo II 1752. fo:(4).'

That 10 April last (quarter sessions for the corporation of Walsall) he saw John Whitehouse, one of the then present overseers of the poor for the part of Walsall parish called the foreign, deliver a list of four substantial householders of the foreign before Robert Aglionby Slaney esquire recorder, Samuel Corbett mayor, and other JPs for the corporation. Whitehouse desired the justices to nominate two of the four listed

'The court inclined to make the rule absolute.

'And by Ryder Ch. J. — It is a settled point, that justices of the peace ought not to be punished criminally, for a mistake arising from an error in judgment: But the conduct of the defendants, in the present case, has been so extremely perverse and obstinate, that it must have proceeded from a partial or corrupt motive.

'The rule was afterwards discharged, upon the defendants paying the costs of this rule, and entering into a rule; that they will at Easter next appoint separate overseers for the division of Walsall Foreign, and sign the rules made by such overseers.'

17   No further proceedings were found in KB 21 or other series. The rule was probably discharged on affdt [17].

to be overseers of the poor for the foreign but the justices refused to take the list and said they knew who were proper persons to serve the office of overseers of the poor, such as Whitehouse and the other overseer Richard Wilkes.[18] The justices said they would choose overseers within the time limited by act of Parliament. Samuel Corbett mayor, Martin Pashley and Charles Turnpenny, standing justices for the corporation, have appointed four overseers of the poor, three of whom live in the borough and one of whom lives in the foreign, to be overseers for the whole parish and not separate according to the usual custom.

[2] Affdt of William Hodgetts baker of Bloxwich, sworn before Thomas Smyth at Bescot 10 June 1752. ITKB

That the town of Walsall is an ancient corporation consisting of mayor, recorder and several aldermen. The mayor for the time being is a JP, and the recorder and two senior aldermen act as standing justices. The jurisdiction extends throughout the whole extensive parish, including the villages of Bloxwich, Bescot, Harden, Coal Pool, Goscote, Caldmore, Wood End and others. Since time out of mind the parish in regard to the poor has been divided into distinct parishes or liberties. The town of Walsall, always called the borough, has maintained the poor of the town. The villages, always called Walsall foreign, have maintained their poor. There have always been separate church wardens and overseers of the poor for the town, and chapel wardens and overseers for the foreign (there being a chapel of ease in the foreign). There have always been separate poor rates for town and foreign,[19] and for the past 20 years separate workhouses for the poor. It has been usual for the foreign annually to return four substantial inhabitants to the justices of the corporation for them to nominate and appoint two overseers of the poor for that part of the parish. Samuel Wilkes and John Whitehouse were the last overseers of the poor for the foreign and the week after Easter past they nominated and returned John Merry, Richard Woodward, John Bate and Ezra Meeson, four substantial householders, unto Robert Aglionby Slaney esquire and recorder, and Samuel Corbett mayor and other justices then present, for them to nominate and appoint two as overseers for the foreign. The justices have refused, and have appointed four overseers, three in the borough and one in the foreign, to serve the whole parish together and not separate according to the ancient or usual custom.

Mich 26 Geo II 1752

[18] 'Samuel Wilkes' in other affdts.
[19] See affdt [6], which is identical in wording to this point.

[3] Affdt of Thomas Tranter yeoman of Bescot, sworn before Thomas Smyth at Walsall 4 Nov 1752. ITKB

That he served Samuel Corbett mayor and Martin Pashley a senior alderman, both JPs, 22 June last with a true copy of the annexed rule and showed them the original.

[*Annexed*]: Copy of the rule of [17 June 1752].

Ea 26 Geo II 1753

[4] Affdt of Thomas Tranter gentleman of Bescot in the parish of Walsall, sworn before Thomas Smyth at Walsall 5 Feb 1753. ITKB [*Verso of this and the following affdt*]: 'Affidt of Service of Rule. Borough and Foreign of Walsall. To move for an attachmt for not returning the Writ of Mandamus according to the within Rule. Wm Beard. ½ G. Wd. Barbor & Bill.'

That he served Martin Pashley the elder 4 Jan last with an original writ of mandamus of which a true copy is annexed, delivering to him a true copy of the writ and endorsement and showing him the original. The deponent also served true copies at their dwellings to Samuel Corbett's wife Sarah and John Coulson's daughter Mary, both of whom promised to deliver the copies to them. The deponent left the original writ with the mayor of Walsall, borough and foreign, Thomas Nicholls. The deponent saw Samuel Corbett later that day and informed him of the service.

[*Annexed copy of writ of mandamus*]: 'Borough and foreign of Walsall in the county of Stafford. George the second by the grace of God of Great Britain France and Ireland king defender of the faith and so forth to the keepers of our peace and to our justices assigned to hear and determine divers felonies trespasses and other misdeeds committed within our borough and foreign of Walsall in our county of Stafford and to every of them greeting. Whereas within the parish of Walsall in our county of Stafford there is and from the time whereof the memory of man is not to the contrary hath been a certain known division or district called Walsall foreign And whereas the households and farmers for the time being inhabiting and residing within that part of the parish of Walsall aforesaid called Walsall foreign as aforesaid have from time to time contributed equally among themselves and have used and been accustomed to contribute equally among themselves for and towards the necessary relief support and maintenance of the poor of and within the said division or district and for that purpose have from time to time had and of right ought to have overseers of the poor appointed of and for the said division or district And whereas it appeareth unto us upon the complaint of divers of the inhabitants of the said part of the parish of Walsall aforesaid called Walsall foreign as aforesaid that there now are several householders and farmers inhabiting and residing within the said division or district substantial and able to contribute equally among themselves for and towards the necessary relief support and maintenance of the poor of and within the said division or districts And whereas there are at present no overseers of the poor nominated and appointed by you or any of you within the division or district aforesaid to receive and provide for the poor legally settled in the said division or districts or to make any equal rate or assessment upon all and singular the householders and farmers aforesaid now inhabiting and residing within the said division or district according to the statute in that case made and provided as well to the great damage and grievance of the said inhabitants of the said division or districts as also to the great damage and grievance of the poor of the same Therefore being willing that due and speedy justice should be done in this behalf (as it is reasonable) we do require and command you and every of you firmly injoining you and every of you that immediately after the receipt of this our writ you or any two or more of you (of whom one is to be of the quorum) according to the directions of the statute in that case made and provided do under your hands and seals or under the hands and seals of two or more of you (one of whom is to be of the quorum as aforesaid) nominate and appoint two or more able and substantial householders inhabiting and residing within that part of the parish of Walsall aforesaid called Walsall foreign as aforesaid to be overseers of the poor of the said division or district to continue and act as overseers of the said division or district for this present year or show to us cause to the contrary thereof least by your default complaint thereof should be again made unto us. And how you shall have executed this our writ make it known unto us at Westminster on Thursday next after the octove of Saint Hilary then returning to us this our writ and this you are not to omit upon peril that may fall thereon. Witness Sir William Lee Knight at Westminster the twenty second day of November in the twenty sixth year of our Reign. By the court. Burrow.'

[5] Affdt of Thomas Tranter gentleman of Bescot in Walsall, sworn before Thomas Smyth at Walsall 7 April 1753. ITKB

That he personally served Martin Pashley and John Coulson 17 Feb 1753, Thomas Nicholls 19 Feb, JPs for the borough and foreign of Walsall in the county of Stafford, with true copies of the annexed rule, at the same time showing them the original.

[*Annexed*]: Side bar rule of [9 Feb 1753].

Mich 27 Geo II 1753

[6] Affdt of Nicholas Parker, George Harrison and John Lightwood gentlemen all of Bloxwich in the foreign of Walsall, sworn before Thomas Smyth at Walsall 13 Nov 1753. ITKB

[All]: [*This affidavit begins with wording identical to that in affdt [2].*] In all acts relative to the poor the foreign and borough have acted as distinct parishes. Since 17 Dec 1746 the churchwardens and overseers within the borough have granted 46 certificates and upwards with paupers directed to the churchwardens and overseers of the foreign. Samuel Wilkes and John Whitehouse were the last overseers of the poor, having left office at Easter 1752. Since then, the justices have refused to appoint overseers for the foreign; the inhabitants of the foreign therefore applied to the court and obtained a mandamus for the justices to do so. The mayor and justices returned the mandamus denying that there is any such division. This is a false return very injurious to residents of the foreign.

[7] Affdt of Thomas Tranter of Bescot[20] in the parish of Walsall, sworn before Thomas Smyth at Walsall 13 Nov 1753. ITKB

That the deponent served notice in writing 13 Nov 1753 to Samuel Corbett, Martin Pashley, John Coulson and Thomas Nicholls, all JPs, that the court was to be moved 19 Nov 1753 that an information might be exhibited against them for a false return to a writ of mandamus.

Hil 27 Geo II 1754

[8] Affdt of Thomas Tranter of Bescot[21] in the parish of Walsall, sworn before Thomas Smyth at Walsall 21 Jan 1754. ITKB [*Verso*]: 'Staffords. Affdt service rule for infn agt Corbett et al. fo:4 [*illegible*] H. A. 2:9 [*illegible*].'

That 10 Dec last the deponent personally served Samuel Corbett, Martin Pashley, John Coulson and Thomas Nicholls esqs with the annexed rule.

[*Annexed*]: Copy of rule of [24 Nov 1753].

Trin 27 & 28 Geo II 1754

[9] Affdt of Charles Bill gentleman of St Dunstan in the West (London), sworn before M. Wright at Serjeants Inn 1 July 1754. ITKB 'The King agt Nicholls & others.' [*Verso*]: 'KB Staffords. The King agt Nicholls & others. Affidt of Service of Rule. To move to make the within Rule Absolute. By Mr Gilbert. 1/2 G. Barbor & Bill.'

---

[20] No occupation given.
[21] No occupation given.

That 29 June 1754 the deponent served William Crowley agent for the defendant with the annexed rule.

[*Annexed*]: Copy of the rule of [28 June 1754].

Trin 28 Geo II 1755

[10] Affdt of William Hodgetts baker of Bloxwich, Timothy Hobbitt custmaker of Caldmore, and Thomas Cowley bucklemaker of Hill Topp, sworn before Thomas Smyth at Walsall 4 June 1755. ITKB [*Thomas Cowley signed with a mark.*]

[William Hodgetts]: That he has known Walsall for 26 years and upwards, having lived in or near the parish for most of that time. [*Hobbitt and Cowley swear to 40 and 3 years respectively.*]

[All]: [*Substantiate account in affdts [2] and [6] respecting composition of the corporation and the division into parish and foreign with respect to the poor, but naming also the villages of Great Bloxwich, Little Bloxwich, Shelfield, Walsall Wood, Birchills and Townend, and adding that the borough and foreign kept separate accounts.*] For more than 50 years borough and foreign have granted certificates with their respective poor to each other and to other parishes, had paupers removed to and from between them, and the foreign has put out parish apprentices. They have had separate workhouses for 20 years.

That the jurisdiction of the justices in borough and foreign is exclusive, the deponents never having heard or known of a single instance where the county justices have acted concerning the poor. [*Substantiate account in affdts [2] and [6] respecting the appointment of overseers for the foreign.*] This was done until 1752 when the justices appointed two overseers for the whole parish. [*Relate application for mandamus, and its terms.*] Nicholls, then mayor of Walsall, Pashley, now deceased, and Corbett and Coulson, the two senior aldermen or capital burgesses, returned the mandamus on the ground that its allegations were false. A rule nisi was granted against them for making a false return to the writ of mandamus. In Hilary Term 1754, having appeared by counsel and prayed that the merits might be tried on a feigned action, which was granted, John Stubbs, Nicholas Parker and Thomas Cox appeared as plaintiffs and Nicholls, Corbett and Coulson as defendants. The issues were tried before Lord Chief Justice Willes and a special jury, and judgment on both issues found for the plaintiffs. Prosecutors of the writ of mandamus applied for a peremptory mandamus in Michaelmas term, for the justices to appoint overseers for the present year, which writ Charles Steward mayor and Samuel Corbett obeyed, appointing Thomas Cowley and George Harrison.

[William Hodgetts and Thomas Cowley]: That although the justices obeyed the writ of mandamus, they refused to sign the poor rate for the foreign. Thus the overseers could not collect the money for the poor unless the inhabitants volunteered contributions; several refused. The year being so far advanced and the inhabitants hoping the justices would appoint overseers and sign rates for the present year, no action was taken to compel the justices to sign the rates. Last Easter Steward was mayor and Corbett and Coulson were the capital burgesses. They are the only acting justices within the borough and foreign. At Easter the deponents according to the usual method delivered a list with the names of John Harrison, John Bate, John Pool, Timothy Hobbitt, Richard Hollyhead and Thomas Rogers, six substantial householders, from which to select overseers. Hobbitt and Harrison were selected by Steward, who signed, but Corbett and Coulson refused to sign the appointments, although they continued to act as the only justices. For two and a half years the inhabitants of the foreign therefore have been without proper maintenance of their poor. They raised money by voluntary subscription, but many more have refused to contribute since the justices refused to appoint. The inhabitants have been obliged to turn out from the workhouse all who can walk, being 30 in number. They are now strolling the countryside begging, the overseers of the borough having refused to relieve them.

[All]: That Corbett and Coulson know the difficulties they have caused. Their motive is to oblige the inhabitants of the foreign to unite the divisions of the parish because there are more chargeable poor in town than in the foreign.

[11] Affdt of service of notice of Thomas Mold the younger victualler of Walsall, sworn before Thomas Smyth at Walsall 4 June 1755. ITKB

That 3 June 1755 the deponent served Samuel Corbett esquire and John Coulson esquire 3 June 1755 with notices signed by Jonas Slaney that the court would be moved against them on Saturday next or as soon after as counsel could be heard for an information for willfully neglecting and refusing to appoint overseers for Walsall foreign.

Affidavits for defence:

Mich 29 Geo II 1755

[12] Affdt of John Coulson esquire and JP, Samuel Corbett baker, maltster and JP, and Samuel Short esquire, the present mayor of the borough and foreign, sworn before Thomas Smyth at Walsall 1 Nov 1755. ITKB

[All]: That by letters patent of 3 Charles I, confirmed by letters patent of 13 Charles II, the inhabitanrts were incorporated as the mayor and commonality of the borough and foreign of Walsall. The mayor and JPs have jurisdiction throughout the whole borough and foreign. Coulson has known and lived in or near the parish for over 33 years, Corbett for 20 years in which he mostly lived there, and Short for 50 years, having lived in the parish or the adjoining parish of Rushall most of that time. Short has occupied lands in the foreign upwards of 30 years. The deponents know that Thomas Cowley, who swore in affdt [9] that he knew the parish for upwards of 30 years, was little more than 34 years old when he swore the affidavit. A true copy of the baptismal records of Cowley is annexed.[22] There are no certain and known boundaries between the foreign and the borough, which have always constituted one entire parish called Walsall. Whenever any of the frequent perambulations of the Vicar or churchwardens are made they are made to the out boundaries of the whole parish, and never of any boundary or division between borough and foreign.

[Samuel Short]: That he has heard several ancient persons now dead say that there was no certain known boundaries between borough and foreign.

[All]: Churchwardens are named for the whole parish and not for divisions of it. Inhabitants of the foreign pay for repairs to the town church. They admit that every year until 1752 separate overseers were appointed by the justices, two for the supposed division called the borough, and two for the foreign. Other towns in Stafford and other counties have appointed separate overseers for certain townships, villages and divisions of certain extent for convenient taxation and poor relief. Yet they do not maintain their poor separately; the monies are jointly applied, notwithstanding the separate appointments of overseers. This is how Walsall should be administered, if separate taxation and overseers can be maintained in the manner suggested in affdt [10]. The separate taxation and management of the poor for the supposed divisions of Walsall are the result of an agreement in 1677 by the inhabitants and not under a statute of 13&14 Charles II or any other statute.

[Samuel Short]: That he has known several instances of the justices refusing to sign certificates from one of the supposed divisions to the other because they are considered as one parish.

[Samuel Short and Samuel Corbett]: That before 1752 they frequently knew Slaney, the recorder of the corporation, to refuse to determine questions between the two districts, considering them as one with respect to their poor.

[22] Not found with the affidavit.

[All]: That there are two parts to the 1677 agreement, one signed by the principal inhabitants of the borough and the other signed by the principal inhabitants of the foreign. They were found among the corporation records and are in the custody of the deponents, ready to be produced; they are in the following words,

'Whereas several differences have arisen betwixt the Burrough and Forren both in the parrish of Walsall concerninge the releif of the poore and other payments beinge two distinct Constablewicks and in two distinct divisions Now to avoyd any further difference, Tis mutually agreed betwixt the partyes concerned both of Burrough and Forren that from this tyme and at all tymes hereafter the Forreners shall not assesse to any Payment any Land that is truly and properly the Land of any that lives within the Burrough though it be held by a Forrener but it shall pay to [*sic*] all payments to the Burrough and be by them soe assessed. And likewise all Lands and Mines that are the Lands of Mrs Persehowse and her Sonnes Mr John Persehowse of Reynold Hall the Land of Mr Hawes at Caldmore the Land of the heires of Bescote and all other lands within the Forren of Walsall that truly and properly belonge to such as are inhabitants within the Forren of Walsall shal be Assessed and pay to [*sic*] all payments to the Forren though held by such as live within the Burrough and not be Assessed and taxed by the Burrough to any payment (only such Howses as are in the Burrough though they belonge to persons livinge in the Forren Yet shall be assessed and pay within the Burrough). And for all other lands that belonge to such as live out of the parrish (except such persons as are above named) as the lands belonginge to the Lord of the Mannor William Ward Esqr or any others that have land within the Forren and are themselves noe inhabitants there shal be assessed and pay to all payments in the place that the Occupants or tennants of the said lands doe inhabite or dwell either in the Burrough or Forren indifferently. And for the Assessment of the Tithes of the said parrish they shal be equally assessed and taxed both by the Burrough and Forren the one halfe to the one and the other halfe to the other whether they be held by a Burroughman or a Forrener. And this Agreemt is to be confirmed and made bindinge by such wayes and meanes as Edward Byrche Esqr shall devise or advise Dated the nineteenth day of May in the Nine and twentieth years of the Raignes of our Soveraigne Lord Kinge Charles the Second of England etc Anno Domini 1677.'

The names subscribed to the part executed by the inhabitants of the supposed division called the borough are Thomas Sheppard, Joseph Freeman, Simon Homer, George Pearson, George Fowler, the mark of Robert Mowsley, John Shotwell, John Blackam, William Pearson, Major William Haddersich, John Sansome, George Turnpenny, Richard

Burton, Phillip Cox, Robert Ebs. The names subscribed to the part executed by the inhabitants of the supposed division called the foreign are the mark of John Ringe, John Harryson, Sampson Barnfield, George Harrison, Zacharas [sic] Greene, John Bayly, John Alport, John Purcell, Richard Wincell, John Bearblock clerk, John Greene, Henry Birch, John Goodwin, William Goodwin, John Smith, Nicholas Chapman, Elizabeth Pershowse, George Hawes, Henry Stone, William Strong, John Allport, John Hawkes, Nicholas Parker, William Hawe, John Pershowse.

That during the deponents' knowledge of the parish and since the making of this agreement until 1752, it has in many instances been complied with, and in many instances varied from and broke through. Whenever a town inhabitant occupied land in the villages of Great Bloxwich, Little Bloxwich, Harden, Goscote, Coal Pool, Shelfield, Walsall Wood, Wood End, Caldmore, Bescot, Birchills and Townend, which Hodgetts, Jobbitt and Cowley suppose to comprise the foreign, their taxation has been for poor relief in the borough.

[Samuel Corbett]: That in 1752, when the deponent was mayor of Walsall, and Charles Turnpenny and Martin Pashley were JPs for the borough, it appeared to all of them that assessment under the agreement had caused great confusion because of the frequent alteration of rateable property in the supposed foreign from the hands of inhabitants of the town to inhabitants of the villages, or the removal of occupiers or owners from the villages to the town, and from the town into the hamlets or townships. Because of the uncertainty over the true boundaries, many properties were unrated or unequally rated. The deponent, Corbett, Turnpenny and Pashley appointed overseers for the whole parish to equalize the assessment.

[All]: [*Substantiate account in affdt [10]of mandamus and peremptory mandamus.*]

[Samuel Corbett]: That he and Charles Steward the then mayor obeyed the peremptory mandamus by appointing Thomas Cowley and George Harrison of the foreign to be overseers there.

[Samuel Corbett and John Coulson]: That they refused to sign a poor rate certificate brought to them because it had been made as the foreign rates usually were. They thought that to sign it would perpetuate the inequality, that they had discretion, and that the mandamus did not compel them to sign rates.

[All]: That they and a great number of inhabitants are dissatisfied with the trial they received at Stafford. The true proper questions in the matter, the boundaries, and the force and validity of the agreement were not entered upon nor decided by the verdict. They are very desirous of having the same reconsidered and put into some new method of trial.

[Samuel Corbett and John Coulson]: That apprehending that appointing separate overseers might prejudice their rights and create difficulties in getting a proper trial, last Easter they were desired by inhabitants of the borough to make separate appointments of overseers for the present year.

[All]: That several inhabitants of the supposed division called the foreign have been oppressed by great inequality in the rates, and want a general rate and general appointment of overseers.

[Samuel Corbett and John Coulson]: That several inhabitants of the supposed foreign and occupiers of rateable property desired them not to make a rate for the foreign. They did not make the single appointment of overseer to distress or throw into confusion the residents of the foreign, as charged in affdt [10].

[Samuel Short and John Coulson]: That in order to have the issue properly tried on a distress for payment of a rate, and that relief may be given to the poor, they appointed an overseer of the poor for the parish of Walsall, borough and foreign, for this year.

[Samuel Corbett and John Coulson]: That they were advised that separate rates could not have been enforced because the boundaries are not known.

[All]: That Walsall is not so large that the poor of the whole parish could not be provided for by appointing one overseer under 43 Eliz.[23] There is no need to call in aid the statute of 13&14 Chas. II[24], or the 1677 agreement. The poor of the borough and foreign were not kept separately until after the agreement of 1677.

[Samuel Corbett]: That in May 1755 he was approached as a justice by several poor persons who said they had been turned out of the foreign workhouse. He ordered Jeremiah Reynolds, governor of the town workhouse, to relieve the poor, which he did. The deponent offered to the inhabitants of the foreign to get a carriage to transport the disabled poor from the foreign workhouse to the town workhouse, but his offer was rejected. He has ordered any in need to be relieved in the town workhouse. The poor of the borough and foreign have not suffered by any wilful neglect or admission on his part or that of John Coulson.

[John Coulson]: That he has not omitted any part of his duty in relieving the poor.

[All]: That the deponents want the poor relieved properly and all disputes determined, and therefore appointed overseers as before set forth, and are ready and willing to do what the court shall direct.

---

23   43 Eliz., c.2 (1601).
24   14 Chas. II, c.12 (1662).

[Samuel Short and John Coulson]: From Michaelmas last they have relieved all such poor of the borough and foreign as have applied.

Hil 29 Geo II 1756

[13] Affdt of John Heeley schoolmaster of Walsall, sworn before Thomas Smyth at Walsall 2 Feb 1756. ITKB

That the deponent saw Short and Coulson in Walsall 2 Feb 1756 by a warrant [*quoted*] appoint Timothy Hobbitt and John Harrison to be overseers of the poor of the foreign for the current year. He delivered the warrant to Hobbitt.

[14] Affdt of Jeremiah Reynolds governor of the workhouse of the town of Walsall, sworn before Thomas Smyth at Walsall 2 Feb 1756. ITKB

That the deponent has been governor of the workhouse for over 13 years. Since the dispute has arisen, many of the poor of the supposed division of the foreign have been maintained in the workhouse, at an expenditure by the inhabitants of the borough of over £70.

Further affidavit for prosecution:

Ea 33 Geo II 1760

[15] Affdt of William Green, William Hodgetts, Thomas Harrison and Thomas Fowler of the parish of Walsall, sworn before Thomas Smyth at Walsall 7 May 1760. ITKB

[All]: [*Repeats contents of affdt[6], except for the allegation of injury caused by the return to the mandamus*]. The return also said that the inhabitants of the supposed foreign had not been used to contribute equally among themselves for poor relief, nor had or ought to have had their own overseers. In a subsequent action the court agreed that the return was a false one, and a peremptory mandamus ordered to appoint overseers, which writ was obeyed. Since then, some borough residents have moved to the foreign, and 19 Feb 1760 several poor resided in the foreign who had immediately before resided in the borough and likely to become chargeable. Several were certificated by Tamworth, Bridgnorth and Willenhall to the borough of Walsall, the others had settlements in the borough. Corbett called them before him as deputy mayor and acting justice 15 Feb to examine them about their settlements. On 19 Feb the deponents Green, Hodgetts and Harrison and these paupers attended Guildhall in Walsall with Corbett and Charles Stewart aldermen. The deponents named, or Green, then overseer for the foreign, applied to Corbett and Steward to examine the paupers and remove them out of the foreign.

[William Green]: Corbett said he would remove them from the foreign if they were from outside Walsall, and not certificated to the borough, but not otherwise, as the borough and foreign were one parish. Steward corrected Corbett by saying that Walsall was two parishes with respect to the poor. Corbett said nothing to this and then asked the two paupers where they belonged. One said he belonged to Bridgnorth and the other to Walsall borough. Corbett told them to go about their business and did not make orders for their removal. When asked by this deponent why he would not do so, Corbett replied 'By Heaven no order of removal shall be made.' The deponent went to Short and Corbett 23 Feb and complained about the burden the extra poor were to the foreign. Short said if there were to be any removal orders made while he was a justice of the peace 'I'll be damned.' Corbett said 'So far you are very right.'

[All]: That a warrant dated 6 May 1760 called for more of the poor resident in the foreign to be examined before Short. The deponents attended with two of the paupers mentioned at the Guildhall before Corbett and Steward, where Fowler requested them to examine the paupers.

[Thomas Fowler]: That he importuned the justices to remove one pauper from the foreign to his place of settlement, the borough. Corbett refused, saying he would not grant a removal order between the borough and foreign so long as he was a justice.

[All]: That Corbett and Short have frequently refused to make removal orders and have combined together not to remove paupers from the foreign to the borough. There are several paupers in the foreign with legal settlements in the borough who are likely to become chargeable.

Affidavits for defence:

Trin 33 & 34 Geo II 1760

[16] Affdt of Samuel Short mayor of the borough and foreign, and Samuel Corbett one of the capital burgesses of Walsall and deputy to Short, both of Walsall, sworn before Thomas Smyth at Walsall 14 June 1760. ITKB [*Verso*]: 'Staffordshire. Affidt of Short and another to show cause agt Inform. In the King's Bench. Affidt of Saml Short and an. fo:10.'

[Both]: That the borough and foreign of Walsall extends throughout the entire parish of Walsall. The JPs for the borough have appointed overseers to act throughout the borough and foreign. There have at times been separate overseers appointed for the borough and foreign and separate assessments for poor relief. Walsall, which these deponents think is largely or entirely in the borough, has 7,000 inhabitants. The medium rates for the last 10 years have averaged 5s in the pound of the value of the houses and ratable property. What is normally called the foreign is chiefly lands whose medium rates have not been more than 2s 6d in the pound of the value of the land. Applications have been made lately to remove several persons residing in the foreign as stated in the affidavits of William Green, William Hogetts, Thomas Harrison, and Thomas Fowler. Boundaries of the borough and foreign have not been fully fixed and inhabitants have complained of the confusion this causes because of unequal assessment rates for the poor. Inhabitants have been unwilling to move poor from one part of the parish to the other.

[Samuel Corbett]: That he admits that he refused to move the poor mentioned in affdt [15] from the supposed foreign to the supposed borough because the boundaries are unclear.

[Both]: That neither remember the deponent Short making use of the expression mentioned in affdt [15]: 'That if there be any orders of removal made while I am a Justice I'll be damned.' Some doubts have been raised as to whether they have legal authority to enforce the statute of 13&14 Charles II for dividing large parishes into small townships for the relief of the poor, but if they have such authority they are willing to act and hope they will not be censured for refusing an order of removal under the circumstances, and that some method will be proposed for ascertaining the boundaries.

Mich 1 Geo III 1760

[17] Affdt of Samuel Short esquire and late mayor now JP, Samuel Corbett late deputy mayor to Samuel Short and now deputy mayor to John Wilson esquire now mayor of the borough and foreign of Walsall, sworn before Thomas Smyth at Walsall 22 Nov 1760. ITKB 'The King against Samuel Short and Samuel Corbett.' [*Verso*]: 'Staffordshire. The King agt Short and an: Affidt. Nov 25 1760 filed by Mr Lane Covent Garden. fo.11.'

[Samuel Short]: That since the rule made in this case [13 May 1760], he and Charles Steward esquire JP 8 July 1760 on the application of the overseers of the poor of Walsall, removed Robert Bayles, Richard Wilcox, Samuel Sarjant and William Ashford and their families from the foreign to the borough. He has always been ready to take examinations and grant orders to remove people from the foreign to the borough, place, township or parish where they belong since the rule of the court was granted, and has made public and general declarations to the overseers to that effect. He has not refused to take examinations or grant orders since the rule was made.

[Samuel Corbett]: That since the rule, he and John Wilson, then JP for the borough and foreign, in the absence of Samuel Short, after examination granted orders 3 July and 6 Aug for the removal of Joseph Lea and Joseph Hodson and their families from the foreign to the borough. [*Affirms his willingness in the same terms as Short.*]

[Both]: That notwithstanding the hardships alleged in affdt [15] to be sustained by the inhabitants of the foreign for want of having the paupers residing there removed to the borough, yet the churchwardens and overseers of the foreign neglected to remove several of the paupers for which such orders of removal were made. They did not remove Ashford, Lea, Hodson and their families until 17 Oct 1760, being after the last quarter sessions held for the borough and foreign 9 Oct 1760.

Sources: KB 1/11 Trin 25 & 26 Geo II 1752, Mich 26 Geo II 1752, KB 1/11/4, Ea 26 Geo II no.2, Mich 27 Geo II 1753, Hil 27 Geo II 1754, Trin 27 & 28 Geo II 1754 no.1. KB 1/12 Trin 28 Geo II 1755, Mich 29 Geo II 1755 no.2, Hil 29 Geo II 1756. KB 1/14 Ea 33 Geo II 1760, Trin 33 & 34 Geo II 1760 no.1, Mich 1 Geo III 1760. KB 21/36 pp. 863, 872, 883. KB 21/37 pp. 26, 45, 137, 162, 248, 384, 390, 405, 454, 466. KB 21/38 pp.354, 369, 389. KB 36/142, /143, /150, /151, /157, /173, /174.

B.5 Information against a justice, refused (24 April 1759)

Defendants: the Reverend George Malbon, JP for Staffordshire, of Uttoxeter; Henry Scott, attorney and deputy sheriff for Staffordshire, of Doveridge (Derbs); Peter Prince, yeoman, of Uttoxeter; Robert Sillito,[25] writing clerk to Henry Scott, of Uttoxeter.

Accusation:
Illegally convicting William Smith labourer of Draycott in the Clay, parish of Hanbury, of a pretended detainer of a house at Draycott, imposing a fine of £5 and committing him to the county gaol until the fine was paid.

Rules and process:
Ea [16 May 1759]: on affdts [1]-[7], rule nisi to [25 May] (Serjeant Nares). ST [25 May 1759]: enlarged rule nisi to FNT (Morton). Trin [26 June 1759]: previous rule discharged (Morton).

---

[25] 'Sillitoe' in most affidavits; he signed 'Sillito'.

Affidavits for prosecution:

Ea 32 Geo II 1759

[1] Affdt of William Smith labourer, late of Edial[26] but now of Draycott in the Clay, parish of Hanbury, sworn before John Hayne at Draycott 24 April 1759. ITKB [*Signed with a mark.*] [*Verso*]: 'fo 26.'

That William Smith yeoman, late of Draycott, died 29 June 1757 seized of lands in Draycott and a house in Draycott or Cotton with the yearly value of £40. The deponent is the nephew and heir to Smith and was advised to assert his rights and get possession if he could in a peaceable manner. Alone and unarmed, he entered the open house 9 March 1759 and found Mrs Bamford, Mrs Woodnought and Mrs Bacon drinking tea and Hannah Moores waiting on them. The deponent informed them that he was there to take possession as heir at law and they consented to leave. No force, arms, or assistance was used. He had peaceful possession until 15 March when the Reverend George Malbon JP of Uttoxeter, Henry Scott attorney of Doveridge, and Robert Sillito of Uttoxeter, writing clerk to them both, came to the house, with others. Malbon asked the deponent, who was at the chamber window, to open the door; he declined to do so and asked Malbon to wait while he sent to Lichfield for his attorney, or else to return another day. Malbon refused and after a half hour returned with about ten men, armed with clubs, staves and hammers, who were hired by Malbon or Peter Prince. Scott, Sillito, Prince and many others also came, unarmed. Malbon demanded that the deponent open the door. The deponent said Malbon could enter but not the mob. Malbon ordered the hired men to break down the door; they entered the house while Malbon remained outside in the court. John Owen thirdborough of Draycott seized the deponent (who did not resist) informing him that Malbon had issued a warrant for his arrest for a £5 fine for forcible entry and detainer; Malbon had not yet entered the house to view the pretended forcible detainer. This shows that Malbon came determined to act, having convicted the deponent without having viewed the supposed detainer and without any way of assessing a proper fine. No one was in the house with the deponent but Mary Woolley, a neighbour's servant, nor were there arms; he used neither force nor threats against Malbon, and would have opened the door if Malbon had consented to enter without the mob. Informed that the warrant was to detain him only until the fine was paid, the deponent paid Owen the £5 on the way to the Stafford gaol,

---

[26] 'Edjall' in the original; Edgehill was an eighteenth-century variant. Edial was in Lichfield St Michael ancient parish and is now in Burntwood parish.

but Owen returned the money at Abbots Bromley because he said he had no authority from Malbon to accept it. Owen delivered this deponent into the custody of the gaoler, who also refused the £5, the next day. The deponent was in the gaol from 16 to 24 March, until the assizes, when Hicklin, undersheriff, under the direction of one or both assize judges, discharged him on the payment of £5.

He is informed that Malbon and Scott, without giving notice to the deponent, caused a jury to be summoned, which met 17 March to enquire about the forcible entry. They gave the jury a genteel entertainment. Scott, attorney for Prince the prosecutor, has some claim to the premises, yet acting as deputy sheriff, he swore the jury in Malbon's presence, examined Sillito before them, and then became a witness himself, sworn by Malbon. The deponent had no opportunity to make his defence. The jury asked that the matter be adjourned in order to hear the deponent, but Scott refused and the jury declared they could not find the deponent guilty of forcible entry. Scott threatened to punish the jury unless they changed their verdict. Scott and Malbon took horse and left, dissatisfied, without a verdict and without adjourning proceedings. The jury left and have not since been called together.

While the deponent was in gaol under the confinement of Alexander Robotham of Draycott, Malbon and Scott refused payment of the £5. The deponent believes that these violent proceedings were to compel him to give up possession and title of the premises and to submit to the claims and pretensions of Prince and Scott without due course of law.

[2] Affdt of John Owen yeoman of Draycott, sworn before John Hayne at Draycott 24 April 1759. ITKB

That the deponent, at the request of Peter Prince, went to Sarah Smith's public house in Draycott 15 March 1759, where he found Malbon, Scott, Sillito and a great number of others. Malbon gave the deponent a warrant to arrest William Smith, labourer, on a conviction of forcible detainer on the complaint of Prince, and to deliver him to the Stafford gaoler until a fee of £5 was paid for the trespass. Malbon told the deponent to try to enter peaceably and if he was not successful, to break down the door. The deponent said he dared not break down the door, and Malbon threatened to send him to Stafford gaol if he failed to arrest Smith. Malbon agreed to indemnify him. They all went to Smith's house, where it did not appear that Smith used force or threats to keep possession. Mr Alexander Robotham and Mr John Archer, neighbours, interposed on Smith's behalf and asked Malbon to let Smith fetch an attorney. Malbon immediately ordered the door to be broken down; some of the persons present did so, and entered the house, without waiting for the deponent's order. The deponent found the house empty except for a servant girl and Smith, who made no resistance; there was no evidence of a forcible entry. Malbon ordered Smith to be taken to Stafford gaol 'the sooner the better'. [*Substantiates the account in affdt [1]of several offers by Smith to pay fine.*] He does not know of any reason for such violent proceedings except to crush Smith, who was in low circumstances, and make him submit to the claims of persons more favoured by Malbon.

[3] Affdt of Mary Woolley spinster, Alexander Robotham yeoman, and Joseph Goodwin bricklayer, all of Draycott, sworn before John Hayne at Draycott 24 April 1759. ITKB [*Mary Woolley signed with a mark.*]

[Mary Woolley]: That she and William Smith were alone and unarmed in the house when Malbon, Prince and the mob came to Smith's house. Smith refused Malbon's request to unlock the door, as he had entered peacefully, and civilly asked Malbon to stay while sending to Lichfield for his attorney. Malbon refused, went away, and returned a half hour later with a mob.

[All]: [*Substantiate account in affdt [1] of entry into the house.*]

[Mary Woolley]: That upon entry, Owen seized Smith as his prisoner.

[All]: That the warrant for arrest must have been made out in advance, as there was no time to draft it after the house was entered.

[Alexander Robotham]: That the deponent, at Smith's request, offered 19 March 1759, when Smith was in gaol, to pay Malbon and Scott the £5. They refused it, and got away as fast as they could to prevent him tendering it. Smith he believes is the nephew and heir of William Smith who died about two years ago. The deponent examined 16 April the warrant of which a true copy is annexed.

[*Annexed copy of warrant and mittimus*]: Malbon to John Owen, headborough of Draycott, and to the keeper of Stafford gaol. 'Whereas upon complaint made this present day by Peter Prince of Draycott aforesaid yeoman I went immediately to the messuage of the said Peter Prince ... and there found William Smith of Edge Hill otherwise Edge Hall in the said county labourer forcibly with strong hand and armed power holding the said house against the peace of our said Lord the King and against the form of the statute', order to arrest and commit Smith to Stafford gaol until he pays a £5 fine. 15 March [1759].

[4] Affdt of Ann Lort, age 60, wife of William Lort, yeoman of Marchington, sworn before Uppingham Bourne at Lichfield 5 May 1759. ITKB [*Signed with a mark.*]

That the deponent has known the Smith family for about 30 years. She knew Ellen, William, and Henry Smith, children of Richard Smith late of Draycott deceased, and Sarah, his first wife. William Smith

survived his father and died without issue in Jan 1757, leaving a messuage and lands. Henry Smith died during William's life after marrying
Elizabeth Alcock, by whom he had a son, William, now living, and one
or more children who died in their infancy without issue; thus William
became heir-at-law to William Smith deceased. Richard Smith married
Ann Fletcher as his second wife by whom Abraham, Hannah and Mary
Smith were born. They all died without issue. There has been a melancholy disorder or distraction in the Smith family for many years.
Richard Smith's brother Samuel made away with himself. Richard himself was at times disordered in his mind. Ellen his daughter made away
with herself; Hannah was quite distracted and died in a melancholy
condition. Abraham Smith, whom the deponent nursed, was melancholy and distracted, and the late William Smith for some years before
his death had the strongest symptoms of the family distemper: he
talked in a wild and incoherent manner and used distorted motions and
gestures. In the three years before his death he often lay in bed for a
week or fortnight, without any apparent illness. From that time he was
not of sound mind or competent understanding to do any act requiring
memory or understanding. Mary, whom the deponent knew for many
years, was melancholy, weak, and illiterate, and easily imposed upon.
The deponent nursed her for the 11 days before her death, and during
that time especially she was not of sound mind or understanding.
Prince was a servant or labourer to William Smith before his death and
later to Mary but of no relation to either of them; he is about 64 years
and is looked upon as a very crafty, designing man. While nursing
Mary, the day before the will was made, the deponent heard Prince
very loud and clamorous in Mary's room, and when she went to her,
she found Mary trembling and frightened. Mary said Prince would
tease her out of her life, that he had been storming and swearing at her
to make her will, and had said that if he left her she would be ruined.
The deponent believes Mary was incapable of giving instructions for
the will, and that she was not of sound mind and under the influence of
Prince, whom she worshipped as a child does a parent. Prince, acting
under the supposed will, made five days before Mary's death, began
the prosecution against William Smith, the nephew, under the warrant
of Malbon, who did not give Smith time to send to Lichfield for his
attorney, although Lichfield is no more than nine miles from Draycott.

[5] Affdt of Alexander Robotham yeoman of Draycott, sworn before
Uppingham Bourne at Lichfield 5 May 1759. ITKB

That 25 April 1759 the deponent delivered notice to Scott that the
court would be moved against him first day of Easter term, for misdemeanour in the execution of his office of deputy sheriff. On 14 March

the deponent and William Smith told Charles Simpson, son of Stephen Simpson, attorney for Smith, that Prince made use of Malbon's name to threaten to proceed against Smith in order to induce him to give up possession. To prevent Malbon proceeding too hastily against Smith, Charles Simpson wrote Malbon to assure him that although Prince threatened proceedings, he was not in possession of the premises when Smith entered into them, that the door was open, and that no force was used. The letter also said that if Prince had any title he had to recover it by ejectment, since a will was of no effect until proved by three witnesses; and that Malbon would agree not to make Smith uneasy in a right the law had cast upon him and that only the law could take from him. The deponent seeks leave to refer to the said letter, which Malbon owned he had received and showed to the deponent. The deponent was born and has lived most of his life in Draycott, and was near neighbour to, and knew well, William Smith the uncle, Mary, and William Smith the nephew now charged with the forcible entry. [*Substantiates account in affdt [4] of William Smith and Mary Smith not being of sound mind prior to their deaths and Prince gaining influence over Mary.*] Prince is an old, designing man, a servant or labourer who gained unbounded influence and power over Mary.

[6] Affdt of Mary Bacon, wife of Richard Bacon weaver of Stubby Lane, Draycott, and Hannah Moores spinster of Draycott, sworn before John Hayne at Draycott 24 April 1759. ITKB [*Hannah Moores signed with a mark.*]
[Both]: [*Substantiate account in affdt [1] that Smith took peaceful possession, and that Bacon, Bamford and Woodnorth freely and voluntarily and without compulsion left the house 9 March.*] That Smith has since been prosecuted by Prince and gaoled by Malbon for pretended forcible entry and detainer. He in fact entered very peaceably. The prosecution is being prompted by Prince or his attorney Henry Scott to have Smith submit to some pretended claim to the property without putting them to the difficulty of making out their respective titles by ejectment or other due course of law.

[7] Affdt of William Burrows yeoman, Richard Bacon weaver, and Robert Robotham yeoman, all of Stubby Lane, Draycott, sworn before John Hayne at Draycott 24 April 1759. ITKB
[All]: That they were summoned by a bailiff of the hundred 17 March to appear before Malbon at Marchington to enquire into the forcible entry. They assembled at the house of John Jones in Marchington, where a genteel entertainment was provided by Scott or Prince. Together with John Blurton, Thomas Newton, John Jones, Robert

Daville, Joseph Cope, Joseph Woodroffe, Edward Fearnihough, Robert Stone and James Trundley, they were sworn as jurymen by Scott, who acted as deputy sheriff. Sillito (clerk to both Scott and Malbon) was sworn by Scott, and Scott by Malbon, to give evidence. [*Substantiate account in affdt [1] of the jury requesting an adjournment to hear Smith's defence, and on being refused, stating they could not find Smith guilty, and of Scott and Malbon leaving.*] None of the jurymen have been summoned to meet again. Scott acted as Prince's attorney while sitting as deputy sheriff in the enquiry and still does, and sets up some pretensions to the premises. Smith entered peacefully and offered no violence or even threatening words to Malbon or others; in their opinion and those of the other jurors he is not guilty of a forcible entry and detainer. The prosecution is designed to get Smith, who is in low circumstances, to give up his title to Prince or Scott without due course of law.

[8] Affdt of Thomas Scragg baker of Yoxall, sworn before Uppingham Bourne at Lichfield 27 April 1759. ITKB

That the deponent served notice in writing to Malbon 25 April that the court would be moved for an information first day of Easter term for illegally imposing a £5 fine on Smith and convicting him of a pretended forcible entry and detainer.

Affidavits for defence:

Mich 31 Geo II 1759

[9] Affdt of Robert Robotham yeoman of Stubby Lane, Draycott, Hanbury, sworn before John Hayne at Uttoxeter 23 May 1759. ITKB 'The King agt Malbon and others.'

That the deponent served on the jury 17 March 1759. Scott came into the jury room twice but did not attempt to intimidate or unduly influence the jury; he informed them they were to give a verdict based on the evidence. Richard Bacon said he would not sign the verdict, nor give a verdict without further evidence, and Scott said 'he did not know but they ought to be fined'.

[10] Affdt of the Reverend George Malbon, JP for Staffordshire, of Uttoxeter, sworn before John Hayne at Uttoxeter 9 June 1759. ITKB 'The King agt Malbon and others.'

That some time in March Prince came to the deponent and told him that he had been dispossessed by Smith, and that Smith and his friends threatened Prince with violence should he approach or attempt to reenter. Prince asked Malbon to come to the house as a JP, and produced a letter from Scott, his attorney, to the same effect. The deponent referred the question to Mr Ley who said he had authority to intervene [*see case and opinion annexed*]. He received a letter 15 March from Charles Simpson, son of Mr Simpson attorney at law, saying he should not proceed in this matter. The deponent sent the letter to Scott for his opinion and Scott saw no reason to change their plans. The letter falsely claimed that William Smith was heir to Mary Smith. At the house, the deponent asked Smith if he could enter but Smith replied he was heir and would hold the land. He then told Smith that as a justice, he was there to execute the statute, that he would enter by violence if necessary and would gaol Smith unless he opened the locked doors. The deponent did not make out a warrant or set a fine on Smith until after he had first viewed the house. He drew this up at the public house and returned to Smith's house in hopes that this would lead to a peaceable settlement. Archer, a principal abetter of Smith, told him not to come out of the house when it appeared that Smith was ready to do so. All peaceful means exhausted, the deponent ordered Owen headborough of Draycott to break open the door. He cautioned all those present to use no violence unless in self defence or in resisting any opposition to their entrance. When the door was opened the deponent saw no arms. The deponent never required anyone to be admitted to the house but himself. No person was hired to break down the door that day.

A jury was summoned pursuant to a precept issued by the deponent to the sheriff. The jury was there until early evening when he asked Scott to inquire about their reaching a verdict. When Scott said they were unlikely to agree, the deponent went home. No jurymen asked for more time to deliberate or for adjournment. He gave no entertainment to the jury, but partook of dinner provided by Prince for the jurors. Prior to this case, the deponent knew neither Smith nor Prince. Throughout this, he has endeavoured to act strictly according to the opinion which is annexed to this affdt and never acted out of ill will.

[*Annexed*]:

'Mary Smith being seized in fee of a messuage and lands in Draycote in County of Stafford by her will devises the term to Peter Prince and his heirs —

'Mary Smith died on Tuesday last. Peter Prince who resided in the same messuage with Mary Smith in her life time and at the time of her death confirmed in possession of the said house and lands until yesterday when one William Smith who is or pretends to be the heir at law of Mary Smith came with two other persons to the said house whilst Peter Prince was attending the interment of Mary Smith and finding the doors only latched and not otherwise fastened, William Smith opened one of the doors and came into the house and was soon afterwards followed by two other persons. And there being three women then in the house William Smith and his followers ordered them to go out adding that if they would not go out quietly they would turn them out. Upon which the women went out. Smith and his assistants augmented to four or five in number locked and bolted the doors and refuse to admit Peter Prince into the house and still keep possession.

'Please to advise by what means Peter Prince can recover the possession of the said house. And whether if a magistrate upon his view finding the possession forcibly detained from Peter Prince has a power to remove the force and restore the possession. If a magistrate has such a power please to direct what steps are necessary to be taken in the execution of it.'

[*Another hand*]: 'I think that Peter Prince took an estate in fee by the will of Mary Smith, and that by his being in possession at the time of her death and continuing so for several days he had such an estate upon and of which a forcible entry or detainer respectively might be made within the statutes; and that the behaviour of William Smith and his followers (who I take it are all principals) amounts to a forcible detainer, on account whereof Peter Prince is intitled to the remedy in that case provided.

'I apprehend that testatrix having acquired the estate by purchase (that is by conveyance in contradistinction to descent) William Smith, who I am told is only of the half blood to her, can have no pretence of title as heir at law, for I think he could never take as heir without the estate having been first cast on a collateral ancestor, and so coming to him in stream of the whole blood. Be that as it will the haeres factus is now as much at least, if not more favoured than the haeres natus.

'As to the remedy, I am of the opinion that one Justice of Peace (or more) the abovementioned particulars having been proved, may go by 15 Richard II, c.2 and 8 Henry VI, c.9 with sufficient power to the place, and if he finds it forcibly detained he shall take the persons so detaining, and after making a record of a conviction of the force he shall commit them to goal till fine made.

'I think the Justice must assess the force (and if more offenders than one severally) for it seems intended as a punishment for the forcible detainer of the circumstances whereof he is the best judge by his view; and without which the parties would be in prison without day.

'As to restitution, it seems probable to me that the record of the force, and the fine will in this case be sufficient to bring the offenders to reason; and then it may be advisable to proceed no farther. The subsequent proceedings are only to ascertain the right; the party is not thereby subject to further punishment; and though it is said in some books that in case of a traverse defendant shall pay the costs, yet as I don't find any particular method marked out, the prosecutor might probably be put to his action to recover them; and the proceedings would be drawn into considerable length consequently subject to cavil and delay — for these reasons I should think it better to stop upon the conviction of the force, and fine, if a proper agreement can be then made but if not the Justice (or Justices) will proceed according to 8 Henry VI, c.9. That is, will inquire of the force by a jury to be returned by the Sheriff; and if the force be found by the jury and traversed by the party the Justice will cause another jury to be returned to try that traverse. If the force found be not denied or if denied found against the defendant, the Justice shall reseise the premises and put the party so held out into full possession.

'If upon recording the force etc the possession should happen to be vacated (I don't think it can be forcibly taken even by the Justice till inquisition made) I think the Justice would be well to order it to be taken by the Constable as his immediate officer, or any other, as being then in the custody of the law. If that is not done by the Justice I think it may be done by any who will, in the nature of occupancy, to be account-able to him who shall be found to have the right of possession.

John Hayne   Thomas Ley
Doveridge March 1759'

[11] Affdt of Peter Prince yeoman, late of Draycott and now of Uttoxeter, sworn before John Hayne at Uttoxeter 9 June 1759. ITKB 'The King agt Malbon and others.'

That the deponent lived as a servant with Smith the elder before his death in Feb 1757. Smith died seized of the lands in question. The land was settled on Mary Smith, who held it peaceably until she died 6 March 1759. The deponent lived with her as a servant from Feb 1757 until her death. By her will, dated 1 March 1759, she devised all her lands to him subject to the payment of her debts and some legacies, and bequeathed him her personal estate and appointed him executor. He continued in possession of the estate from Mary's death until 9 March when he went to the funeral. Smith and Thomas, Francis, and John Mallabar came to the house while the deponent was at church and with threats Smith forced three women out of the house. When the deponent returned Smith called from the window that he was Mary's heir and told him not to enter the house. The next day Scott advised him to apply to Malbon for possession of the house. [*Substantiates account in affdt [10] of Malbon seeking Ley's opinion.*] Malbon came to the house 15 March, when Smith appeared at an upper window, but the deponent did not hear what Malbon and Smith said. They went to a tavern for an hour, returning with Owen, headborough of Draycott, and others. The deponent heard John Archer say Smith should keep where he was.

Malbon ordered Owen and others to break open the door, and on the deponent's advice decided to break open the back door since entry would be easier than from the front door. A jury met 17 March to enquire of the forcible detainer and the deponent had two joints of butcher meat brought to the public house for dinner for Malbon and the jury.

The deponent has lost food and valuables which he kept in the house before Smith took possession. Smith was only a half-blood nephew to Mary Smith and not the heir at law, nor did he have title to the property.

[12] Affdt of Richard Parker servant to the Reverend George Malbon of Uttoxeter, sworn before John Hayne at Uttoxeter 9 June 1759. ITKB 'The King agt Malbon and others.'

That the deponent attended his master 15 March 1759 as did Scott and Sillito. When they came to Smith's house, Malbon said who he was and that he was there on the complaint of Peter Prince. Malbon asked Smith to open the door. [*Substantiates account in affdt [1] that Smith wanted to consult Simpson or that Malbon could come back, that Malbon left for a public house and returned with a group of people, but does not mention they were armed.*] Smith agreed to open the door but John Archer called out to Smith not to. He did not. [*Substantiates account in affdt [11] of entry into the house.*] Smith was taken to Stafford gaol. Malbon gave orders against ill treatment. Malbon did not say it would be necessary to admit them into the house, nor did the deponent hear Smith invite Malbon to enter alone.

[13] Affdt of James Findley gentleman of Uttoxeter and Robert Stone yeoman of Fauld in Hanbury, sworn before John Hayne at Uttoxeter 9 June 1759. ITKB 'The King agt Malbon and others.'

[Both]: That they were summoned 17 March 1759 to serve on the jury. Scott and Sillito gave evidence and Scott said that if they needed more evidence Malbon would swear whomever they wished to hear. Scott did not pretend to act as deputy sheriff nor did he attempt to influence the verdict. Scott did urge them to agree on a verdict because Malbon wanted to go home. The juror Richard Bacon asked John Blurton whether he would give a verdict and Blurton replied 'you know I have promised to give no verdict unless you will'. Bacon declared he would give none. Scott may have blamed these two jurors and then left the room.

[14] Affdt of Henry Scott gentleman of Doveridge (Derbs), sworn before John Hayne at Uttoxeter 9 June 1759. ITKB 'The King agt Malbon and others.'

That Prince informed the deponent 10 March of the entry and detainer and asked him, as an attorney, how he might get possession again. The deponent advised him to apply to a magistrate, so he sent a letter of request to Malbon, suggesting he might take counsel's advice, and Malbon requested an opinion from Thomas Ley barrister of Doveridge. The deponent drew a statement of the case and he and Prince left it with Ley, who replied that evening or the next morning. He then sent it to Malbon. Malbon later asked the deponent to accompany him to view the detainer the next morning; at that time Malbon showed the deponent a letter he had received from Charles Simpson.

[*Substantiates account in affdt [15] of first meeting with Smith.*] At the public house, a record of the forcible detainer of the house was drawn and signed, a fine was set upon Smith, and an arrest warrant granted by Malbon. The deponent stayed across the street until Smith was brought out of the house. The deponent did not give instructions to anyone to break down the door. The deponent did not promise to pay John Owen the charges of taking Smith to gaol. The deponent went with Malbon and others 17 March, but not as deputy sheriff, to John Jones's public house in Marchington where a jury was summoned to meet to inquire of the forcible detainer. As an assistant to Malbon the deponent read out of a book called Burn's *Justice* the oath for such jurors. He also read to Sillito the oath to be administered to witnesses. He informed the jury that there were others in the house who could testify if the jury so desired. The foreman William Burroughs desired the deponent to give evidence and he was sworn by Malbon. After waiting several hours for the jury to return a verdict the deponent asked them to reach one. [*Substantiates affdt [13].*] The deponent may have said that they were blameable for coming with a predetermined verdict and liable to be fined or taken notice of, but he did not attempt to unduly influence the jury. Malbon and the deponent left when the jury did not reach a verdict.

The deponent claims no interest or title in the property, but by indentures of lease and release of 7 and 8 Nov 1735 certain closes called the two little meadows and a piece of land called the Long Acres in Draycott, part of the late William Smith's estate, were among the lands limited after William Smith's death to John Archer in trust for a term of 300 years for raising money to pay certain debts of Smith, and other monies totaling £35 to be paid to nephews and nieces of Smith. After William Smith's death, the deponent advanced £50 to John Archer at Mary Smith's request, to be applied for these purposes. At the direction of Mary Smith, on 13 July 1757 John Archer assigned the deponent the two closes and the Long Acres for the residue of the 300 year term as security for the £50 and interest. He later advanced Mary Smith £40, and she agreed by an endorsement of 23 Dec last that the said lands be

charged with the payment of £40 and interest. These are his only interests in the land. He did not provide any entertainment for the jury, nor
give any orders relating to such a matter.

[15] Affdt of Robert Sillito yeoman of Uttoxeter, sworn before John
Hayne at Uttoxeter 9 June 1759. ITKB 'The King agt Malbon and others.'
[*Verso*]: '9 June 1759. Affid of Robt Sillito Clerk to Mr Malbon. 6 fo:25.'
    That the deponent took Prince's sworn complaint 14 March and went
to the house in Draycott 15 March with Scott, Richard Parker (servant
to Malbon) and Luke Turner. [*Substantiates account in affdt [10] of Smith
refusing Malbon entry and Malbon threatening to commit him to gaol.*] At the
public house, the deponent was instructed to write down a record of the
forcible detainer, part of which Malbon dictated from Burn's *Justice.*[27]
A fine of £5 was imposed on Smith. He also wrote the warrant, which
was given to the headborough to execute immediately. Malbon, the
headborough, and others assisting him went to the house while the
deponent stayed at the ale house with Scott, then followed and found
Malbon once again arguing with Smith. He was about to open the door
when John Archer cried out not to let Malbon in. [*Substantiates account
in affdt [11] of entry into house.*]
    The deponent was asked who would pay the headborough. He
replied no one had to, but Prince agreed to pay him a reasonable charge.
He never heard Scott promise to do so, nor Malbon insist the mob be
admitted. The deponent went to aid Malbon 17 March at a public house
at Marchington where a jury had been summoned. [*Substantiates
account in affdt [14] of being sworn and the charge to the jury as well as
exchange between Robotham and Brown in affdt [9].*] Neither Malbon nor
Scott tried to influence the jury. At 5pm, with still no verdict, Malbon
went home.

[16] Affdt of Judith Bamford, wife of Nock Bamford of Abbots Bromley,
sworn before John Hayne at Abbot's Bromley 11 June 1759. ITKB 'The
King agst Malbon and others.'
    That William Smith the elder owned the property before he died, and
Mary Smith, sister by half blood, held them until her death 6 March
1759. The deponent went to attend Mary's funeral 9 March, but as it was
raining, went to the late Mary's house instead with Mary Bacon, Mary
Woodnorth and Mary Smith's maid servant. Smith came in and said he
was there to take possession. Thomas Francis Mallabar and John

---

[27] See Richard Burn, *Justice of the Peace and Parish Officer* (2nd ed., London,
    1756), title 'Forcible Entry and Detainer', for the law, and an example of a
    mittimus, doubtless the model used by Malbon's clerk.

Mallabar[28] came into the house and Smith told the women to leave. The deponent pointed out it would be unkind to turn women out in the rain. Smith and the two other men threatened to carry them out, so the women left.

[17] Affdt of Mary Woodnorth, wife of John Woodnorth plumber of Abbott's Bromley, sworn before John Hayne at Uttoxeter 11 June 1759. ITKB 'The King agst Malbon and others.'

That Smith entered and told the women he understood his aunt had left him nothing by her will but that as heir he had come to take possession. [*Substantiates account in affdt [16] that they did not attend the funeral because of the rain, and that Smith threatened to carry them out.*]

[18] Affdt of Luke Turner farmer of Doveridge (Derbs), sworn before John Hayne at Uttoxeter 11 June 1759. ITKB 'The King agt Malbon and others.'

[*Substantiates account in affdt [14] that Scott went no closer to the house than the lands across the street, and stayed there until Smith was taken into custody by the headborough.*]

Sources: KB 1/13 Ea 32 Geo II no. 2. KB 1/13 Mich 31 Geo II. KB 21/38 pp. 230, 238, 259.

B.6 Information exhibited against two justices (29 April 1771)

Defendants: Richard Palmer, esquire and maltster; and Joseph Taylor, esquire and tanner, both justices of the borough of Walsall.

Information:
Trin 12 Geo III 1772 [1 June 1772]

[1] Joseph Hughes of Walsall appeared before Palmer and Taylor 21 Jan [1771], offering to inform against Charles Day of Bentley, Richard Read of Walsall, and William Whitehouse of Walsall for hunting and killing a hare with greyhounds 20 Jan in the borough of Walsall, and Palmer and Taylor refused to accept his information; [2] 22 Jan [1771] Hughes again offered, at the town hall, and they again refused.

Rules and process:
Trin [31 May 1771]: on affdts [1, 2], rule nisi for an information to [7 June] (Dunning); summons. ST [10 June 1771]: enlarged rule nisi

---

[28] Spelled 'Malliber' in this affidavit.

to FNT (Morton). Mich 1771: affdts [3] to [8] filed. ST [7 Nov 1771]: rule discharged, on Palmer and Taylor's agreeing to pay prosr's costs, to be taxed if necessary; otherwise rule absolute for an information (Wallace for defdts; consent of Dunning for prosr). Ea [1 June 1772]: on affdt [9], rule absolute for an information (Dunning). Mich 1772: pray a day to answer; imparl. ST [27 Nov 1772]: rule nisi to FNT for a stay of the prosn, on Barlow's[29] undertaking to pay all costs already taxed and all other prosr's costs still to be taxed (Baldwin). Hil [26 Jan 1773]: stay of proceedings, Barlow undertaking to pay costs to be taxed by the master of the crown office (Baldwin).

Affidavits for prosecution:

Trin 11 Geo III 1771

[1] Affdt of Joseph Hughes nailer, William Hughes nailer, and William Bagnall chapefiler, all of Walsall, sworn before Thomas Holbeche at Walsall 29 April 1771. ITKB [*William Bagnall signed with a mark.*]

[Joseph Hughes]: That on Sunday, 20 Jan 1791, he saw Richard Read chapefiler of Walsall, Charles Day labourer of Bentley, and William Whitehouse chapeforger of Walsall, chasing a hare for two hours with two greyhounds. The dogs killed the hare and William Whitehouse took it up. He went to Palmer 21 Jan to lay an information; he also told Palmer that Read said that he and Whitehouse were acting on the instructions of another justice, Joseph Taylor tanner and JP, who paid them with 2s, meat and drink. Palmer then refused to take the information before speaking to Taylor. The next day when the deponent tried again to lay the information, Palmer said that he was too late, for Taylor had already taken the information of Nicholas Sly, a sometime employee of John Taylor. Palmer laughed at the deponent's anger and called it a 'hum bug affair'.

[William Hughes]: [*Substantiates Hughes's account above.*]

[All]: That in the evening of 22 Jan they all went to the town hall or courthouse to confront the two justices. Palmer repeated that the information had already been taken and that he would have nothing to do with the matter. Taylor remarked that it was too bad they did not have a hare and asked the town clerk whether he had any press warrants: 'It is very fitting these fellows should be pressed.' Three weeks later Joseph Hughes learned from Nicholas Sly that he had not laid an information but was to do so if Hughes and the others aimed at doing so, to save Taylor paying the money.

---

[29] Henry Barlow, probably the defendants' clerk in court: Hands, preface.

[2] Affdt of John Hickman gentleman of Droitwich (Worcs), sworn before William Jones at Droitwich 27 May 1771. ITKB

That he delivered notices on 20 May signed by Thomas Holbeche gentleman, to Taylor and Palmer that the court would be moved for an information on the first day of Trinity term.

Affidavits for defence:

Mich 12 Geo III 1771

[3] Affdt of Richard Palmer, maltster and JP of Walsall, sworn before Thomas Hodgkins at Walsall 17 Oct 1771. ITKB

That he was an acting magistrate and the deputy of John Bradnock, bucklemaker and mayor of Walsall, who was absent. He admits that Hughes came to his house to lay an information against Day, servant of John Taylor, and Richard Read. He does not recall a third accused. Hughes did not tell him that Read had been asked by Taylor to fetch Day and his hounds. The deponent refused to take the information until he had first consulted with Taylor who, later in the day, informed him that an information had already been taken from Sly; he therefore did not take an information from Hughes. On the evening of 22 Jan in the courthouse Hughes insisted he take an information but the deponent once again refused for the reasons already stated. He reaffirms the fact that he did not refuse to take the information in order to frustrate or prevent the laws of this country being put into execution.

[4] Affdt of Charles Day, labourer and manager of John Taylor's farm of Bentley, sworn before Thomas Hodgkins at Walsall 18 Oct 1771. ITKB
[*Signed with a mark.*]

That the deponent was first informed of the hare when he was accosted in the street by Read. Taylor was annoyed to be disturbed by such a trifling matter on a Sunday and would have nothing to do with it. Around 11am the deponent returned to the farm to find the hounds out and several people about. His wife told him that they were trying to kill a hare. He gathered his master's hounds but owing to a great noise 100 yards behind them they broke loose. At about 12:15pm the hare had been killed but the deponent does not know how. Joseph Hughes swore repeatedly that the hare belonged to him because he had started it. The deponent denies that he, either alone or with Read or Whitehouse, traced any hare for two hours or more, as he understands Joseph Hughes has sworn.

[5] Affdt of Joseph Joesbery chapemaker, Joseph Somerfield filecutter and William Smith chapefiler, all of Walsall, sworn before Thomas Hodgkins at Walsall 18 Oct 1771. ITKB

[Joseph Joesbery]: That he saw Joseph Hughes following the tracks of a hare in the snow between 11am and 12pm on a Sunday in January. Hughes swore that no one else would get the hare, and rubbed out the tracks with his foot. The deponent did not see him kill the hare. Later he saw Joseph Hughes returning home, angry at being cheated of his hare. Hughes said that he had tried to borrow Jacob Smith's hounds. He believes Hughes formerly lived in Brocton but had been forced to leave because of his poaching.

[Joseph Somerfield]: [*Substantiates Joesbery's account above.*]

[William Smith]: That he saw Joseph Hughes tracing the hare over a period of three hours, and that he said that if he caught the hare Jacob Smith would reward him with money, victuals and drink. The next morning Hughes asked the deponent to go hunting with him, and told him that he had found the hare in a bramble, but when he returned with a borrowed greyhound to kill the hare, it was gone.

[6] Affdt of Richard Reed, tenant, chapefiler and occupier of Reed's Wood, sworn before Thomas Hodgkins at Walsall 18 Oct 1771. ITKB [*Signed with a mark.*]

That on Sunday, 20 Jan 1771, the deponent went to care for his rabbits in Reed's Wood. He saw a hare running loose but could not catch it so he went into Walsall for John Taylor's greyhounds. He asked Day to tell him whether he wished to send his hounds. After visiting John Arrowsmith, a relation, the deponent returned to the warren to find ten or more people, including Joseph Hughes, chasing the hare. About 12:15pm the hare was killed, to Hughes's great annoyance. The deponent denies that Taylor directed him or Whitehouse to go to Day and take hounds to kill the hare. He also denies that he said as much to Hughes.

[7] Affdt of Nicholas Sly spurmaker of Walsall, sworn before Thomas Hodgkins at Walsall 18 Oct 1771. ITKB [*Signed with a mark.*]

That on 20 Jan 1771 the deponent went to the house of William Hughes, who told him that his brother, Joseph Hughes, had been chasing a hare for some hours and had gone to Jacob Smith's house to get hounds. Later he heard Joseph Hughes talking with Joseph Somerfield about the hare, saying that if Somerfield caught it, he would catch another. In the wood where the hare was killed, the deponent heard Hughes say that he wanted to give the hare to Jacob Smith for whom he sometimes worked as a labourer and sometimes dealt with in trade. The following day Hughes inquired at the deponent's house for the name of Taylor's servant; Richard Read and William Whitehouse, both chape-forgers of Walsall, were also mentioned. When the deponent's wife said, 'surely he was not offering to hurt those poor men', Hughes replied that any hurt would lie on Read, Day, and chiefly on Taylor himself 'because he was the man that had the money'. The deponent told Taylor of this conversation soon after and then went to Wednesbury on business with Hughes and William Bagnall chapefiler. He denies that William Hughes ever asked him whether he gave his information to John Taylor, or that he answered that he was only to do so if Joseph or William aimed to do it. He has heard Joseph Hughes brag about sporting and catching game.

[8] Affdt of John Taylor tanner of Walsall, sworn before Thomas Hodgkins at Walsall 19 Oct 1771. ITKB

That the deponent is qualified by law to kill game. When he was informed of the hare by his servant Day, he ordered that nothing be done about it. He denies that he ever ordered out his only hound. He admits meeting Joseph Hughes at the town hall on the following evening. Hughes is a man of indifferent character and a reputed poacher. The deponent thought such persons should not be encouraged and dismissed him. He did not tell Palmer not to take Hughes's information. He asserts that the prosecutor is supported in his cause by Jacob Smith chapman of Walsall, and by several others. They have proposed articles of accommodation, but have rejected his counter proposals. They are carrying on this prosecution to oppress him.

Further affidavit for prosecution:

Ea 12 Geo III 1772

[9] Affdt of John Hickman gentleman of Droitwich (Worcs) and Joseph Hughes nailer of Walsall, sworn before William Holland at Walsall 11 April 1772. ITKB

[John Hickman]: That he presented the order annexed to Palmer and Taylor 10 April 1772.

[Joseph Hughes]: That he was present and demanded payment of £22 6s 3d but Palmer absolutely refused to pay and neither has since paid any part.

[*Annexed*]: Copy of order of [7 Nov 1771]. 'I appoint Thursday the 23d of Jan 1772, at seven in the evening. James Burrow.' [*Costs allowed of £22 6s 3d.*]

Further affidavit for defence:

Hil 13 Geo III 1773

[10] Affdt of William Finch gentleman of Clement's Lane (London), sworn before J. Aston at Serjeants' Inn 26 Jan 1773. ITKB 'The King agt Richard Palmer Esq and John Taylor Esq.' [*Verso*]: '21 Staffordsh. The King agt Rd Palmer Esq & ano., Afft of Service. Lane.'
    That 3 Dec last he served Sleigh, attorney for the prosecution, with a copy of the order of [27 Nov 1772], by giving his clerk a copy. On the motion of Baldwin.

Sources: IND 1/6661, Mich 13 Geo III. KB 1/18 Ea 12 Geo III, Trin 11 Geo III, Mich 12 Geo III, no.1. KB 1/19 Hil 13 Geo III, no.1. KB 11/48 Trin 12 Geo III 1772 #12. KB 21/40 [unpaginated] Trin 11 Geo III. Mich, Ea 12 Geo III. Mich, Hil 13 Geo III. KB 29/432 Mich 13 Geo III.

B.7 Information against a justice, refused (27 May 1772)

Defendant: Fettiplace Nott esquire of Lichfield, JP for Staffordshire.

Accusation:
Convicting the Reverend John Landor of Colton on the Turnpike Act, 7 Geo III, c.42, without first summoning him to show cause against such conviction.

Rules and process:
27 May–13 June 1772: affdts [1] to [3] taken, filed Trin. Trin [19 June 1772]: on affdts [1] to [3], rule nisi to [2 July]. ST 19–29 June 1772: affdts [4] to [6] taken, filed Trin. ST [8 July 1772]: rule discharged.

Affidavits for prosecution:

Trin 12 Geo III 1772

[1] Affdt of the Reverend John Landor of Colton, sworn before E. Willes in his chambers at Serjeants' Inn 27 May 1772. ITKB
    That the deponent or his servant, Christopher Ball, was convicted 25 Feb 1772 by Fettiplace Nott JP, upon the information of George Walker, for having drawn a wagon with five horses upon the turnpike which runs from Lichfield to Yoxall 24 Feb 1772. The penalty was a black mare belonging to the deponent worth £20. It was seized by Benjamin Collett and delivered to the constable of King's Bromley, John Cooper. Nott

ordered it to be forfeited to George Walker labourer on his warrant, even though he was not present at the seizure. The deponent was never called to show cause against the conviction and thus was deprived of his right to appeal to general quarter sessions under 7 Geo III.

[2] Affdt of Christopher Ball servant and waggoner of Colton, sworn before George Cookes at Stafford 11 June 1772. ITKB [*Signed with a mark.*]
  That the deponent was driving a waggon through King's Bromley 24 Feb when Benjamin Collett, labourer, seized a black mare belonging to Landor which was loose and unlinked before the other four horses. The deponent was never summoned before Nott to show cause against the conviction. [*Substantiates details in affdt [1].*]

[3] Affdt of Francis Brookes gentleman of Stafford, sworn before W. Keen at Stafford 13 June 1772. ITKB [*Verso*]: 'In the King's Bench. The King agt Nott: Affidt of Francis Brookes of Service of notice. Higgins.'
  That on 12 June 1772 he personally served the annexed notice on Nott.
  [*Annexed*]: King's Bench will be moved against Fettiplace Nott esquire at the instance of John Landor clerk of Colton on the first day of next Trinity term for convicting him of drawing five horses upon the turnpike road between Lichfield and Yoxall without summoning Landor to show cause against such conviction contrary to 7 Geo III. [Signed] Francis Brookes, 11 June 1772.

Affidavits for defence:

Trin 12 Geo III 1772

[4] Affdt of Fettiplace Nott, esquire and JP for Staffordshire, of Lichfield, sworn before Charles Howard at Lichfield 29 June 1772. ITKB 'The King agt Fettiplace Nott esq.' [*Verso*]: 'B.R. The King agt Nott Esq: Affidt of Mr Nott fo: 17 R. & S. S. Baxter.'
  That Collett and Richard Lawrence, clerk and Landor's head servant, appeared before the deponent 24 Feb 1772. They said that Collett had seized a mare, now with the constable, and that they wished to settle the matter and sought his interposition as a magistrate. Collett said Landor was absent from home so the deponent told them to return on the morrow with an informer and proof of the facts. The following day they returned with George Walker as informer and the deponent took his information, proceeded to conviction, and gave a warrant to the constable which by inadvertence and mistake commanded him to deliver the mare to Walker instead of Collett.

He believes that Lawrence redeemed the horse from either Collett or Walker for £9 4s and did so as an act of service to John Landor. He asserts that he was merely doing his duty and he feels that he needed to summon neither Landor nor Ball owing to the presence of Lawrence, and that he was acting in Landor's best interests, at the request of his head servant.

[5] Affdt of John Cooper the younger, farmer and son of the constable of King's Bromley, sworn before Charles Howard at King's Bromley 27 June 1772. ITKB 'The King agt Fettiplace Nott esquire.'

That Collett entrusted him with a mare that he had seized from a wagon belonging to Landor. In the evening, Lawrence came and told the deponent that he had already been before William Inge and Nott, justices, and he instructed the deponent to care properly for the mare.

[6] Affdt of William Inge esquire and JP for Staffordshire, of Thorpe Constantine and Lichfield, sworn before Charles Howard at Lichfield 29 June 1772. ITKB 'The King agt Fettiplace Nott esq.'

That Lawrence and Collett came to the deponent 24 Feb 1772. Lawrence declared that Collett had properly seized a mare of Landor's because it was improperly drawing a narrow wheeled wagon on a turn-pike. Collett was willing to compromise but wanted a justice to super-vise any settlement for his own protection. Both men wanted a settlement because otherwise Christopher Ball might lose his place. The deponent declined to intervene as he was entertaining guests, but he suggested that they see Nott.

Sources: KB 1/19 Trin 12 Geo III no. 1. KB 21/40 [unpaginated], Friday after the Morrow of Holy Trinity, 12 Geo III [19 June 1772], and Wednesday next after three weeks from Holy Trinity [8 July 1772].

B.8 Informations against a justice, refused (13 May 1784)

Defendant: John Gough esquire, JP for Staffordshire, of Perry Hall, Handsworth.

Accusation:
Misdemeanours Feb to June 1784 in his office of a magistrate, in the case of Charles Dudwell in administering the poor law, and in the cases of Thomas Kendrick and John Fowke with respect to commital proceedings.

Rules and process:
13 May to 7 June 1784: affdts [1] to [14] taken. Trin [11 June 1784]: on reading affdts [1] to [14], rule nisi to [21 June 1784] for information against Gough (Lane). 19, 21 June 1784: defence affdts [15], [16] taken. ST [21 June 1784]: peremptory rule nisi to second day next term (Bower). Mich [21 Nov 1785]: peremptory rule nisi to fourth day next term (Bower). Hil [26 Jan 1786]: on hearing counsel both sides, rule discharged (Bower for defdt, Bearcroft for prosr).

Affidavits for prosecution:

Trin 24 Geo III 1784

[*Re Dudwell*]:

[1] Affdt of John Inman gentleman, Richard Phillips and Samuel Bickley farmers, all of Wednesfield, sworn before Henry Smith at Wednesfield 14 May 1784. ITKB [*Verso*]: '14 May 1784 The King Prosn of Dudwell agt Gough Esq: 1st affid of Inman Phillips & Bickley. psn affts. fo:9.'
[John Inman and Richard Phillips]: That they are chapelwardens and Bickley is overseer of the poor. Gough acted without their application against Dudwell and without any just cause or complaint whatsoever either on account of his child or otherwise but merely to gratify the unbounded caprice of the said John Gough who has for some time past most cruelly wantonly and oppressively exercised his power and authority of a magistrate and tyrannized over many of His Majesty's subjects by committing them and releasing them at his pleasure.
[Richard Phillips]: That he received 14 April from Dudwell the £2 8s that was the outstanding amount on Dudwell's account. He gave Mary Dudwell a receipt for this amount.
[John Inman]: That he was present at a meeting 4 May, convened by John Alcock, a constable and a tenant of Gough's, wherein it was unanimously decided that Wednesfield had no claim upon Dudwell.

[2] Affdt of Charles Dudwell, prisoner in Wolverhampton house of correction, sworn before Henry Smith at Wolverhampton 16 May 1784. ITKB [*Verso*]: '16 May 1794 The King Prosn of Dudwell agt Gough Esq: 1st affid of Dudwell fo:20.'
That the deponent was apprehended 3 May by the constable of Wednesfield, John Alcock, and taken to the Old Fallings, the seat of John Gough, and left in the yard under the care of William Shaw. Gough appeared in the yard with a warrant of commitment (annexed)

to the Wolverhampton house of correction for the deponent's 'impu-dence', and said that he would commit him 'to the House of Correction till Monday and would then commit this deponent to Stafford and from thence to Hell'. Gough refused to take bail from his master, Richard Fryer. He was taken to Wolverhampton and committed to the custody of James Swain, the keeper.

Since then he has been confined under irons, locked to the floor, slept on a bed of straw and in all respects treated like a felon. When he came before Gough no one appeared to make a charge against him, and he had settled accounts with the chapelwardens 14 April for keeping the child at nurse at a cost of 2s a week. He married his wife, Mary Dudwell, twelve years ago, but as she was lewd and disorderly they parted upon mutual consent one year after marriage and have not had any inter-course or connection since, or cohabited. In the summer of 1783 she bore a child in Wednesfield, and was willing to appear before Gough to swear that this deponent was not the father.

In October he was committed to the Wolverhampton house of cor-rection by Gough, and was released the following day on agreeing to pay for the child's care. Then Gough prevailed upon Fryer to turn him out of his service. He sought work in London but took ill and was forced to sell his clothes before returning to Wednesfield in April. Upon his return his brother, Richard Dudwell, shoemaker, sent £2 8s to pay the parish for the upkeep of the child. He believes no complaint has been made.

[*Annexed*]: Staffordshire. Warrant of committal of Charles Dudwell to Wolverhampton house of correction for further examination for refus-ing to give security to indemnify the parish for the maintenance of his child, 3 May 1784. J Gough.

[3] Affdt of Richard Fryer gentleman of Wolverhampton, sworn before Henry Smith at Wolverhampton 16 May 1784. ITKB

That Dudwell was his servant for eleven years until last November, and always behaved himself with the strictest sobriety and honesty and was always diligent and mindful of this deponent's business. He believes that Dudwell never lay out of the deponent's house one night, and he was discharged only to oblige Gough. When Dudwell returned in April the deponent took him back. When Alcock came for Dudwell 3 May the deponent went in Dudwell's place to satisfy Gough, and showed him the receipt from the parish. Gough demanded to see Dudwell and refused to allow the deponent to be bound for his appear-ance, although Gough must have known that he had property worth £500 a year. He then committed Dudwell to the house of correction.

[4] Affdt of Mary Dudwell, age 30, wife of Charles Dudwell, and Charlotte Stringer, age 23, spinster, both of Wolverhampton, sworn before Henry Smith at Wolverhampton 3 June 1784. ITKB [*Mary Dudwell and Charlotte Stringer signed with a mark.*] [*Verso*]: '3d June 1784 The King Prosn of Dudwell agt Gough Esq: affid of Dudwell's wife & Charlotte Stringer fo:10.'

[Mary Dudwell]: [*Substantiates account in affdt [2] of their parting.*] That she and her husband had one daughter, Elizabeth, while they were married, but they have not cohabited for 11 years. She had another daughter last June, now put out at nurse by Charles Dudwell. She is providing for herself and is not chargeable, and at the time of her husband's imprisonment he was maintaining both children. When she heard that he was in the Wolverhampton house of correction she and Stringer went to see John Gough on 10 May.

[Both]: That Gough admitted that there was no cause to confine Dudwell but that he had been affronted by Richard Fryer, Dudwell's master, and was determined to get revenge.

[5] Affdt of Charles Dudwell, age 33, prisoner in Stafford house of correction, sworn before Henry Smith at Stafford 5 June 1784. ITKB

That the deponent was moved by John Alcock to Stafford 27 May, and committed on the annexed warrant. He was originally committed 3 May to Wolverhampton house of correction until further examination, which has not taken place. He lived nine years in Wolverhampton, did not desert his wife and child, and would not have left Wolverhampton had Gough not prevailed upon Fryer to discharge him. Neither his wife nor child were chargeable to the township when he was apprehended.

[*Annexed*]: Warrant by Gough to constable of Wednesfield and to keeper of the Stafford House of Correction, 19 May 1784, for the committal of Dudwell until next quarter sessions.

[6] Affdt of John Inman, age 41, gentleman, and Samuel Bickley, age 25, farmer, both of the liberty of Wednesfield, sworn before Henry Smith at Wednesfield 6 June 1784. ITKB [*Verso*]: '6 June 1784. The King Prosn of Dudwell ag Gough Esq: 2d affid of Inman & Bickley. The prosn affts. fo:7.'

[Both]: That Bickley is overseer of the poor; Inman and Richard Phillips, who is absent because he is visiting Beverley (Yorks), are chapelwardens. Gough has caused Charles Dudwell to be imprisoned in Stafford house of correction for leaving his wife and child, Sarah, unprovided for, and the child chargeable. They have made no such complaint to Gough: Dudwell is now confined without any just cause and is an injured man.

[7] Affdt of William Shaw, age 45, yeoman of Wednesfield, sworn before Henry Smith at Wolverhampton 6 June 1784. ITKB [*Signed with a mark*.] [*Verso*]: '6 June 94 The King Prosn of Dudwell ag Gough Esq: Shaw's Affidt fo:5.'

That Dudwell and his wife have not cohabited, and Dudwell has lived as a servant to Richard Fryer gentleman of Wolverhampton for many years. Since 15 April this deponent's wife has acted as nurse to Sarah at a cost of 1s 6d per week.

[8] Affdt of John Parrott gentleman of Wolverhampton, sworn before Henry Smith at Wolverhampton 7 June 1784. ITKB [*Verso*]: '7 June 1784. The King Prosn of Dudwell ag Gough Esq: Affid of Ser of Notice of Motn fo:5.'

That the deponent attempted to serve Gough 29 May with the notice annexed at his house at Perry. Gough threatened to set his hounds upon him; he then went to Old Fallings and served the notice on Gough's servant, Jeremy Tonks. The deponent again tried 2 June to serve Gough personally, and when he refused the notice the deponent left it on the floor, and told Gough he had done so.

[*Annexed*]: Notice by Benjamin Price, solicitor for Dudwell, that motion for an information will be made 11 June 1784, first day Trinity term. 26 May 1784.

[*Re Kendrick*]:

[9] Affdt of Thomas Kendrick locksmith of Willenhall, sworn before Henry Smith at Wolverhampton 13 May 1784. ITKB [*Signed with a mark*.] [*Verso*]: '13 May 1784. The King Prosn of Kendrick agt Gough Esq: Affidt of Thos Kendrick fo:8.'

That he was informed 2 Feb by Edward Ash, deputy constable of Willenhall, that John Gough had issued a warrant for the deponent's appearance at Perry Hall. Gough said that the deponent had accused Elizabeth, the wife of John Walters, of stealing linen from Marson of Willenhall.

He was committed and conveyed to Wolverhampton house of correction and kept in irons until 16 April when James Swain discharged him at the direction of Gough. He denied before Gough that he ever accused Walters, and says that no other charge was made against him. He told Swain that he would seek redress for his false imprisonment and demanded that Swain keep the notice of commitment. Immediately upon his release he demanded to see it but Swain said that Gough had recalled the original and had sent a fresh one.

[10] Affdt of Edward Ash farmer and deputy constable of Willenhall, sworn before Henry Smith at Wolverhampton 13 May 1784. ITKB [*Verso*]: '13th May 1784. The King Prosn of Kendrick agt Gough Esq: Ash's Affidt 2 fo:5.'

That the deponent received a warrant dated 30 Jan from John Gough 1 Feb, directing him to bring Kendrick before Gough by 11am on the morrow at the Boar's Head in Perry to answer Walters for accusing his wife; the deponent brought Kendrick before Gough, who committed him to Wolverhampton House of Correction. He delivered him into Swain's custody.

[11] Affdt of William Swain locksmith and son of James Swain keeper of the Wolverhampton house of correction, sworn before Henry Smith at Wolverhampton 16 May 1784. ITKB [*Verso*]: '16 May 1784. The King Prosn of Kendrick agt Gough Esq: Swain's Affidt fo:8.'

That Thomas Kendrick was delivered for imprisonment 2 Feb and after several days one Mr Dawes delivered a fresh commitment and said that Gough requested the return of the original. Before returning the original the deponent made a copy annexed which is marked No. 1. The copy of the second commitment is marked No. 2, and is a true copy of the original in the hands of James Swain.

[*Annexed*]:

'*Number 1*. Staffordshire. To the keeper of the Wolverhampton house of correction receive into your custody the body of Thos Kendrick herewith sent you being charged upon the oaths of Ann Hodson and William Walters with charging Elizabeth Walters with stealing some child bed linen and some other clothes the property of Richard Marson of Willenhall and for refusing to find sufficient surety for his good behaviour towards Elizabeth Walters and him safely keep in your custody till the next quarter sessions. Given under my hand and seal 2 Feb 1784. J Gough'

'*Number 2*. To the constable of Willenhall in the said county and to the keeper of his Majesty's Wolverhampton house of correction in the said county. I do hereby in his Majesty's name command you the said constable forthwith safely to convey and deliver into the custody of the said keeper the body of Thos Kendrick being charged before me one of his Majesty's JPs in and for the said county upon oath of Ann Hodson and William Walters with accusing Elizabeth Walters with stealing some child bed linen and some other clothes the property of Richard Marson of Willenhall and for refusing to find sufficient surety for his good behaviour towards Eliz Walters. And you the said keeper are hereby required to receive the said Thomas Kendrick into your custody in the said house of correction and him there safely to keep until he shall thence be delivered by due order of law. Herein fail not. Given under my hand and seal 2 Feb 1784. J Gough'.

[12] Affdt of John Parrott gentleman [*affidavit and notice identical to [8], except for name of prosecutor*]. ITKB [*Verso*]: '7 June 1784. The King Prosn of Kendrick agt Gough Esq: affid of Ser of Notice of Motn fo:5.'

[*Re Fowke*]:

[13] Affdt of John Fowke labourer, and John Parrott gentleman, both of Wolverhampton, sworn before Henry Smith at Wolverhampton 16 May 1784. ITKB [*John Fowke signed with a mark.*] [*Verso*]: '11. 16 May 1784. The King Prosn of Fowke ag Gough Esq: Affid of Fowke & Parrott fo:10 Enlarged. 3.'
   [John Fowke]: That he is indebted to Alexander Harbetch, screwfiler of Wolverhampton, for the sum of £2 14s for the ley of cows. His financial troubles have been caused by his landlord's distraint of all his cattle for rent. Harbetch applied to Gough to enforce payment; Gough caused the deponent to appear before him on 5 May, when he committed him to Wolverhampton house of correction. On that and the following day the deponent was chained to the wooden floor. He was later allowed some straw but was always held in irons and treated like a common felon. He was set at liberty by Gough 13 May.
   [John Parrott]: That he visited Swain 10 May to secure a copy of Gough's annexed warrant .
   [*Annexed*]: Warrant to the constable of Wolverhampton and keeper of the Wolverhampton house of correction to deliver Fowke into custody and keep for further examination on the oath of Harbetch for Fowke's fraudulent taking of two cows without paying for their upkeep as required by prior agreement.

[14] Affdt of John Parrott gentleman [*affidavit and notice identical to [8], except for name of prosecutor*]. ITKB [*Verso*]: '7 June 1784. The King Prosn of Fowke ag Gough Esq affid of ser of not of motn fo:5.'

Affidavits for defence:

Trin 24 Geo III 1784

[15] Affdt of Joseph Smith yeoman of Handsworth, sworn before R. Grant at Birmingham 19 June 1784. ITKB [*Verso*]: 'Affidavit of Jos Smith. S Purlewent Linc Inn.'

That Inman appeared 11 June before Gough and swore that the township had no claim against Charles Dudwell, whereupon Gough immediately signed a discharge which was executed 13 June. By order of Gough the deponent paid the fees owing to the keeper of the house of correction.

[16] Affdt of John Hood gentleman of Lincoln's Inn, sworn in court 21 June 1784. ITKB [*Verso*]: '30. X. Staffords. Affidavit of John Hood For Informn agt John Gough Esq. S Purlewent. No. 8. Linc Inn.'
    That immediately after the deponent learned that motions had been made for leave to file an information or informations against Gough, and that a rule nisi had been granted, he applied to the clerk of the rules in the crown office for copies of the affidavits filed. On 14 June he obtained copies of the fourteen affidavits filed 12 June and sent them by the earliest conveyance; Gough could not possibly receive them until 16 June.

Sources: KB 1/23 Trin 24 Geo III no.1. KB 21/43 (incomplete pagination), Trin 24 Geo III, Mich 26 Geo III, Hil 26 Geo III.

B.9 Information against a justice, refused (17 Oct 1785)

Defendant: John Gough esquire, JP for Staffordshire, of Perry Hall, Handsworth.

Accusation:
Misdemeanour in office of a magistrate in improperly committing Mary Foster to Wolverhampton house of correction.

Rules and process:
Mich 1785: affdt [1] filed. ST [9 Nov 1785]: rule nisi to [21 Nov] (Bearcroft). ST [21 Nov 1785]: enlarged peremptory rule to fourth day NT (Bower for defdt). Hil [26 Jan 1786]: on hearing counsel on both sides, rule discharged (Bower for defdt, Bearcroft for prosr).

Affidavit for prosecution:

Mich 26 Geo III 1785

[1] Affdt of Joseph Foster, age 47, chapemaker (buckle chapefiler), his wife, Mary Foster, age 46, both of Stafford, and Thomas Green, age 28, farmer and former constable of Darlaston, sworn before Henry Smith at Darlaston 17 Oct 1785. ITKB [*Mary Foster signed with a mark.*]

[Mary Foster]: That during the month of June, Mary Fisher, wife of John Fisher of Darlaston, borrowed a silk bonnet from her sister Ann, wife of William Yardley of Darlaston, at the request of the deponent, who wished to use it as a pattern.

[Thomas Green]: That as constable, he brought Mary Foster before Gough at Perry Barr 8 July, on his summons [*annexed, no. 1*], on a complaint of obtaining the bonnet from Mary Fisher on false pretenses.

[All]: That at the hearing of 8 July, Mary Fisher confessed that the bonnet was borrowed for the reason given and Gough released Mary Foster, dismissing the complaint.

[Thomas Green]: That he apprehended Foster 20 July on Gough's second warrant [*annexed, no. 2*] for defrauding Mary Fisher of the bonnet on false pretenses.

[All]: That Gough insisted 20 July that Mary Foster give up the bonnet and pay 18*s* costs. When she refused he committed her to Wolverhampton house of correction and issued a warrant for distraint of the costs and the costs of levying. That on that warrant [*annexed, no. 3*] Green delivered Mary Foster to the house of correction at Wolverhampton where she stayed until 25 July, when she was again taken before Gough for further examination. On this occasion William Griffiths gunlockfiler of Darlaston went with the Fosters as a neighbour and friend; Gough turned him out, saying he was there to swear falsely. Gough asked John Foster whether he had sought the advice of legal counsel; on being told he had, Gough blamed him, dismissed the complaint, and released Mary Foster.

[Thomas Green]: That Gough then asked whether the warrant for distress had been executed; told that it had not, he asked for its return and kept it.

[Mary Foster]: That when she had done with the bonnet she returned it to Yardley as she had always intended.

[*Annexed*]: No.1 Gough to the constable of Darlaston, 4 July 1785, to summon Mary Foster for obtaining the bonnet with false pretenses, intent to defraud Mary Fisher; No. 2, 19 July 1785 to bring her before him on the oath of Mary Fisher for defrauding her of the bonnet and refusing to deliver it up; No. 3, 20 July 1785 warrant of commitment to Wolverhampton house of correction until further examination on Monday 25 July.

Sources: KB 1/24 Mich 26 Geo III no. 2. KB 21/44 Mich, Hil 26 Geo III.

B.10 Information against a justice, refused (25 Oct 1785)

Defendant: John Gough esquire, JP for Staffordshire, of Perry Hall, Handsworth.

Accusation:
Misdemeanour in his office of magistrate, in improperly confining James Walters locksmith, William Offley latchmaker, and Lewis Wootton whitesmith, and committing Offley and Wootton to Wolverhampton house of correction, Oct 1785.

Rules and process:
Mich 1785: affdt [1] filed. ST [8 Nov 1785]: on affdt [1] rule nisi to [21 Nov] (Leycester). ST [21 Nov 1785]: enlarged peremptory rule to second day NT (Bower, for defdt). Hil 1786: affdt [2] filed. ST [26 Jan 1786]: on hearing counsel on both sides, rule discharged (Bower for defdt, Bearcroft for prosr).

Affidavit for prosecution:

Mich 26 Geo III 1785

[1] Affdt of John Walters age 44 locksmith, James Walters age 18 locksmith and son of John Walters, William Offley age 20 latchmaker, Lewis Wootton age 24 whitesmith, Joshua Fletcher age 67 padlock maker, all of Willenhall, sworn before Henry Smith at Willenhall 25 Oct 1785; and Richard Hadley age 40 coffin handle maker [and constable of Willenhall] sworn before Henry Smith at Wolverhampton 26 Oct 1785. ITKB [*William Offley and Lewis Wootton signed with a mark.*]
　　[John Walters, James Walters, Offley, Wootton]: That returning from Walsall Wake about 9pm 28 Sept last with Samuel Tonks, William Lyons, Richard Clewly, Isaac Clewly, Sarah Atkins, Elizabeth Atkins, Elizabeth Robinson and other neighbours, they met the Walsall carrier's waggon near Park Brook. The waggoner shortly after called out that he had been robbed. Walter Lane the elder, Walter Lane the younger and some others then ran by as if escaping. The deponent John Walters said it was a pity that all thieves could not be caught, on which Lane the elder seized him by the coat and asked what he meant. Lane struck Richard Clewly and Lane the younger knocked Isaac Clewly down; he was kicked by one of Lane's party. William Lyons, enraged by this, said 'who was tried at Derby for stealing the silver tankard', alluding to Lane the younger, who knocked him to the ground. None of these deponents fought.
　　[Richard Hadley]: That he took James Walters, Wootton and Offley before Gough 1 Oct, on his summons from Lane the elder's complaint.

Gough kept the summons, and would not hear them as they were ten minutes early; he said this deponent should not see and hear what he did.

[John Walters, James Walters, Wootton, Offley, Hadley]: That Gough refused to hear Elizabeth Atkins, Sarah Atkins, and Elizabeth Robinson for the deponents, or their own statements.

[James Walters, Wootton, Offley]: That Gough held them at the Boar's Head, which he owns, under the guard of two of his servants, and later two others. Next morning Joseph Scott, constable of Barr, stood guard, until 3 Oct. Brought before Gough, they were sent back to the pub as Lane the elder was absent. Brought before Gough again, they were again sent back to custody till next morning. Gough refused testimony from the deponent Fletcher or Thomas Myott farmer of Willenhall.

[John Walters]: That Lane the elder offered 4 Oct to drop the complaint on payment of 17s; deponent agreed, having been held four days, with Gough threatening prison and refusing their witnesses. He claimed 5s from Lane the elder and 2s from deponent, which he paid. Offley and Wootton were held, unable to pay their share of the £3 12s 6d constable's charges, much more than they ate or drank, and more than this deponent could raise.

[John Walters, James Walters, Wootton and Offley]: That they were held until 5 Oct.

[John Walters]: That he could raise only £1 6s; Gough discharged him for that sum.

[Wootton and Offley]: That Gough ordered them to Wolverhampton house of correction unless each paid one guinea. Wolverhampton quarter sessions freed them 6 Oct.

[Joshua Fletcher]: The evening of 5 Oct he received from Joseph Scott two warrants of commitment; true copies are annexed. Scott also delivered to him the prisoners, and a written order from Gough [No. 3]. They were unable to pay the guinea each; he delivered prisoners and warrants to the keeper of Wolverhampton house of correction.

[*Annexed*]: No. 1. Gough to Joshua Fletcher constable of Willenhall, 5 Oct 1785. Lewis Wootton of Willenhall to provide sureties to keep the peace against Walter Lane, the elder, or to be remanded to Wolverhampton house of correction until such sureties are provided.

No. 2. The same, re John Offle (William Offley).

No. 3. Gough to Joshua Fletcher constable of Willenhall, 5 Oct 1785: 'If these two prisoners that are brought to you can find and pay to Joseph Scott or you one guinea each, you may release them as Walter Lane is agreeable to have them released if they pay the expenses.'

Affidavit for defence:

Hil 26 Geo III 1786

[2] Affdt of Walter Lane cabinet locksmith and his wife Elizabeth, both of Wednesfield, Mary Dry, wife of James Dry tailor of Willenhall, Abel Gravenor woodcutter of Willenhall, John Gough esquire JP, William Dawes yeoman, and Joseph Scott constable of Perry Barr, all of Perry Barr, sworn before Charles Woodward at Perry Hall 13 Jan 1786. ITKB 'Between James Walters and others and John Gough esquire.' [*Elizabeth Lane, Mary Dry, Abel Gravenor and William Dawes signed with a mark.*]

[Walter Lane and Elizabeth Lane]: That while on the road from Walsall to Willenhall the evening of 28 Sept 1785, they saw several persons, among them James Walters, William Offley, and Lewis Wootton, assaulting Abel Gravenor near Bentley in Aldridge, half a mile beyond Park Brook. The deponent Walter Lane called out 'in the name of God are you killing the man' on which several knocked the deponent down and much abused him on the road to the bridge which crosses the Willenhall road to Darlaston. James Walters said 'Damn his eyes we will either have his life or his money'; Lewis Wootton knocked the deponent down and William Offley called out 'damn him, skin him.' James Dry and his wife were also present. Walters, Offley and Lewis Wootton continued to abuse the deponent Lane all the way to Willenhall chapel. The deponents stayed the night at Dry's house fearing further harm to the deponent Walter Lane. The deponents were not at the affray at Park Brook, nor are guilty of any of the charges in the affidavit of John Walters.

[Walter Lane]: That he swore an information 30 Sept 1785 before John Gough to obtain a warrant against Walter, Wootton and Offley, who were brought before Gough 1 Oct and ordered to provide sureties to keep the peace. When they said they could not do so until Monday, Gough ordered them kept at the Boar's Head Inn in Perry Barr in the custody of Joseph Scott until Monday 3 Oct in order to save the expense of sending them to the Wolverhampton house of correction and bringing them back. Gough did refuse to hear the evidence of Elizabeth Atkins, Sarah Atkins, and Elizabeth Robinson for the defendants because Mary Dry who had been present said that none of them were present at the most serious assault, at the bridge, which deponent believes to be true. In the evening of 3 Oct John Walters father of James Walters told him that John [*sic*] Fletcher and Thomas Myott were at the Boar's Head and would become bondsmen. He went to the Boar's Head but found that Fletcher and Myott were gone and none of the parties had got sureties. On 4 Oct, he, Walters, Offley, and Wootton agreed that if the three would sign a public apology (annexed, C) and pay the expenses of the advertisement, attendance of Scott and Dawes, and house expenses at the Boar's Head (between £3 and £4), and deponent's expenses of 17s, he would stop all further proceedings. John Walters, father of James Walters, paid his son's expenses. Offley and Wootton, being unable to pay their expenses, were remanded by Gough to the Wolverhampton house of correction. When he attended Michaelmas quarter sessions to proceed with articles of the peace or an indictment against Offley and Wootton, he found that they had been discharged by the court.

[Mary Dry]: That as she rode on before the wife of Walter Lane the elder to Willenhall 28 Sept she got down from the horse to examine two long pieces of iron lying in the road; a waggoner who came up told her some one had pulled it off his waggon. She rode a half mile further and came across the affray at Bentley. [*Substantiates Walter Lane and Elizabeth Lane's account of the assaults there and a mile further down the road.*] She is confident that no other women whatsoever were near enough to see or properly know the circumstances. That evening she heard somebody say 'damn him, we'll skin him' and saw James Walters about her husband's house. Elizabeth Atkins declared to this deponent that she was not present at the assault nor knew anything about it, but came to the justice with the prisoners to keep them company.

[Abel Gravenor]: That going from Walsall races he and Walter Lane were beaten 28 Sept by Walters, Offley and Wootton. [*Substantiates Walter and Elizabeth Lane's testimony, and that of Mary Dry that no other women were present.*]

[John Gough]: That Walter Lane applied for the warrant 30 Sept, when deponent took his information. Before the defendants appeared 1 Oct, Lane made another information: both are annexed marked B. When they were brought before him that day, he refused to examine Elizabeth and Sarah Atkins and Elizabeth Robinson as witnesses on behalf of Walters et al because Mary Dry swore and deponent believed that they were not present when the second assault occurred. He may have told Richard Hadley what was deposed, because he did conceive him to be a very busy and inquisitive person, but Hadley was present all the time the deponent first had Walters, Wootton and Offley before him, and never came again with them. When they could not find sureties he ordered them detained at the Boar's Head in Perry until they could find sureties or settle, Willenhall being eight miles from this deponent's house, and the Boar's Head only a mile. They came before him twice Monday 3 Oct, Walter Lane not being present. Two men who might have been Fletcher and Myott came with them, but offered no defence nor offered to become bound for the defendants. The prisoners asked to remain at the Boar's Head until they compromised the matter or found sureties. Whoever wanted to speak to them had free access. On the agreement of 4 Oct Walters was released, but Wootton and Offley not being able to raise money for expenses, or give sureties, were committed. He sent word to Lane that he could attend quarter sessions, which were the next day, to exhibit articles or prefer an indictment. He has acted according to what in his conscience he thought the duty of his office, without favour, malice or affection.

[Joseph Scott and William Dawes]: They twice took Walters, Wootton and Offley before Gough 3 Oct; on one occasion Fletcher and Myott were present, although not Walter Lane, which is why Gough refused to examine them. Neither offered in their presence to become bound. The three were sent back by Gough until they could provide sureties. The agreement of 4 Oct included payment of expenses of £3 12s 6d. Walters's father paid a third. Wootton and Offley stayed at the Boar's Head at their request while finding sureties; Gough otherwise would have committed them on the Monday. Walters, Wootton and Offley were repeatedly taken before Gough because they repeatedly expressed their expectation of someone coming to be security for them. Their expenses were high because many friends visited them at the Boar's Head, and ate and drank at their expense.

[*Annexed documents*]:

B: Information and complaint of Walter Lane that he was assaulted by John Offle (William Offley) padlock maker, James Walters locksmith, and Lewis Wootton boltmaker, praying sureties of the peace because he fears they will do so again. Sworn before Gough 1 Oct 1785.

Information and complaint of Walter Lane that John Offle (William Offley) James Walters, and Lewis Wootton violently assaulted the complainant 28 Sept 1785 without any just cause or provocation. Sworn before John Gough 30 Sept 1785.

C: 'We whose Nemes [*sic*] under are manetion [*sic*], Lewis Wotton [*sic*], William Offley, James Werters [*sic*] for assaulting Walter Lane on the 28 of Sept 1785 on the King's Highway in the parish of Wednesfield in the County of Stafford do hereby acknolege [*sic*] themselves in a Fault and beg his Pardon and pay the Charges.' [*Signed and witnessed by* Joseph Scott *and* Robert Scott.]

Sources: KB 1/24 Hil 26 Geo III, Mich 26 Geo III no. 2. KB 21/44 Mich, Hil 26 Geo III.

B.11 Information against a justice, refused without costs (7 May 1787)

Defendant: John Marsh esquire, JP of Staffordshire, of the Lloyd in the parish of Penn.

Accusation:
Misdemeanour in the office of magistrate, in unlawfully convicting and imprisoning William James.[30]

Rules and process:
Ea 1787: affdts [1], [2] filed. ST [18 May 1787]: on affdts [1] and [2], rule nisi to FNT for an information (Bower). Trin 1787: affdts [3], [4] filed. ST [15 June 1787]: rule discharged without costs (Bower for prosr, Leycester for defdt).

Affidavits for prosecution:

Ea 27 Geo III 1787

[1] Affdt of William James toymaker of Birmingham, sworn before W. H. Ashhurst[31] at his chambers in Serjeants' Inn, Chancery Lane (London) 7 May 1787. ITKB [*Verso*]: 'In the Ks Bench Affidt of Wm James For a certiorari to remove conviction Fosr Bower, Bolton Agent Temple.'

That there is an annual fair in Wolverhampton which lasts for eight to ten days and a market every Wednesday. On Wednesday 12 July 1786 the deponent offered for sale metal toys, mostly crafted by himself, at the fair and market. Once he opened his stall he was approached by two unknown men who asked to see his licence. He replied that he need not have one if the goods were of his making or sold on a fair day. He showed them a copy of the Hawkers and Pedlars Act[32] and offered to point out the appropriate clause. They left and later returned, asking that he accompany them before a justice of the peace. He refused; they returned once again, seized him, and took him before Marsh.

The deponent protested that he never sold retail except at fairs or on market days, which he had the right to do under clause 10 of the Act. Marsh ignored his protests and convicted the deponent in £10, offering to mitigate the penalty to £5, but because the deponent would not pay and had no goods or chattels in Marsh's jurisdiction, he committed him to Wolverhampton house of correction for six months. After serving three months the deponent was released upon the instructions of Marsh. He then sued Marsh for trespass, assault and false imprisonment at the last assizes, but was nonsuited when Marsh produced the record of conviction annexed in which he falsely stated the circumstances.

---

30 Note that the verso of affdt [1] shows that it was originally filed as an application for certiorari on the conviction.
31 A puisne justice of King's Bench 1770 to 1799.
32 25 Geo III, c.78.

[*Annexed*]: Record of conviction of James by John Marsh JP 12 July 1786 on the information of James Hordern, draper of Wolverhampton, who swore that James, a hawker, pedlar and petty chapman, travelled on foot from town to town selling iron and steel wares, and on 12 July set up a stall in Wolverhampton, a market town, without the licence required by the act of 25 Geo III. James is not a worker of metals, nor is his normal abode in Wolverhampton; he offered the defence that he had made some of the goods and was thus entitled to sell all his wares. On the testimony of William Fregleton, mercer of Wolverhampton, a credible witness, James is convicted and fined £10.

[2] Affdt of Joseph Lane yeoman of Birmingham (Warws), sworn before John Richards at Birmingham 10 May 1787. ITKB [*Verso*]: '49 East 87 Staffordshire In the Ks Bench. Affidt of Service of Notice of Motn for an informatn agt John Marsh Esq 18 May R nisi Bolton Agent Temple fo:4.'
    That the deponent served Marsh with a copy of the annexed[33] notice 2 May 1787.
    [*Annexed*]: Notice 2 May 1787 by John Richards, attorney for William James, to John Marsh that the court will be moved 14 May for a rule nisi for unlawfully convicting James and causing him to be imprisoned for not paying the fine.
    Notice 4 May 1787 by Richards to Marsh [*to the same effect*].

Affidavits for defence:

Trin 27 Geo III 1787

[3] Affdt of John Marsh esquire and JP for Stafford of the Lloyd in the parish of Penn, Thomas Clarke locksmith of Chapel Ash in Wolverhampton, John Hanbury draper of Wolverhampton, and Charles James perukemaker of Wolverhampton, sworn before William Chrees at Wolverhampton 2 June 1787. ITKB [*Verso*]: '20 Trin 87 Staffords. Affs to sh c agt rl ni for infn ag John Marsh Esq 15 June R discharged without costs Price fo:12.'
    [John Marsh]: That on 12 July 1786 he was sitting, pursuant to his office, at the Cock and Bell. The three other deponents were present when William James was brought in to answer the information of Hordern. James relied on the defence that he made some of the goods and therefore could sell all of them. After the conviction the deponent advised James that he could appeal the decision to quarter sessions and for surety could leave his goods in the constable's hands. This advice went unheeded.

---

[33] Two notices of different dates are filed.

[All]: That James did not say that he only sold others' wares at fairs or on market days nor did he claim an exemption under section 10 of the Act. During the proceedings James behaved in a very daring and insolent manner and sat with John Marsh with his hat on, drinking liquor and treating him with much indignity, insisting that he had a right to do so, as it was a public house. Because William James refused to pay the penalty Marsh committed him to the house of correction.

[4] Affdt of John Marsh esquire and JP of the Lloyd in the parish of Penn, sworn before William Chrees at the Lloyd 12 June 1787. ITKB

That when William James was brought before him he did not know that James had claimed the benefit of section 10 of the Hawkers and Pedlars Act, nor did he know of the transactions James had with the two persons in Wolverhampton market nor who the two men were.

Sources: KB 1/25 Ea 27 Geo III, Trin 27 Geo III bdl 20. KB 21/44 pp. 340, 364.

B.12 Information moved against two justices, exhibited against one (9 Nov 1791)

Defendants: Sir Nigel Bowyer Gresley baronet of Drakelow (Derbs), and the Reverend James Falconer DD of the Cathedral Close Lichfield, JPs for Staffordshire.

Information:
Hil 32 Geo III 1792 [23 Jan 1792]

[1] At Tatenhill 19 Sept [1791], in licensing sessions, corruptly and maliciously refused a licence without cause to Edward Allsopp innholder of Tatenhill, who had held one for ten years, Allsopp being ready to enter a recognizance with sufficient sureties; [2] [*Gresley only*]; [3] [*Gresley only; no mention of recognizances and sureties*]. [34]

---

[34] The full version of this lengthy information appears as a precedent in the Appendix of forms in Hands, 97–103. *The Times* reports the rule nisi on 21 Nov 1791. Samuel Pipe-Wolferstan reported in his diary that he had had news of Stafford assizes from a friend, including 'Hand v Sir Nigel Gresley etc' (SRO, D1527, 23 March 1792). ASSI 4/8 Lent 1792 notes a verdict for a plaintiff in an action in King's Bench, for trespass: Hand v Gresley, damages £5 5s., costs 40s. But there is no record of a trial or verdict for the Allsopp case, which presumably was settled.

Rules and process:
Mich [18 Nov 1791]: on affdts [1] to [9], rule nisi to [26 Nov 1791] (Shepherd). ST [26 Nov 1791] enlarged rule nisi to fifth day NT, on undertaking of defdts to appear immediately, and that prosr may give rules to plead as if such appearance had been this term (Shepherd for prosr, Leycester for defdts). Hil [3 Feb 1792]: on defence affdts [10] to [14], rule against Falconer discharged; rule absolute against Gresley (Erskine for prosr, Bearcroft for defdt). ST: summons to Gresley. ST [4 Feb 1792]: first rule to plead (side bar) to [7 Feb]. ST: appears; prays a day to answer; leave to imparl; pleads not guilty; venire facias juratores. ST [10 Feb 1792]: rule for a special jury, instance of defdt (Leycester). ST 14 Feb 1792: notice of trial for the King (Dealtry).

Affidavits for prosecution:

Mich 32 Geo III 1791

[1] Affdt of Edward Allsopp and his wife Elizabeth tavernkeepers of Barton Turn, township of Barton under Needwood in the parish of Tatenhill, sworn before Henry Smith at Barton Turn 9 Nov 1791. ITKB [*Verso*]: '59 Mic 91. Staff 9 Affits for Infn ag Sir Nigel Bowyer Gresley Bart & anot. Affidavit of Edward Allsopp & Elizabeth his wife. 19 Not R nisi Leeson fo:23.'
   [Edward Allsopp]: That he was a tavernkeeper in his present public house[35] for 18 years and for 10 years before that in Burton upon Trent. In Nov or Dec 1790, the master of a canal boat left five or six empty rum puncheons in his yard and told William Brown, the deponent's servant, that they were for Gresley, who resided four miles away. The deponent's yard is not a public wharf, nor was he paid for storing the casks. Brown informed Gresley's servant but they were not picked up for over a month. In the meantime, to the best of the deponent's knowledge, one was blown into the canal, and could not be found. On hearing of this Gresley instructed his servant to demand payment; the deponent refused.
   [Elizabeth Allsopp]: That in April 1791 Gresley came when her husband was away and demanded payment. She refused because they did not keep a public wharf and the cask was not lost owing to their neglect. Gresley replied that they would never have another licence.
   [Edward Allsopp]: That when he was denied his licence on 19 Sept by Gresley and Falconer, the only justices present, he said, 'Gentlemen

---

[35] William Yates's 1775 map of the county, surveyed from 1769, identifies it as a coffee house.

I am informed I am not to have a Licence pray what have I done'; Gresley answered 'that he was never so ill-used by any person as by [Allsopp's] wife and therefore he would not sign the licence' and Falconer said 'Mr. Desbrow speaks very slightly of your wife and therefore I will not sign the licence and you don't take care of people's goods and you don't deserve a licence'.

[Elizabeth Allsopp]: That she went to see Mr Desbrow, a justice at Walton upon Trent (Derbs), who denied he had spoken slightingly of her and said that he knew of no tavernkeepers to whom he would sooner give a licence. He gave her an unsealed letter for Falconer to this effect, which she showed to her husband and to John Meek, gentleman of Dunstall, before posting. Desbrow had declined making an affidavit in this cause.

[Edward Allsopp]: That he believes that Gresley and Falconer cannot give evidence of any instances of misconduct by the deponents in their 18 years of business.

[2] Affdt of John Meek, age about 57, gentleman of Dunstall in the parish of Tatenhill, sworn before Henry Smith at Barton Turn 9 Nov 1791. ITKB

That he has known Edward Allsopp and his wife Elizabeth for over 30 years. For the past 18 years, until Sept 1791, Allsopp kept a public house at Barton Turn and before that kept a public house at Burton upon Trent. Allsopp and his wife Elizabeth are of good character and reputation and conduct themselves with propriety.

Sometime about April 1791, the deponent called at the house of Allsopp and found Gresley talking with Elizabeth; he insisted he be paid for the lost cask. Elizabeth replied that such repayment would be a 'great hardship' to her husband.

Gresley told the deponent about the cask and his expected repayment, and then asked Elizabeth if ale was sold at the house. She said yes. Gresley replied 'you shall never have another licence unless your husband finds or pays for the lost cask'.

On 20 Sept 1791, Elizabeth showed the deponent a letter which she said was written by Mr Desbrow of Walton upon Trent to Falconer. [*Substantiates account of the letter given in affdt [1].*]

[3] Affdt of William Brown maltster and his wife Mary of Burton Extra, otherwise known as Bound End in the parish of Burton upon Trent, sworn before Henry Smith at Burton upon Trent 9 Nov 1791. ITKB

[William Brown]: That he lived as a servant with Edward Allsopp at Barton Turn from 25 March to Michaelmas last. In Nov or Dec 1790, a man brought five empty casks or puncheons by boat along the canal adjoining Allsopp's yard, placing the casks in the yard. The man told the deponent they were for Gresley, giving him a written note which he gave to a servant of Gresley a few days later, asking the servant to inform him.

[Mary Brown]: That she lived as a servant with Allsopp at Barton Turn for three years until Michaelmas last. In April 1791, she saw Gresley talking with Elizabeth and John Meek about a lost cask. She heard Meek say Allsopp did not keep a public dock and had tried to find the lost cask. She twice heard Gresley tell Elizabeth that if her husband did not find or pay for the cask 'he shall never have another licence'.

[4] Affdt of Elizabeth Arkers spinster of Barton Turn, township of Barton under Needwood in the parish of Tatenhill, sworn before Henry Smith at Barton Turn 9 Nov 1791. ITKB

That in Nov 1790 she became Edward Allsopp's servant and continues to live with him in that capacity. In April 1791 Gresley came to her master's house and told Elizabeth Allsopp that if her husband did not find or pay for the lost cask 'he should never have another licence'.

[5] Affdt of Henry Evans merchant of Burton upon Trent, sworn before Henry Smith at Burton 9 Nov 1791. ITKB

That the deponent has known Allsopp and his wife for over 28 years. For the last seven years the deponent has been bookkeeping and accounts clerk at Burton Company, of which he is a partner. During the whole time he has known the Allsopps they have conducted themselves with propriety and are of good character and reputation.

[6] Affdt of Owen Lloyd clerk of Stapenhill (Derbs), sworn before John Fowler at Burton upon Trent 9 Nov 1791. ITKB

That the deponent has been vicar of Stapenhill for the last 24 years and that he has resided there 21 years, within one mile of Burton. Since becoming vicar he has known Edward Allsopp and his wife Elizabeth for six years as publicans in Burton, and for the last 18 years at Barton Turn.

The whole time they have behaved with propriety and are of good character and reputation, and proper persons to hold a licence to sell ale and beer.

[7] Affdt of William Whitaker clerk, minister of the chapel of Barton under Needwood, John Turner and William Nichols, churchwardens of same, John Biddulph esquire, Thomas Webb gentleman, Moses Birch surgeon, John Holland gentleman, John Whiting farmer, William

Mousley draper, all of Barton under Needwood in the parish of Tatenhill; and William Wetton gentleman of Dunstall in the parish of Tettenhall [*sic*], sworn before Henry Smith in the township of Barton under Needwood 9 Nov 1791. ITKB

[All]: That they have known Allsopp and his wife as publicans at Barton Turn for upwards of 18 years. They have behaved with great propriety and are of good character and reputation, proper persons to sell ale and beer. It would be a convenience to the neighbourhood and travelers if Edward Allsopp was permitted to continue keeping a public house at Barton Turn.

[8] Affdt of the Reverend Thomas Gisborne clerk of Yoxall Lodge in Needwood Forest, sworn before Henry Smith at Yoxall Lodge 9 Nov 1791. ITKB

That the deponent has known Allsopp and his wife for over six years and for the whole time they have behaved with great propriety and have been of good character.

[9] Affdt of William Osborne the younger, gentleman of Burton upon Trent, sworn before Henry Smith at Burton 9 Nov 1791. ITKB

That the annexed notices were given to Gresley and Falconer on 13 Oct 1791 at Wychnor Bridges.

[*Annexed*]: Notice to Falconer by Daniel Dalrymple and William Osborne the younger, attorneys for Edward Allsopp, 12 Oct 1791 that they would move King's Bench for a criminal information in Michaelmas 1791 for refusing on 19 Sept 1791 to grant a licence to Allsopp to sell victuals ale and beer. [*Similar notice by Edward Allsopp 12 Oct 1791*, and *two notices to Gresley otherwise identical to the others.*]

Affidavits for defence:

Hil 32 Geo III 1792

[10] Affdt of Sir Nigel Bowyer Gresley baronet and JP for Staffordshire of Drakelow (Derbs), sworn before Thomas Hinckley at Lichfield 11 Jan 1792. ITKB 'The King agst Sir Nigel Bowyer Gresley baronet and another.' [*Verso*]: '2 Hil 92 Staff. In the King's Bench. 4 Affids sh c agt Infn Sir Nigel Bowyer Gresley Bart & anot. The King agst Sir N.B. Gresley & another: affidavit of deft Gresley 27 Jany Dichd agt James Falconer DD Abs Sir N.B. Gresley.'

That the deponent had six casks left on Edward Allsopp's wharf, believing it to be a public wharf. Later, one cask was found to be missing. He suspected that it had been stolen or hidden, having some time before lost nearly eleven tons of coal out of 20 left there. The circumstances and the impertinence of Elizabeth Allsopp caused the deponent to tell her that 'she seemed to be above keeping an inn and if so they had better be without it'; she replied that she did not care if they lost their licence. The deponent responded that he would not renew it next licensing day; he does not recall that he ever threatened not to renew if the missing cask were not returned. If he did so, it was in the anger of the moment. He did not refuse the licence solely because of the cask. At the last assizes for Staffordshire Justice Heath charged the grand jury to reduce the number of public houses, to which he ascribed many of the offences to be tried, and to be very circumspect in granting licences. The deponent and Dr Falconer met at Wychnor Inn 19 Sept for licensing, where they discussed Heath's charge and the deponent acquainted Falconer with Elizabeth Allsopp's impertinence and the fact that she did not care if the licence was lost. They concluded that it was a licence proper not to be renewed. Edward Allsopp said he was contented to have no licence and left. The deponent and Falconer thought that eight public houses in an area with only four small villages, and few other people (because bounded by Needwood and the Trent) were too many. Denying this licence accorded with the deponent's constant policy to reduce the number of public houses.

[11] Affdt of the Reverend James Falconer Doctor in Divinity, Cathedral Close, Lichfield and JP for Staffordshire, sworn before Thomas Hinckley 11 Jan 1792. ITKB 'The King agst Sir Nigel Bowyer Gresley baronet and another.' [*Verso*]: 'Staff. In the King's Bench. The King agst Sir N.B. Gresley Bart & ano: affidavit of Deft Falconer. Hodges fo:21.'

That at the last Staffordshire assizes there was a long calendar of prisoners to be tried, and the deponent believes Justice Heath observed that the great number of public houses was the source of most of the evils in society and strongly recommended reducing the number of licences.

The public house of Edward Allsopp at Barton Turn is bounded on one side by Needwood Forest and on the other side by the River Trent. There is no great road through the township except that from Barton to Lichfield, and the Allsopp house stands alone. [*Substantiates affdt [8] that there are eight public houses and describes where they are.*] The deponent believes that there are more public houses than are needed for the convenience of the public or the neighbourhood, and that public houses on the border of the Forest have frequently harboured deer stealers and poachers.

The deponent and Gresley met on 19 Sept 1791 at Wychnor Bridges Inn, discussed Justice Heath's comments [*above*], and agreed to comply with them. Gresley then said that Allsopp's wife had told him she did not care whether a licence was granted or not, and that 'she rather wished not to continue in the business'. The deponent then said 'it was a proper house to decline licensing'. This was the first time that the deponent heard of the differences between Gresley and Allsopp.

Edward Allsopp told the deponent and Gresley that 'he was well satisfied without a licence as with one' or words to that effect. No further application for licence was made to the deponent. At the same meeting he and Gresley refused to grant licences to a public house at Haunton and another at Edingale.

At the time of the meeting he believed that the complaint of Desborow was made against Elizabeth, but had since found that the complaint was against another person. He did not discover his mistake nor receive Desborow's letter until some days after 20 Sept 1791, when the time for licensing had passed. It was only Heath's recommendations and Gresley's account of Elizabeth's indifference to keeping the public house that caused him to refuse the licence. He was not prompted by personal motives, and acted honestly and sincerely according to his duty as magistrate.

The deponent believes Allsopp would not have brought the action had John Meek, Allsopp's partner as maltster and cheesefactor, not persuaded him to do so. The deponent has acted as JP for Staffordshire for upwards of 16 years.

[12] Affdt of John Jackson the younger, bookseller and stationer of Lichfield, sworn before William Gill the younger at Lichfield 31 Dec 1791. ITKB 'The King agst Sir Nigel Bowyer Gresley baronet and another.' [*Verso*]: 'Staff. In the King's Bench. The King agt Sir N B Gresley Bart and anor: Affidavit. Hodges fo. 6.'

That sometime in Nov 1791 the deponent was travelling between Burton and Lichfield with Edward Allsopp. The conversation was chiefly about Allsopp's motion in King's Bench. Allsopp said he had friends, including John Meek, who 'would see him through the business or he should not have begun it'. The deponent believes that Meek and Allsopp are partners as maltsters and cheesefactors. He has seen notes in trade under the name 'Allsopp and Co.' which is understood in the neighborhood to consist of Meek and Allsopp, both trades being carried on at the house of Allsopp at Barton Turn.

During another conversation, Allsopp told the deponent that the chief use of Allsopp's house as a public house was 'for the accommodation of persons bringing things to his house as it would otherwise be an expense to him in treating such persons', and that otherwise he did not care for his licence.

[13] Affdt of the Reverend Thomas Gisborne clerk of Yoxall Lodge in Needwood Forest, sworn before John P. Dyott at Yoxall Lodge 27 Dec 1791. ITKB 'The King agst Sir Nigel Bowyer Gresley baronet and another.' [*Verso*]: 'Staff. In the King's Bench. The King agst Sir N.B. Gresley Bart & another: Affidavit. Hodges fo. 4.'

That a few years ago, because of gross irregularities in some of the public houses in the township of Barton and because of the number of public houses, the deponent asked the magistrates of Staffordshire to withhold licences from certain public houses, which they did. At the same time the deponent was told by the principal inhabitants that Allsopp's public house was of very little use to the township. The deponent believes there are now enough public houses to serve the inhabitants and occasional travellers.

[14] Affdt of Henry Mould victualler of Burton upon Trent, sworn before John Fowler at Burton upon Trent 16 Jan 1792. ITKB 'The King against Sir Nigel Bowyer Gresley barnonet and another.' [*Verso*]: '5 Hil 92 Staff. Addl Afft to sh c. agt Infn agt Sir Nigel Bowyer Gresley Bart and anr: The King agt Gresley and anr. Affidavit of Henry Mould. 27 Jany. Disch. agt James Falconer DD. Abs & Sir N B Gresley. Hodges Clements Inn fo. 3.'

That on 19 Sept 1791 the deponent was present at Robert Shorthouse's public house at Wychnor Bridges at the licensing sessions for the Hundred of Offlow North. He heard Edward Allsopp say he 'did not care a half penny' whether he had a licence or not.

Sources: IND 1/6664 Hil 32 Geo III fol.9. KB 1/27 Hil 32 Geo III no. 1, bdl 2, Mich 32 Geo III no. 1, bdl 59. KB 11/57 Hil 32 Geo III 1792 #15. KB 15/5 Hil 32 Geo III. KB 15/16 Hil 32 Geo III. KB 21/45 pp. 517, 534, 549, 560, 568. KB 28/360 roll 14. KB 29/451 Hil 32 Geo III.

B.13 Information against a justice, refused (12 Jan 1795)

Defendant: Bernard Coombe, surgeon, apothecary, and chief magistrate of the borough of Newcastle under Lyme.

Accusation:
Acting under 34 Geo III, c.13 without authority, and 'other misconduct and illegal practices' in execution of his office.

Rules and process:
Hil [6 Feb 1795] on affdts [1] to [5], rule nisi to FNT (Manley). Ea [6 May 1795] enlarged rule nisi to [11 May], on condition that if an information

is filed, defdt will appear to it within four days (Manley for prosr, Leycester for defdt). ST [15 May] on defence affdts [6] to [8], rule discharged (Manley; Leycester).

Affidavits for prosecution:

Hil 35 Geo III 1795

[*Wrapper*]: '12 Hil 95 England Bucks 3 Affts for Ha Cor for John Liversage 26 Jan, Ha Cor. Heath fo. 24.'

[1] Affdt of John Liversage, shoemaker of Newcastle under Lyme, sworn before Joseph Gibson at Newcastle 4 Feb 1795. ITKB [*Verso*]: 'King's Bench Staff. Affidt of John Liversage. Leigh fo:34.'

That in the Red Lion 1 Dec 1794, William Ensor ironmonger asked the deponent, who was drunk, to enlist; he was enticed with a guinea which he was told he could return in the morning. While waiting to see Ensor the following morning to return it, the deponent got drunk in the Red Lion. Once in Ensor's shop, he took the oath, which was administered by Coombe, who read the attestation and completed the signature of the deponent, who was too drunk to write. The articles of war were not read to him, and he remembers nothing else of that day until he arrived home and his brother, Robert Liversage, informed him that he had enlisted. He, his brother and several others went to Ensor's shop to remedy the situation. There they offered John Edensor [*sic*], William's stepson (for whom he was recruiting), his one guinea back in addition to 20s for the smart. Ensor refused the money, declaring 'it was not money but the man he wanted and the man he would have', and that he would not release the deponent for £50.

Edensor refused a similar offer 3 Dec, made before Joseph Adams esquire mayor, who then discharged the deponent from enlistment. Edensor arrived 5 Dec with soldiers under the command of two recruiting officers, William Ball esquire, and Gerard[36] Gosling esquire, and took the deponent to the office of the town clerk. On the way Ensor ordered a soldier to ready a chaise to transport the deponent to Stafford. Ball said that the deponent would be treated as a deserter, and threatened to horsewhip any attorney summoned by the deponent. As the town clerk was not present, the deponent was taken to the Red Lion where Coombe said he would wager £5 that the deponent was a soldier. At a hearing before Coombe and Adams that evening the deponent was represented by an attorney, as were Ensor, Edensor, Ball and Gosling,

---

[36] Spelled 'Gerrard' in other affdts.

who swore that the deponent was a soldier and thus subject only to military law. On behalf of the deponent it was argued that he was drunk, that the oath was administered too soon (by the terms of the Act), and that Coombe was not empowered to administer the oath as he was not the chief magistrate. Coombe said that if this was the law he would shield himself with custom, and he, Gosling, and Ball agreed to share the expense of any consequences. The mayor argued again that the deponent should be discharged, but the deponent was imprisoned. He was taken to the Red Lion 6 Dec, and only his wife was allowed to accompany him. There the town clerk Thomas Sparrow told the deponent that he 'must submit and go for a soldier'. He refused and was insulted by Coombe and by Ball, who called him a 'damned rascal' and threatened to have him flogged to death. On 8 Dec the deponent was forced, against his will, into a chaise, and carried and marched to Stamford (Lincs) where he told his story to the colonel, Newton Treen esq. When the deponent refused to put on a uniform (unless the law would compel him) because he was the sole provider for his wife and young family, he was put in irons and placed in close confinement. For four weeks and three days he was kept in a cell without light or fire, sleeping on bare boards without so much as a single blanket. He was given no meat or drink, and sometimes prevented from receiving food or drink from others, so that his life was in danger from cold and hunger. He was then transferred to a gaol in Buckingham, until he arrived in London on the writ of habeas corpus issued from King's Bench.[37]

[2] Affdt of Mary Liversage, wife of John Liversage shoemaker of Newcastle under Lyme, sworn before Joseph Gibson at Newcastle under Lyme 12 Jan 1795. ITKB [*Verso*]: 'England, Bucks. Heath fo. 35.'

That late on 1 Dec 1794, the deponent's husband, John Liversage, came home ill and in a drunken stupor. The next morning Liversage told her that William Ensor had paid him a guinea and he claimed to have enlisted Liversage in the army. The deponent's husband left before dawn to persuade Ensor to take back the guinea. He believed Ensor was not a soldier and was incapable of enlisting men. Between 8 and 9am the deponent found her husband exceedingly drunk at a pub next door to William Ensor's house, in company with John Edensor, a stepson of Ensor, who has authority to raise men for the Stamford volunteers. She warned Edensor not to swear her husband in his present condition. She returned one hour later and her husband informed her that 'they have sworn me'. She learned that Bernard Coombe, a JP, had

---

[37] Probably directed to the gaoler at Buckingham.

been brought over to administer the oath. Her husband was so drunk he could only sign part of his name. Coombe wrote the remainder.

Despite offering the return of the guinea that Liversage had received and a further 20s he offered to Ensor and Edensor, and despite the chief magistrate of the borough hearing all parties and discharging Liversage from being a soldier, Ensor, Edensor, Ball, and Gosling took Liversage into custody 5 Dec 1791. That evening, Joseph Adams esquire mayor of the borough, and Coombe ordered the deponent's husband to be brought before them. An attorney for Ensor, Ball, Edensor and Gosling, and another for Liversage, attended. The timing of the enlistment, the chief magistrate's discharge of Liversage, the offering of one guinea and the offer of 20s were offered as reasons for a discharge by the deponent's husband. It was contended by Ball and Gosling that because Liversage was sworn, the magistrate had no jurisdiction in the matter to which it was answered that the swearing did not appear to be legal because Coombe was not the chief magistrate of the borough. The mayor was satisfied with his former determination and Liversage remained in custody.

Gosling and Ball praised the ruling: if Liversage were discharged, most other men enlisted would have to be released. Liversage was imprisoned until 8 Dec, during which time he was often told to serve in the forces, and refused. He was called a 'damned rascal' and was told he deserved to be flogged to death. He was carried out of the borough to Stamford (Lincs) under the command of Newton Treen, imprisoned, fed only bread and water, and put in irons.

[3] Affdt of Joseph Jordan joiner, William Bailey hatter, Robert Liversage shoemaker, William Brett shoemaker, Elizabeth Liversage spinster, and Joseph Tittenson shoemaker, all of Newcastle under Lyme, sworn before Joseph Gibson at Newcastle 12 Jan 1795. ITKB [*Robert Liversage signed with a mark*].

[Joseph Jordan]: That between 7 and 8pm 2 Dec 1794 he was at the house of William Eccles called 'The Sign of the Red Lion' in Newcastle under Lyme in the company of John Liversage and others. Liversage had received a parcel of boiled dried herring on a plate and offered some to him. Liversage said he had been exceedingly drunk the night before and was so ill he could not eat. Liversage appeared disordered and drunk, his eyes inflamed, and his conversation confused and irregular.

[William Bailey]: That later that morning Liversage appeared to be greatly intoxicated. [*Corroborates Jordan's affdt.*] Liversage asked the deponent to drink with him. He and Liversage each had several glasses of good rum, and Liversage then drank a considerable quantity of ale.

He left the pub briefly, then returned, announcing that he had been made a soldier at the shop of William Ensor.

[Robert Liversage]: That he found John Liversage very drunk in the company of soldiers at the pub on 2 Dec 1794. The deponent and friends put him to bed at another pub where he slept for several hours. John Liversage then persuaded the deponent and others to go with him to William Ensor and John Edensor to return Ensor's money and 20s for expenses but they refused to take it.

He was informed 5 Dec 1794 that the soldiers had seized Liversage and taken him to the office of Mr Sparrow, town clerk. He heard Ensor declare he would commit John Liversage to Stafford. To suggestions that Liversage have an attorney, William Ball replied that he would horsewhip him, for he was a deserter.

[William Brett]: That he was present at the Red Lion on Friday evening 5 Dec 1794 when Liversage was imprisoned by Ensor, Edensor and Ball. The deponent believes Ball is an officer in his Majesty's service now recruiting in Newcastle under Lyme. Also present were Gerrard Gosling, who he believes is an officer in the Staffordshire [*sic*] Volunteers, Bernard Coombe JP, and an attorney for Liversage and another for the soldiers. [*Substantiates account in affdt [2] of the arguments made by John Liversage, Gosling and Ball and of the mayor upholding his decision.*] Liversage remains in prison in Stamford (Lincs).

[Elizabeth Liversage]: [*Substantiates affdt [2] with respect to the 'trial'.*]

[Joseph Tittenson]: That he was at the Red Lion between 9 and 10am 2 Dec 1794 and drank several pints of strong ale with Liversage. He also saw Liversage drink ale with other persons. Liversage confirmed his exceeding drunkenness the night before and appeared to be 'out of his mind' that morning. [*Substantiates William Bailey's account of Liversage returning to the pub as 'a soldier' and confirms William Brett's account of the hearing.*]

[All]: That William Ensor is a shopkeeper and housekeeper and they do not believe that at the time of enlisting John Liversage he was a soldier or that he was in his majesty's service. It has recently been a common practice in Newcastle under Lyme to swear men in immediately on enlistment and when they are in a state of intoxication.

[*Note at the bottom of the affdt*]: 'The said Robert Liversage having signed the affdt in my presence and seemed perfectly to understand the contents thereof before he was so sworn thereto. Joseph Gibson.'

Ea 35 Geo III 1795
[*Wrapper*]: 'East 95 King's Bench Staff. 2 addl afftd for infn & Bernard Coombe. Liversage agt Coombe: Affidt of Service of Notice of Motion. 6 Feb Rule Nisi. Leigh for Heath fo:4.'

[4] Affdt of Joseph Heath gentleman of Newcastle under Lyme, sworn before the court 26 Jan 1795. ITKB [*Verso*]: 'England Bucks. Heath fo:3.'

That 25 Jan 1795 the deponent received a letter in town dated at Buckingham 20 Jan informing him that John Liversage was in prison in the gaol at Buckingham, and that having heard nothing to the contrary believes Liversage still to be in the gaol.

[5] Affdt of Joseph Page gentleman of Newcastle under Lyme, sworn before Joseph Gibson at Newcastle 4 Feb 1795. ITKB [*Verso*]: 'Served the original of this copy upon the within named Bernard Coombe. 31st of Janry 1795. Page.'

That the annexed notice was given by the deponent to Coombe 31 Jan 1795.

[*Annexed*:] Notice by J. Heath, attorney for Liversage, 29 Jan 1795, that he would move King's Bench for a criminal information on 7 Feb, against Coombe, for acting under 34 Geo III, c.13 without authority, and for 'other misconduct and illegal practices' in the execution of his office.

Affidavits for defence:

Ea 35 Geo III 1795

[6] Affdt of Bernard Coombe, surgeon and apothecary of Newcastle under Lyme, sworn before Nathaniel Beard at Newcastle18 April 1795. ITKB 'The King against Bernard Coombe.' [*Verso*]: 'Staff. In the King's Bench. Rex v. Coombe: Affidavit of Defendant to shew cause agt the rule. Kinderley & Long fo:17.'

That he is a member of the corporation and that he unwillingly agreed to act as a justice, with no other motive than promoting the public service and discharging the duties of his situation. William Ensor asked the deponent 2 Dec to come to his house immediately to swear in and attest John Liversage for Edensor for the Stamford volunteers, as he feared his relatives might stop him. He refused to go as he was busy but did so after Thomas Fallows and another made further requests. The deponent read the written attestation which had been filled in and made sure that Liversage understood it; the attestation included sections 2 and 6 of the articles of war. Liversage said that he had written his Christian name and had asked Ensor to write his last name for him. Liversage took the oath and appeared perfectly sober. The deponent later heard that he had not taken the oath 24 hours before the attestation and that Adams therefore had discharged him. Thomas Sparrow, town clerk, thought the enlistment was legitimate because the practice of the borough had been to admit voluntary attestations within the 24 hours prescribed by statute. To settle doubts, the deponent called a meeting with the mayor, who left without giving an opinion. The deponent, Major Gosling, and Lieutenant Ball concluded that Liversage had entered the army voluntarily and was therefore subject only to military law. If he misinterpreted the Act it was not out of partial or corrupt motives, or by design, but by mistake. He admits he called Liversage a scoundrel for saying the deponent had forged the volunteer's name; the deponent denies offering to make a wager or saying that he would shield himself by custom.

[7] Affdt of William Ensor ironmonger of Newcastle under Lyme, sworn before Nathaniel Beard at Newcastle 9 May 1795. ITKB 'The King against Bernard Coombe.'[*Verso*]: '57 East 95. Staff In the King's Bench. 3 Affts to sh. c. agt inf v Bernard Coombe. Holland. The King v Coombe: Affidt of Wm Ensor to shew cause agst the rule. Brief'd [*illegible*] 3 [*illegible*] sheets each. 11 May 1795 WB 15 May Rule dischd. Kinderley & Long fo:32.'

That Colonel Newton Treen esquire promised to make the deponent's stepson, William Edensor, an ensign if he were to raise 30 men, and towards this goal Edensor gave the deponent a beating order. At about 8pm on 1 Dec John Liversage came to the deponent and to Edensor in the Red Lion and asked to enlist. Edensor offered Liversage a half-crown to serve his Majesty, but told him that if he repented in the morning he might return it. Liversage refused the coin, but demanded and accepted a guinea to serve in the Stamford volunteers. Liversage appeared perfectly sober. At about 10am the following morning he showed up at the deponent's ironmongery and had the attestation filled in and signed, and then attested before Coombe. Once the oath was taken, Liversage, appearing perfectly sober, was paid the remainder of his bounty of three guineas. [*Substantiates Ann Eccles's account in affdt [8] of Ensor and Edensor refusing to take back the money from Liversage's sister and brother.*] At around 2pm 3 Dec, the deponent and his stepson were summoned by the mayor, who discharged Liversage because the bounty had been returned and Coombe had attested him within 24 hours of enlistment. Edensor objected that no discharge was possible as a return had been made to the colonel and that only the colonel was empowered to make such discharges. The bounty and 20s was tendered to Edensor, who refused it; Adams then discharged Liversage. Coombe convened a meeting 5 Dec. [*Substantiates affdt [6].*] Coombe used no intemperate language, nor did he make any wager, nor was the argument that Liversage had been drunk advanced at any time.

[8] Affdt of Thomas Fallows journeyman and clockmaker, and Ann Eccles spinster, both of Newcastle under Lyme, sworn before Nathaniel Beard at Newcastle 9 May 1795. 'The King against Bernard Coombe.' [*Verso*]: 'Staff. In the King's Bench. Holland. Affs of Thomas Fallows & Ann Eccles, to shew cause agt the Rule. Briefed 2 parts 3 sheets each 11 May 95 W.B. Kinderley & Long fo:27.'

[Thomas Fallows]: That he was drinking at the Red Lion 1 Dec when Liversage entered, drank half a pint of ale, and went out into the yard. The deponent followed and saw him talking with Ensor and Edensor and saying 'I am come to be a soldier'. Edensor tried to pay him with a half crown but Liversage demanded a guinea. Later in the evening he called the deponent into the parlor and produced a guinea, paid to him by Ensor, and said 'I am a soldier and you shall have a pot of ale'. The following morning the deponent entered the ironmongery to find Ensor talking to Liversage, who said 'I wish to be sworn'. Ensor produced an attestation and Liversage signed his Christian name but asked the iron-monger to sign his last name as he was better with writing. Liversage now asked for Coombe to come to do the swearing in as he did not want his friends to see him. When the justice did not come, Liversage sent this deponent to fetch him. [*Substantiates account in affdt [7] of administration of the oath.*] The deponent saw the new recruit later in the day, very intoxicated, with colours in his hat, a sword in his hand, accompanied by a drummer, beating up for recruits. When he enlisted and took the oath he appeared perfectly sober.

[Ann Eccles]: That Liversage and William Fox arrived at the Red Lion at 7pm and had one pint of ale. At 9pm Liversage demanded that she fetch Edensor, which she was only able to do after several inquiries. Edensor accompanied Liversage to William Ensor's shop. A half hour later Liversage returned with his wife and shook hands with a Sergeant Hearns, declaring, 'I am a soldier'. He bought drinks for Hearns, him-self, and his wife, who said to him 'Now thou will have what thou hast long wanted ... a damned good flogging'. John Liversage returned to the shop of William Ensor to be attested. Liversage was sober, and John Austin, whom the deponent believes was enlisted by Liversage the pre-ceding evening, paid him 20s smart money in her presence, receiving back 15s.

The deponent saw Liversage 2 Dec at 5pm with a cockade in his hat, a sword in his hand, accompanied by a drummer, who was beating around town. At 8pm she saw Liversage, his brother, and his sister in the bar. The brother had three guineas and two and a half guineas and said to Ensor, 'will you take your money back or not, that is the whole of the money he had from you'. Ensor replied, 'I will have nothing to do with it'. Edensor also refused, saying he had made his return.

Liversage's brother put the money in his pocket, and his sister said to John 'I have paid the smart for you six times, see what a disagreeable situation you are in, if it was not for your family you should go'.

Sources: KB 1/28 Hil 35 Geo III, pt. 1, bdls 12[38], 32; Ea 35 Geo III, pt.2, bdl 57. KB 21/46 pp. 324, 357, 367.

[38] This bundle is marked 'Bucks'.

Section C

Of all criminal proceedings in King's Bench, those begun by the attorney general (or, in some circumstances, by the solicitor general) attracted most attention. They were 'ex officio' because it was a prerogative of his office to bring an information without having to seek the permission of the judges by filing affidavits. Such prosecutions often held great constitutional significance, and were supposed to be used only against great offences. Blackstone explained,

> The objects of the king's own prosecutions, filed *ex officio* by his own attorney general, are properly such enormous misdemeanours, as peculiarly tend to disturb or endanger his government, or to molest or affront him in the regular discharge of his royal functions. For offences so high and dangerous, in the punishment or prevention of which a moment's delay would be fatal, the law has given to the crown the power of an immediate prosecution, without waiting for any previous application to any other tribunal: which power, thus necessary, not only to the ease and safety, but even to the very existence of the executive magistrate, was originally reserved in the great plan of the English constitution, wherein provision is wisely made for the due preservation of all its parts.[1]

In both the eighteenth and nineteenth centuries the ex officio information was politically contentious and fell into disuse, although not abolished until 1967.[2]

The attorney general could proceed without sworn affidavits and indeed without any oath, motion in court, or opportunity for the defendant to show cause before trial. The contrasting case to which critics constantly pointed was trial on indictment, where at least twelve grand jurors, composing at least the majority of the grand jury, had first to find a true bill, usually after committal proceedings before a magistrate.

[1] Blackstone, iv, 308–9.
[2] J. Ll. J. Edwards, *The Law Officers of the Crown* (London, 1964), 262–7. When ordinary criminal informations were abolished in 1938, the ex officio information was explicitly preserved. It was last used in England in 1910, and finally ended by legislation in 1967; it survived in Canada until 1955; in New Zealand, by implication, until 1961. J. Ll. J. Edwards, *The Attorney General, Politics and the Public Interest* (London, 1984), 439 n67.

Informations avoided the hearings before both magistrates and grand juries, and the process was both swift and dramatic, points which recommended it to governments. An ex officio information forced the defendant to respond in Westminster Hall, although the trial itself was carried out in the county of the offence. Such a prosecution could be initiated, then left in suspension as a threat indefinitely, even after conviction but before judgment. Unlike an indictment removed on certiorari (Section F), an information ex officio could not be quashed. Because no affidavits were filed (as with ordinary criminal informations, including those against magistrates), the accused had no idea of the evidence until the prosecution's case was opened. The attorney general could insist that the trial be 'at bar' (before the judges in Westminster Hall, rather than at nisi prius in the county) and (as in other cases he prosecuted) he had right of last reply in argument. And an acquitted defendant could not have costs against the king.

All these were such clear advantages to the government that they were perceived as oppression by those in opposition, and especially by those prosecuted. It is true that any information in King's Bench, including one by the attorney general, carried with it the right of the defendant as well as the prosecutor to call for a special trial jury. But as Bentham noted, the treasury solicitor took care to pack juries in such cases.[3] For all these reasons the ex officio criminal information was politically controversial in the seventeenth, eighteenth, and nineteenth centuries, in both England and the colonies.[4]

Records in King's Bench
Ex officio informations can be distinguished by the words with which they begin: 'Be it Remembered that Sir John Mitford Knight [*the current attorney general*] Attorney General of our present Sovereign Lord the King who for our said Lord the King in this behalf prosecuteth in his proper person cometh here into the Court of our said Lord the King before the King Himself at Westminster on Wednesday next after fifteen days of Easter in the same Term [*the date given is by convention the first day of term*] and for our said Lord the King giveth the Court here to understand and be informed that...'[5] They are signed lower right by the attorney general, and 'Ex[hibite]d' is subscribed lower left. Like

---

[3]   See the Introduction.
[4]   For the history and significance of ex officio informations in the eighteenth and early nineteenth century see Hay, *The Judges and the People*.
[5]   Case C.14, KB 11/61 Ea 40 Geo III [1800] #8; KB 28/394 roll 16. See also Hands, 199, 228; Gude, ii, 249.

ordinary criminal informations, but unlike qui tams, they have no endorsement.

Because the attorney general was not obliged to file affidavits as the basis of a motion for an information, details of such cases are sparse. For two cases in this section affidavits were filed: supporting an application for pauper status (C.6); and for pauper status, for dispensing with personal appearance, and in mitigation of sentence (C.13).[6] In a third case (C.15) a prosecution affidavit survives in a KB series that appears to be affidavits used by the treasury solicitor when drafting informations in excise cases.

Prosecution affidavits were of course used in all the cases to draft the information, and to inform the prosecution in court, although they were not filed. They sometimes can be found in other archives (see case C.13). The clerks drew the ex officio informations on the instructions of the attorney general in excise and customs prosecutions, such as cases C.14 and C.15, and probably in others. Examples are preserved in one of the King's Bench series, the affidavits marked 'drawn', and signed by Henry Dealtry (secondary on the crown side) and Henry Barlow (clerk of the rules and affidavits). In several instances no information was drawn. A Kent affidavit in Pittock v Crump (Hil 1801) is endorsed with a note from the attorney general, 'I think this is not a case for an information in the name of the Attorney General'; in an Essex case, Steel v Rich (Ea 1801), the attorney general, Edward Law, wrote 'Upon the whole of the circumstances stated to me I am of opinion that this information cannot be supported.'[7]

The process followed for informations ex officio was the same as that for cases in Sections A and B. Unlike ordinary informations and informations against magistrates, informations ex officio often were prosecuted rigorously. The cases here were mostly dropped as part of a political compromise, once notice of trial had been given (see the notes to C.1 and C.8), but in three cases fines were imposed (C.1, C.6, C.9) and in a fourth (C.13), nine men and women were given harsh sentences of hard labour, four with exposure in the pillory (see below). In contrast, no defendants to ordinary criminal informations (Section A) or those exhibited against magistrates (Section B) were ever tried or sentenced.

---

[6]   The applications for pauper status, successful in one case (C.13), are the only such cases in this volume. The right to plead *in forma pauperis*, which relieved the party of all court costs and gave the right to petition for and receive representation by counsel, required an affidavit that one was not worth £5, and a motion in court. See Chitty, i, 412–14. In C.6 it appears that the defendant or his advisors thought the limit was £100.

[7]   KB 32/3 41 Geo III Hil and Ea 1801.

Apart from two (C.14, C.15) for attacks on excisemen in 1800, which probably represent a general tightening of the system during the war and resentment of Pitt's new duties, the only use of the ex officio information in Staffordshire in these years was against Jacobite rioters or Tory-Jacobite sympathizers at mid-century. Two brief points can be made here about these cases. One is that the government clearly resorted to informations because Staffordshire grand juries were unreliable: the crown simply could not get true bills from the Tory (and often Jacobitical) gentlemen of the county. (No such problem occurred with proceedings against Jacobins in the 1790s: all these were prosecuted on indictment at quarter sessions and assizes).

Secondly, the Jacobite cases show the usefulness to the government of bringing the convicted up to London for judgment. In the case of some unhappy rioters from Walsall, who had seditiously hanged, shot and burned George II in effigy, the government brought them to Westminster Hall to hear their sentences (C.13). The ringleader was condemned to be put in the pillory for one hour between the hours of 12 and 2 at Charing Cross, at the Royal Exchange six days later, and again in Chancery Lane the following day, and then to be incarcerated in Clerkenwell House of Correction for two years. Three of the eight other defendants were also sentenced to two sessions in the pillory, and all of them were given terms of imprisonment. In Staffordshire the pillory would have been a triumph for the defendants, who would have been considered heroes by all Jacobite supporters; in London, they were at the mercy of the Whig mob.[8]

CASES

C.1 Information ex officio (23 Oct 1747)

Defendants: Joseph Loxdale, gentleman and alderman of Stafford; William Barnett, shoemaker; John Birtles*, cheesemonger; Benjamin Blackbourne, labourer of Rickerscote; Samuel Brown*, labourer of Burleyfield; Thomas Calkin*, gunsmith; John Creamer*, blacksmith; Joseph Calkin, gunsmith; Richard Dimmock, tailor; Thomas Dudley*, carpenter; Richard Dyott*, gentleman; William Ford, shoemaker; John

---

[8]   Case C.13, which was consulted in later cases in the crown office as a precedent for carrying out sentence in a different county from the trial. For the reasoning behind the use of ex officio informations in these Jacobite cases see D. Hay, 'The Last Years of Staffordshire Jacobitism,' *Staffordshire Studies*, 14 (2002), 53–88.

Godwin, butcher; Thomas Godwin* the younger, shoemaker; Michael Grey*, wheelwright; Thomas Grey*, bricklayer; Wick Hill, tinman; Joseph Hill, threadman; Thomas Heath* the younger, shoemaker; Thomas Hitchcock*, grocer; Mark Lewis, labourer of the Green; James Meeson, labourer of the Green; William Nevett, weaver of the Green; Thomas Nevett, weaver of the Green; Charles Perkins*, butcher of the Green; Thomas Phillips the elder, glazier of the Green; Edward Renshaw+, mason; Thomas Rose the younger, labourer; Thomas Smallbridge*, dyer of Stafford Green; Joseph Snape, weaver and comber of Stafford Green; Theophilus Smith the younger, plumber and glazier; Joseph Startin+, shoemaker; James Tunks [?], maltster late of Stafford ; Thomas Warner*, threadman; Roger Williams*, shoemaker; William Young, labourer [*entered twice*]; [*all of Stafford, except where noted*].

Information:
Mich 21 Geo II [1747] [Exhibited 23 Oct 1747; FDT]
[1] That the defendants, and others to the number of 150 and more, armed with sticks, clubs, staves, stones, with a drum beating before them, riotously, routously and tumultuously assembled with an intent to break the peace and to aggrieve William Chetwynd esquire, member of parliament for the borough of Stafford, and with the intention to demolish his house, at 6pm 1 July [1747] in Greengate Street for a period of more than an hour and a half, forced open the gate, threw large stones in the windows and broke most of them, hit and injured Stephen Stanley in the face and almost struck Chetwynd who was in the house with his family, terrified them and broke doors and furniture, to the peril of life, forcing Chetwynd to hide in an upstairs room; [2] *the defendants, and others to the number of one hundred and fifty and more, being armed, riotously, routously assembled (etc)* broke into courtyard, broke windows, *broke and entered*, and broke doors, wainscotting, and furniture, *to the dread of Chetwynd and his family*; [3] [*as italicized passage in second count*] and remained for one and a half hours; [4] the defendants and others to the number of 150 and more, armed with a drum, in Greengate Street, being a highway, riotously and routously assembled (etc), and rioted for one and a half hours, breaking windows, hallooing, etc.[9]

[9] For a paper copy of this information, probably used at trial, see SRO, D1798/618/163.

Rules and process:
Mich [23 Oct 1747; FDT]: information exhibited (attorney general, Sir Dudley Ryder); summons. ST: pray a day to answer; li lo; imparl. Hil [23 Jan 1747/8; FDT]: first rule to plead. ST: [27 Jan 1747/8]: second rule to plead. ST [1 Feb 1747/8]: peremptory rule to plead (attorney general, Sir Dudley Ryder). ST: plead not guilty, venire facias juratores.[10] Hil Vac 18 Feb 1747/8: notice of trial for the King (Masterman); countermanded 25 Feb 1747/8 (Masterman). Trin [27 June 1748]: rule for a special jury, instance of defdts (Levett). Trin Vac 1 July 1748: notice of trial for the King (Masterman). Summer assizes Stafford: verdict against defdts [*marked with an asterisk*]. Mich [4 Nov 1748]: rule nisi on the postea for judgment [*against all defdts marked with cross or asterisk*.] ST: postea and judgment against. Hil [1748/9]: convicted, fined 6s 8d.[11]

Sources: IND 1/6659 Mich, Hil 21 Geo II, Mich 22 Geo II. KB 11/38 Mich 21 Geo II [1747] #16. KB 15/2 Mich 21 Geo II, b66v. KB 15/14 Hil Vac, Trin Vac KB 21/36 pp. 271, 276, 281, 358, 377, 415. KB 28/184 Hil 21 Geo II [1747/8], roll 5. KB 29/407 Mich, Hil 21 Geo II. KB 36/127.

[10] KB 29/407 Hil, with subscribed notation of a capias against defendants marked with an asterisk; superscribed notation of the verdict. See next note.
[11] *Aris's Birmingham Gazette*, 22 Aug 1748: 'On Saturday the 13th Instant at the Assizes held at Stafford, came on before the Honourable Mr. Justice Burnett, the Trial of an Information against Joseph Loxdale and others, by a special Jury of Gentlemen of that County, for a Riot committed at the Borough of Stafford, and for forcibly breaking into, defacing, and demolishing the House of William Chetwynd Esq; on the Election Day, when the said William Chetwynd and John Robins Esqrs. were returned Members to represent that Borough in Parliament; and after some Hours had been spent in examining a great Number of Witnesses for the Crown, and the Facts fully proved against eighteen of the Defendants in that Information, the Counsel for the Rioters proposed that these eighteen Persons should be found Guilty, and that Mr. Chetwynd should have Satisfaction for the Damage done to his House, if the Counsel for the Crown would consent to withdraw the other Informations which were then to have been tried against several other Persons concerned in that Riot, which Proposal was agreed to by the Counsel for the Crown, and those eighteen Persons convicted by the Jury; upon which Mr. Chetwynd very generously refused to take any Satisfaction for the Damage done to his House.' See also *ABG*, 15 Aug 1748: 'On Saturday the Assizes ended at Stafford, when the Trials concerning what happened at the late Election at Stafford, and at Lichfield Races, were compromised, in which was included the intended Trial at Warwick.'

C.2 Information ex officio (23 Oct 1747)

Defendants: Thomas Hitchcock, chandler, and Thomas Grey, bricklayer, both of Stafford.

Information:
Mich 21 Geo II [1747] [Exhibited 23 Oct 1747; FDT]
[1] With 150 others unknown, and armed with sticks, clubs, staves and stones, riotously attacked Chetwynd's house 1 July [1747][*see the preceding case*], and assaulted Thomas Smallwood, by stoning, blows with truncheons, and pelting with filth; thus covered with blood, mire, dirt and filth, he was dragged out of the house and forced, on his knees, to beg the pardon of John Robins, esquire[12] of the borough of Stafford; [2] [*as [1], without mention of Smallwood being dragged out of the house, or an attack on the house*]; [3] [*mentions only 'diverse others', and the assault*]; [4] [*mentions only defdts, violent assault*]; [5] false imprisonment.

Rules and process:
[*Identical to that for case C.1 to the point of notice of trial, 1 July 1748. For the reasons given in the newspaper account quoted in that case, there is no verdict, no rule nisi on the postea, no postea and judgment, no record of conviction, and no fine.*]

Sources: KB 11/38 Mich 21 Geo II [1747] #21. [*And the sources for case C.1.*]

C.3 Information ex officio (23 Oct 1747)

Defendants: Thomas Phillips, glazier; William Ford, shoemaker; Thomas Godwin the younger, shoemaker; Thomas Calkin, gunsmith; all of Stafford.

Information:
Mich 21 Geo II [1747] [Exhibited 23 Oct 1747; FDT]
[1] With 150 others unknown, after the reading of the *Riot Act* 1 July [1747] at the instance of Chetwynd to prevent demolition of his house and the murder of himself and his family, assaulted constables Thomas Lee and John Collins with the intent to rescue, and rescued, an unknown rioter (seized by the constables as among the most active) from their custody; [2] violent assault on the constables, acting in execution of their office, and rescue; [3] violent assault on the constables;

---

[12] Elected, with Chetwynd, as one of the members for Stafford. See also case A.10.

[4] violent assault on Lee and Collins [*not named as constables*].

Rules and process:
[*As in case C.2.*]

Sources: KB 11/38 Mich 21 Geo II [1747] #22. [*And the other sources for case C.1.*]

C.4 Information ex officio (23 Oct 1747)

Defendant: John Birtles, cheesemonger of Stafford.

Information:
Mich 21 Geo II [1747] [Exhibited 23 Oct 1747; FDT]
[1] With more than 150 others, unknown, riotously and routously assembled, committed assault and affray, 1 July [1747] at Stafford, on Peter Dudley, knocking him to the ground twice, and taking his gold-laced hat; [2] riotous assault and affray; [3] [*Birtles only*] violent assault.

Rules and process:
[*As in Case C.1, with the exception of the fine.*]

Sources: KB 11/38 Mich 21 Geo II [1747] #19. [*Other sources as in C.1.*]

C.5 Information ex officio (23 Oct 1747)

Defendant: Michael Grey, wheelwright of Stafford.

Information:
Mich 21 Geo II [Exhibited 23 Oct 1747; FTD]
[1] With more than 150 others unknown, riotously, routously assembled and committed assault on John Deakin 1 July [1747] at Stafford; [2] violent assault [*Grey only.*]

Rules and process:
[*As in Case C.2.*]

Sources: KB 11/38 Mich 21 Geo II [1747] #23. [*Other sources as in C.2.*]

C.6 Information ex officio (23 Oct 1747)

Defendants: Thomas Hadley, gunsmith of Birmingham (Warws), and Patrick Fitzgerald, late chapman of Handsworth.

Information:
Mich 21 Geo II [1747] [Exhibited 23 Oct 1747; FDT]
[1] Committed assault and affray, with sticks and butt ends of whips, on John Fowler, postman, at 8pm 2 Sept [1747] while in execution of his office, to his terror and danger of his life, and violently hindered, obstructed and opposed him while he was carrying the post from Birmingham to Shifnal (Salop), on Handsworth Heath; [2] violent assault while in execution of his office; [3] violent assault causing injury for one month; [4] violent assault.

Rules and process:
[*All for Hadley only*]: Hil [1747/8]: li lo. Ea [1748]: prays a day to answer; imparl. Ea [9 May 1748]: first rule to plead. ST [13 May 1748]: second rule to plead. ST [23 May 1748]: peremptory rule to plead. Trin [1748]: pleads not guilty. ST: venire facias juratores.[13] Trin Vac, 5 July 1748: notice of trial for the King (Masterman); rule nisi on the postea, on conviction. Hil [4 Feb 1748/9]: motion for judgment, by the court. Trin [8 June 1749]: affdt of Hadley for pauper status. ST [10 June 1749]: 'it is ordered that one of the justices of this court to attend Mr Justice Burnett who tried this cause and request him to make his reports of the facts as they appeared to him upon the trial of the issue joined in this cause.' (Evans). ST [12 June 1749]: order that a writ of habeas corpus issue directed to the sheriffs of London to bring into this court the body of the defdt (Bathurst). ST [13 June 1749]: defdt having been brought into court by sheriff of London on habeas corpus, remanded until tomorrow (Bathurst). ST [14 June 1749]: order for fine of £20 for the Staffordshire offence (attorney general); and £10 for the Warwickshire offence, and recognizance of £100 with two sureties of £50 each for his appearance in KB the last day of Trin term next, and good behaviour in the meantime. On payment of fines and on entering into recognizances, to be discharged (attorney general). Trin [4 July 1750]: appearance on recognizances recorded, and recognizances discharged.

---

[13] KB 29/407 Ea 21 & 22 Geo II, subscribed 'capias' for Staffordshire and Warwickshire, superscribed 'convicted'. The capias is recorded in KB 29/408 Trin 22 Geo II.

Affidavit for defence, claiming pauper status:

Trin 22 & 23 Geo II 1749

[1] Affdt of Thomas Hadley, gunsmith of Birmingham (Warws), sworn before M. Wright at Serjeants' Inn 8 June 1749. ITKB 'The King agst Thomas Hadley.' [*Verso*]: 'Stafford. The King agst Hadley. Affidt Defendt.'

That two[14] informations have been sworn against him for an assault on John Fowler, postman. Since then several of his creditors came upon him and distressed him to that degree that his trade and business is very much decayed and fallen away. He has lately taken a true and exact account of all goods, stock and debt due him and his debts to others. He has not £100 in the world, and has a wife and nine children who have nothing to support themselves but what the deponent can provide by his trade and his own labour and industry.

Sources: IND 1/6659 Ea 21 Geo II, Trin 21 & 22 Geo II. KB 1/10/2 Trin 22 & 23 Geo II 1749. KB 11/38 Mich 21 Geo II [1747] #34. KB 15/2 b68 Hil 21 Geo II. KB 15/14 Trin Vac 22 Geo II. KB 21/36 pp. 315, 317, 414, 466, 469, 471, 472, 583. KB 29/407 Ea 21, Trin 21 & 22 Geo II. KB 29/408 Trin 22 & 23 Geo II. KB 36/130.

C.7 Information ex officio (23 Oct 1747)

Defendants: Daniel Astle*, yeoman of Yoxall; Thomas Scragg*, baker of Yoxall; Christopher Tole, dancing master of Burton upon Trent; William Dickenson*, wheelwright of Fazeley; Richard Aston, glazier of Lichfield; William Emery, breeches-maker of Lichfield; William Heath, barber of Lichfield; Thomas Jobbet*, tailor of Lichfield; Thomas Mallet*, yeoman of Lichfield; William Taylor*, dyer of Lichfield; Richard Woodroffe, skinner of Lichfield; Henry Bannister*, labourer of Shenstone; William Gee*, labourer of Beaudesert Hall[15]; Charles Leeson*, baker of Burton on Trent; Robert Shilton* the younger, clothier of Burton upon Trent; Richard Pyott*, waggoner of Aldridge.

---

[14] No other information against Hadley has been found for Staffordshire; it is likely that the same charge was also laid in Warwickshire, because Handsworth Heath was divided by the county boundary: see KB 21/36 p. 414, where a rule on the postea or conviction is noted for each of Staffordshire and Warwickshire; similar entries at pp. 315, 317, 466, 469, 471–2.

[15] The seat of Henry Paget, ninth baron and second earl of Uxbridge, d.1769.

Information:
Mich 21 Geo II [1747] [Exhibited 23 Oct 1747; FDT]
[1] That defdts, and others unknown to the number of 200 and more, armed with whips, sticks, staves, and other weapons at 5pm 3 Sept [1747] at the parish of Whittington assaulted Thomas Bradney esquire of Wolverhampton, on horseback, pursuing him returning from the race course on Whittington Heath, and beat and whipped him so that he lost much blood, to his great terror, peril, and danger of losing his life; [2] defdts and over 200 others unknown, armed [*as above*] unlawfully, riotously and routously assembled, in a violent assault and affray, violently assault beat [*etc*]; [3] [*defdts only*] assault and affray, violently beat [*etc*]; [4] defdts and over 200 and unknown, armed [*as above*] riotously, and routously assembled for one hour.

Rules and process:
Mich [23 Oct 1747; FDT]: information exhibited (attorney general, Sir Dudley Ryder); summons. ST: pray a day to answer; li lo; imparl. Hil [23 Jan 1747/8; FDT]: first rule to plead. ST [27 Jan 1747/8]: second rule to plead. ST [3 Feb 1747/8]: peremptory rule to plead (attorney general, Sir Dudley Ryder). ST: plead not guilty. ST: venire facias juratores. Hil Vac 18 Feb 1747/8: notice of trial for the King (Masterman); countermanded 25 Feb 1747/8 (Masterman). Trin [27 June 1747/8]: rule for a special jury, instance of defdts (Levett). Trin Vac 1 July 1748: notice of trial for the King (Masterman).[16] Mich [4 Nov 1748]: rule nisi on the postea for judgment [*against all defdts marked with an asterisk.*]

Sources: IND 1/6659 Mich, Hil 21 Geo II, Mich 22 Geo II. KB 11/38 Mich 21 Geo II [1747] #17. KB 15/2 Mich 21 Geo II, b67. KB 15/14 Hil Vac 21 Geo II, Trin Vac 22 Geo II. KB 21/36 pp. 271, 276, 281-2, 358-9. KB 29/407 Mich, Hil 21 Geo II. KB 36/127.

C.8 Information ex officio (23 Oct 1747)

Defendants: [*as in C.7, but beginning with Christopher Tole*].

Information:
Mich 21 Geo II [1747] [Exhibited 23 Oct 1747, FDT]
[1] With over 200 others unknown at 5 pm 3 Sept [1747], with whips, sticks, clubs, staves and other weapons, riotously and routously assembled, committed an assault and affray on Granville Leveson Gower,

---

[16] See note to case C.8.

Viscount Trentham, at Whittington Heath, pursuing him as he returned from the horse races; [2] [*as in first count*], violent assault and affray; [3] [*violent assault by named defendants only*]; [4] riot for one hour. [*Verso*]: 'Tole and others for assaulting the Duke of Bedford [*sic*].'[17]

Rules and process:
[*As in case C.7.*][18]

Sources: KB 11/28 Mich 21 Geo II [1747] #18. [*Other sources as in case C.7.*]

C.9 Information ex officio (23 Oct 1747)

Defendants: Christopher Tole and others [*as in case C.8*].

Information:
Mich 21 Geo II [Exhibited 23 Oct 1747]
[*As in case C.8, but for an attack on the Duke of Bedford.*] [*Verso*]: 'Tole and others for assaulting the Duke of Bedford'.

Rules and process:
[*Identical to that in case C.1, but capias, verdict and sentence are not recorded for defendants Aston, Emery, and Heath.*][19]

Sources: KB 11/38 Mich 21 Geo II [1747] #20. KB 28/184 Hil 21 Geo II [1747/8], roll 6. [*Other sources as in case C.8.*]

---

[17] For the information actually exhibited for the assault on the Duke of Bedford, see C.9.
[18] *ABG*, 22 August 1748: 'On the same day [13 August] came on the Trial of the Informations against Toll [*sic*] and others for insulting and striking his Grace the Duke of Bedford and other Gentlemen upon Whittington Heath, at the last Lichfield Horse Races, when it was likewise proposed by the Counsel for the Defendants, that the several Rioters in that Information, to the Number of thirteen, should submit to be found Guilty, if the Counsel for the Crown would consent to withdraw the Informations against several other Persons concerned in that Riot, which was agreed to by the Counsel for the Crown, and those Defendants, who were the principal Persons concerned in that Riot, were also convicted by the Jury.'
[19] See the preceeding note.

C.10 Information ex officio (23 Oct 1747)

Defendants: John Burrows, ironmonger of Walsall; Herbert Hancock, currier of Dudley (Worcs).

Information:
Mich 21 Geo II 1747 [Exhibited 23 Oct 1747, FDT]
[1] Defdts, with more than 100 others unknown, armed with whips, sticks, clubs and staves, at 5pm 3 Sept [1747], being riotously, routously, and tumultuously assembled, pursued and committed an assault and affray on the Duke of Bedford, at Whittington Heath while returning from the horse race, and beat him on the head, neck, shoulders, arms and back with whips, sticks, truncheons, clubs or bludgeons, causing the Duke terror and dread for his life; [2] [*as in [1], but details of violent assault not mentioned*]; [3] [*mentions only defdts, violent assault*]; [4] defendants and over 100 others assaulted for over one hour.

Rules and process:
Mich [23 Oct 1747; FDT]: information exhibited (attorney general). Hil [1747/8]: pray a day to answer; li lo; imparl. Ea [27 April 1748]: first rule to plead. ST [2 May 1748]: second rule to plead. ST [18 May 1748]: peremptory rule to plead (attorney general). Trin [1748]: plead not guilty. ST [29 June 1748]: rule for a special jury, instance of defdts (Spiltimber). ST: venire facias juratores. Trin Vac, 1 July 1748: notice of trial for the King (Masterman).[20]

Sources: IND 1/6659 Hil 21 Geo II, Trin 21 & 22 Geo II. KB 11/38 Mich 21 Geo II [1747] #36. KB 15/2 b66v Hil 21 Geo II. KB 15/14 Trin Vac 22 Geo II. KB 21/36 pp. 302, 307, 323, 364. KB 29/407 Hil 21 Geo II, Trin 21 & 22 Geo II. KB 36/127.

C.11 Information ex officio (28 Nov 1747)

Defendants: John Tompson the younger, surgeon of Ashbourne (Derbs) and Francis Garrat, clerk of Burton upon Trent.

---

[20] See note 18 to case C.8.

Information:
Mich 21 Geo II [1747][21] [Exhibited 28 Nov 1747, LDT][22]
[1] With more than ten others unknown, riotously and routously assembled, and committed a violent assault and affray on Daniel Sleamaker, sergeant (of the regiment of dragoons commanded by Lord Mark Kerr), whom they knocked down and kicked, at Burton upon Trent 28 July [1747] in the White Hart (the public house of Mary Richardson, widow), and a second assault, almost causing loss of an eye, thus preventing the sergeant from carrying out his regimental duties; [2] riotously, routously assembled, and violent assault; [3] [*named defdts only*], violent assault and affray.

Rules and process:
Mich [28 Nov 1747]: information exhibited. Hil [1748]: pray a day to answer; li lo; imparl. Ea [27 April 1748]: first rule to plead. ST [2 May 1748]: second rule to plead. ST [16 May 1748]: peremptory rule to plead (attorney general). ST: plead not guilty. Trin [1748] rule for a special jury, instance of defdts (Levett). Trin Vac, 1 July 1748: notice of trial for the King (Masterman).

Sources: IND 1/6659, Hil and Ea 21 Geo II. KB 11/38 Mich 21 Geo II [1747] #37. KB 15/2 b66v Hil 21 Geo II. KB 15/14 Trin Vac. KB 21/36, pp. 302, 307, 320, 359. KB 29/407 Hil 21 Geo II. KB 36/125, /127.

C.12 Information ex officio (28 Nov 1747)

Defendant: John Tompson the younger, surgeon of Ashbourne (Derbs).

Information:
Mich 21 Geo II [1747] [Exhibited 28 Nov 1747, LDT]
[1] Seditious libel: a favourer of James, with others at Burton upon Trent, 28 July [1747], said 'Down with the rump, damn all Hanoverians, Prince Charles for Ever'; [2] said 'Damn all Hanoverians'; [3] said 'Prince Charles for Ever'.

Rules and process:
Mich [28 Nov 1747]: information exhibited; summons. Hil [1748] prays a day to answer; li lo; imparl. Ea [27 April 1748]: first rule to plead. ST

---

[21] This and the following information were filed following an unsuccessful prosecution on indictment at Staffordshire summer assizes, 1747: TNA, SP 44/133 p. 373v; attorney general to Duke of Newcastle 23 Nov 1747.

[22] This and the following information are unusually dated the last day of term.

[2 May 1748]: second rule to plead. ST [16 May 1748]: peremptory rule to plead (attorney general). ST: pleads not guilty; venire facias juratores. Trin [1748]: rule for a special jury, instance of defdt (Levett[23]). Trin Vac, 1 July 1748: notice of trial for the King.

Sources: IND 1/6659, Ea 21 Geo II and Trin 22 Geo II. KB 11/38 Mich 21 Geo II [1747] #38. KB 21/36, pp. 302, 307, 320. KB 15/2 b66v Hil 21 Geo II. KB 15/14 Trin Vac 22 Geo II. KB 29/407 Hil 21 Geo II. KB 36/125, /127.

C.13 Information ex officio (23 Oct 1750)

Defendants: Thomas James*+ the elder, engraver of buckles; Ann James*+, his wife; Thomas James* the younger, bucklemaker; John Cotterell*+, spurrier; Steward James, alias Steward James, bucklemaker; Samuel Higgins[x]#, bucklemaker; James Littlefoot[x], bucklemaker; Thomas Wiggin[24] [x]#, bucklemaker; Elianor Wiggin*+, his wife; William James*+, bucklemaker; Stephen Higgins[x]#, bucklemaker; Richard Chatterton[x], bucklemaker; John Guy*+, alias John Hinton, bucklemaker; Robert Spink[x], alias Devil Bob, chapemaker; James Ross*, alias Rossar, awl blade maker; all of the borough of Walsall. [*Those marked x absconded.*[25]]

Information:
Mich 24 Geo II [1750] [Exhibited 23 Oct 1750][26]
[1][a] With 200 and more others unknown, armed with guns, pistols, sticks, clubs, staves etc., disaffected and for the Pretender, seditiously intending to disgrace, scandalize and vilify the King, and to represent the King hanging from a gibbet or gallows by a rope about his neck, 29 May [1750], being the anniversary of Charles II, riotously, routously and tumultously assembled etc. at Walsall; erected on Hill Top or Hill Street an 18-foot gibbet and seditiously hung on the gallows an effigy with a brown paper coat, shoes, stockings, and breeches and a wig on

---

[23] 'Ford' in KB 36/126.
[24] 'Wiggen' in the information; they signed 'Wiggin' in the affidavits. His wife signed 'Elianor'.
[25] For the other marks, see *Rules and process*.
[26] KB 11. For a paper copy of this information, perhaps used at trial or by the defence, or a draft, see Birmingham City Archives, 328834. The version of the information given in the crown roll, KB 28/196 Hil 24 Geo II, 1750, is much abbreviated.

its head and a long tail fixed and tied thereto and a pair of horns on its forehead and a bunch of turnips under one of its arms and an orange in one of its hands; and [b] affixed two paper writings on the upright post: 'Evil to him that evil thinks'; and 'It is I that makes this nation stink of Turnips', and two more paper writings on his breast: 'George Rex the Second'; and 'Evil to him that evil thinks', 'This is he that makes the land to stink of turnips'; and [c] shot with guns and pistols at the effigy, shouting, hallooing and huzzaing; [d] that William James damned the effigy, 'Damn you there is another heir to the Crown'; and [e] that the Wiggins, while the effigy hung up, did violently and unlawfully hinder and prevent some persons unknown from attempting to take it down. [f] That after seven hours (by 7pm) they took down and burnt the effigy after taking it around the most public streets and the market cross, [g] crying 'Down with the Rump, Down with the Hanoverian line, Prince Charles for ever.' [2] [[a] to [b], [d] to [e]]. [3] [[a] to [b], description of effigy much abbreviated, followed by [c] to [d]]. [4] [[a] to [b], much abbreviated, and that Ann James fixed on the horns]; [5] [[a] to [c] abbreviated, and followed by [e] to [f]]; [6] riot only.

Rules and process:
18 Aug 1750, recognizances for £100 each of eight defdts marked*, with four sureties each of £50, returned to Staffs summer assizes to appear in King's Bench first day Mich term to answer to an information.[27] Mich [23 Oct 1750] information exhibited. ST [15 Nov 1750]: attorney general consents that [personal] appearance of [*defdts marked*, and John Aaron Broad*] may be dispensed with, Mr Walrond[28] undertaking to appear to such informations as may be filed, and to enter into recognizances (Ford for the defdts; attorney general for the King). ST [26 Nov 1750]: rule nisi for defdts [*now including Thomas Wiggin*] to defend as paupers [*see affdts [1] to [4]*] (Ford).[29] Hil [23 Jan 1750/51]: enlarged rule nisi to defend as paupers (attorney general). ST [7 Feb 1750/51]: rule absolute to defend as paupers. ST 19 Feb 1750/51: notice of trial [*defdts marked*] for the king (Masterman). ST: venire facias juratores.[30] Stafford Lent assizes 1751: verdicts against six of the eight defdts marked *; Thomas

---

[27] The sureties were Humphrey Moore, bucklemaker, William Kendrick, innholder, John Perkes, bucklemaker, and William Green, bucklemaker.
[28] Their clerk in court.
[29] Gude, i, 340, ii, 18, 652.
[30] KB 29/410 Hil 24 Geo II: superscript: 'for defendants' Thomas James [the younger] and James Ross; subscript: 'without day' for James [the younger] and Ross; 'for King', and capias, for all others.

James the younger and John Ross acquitted.[31] Ea [24 April 1751]: order that [*defdts marked +, identified as* 'paupers'] having surrendered in discharge of their recognizances, be committed to custody of the marshal of the Marshalsea until discharged by law (Moreton). ST [24 April 1751]: rule on the postea, for a conviction.Trin [25 June 1751]: [*defdts marked +*] convicted. Thomas James to be pilloried for one hour between the hours of twelve and two at Charing Cross 16 July, at the Royal Exchange 22 July, and at Chancery Lane 23 July, and sentenced to the Clerkenwell house of correction at hard labour for two years; William James, John Cotterell and John Hinton alias Guy to be pilloried at Charing Cross 17 July, and two years hard labour in the house of correction and pilloried at the Royal Exchange 22 July; Ann James and Elianor Wiggin sentenced to one year hard labour in the House of Correction (motion of solicitor general). 24 July 1751, recognizances for £10 of defdts marked # returned to Staffs summer assizes; that they personally appear in King's Bench first day next Mich term to answer to an information.[32] Mich [23 Oct 1751]: defendants [*marked #*] appear, and confess (Gilbert). ST [26 Oct 1751]: hard labour for three months, Clerkenwell house of correction (solicitor general).[33]

Defence affidavits to dispense with personal appearance and for pauper status:[34]

[31] *ABG* 18 March 1751: 'On Saturday the Assizes ended at Stafford … Thomas James Sen. and Anne his Wife, John Cotterell, Eleanor Higgins, John Guy, and William James, charged on the Oaths of several Persons of being guilty, together with divers other Persons, of commiting a treasonable Riot in the Borough of Walsall on the 29th of May last, and other treasonable Practices, were found guilty, and are to appear in the King's Bench the first Day of next Easter Term, to receive Judgment. Thomas James Jun. and John Ross, charged with the same Offence, were found not guilty.'

[32] Each man acted as a £5 surety for each of the others.

[33] This and the preceding entry appear in the draft minute book (KB 36/139) but not in KB 21. The record of the case in the crown roll, KB 28, fills both sides of seven membranes.

[34] Because the attorney general enjoyed the privilege of filing informations ex officio, it was not necessary to file affidavits with the court in support of the information (see introduction to this chapter). Affidavits were, of course, taken in order to prepare and to prosecute the case, and these can sometimes be found in other sources. Some of the prosecution affidavits in this case are printed in R. W. Gillespie, *Walsall Records* (Walsall, 1914), Appendix. The originals are found in TNA, SP 36/113 fols. 88–101, 129–144, 160–66, and copies of the evidence are found in Birmingham City Archives, 328833;

Mich 24 Geo II 1750

[1] Affdt of Jonathan Hawe, gentleman of Walsall, attorney for the defendants Thomas James, his wife Anne, William James, Thomas James the younger, Thomas Wiggin, Elianor his wife, John Cotterell, John Hinton alias Guy, James Ross alias Rossar and John Aaron Broad, sworn before John Dearle at Stafford 3 Oct 1750. ITKB 'The King against Thomas James Ann his wife William James the younger Elianor Wiggin wife of Thomas Wiggin John Cotorell John Hinton otherwise Guy James Ross otherwise Rossar and John Aaron Broade.' [*Verso*]: 'Hawe. The King a James: Afft. Crawley 2 Affdts fo 17 fo 9. Staffordshire. Afft of Hawe and The Same for to move to dispense with Appearance of Thomas James et al. fo 17.'

That he was present at last Stafford assizes when the defendants entered into recognizances before Sir Thomas Parker, knight, chief baron of the court of Exchequer, for their appearance in King's Bench the first day of Michaelmas term to answer an ex officio information. He does not believe the court intended to require a personal appearance, if it was practicable for them to be represented by attorney. Parker directed that the word 'personally' not be inserted as a condition of the recogizances. Ford, counsel for the defendants, objected to the words 'and not to depart the said court without leave'; Mulso, clerk of assizes, or his son the deputy clerk, replied that those words were always used.

All the above named defendants, except John Aaron Broad, who was bound by recognizance to appear at the last Staffordshire assizes, were committed to Stafford gaol, some in June, others in July 1750. They were there detained until the last Staffordshire assizes when the recognizances were entered into. Osborne was one of the counsel for the imprisoned defendants, and at the assizes he moved that those defendants might be tried, bailed, or discharged; Parker ordered Mulso or his son to make an entry of the motion. The deponent believes the intention of the assize court was that the defendants not be obliged to appear in King's Bench in person if they could be represented by an attorney. If the deponent had known that the defendants' personal appearances were intended by the wording, he would have advised them not to enter into the recognizances, as they had by law a right to be discharged without doing so, as there was no indictment found against them, nor (as he heard and believes) even preferred to the grand jury.

some affidavits are also copied in SRO, D1287/10/2. The affidavits calendared here were filed by the defendants to support their motion for pauper status. See D. Hay, 'The Last Years of Staffordshire Jacobitism,' *Staffordshire Studies*, 14 (2002), 77–84, for an account of this case.

[2] Affdt of John Hawe gentleman of Walsall, sworn before Uppingham Bourne at Lichfield 10 Oct 1750. ITKB 'The King agt Thomas James and others.'

That the deponent delivered 10 Oct 1750 a copy of the annexed notice to Joseph Simpson esquire, son of Stephen Simpson of Lichfield, whom he believes acts as solicitor for the King against the defendants.

[*Annexed*]: Notice to Stephen Simpson solicitor for the King by Jonathan Hawe, solicitor for the defendants [*listed in* [4]] 10 Oct 1750. [*Verso*]: 'Annext at the time of swearing before me. Uppingham Bourne fo 8.'

Whereas the defendants are bound by recognizances to appear in the court of King's Bench at Westminster on the first day of Michaelmas next to answer an ex officio information, the court of King's Bench will be moved that day that the personal appearance of the defendants may be dispensed with on their appearing by their clerk in court according to the intent of their recognizances taken at the last Staffordshire assizes.

[3] Affdt of Thomas James the elder, bucklemaker, and Anne his wife; William James, bucklemaker; Thomas James the younger, buckle-maker; Elianor Wiggin, wife of Thomas Wiggin, bucklemaker; John Cotterell, spurrier; John Hinton alias Guy, bucklemaker; James Ross alias Rossar, awl blade maker; and John Aaron Broad barber, all of Walsall, sworn before Roger Holmes at Walsall 10 Nov 1750. ITKB 'The King against James and others.' [*Verso*]: 'Staffordshire. Afft of James & al to dispense wth their Appearances Fo 32.'

[Thomas James the elder and Anne his wife; William James; Thomas James the younger; Elianor Wiggin; and John Cotterell]: That under a warrant dated 18 June 1750 and authorized by Joseph Spurrier, late mayor of Walsall, and by Sir Richard Wrottesley, baronet, and John Wyrley, both JPs, the deponents were sent to Stafford gaol, charged with being involved in riotous proceedings in Walsall on 29 May 1750, making an effigy of King George II, shooting at the effigy, and other treasonable speeches and practices. All were confined with heavy irons until the last Staffordshire assizes except Anne James whose irons were removed on 10 July 1750 and Elianor Wiggin who never had irons placed on her.

[John Hinton alias Guy]: That on a warrant or seal signed by Wrottesley and Wyrley he was committed to the gaol for the same offences as the above deponents. He was chained to James Ross alias Rossar.

[James Ross alias Rossar]: That he was committed to Stafford gaol for the same offence as the above deponents by a warrant signed by Spurrier, Wrottesley, and Wyrley.

[John Aaron Broad]: That in June 1750 he was brought before Spurrier, Wrottesley, and Wyrley and charged with lending a wig block for dressing an effigy on 29 May 1750 in Walsall. He was a stranger to these events and the block was lent without his knowledge. The mayor and justices were satisfied of his innocence after examining Benjamin Walton, the deponent's apprentice. Still they insisted he enter into recognizances with two sureties of £10 each for his appearance at last assizes.

[All]: That they are innocent of all charges against them and that they abhor practices such as those charged against them. They believed that by entering the recognizances they would not have to appear personally in court but could appear through their attorney. On 29 May, the day marking the restoration of Charles II to the throne, it has been customary for several years last past at Walsall to rejoice, ring bells, fix up effigies for shooting, and other such demonstrations of joy. They deny that the effigy in question was intended to represent George II.

[Thomas James the elder]: That he is 54 years of age and scarcely able to provide sustenance for his family. With all his debts paid he is not worth £3. The masters for whom the deponent previously worked have all employed other men while he has been in gaol, and he has not had a fortnight's work since the last assizes. If he is forced to appear at the next assizes, he must sell his household goods to pay for passage to London, which will prove his ruin.

[Anne James]: That she has nothing in her own right or held in trust for her. She is 57 years of age, gross, and infirm. If she has to appear personally in court it will be hazardous to her life.

[William James]: That he is 56 years of age and scarce able to get a subsistence for himself, his wife and three small children. After his debts are paid he is not worth 20s. During his imprisonment his children were left to beg. Having to make a personal appearance in court will prove his ruin.

[Thomas James the younger]: That after all his debts are paid he is not worth £4. While in gaol the masters for whom he worked have employed others. Having to make a personal appearance will cost him all his business and his chance of paying his debts.

[Elianor Wiggin]: That her husband has been in Stafford gaol for two months. He is very poor and has four children aged one to seven years. After her husband's debts are paid he is worth no more than £5. She has nothing in her own right or in trust for her, and she has been unable to support her children, having no income save the gains of two small apprentices who earn 5s a week but there is not always work for them. If she is forced to make an appearance at court she does not know what will become of her children and the two apprentices; she and her husband will be ruined.

[John Cotterall]: That he is about 56 years old and after all his debts are paid he is not worth £5. He cannot make more than 4s a week at his trade. If he is forced to make an appearance he believes he will have to beg for relief on the road.

[John Hinton alias Guy]: That after paying all his debts he is not worth 40s. If he is forced to make an appearance he will have to ask for relief to support him on the road.

[James Ross alias Rossar]: That he is not worth £3 when all his debts are paid.

[John Aaron Broad]: That he is very poor, scarcely able to get a subsistence for his wife and five small children, aged one month to ten years. When all his debts are paid he is not worth one shilling. If he is forced to make an appearance in court his family will become chargeable to the parish of Walsall; he has no money to support his expenses to and from London.

[4] Affdt of William Crawley, agent for defendants [*as listed in affdt [3]*], sworn in court 26 Nov 1750. ITKB 'The King agt Thomas James the elder and Ann his wife William James Thomas James the younger Elianor Wiggin wife of Thomas Wiggin John Cottorell John Hinton otherwise Guy James Ross also Rossar and John Aaron Broad.'

That on Saturday last the deponent delivered a notice at the chambers in Lincoln's Inn of John Sharpe esquire, treasury solicitor, that the court would be moved on this day or soon as counsel can be heard that the defendants be admitted to defend as paupers.

[5] Petition of Thomas James, his wife Anne, William James, Thomas James the younger, Thomas Wiggin, Elianor Wiggin, John Cotteral, John Hinton alias Guy, James Ross alias Rossar and John Aaron Broad [*no date*]. [*Ann James, Elianor Wiggin, and John Hinton alias Guy signed with a mark.*]

To the right honourable Sir William Lee knight chief of the court of King's Bench at Westminster and to the other members of the court. As your petitioners are extremely poor (as by affidavit annexed [6] appears), they humbly beseech that they allowed to defend the information as paupers.

[6] Affdt of all defendants, sworn before John Dearle (Thomas, Ann, and William James) and Roger Holmes (the other deponents) at

Stafford 19 Nov 1750 and at Walsall 20 Nov 1750 respectively. ITKB 'The King against James and others.' [*Verso*]: 'Staffordshire. The King agt James & others. Affidt & Petition Defts to be admitted Paupers.'

[All male defendants]: That they are not worth £5 in the whole world.

[All female defendants]: That they have nothing in their own right and nothing held in trust for them.

Prosecution affidavits against pauper status:

Hil 24 Geo II 1751

[7] Affdt of Andrew Wall, innholder of Walsall, sworn before Roger Holmes at Walsall 26 Jan 1750/1. ITKB 'The King against Thomas James and others.' [*Verso*]: 'Staffords. Affidts Thacker, Wall & Smith to discharge Rule for admitting James & others Paupers. 3 affts fo11. fo.3.'

That it is the general report in Walsall that several gentleman are taking up a collection to defray the expenses of the defendants. He believes the report to be true because the defendants would not otherwise be able to afford an attorney or court fees. On 29 Oct 1750 Nicholas Summerfield, a scot who sometimes carries a pack, told him that the gentlemen who met at Wolseley Bridge had raised £300 for the defendants' legal expenses. Summerfield was present at the time of the meeting. Sir John Astley was among those present. But where Summerfield now is the deponent cannot set forth.

[8] Affdt of Robert Thacker, gentleman of Lichfield, sworn before Uppingham Bourne at Lichfield 18 Dec 1750. ITKB 'The King against Thomas James and others.'

That he was at the Red Lyon public house in Sutton Coldfield 1 Aug 1750 with John Scott, whose mother keeps the excise office there. The deponent, having heard collections were being taken up for the Walsall rioters in Stafford gaol, asked Scott if anyone was taking collections in Sutton Coldfield. At first Scott said no, but then said two men had been collecting money for them but declined to mention who they were. Scott said he had contributed 2s for the defence of a woman defendant whom he knew but knew of no other persons who had contributed money for that purpose.

[9] Affdt of Edward Smith, city officer of excise, late of Walsall, now of Lichfield, sworn before Uppingham Bourne at Lichfield 18 Dec 1750. ITBK 'The King against Thomas James and others.'

That when he lived in Walsall it was common knowledge that a fund was being raised privately for the defence of Thomas James et al. The deponent moved to Lichfield on 17 July 1750 and since has heard frequently, and believes, that the money for the defence has been raised.

Further defence affidavits for pauper status:

Hil 24 Geo II 1751

[10] Affdt of Thomas James and other defendants [*listed in [3]*], sworn before Roger Holmes at Walsall 31 Jan 1750/1. ITKB 'The King against Thomas James and others.'
   That they know of no money collected for their defence, but they know of some money given by a few persons to them while at the Stafford gaol, with the exception of John Aaron Broad who was not in Stafford gaol, for their charitable support and relief and for their families to buy bread.

[11] Affdt of Sir John Astley, baronet, sworn before M. Wright at his chambers in Serjeants' Inn, Chancery Lane, London 21 Feb 1750/1. ITKB 'The King against James and others.'
   That he was mentioned in Andrew Wall's affdt [7] but was not present at Wolseley Bridge when the £300 or any sum at all was raised for the expenses of the defendants. He knows of no fundraising by any gentlemen for this purpose.

Defence affidavit in mitigation for Marlow, Samuel and Stephen Higgins, and Thomas Wiggin:

Mich 25 Geo II 1751

[12] Affdt of Thomas Marlow, stirrup maker, Samuel Higgins, Stephen Higgins and Thomas Wiggin, all of Walsall, sworn in court 26 Oct 1751. ITKB 'Between the King Plt and Samuel Higgins, Stephen Higgins and Thomas Wiggin Defts.'
   [Marlow]: That he knows Samuel Higgins, Stephen Higgins and Thomas Wiggin, defendants, and says they are all poor and unable to support themselves except by their daily labour. The defendants are charged with rioting on 29 May 1750 but surrendered voluntarily to the mayor and justices of the peace without need of a warrant to be taken out against them. He has heard the Stafford gaol keeper say that while the defendants were in gaol they helped voluntarily to recapture five of seven prisoners who broke gaol; two of them were capital convicts.
   [Higgins, Higgins and Wiggin]: That although the deponents were unfortunately present at the riot *they did not dress up any effigy nor did*

they see it until it was brought out onto the street.[35] Nor did they knew who the effigy resembled. *The deponents voluntarily surrendered to the mayor, who with John Wyrley*[36] *and Sir Richard Wrottesley committed the deponents to Stafford gaol. They have been in gaol from Sept 1750 to 27 July 1751* when they were let out on bail. *Wiggin was forced to stay for six weeks longer for his fees,* while having four helpless children in the utmost distress.

When the *gaol was broke open and seven* felons escaped, the deponents helped the under keeper capture five of them, two of whom were sentenced to death. They know of no information ever being read to them nor do they know the particulars of the charges against them. They have pleaded guilty and are relying on the mercy of the court. They have no money and no friends in London and their families are starving.

Sources: ASSI 2/15, Staffs summer assizes 24 Geo II, 1750. ASSI 2/16, Staffs summer assizes 25 Geo II, 1751. KB 1/10 Mich, Hil 24 Geo II, Mich 25 Geo II. KB 11/39 Mich 24 Geo II [1750] #36. KB 15/14 Hil 24 Geo II. KB 21/36, pp. 607, 616, 626, 643, 657, 658, 717. KB 28/196 Hil 24 Geo II, 1750, roll 32. KB 29/410 Mich, Hil 24 Geo II. KB 36/139 Mich 25 Geo II.

C.14 Information ex officio (30 April 1800)

Defendant: Joseph Haynes labourer of Brettle Lane, Kingswinford.

Information:
Ea 40 Geo III [1800] [Exhibited 30 April 1800, FDT]
[1] violent assault and obstruction of an excise officer, James Evans, at Brettle Lane 20 Feb [1800]; [2] violently hindered and obstructed an excise officer; [3] violent assault on an excise officer on duty; [4] violent assault on an excise officer [*no mention of his being on duty*] (attorney general).

Rules and process:
Ea [30 April 1800]: information exhibited. ST: summons; entry of an appearance. Trin [20 June 1800]: first rule to plead. ST: pleads not guilty. ST [2 July 1800]: rule for a special jury, instance of prosr (Jackson). ST 7 July 1800: notice of trial for the King (Dealtry and Barlow).

Sources: IND 1/6664, Ea, Trin 40 Geo III. KB 11/61 Ea 40 Geo III [1800] #8. KB 15/17 Trin 40 Geo III. KB 21/47 pp. 381, 405. KB 28/394 roll 16. KB 29/459 Ea 40 Geo III.

---

[35]   This and the other italicized passages are underlined in the original.
[36]   'Worley' in original.

C.15 Information ex officio (13 June 1800)

Defendant: John Bucknall, late dealer in spirits of Newcastle under Lyme.

Information:
Trin 40 Geo III 1800 [Exhibited 13 June 1800, FDT]
[1] Intending to cheat and defraud the excise of six gallons (forfeited British spirits), violent assault and obstruction in their duty of Richard Pearson and Samuel Barber, excise officers, who had attempted to seize the spirits 9 June [1800] at Newcastle under Lyme; [2] violent obstruction of Richard Pearson in his duty, s.d.; [3] violent assault on Richard Pearson, excise officer, s.d.; [4] violent assault and obstruction of both officers on duty, s.d.; [5] violent assault on both officers, s.d.; [6] violent assault on Richard Pearson, excise officer, 10 June [1800] (attorney general).

Rules and process:
Trin [13 June 1800]: information exhibited; summons. Mich [1800]: entry of an appearance. Hil [23 Jan 1801]: first rule to plead. ST [27 Jan 1800]: second rule to plead. ST [31 Jan 1801]: peremptory rule to plead within 10 days. ST: pleads not guilty. ST [12 Feb 1801]: rule for a special jury, instance of prosr (Jackson). Hil Vac, 27 Feb 1801: notice of trial for the king (Dealtry and Barlow); countermanded 7 March 1801 (Dealtry and Barlow).

Affidavit for prosecution:

Trin 40 Geo III 1800

[1] Affdt of Richard Pearson officer of excise and Samuel Barber officer of excise both of Newcastle under Lyme, sworn before Thomas Sparrow at Newcastle under Lyme 17 June 1800. ITKB [*Verso*]: '3 Excise Trin 1800. Staff. Afft of Richard Pearson and drawn against John Bucknall late of Newcastle under Lyme, Dealer in Spirits. Dealtry & Barlow. fo. 6.'
    [Pearson]: That 9 June 1800 the deponent, as an excise officer, went to the premises of Bucknall to survey the liquor there and take account of his stock. He found an illegal excess of six gallons British compound spirits without a permit or certificate to protect them. The spirits were liable to be seized and forfeited. Bucknall began to abuse and threaten the deponent in a violent and outrageous manner and actually threatened to shoot the deponent, and by force and violence prevented the

deponent and Samuel Barber from seizing the spirits. Bucknall forced them to leave the house.

[Pearson and Barber]: That the next morning they went to Bucknall's premises and seized the liquor (Bucknall not then being at home) and conveyed it to the proper excise officer in Newcastle. They then went to Barber's house where they were followed by Bucknall who entered, and armed with a brace of pistols, threatened to shoot the deponents. The deponents closed with him and then carried him before the mayor of Newcastle who detained him in custody. They consider themselves in danger from Bucknall.

Sources: IND 1/6664 Mich, Hil 41 Geo III. KB 1/32 Trin 40 Geo III. KB 11/61 Trin 40 Geo III 1800 #6. KB 15/17 Hil Vac 41 Geo III. KB 21/47, pp. 444, 449, 454, 472. KB 28/396 Hil 41 Geo III, roll 8. KB 29/459 Trin 40 Geo III. KB 29/460 Mich, Hil 41 Geo III. KB 32/2 Trin1800.

Section D

By the terms of a large number of statutes it was possible for a 'common informer', any private citizen, to begin a 'penal action' or a 'popular action' against an offender. It was so called because it had elements of both a criminal prosecution and a civil suit, and because anyone could bring one: 'they are given to the people in general'.[1] The informer who secured a conviction shared the penalty with the crown, and in such instances the information before 1731 began with the words, *qui tam pro domino rege, quam pro se ipso, sequitur* (who as well for our Lord the King, as for himself, sues). Such qui tam informations as were still possible under statute were abolished by the Common Informers Act, 1951,[2] but in the eighteenth century they were very common, and certain kinds could be begun not only before justices of the peace in summary proceedings (the most common venue), but also in the high courts, including King's Bench. Common informers provided a cheap enforcement mechanism for government and for private persons, but they were much hated by those on whom they informed, in part because informers sometimes incited the offence, or perjured themselves for profit.[3]

Without exception, the Staffordshire qui tams in King's Bench in these years were prosecutions under the game laws; game cases were still said to be the most common kind of qui tam proceedings in King's Bench in the early nineteenth century. All game cases were eligible for King's Bench proceedings by an Act of 1721, which provided that

> where any person for any offence against any law in being for the better preservation of the game, shall be liable to pay any pecuniary penalty or sum of money, on conviction before a justice of the peace, the prosecutor may either proceed to recover the same in such

---

[1] Blackstone, iii, 160; the term is also found in the statute 4 Hen VII, c.20 (1488). See also [Anon.], 'The History and Development of Qui Tam', *Washington University Law Quarterly*, (1972), 81 ff.

[2] 14 & 15 Geo VI, c.39 (1951).

[3] The cases in Section E arose when defendants sought to overturn their convictions.

manner, or he may sue for the same by ... information ... at Westminster, with double costs.[4]

After 1753 the proceedings had to be brought before the end of the second term after the offence was committed, a time limit changed in 1762 to six months.[5] By the 1721 Act the informer took half the penalty, and the other half went for the relief of the poor of the parish; by the 1762 Act the informer kept the entire penalty. (In the former case, the information refers to the informer as he 'who as well for the poor of the parish of Kingswinford as himself in this behalf prosecuteth in his proper person').[6] The most important change, however, was simply the right conferred by the 1721 Act to proceed in King's Bench and the other courts at Westminster, where the complexity of the procedure, and attendant fees, vastly increased the expense to defendants where convictions were secured, and always burdened them with all the delay, inconvenience and expenditure of a serious lawsuit. For plaintiffs, however, the use of qui tam in King's Bench was a relatively inexpensive, speedy, and useful process in a sure case. Not surprisingly, given the unpopularity of the game laws, the use of the qui tam information in King's Bench aroused enormous resentment, in part because conviction or a forced settlement was highly likely: it is clear that almost all of the Staffordshire cases had such an outcome.[7]

In qui tam proceedings on the game laws the poacher sometimes outwitted the squire. The qui tam action, if successful, conferred property on the informer; therefore, once the process was begun, no other person could take action against the offender. The poacher could block a gamekeeper who was about to lay an information by asking a friend to do so instead. Collusion on qui tams among poachers probably took place

---

[4] 8 Geo I, c.19 (1721). See also Gude, i, 166ff, who mentions that most penal actions in King's Bench in the 1820s were still on the game laws, and who is also the source for the following account of proceedings. The same penalties could be sued for civilly, under the same terms.

[5] 26 Geo II, c.2 (1753); 2 Geo III, c.19 (1762).

[6] The information in case D.9. All cases in this section were under the 1721 Act.

[7] It was possible in qui tam for the real complainant to remain anonymous, with the informer named on the information acting as his or her agent, as Bentham noted: Jeremy Bentham, *Works* (ed. Bowring, 1838–43; repr. New York, 1962), iv, 390, note. In the case of game offences, however, the complainant was assumed to be the owner or lord of the manor of the land where the offence was committed.

almost entirely before justices of the peace, rather than in King's Bench, but one case here (D.9) may be such an instance.[8] On the other hand, another case (D.30) was prompted by the prosecutor's outrage at just such collusion.

Obtaining an information qui tam
Qui tam proceedings in King's Bench were begun by the affidavit of a witness, which was filed by a clerk in court, and left with him (or counsel in difficult cases) as a basis for drawing the information.[9] These affidavits do not appear to have survived, perhaps because they were not required for subsequent argument before the court (as was the case with other kinds of informations).[10] The informations, now filed in KB 11,[11] were engrossed on parchment by the clerk in court; the informer

[8] On collusive proceedings before Staffordshire justices, see D. Hay, 'Poaching and the Game Laws on Cannock Chase', in D. Hay, P. Linebaugh, E. P. Thompson, *Albion's Fatal Tree: Crime and Society in Eighteenth-Century England* (London, 1975), 198. Collusive actions did not bar *bona fide* proceedings in law, although they may often have done so in practice: Blackstone, i, 160.

[9] Gude, i, 561.

[10] See Sections A, B. Affidavits have been identified only in cases D.10 and D.23; in both, they support later process, rather than the drawing of the original information. Some original affidavits are to be found from time to time: e.g. KB 1/9/6, Trin 21 & 22 Geo II, information by James Gardner, 18 Nov 1748, an Essex case. See note 11.

[11] Early in the twentieth century it was proposed to destroy all 'informations' respecting 'Customs, 1727 to 1843', 'Excise, 1717 to 1830', and 'Game, 1747 to 1820': *Reprint of Statutes, Rules and Schedules Governing the Disposal of Public Records by Destruction or Otherwise, 1877–1913* (London, HMSO, 1914), 108. All three kinds of cases were prosecuted as qui tams. Examples of the first two are found in KB 32, and the examples of Staffordshire game cases reprinted in this volume cover the period 1742 to 1791. It is possible that others were destroyed, although all cases that I have found mentioned in private correspondence in the Staffordshire Record Office appear to survive in the records of the court. It is possible that the destruction schedule uses the word 'informations' in the common sense of 'affidavits', which could account for the lack of qui tam affidavits in the surviving records of the court. On the other hand, there is a reference in the schedule to the informations having been entered on the Crown Rolls, as a justification for their destruction, and affidavits were not so entered; rather the text of the parchment informations was copied there. Yet the parchment informations survive in KB 11.

signed at the foot, and personally delivered it in open court to the
master of the crown office, who endorsed the date it was received, a
date in term time, which by statute was the date on which process could
commence.[12] The endorsement usually, but not always, coincides with
the date given for the appearance of the informer, recorded at the beginning of the information.[13] Many of the 35 exhibited informations from
Staffordshire are very prolix, and the parchment correspondingly large,
as each offence required both a statement that the accused was unqualified to hunt game, as well as a detailed description of the acts that
brought the accused within the statute. The name of the informer, or
prosecutor, is included in the information, but that person could not be
a material witness because being named as the informer rendered him
incompetent to testify, as he had an interest in the penalty.

Process on an information
The informer's clerk in court then issued an attachment[14] (noted in KB
29), directed to the sheriff of the county where the defendant might be
found; the defendant was thereby arrested, and the sheriff could take
bail for £10.[15] If the defendant did not offer bail, he was gaoled; if bailed,
but he did not enter an appearance in court four days after the return of
the writ, the informer could take an assignment of the bail bond. If
gaoled, the defendant was brought into court by writ of habeas corpus.[16] In 22 of the 35 cases in this section, no process after the initial
attachment is recorded. In one of these cases (D.22) we know the reason:
the defendant absconded. It was probably a common response to an
information qui tam in the crown office.

---

[12]   31 Eliz., c.5 (1588); Gude, i, 168. The endorsement in case D.9 reads in part,
       'this Information was delivered here into Court upon Tuesday next after 15
       days from the Feast of St Martin (that is to say) 27 November in the 18th year
       of the Reign of King George the Second ... to be determined upon Record.
       [signed] James Burrow.'
[13]   See case D.5, in which the endorsement is one week later than the date given
       for the appearance of the informer; however, this may be a clerk's error.
[14]   Gude, ii, 154, no.10. See also the notes to case D.1.
[15]   But in the last five cases a summons rather than an attachment is recorded
       on the controlment rolls (KB 29): see cases D.31 to D.35. Rather than a
       change in process (there is no relevant general rule of court between the
       time of case D.30 and D.31), clerical error seems likely: for D.34 an attach-
       ment is found in KB 16.
[16]   In the same manner as in process on an information: see Sections A, B.

A defendant wishing to reply to the information entered an appearance through a clerk in court, who then supplied (for the usual fee) the defendant with an office copy of the information. It was possible at this point to offer to compound — to compromise the suit with the informer for a lesser sum than might result from a full trial. Compounding required permission of the court (recorded in KB 21): this is recorded for three cases (D.1, D.3, and D.10).[17] A defendant might also retract a plea of not guilty (D.35). The most common response was to pray an imparlance, deferring the case to the next term. Meanwhile a prosecutor could obtain a side bar rule to correct an error in the name of the defendant (D.23).

If a defendant's plea of not guilty (D.10, D.23, D.35), or special plea of formerly convict, etc. (D.9) was not replied to, the defendant was entitled to costs (D.23, and see below). Judgment also went to him if the informer did not proceed to trial. On the other hand, if the defendant did not appear to plead, the informer intent upon a judgment proceeded with two four-day rules to plead, and a peremptory four-day rule to plead (KB 21), as in proceedings on other kinds of informations (D.1, D.2, D.3, D.9, D.23, D.29, D.35). Subsequent process also was virtually identical to such proceedings.[18]

Trial and judgment
After trial of the cause in the county at nisi prius, the solicitor for the successful informer had the postea returned, and the clerk in court signed judgment. Only two cases appear to have reached this stage: in D.2 the defendant was convicted by default, and in D.29 there was a verdict at nisi prius. An appointment with the master was had to tax the costs (recorded in KB 21): see D.2. In game cases the informer was entitled to double costs by 8 Geo I, c.19, which in law was interpreted to mean the common costs, and then, after deducting fees to counsel, half the common costs again.[19] Costs and the penalty, if not paid by the defendant, were then pursued by means of a *capias ad satisfaciendum* to

---

[17] In some cases there is also an affidavit: see case D.10. By a rule of court of 1766, whenever leave was given by the court to compound, 'the King's half of the composition shall be paid into the hands of the master of the crown office, for the use of his majesty.' In 1793 a new rule also required express agreement of the defendant to pay the money, since defendants had been evading or delaying payment. Gude, i, 370, 380.

[18] Gude, i, 170; see Section A.

[19] Gude, i, 171, 562.

arrest the defendant, or a *fieri facias* to seize his goods, the usual writs used in recovering judgment debts in civil cases.[20]

Costs in such cases could be substantial. In the mid-eighteenth century a critic suggested that a simple case could burden the defendant with costs of £50 to £80 or more.[21] There was a strong motive for defendants to settle, or to flee, before trial.

CASES

D.1 Information qui tam (16 Nov 1742)

Defendant: Benjamin Winwood, baker of Wordsley in the parish of Kingswinford.

Information:
Mich 16 Geo II [1742] 16 Nov [1742][22]
Possession of one net or tunnel (forfeits £5), at Enville, 30 Aug [1742]. Samuel Law, yeoman of St Clement Danes (Middx), informer for himself and the poor of Enville.[23]

---

[20] Gude, i, 164, 171. The records of these further proceedings are not found in the crown side records of King's Bench.

[21] Hay, 'Poaching and the Game Laws on Cannock Chase', 237. In the early nineteenth century Gude cites cases of taxed costs of £20 6s (plaintiff's costs on a compounded case), and £76 17s (defendant's costs on a verdict obtained). Gude, i, 562, 564. The annual income of a labourer at the end of the eighteenth century was about £20.

[22] The date given here is that on which the informant was said to 'give the court to understand and be informed', according to the text of the information: i.e., the date on which it was said to be 'exhibited.' ('Ex'd' is written in the lower left corner of all informations.) In the endorsement is given the date when they were 'delivered into court'; this was the day it was 'actually exhibited' (Gude, i, 167ff; ii, 238, 240). In all but one (D.5) of the *qui tam* informations examined here, it corresponds to the date given in the text of the information. The master of the crown office was required to note on all informations exhibited on penal statutes the day, month and year on which it was exhibited (Gude, i, 23).

[23] The informer's name in D.1, D.2 and D.3 is sometimes given in KB 21/35 as Dovey.

Rules and process: Mich [1742]: attached[24]; prays a day to answer; leave to imparl. Hil [21 Jan 1742/3]: first rule to plead. ST [28 Jan 1742/3]: second rule to plead. ST [5 Feb 1742/3]: peremptory rule to plead (Ford). ST [7 Feb 1742/3]: prosr at liberty to compound the penalty with defdt (Frederick).

Sources: KB 11/36/3 Mich 16 Geo II [1747] #10. KB 15/2 b53 Mich. KB 21/35 pp. 531, 537, 547, 550. KB 29/402 Mich 16 Geo II.

D.2 Information qui tam (16 Nov 1742)

Defendant: Edward Houghton [Haughton], victualler of Amblecote [*see also D.19*].

Information:
Mich 16 Geo II [1742]
[*The body of the information is identical to D.1.*]

Rules and process: Mich [1742]: attached; prays a day to answer; leave to imparl. Hil [21 Jan 1742/3]: first rule to plead. ST [28 Jan 1742/3]: second rule to plead (Ford). ST [10 Feb 1742/3]: peremptory rule to plead. ST: convicted by default; capias ad satisfaciendum.

Sources: KB 11/36/3 Mich 16 Geo II [1742] #11. KB 15/2 b53. KB 21/35 pp. 531, 538, 558. KB 29/402 Mich 16 Geo II, Hil 17 Geo II.

D.3 Information qui tam (16 Nov 1742)

Defendant: Joseph Butler, butcher of Cradley (Worcs).

Information:
Mich 16 Geo II [1742]
[*The body of the information is identical to D.1.*]

Rules and process: Mich [1742]: attached; prays a day to answer; leave to imparl. Hil [21 Jan 1742/3]: first rule to plead. ST [28 Jan 1742/3]: second rule to plead. ST [7 Feb 1742/3]: prosr at liberty to compound

---

[24] The attachment is recorded in the controlment rolls, KB 29, and differs from that given in Gude, ii, 154 in specifying that the defdt is to answer 'as well to our Lord the King as to Samuel Law for a certain trespass and contempt whereof he is impeached.'

the penalty with defdt (Gapper). ST [8 Feb 1742/3]: peremptory rule to plead (Ford).

Sources: KB 11/36/3 Mich 16 Geo II [1747] #12. KB 15/2 b53. KB 21/35 pp. 531, 538, 550, 554. KB 29/402 Mich 16 Geo II.

D.4 Information qui tam (16 May 1743)

Defendant: Richard Guest, nailer of Sedgley.

Information:
Ea 16 Geo II [1743] 16 May [1743]
Had and used gins and snares (forfeits £5), at Sedgley, 17 April [1743]. Samuel Law [*as in D.1*], informer for himself and the poor of Sedgley.

Rules and process: Ea [1743]: attached.

Sources: KB 11/36/3 Ea 16 Geo II [1743] #16. KB 29/402 Ea 16 Geo II.

D.5 Information qui tam (24 Jan 1743/4)

Defendant: Ward Bagley, baker of Dudley (Worcs).

Information:
Hil 17 Geo II [1743/4] [24 Jan 1743/4] [*Endorsed* 31 Jan][25]
[1] Killing one hare (forfeits £5); [2] possession of one gun (forfeits £5), at Sedgley, 21 Nov [1743]. Samuel Law [*as in D.1*], informer for himself and the poor of Sedgley.

Rules and process: Hil [1743/4]: attached.

Sources: KB 11/36/8 Hil 17 Geo II [1743/4] #18. KB 29/403 Hil 17 Geo II.

---

[25] The engrossed information was personally delivered in open court into the hands of the master of the crown office, who endorsed the day it was received; in most cases (although not this) the endorsement date is the same as the date on which the informer is said, in the text of the information, to come into court. See Gude, i, 167ff.

D.6 Information qui tam (31 Jan 1743/4)

Defendant: Thomas Davis, hatter of Stourbridge (Worcs).

Information:
Hil 17 Geo II [1743/4] 31 Jan [1743/4]
[1] Selling one hare to Samuel Wilson of Amblecote (forfeits £5); [2] and offering for sale one other hare to Samuel Wilson (forfeits £5), at the township of Amblecote, Old Swinford, 12 Dec [1743]. Samuel Law [*as in D.1*], informer for himself and the poor of Old Swinford.

Rules and process: Hil [1743/4]: attached.

Sources: KB 11/36/8 Hil 17 Geo II [1743/4] #17. KB 29/403 Hil 17 Geo II.

D.7 Information qui tam (13 February 1743/4)

Defendant: John Crutchley, labourer of Wombourn.

Information:
Hil 17 Geo II [1743/4] 13 Feb [1743/4]
[1] Kept and used a gun (forfeits £5); [2] and one spaniel (forfeits £5), at Sedgley, 21 Dec [1743]. Samuel Law [*as in D.1*], informer for himself and the poor of Sedgley.

Rules and process: Hil [1743/4]: attached.

Sources: KB 11/36/8 Hil 17 Geo II [1743/4] #19. KB 29/403 Hil 17 Geo II.

D.8 Information qui tam (13 Feb 1743/4)

Defendant: William Guest, brickmaker of Chaddesley [Corbett] (Worcs).

Information:
Hil 17 Geo II [1743/4] 13 Feb [1743/4]
[1] Kept and used a gun (forfeits £5); and [2] a spaniel (forfeits £5), at Sedgley, 21 Dec [1743]. Samuel Law [*as in D.1*], informer for himself and the poor of Sedgley.

Rules and process: Hil [1743/4]: attached.

Sources: KB 11/36/8 Hil 17 Geo II [1743/4] #16. KB 29/403 Hil 17 Geo II.

D.9 Information qui tam (27 Nov 1744)

Defendant: Thomas Worrall, yeoman of Stourton in the parish of Kinver.

Information: Mich 18 Geo II [1744] 27 Nov [1744]
[1] Possession of one setting dog (forfeits £5); [2] and one net (forfeits £5), at Kingswinford, 31 July [1744]. Samuel Law [*as in D.1*], informer for himself and the poor of Kingswinford.

Rules and process: Hil [1744/5]: attached; prays a day to answer; leave to imparl; imparls. Ea [1 May 1745]: first rule to plead. ST [4 May]: second rule to plead. ST [16 May]: peremptory rule to plead (Heckford). ST [1745]: special plea.[26] Trin [14 June 1745]: unless the [master of the crown office] shall reply to the special plea on Monday next let judgment be entered for the defendant. Trin [18 June 1746]: unless the [master] shall peremptorily reply to the defdt's special plea let judgment be entered into for the defdt (Wheler).[27] Trin [1746]: judgment for want of a replication to the special plea of the defdt. [Goes] without day. Hil [10 Feb 1746/7]: [the master] to tax costs, to be paid by informer to defdt, Worrall (side bar rule). Trin [25 June 1747]: defdt to show cause by [1 July 1747] why the rule made in this cause that it should be referred to [the master] to tax the costs to be paid by the informer to defdt should not be discharged upon notice of this rule to be given to defdt in the meantime (Evans).[28] Mich [19 Nov 1747]: court will

---

[26] Worrall pleaded that he had already been convicted of the offence before a justice of the peace on 9 Aug, in a penalty of £5; his plea of previous conviction is reproduced in Gude, ii, 615-17.

[27] For this 'rule to reply to a special plea' see Gude, ii, 650, no.20.

[28] This case was reported on the issue of costs: *Law qui tam etc.* v *Worrall*, 1 Wils. K.B. 177, 95 ER 559 (and cited in Gude, i, 170). The report reads in its entirety: 'Information on the Stat. 8 Geo. 1, for killing game; the defendant pleaded a conviction before a justice of peace for the same fact, and the defendant had judgment for want of a replication, and obtained a side-Bar rule for costs, which Mr. Evans now moved to set aside, alledging that the statute did not give the defendant costs, and that the Stat. 18 Eliz. c. 5, does not extend to the subsequent statutes. But per Cur. — The words of the stat. 18 Eliz. c. 5, are as general as any statute relating to costs, and seem to extend to every informer upon any penal statute who shall delay his suit, discon-

consider the matter (Evans). Hil [1747/8] previous rule discharged; costs to be taxed (Ford).

Sources: IND 1/6659 Hil 18 Geo II, Trin 19 & 20 Geo II. KB 11/36/11 Mich 18 Geo II [1744] #20. KB 15/2 b57v. KB 21/35 pp.838, 842, 850. KB 21/36 pp.115, 133, 184, 230, 261, 278. KB 29/404 Mich 18 Geo II. KB 36/113.

D.10 Information qui tam (7 Feb 1744/5)

Defendant: John Budworth, yeoman of Marchington in the parish of Hanbury.

Information: Hil 18 Geo II [1744/5] 7 Feb [1744]/5]
[1] Kept 2 guns (forfeits £5); [2] and 2 other guns (forfeits £5); [3] and 13 nets (forfeits £5); [4] and 13 other nets (forfeits £5) at Hanbury, 29 Dec [1744]. Robert Rattenbury barber of St Clement Danes (Midd), informer for himself and the poor of Hanbury.

Rules and process: Hil [1744/5]: attached. Trin [1745]: imparls, pleads not guilty. ST: venire facias juratores. ST [3 July 1745]: with consent of counsel on both sides, liberty to compound on reading affdt [1] (Gilbert for defdt).

Affidavit:

Trin 18 & 19 Geo II

[1] Affdt of Michael Barbor gentleman, agent for the informer, of Lyons Inn (Mddx), sworn by the court in court 3 July 1745. ITKB [*Verso*]: 'Rattenbury who as well &c agt Budworth: Affidt to compound with deft. Compounded. Mr Gilbert.'
    That the information is for keeping and using guns and nets for the destruction of game within a lordship or manor belonging to George Venables Vernon esquire to which the defendant has appeared and pleaded not guilty. The deponent has since received information from Vernon's attorney and believes it to be true that the defendant has made

tinue, be nonsuit, or shall have the matter pass against him by verdict or judgment, such informer shall pay costs; and there have been a great number of cases like this where costs have been given; and cited Carter qui tam v Tooting, Mich. 12 Geo. 1 [*not otherwise reported*].' See also Gude, i, 170.

his submission and that Vernon is willing to compound for the offence mentioned in the information. Rattenbury the informer is also willing to compound.

Sources: IND 1/6659 Trinity 18 & 19 Geo II. KB 1/8 Trin 18 & 19 Geo II. KB 11/36/12 Hil 18 Geo II [1744/5] #4. KB 15/2 Trin 18 & 19 Geo II. KB 21/36 p.28. KB 29/404 Hil 18 Geo II, Trin 19 Geo II.

D.11 Information qui tam (12 Feb 1744/5)

Defendant: Joseph Clement, carpenter of Rowley Regis.

Information: Hil [1744/5] 12 Feb [1744/5]
[1] Kept one gun (forfeits £5); [2] and two dogs (forfeits £5), at Rowley Regis, 11 Jan [1744/5]. Samuel Law [*as in D.1*], informer for himself and the poor of Rowley Regis.

Rules and process: Hil [1744/5]: attached.

Sources: KB 11/36/12 Hil [1744/5] #18. KB 29/404 Hil 18 Geo II.

D.12 Information qui tam (12 Feb 1744/5)

Defendants: Cornelius Jesson the younger, Henry Jesson, Charles Jesson, George Scraggs, William Mulliner, all labourers of Wombourn.

Information: Hil 18 Geo II [1744/5] 2 Feb [1744/5]
Kept and used two greyhounds (forfeit £5 each), at Himley, 24 Jan [1744/5]. Samuel Law [*as in D.1*], informer for himself and the poor of Himley.

Rules and process: Hil [1744/5]: attached.

Sources: KB 11/36/12 Hil 18 Geo II [1744/5] #19. KB 29/404 Hil 18 Geo II.

D.13 Information qui tam (12 Feb 1744/5)

Defendant: John Crane, threadman of Rowley Regis.

Information:
Hil 18 Geo II [1744/5] 12 Feb [1744/5]
[1] Kept and used one gun (forfeits £5); [2] and two dogs (forfeits £5), at

Rowley Regis, 11 Jan [1744/5]. Samuel Law [*as in D.1*], informer for himself and the poor of Rowley Regis.

Rules and process: Hil [1744/5]: attached.

Sources: KB 11/36/12 Hil 18 Geo II [1744/5] #20. KB 29/404 Hil 18 Geo II.

D.14 Information qui tam (12 Feb 1744/5)

Defendant: William Clement, carpenter of Rowley Regis.

Information:
Hil 18 Geo II [1744/5]
[*The body of the information is identical to D.13.*]
Rules and process: Hil [1744/5]: attached.

Sources: KB 11/36/12 Hil 18 Geo II [1744/5] #21. KB 29/404 Hil 18 Geo II.

D.15 Information qui tam (12 Feb 1744/5)

Defendant: Samuel Willetts, butcher of Rowley Regis.

Information:
Hil 18 Geo II [1744/5] 12 Feb [1744/5]
Kept and used a gun (forfeits £5), at Rowley Regis, 4 Jan [1744/5]. Samuel Law [*as in D.1*], informer for himself and the poor of Rowley Regis.

Rules and process: Hil [1744/5]: attached.

Sources: KB 11/36/12 Hil 18 Geo II [1744/5] #22. KB 29/404 Hil 18 Geo II.

D.16 Information qui tam (25 Nov 1745)

Defendant: John Godwin, glassmaker of Kingswinford.

Information:
Mich 19 Geo II [1745] 25 Nov [1745]
[1] Shot and killed one partridge (forfeits £5); [2] and kept and used a gun (forfeits £5), at Kingswinford, 3 Oct [1745]. Samuel Law [*as in D.1*],

informer for himself and the poor of Kingswinford.

Rules and process: Mich [1745]: attached.

Sources: KB 11/37 Mich 19 Geo II [1745] #27. KB 29/405 Mich 19 Geo II.

D.17 Information qui tam (12 Feb 1745/6)

Defendants: John Plant, groundcollier and John Wakeman trumpmaker, both of Old Swinford.

Information:
Hil 19 Geo II [1745/6] 12 Feb [1745/6]
Caught one hare (forfeit £5 each), at the township of Amblecote, Old Swinford, 17 Dec [1745]. Samuel Law [*as in D.1*], informer for himself and the poor of Old Swinford.

Rules and process: Hil [1745/6]: attached.

Sources: KB 11/37 Hil 19 Geo II [1745/6] #14. KB 29/405 Hil 19 Geo II.

D.18 Information qui tam (12 Feb 1747/8)

Defendant: Thomas Poole the younger, gentleman of Weston (Ches).

Information:
Hil 21 Geo II [1747/8] 12 Feb [1747/8]
[1] Kept and used a greyhound (forfeits £5); [2] and coursed and killed one hare (forfeits £5), at Keele, 1 Jan [1747/8]. William Broome vintner of St Mary, Westminster (Middx), informer for himself and the poor of Keele.

Rules and process: Hil [1747/8]: attached.

Sources: KB 11/38 Hil 21 Geo II [1747/8] #6. KB 29/407 Hil 21 Geo II.

D.19 Information qui tam (2 Feb 1748/9)

Defendants: Edward Haughton, victualler [*see also D.2*] and John Squire, labourer, both of the township of Amblecote, Old Swinford.

Information:
Hil 22 Geo II [1748/9] 2 Feb [1748/9]

[1] Kept and used one gate net (forfeit £5); [2] and kept and used 2 dogs (forfeit £5 each), at Old Swinford, 1 Nov [1748]. Thomas Leek yeoman of St Clement Danes (Middx), informer for himself and the poor of Old Swinford.

Rules and process: Hil [1748/9]: attached. Trin [1749]: leave to imparl [*John Squire only*].

Sources: KB 11/38 Hil 22 Geo II [1748/9] #23. KB 15/2 b71v Trin 22 & 23 Geo II. KB 29/408 Hil 22 Geo II.

D.20 Information qui tam (12 Feb 1749/50)

Defendants: Samuel Barrett, feltmaker and John Mare, towdresser, both of Newcastle under Lyme.

Information:
Hil 23 Geo II [1749/50] 12 Feb [1749/50]
[1] Kept and used one gun (forfeit £5 each); [2] and kept and used four spaniels (forfeit £5 each) at Swynnerton, 21 Nov [1749]. William Tinling gentleman of St Andrew Holborn (Middx), informer for himself and the poor of Swynnerton.

Rules and process: Hil [1749/50]: attached.

Sources: KB 11/39 Hil 23 Geo II [1749/50] #10. KB 29/409 Hil 23 Geo II.

D.21 Information qui tam (20 May 1751)

Defendants: George Gilbert, butcher and Edward Ratcliffe, labourer, both of Waterfall.

Information:
Ea 24 Geo II [1751] 20 May [1751]
[1] Kept a greyhound and used it to kill game (forfeit £5); [2] had a greyhound with them, used to kill game (forfeit £5), at Ellastone, 28 Jan [1750/1]. William Gregory the younger gentleman, of St Dunstan in the West (Middx), informer for himself and the poor of Ellastone.

Rules and process: Ea [1751]: attached.

Sources: KB 11/40 Ea 24 Geo II 1751 #6. KB 29/410 Ea 24 Geo II.

D.22 Information qui tam (29 Oct 1751)

Defendant: John Hodgkiss alias Hodgkins, sawyer of Kidderminster (Worcs).

Information:
Mich 25 Geo II [1751] 29 Oct [1751]
Had and used an engine to destroy the game (forfeits £5) at Enville, 23 Oct [1751]. Thomas Downes gentleman of St Clement Danes (Middx), informer for himself and the poor of Enville.

Rules and process: Mich [1751]: attached.[29]

Sources: KB 11/40 Mich 25 Geo II [1751] #1. KB 29/411 Mich 25 Geo II.

D.23 Information qui tam (12 Feb 1752)

Defendant: John Baker, chapman of Wolverhampton.

Information:
Hil 25 Geo II [1752] 12 Feb [1752]
[1] Killed one hare (forfeits £5), and exposed it to sale (forfeits £5), at Kingswinford 26 Nov [1751]. William Parker yeoman of St Clements Danes (Middx), informer for himself and the poor of Kingswinford.

Rules and process: Hil [1752]: attached. Ea [1752]: imparls. Hil [23 Jan 1753]: first rule to plead. ST [27 Jan 1753]: second rule to plead. ST [5 Feb 1753]: peremptory rule to plead (Ford). ST: pleads not guilty. Trin [1753]: venire facias juratores. Hil [5 Feb 1754]: on reading affdt [1] and entry of the issue upon record, rule nisi for judgment against prosr as in case of a nonsuit[30] (Nares). ST [8 Feb 1754]: side bar rule for change of name in information, from John to William. Hil Vac 13 March 1754: notice of trial for the prosr (Masterman). Ea [1754]: nonsuit; goes without day.

---

[29] Hodgkiss absconded, and the agent of Lord Stamford offered a reward of five guineas for information leading to his arrest on the attachment: *Aris' Birmingham Gazette*, 16 March 1752.
[30] Gude, i, 170.

Affidavits for defence:

Hil 27 Geo II 1754

[1] Affdt of William Crawley agent for the defendant, sworn in court by the court 5 Feb 1754. ITKB 'Between William Parker who etc Plt and John Baker Dft'. [*Verso*]: 'Staffords. Parker who &c agt Baker: Affidt of Issue being joined in Hil 1753 & no Notice of tryal being yet given.'

That in Hil term 1752 an information was exhibited by the prosecutor against the defendant, to which the defendant appeared. In Hil term 1753 issue was joined therein but no notice of trial has since been given nor has any other proceeding been taken by the prosecutor.

[*Annexed*]: [*Verso*]: 'In Kings Bench. Parker who &s agt Baker: Copy Notice of Motion for the like Judgment as in the Case of a Nonsuit. Please to move on this Notice which will be admitted to be delivered by Plts Clk in Court. Crawley.'

Notice to Thomas Masterman, clerk in court for the prosecutor, from Henry Walrond, clerk in court for the defendant, that he would move 4 Feb 1754 or as soon after as counsel could be heard that the defendant may be given the like judgment as in a nonsuit pursuant to the late act of Parliament.

[2] Affdt of William Crawley agent for the defendant, sworn in court by the court 12 Feb 1754. ITKB 'Parker who etc agt. Baker'.

That 5 Feb last the deponent delivered to Clowdesly's clerk at his chambers a true copy of the annexed rule. Clowdesly is the agent for the prosecutor in this cause and has signed the annexed undertaking to pay the defendant all such costs as he might be entitled to by law as a result of this prosecution against him.

[*Annexed*]: Rule of [5 Feb 1754].

[*Annexed*]: 'Staffordshire, William Parker who &c agt John Baker. In consideration that Mr William Crawley agent for John Baker the defendant in this cause hath at my request consented and agreed not to apply for any rule or order on the prosecutor in this cause to deliver to the said Deft or to his Clerk in Court Agent or Solicitor a Note of the place of abode of the Informer in this Cause, I do hereby undertake consent and agree on behalf of the said Informer and Prosecutor in this Cause to pay to the said Defendt or to his Order all such Costs as the said Defendt shall or may be intitled to by Law on account of this Prosecution against him. Dated this Nineteenth day of February 1753. Ha[rr]y Clowdesley.'

Sources: IND 1/6659 Ea 25 Geo II. KB 1/11 Hil 27 Geo II. KB 11/40 Hil 25 Geo II [1752] #5. KB 15/3 a6 Hil 26 Geo II. KB 15/14 Hil Vac 27 Geo

II. KB 21/37 pp.3, 12, 20, 167, 173. KB 29/411 Hil 25 Geo II. KB 29/412 Trin 26 Geo II. KB 29/413 Ea 27 Geo II.

D.24 Information qui tam (11 Nov 1752)

Defendant: John Mash the younger, locksmith of Little London, liberty of Willenhall.

Information:
Mich 26 Geo II [1752]11 Nov [1752]
[1] Killed one hare (forfeits £5); [2] used a brass wire to kill one hare (forfeits £5), at Bushbury 28 Sept [1752]. Cornelius Chapman yeoman of Staples Inn (London), informer for himself and the poor of Bushbury.

Rules and process: Mich [1752]: attached.

Sources: KB 11/40 Mich 26 Geo II 1752 #2. KB 29/412 Mich 26 Geo II.

D.25 Information qui tam (25 Nov 1752)

Defendant: Richard Alcock, labourer of Stoke upon Trent.

Information:
Mich 26 Geo II [1752] 25 Nov [1752]
Used a stick to kill the game (forfeits £5), at Stoke, 23 Oct [1752]. Cornelius Chapman [*as in D.24*], informer for himself and the poor of Stoke.

Rules and process: Mich [1752]: attached.

Sources: KB 11/40 Mich 26 Geo II 1752 #4. KB 29/412 Mich 26 Geo II.

D.26 Information qui tam (25 Nov 1752)

Defendant: Joseph Bradley, labourer of Newcastle under Lyme.

Information:
Mich 26 Geo II [1752] 25 Nov [1752]
Kept and used a gun, (forfeits £5), 23 Oct [1752] at Stoke upon Trent. Cornelius Chapman [*as in D.24*], informer for himself and the poor of Stoke.

Rules and process: Mich [1752]: attached.

Sources: KB 11/40 Mich 26 Geo II [1752] #3. KB 29/412 Mich 26 Geo II.

D.27 Information qui tam (25 Nov 1752)

Defendant: John Mare, labourer of Newcastle under Lyme.

Information:
Mich 26 Geo II [1752] 25 Nov [1752]
Kept and used a gun (forfeits £5) at Stoke, 23 Oct [1752]. Cornelius Chapman [*as in D.24*], informer for himself and the poor of Stoke.

Rules and process: Mich [1752]: attached. Ea [1755]: prays a day to answer; leave to imparl; imparls.

Sources: IND 1/6659 Ea 28 Geo II. KB 11/40 Mich 26 Geo II 1752 #5. KB 15/3 a15v Ea 28 Geo II. KB 29/412 Mich 26 Geo II. KB 29/414 Ea 28 Geo II.

D.28 Information qui tam (28 Nov 1753)

Defendant: Daniel Blakemore, butcher of Worfield (Salop).

Information:
Mich 27 Geo II [1753] 28 Nov [1753]
[1] Kept and used a setting dog to take a partridge (forfeits £5); [2] and used a dog to destroy the game (forfeits £5); [3] and offered the partridge for sale (forfeits £5) at Kingswinford, 6 Sept [1753]. John Blackburn gentleman of Clements Inn (Middx), informer for himself and the poor of Kingswinford.

Rules and process: Mich [1753]: attached.

Sources: KB 11/41 Mich 27 Geo II 1753 #11. KB 29/413 Mich 27 Geo II.

D.29 Information qui tam (20 Nov 1756)

Defendant: John Clewes, yeoman of Norton in the Moors.

Information:
Mich 30 Geo II [1756] 20 Nov [1756]
[1] Possessing one snare, (forfeits £5); [2] and used another snare to kill one hare (forfeits £5), at Wolstanton, 5 Aug [1756]. James Innell yeoman of Lincoln's Inn, informer for himself and the poor of Wolstanton.

Rules and process: Mich [1756]: attached; prays a day to answer; leave to imparl; imparls. Hil [24 Jan 1757]: first rule to plead. ST [28 Jan 1757]: second rule to plead. ST: pleads not guilty; venire facias juratores. Hil Vac 15 Feb 1757: notice of trial for the prosr (Althorpe). ST 23 Feb 1757: countermanded (Althorpe for prosr). Trin Vac 22 July 1757: notice of trial for the prosr (Althorpe). Mich [1757]: postea and judgment against; impeached; capias.

Sources: IND 1/6659 Mich, Hil 30 Geo II, Mich 31 Geo II. KB 11/42 Mich 30 Geo II 1756 #8. KB 15/3 a21b, a22. KB 15/14 Hil Vac 30 Geo II, Trin Vac 30 & 31 Geo II. KB 21/37 pp.579, 587. KB 29/416 Mich 30 Geo II, Hil 30 Geo II.

D.30 Information qui tam (8 Nov 1760)

Defendants: Joseph Harding the elder, maltster of Chorley (Farewell parish) and Robert Derry, labourer of Cannock.

Information:
Mich 1 Geo III [1760] 8 Nov [1760]
[1] Used a net (forfeit £5); [2] and killed one hare (forfeit £5); [3] had in their custody one hare (forfeit £5); [4] exposed the hare for sale (forfeit £5); [5] kept and used a greyhound (forfeit £5); [6] and used a grey-hound to kill game (forfeit £5) on 26 Sept [1760] at Cannock. Enoch Dunkerly weaver of the Inner Temple (London), informer for himself and the poor of Cannock.

Rules and process: Mich [1760]: attached. Hil [1761]: pray a day to answer; appearances entered.[31]

---

[31]   The actual prosecutor, Lord Uxbridge, originally contemplated a civil action or an information before a magistrate, but when Harding caused a friend to lodge such an information, with the intention of forestalling the prosecution, and boasted of it, the steward advised that the poachers were probably liable to more than one penalty. (The information shows that they were sued for six.) Lord Uxbridge's London lawyer prepared process for the qui tam prosecution, and sent it to the steward in Staffordshire. He had Harding and Derry arrested on the attachment, and obtained bail bonds from them 20 Dec. See D. Hay, 'Poaching and the Game Laws on Cannock Chase', 211 and the sources cited there. Harding was perhaps the yeoman of Farewell prosecuted by the clerk of the peace in Lent 1752 for perjury; he was acquitted. ASSI 2/16 Staffs summer 1751, Lent 1752; ASSI 5/72 Lent 1752.

Sources: IND 1/6660 Hil 1 Geo III. KB 11/44 Mich 1 Geo III 1760 #1. KB 29/420 Hil 34 Geo II [*sic*][32], Mich 1 Geo III.

D.31 Information qui tam (6 July 1772)

Defendant: Oliver Pearson, sawyer of Stourbridge (Worcs).

Information:
Trin 12 Geo III [1772] 6 July [1772]
[1] Used one gin (forfeits £5); [2] exposed one hare for sale (forfeits £5) at Kinver, 22 April 1772. William Fletcher gentleman of St Andrew, Holborn (Middx), informer for himself and the poor of Kinver.

Rules and process: Trin [1772]: summons. Hil [1773] prays a day to answer; leave to imparl; imparls.

Sources: IND 1/6661 Hil 13 Geo III. KB 11/48 Trin 12 Geo III [1772] #10. KB 15/4 Hil 13 Geo III. KB 29/431 Trin 12 Geo III. KB 29/432 Hil 13 Geo III.

D.32 Information qui tam (29 Nov 1779)

Defendant: William Machin, potter of Tunstall, Furlong Lane township.

Information:
Mich 20 Geo III [1779] 29 Nov [1779]
[1] Kept one snare (gin) (forfeits £5); [2] and another (forfeits £5), at Rudyard, Leek. Cornelius Dyer yeoman of the Inner Temple, London, informer for himself and the poor of Leek.

Rules and process: Mich [1779]: summons.

Sources: KB 11/51 Mich 20 Geo III [1779] #18. KB 29/439 Mich 20 Geo III.

D.33 Information qui tam (29 Nov 1779)

Defendant: Edward Till, potter of Tunstall.

---

[32] The information appears in KB 29 as Michaelmas 34 George II, but one entry of process appears as Hilary of that regnal year; George II died 25 October so there was no such term.

Information:
Mich 20 Geo III [1779]
[*The body of the information is identical to D.32.*] Cornelius Dyer [*as in D.32*], informer.

Rules and process: Mich [1779]: summons.

Sources: KB 11/51 Mich 20 Geo III [1779] #17. KB 29/439 Mich 20 Geo III.

D.34 Information qui tam (23 Jan 1783)

Defendant: Andrew Cherington, baker of Brewood.

Information:
Hil 23 Geo III [1783] 23 Jan [1783]
[1] Kept and used a gun (forfeits £5), [2] and another gun (forfeits £5), [3] and a spaniel (forfeits £5) on 14 Nov [1782] at Brewood. Cornelius Dyer [*as in D.32*], informer.

Writ of attachment: 23 Jan [1783] to the sheriff of Staffs, for the appearance of Cherington on [15 May 1783; FDT Ea] to answer to Cornelius Dyer of Inner Temple, London, yeoman for contempts against *An Act for the Better Preservation of the Game*. [*Verso*:] On 2 Geo III; Dyer prosecutes on the information he has exhibited for the recovery of three penalties of £5. [*Another hand*]: 'not found in my bailiwick, Richard Gildart esq sheriff. Fra: Barlow Clerk in Court 592.'

Rules and process: Hil [1783]: summons.

Sources: KB 11/52 Hil 23 Geo III [1783] #4. KB 16/19/3 23 Geo III 1782/3. KB 29/442 Hil 23 Geo III.

D.35 Information qui tam (26 Nov 1791)

Defendants: Baggot Ball, twister, William Plant, labourer, William Cumberlidge, labourer, all of Leek.

Information:
Mich 32 Geo III [1791] 26 Nov [1791]
[1] Had and kept and used to kill the game, a snare (forfeit £5 each); [2] 'had, kept, used, set and placed' a snare (forfeit £5 each); [3] 'did use, set, fix and place' a snare (forfeit £5 each) on 16 Nov [1791], at Leek.

Robert Carvell yeoman of the Inner Temple (London), informer for himself and the poor of Leek.

Rules and process: Mich [1791]: summons. Hil [1792]: appearance entered; Cumberlidge prays a day to answer; leave to imparl. Ea [25 April 1792]: first rule to plead. ST [30 April 1792]: second rule to plead. ST: all plead not guilty. Trin 28 June 1792: notice of trial to Cumberlidge for the prosr (Belt). Trin Vac 31 July 1792: notice of trial countermanded (Belt). Mich [1792]: entry of a retraxit for Cumberlidge.

Sources: IND 1/6664 Hil, Ea 32 Geo III, Mich 33 Geo III. KB 11/56 Mich 32 Geo III [1791] #15. KB 15/5 Hil, Ea 32 Geo III, Mich 33 Geo III. KB 15/16 Trin, Trin Vac 32 Geo III. KB 21/45 pp.580, 587. KB 21/46 p.38. KB 29/451 Mich, Hil 32 Geo III. KB 29/452 Mich 33 Geo III.

Section E

SUMMARY CONVICTIONS REMOVED BY CERTIORARI

In its role as a court of review King's Bench exercised extensive supervisory powers, at least in theory, over the acts of justices of the peace and other magistrates. That control was largely exercised through the court's decisions on informations exhibited against magistrates (see Section B), and through the use of the writ of certiorari to bring into King's Bench cases that had begun (and may have resulted in conviction) as summary proceedings before them. The latter are the subject of this section.[1]

The writ of certiorari was, with habeas corpus, one of the two most important prerogative writs by which the court of King's Bench could control almost all inferior jurisdictions, although it acted only on the request of a litigant. The general procedural issues involved, including the choice of an order in term or a judge's fiat between terms to obtain the writ, are treated in Section F, cases in which the writ was used to remove indictments from quarter sessions and assizes, its most common use in criminal cases.[2] What follows here is a summary of the rules specific to the removal into King's Bench of summary convictions made by magistrates.

Summary convictions

The summary jurisdiction of magistrates was conferred by statutes, of which there were hundreds, covering a wide range of offences, although few thefts. Apart from some minor thefts of such things as wood, turnips and potatoes (see case E.6), most larceny had to be tried at quarter sessions or assizes before a jury. Poaching prosecutions (E.8), proceedings under the poor laws, master and servant disputes, and

---

[1] Certiorari was also used to question magistrates' orders on the poor laws (usually settlement or bastardy disputes), a group of cases not included in this volume. For the procedure in such cases see Hands, 27–31 and Gude, i, 213–221. The returned writs of certiorari with orders are now to be found in KB 16, whereas returned certioraris with convictions are in KB 11.

[2] In five cases (E.2, E.3, E.4, E.5, E.7) there was a rule in court; in the three others the defendants presumably obtained a judge's fiat for the writ. See the introduction to Section F.

licensing and nuisances (E.3, E.4, E.7) were the most common kinds of summary convictions heard by the magistrates.[3] They were very numerous: using the narrow definition of 'crime' given in the General Introduction, probably over 80% of criminal proceedings in Staffordshire were concluded before magistrates in a summary way, amounting to perhaps 8,000 cases in the years covered by this book.[4] It is striking, therefore, that only 14 defendants convicted in 11 summary hearings before nine magistrates sought to reverse their convictions by removing them on certiorari into King's Bench. Six succeeded in having their convictions quashed. Two of these cases were reported, becoming part of English case law (E.3, E.4).

Most of the cases in this section began as qui tam actions (see section D) or similar proceedings before magistrates, in which an informer sought that part of the penalty (usually half in qui tam actions) that statute awarded him on his convicting the accused. Convictions under the highway and turnpike acts (E.1, E.2, E.5) were particularly contentious, because the statutes provided that the informers could seize as their reward some of the horses on the wagon, with all their harness. The purpose was to deter waggoners from damaging the public road with too heavy loads or too narrow wheels.

Many statutes creating summary offences also allowed an appeal to quarter sessions; they might or might not expressly forbid recourse to certiorari. A typical appeal to quarter sessions is that of Simon Ironmonger, recorded in the Stafford quarter sessions order book in 1771. He appealed a conviction by the Reverend John Carver, JP, who ordered that he forfeit one grey horse and one black mare to Thomas Allen 'by whom they were seised and estrained for being Drawn with six horses mares or geldings upon the turnpike road leading from Wolverhampton towards Cannock in the said county in a waggon belonging to the said Simon Ironmonger having the fellies [*also* felloes, *the outer circles*] of the wheels thereof of less breadth or gage than nine inches ... contrary to the form of the statute.' After hearing evidence and counsel on both sides, the bench of magistrates confirmed the conviction.[5] Ironmonger did not choose to remove the conviction

---

[3] An analysis of the cases in this section appears in D. Hay, 'Dread of the Crown Office: the English Magistracy and King's Bench, 1740–1800', in Norma Landau, ed., *Law, Crime and English Society 1660–1840* (Cambridge University Press, 2002), 19–45.

[4] D. Hay, 'Legislation, Magistrates and Judges: High Law and Low Law in England and the Empire', in David Lemmings, ed., *The British and their Laws in the Eighteenth Century* (London: Boydell, 2005), 63.

[5] SRO Q/SO 16, Ep 1771.

by certiorari. In such cases, the writ could not be applied for before the appeal had been decided, or the time limit for appeals had been exhausted, when such limits were established by the relevant statute.[6]

Limits on certiorari on convictions, by common law and statute
By 1740 the case law stated that certiorari could not be had to test the merits of the case, but only to challenge the jurisdiction of the justices, or the form of the conviction. In practice, the judges interpreted both so broadly that they gave themselves ample room to reflect their own policy preferences, if they so wished. There were comments in the cases, as in general public discussion, about the advantages and disadvantages of summary conviction as a mode of proceeding, particularly in certain kinds of cases. There were also restrictions on certiorari enacted in the statutes creating such offences, but a simple declaration that the magistrate's decision was to be final did not exclude the possibility of certiorari: the court required explicit wording to that effect, and frequently ignored statutory bars to certiorari.[7] A 1752 act against bawdy-houses, 25 Geo II, c.36, did so, as did the excise acts, and some statutes for wage recovery. Thus 29 Geo II, c.33 (1756) revised 12 Geo I, c. 34 (1725) providing summary conviction for truck payments in the woollen industry; the 1756 statute again allowed an appeal to sessions, but barred certiorari. The reason: 'several prosecutions have been carried on against offenders for offences committed in breach of the said act, in manner therein prescribed, but the trials thereupon have been removed by Certiorari into some or one of his Majesty's courts of record at Westminster, and such prosecutions have been dropped upon account of the expense of carrying them on.'
  Some statutes sought to make it most costly or inconvenient to use certiorari to remove justices' convictions and orders, particularly when applicants were 'in hopes thereby to discourage and weary out' the parties, 'injured by great delays, expences and incertainties'. The words originally appeared in the 1692 Game Act, and were repeated in a more general act of 1732 applying to all convictions: those statutes and also the Game Act of 1706 all required that a £50 recognizance with sureties, or a bond for the same amount in game cases, be entered into by applicants for certiorari, with the conditions that they proceed at their own cost, without delay, and that they pay the winning party, if the original order was maintained, their full costs within a month. There were

---

[6]   Hands, 33.
[7]   Hands, 32–33; Hay, *The Judges and the People*.

similar requirements enacted by the Deerstealing Act of 1776, but the
bond for the latter was £100.[8]

Obtaining certiorari on a conviction
By 13 Geo II, c.18 (1739), which came into effect 24 June 1740, certiorari
to remove a conviction before a magistrate could be had only within six
months, and required proof on oath (i.e., by a sworn affidavit) that six
days' notice in writing had been given to the justice or justices to allow
them to show cause.[9] An affidavit of service of notice, stating also the
ground of complaint ('although a slight one may be sufficient'), came
before the court, or before a single judge of King's Bench in the vacations between terms. The objection had to be to the jurisdiction of the
justice, 'or to the form of the ... conviction', and not the merits, 'unless
in a case where it is intended to move for an information against the
convicting justice and then the court will grant a certiorari if not taken
away by statute before it grants or refuses an information.'[10]

---

[8]   5 Geo II, c.19 (1732); 4 & 5 Will & Mary, c.23 (1692); 6 Anne, c.16 (1706; also cited
      as 5 Anne st. 2, c.14); 16 Geo III, c.30 (1776); all cited in Bacon, *Abridgement*, ii,
      17–19. See also SRO Q/SB Tr 1790/123 for the recognizance of Henry Goodall,
      yeoman of Packington, convicted by John Daniel of taking a partridge in the
      manor of Weeford. No certiorari issued in this case, nor in a deerstealing case
      reported in a letter of 8 Feb 1772. Two servants of a gentleman, Ralph Weston,
      were accused of poaching deer, a case requiring careful consideration by the
      justices meeting at Wolseley Bridge, who were told by Weston that he
      intended to remove the case into King's Bench on certiorari. 'Upon this the
      gentlemen were of opinion that they ought to convict & Mr Weston thereupon
      payd into the hands of Mr Anson for his two servants sixty pounds – 'tis said
      that Mr Weston's intention is to remove the record of conviction into the King's
      Bench and have the validity of it argued there ... ' (SRO D603, George Ridgway
      to Lord Paget, 2 Feb 1772). He does not appear to have done so. The £30 fine
      was the punishment under earlier acts as well as the 1776 statute, which added
      the punishment of transportation for seven years on a second offence.
[9]   The clerks of the crown office noted the statute in KB 15/50 fol. 5, under
      'Rules to be observed as to the return of writs'. In 1801 the statute was held
      to apply only to summary proceedings, not indictments: Chitty, 382, citing
      R v Battams and others (1801) 1 East 298, 102 ER 116. The notice had to be
      given before moving for the rule nisi: *R v The Justices of Glamorganshire* (1793)
      5 TR 279, 101 ER 157.
[10] Hands, 34–5. The last two phrases in inverted commas are manuscript addi-
      tions in the crown office copy in my possession; the last of them appears ver-
      batim in Gude, i, 222. The following description of process is from Hands,
      32–36 and Gude, i, 221–24.

The court in term time (in five of these cases) or a single judge in vacation (three cases) then decided whether to grant a rule or a fiat for the writ to issue.[11] If the answer was yes, the clerk in court made out the writ (engrossed on parchment) and the necessary recognizance; the process was noted on the controlment roll (as 'record of conviction'), and the clerk delivered writ and recognizance to the solicitor, who found two sureties to enter into it. He in turn delivered writ and recognizance to the justice, or one of them. The justice returned the writ and conviction to the crown office, and on failing to do so could be compelled by a side bar rule to return it in six days, or face an attachment for contempt. The solicitor moved for a rule nisi to quash the order, and the rule nisi was served on the prosecutor, to show cause, and an affidavit of doing so prepared to read if no cause was shown. If no cause was shown the court quashed the conviction. If the prosecutor chose to contest the case, the clerk in court for the defendant entered a comparentia (appearance) to the conviction, and a rule for a concilium, which was served on the prosecutor (cases E.1, E.7, E.8). The arguments of counsel, supplied in writing to the judges two days before, were heard on one of what were called 'crown paper days', 'the counsel for the defendant beginning the argument. In these cases only one counsel on each side is heard.'[12] A conviction judged insufficient in law was quashed (cases E.1, E.3, E.8). Otherwise the judges confirmed it and the prosecutor was entitled to his costs.

[11] Manuscript addition to my copy of Hands, 35, and in identical wording in Gude, i, 222: 'These previous steps are not necessary when the application for the certiorari is made by the party in whose favour the order has been made.'

[12] Compare Gude and the manuscript interpolations in Hands; the quoted words are found only in the latter. Gude reports that the crown paper days in the term were Wednesdays and Saturdays, except within the first four or last four days of the term. The clerks made office copies of the 'paper book' for the solictors to prepare the briefs and for the judges. See Gude, i, 94–95, describing the process in Middlesex indictments, which appears to have been the same as that used for convictions removed on certiorari, based on a rule of court of Hilary 1738 (Gude, i, 366).

CASES

E.1 Certiorari on a conviction, by defendant (25 April 1748)

Defendant: John Stones alias Stonehall, common carrier.[13]

Writ and return:
Ea 21 Geo II 1748

Writ for return by [25 April 1748], witness Sir William Lee,[14] by the court, Burrow;[15] [*verso*]: 'At instance of the defendant'; endorsement of execution, W. Chetwynd.

Information by Thomas Snape [*signed with a mark*] of Hilderstone and Joshua Tinker of Sandon, informers, 17 Feb 1747/8, against Stonehall for a wagon with too narrow tires, between Lane End and the Mear, in the parish of Caverswall, 16 Feb 1747/8. The informers seized the horses and put them in the custody of the constable of Caverswall.

Conviction 18 Feb 1747/8: forfeits three horses with the gearing, on appearing before William Chetwynd, JP, and offering no good defence for having too narrow tires on the wagon. [*At bottom*]: 'Quashed by Rule of Court of Easter Term'.

Warrant (copy) by Chetwynd, 17 Feb [1748], to constable of Caverswall to deliver the horses to Snape and to inform Stonehall [*the copy notes that the constable, Thomas Tomkinson, gave the warrant to Snape, who refused to return it*].

Rules and process:
Ea [11 May 1748] order for a concilium (Jodrell). ST [21 May 1748]: conviction quashed for insufficiency in law (Jodrell; by the court.)[16]

Sources: KB 11/38 Ea 21 Geo II [1748] #9. KB 21/36 pp. 316, 325. KB 29/407 Ea 21 Geo II. KB 36/125.

---

[13] No residence is given.
[14] Chief justice of King's Bench 1737–1754.
[15] James Burrow, master of the crown office.
[16] The basis of the decision is not known, but the conviction does not give occupations for the informers, nor cite or recite the terms of the relevant statutes that allowed the informer to seize all horses above three in number, with their harness, between 29 Sept and 15 April, on specified kinds of wagons: 5 Geo I, c.12 (1718), 14 Geo II, c.42 ss.2, 6 (1740), 15 Geo II, c.2 (1741).

E.2 Certiorari on a conviction, by defendants (16 June 1748)

Defendants: James Hand, husbandman of Sandon, and Charles Stockley, son of John Stockley, common wayfarer.

Writ and return:
Trin 21 & 22 Geo II 1748

Writ 16 June [1748] by Sir William Lee for immediate return of convictions of Hand and Stockley.
  Information 4 April 1748, before Walter Chetwynd, against James Hand, Charles Stockley, and William Heath[17] for assaulting violently with clubs and staves and obstructing the informers when they were seizing three horses on a wagon of six belonging to John Stockley, at Sandon, and rescuing the horses 4 April 1748. Joshua Tinker, Thomas Snape, Joseph Snape, informers. [*Thomas and Joseph Snape signed with a mark.*]
  Warrants by Walter Chetwynd, JP: [a] 4 April [1748] for the arrest of the three named defdts; [b] 21 April [1748] for the arrest and committal of the three named defdts to gaol for three months; [c] for the constable of Sandon to levy £10 by distress of goods and clothes of Hand.[18]

Rules and process:
  Trin [1 June 1748]: rule for a writ of certiorari for Hand and Stockley (Ford; by the court).[19]

Affidavits for defence:

Trin 21 & 22 Geo II 1748

[1] Affdt of Francis Lycett yeoman of Mothersea in the parish of Stone, sworn before John Dearle at the borough of Stafford 30 May 1748. 'In the Court of King's Bench at Westminster.' [*Verso*]: 'Staffordsh. Affdts of Lycett and Weston for certiorari for convns agt Hand et al. Bh. fo 4.'
  That he personally served Walter Chetwynd esquire JP for Stafford with a true copy of the annexed notice 30 May 1748 and at the same time acquainted him with its contents.
  [*Annexed*]: notice to Walter Chetwynd:

---

[17] William Heath, the driver, named on the information, did not seek certiorari.
[18] The penalties are those of 5 Geo I, c.12 (1718).
[19] [*In margin*]: 'Bach 1'.

That the court of King's Bench will be moved first day of Trinity Term for a writ of certiorari to remove to the court all records of conviction of James Hand and Charles Stockley, convicted before you. 28 May 1748. William Sutton, solicitor for James Hand and Charles Stockley.

[2] Affdt of Ralph Weston gentleman of Rugeley, sworn before Michael Robinson at Rugeley 12 June 1748. 'In the King's Bench at Westminster.' [*Verso*]: 'Staffordshire. Afft of Weston for cert for convns agt Hand and another. fo 2.'

That all records of conviction of James Hand and Charles Stockley before Walter Chetwynd esquire JP for Stafford and which are intended to be removed into King's Bench, were made before Walter Chetwynd in April last and not before.

Sources: KB 1/9/6 Trin 21 & 22 Geo II. KB 11/38 Trin 21 & 22 Geo II [1748] #2. KB 21/36 p. 345. KB 29/407 Trin 21 & 22 Geo II.

E.3 Certiorari on a conviction, by defendant (17 Jan 1758)

Defendant: Thomas Little of the parish of St Mary, city of Lichfield.

Writ and return:
Hil 31 Geo II 1758

Writ 27 Jan [1758] to be returned immediately. [*Verso*]: by rule of court; returned by William Bailye, JP, in the city and county of Lichfield.[20]

Conviction on an information qui tam by William Bailye, senior bailiff and justice, for selling silk handkerchiefs and trading as a hawker, pedlar, and petty chapman without a license 24 Oct 1757 at St Mary, city of Lichfield, against the statute of 1698; accused freely confessed to offering silk handkerchiefs to Thomas Preston; forfeits £12.[21] Thomas Preston, gentleman, informer.

[*At bottom*]: 'Quashed by rule of court of Trinity term in the thirty-first year of King George the Second.'

---

[20]   This, like the following case, is a summary conviction by a Lichfield magistrate, and therefore does not appear in the record of Lichfield quarter sessions: Lichfield Record Office, document 68.

[21]   The penalty of s.3 of 9 William III, c.27 (1697), also cited as 9 & 10 William III, c.27 (1698).

Rules and process:
Hil [27 Jan 1758]: rule for a certiorari (Walker). Trin [1758]: dismission of conviction.[22]

Affidavits for defence:

Hil 31 Geo II 1758

[1] Affdt of Thomas Little, servant to William Gibson linen draper of Birmingham (Warws), sworn at Birmingham before R. Woodward 17 Jan 1758. ITKB [*Verso*]: 'Granted.'
    That the deponent was taken into custody 24 Oct 1757 by Thomas Preston, inspector of licences for hawkers and pedlars, and James Wright a peace officer in and for the city and county of Lichfield, and carried before William Bailey [*sic*] esquire, bailiff and JP, charged with an offence against the laws and statutes now in force for licencing hawkers and pedlars. The deponent swears that William Bailey examined him touching the offence alleged against him and convicted the deponent. The deponent is rather induced to believe that the conviction was obtained for the sum of £12, being the penalty forfeited, on the goods of William Gibson, then in the possession of the deponent.

[2] Affdt of John Strayen yeoman of Birmingham (Warws), sworn at Birmingham before Jonathan Wheeler 17 Jan 1758. ITKB
    That the deponent delivered 16 Jan to William Bailey [*sic*] esquire JP for the county of Lichfield, a copy of the annexed notice.
    [*Annexed*]:
    Notice to William Bailey [*sic*] esquire and JP 10 Jan that King's Bench will be moved 23 Jan 1758 for a writ of certiorari for removing the

---

[22] The case, *R* v *Little*, is reported in 1 Burrow 609, 97 ER 472, and 2 Kenyon 317, 96 ER 1195, and reprinted in Richard Burn, *Justice of the Peace* (12th edn, 1772), ii, 348–9. Little's counsel argued that he was not described in the conviction as going from town to town on foot or by horse, the definition of a hawker in the statute, and that he confessed only to offering silk handerchiefs for sale, not to the offence. Chief Justice Lord Mansfield and the other judges present concurred: the conviction did not aver that he was such a hawker, pedlar or petty chapman as should take out a license. The Chief Justice observed, 'Convictions ought to be taken strictly; and it is reasonable that they should be so, because they must be taken to be true against the defendant.' But see case E.4.

records of conviction of trespass and contempt whereof Thomas Little is convicted.[23]

Sources: IND 1/6659 Trin 31 Geo II. KB 1/13 Hil 31 Geo II. KB 11/43 Hil 31 Geo II 1758 #24. KB 21/38 p. 86. KB 29/417 Hil 31 Geo II.

E.4 Certiorari on a conviction, by defendant (26 Jan 1764)

Defendant: William Smith, petty chapman of Midlem [?Middleham] (Yorks).

Writ and return:
Hil 4 Geo III 1764

Writ 31 Jan [1764] to Samuel Palmer and John Hartwell, JPs of the city of Lichfield, for immediate return. [*Verso*]: by rule of court; returned by Samuel Palmer and John Hartwell.
   Conviction on an information qui tam 17 Nov [1763] in the parish of St Mary before Samuel Palmer and John Hartwell for exercising the trade of a petty chapman while unlicenced by exposing to sale a piece of muslin, against the statute;[24] having been apprehended by Isaac Snape, constable, on 16 Nov, the accused now freely confesses, forfeits £12.

Rules and process:
Hil [10 Feb 1764]: rule for a certiorari (side bar); summons. Ea [18 May 1764]: order for a consilium (Harrison).[25] ST [23 May 1764]: conviction affirmed (Price).

Affidavits for defence:

Hil 4 Geo III 1764

[1] Affdt of Joseph Thorpe lastmaker of Derby (Derbs), sworn before William Merrill Lockett at Derby 26 Jan 1764. ITKB
   That the deponent served Samuel Palmer and John Hartwell 23 Jan 1764 with a true copy of the annexed notice.
   [*Annexed*]: Notice by William Smith hawker and pedlar of Midlem (Yorks) to Samuel Palmer and John Hartwell gentlemen 19 Jan 1764 that

---

[23] The notice appears to be signed 'William Brookesby Welbank, attorney for Thomas Little.'
[24] 9 Wm. III, c. 27 (1697).
[25] The case was reported: *R* v *Smith* (1764), 3 Burrow 1475, 97 ER 934. See also the note of the hearing made by Lloyd Kenyon, below.

the King's Bench will be moved 31 Jan for a writ of certiorari for removing the conviction into that court.

[2] Affdt of William Smith hawker and pedlar of Midlem (Yorks), sworn before J. Yates at his house in Lincoln's Inn 30 Jan 1764. ITKB [*Verso*]: 'Litchfield. Mr. Ashhurst. To move for a certiorari to be directed to Samuel Palmer Gen. and John Hartwell Bailiffs and two of His Majesty's justices of the peace for the city and county of Lichfield according to the notice within. ½ G. W. H. Ashhurst. Barbor.'

That on 17 Nov 1763 at Lichfield the deponent was convicted before Samuel Palmer and John Hartwell, both JPs, of trespasses and contempts against the *Act for Licencing Hawkers and Pedlars*. The sum of £12 and expenses was levied on the deponent's goods and chattels for the offence.

[*In addition to the published report of the case, an unpublished note was made in 1764 by the law student Lloyd Kenyon, who became chief justice of King's Bench 1788–1802*]:

[*In margin*]: 'What is a sufficient conviction under the Act against Hawkers and Pedlars.'[26]

'Easter Term Geo 3, 1764. R v Wm Smith. The defendant was convicted by 2 JPs of the City of Lichfield in a penalty of £12 on the 8th section of the Hawkers and Pedlars Act 9 & 10 W.3.

'Mr Harrison took his exceptions to it. — 1. That the name of witness exhibiting the charges was not set forth — 2. It did not charge that he had no license.

'The conviction set forth that Smith being apprehended by the constable exposing goods to sale as a hawker and pedlar without license was brought before the justices and being charged upon oath with *exposing to sale as a hawker and pedlar and particularly a piece of muslin*, he was asked by one of the justices what he had to say why he should [not] be convicted, and the said Smith then and there freely and voluntarily confessed that he did expose the goods aforesaid to sale in manner [aforesaid] we the said justices required him to produce his license which he neglected to do. We therefore convict him of the offence and adjudge him to have forfeited £12 according to the statute.

'He insisted that the confession went no further than the charge, and therefore had not cured the defect.

---

[26] Contractions expanded and spelling modernized. Lancashire RO, Kenyon papers, notebook of cases 1763 to 1766 ('Ll. Kenyon 19 May 1761'), fol. 36.

'2. He insisted that as by s.3 of the Act if a constable peace officer demands sight of a hawker's license and he refuses to produce it, that he shall forfeit £5. Therefore they ought to have proceeded on that section and not on s.8.

'Mr Price in support of the conviction relied upon the rule laid down by Holt CJ in the case Rex v Chandler, Ld Raymond 581 and which has ever since been adhered to, that the court will support convictions under new acts of parliament if the party appears to be brought within them, though the conviction not be formal in every particular. Now the party is brought within 8th section, and as to 3rd section, that has another purpose, viz. when a constable [*illegible*] to see the license.

'Curiam [*illegible*] the conviction.

'At the rising of the court the attorney general took up the matter [and] observed that the conviction was bad upon two of the objections. 1. He is only said to be a hawker and pedlar, and not said *to be a person travelling from place to place*, which is part of the description of the offender necessary to give the justices jurisdiction, and nothing can be intended in a conviction that is necessary to give jurisdiction. 2. The justices have not ordered the penalty to be distributed, and all convictions being in the nature of judgments must be precise and certain. R v Vipont Easter 1 George 3 BR.[27]

'But Lord Mansfield, Wilmot, and Yates JJ (absent Denison) agreed that the conviction was good. 1. Hawker and pedlar is a sufficient description, and imports his travelling from place to place; 2. The Act distributes the penalty.'

Sources: KB 1/15 Hil 4 Geo III no. 2. KB 11/45 Hil 4 Geo III 1764 #22. KB 21/39 Hil, Ea 1764. KB 29/423 Hil 4 Geo III.

E.5 Certioraris on two convictions, by defendants (29 April 1765)

Defendant: Samuel Lowe, farmer of West Bromwich, and Mary Crockett, widow of Handsworth.[28]

Writ and return:
Ea 5 Geo III 1765

---

[27] R v *Vipont* (1761) 2 Burrow 1163, 97 ER 767.
[28] Each defendant is named separately in otherwise identical convictions, by writs of certiorari of the same date. The affidavit and notice, and rule in Easter term, are identical (except for the name of the defendant) in the two cases.

Writs 6 May [1765], to John Wyrley also known as John Wyrley Birch, to be returned immediately.

Convictions on both informations qui tam 14 Dec [1764] before John Wyrley alias John Wyrley Birch JP for using a waggon with five horses with fellies of wheels too narrow for the turnpike, near West Bromwich 5 Dec [1764]; appears at Hampstead 14 Dec and pleads not guilty; convicted and forfeits £5, to be distributed as the statute[29] directs. John Wyatt, carpenter and surveyor of the turnpike, of Birmingham (Warws), informer.

Rules and process:
Ea [6 May 1765]: certiorari ordered (Kenyon); summons.

Affidavit for prosecution:

Ea 5 Geo III 1765

[1] Affdt of James Gardner cordwainer of Dudley (Worcs), sworn before Thomas Lewis at Dudley 29 April 1765. ITKB

That this day day he served John Wyrley otherwise John Wyrley Birch JP with the annexed notice.

[*Annexed*]: Notice 29 April 1765 by Thomas Lewis of Dudley, attorney for Samuel Lowe, of a motion to be made in King's Bench 6 May for a writ of certiorari to remove his conviction dated 14 Dec, by which he was convicted on the oath of John Wyatt of Birmingham, surveyor of the turnpike, of having on 5 Dec a wagon belonging to one Mary Crockett drawn with more horses than four and fellies of the wheels narrower than six inches, on the Birmingham to Wolverhampton turnpike, penalty £5.

Sources: KB 1/16/2 Ea 5 Geo III. KB 11/45 Ea 5 Geo III #15, #17. KB 21/39 Ea 5 Geo III. KB 29/424 Ea 5 Geo III.

E.6 Certiorari on a conviction, by defendants (28 Nov 1783)

Defendants: John Cotterell the elder, John Cotterell the younger, and Thomas Cotterell, all of Willenhall.[30]

Writ and return:
Hil 24 Geo III 1784

---

[29]   26 Geo II, c.30 (1753), ss.1, 16, 17.
[30]   No occupations are given.

Writ 28 Nov 1783 for return [9 Feb 1784] of conviction under 23 Geo II.[31] *Conviction* before Willis Kempson JP 15 Oct for theft of 60 bushels of potatoes value £4 and 20 bushels of turnips value 15s, the property of Richard Gildart esquire, 12 Sept to 13 Oct at Willenhall, against the statute. Penalty £4 15s to the owner for damage, and 10s for the poor.

Rules and process:
Hil 1784: recognizances continued. Ea [8 May1784]: order to Willis Kempson esquire to return within six days a writ lately issued out of this court (side bar).

Sources: KB 11/53 Hil 24 Geo III #38. KB 21/43 Easter 24 Geo III 1784. KB 29/443 Hil 24 Geo III.

E.7 Certiorari on a conviction, by defendant (1 Nov 1786)

Defendant: John Rooker, yeoman and shopkeeper of Walsall.

Writ and return:
Hil 27 Geo III 1787

Writ 13 Nov 1786 to John Marsh esquire JP to return immediately the conviction of John Rooker on An act for Granting to His Majesty Additional Duties on Hawkers, Pedlars, and Petty Chapmen and for Regulating their Trade. [*Verso*]: returned by Marsh.
   Schedule of the return of the writ, by John Marsh, at Wolverhampton 22 Nov 1786.
   Record of conviction before John Marsh JP at Wolverhampton, for going about on a horse, hawking linen and cotton goods and other goods 12 July 1786 without a license, at Wolverhampton, against the statute 25 Geo III;[32] summoned; defence offered that he goes only to farms and markets for which no license is required; forfeits £10.
   William Fregleton, draper of Wolverhampton, informer; Richard Meeson, yeoman of Wolverhampton, witness.

---

[31] The turnip-stealing clause of this act had been repealed by 13 Geo III, c.32 (1772), which gave the JP discretion to divide the penalty between the owner and the overseer of the poor, or to give the entire penalty to either. On default of payment the thief could be imprisoned for up to one month at hard labour. There is no schedule with the writ.
[32] 25 Geo III, c. 78 (1785).

Rules and process:
1 Nov 1786: notice to Marsh of motion for certiorari. Mich [13 Nov 1786]: on affdts [1], [2] certiorari ordered.[33] ST [24 Nov 1786]: rule for return of the certiorari and conviction within six days (side bar). Hil [10 Feb 1787]: concilium ordered. ST: comparentia and dismission of record.

Affidavits for defence:

Mich 27 Geo III 1786

[1] Affdt of John Perks gentleman[34] of Walsall, sworn before H. W. Whateley at Walsall 11 Nov 1786. ITKB 'John Rooker agt John Marsh Esqr.' [*Verso*]: '26 Staffordshire. The King agt. John Rooker Affidt for cer John Rooker v Marsh Esqr Affidt as to the Date of the Conviction. 13 Novr. Certior fo:9 Griffith.'
    That the warrant of conviction of John Rooker as a hawker and ped-lar by John Marsh is dated 19 July 1786; the deponent saw and exam-ined the original in the hands of John Hanbury, the constable who levied the penalty.

[2] Affdt of John Perks yeoman of Walsall, sworn before Samuel Wilson at Walsall 1 Nov 1786. ITKB
    That he served John Marsh esquire JP for Stafford personally 1 Nov 1786 with the annexed notice by Richard Jesson gentleman of Walsall, attorney for John Rooker shopkeeper of Walsall. On 25 Oct 1786 the deponent did demand of John Hanbury constable of Wolverhampton who levied the penalty of £10 on the goods and chattels of Rooker under the warrant of distress issued by Marsh but which [*sic*] he refused to deliver.
    [*Annexed*]: [*Verso*]: '1st Novr 1786 Served John Marsh Esqr. J. Perks.' Notice by Richard Jesson attorney for John Rooker that King's Bench will be moved 8 Nov 1786 for a writ of certiorari for removing his convictions on the Act.

Sources: IND 1/6663 Hil 27 Geo III. KB 1/25 Mich 27 Geo III no. 1 bdl 26. KB 11/54 Hil 27 Geo III 1787 #16. KB 15/5 Hil 27 Geo III. KB 21/44 pp. 228, 244, 295. KB 29/446 Hil 27 Geo III.

---

[33] The barrister or clerk making the motion is not named.
[34] Gentleman in affidavit [1], yeoman in affidavit [2].

E.8 Certioraris on convictions, by three defendants (28 Nov 1786)

Defendants: Richard Dean, James[35] Henshaw, John Sadler, all labourers of Wombourn.

Writs and returns:
Hil 27 Geo III 1787

Writs [all identical] 28 Nov [1786] to John Durant, clerk, and Thomas Fenton esquire, clerk of the peace for Staffs, for return by [20 Jan 1787; FDT] of the three convictions against the statute.[36] *[Verso]: [all three]* returned by Thomas Fenton at Newcastle under Lyme 20 Jan [1787].
    *Convictions [all identical]*13 July [1786] before John Durant JP on an information of 12 July at Clent for taking or attempting to take fish of Sir John Wrottesley baronet in Smestal Stream 10 July, the defdt is brought on warrant and freely confesses; forfeits £5. William Sims gamekeeper to Wrottesley, informer. *[Verso]*: filed Mich 5 Oct 1786.[37]

Rules and process:
Hil [29 Jan 1787]: ordered that there be a concilium in each case (Bower). ST [7 Feb 1787]: convictions quashed as insufficient in law; comparentia and dismission of record (Bower).

Sources: IND 1/6663 Hil 27 Geo III. KB 11/54 Hil 27 Geo III, #5, #6, #7. KB 15/5 Hil 27 Geo III. KB 21/44 Hil 27 Geo III pp. 268, 284. KB 29/446 Hil 27 Geo III.

---

[35] KB 21/44 p. 268 gives John, the other sources James.
[36] 5 Geo III, c. 14 (1765).
[37] See SRO QS/B 1786 Mich/170 for a receipt 24 Jan 1787 from Chrees Wightwick solicitor for Richard Dean to the clerk of the peace for the writs, records of conviction and recognizances of the defendants.

Section F

Blackstone summarized the main uses of the writ of certiorari for removing indictments, noting that it was after an indictment[1] was found a true bill by the grand jury at quarter sessions or assizes

> that writs of *certiorari facias* are usually had, though they may be had at any time before trial, to certify and remove the indictment,[2] with all the proceedings thereon, from any inferior court of criminal jurisdiction into the court of king's bench, which is the sovereign ordinary court of justice in causes criminal.[3] And this is frequently done for one of these four purposes; either, 1. To consider and determine the validity of appeals[4] or indictments and the proceedings thereon; and to quash or confirm them as there is cause: or, 2. Where it is surmised that a partial or insufficient trial will probably be had in the court below, the indictment is removed, in order to have the prisoner or defendant tried at the bar of the court of king's bench, or before the justices of *nisi prius*; or, 3. It is so removed, in order to plead the king's pardon there; or, 4. To issue process of outlawry against the offender, in those counties or places where the process of the inferior judges will not reach him.[5]

[1] One case in this section, F.2, is an information qui tam exhibited at Stafford quarter sessions: the notes to that case explain why it is included in this section.

[2] Certiorari could also be used to remove committal proceedings, which might be done during habeas corpus proceedings (Chitty, 373): see case G.7.

[3] Most authorities suggested that certiorari would not be granted once issue was joined and the venire for the jury had been awarded. In theory an indictment could be removed even after conviction, but such a remedy was greatly discouraged by the judges, because they did not wish verdicts to be questioned, and deplored the expense and inconvenience. Bacon, ii, 11; Hay, *The Judges and the People*.

[4] Appeals of felony, a rarely used alternative to prosecutions on indictment, abolished by 59 Geo III, c.46 (1819).

[5] Blackstone, iv, 320, citing Sir Matthew Hale, *Pleas of the Crown* (London, 1716), ii, 210–11. No instance of the third purpose appears in the records examined.

Blackstone's first category, where the object was to quash an indictment by pleading a demurrer to it, was apparently part of the strategy in one Staffordshire case, although it eventually went to trial (F.1). Two others (F.10, F.22) fall in his fourth category, outlawry, although the first of these was originally brought for the second purpose mentioned by Blackstone, of having the case tried at nisi prius at Stafford assizes.[6] All the other cases in this section were probably begun for the same reason. The dangers of a 'partial or insufficient trial' that justified removal from quarter sessions or from the criminal court at assizes were summarized in the case law. Ordinarily a case at the Old Bailey or assizes was not easily removed, but grounds had included the fact that a prosecutor's attorney was also the undersheriff and had attended the grand jury, that the defendant was of good repute and the prosecution brought on slight grounds, or that it was malicious. Certiorari was also used to obtain the opinion of the other judges in King's Bench in difficult cases, to allow trial in an adjoining or some other county if it could be shown that a fair and impartial trial could not be had in the original one, or to get a new trial on the merits.[7] None of these reasons arise explicitly in the Staffordshire cases, but others do.

Certiorari gave the prosecutor an opportunity to seek a warrant for arrest, if the defendant was not already in custody, and if the offence was serious enough: a Waterfall cleric unwilling to support his grandchildren was the object of one such attempt (F.5).[8] It could also be used by either party to get a view, when a nuisance was prosecuted at assizes (F.17, F.23).[9] But the most likely motives for seeking certiorari were two. The first was to have the case heard by a special jury (also mentioned in F.17). Doing so offered a prosecutor or a defendant, depending on the case, procedural advantages not otherwise open to them. Equally important was the desire to increase the cost of proceedings and thereby deter or embarrass the other litigant.

Special juries
Most of the indictments in this section were first found true bills at quarter sessions, before a bench of Staffordshire justices, but six (F.10, F.16,

---

[6] The purpose was to allow the arrest of someone who had escaped into another county: a magistrate's warrant could be used in one other county (by 'backing', i.e. endorsing it), but not more, or where the county was unknown. But 'every difficulty is obviated by removing the proceeding into the supreme court of criminal jurisdiction.' Chitty, 372.

[7] Chitty, 371–2, 379–80; Bacon, ii, 10–11. See Hay, *The Judges and the People*.

[8] Hands, 42–43; see the notes to F.5.

[9] Chitty, 373; Bacon, ii, 11.

F.17, F.19, F.22 and F.23) were assize cases, which ordinarily would have been heard by the assize judge in the crown court before an ordinary jury. A rule for a special jury was entered in five of these cases (F.22 was a proceeding to outlawry, and no trial was involved). All but one of the special juries were requested by the defendant; the exception was a deer killing case, where a special jury would be likely to favour the prosecutor, who requested it (F.10). In three of the cases removed from quarter sessions there was a rule for a special jury. Two were prosecutions of a butcher and the mob he led to rescue five horses distrained for farm rent owed by a widow (F.12, F.13) and the request was by the prosecutor. In the third a gentleman was one of the defendants, accused of assaulting a clergyman, and here it was the defence that requested a special jury. The advantage of a special jury of gentlemen to one party or the other clearly was a strong influence in decisions to seek certiorari.[10]

The expense of certiorari
Other calculations also lay behind the use of the writ. Gude observed:

> It often happens, that a writ of *certiorari* issued out of the Court of King's Bench, is used by prosecutor and defendant to inconvenience and oppress each other, and is subject to great abuse; for instance, after the defendant [in the lower court] has had much trouble in serving the prosecutor personally with notice of trial, and at a great expence delivered his briefs to counsel, *subpoenaed* his witnesses, taken out his *venire*, and in other respects prepared himself for trial, all his preparations are rendered abortive by the writ of *certiorari* being lodged at the very moment before the trial is called on, and the defendant, after incurring an enormous expense, is compelled to appear in the Court of King's Bench and plead again *de novo*.[11]

Once in King's Bench, fees and costs mounted even more rapidly. As a consequence, the choice to use certiorari often depended on whether the opposed party had enough property to lose, and was likely to be deterred by the threat of litigation at Westminster.

A case that in the end did not result in an application for the writ nonetheless shows the reasoning that lay behind most decisions to use certiorari. An assault on his gamekeeper by two poachers, John and Thomas Wootton of Rugeley, led the earl of Uxbridge first to seek a criminal information in the crown office in 1759, but his London lawyer replied:

---

[10] A simple statement by a defendant that he wished to be tried by a special jury was not, however, a sufficient ground: Gude, i, 136. On special juries see the General Introduction.

[11] Gude, i, 127, my interpolation.

I am assured by the officers there (whose interest it is not to refuse business) that in this case the court will not grant an information, for such an assault as that sworn to by Francis Dickens, but if moved will refer him to his remedy by indictment at the assizes or sessions, where upon his positive oath the grand jury cannot well do otherwise than find the bill of indictment immediately after which they can remove it by certiorari in the crown office.[12]

Uxbridge's steward remembered that that had been the course in another case in the county some years before (case F.3). He also consulted a local lawyer who once had prosecuted Uxbridge's gamekeeper on a criminal information (case A.6), but noted that 'the same much exceeded a common battery.' Yet an indictment, removed by certiorari, also would be 'tried in the information way.'

An indictment for special assault and affray on the gamekeeper ('in performance of his duty ... large sticks ... violent strokes blows wounds and bruises') was preferred at Lent assizes, found a true bill, but then the relative advantages and disadvantages of using certiorari began to be calculated. The indictment could be removed into the crown office on certiorari, or simply prosecuted in the ordinary way at assizes, 'which as the fellows are scarcely worth sixpence may sufficiently chastise or drive the country of them.' The Woottons were weavers, and the expense of certiorari made no sense, as they could not possibly pay costs. Uxbridge therefore decided to prosecute them on the indictment at summer assizes, where they confessed and paid a 10s fine.[13]

In contrast, some of the expense that certiorari could inflict can be seen in an affidavit to increase costs in an assault prosecution against a Nantwich gentleman by a Lichfield butcher (F.19). The defendant was wealthy, an attorney, and probably planned his defence in the terms suggested by Gude, using certiorari to 'inconvenience and oppress' the butcher, perhaps enough to have him drop the prosecution.[14] The bluff

---

[12] He noted the only other remedy offered by the crown office was to exhibit articles of the peace, but since the prosecutor needed to swear that he went in daily fear of his life, the better course was to pursue an indictment at the next assizes. Articles of the peace have not been included in this volume; for the procedure, see Hands, 75–85; Gude, i, 245–50.

[13] This account is from SRO, D603, Parry to Uxbridge 30 Jan 1759; Ridgway to Uxbridge 24 Feb, 3, March, 12 March, 28 March, 12 May, and 23 May 1759; Ridgway to Parry, 28 March 1759. For the case in context, see D. Hay, 'Poaching and the Game Laws on Cannock Chase,' in D. Hay, P. Linebaugh, E. P. Thompson, eds., *Albion's Fatal Tree: Crime and Society in Eighteenth-Century England* (London, 1975; New York, 1976), ch.5 at 237.

[14] Gude, i, 127.

in this case failed, and the defendant had to pay the very much higher costs that had been incurred by going into King's Bench. But such a calculation, combined with the desire for a special jury, probably lay behind most cases.

Obtaining the writ
Certioraris to remove indictments had been granted for centuries for these purposes, and parliament sought to curb their most egregious uses by defendants through legislation, notably in statutes of 1554, 1623, 1694, and 1696.[15] The first required the chief justice or another judge to sign the writ. That of 1623 required the defendant to enter into a recognizance of £10 to remove indictments of riot, forcible entry, or assault and battery from quarter sessions. The 1694 and 1696 statutes were more important, directed against 'divers turbulent contentious, lewd and evil disposed persons' who used certiorari to escape trial in the counties at quarter sessions. Their effect was to require a defendant seeking to remove an indictment for misdemeanour from quarter sessions to find two sureties of £20 each for a recognizance to guarantee that the defendant would appear and plead in King's Bench, pay for the process, and not depart until discharged. On conviction such a defendant was taxed costs, and could not be discharged of the recognizance until the costs were paid. At assizes or in King's Bench itself, the judges could set what sum they wished.[16] The 1694 statute also required that certioraris only be granted by motion or rule in open court in term time, or by a judge's fiat in the vacations, thereby giving the judges the power to determine which defendants obtained the writ. In this volume there are 14 by defendants (of which 3 were from assizes). Defendants (but not prosecutors) were also precluded by other statutes from removing indictments for offences against the highway acts, for the non-repair of

---

[15] 21 James I, c.8 (1623), 5 & 6 Wm & Mary, c.11 (1694), 8 & 9 Wm III, c.33 (1696). There were also many later statutes making minor changes.

[16] My copy (see the General Introduction) of Hands, 38, has an added manuscript note, 'If the certiorari be directed to justices of oyer and terminer or justices of gaol delivery [i.e., the judges who heard criminal cases at assizes in the counties and the Old Bailey in London] the recognizance is not taken under the statute, but may be in such sum as the judge shall direct. If no directions are given it is usual to take it by two bail in £50 each.' In any case where the bailsmen appeared insufficient, the prosecutor could force the defendant to add sufficient bail by serving a summons to his solicitor for a procedendo: Hands, 39 ('clerk in court' replaced in manuscript by 'solicitor').

bridges, for keeping disorderly houses, and obtaining money or goods by false pretences.[17]

On the other hand, a prosecutor, whether the attorney general or a private prosecutor, could demand a writ of certiorari. In these years in Staffordshire, ten prosecutors obtained certiorari, three of them to remove assize indictments. There was a distinction here, clarified by a case in 1769. The attorney general could demand the writ, and the court was bound to grant it; a private prosecutor could get it 'of course' (without making a case to the judges) but a defendant could contest the issue of the writ, and reverse it on a procedendo, which sent the case back to the original jurisdiction. In contrast to a prosecutor, a defendant seeking the writ was obliged to show special grounds for it.[18] However, a defendant who happened to be an officer of the crown or for whom the crown for any reason took up the defence (excise men, for example), could have certiorari without laying any special ground.[19]

The writ could be had either by an order of the court in term time or, in the vacations between terms, by a fiat from a judge. A defendant seeking certiorari had to make an affidavit.[20] If application for the writ was made in term time, there was a motion for a rule nisi (a rule to show cause why the writ should not issue), and the affidavits were filed (they are now in KB 1). If in vacation, the affidavit was laid before the judge in chambers; the affidavits do not survive for such cases, nor do the

---

[17] Chitty, 377; there were also other statutory restrictions for particular offences.

[18] *R* v *Lewis and others* (1769), 4 Burr. 2456, 98 ER 288, summarized in Bacon, *Abridgement* (5th ed., 1798), i, 559. The account in Hands, 37 is inaccurate: 'This writ the King has a right to demand; but to a common prosecutor, who only uses the King's name as of course, the court may either grant or refuse it at their discretion, to a defendant, who must shew a special ground for it to the court.' In the crown office copy I possess the passage is amended in manuscript to read, 'This writ the King has a right to demand; as has also a common prosecutor, who uses the King's name, but the court may either grant or refuse it at their discretion, to a defendant, who must shew a special ground for it to the court.' Some of the history of the case law giving grounds is summarized in D. C. M. Yardley, 'The grounds for certiorari and prohibition', *The Canadian Bar Review*, xxxvii (1959), 294–355; see also Hay, *The Judges and the People*.

[19] Footnote to *R* v *Battams and others* (1801) in 1 East 298, at 303 note (c), 102 ER 116 at 118.

[20] Chitty, 382; Hands, 38; Gude, i, 136–7.

fiats.[21] In contrast, a prosecutor applying for the writ could simply ask his clerk in court for it: there was no need for affidavits, recognizances, orders, or fiats.[22] The combined effect of these rules is that only two of the 24 cases of certioraris on indictments should have originating affidavits (cases F.1, F.17). The latter does have such an originating affidavit; in F.1, it seems likely that six affidavits by the defendants on which they tried to prosecute the prosecutor in a criminal information (see case A.3 [1] to [6]), were also used as the basis of their application, as defendants, for writ of certiorari to remove into the court his indictment against them. In several other cases, affidavits required in later stages of process were found: case F.1 (service of the rule nisi, and supporting subsequent proceedings for contempt); case F.11 (99 affidavits in a bitterly fought arbitration between family members); case F.19 (to increase costs); and case F.23 (seeking mitigation of punishment after conviction). The consequence, then, is that for most cases of certioraris on indictments, no affidavits survive, and the most striking exception (case F.11) is an instance of an arbitration proceeding through reference to the master (see below).

It was also possible in some instances (fraud in obtaining it, or if obtained by a defendant who failed to comply with the condition of the recognizance) to cancel the effect of the writ of certiorari by a successful motion for a procedendo, which instructed the justices to whom the certiorari had been directed, to ignore it, and to proceed to judgment.[23] No such motions have been found for the cases in this section.

From 1740 until 1801 all applications for certiorari to remove indictments from justices at quarter sessions, like summary convictions removed from justices of the peace (see Section E), had to be moved within six months of the proceedings, and on proof by affidavit that the justices had been given six days notice in writing.[24]

---

[21] TNA Research Guide, King's Bench, section 5; *Reprint of Statutes, Rules and Schedules Governing the Disposal of Public Records by Destruction or Otherwise 1877–1913* (HMSO, 1914), 109.

[22] Chitty, 386.

[23] Chitty, 397; Gude i, 138–9, 147, ii, 621. In *R v Lewis* (above), the defendants attempted, unsuccessfully, to do this, in part on the grounds that the case should have been decided in the Welsh courts. In that judgment Yates J also pointed out that once a certiorari had been filed, any motion for a procedendo had to be preceded by a motion 'to take the certiorari off from the file.'

[24] 13 Geo II, c.18 s.5 (1739). The clerks of the crown office noted the statute in KB 15/50 fol.5, under 'Rules to be observed as to the return of writs'. The notice had to be given before moving for the rule nisi: *R v The Justices of*

Proceeding to trial

Once the clerk in court received the fiat or rule on behalf of a defendant, he made out the writ, and delivered it to the solicitor, with the required recognizance. A certiorari granted on a fiat from a judge (that is, between terms) is dated the last day of the preceding term, for return the following term.[25] For several cases here the result is that the certiorari is dated (tested, to use the legal terminology) before the indictment was presented. However, it was possible for a prosecutor to obtain the writ even before the indictment was preferred; it could then be used the instant the grand jury found a true bill.[26] Some of these cases may be instances of that strategy. On the other hand, of the few certioraris granted after a motion in court (cases F.1, F.2, F.5, F.17, F.22) three are dated the day the motion was granted, one the next day, and one a week later.[27] Certioraris issued in term command a return 'immediately' and the writ is subscribed 'by rule of court.'[28]

In cases of delay there was available 'the usual side bar rule ... to return the writ', a simple application by the clerk in court.[29] Once the writ was returned with the indictment or (rarely)[30] a certified copy, a prosecutor could compel the defendant to proceed to trial by serving on his clerk in court a side bar rule to estreat the recognizance (cases F.8, F.12, F.13, F.14, F.15).[31] Subsequent proceedings (imparlance, rules to plead, notice of trial, etc) were similar to those on criminal informations (see Section A), but much more common.[32] In the 24 cases in this section

> *Glamorganshire* (1793) 5 TR 279, 101 ER 157. In 1801 the statute was held to apply only to summary proceedings, not indictments: Chitty, 382, citing *R* v *Battams and others* (1801) 1 East 298, 102 ER 116.

[25] Gude, ii, 188.

[26] Chitty, 386.

[27] Gude, ii, 187–88 suggests that those issued in term should be tested (dated) the first day of term, and endorsed 'by rule of court.' So too does an undated book of practice in the crown office: 'It is ... usual to make the certiorari bear teste on the first day of the term although it may not have been granted in the court till after that day.' (KB 15/50 fol.4).

[28] Chitty, 390; my copy of Hands, 354, 359 manuscript note: 'The judge does not sign the writ only the fiat. If granted by the Court add 'By rule of Court'.'

[29] *R* v *Battams and others* (1801) 1 East 298, 102 ER 116; Gude, i, 140–41.

[30] Cases F.1, F.2.

[31] The form is given in Gude, ii, 651 no.23.

[32] A manuscript entry to my crown office copy of Hands, 40 adds 'except that in cases of indictments removed by defendants either party may give notice of trial and make up the record, whereas on informations a defendant cannot make up the record until the prosecutor has made default.'

half went to trial (cases F.1, F.4, F.5, F.9, F.10, F.12, F.13, F.14, F.15, F.17, F.19, F.23). There was also one guilty by default (F.11) and another guilty by consent (F.20).

Costs

If the defendant had removed the indictment into King's Bench on cer-tiorari, and was then convicted at trial, and the prosecutor was the injured party or a civil officer, the prosecutor was entitled to costs and the defendant's recognizance was not discharged until they were paid. But this provision of the statute 5 & 6 Wm & Mary, c.11 applied only to indictments for misdemeanours removed from quarter sessions. The prosecutor was not entitled to costs when the indictment was for felony or removed from the judges of oyer and terminer and gaol delivery (i.e., from the assizes).[33]

Reference to the master of the crown office

In any proceedings in misdemeanour where the defendant had been convicted on a verdict or by default, but had not yet suffered judgment, this procedure was often advised. On the recommendation of the court the defendant 'often consents to go before the master; that is, to refer the whole of the matter to him, and comply with what he shall think fit to direct the parties to do.'[34] The solicitors attended the master with the briefs and the affidavits made in aggravation or mitigation, and any other affidavits or matters the solicitors put before him; if the defendant complied with what the master ordered, the court refrained from pass-ing sentence. There are two such cases in this section, F.11 and F.14. In neither has the outcome been found. It appears that the prosecutors in F.11 did not proceed after filing the affidavits in aggravation. The defendant, a man of wealth and standing, the sheriff of Caernarfon, had made a personal appeal directly to the master of the crown office, declaring his absolute unwillingness to settle. Perhaps the prosecutor had been told that as a result compensation was highly unlikely. He did believe that the defendant, by suffering judgment by default, had blocked subpoena and examination of several important prosecution witnesses.[35]

Quashing an indictment

If the certiorari had been obtained by a defendant seeking to have the indictment quashed as insufficient (the first purpose enumerated by

[33] Hands, 43–44 and manuscript addition in my copy.
[34] Chitty, 693–4.
[35] See F.11, affdts [61], [66], [83], [88].

Blackstone), he or she demurred to it by getting a side bar rule for permission to enter a retraxit, getting a demurrer drawn, engrossed and filed. If the prosecutor contested it (by joinder), the cause was argued in a concilium, such as described for cases in Section E.[36] There are no such cases in this section.

Outlawry

Where a defendant in either civil or criminal proceedings failed to respond to the court's process, the ancient process of outlawry could be invoked; it was abolished in civil proceedings by statutes of 1852 and 1879, and in criminal cases by an act of 1938, although practically never used long before that date.[37] The stages of the process are described, and the writs reproduced, by Blackstone; legislation in 1692 allowed the defendant to appear by attorney, which had not formerly been the case, and provided for public proclamation of the proceedings, 'because the consequences to persons outlawed in criminal causes are more fatal and dangerous to them and their posterities, than in any other causes.'[38] Outlawries could be reversed on appearance by the defendant; it was also easy to overturn them because the process was so exacting. Only two criminal outlawries, both against deerstealers by the keepers of Needwood Forest, appear to have taken place in Staffordshire in the period covered by this volume (cases F.10, F.22); see the former for details of the procedure, and for the additional information provided by the rare survival of a defence brief.

CASES

F.1 Certiorari on an indictment from quarter sessions, by defendants (6 Nov 1744)[39]

Defendants: Joseph Turton the elder, chapman; Joseph Turton the younger*; Thomas Turton*; George Roberts, chapman; Joseph Green,

---

[36] Hands, 40-41.

[37] The Administration of Justice (Miscellaneous Provisions) Act, 1 & 2 Geo VI, c.63 (1938) s.12 abolished outlawry for criminal proceedings. The Common Law Procedure Act 15 & 16 Vict, c.76 (1852) ended it on mesne process in debt cases, and the Civil Procedure Acts Repeal Act 42 & 43 Vict, c.59 (1879) s.3 abolished it as a process on judgment.

[38] Blackstone, iv 319ff (criminal) and iii 283–4 (civil). 4 Wm & Mary, c.18 ss.3–5, and c.22 s.4 (both 1692).

[39] See also case A.3, R v Barr et al., which is closely related litigation.

baker; Richard Fowler, hatter; Thomas Ash, lockman; Thomas Pye, saddle tree maker; James Parker the younger, labourer; all of Wolverhampton, and persons unknown.
  *sons of Joseph the elder, according to the writ.

Writ and return:
Mich 18 Geo II 1744

Writ 7 Nov [1744] for return immediately; return by R. Rider.[40]
  Schedule[41] and copy by Theo. Levett, clerk of the peace, of the indictment found at Staffs Mich quarter sessions 2 Oct [1744] for [1] riotously entering the dissenting meeting house then in possession of Alexander Barr at Wolverhampton and forceable entry and detainer from 5 Feb to 5 Aug [1744]. Alexander Barr, prosecutor; John Adams, witness. A true bill.[42]

Rules and process:
2 Oct 1744: indicted at Staffs Mich quarter sessions. Mich [6 Nov 1744]: order for certiorari (Jarvis). ST 7 Nov [1744]: certiorari issues. ST: summons; defdts pray a day to answer, imparl. ST [21 Nov 1744]: rule nisi to FNT to quash the indictment as insufficient (Kay).[43] Hil 1744: affdt [1] of 12 Jan 1744/5 of service of the rule. ST [9 Feb 1744/5]: side bar rule to compel defdts to plead. Hil [1745]: plead not guilty. Hil Vac 15 Feb 1744/5: notice of trial (Matthews for defdts). Ea [22 May 1745]: rule on the postea on conviction to [27 May], for judgment for the King; affdt

---

[40] Probably Richard Rider, a justice who committed two prisoners for trial in Lent 1746: WSL, Gaol Calendars.

[41] The schedule was the statement of the proceedings in the lower court returned with the indictment; the formal statement extracted from it, entered on the rolls of the court, was termed the caption. As well as the information given in the text, both also contain the names of justices at quarter sessions (or assize judges) and usually grand jurors: see Gude, i, 139 and ii, 169–70, 173–4 for the form, and Chitty, 326ff for the law. It was not necessary to name all the justices, and grand jurors might be omitted: Chitty, 331, 333.

[42] The original indictment is in SRO Q/SR Mich 1744. In all other cases the indictment has been returned with the writ and schedule; see also the next case, certiorari on an information.

[43] The defendants apparently intended to enter a demurrer on the grounds of insufficiency in the indictment, but appear not to have proceeded with it. See Hands, 40–41, Gude i, 93–5.

[2] to dispense with appearance of defdts; rule absolute to dispense with personal appearance of defdts on giving judgment (Kay). ST [27 May 1745]: rule nisi, FNT, for arrest of judgment (Cary). Trin: affdt [3] of 10 June 1745 of service of last rule. ST [27 June 1745]: rule nisi, FNT, for arrest of judgment (Cary);[44] defdts' recognizances respited. Mich [26 Nov 1745]: further rule nisi, FNT, for arrest of judgment (Gundry).[45] Hil [12 Feb 1745/6]: defdts' recognizances respited. Ea [14 May 1746]: rule nisi, FNT, for arrest of judgment (Cary). Trin [11 June 1746]: defdts' recognizances respited. Trin [18 June 1746]: rule nisi, FNT, for arrest of judgment (Ford). Mich [26 Nov 1746]: rule nisi, FNT, for arrest of judgment (Cary). Trin [30 June 1747]: defdts' recognizances respited. Trin [7 July 1747]: by consent of counsel on both sides, cause referred to final arbitration by James Wightwick esquire of Tunstall[46] near Wolverhampton and John Finch gentleman of Dudley, to make their award on or before 1 Nov (Cary for defdts, Ford for prosr). 31 Oct 1747: arbitrators' award [*annexed to [4]*]. 16 Jan 1747/8: affdt of Green [4] taken. Hil [29 Jan 1747/8]: on reading affdt of Green [4] and rule [of 7 July 1747], rule nisi to [11 Feb 1747/8] for an attachment against Barr for contempt (Cary); [2 Feb 1747/8]: rule nisi to [11 Feb 1747/8] for discharge of defdts' recognizances (Whitaker); defdts' recognizances respited. ST 1 Feb 1747/8: affdt [5] of service of notice of rules for attachment for contempt and discharge of defdts' recognizances. 8 Feb 1747/8: affdt of Barr [6] taken. Hil [11 Feb 1747/8]: on reading affdt of Barr [6], enlarged rule nisi, to FNT, for an attachment of Barr for contempt (Whitaker). Ea [5 May 1748]: defdts' recognizances discharged (Cary). ST [18 May 1748]: order for writ of attachment against Barr for contempt (Sir John Strange).[47] Tr [28 June 1748]: recognizance of Joseph Turton discharged.

44 There is a marginal note in the KB 36/114 entry: 'Entd. arrested'.
45 Marginal note in KB 36/115: 'Mn. 24'.
46 Probably either James Wightwick esquire (d. 1749) of Dunstall, a house near Wolverhampton (Yates' map of 1775; *VCH Staffs*, xx, 18); or James Wightwick esquire of Tunstall in Adbaston parish, who lived there 22 Oct 1737 (Salop Archives, 1067/4).
47 The writ, endorsed by J. Matthews, clerk in court for the prosecutor, issued 20 May for the return of Barr by 10 June; the sheriff of Staffordshire, John Jervis, issued a warrant 23 May; he returned the writ 'not found in my bailiwick.' A similar writ issued 29 June for return by 24 Oct; Jervis issued a warrant 12 Aug, and returned the writ 'not found.' On 12 April 1749 a third writ of attachment was sent to John Wyrley, sheriff, who issued warrants to his officers 17 April; he too returned the writ 'not found.'

Affidavits for defence:

Hil 18 Geo II 1744/5

[1] Affdt of Francis Morton gentleman of Wolverhampton, sworn before W. Perks at Wolverhampton 12 Jan 1744/5.
   That 18 Dec last the deponent served the prosecutor Alexander Barr with the [*annexed*] rule.
   [*Annexed*]: Rule nisi [21 Nov 1744] to FNT to quash the indictment as insufficient.

Ea 18 Geo II 1745

[2] Affdt of William Curlewes ironmonger of Cannon Street (London), sworn before T. Denison at Serjeants' Inn 23 May 1745. ITKB 'The King against Turton and others.' [*Verso*]: 'Staffordshire. The King agt Turton & others: Affidt of Wm Curlewes to dispense with personal appear of deft.'
   That the deponent is acquainted with Joseph Turton the elder, and his sons Joseph Turton the younger, and Thomas Turton, all of Wolverhampton. The other defendants George Roberts, Joseph Green, Richard Howler, Thomas Ash and James Parker also live in Wolverhampton, which is more than one hundred miles from London.

Trin 18 & 19 Geo II 1745

[3] Affdt of Francis Morton gentleman of Wolverhampton, sworn before John Jesson at Wolverhampton 10 June 1745. ITKB 'Staffordshire. The King against Turton and others.' [*Verso*]: 'King v Turton: Rule and affdt of service. Staffordshire. The King agt Turton and others: Affidt Service Rule. [*Illegible*].'
   That on 4 June instant the deponent served the prosecutor Alexander Barr with the [*annexed*] rule.
   [*Annexed*]: Rule nisi [27 May 1745] to FNT for arrest of judgment.

Hil 21 Geo II 1747/8

[4] Affdt of John Green yeoman of Wolverhampton, sworn before W. Perks at Wolverhampton 16 Jan 1747/8. ITKB [*Verso*]: 'Staffordshire. Afft of Green for attachmt agt Barr. fo:28 The King v Turton Rule An'd & Affidts. Sheffield.'
   That the deponent witnessed the [*annexed*] award signed by James Wightwick esquire and John Finch gentleman 31 Oct last. The deponent

delivered a copy to Alexander Barr 12 Nov and another to Joseph Turton 13 Nov. On 26 Dec the deponent, Turton, and Joseph Swain went to Barr's house in John's Lane Wolverhampton near the protestant dissenting meeting house. The door was locked and no one answered. Turton declared he had come to perform his part of the award in paying £70 to Barr, a sum which he carried in a linen bag. Turton was told that Barr was at the house of Thomas Hill of the Three Crowns in Dudley Street, where the three went at about 3pm with James Marshall and Daniel Hickcox[48] (two other trustees of the congregation of the dissenting meeting house in Wolverhampton), Swain and the deponent. They offered to pay Barr the £70. Barr said he would not accept the money without advice from his attorney, Mr Asteley. Turton replied that this was the day for the trustees to take possession of the meeting house. Barr replied that he had not received the award until eleven days after it was made, declared that 'you are all a pack of sorry fellows' and that James Marshall was a 'scrubby Scotchman', and left.

[*Annexed*]: Answer of James Wightwick esquire of Tunstall and John Finch gentleman of Dudley 31 Oct 1747 to the order of King's Bench dated [7 July 1747] that they resolve all differences of law and equity between Alexander Barr (prosecutor) and Joseph Turton and others (defendants) by 1 Nov 1747. The arbitrators order that Alexander Barr shall on or before 26 Dec 1747 deliver up to the defendants possession of the tenement or dwelling house, dissenting meeting house, and gardens and outbuildings now in the possession of Alexander Barr, without any wilful hurt or prejudice in the meantime done by Alexander Barr to the said property, and to deliver up all deeds, writings and books of account relating to the dissenting meeting house, which he admitted to be in his custody in his answer to a bill filed against him in the court of chancery on the complaint of Turton and others. Barr shall also give the defendants a general release of all lawsuits. The defendants are ordered to pay to Barr on or before 26 Dec the sum of £70. All actions or suits between the parties shall be ended as of the day of this order dated 31 Oct 1747, parties to pay their own costs.

James Wightwick	Joseph Swain
John Finch	John Green
[Arbitrators]	[Witnesses]

Hil 21 Geo II 1747/8

[5] Affdt of Daniel Hickcox mercer of Wolverhampton, sworn before W. Perks at Wolverhampton 1 Feb 1747/8.

---

[48] 'Hiccox' in original.

That on 1 Feb the deponent served the prosecutor Alexander Barr with the [*annexed*] rules.

[*Annexed*]: Rules nisi to 11 Feb for an attachment against Barr for contempt, and for discharge of recognizances of defendants.

Affidavit for prosecutor to oppose attachment for contempt:

Hil 21 Geo II 1747/8

[6] Affdt of Alexander Barr dissenting minister of Wolverhampton, sworn before W. Perks at Wolverhampton 8 Feb 1747/8. ITKB 'The King agt Joseph Turton and others at the prosecution of Alexander Barr.'

That the deponent was served a copy of the [*annexed: see [5]*] two rules on 1 Feb. His attorney Mr Asteley is disordered in his senses and incapable of acting in the matter; the deponent has lately employed another attorney, Mr Sparry gentleman of Blewet's Buildings, Fetter Lane, London, in his stead.

As Sparry is unfamiliar with the proceedings in the case, the deponent has insurmountable difficulty in showing cause in the time prescribed by the rules. He asks for a reasonable enlargement of time for that purpose.

Sources: IND 1/6659, Mich, Hil 18 Geo II. KB 1/8 Hil 18 Geo II no. 2, Ea 18 Geo II, Trin 18 & 19 Geo II. KB 1/9 Hil 21 Geo II. KB 11/36/11 Mich 18 Geo II #23. KB 15/14 Hil Vac 18 Geo II. KB 16/13/5, 16/13/6. KB 21/35 pp. 774, 785, 827, 839, 854, 855, 858; KB 21/36 pp. 16, 18, 57, 78, 112, 125, 137, 161, 233, 239, 278, 279, 293, 310, 324. KB 29/404 Mich 18 Geo II #23. KB 36/113, /125, /126. SRO, Q/SR, Mich 1744.

F.2 Certiorari on an information from quarter sessions, by prosecutor (9 Nov 1748)

Defendant: James Robison, linen draper of Newcastle under Lyme.

Writ and return:
Mich 22 Geo II 1748

Writ 9 Nov [1748] for immediate return; by rule of court, return by John Robins, JP.

Affidavit of John Tilstone 22 Oct 1748, sworn in court, that offences were committed in Staffs and within a year before the information exhibited. [*Signed with a mark.*]

Caption by the court, that John Tilstone exhibited the attached information against James Robison at quarter sessions Wednesday 4 Oct 1748.

Copy of an information qui tam made by William Brookes, deputy clerk of the peace, of an information exhibited at Staffs quarter sessions Mich 1748: that Robison exercised the trade of hatmaker, not being qualified by 5 Eliz c.4, from 1 Nov 1747 to 4 Oct 1748, and forfeits £22 (40s for every month, half to the king, half to the informer); same sum for each offence of exercising trades of feltmaker, linen looper and buttoner of hats, dresser of hats and haberdasher. John Tilstone, feltmaker, informer; William Bucknall, prosecutor. [*Tilstone signed with a mark.*][49]

Rules and process:
Mich [2 Nov 1748]: order for a certiorari to the justices (Ford). ST: attached. Hil [1748/9]: prays imparlance; leave to imparl; imparls. Ea [12 April 1749]: first rule to plead. [17 April 1749]: second rule to plead. ST [5 May 1749]: peremptory rule to plead. Trin [1749]: pleads not guilty; venire facias juratores. Trin Vac 21 June 1749: notice of trial for the King (Hughes).

Sources: IND 1/6659, Hil 22 Geo II, Trin 22 & 23 Geo II. KB 11/38 Mich 22 Geo II [1748] #25. KB 21/36 p. 430. KB 29/408, Mich and Hil 22 Geo II. KB 29/408 Hil 22 Geo II, Trin 22 & 23 Geo II. KB 36/127, /129.

F.3 Certiorari on an indictment from quarter sessions, by prosecutor (12 Feb 1752)

Defendant: Richard Drakeford, gentleman of the borough of Stafford.[50]

---

[49] This case is the only one of its kind, an information qui tam exhibited before quarter sessions (rather than in King's Bench or before a magistrate, like those in Sections D and E) and then removed by certiorari into King's Bench. It initially confused a clerk, who entered a venire ('Cause to come ... whereof he is impeached') on the controlment roll (KB 28 for Hil 22 Geo II), then crossed it out, as a writ of attachment had been recorded on the roll for the preceding term. The case might have been placed in section E, but it is not a summary conviction before a magistrate removed by certiorari. Because it was exhibited at quarter sessions it originally was to be tried by jury, like an indictment, and was then removed by certiorari into King's Bench in order to be tried by jury at nisi prius.

[50] Probably the town clerk of Stafford.

Writ and Return:
Ea 25 Geo II 1752

Writ 12 Feb [1752][LDT] to be returned [13 April 1752, FDT Ea];
returned by John, Lord Ward.

Schedule by William Brookes, deputy clerk of the peace of Staffs, that
the annexed indictment was presented at Staffs quarter sessions
[7 Jan]1752.

Indictment for assault and battery 2 Jan [1752] at the parish of St Mary,
borough of Stafford on Abraham Hoskin,[51] gentleman, prosecutor and
witness. A true bill.

Rules and process:
Hil [1752]: asks leave to imparl. Ea [1752]: summons; leave to imparl;
imparls. Trin [29 May 1752]: first rule to plead. ST [2 June 1752]: second
rule to plead. ST [9 June 1752]: peremptory rule to plead[52] (Whitby). ST:
pleads not guilty; venire facias juratores. Trin Vac 13 July 1752: notice
of trial for the King (Hughes).[53]

Sources: IND 1/6659 Ea 25 Geo II, Trin 25 & 26 Geo II. KB 11/40 Ea 25
Geo II #7. KB 15/2 b80v, b81. KB 15/14 Trin Vac 25 Geo II. KB 21/36 pp.
832, 839, 850. KB 29/411 Ea 25 Geo II, Trin 25 & 26 Geo II. KB 36/142.
SRO, Q/SO 15 Ep 1752.

F.4 Certiorari on an indictment from quarter sessions, by defendant (3 July 1754)

Defendant: Thomas Knight, weaver of Haughton.

Writ and return:
Mich 28 Geo II 1754

---

[51] Drakeford and Abraham Hoskins (note spelling) of Burton upon Trent and
      later of Shenstone Park probably both held property in Castle Church near
      Stafford at this date: *VCH Staffs*, v, 91–3; viii, 153; ix, 83–4, 87.
[52] '38' in margin.
[53] According to a letter from the estate steward and attorney George Ridgway
      to his employer the second earl of Uxbridge, the prosecution of Drakeford
      by Hoskins (note spelling) eventually came to trial at nisi prius. SRO D603,
      24 Feb 1759. No postea or other record of a verdict has been found.

Writ 3 July [1754][LDT] to be returned [2 Nov 1754, FDT Mich].[54]

Return and schedule by William Brookes, deputy clerk of the peace of Staffs, that the annexed indictment was presented at Staffs quarter sessions 16 July [1754].

Indictment for fishing on 4 June [1754] a pond called Turnpitt in the parish of Haughton belonging to Francis Eld esquire and took five carp value 1s, five tench value 1s, five bream value 1s, five pike value 1s, five perch value 1s, and in another pond five other fish value 1s. Samuel Hanning, prosecutor and witness; Thomas Turner, witness. A true bill.[55]

Rules and process:
Mich [1754]: summons; prays a day to answer. Hil 28 Feb 1755: notice of trial for the defdt (Althorpe). ST: venire facias juratores. Ea [18 April 1755]: motion for judgment on 23 April. ST: postea and judgment for defdt, by the controllment of last term.

Sources: IND 1/6659 Ea 28 Geo II. KB 11/41 Mich 28 Geo II #19. KB 15/14 Hil 28 Geo II. KB 21/37 p. 343. KB 29/414 Mich, Hil 28 Geo II.

F.5 Certiorari on an indictment from quarter sessions, by prosecutor (8 Nov 1757)

Defendant: Robert Robinson, clerk of Waterfall, formerly of Sheen.[56]

Writ and return:
Mich 31 Geo II 1757

Writ 8 Nov [1757] for return immediately after receipt. [*Verso*]: by rule of court; returned by Brooke Boothby.

Schedule by William Brookes, deputy clerk of the peace, that the indictment was presented at Staffs quarter sessions 12 July [1757].

Indictment not caring for his destitute and orphaned grandchildren, James Robinson aged nine and Peter aged seven years, against the

---

[54] The writ notes that Knight was indicted under the Act for the More Easy Discovery and Conviction of such as shall Destroy the Game of this Kingdom, 4 & 5 Wm & Mary, c. 23 (1692).

[55] A copy of the indictment in SRO, Q/SR, Trans 1754, is marked 'removed by certiorari'.

[56] Curate of Longnor 1735 to 1768, incumbent of Sheen 1751 to 1760, when he lived on his estate in Waterfall. *VCH Staffs*, vii, 46, 247–8.

statute 43 Elizabeth,[57] as he holds freehold land of a value greater than
£100, and considerable church preferment, he was ordered at 11 Jan
1757 quarter sessions to pay 4s weekly to relieve and maintain the two
children; refused to pay on 21 Jan [1757], and continues in contempt of
the order. Prosecuted by the churchwardens and overseers of Waterfall.
Witnesses, Francis Berrisford and George Smith. A true bill.

Rules and process:
Mich [8 Nov 1757]: order for certiorari (by the court; motion of
Howard); writ of certiorari and writ of capias ad respondendum[58] to
bring him before the court 25 Nov, both issue 8 Nov [1757]; capias
returned 'not found' by William Acton Moseley, sheriff. ST [28 Nov
1757]: writ of alias capias to bring Robinson before the court on [28 Jan
1758], returned 'not found' by Moseley 24 Dec 1757. Hil [1758]: prays
imparlance; leave to imparl. Ea [1758]: pleads not guilty; venire facias
juratores; capias. Trin 28 June 1758: notice of trial for the King (Bach).
Mich [6 Nov 1758]: rule nisi for judgment (side bar) for the King. ST:
postea and judgment against, convicted. Hil [29 Jan 1760]: recognizances respited. ST [1 Feb 1760]: by consent of counsel on both sides,
order that on the defdt's paying the prosr £52 10s for costs and also the
further sum of £80 for the maintenance of the grandchildren, parish to
give a certificate acknowledging them as their parishioners (motion
and consent of Morton for defdt, consent of Aston for prosr). ST [12 Feb
1760]: ordered that a writ of attachment for contempt issue unless the

---

[57]   Poor Relief, 43 Eliz, c. 2 (1601).
[58]   If the prosecutor wished, the sheriff would return the usual venire (ordi-
       narily followed by the sequence of distringas, alias, and pluries) *non est
       inventus*, and the clerk in court then immediately made out a capias and the
       sheriff took the defendant into custody. (Hands, 42–3, although Chitty, i,
       396–7, citing this passage, does not say that a return of *non est inventus* could
       be requested by the prosecutor.) The defendant, to be freed, had to 'cause an
       appearance to be entered, upon which his Clk in Ct will issue a supersedeas.
       If the Indt be for some great crime, as perjury, obtaining money under false
       pretences, &c and the deft has not been held to bail below, a judge on cer-
       tificate of the Indt being returned will grant a warrant to apprehend and
       hold him to bail. App[endix] 379.', Hands, 42–3, 379, Gude ii, 143. The
       quoted words are interlineations that replace Hands's original words in my
       crown office copy of Hands, 43; the preceding page is also corrected to show
       that it is the clerk in court, not the court, that issues an alias and pluries. See
       also Chitty, 340, for the usual procedure in warrants following certioraris.
       The original venire in this case is noted in KB 29/417 Mich 31 Geo II.

defdt pay the prosr or his agent the sums of £52 10s and £80 ordered by this court on [1 Feb 1760] within six weeks and the further sum of 10s a week for the maintenance of the defdt's grandchildren until the money is paid or the said children taken away. Trin Hil [30 Jan 1761]: recognizance respited. [4 June 1761]: on reading affdt of the defdt, fined 6s 8d and recognizance discharged.

Affidavit for prosecution:

Mich 33 Geo II 1759[59]

[1] Affdt of John Alcock yeoman, Henry Alcock yeoman, George Smith farmer, and William Stubbs farmer, all of Waterfall, and Francis Beresford farmer of Colton, sworn before John Goodwin at Waterfall 8 Feb 1759. ITKB 'The King against Robert Robinson Clerk' [*Verso*]: 'Staffordshire. Copy Affdt of John Alcock & others agt Robert Robinson clerk. 4 Augt ['21st July' *is struck out*] 1759 sent copy to Mr Robinson fo. 43 & 2 st. 1.10.8 Fawkes & Richardson'.[60]

[John Alcock]: That James, Peter, Charles, Mary and John Robinson, children of Smith Robinson deceased, who was the eldest son of the defendant Robert Robinson, being destitute of subsistence since Sept 1756, were brought from Manchester (Lancs) to Waterfall to be maintained and provided for when the deponent was overseer of the poor.

[Henry Alcock]: That he is the son of John Alcock and was churchwarden for the parish of Waterfall at the time the children were brought into Waterfall to be maintained. As they were unable to work and the defendant was able to maintain them, the deponent and others went to his house in Sheen to request him to do so. He was not at home; they therefore asked his wife to communicate their request to him for his answer.

---

[59] Affidavits [1] to [6], except the original of [1], are filed in KB 1/14/3 Mich 33 Geo II [1750] no. 3, although the endorsement of [4] clearly indicates Trinity Term 1759. It is not clear whether the affidavits without term endorsements also were originally filed in other terms, and then refiled in Michaelmas 1759 (see next note) or whether they were only filed in Michaelmas 1759, although taken much earlier.

[60] This is an 'office copy' of the original affidavit, which is filed in KB 1/13/2 Mich 31 Geo II [1757], endorsed 'Staffordshire. Affdt of John Alcock and others agt Robert Robinson clerk. 43.' It is unclear why the clerks filed or refiled it in the Michaelmas 1757 bundle, except that that was the session in which the certiorari originally issued.

[John Alcock]: That after Henry Alcock's visit, Robinson came to the deponent's house. He tried to convince him to maintain his grandchildren without recourse to law, pointing out that he would be well-spoken of if he did it voluntarily, but that if he were forced to do it the country would say he could not help it. Robinson said that the parish would not have to pay a half penny for maintenance. Soon afterwards Thomas Gould told the deponent that Robinson desired him to keep his grandchildren for as little expense as possible, and that he would pay the deponent soon for the expenses incurred by the parish. When Robinson failed to come, the deponent sent letters but never received a reply. The deponent, being infirm, sent his son Henry to visit Robinson to ask in an amicable manner whether he intended to maintain his grandchildren.

[Henry Alcock]: That Robinson told him that he would not maintain his grandchildren unless the parish forced him by law to do so. As a result, application was made to the next general quarter sessions to be held at Stafford on 11 Jan 1757 to oblige Robinson to maintain his grandchildren. The court granted three orders on 11 Jan for Robinson to pay 2s per week for each child.

[John Alcock]: That he received notice dated 2 April 1757 of Robinson's intention to appeal the decision at the next quarter sessions. He did not pay the five weekly sums as ordered by the court. On 21 April 1757 Robinson tendered money to the deponent at the rate of 5s per week, but no more. He declined the money because he had already put out 10s a week for the grandchildren's maintenance from 1 Jan 1757 to 14 May when the deponent left office as overseer, in all £8. The deponent told Robinson that he, Robinson, knew that his estate had been entailed on Smith Robinson his son, and that as he had cut him off, it appeared he intended to throw Smith Robinson's children on the parish.

[George Smith]: That he became overseer of the poor on 14 May 1757 and held the position for one year, during which he paid 10s a week for relief of the children, totaling £26.

[William Stubbs]: That he is now overseer of the poor and since he entered office on 14 May 1758 he has paid 10s a week for the relief of Robinson's grandchildren, totaling £19 10s.

[John Alcock, Henry Alcock, George Smith and William Stubbs]: That two fifths of the total sum applied to relief of Robinson's grandchildren was applied to the maintenance of James and Peter Robinson, two infant children, amounting to £21 8s.

[Henry Alcock]: That he, acting on behalf of his father, disbursed £18 14s obtaining the court orders and opposing the defendant.

[George Smith]: That he believes the defendant left the county before any proceedings began to enforce the orders. The defendant moved to

Norton (Derbs). As overseer of the poor, the deponent paid £21 9s toward the defendant's indictment and prosecution.

[William Stubbs]: That he is liable to pay a further £43 3s in the future prosecution of this case, bringing the total to £104 14s. The defendant has not paid his 10s a week.

[Francis Beresford]: That the defendant is in possession and receipt of the rents and is reputed to be the owner of a freehold estate in Waterfall, worth £100 a year or more. The defendant also has a preferment in the church of £100 a year or more.

Affidavits for defence:

Mich 33 Geo II 1759

[2] Affdt of Thomas Gould yeoman of Sheen and Sampson Parkes yeoman of Waterfall, sworn before James Davis at Oddo in Winster (Derbs) 11 Jan 1759. ITKB 'The King against Robert Robinson Clerk'. [*Verso*]: 'The King agt Robinson clk. Affidt of Thos Gould and Sampson Parkes fo. 16. Fawkes & Richardson.'

[Thomas Gould]: That on 23 April 1757, under directions given by Robinson, he tendered to John Alcock, the churchwarden and overseer of the poor of Waterfall, the sum of £3 15s at the rate of 20s a month for three months commencing 11 Jan 1757 and ending on or about 5 April; he also tendered 20s for the current month. He understood the payment to be a penalty by law directed to be made in lieu of the performance of certain orders of the court of Epiphany quarter sessions and that the money was to go towards the maintenance of the children of Smith Robinson and Robert Robinson. John Alcock refused to accept the money.

[Sampson Parkes]: That four months after Epiphany quarter sessions 1757, under orders from Robinson, he tendered to the church warden and the overseer of the poor of Waterfall the sum of £4 as and for the penalty of 20s a month in lieu of the performance of the aforementioned orders. After the fifth month he tendered five months' payment of 20s a month, a total amounting to £5, as and for the like penalty. The officer of the parish refused to accept the money.

[3] Affdt of Robert Robinson clerk of Norton (Derbs) and Thomas Gould yeoman of Sheen, sworn in court, by the court 23 Jan 1759. ITKB 'The King agt Robert Robinson Clerk'. [*Verso*]: 'Staffordshire. The King agt Robinson clk. Affid of deft & anr fo: 7 Fawkes & Richardson.'

[Robert Robinson]: That after the death of his son Smith Robinson, the deponent made overtures to the widow's father for maintaining the widow and her five children. For any contribution the widow's father made, the deponent would contribute twice as much, but the father refused to contribute anything. The deponent was served with three orders of quarter sessions to pay 2s a week to each child. He was informed that the justices had ordered him to pay more than they could by law; he therefore requested the churchwarden and overseer of the poor of Waterfall to pay 20s a month for maintenance, which they refused. He has four other children who are entirely maintained by him: Martha, Mary, Peter and Bullwer.

[Thomas Gould]: That about a fortnight after making the tender of £3 15s to John Alcock, he applied to Elizabeth, the widow, in order to agree about some provision to be made for the children and on the defendant's behalf proposed to pay £13 a year. Elizabeth seemed satisfied with that and later told the deponent that she had applied to the overseer for a certificate in order to enable her to return to Manchester to follow her business there, but that he refused to grant her one, telling her they were determined to plague the defendant as much as they could by the orders they had obtained against him. The deponent is acquainted with John Royle,[61] who has a clear income of £40 a year.

[4] Affdt of Robert Robinson of Norton (Derbs), sworn before Thomas Froggatt at Bakewell (Derb) 28 June 1759. ITKB 'The King agt Robert Robinson Clerk'. [*Verso*]: 'Staffordshire. The King agt Robinson. The Defdts 2d affdt. Trini. 1759 Fawkes & Richardson 5.'[62]

That the deponent did not tender more than 20s a month to the overseers of the parish of Waterfall for the maintenance of the children because counsel advised him that such tender was agreeable to 43 Elizabeth. No wilful contempt of the orders of sessions was intended. He continued to reside in the parish of Sheen six months or more after the order of session and he did not remove himself out of Staffordshire with any intention of preventing the overseer of the parish of Waterfall from enforcing the orders by distress on his goods, but on necessary business. On the finding of the indictment he was arrested on a Saturday afternoon and kept in prison three weeks. His circumstances would be greatly diminished with the combination of his old age, the labour and expense caused by his prosecution, and charges which may arise from keeping a curate. His family will be impoverished if he is

---

[61] 'Royl' in some affidavits.

[62] Although the affidavit is clearly endorsed Trinity term 1759, which corresponds to the date it was taken, it is filed in KB 1/14/3 Mich 33 Geo II [1759] no. 3, with an office copy endorsed 'Staffordshire. X The King agt Robinson Clk Office copy of the Defts 2d affid. Fo: 5. Fawkes & Richardson.'

compelled to make all the payments in compliance with the orders. The real estate in his possession in the parish of Waterfall, which he holds in right of his wife, does not exceed the yearly value of £90 a year and the inhabitants of Waterfall force him to contribute to their expenses in carrying on these prosecutions against him. He is put to the burden of defending himself while at the same time contributing to the expenses of the inhabitants who prosecute him. The expenses are increased more than they would be if he had no lands in the parish of Waterfall.

Mich 33 Geo II 1759

[5] Affdt of Robert Robinson clerk of Norton (Derbs) defendant, Peter Robinson, oldest son of the defendant and 21 years of age and upwards, and Thomas Gould yeoman of Sheen, sworn before Thomas Froggatt at Bakewell (Derbs) 31 Oct 1759. ITKB 'The King agt Robert Robinson Clerk'. [*Verso*]: 'fo 29.'

[Robert Robinson]: That he bound his late son Smith Robinson apprentice to one Nadin of Blakeley (Lancs), a Manchester trader, whom he served about two years. Afterwards the deponent set up his son in trade at Manchester where he continued for more than two years, in which he wasted and consumed his substance, married a wife with whom he had no fortune, and died destitute leaving his widow and five children. They were brought by a pass to Waterfall where they were received and taken in by the then officer John Alcock who applied to the deponent for their maintenance. The deponent told Alcock that Smith had gained a settlement either in Blakeley or Manchester, and that the deponent would pay to try the right of settlement with either of those places, and would not put Waterfall to any expense for so doing. The deponent did not say, as Alcock has sworn, that the inhabitants of Waterfall would not have to pay a farthing for the maintenance of the children. He several times requested the Waterfall overseers to provide for them. The deponent was informed that John Royl of Blakeley, father to the mother of the children, was able to maintain them. Royl has an income of £40 a year, his other children are provided for, and as grandfather to the children is equally liable with the deponent to contribute to their maintenance. The deponent sent Thomas Gould to Manchester to make an offer to Royl that the deponent would pay two-thirds of the maintenance of the children if Royl would pay the other third, but Royl refused to contribute in any manner. Alcock refused to move the widow and children into Lancashire at the deponent's expense, which he suggested to compel Royl to contribute to their maintenance. Alcock declared that the deponent was liable to maintain the children and therefore he was not concerned about removing them. The deponent denies directing Thomas Gould to tell Alcock to keep the children at as little expense as possible, and that the deponent would pay, or that the deponent remembers Alcock telling the deponent that having cut off the entail on his son's estate, he (Robinson) wanted to throw his grandchildren upon the parish. The estate was not in fact entailed; it was well known the deponent was willing to contribute two-thirds of the upkeep of the children; the overseer and inhabitants absolutely refuse to compel Royl to contribute anything, and have tried to ruin the deponent and his family through such scandalous and vexatious and litigious behaviour.

The deponent's yearly rents amount to £96 (subject to outgoings), his church preferment is no more than £70 per annum clear of all deductions, and the deponent is only in possession of his living of Norton (Derbs). The deponent must maintain his son Peter Robinson at university at a cost of £50 a year, as well as the deponent's wife and three other children. He denies leaving Staffordshire to prevent the officers of Waterfall from enforcing the orders of sessions. He continued to reside in Sheen nearly three months after his appeal to the orders was rejected. He moved out of Staffordshire at the beginning of July 1757 and the appeal was heard on or about 19 April 1757; the officers could have enforced the order while he resided in the county without the oppressive method of indictment. The deponent moved to Norton (Derbs) because he was under the obligation of an oath and the injunction of his diocesan to do so. The deponent says that the parish officers and inhabitants of Waterfall in the last year assessed the deponent's estate for the poor rate at the sum of £12, most of which the deponent believes is to be put towards the prosecution of this suit; he was obliged to excuse his tenant £12 of the rent due him. The deponent states that he told Alcock he would not maintain the widow and children but that if she was persuaded to return to Manchester with them the deponent would contribute twice as much as her father for their maintenance.

[Thomas Gould]: That he went to Manchester at the burial of Smith Robinson, and on two or three occasions at the request of the defendant, to ask John Royl to share in the maintenance of their grandchildren. The deponent proposed that the defendant should pay two thirds of the maintenance and Royl the other third. Royl refused. The deponent heard the defendant urge the overseer and inhabitants to send the widow and children back into Lancashire to give an opportunity to try the right of the settlement of the children and to compel Royl to contribute to their maintenance. The deponent heard the defendant offer to pay the expenses of such a proceeding himself but Alcock refused to comply. The deponent heard John Alcock say that they (Alcock and the inhabitants) knew they could make the defendant maintain the

children and intended to so without regard to any other business. He
denies that he ever told Alcock that Robinson would pay for their maintenance. He has often attempted to accommodate the parties; some of
the inhabitants were for an agreement, others against. Last Christmas
the deponent went with the defendant to a meeting with the inhabitants
of Waterfall where it was agreed to submit the matter of maintenance
to a reference. The agreement broke off when one of the inhabitants not
at the meeting, Ralph Oakden, refused to agree to a reference. Last 18
Oct by order of Robinson the deponent with Peter Robinson applied to
Joseph Harvey, overseer of the poor, to pay the monies owed by virtue
of the three orders of sessions. The deponent wanted a certificate allowing the widow and children to be moved to Manchester, after which the
defendant would pay the widow 5s a week for maintenance. The
widow and children would no longer be chargeable to the parish of
Waterfall. Joseph Harvey and the inhabitants refused to accept the proposal from the deponent, insisting the defendant pay half the prosecution costs amounting to upwards of £200. The certificate was also
refused and the inhabitants stated they could do better for the children
by placing them out themselves.

[Peter Robinson]: That he heard Thomas Gould make the above proposals and heard the refusals by the inhabitants.

Affidavit for prosecution:

Mich 33 Geo II 1759

[6] Affdt of Joseph Harvey yeoman and overseer of the poor, and Ralph
Oakden gentleman, both of Waterfall parish, sworn before John
Goodwin at Ashbourne (Derbs) 7 Nov 1759. ITKB 'The King plt against
Robert Robinson Clerk deft.' [*Verso*]: 'The King & Robinson Clk Warrt
fo:4.'[63]

That on 5 Nov instant they made overtures of an agreement to the
defendant Robert Robinson. If the defendant would comply with the
orders stipulated by quarter sessions and maintain his five grandchildren by paying 10s a week from the date of the said order and pay
half of the costs and expenses of prosecuting the case, then the overseer
of the poor and the parishioners would allow a certificate to be issued.
This would legally settle Elizabeth Robinson and the five children
within the parish of Waterfall. The defendant refused to give the

[63] With the original is also filed an office copy, endorsed 'Office copy fo:4 & st
£0:4:2.'

deponents a determinate answer and informed them that the matter would be decided the next day in London.[64]

Affidavits for defence:

Trinity 1 Geo III 1761

[7] Affdt of Robert Robinson clerk of Norton (Derbs), sworn before James Dawson at Norton (Derbs) 25 May 1761. ITKB 'The King agt Robert Robinson Clerk'. [*Verso*]: 'Derbyshire [*sic*] Affidt of Robt Robinson Clerk. Fawkes and Richardson fo.3'.

That the deponent, in obedience to the court's rule of [12 Feb 1760], paid to the prosecutor's agent on 25 March 1760 the several sums of £52 10s and £80. He paid to John Smith, overseer of the poor, £3, which was full satisfaction for six weeks' maintenance of the children.

[8] Affdt of Roger Peel gentleman of Furnival's Inn (London), sworn before J. Dawson at his chambers in Sergeants' Inn, Chancery Lane 27 May 1761. ITKB 'The King agt Robert Robinson Clerk'. [*Verso*]: 'Staffordshire 1761 Rev [?] Grant [*illegible*] <u>Assignee</u> [*illegible*] The King agt Robinson Clk Afft. To move that a small Fine may be set upon the Defendt and that his Recognizance may be discharged. Fined 0:6:8 Mr Morton Fawkes & Richardson 1 Ge.'

That on 21 May last the deponent served John Want, agent for the prosecutor, with a notice that a small fine might be set upon the defendant for the offence of which he stands convicted and that his recognizance be discharged by leaving the notice with Mr Want's clerk at Want's dwelling house in Dean Street Fetter Lane.

Sources: IND 1/6659 Hil, Ea 31 Geo II, Mich 32 Geo II. IND 1/6660, Trin 1 Geo III p. 13. KB 1/13 Mich 31 Geo II. KB 1/14 Mich 33 Geo II no. 3. KB 1/15 Trin 1 Geo III. KB 11/42 Mich 31 Geo II [1757] #20. KB 15/3 a25 Hil, and 25v, Ea 31 Geo II. KB 15/14 Trin 1758. KB 16/15/2. KB 21/38 Mich 31 Geo II pp. 59, 160, 317, 442, 515. KB 29/417 Hil, Ea 31 Geo II. KB 36/172.

---

[64] i.e., in King's Bench.

F.6 Certiorari on an indictment from Lichfield quarter sessions, by defendant (9 Feb 1759)

Defendant: Alexander Gordon, yeoman in the parish of St Mary, city of Lichfield.

Writ and return:
Ea 32 Geo II 1759

Writ 9 Feb [1759], to be returned by [30 April; FDT Ea]; by rule of court [*no endorsement*].

Schedule by Joseph Adey, clerk of the peace and town clerk of the city of Lichfield, that the annexed indictment was found a true bill at the general quarter sessions 11 Jan [1759].[65]

Indictment for exercising the trade of a linendraper from 9 Oct [1758] to 11 Jan [1759] without having served an apprenticeship, against the statute 5 Elizabeth.[66] Thomas Kennedy prosecutor; John Beresford and Margaret Lea, witnesses. A true bill.

Rules and process:
Ea [1759]: summons. Mich [1759]: leave to imparl. Hil [1760]: pleads not guilty; venire facias juratores.[67]

Sources: IND 1/6659 Hil 33 Geo II. KB 11/43 Ea 32 Geo II #36. KB 15/3 a32. KB 28/229 Ea 32 Geo II. KB 29/418 Ea 32 Geo II. KB 29/419 Hil 33 Geo II.

F.7 Certiorari on an indictment from Lichfield quarter sessions, by defendant (4 July 1759)

Defendant: Alexander Gordon, yeoman in the parish of St Mary in the city of Lichfield.

---

[65] See also Lichfield Record Office, D 25/1/1, 11 Jan 1759, noting the true bill, and 5 April 1759, 'Memorandum that the indictment found against Alexander Gordon was removed by writ of certiorari into his majesty's court of King's Bench bearing teste the ninth date of February last past and returnable in fifteen days from the feast day of Easter, and the said writ was allowed and return made by Mr Bailiff Grundy bearing date 29 March 1759.'

[66] The Statute of Artificers, 5 Eliz, c. 4 (1562).

[67] The entry in KB/29/418 Ea 32 Geo II has a marginal note to 'Ro. 32' of the Crown Rolls (KB 28). There are no further entries of process on KB 28/229 32 Geo II Ea. See also the next case, F.7.

Writ and return:
Mich 33 Geo II 1759

Writ 4 July [1759][LDT], to be returned [3 Nov 1759; FDT Mich]; returned [*endorsed*] by Joseph Adey, clerk of the peace and town clerk of the city of Lichfield.

 Schedule by Joseph Adey, clerk of the peace and town clerk of the city of Lichfield, that the annexed indictment was found a true bill at the general quarter sessions 12 July [1759].[68]

 Indictment for exercising the trade of a linendraper from 31 May to 12 July [1759], one whole month, in the city and county of Lichfield, without having served an apprenticeship, against the statute 5 Elizabeth. Thomas Chatterton, prosecutor; Mary Eccles and Susannah Past, witnesses. [*Verso*]: A true bill.

Rules and process:
[*None found after initial summons: but see the preceding case.*][69]

Sources: KB 11/43 Mich 33 Geo II #19. KB 29/419 Mich 33.

F.8 Certiorari on an indictment from Walsall quarter sessions, by defendant (29 Nov 1762)

Defendant: Myer Abrams alias John Tompson,[70] dealer of Walsall borough.

Writ and return:
Hil 3 Geo III 1763

Writ 29 Nov [1762][LDT] to Walsall borough magistrates for return by [20 Jan 1763, FDT]; returned by Richard Palmer, mayor.

 Schedule that the annexed indictment was presented at Walsall borough and foreign general quarter sessions 6 Oct 1762 before Richard Palmer, mayor, Thomas Gilbert esquire, recorder, and John Bradnock and Charles Stewart, justices.

 Indictment that Myer Abrams deceitfully exposed to sale to Elizabeth wife of Robert Cope of Walsall, victualler, a powder counterfeited to

---

[68] Lichfield Record Office, D 25/1/1, 12 July 1759, true bill 'removed by writ of certiorari ret. on morrow of All Souls. Thomas Chatterton Prosr'.

[69] Gordon appears to have proceeded only on the one indictment.

[70] 'Thompson' in some of the process entries.

look like snuff, whereas only a small part of it was snuff, 31 Aug 1762 at Walsall, defrauding her of 40s 6d. Robert Cope, prosecutor; Elizabeth Cope, Joseph Woollett, John Spurrier, witnesses. A true bill.

Rules and process:
Hil [25 Jan 1763]: rule nisi for defdt to appear, plead and try the misdemeanour at nisi prius, else recognizances to be estreated (side bar, by the court). ST: summons. Trin [8 June 1763]: recognizances respited. Trin [following year, 8 June 1764]: recognizances respited. ST [6 July 1764]: recognizances respited.

Sources: KB 11/45/2 Hil 3 Geo III #13. KB 21/39 Hil 1763, Trin 1763, Trin 1764. KB 29/422 Hil 3 Geo III. KB 36/190.

F.9 Certiorari on an indictment from quarter sessions, by prosecutor (12 Feb 1766)

Defendants: Joseph Proud, yeoman of Bilston, and Rice Foulkes, gentleman of Gwymygron (Flints).

Writ and return:
Ea 6 Geo III 1766

Writ 12 Feb [1766][LDT], to be returned [14 April 1766, FDT Ea].
   Return by Ralph Sneyd 27 Mar 1766, inclosing
   Indictment [1] for assaulting John Jeffreys, clerk, at Bilston, 31 Aug 1765, and false imprisonment and detainer until this date; [2] for assault and false imprisonment at Bilston 1 Jan 1766 until taking of this inquisition. Eleanor Rogers, prosecutor and witness; John Daveston, witness. A true bill.
   Record by T. Fernyhough, clerk of the peace (Staffs) that at Ep 1766 quarter sessions, 14 Jan 1766, on this presentment, the sheriff was commanded to summon Proud and Foulkes to the next general quarter sessions.

Rules and process:
Ea 1766: summons; appears; prays a day to answer. Trin [30 May 1766]: first rule to plead (side bar). ST: leave to imparl; pleads not guilty; venire facias juratores. ST [17 June 1766]: rule for a special jury, instance of defdt (Price). Trin Vac 19 June 1766: notice of trial for the King (Barlow). Staffs summer assizes 1766: not guilty.

Sources: ASSI 4/4 summer 1766. IND 1/6660, Ea, Tr 6 Geo III. KB 11/46

Ea 6 Geo III #5. KB 15/3 a55. KB 15/15 Trin Vac 6 Geo III. KB 21/39 Trin 6 Geo III. KB 29/425 Ea, Trin 6 Geo III.

F.10 Certiorari, conviction and outlawry on an indictment from the assizes, by prosecutor (8 May 1769)

Defendants: William Lant, victualler; Edward Thompson, tailor; Martin Hicklin, labourer; Samuel Hicklin, labourer; all of Yoxall.[71]

Writ and return:
Trin 9 Geo III 1769

---

[71] The indictment also names Francis Thompson, tailor, but that charge was found no true bill. At trial the defence case was that Turner was trying to enforce forest law in land out of his jurisdiction and that the indictment did not charge an attack on a forest officer; that the defendants were driving out and killing deer that were harming crops in the Sale Hill, land belonging to Henry Arden esquire that was not part of the Forest; that the so-called Forest of Needwood had in fact been disafforested long in the past; that Turner and his men unlawfully attacked the defendants without warning; and that none were killed only because his shotgun and the pistol carried by one of his servants misfired. The defence brief referred to Turner's constantly carrying guns, 'his usual weapons since a man was found dead in the Forest supposed to be killed by him.' His men were armed with another gun and with pike staves 'having an iron spike at one end and a spear at the other.' The defendants hoped 'they shall not now be punished for proving the better men or even for beating their assailants in their own defence tho' with their own weapons.' 'This prosecution is carried on with great asperity, against the poor defendants ... of whom Samuel and Martin Hicklin have already suffered two months imprisonment for the supposed offence in this indictment, and who had before this day been tried for murder, had Mr Turner either died in time of the wounds he received ... or by the surgeons exerting their skill.' The prosecution led evidence that Turner and his men were accustomed to recover deer in the purlieus of the forest, that they were attacked by the defendants who were discovered killing deer at one o'clock in the morning, that the defendants were warned in the King's Peace before the fracas, and that after the initial fight Turner was attacked and beaten a second time, leading to very serious head injuries. Dr Erasmus Darwin of Lichfield testified that he had recommended trepanning (opening the skull to relieve pressure), which Turner underwent twice. BCA 328828, defence brief, Stafford Assizes 3 April 1770, The King against Lant and others.

Writ 8 May [1769][LDT], to be returned [22 May 1769, FDT Trin]; returned by George Perrot.[72]

Schedule by Price,[73] that this indictment was presented and found a true bill at Staffs Lent assizes 28 March 1769.

Indictment Staffs Lent assizes 1769 for [1] violent assault with clubs, staves etc 21 Nov [1768]; [2] common assault, on Thomas Turner at Yoxall.[74] [*Verso*]: James Mosedale,

James Stoddard and Thomas Hollis. A true bill [*except* Francis Thompson].

Rules and process:
Trin [1769]: summons; appeared; leave to imparl. Hil [23 Jan 1770]: first rule to plead. ST [27 Jan 1770]: second rule to plead; plead not guilty; venire facias juratores. ST [10 Feb 1770]: rule for a special jury, instance of prosr (Ambler). Hil Vac 19 Feb 1770: notice of trial for the King (Barlow). Lent assizes 28 March 1770 Staffs: both Hicklins and Edward Thompson found guilty, Lant not guilty. Ea [1770]: postea and judgment against Edward Thompson, Martin Hicklin, Samuel Hicklin; rule nisi for judgment. ST 15 May 1770: capias for Edward Thompson and the Hicklins, returnable [25 May]. ST 28 May 1770: alias capias returnable [2 July]. Trin 4 July 1770: capias cum proclamatione and exigent, both returnable [3 Nov 1770].[75] Mich [6 Nov 1770]: exigent with allocatur against Thompson and both Hicklins; outlawed 6 Dec 1770. Hil 23 Jan [1771]: capias utlagatum to [15 April]. Ea 17 April [1771]: capias utlagatum to [27 May 1771]. Trin 26 June [1772]: capias utlagatum to [3 Nov 1772].[76]

[72] Baron of the court of exchequer 1763–75.
[73] No given name, but probably Meredith Price esquire, clerk of assize for the Oxford circuit: see case G.3.
[74] Although the indictment does not identify Turner as a keeper or the offence as an attack on a keeper, the defence brief identifies him as 'keeper of Shirrall Lodge'; see also case F.22, another outlawry.
[75] The return of the capias cum proclamatione by sheriff John Marsh notes that the proclamation was made 16 Aug, 2 Oct (at quarter sessions), and on the church door at Yoxall 7 Oct; his return of the exigent notes exactions 16 Aug, 13 Sept, and 11 Oct 1770. KB 16/17, 11 Geo III 1770–1771.
[76] Since the convicts had been exacted at only three of the five county courts required by common law, the allocatur provided for further exactions until Hilary term. The return by John Marsh noted exactions at county courts on 8 Nov and 6 Dec: the last failure to appear resulted automatically in a judgment of outlawry, entered up by the prosecutor's clerk in court, F. Barlow. KB 16/17, 11 Geo III 1770–1771; the outlawry is also subscribed on the

Sources: ASSI 4/4 1770. IND 1/6661 Trin 9 Geo III, Hil and Ea 10 Geo III. KB 11/47 Trin 9 Geo III #4. KB 15/3 a66b, Trin 9 Geo III. KB 15/15 Hil Vac 10 Geo III. KB 16/17, 11 Geo III 1770-1771. KB 21/40 Hil, Ea 10 Geo III. KB 29/428 Trin 9 Geo III. KB 29/429 Mich, Hil, Ea, Trin 10 Geo III; KB 29/430, Hil, Ea 11 Geo III; KB 29/431 Trin 12 Geo III.

F.11 Certioraris on indictments from quarter sessions, by defendants (12 Feb 1771)

Defendants: William Archer esquire and his wife Ann, of Castle Church.

Writ and return:
Ea 11 Geo II 1771

Writ 12 Feb [1771][LDT] to be returned by [15 April, FDT Ea];[77] returned by William Inge.

controlment roll for Hil 1770, KB 29/429, below the entry of the venire for the jury. [*In margin*]: 'Roll 15.' For the process, see Gude, i, 261; for the form of the allocatur, see A.B. Corner, *Forms of Writs and other Proceedings on the Crown Side of the Court of Queen's Bench, with practical directions* (London, 1844), 79, no.CI. Gude states that in cases of proceeding to outlawry *after* conviction for misdemeanour (of which this case is an instance), one capias, returnable on the first day of the ensuing term, suffices, and that on return of that writ non est inventus, only the writ of exigent is required, 'as the statutes at common law do not require proclamation after conviction'. It is not clear why in this case the prosecutor instead used the process Gude describes for outlawry where the accused has made no appearance. Gude comments also, 'It is proper to observe that every possible care be taken to the issuing and returns of the writs, as to their correctness and regularity, and it may be prudent to have the returns of the several writs, and the draft of record of outlawry, settled by counsel previous to its being inrolled, as it is necessary to be scrupulously exact and strict in the whole of the proceedings, otherwise the outlawry may be reversed.' Compare Hands, 46, and Blackstone, iv, 320: '... outlawry may be frequently reversed by writ of error; the proceedings therein being (as it is fit they should be) exceedingly nice and circumstantial; and, if any single minute point be omitted or misconducted, the whole outlawry is illegal, and may be reversed: upon which reversal the party accused is admitted to plead to, and defend himself against, the indictment.'

[77] Subscribed, 'Johnson (for Brookes)'. Both indictments are returned under the one writ. The Archers traversed to Easter sessions, when the indictments were removed by writ: SRO, Q/SO 16, Epiph, Ea 1771.

Schedule that the indictments were presented at Stafford Epiphany quarter sessions, 15 Jan [1771].

Indictments[78]

of William Archer charged with common assault on Elizabeth Archer, spinster, 1 Oct, 10 June, 1 Nov, and 15 Dec [1770]. John Barker, prosecutor; Elizabeth Archer and Richard Thrustons, witnesses. [*Verso*]: A true bill.

of Ann Archer for the same offence, but committed 1 May, 1 Oct, and 10 Nov [1770]. John Barker, prosecutor; Elizabeth Archer, witness. [*Verso*]: A true bill.

Rules and process:

Ea [1771]: summons. Trin [1771]: defdts imparl. ST [31 May 1771]: on reading affdts [13] and [14] of William Archer and Ann Archer, rules nisi to [7 June 1771] to dispense with personal appearance of the defdts on undertaking of Barlow to pay such fine as shall be imposed by the court, the defdts having been convicted by default, notice to be given to prosx, her clerk in court, or attorney (Bearcroft). ST [14 June 1771]: reference to Burrows [master of the crown office] to determine whether any and what satisfaction to be made to the prosecutrix; defdts' personal appearance to be dispensed with in the meantime (Bearcroft for defdts; Dunning for prosx). ST: confessed; fined.[79] Trin [26 June 1772]: recognizances respited. Hil [3 Feb 1773]: recognizances respited. Trin [25 June 1773]: recognizances respited.[80] Trin [12 June 1777]: recognizances

---

[78] The affidavits in this case (calendared below) have captions against Ann, against William, or against both, since two indictments were removed by the one writ of certiorari. The clerks nonetheless filed all the affidavits together, and the prosecutions involved identical stages.

[79] KB 39/6 Trin 11 Geo III and KB 21/40 Trin 11 Geo III note a confession and small fine, part of the usual proceedings for a settlement with the agreement of the court, a formal compounding process for an agreed sum. The details of a settlement have not been found, and it clearly had not been agreed by Nov 1771 (see William Archer's letter, [66] below). It appears likely that the attempt to make the Archers pay compensation was abandoned after the filing of prosecution affidavits in aggravation [71] to [98] in 1772 (see affidavit [99] of William Johnston, 28 Jan 1778).

[80] There is no entry in KB 21/41for recognizances respited from this date until 1777 (Trin 17 Geo III), nor do there appear to be such entries for other cases. The early part of this Crown Side Rule Book is in a variety of hands and inks, with some struck out mistakes, suggesting that the clerks were not recording all rules consistently during this period.

respited. Hilary [29 Jan 1778]: recognizances respited. ST [30 Jan 1778]: on reading the affdt of William Johnson gentleman, rule nisi to 6 Feb to prosecutrix for discharge of the recognizances (Cowper). ST [5 Feb 1778]: recognizances respited. Ea [6 May 1778]: recognizances respited until further notice (Cowper for defdts, Dunning for prosx).[81]

Affidavits for defence:

Ea 11 Geo III 1771[82]

[1] Affdt of William Burton labourer and his wife Elizabeth of Pattingham, sworn before W. Perks at Wolverhampton 17 May 1771. ITKB The King v William and Ann Archer. [*Verso is a wrapper for the bundle*]: '67. The King agt William Archer & Wife. Affidt of Mr & Mrs Burton for defts 10 Affts fo.55 Easter Term 1771 Johnston fo.4.'
   [William Burton]: That he was a servant for William Archer for a year and a half.
   [Elizabeth Burton]: That she was a servant for William Archer for almost three years.
   [Both]: That Elizabeth Archer was always treated with tenderness.
   [Elizabeth Burton]: That Elizabeth's ears were boxed by William Archer only when she misbehaved.
   [William Burton]: That he never saw William Archer strike Elizabeth Archer.

[2] Affdt of Dorothy Kirby spinster and sister of Ann Archer of Doveridge (Derbs), sworn before John Hayne at Doveridge (Derbs) 10 May 1771. ITKB The King v William and Ann Archer.
   That the deponent lived with the Archers for months at a time and never saw them strike Elizabeth. Elizabeth was not unhappy with her situation other than what arose from a proud, obstinate temper. Elizabeth told the deponent she believed her uncle would always be her friend if she behaved well, and that she was in a better situation than her brothers and sister, as her uncle gave her board and clothes. Whatever correction William and Ann gave her was to promote virtue and correct vice, with the tenderness of a parent to a child.

---

[81] Counsel for the defdts apparently moved for a discharge, unsuccessfully (see affidavit of William Johnson.)
[82] Some of these affidavits were sworn after the end of Easter term (16 April 1771 to 13 May 1771), but are filed with the affidavits of that term, as part of bundle 67. Similarly, affidavits sworn after the end of Trinity term but before Michaelmas are filed in Trinity term bundles.

[3] Affdt of Sarah Scott, wife of Benjamin Scott brass founder of Wolverhampton, sworn before W. Perks at Wolverhampton 14 May 1771. ITKB The King v William and Ann Archer.

That the deponent lived with William for more than six years. He provided Elizabeth all necessities and sent her to an eminent boarding school in Wolverhampton where William then lived. She was under the care of Mrs Brett, Mrs Eykyn and Mrs Stedman (Mrs Brett's successors) as a day scholar for six years. Elizabeth was frequently kept after school for not doing her work and learning her book. Elizabeth stayed with William more than 12 years; he always treated her with the utmost tenderness.

[4] Affdt of Clement Kynnersley[83] esquire of Loxley, sworn before John Hayne at Uttoxeter 13 May 1771. ITBK The King v William and Ann Archer.

That William is a remarkable sober religious man, a good husband, and tender father. Ann is of a mild and tender disposition, a most humane, moral and religious woman. All reports to the contrary arise from the strong antipathy of bad to good.

[5] Affdt of Elizabeth Foden wife of Thomas Foden maltster of Stafford, sworn before John James Stevens at Forebridge 3 June 1771. [*Signed with a mark.*] ITKB The King v Ann Archer.

That she lived as a servant with the Archers from June 1767 to Oct 1770. Ann struck Elizabeth only once, on the head, and ordered her out of the house. Ann was greatly provoked; Elizabeth is of a very stubborn idle temper and disposition. She was healthy, and never needed a surgeon or apothecary.

[6] Affdt of Richard Thrustans cutler of Forebridge, sworn before John Dearle at Stafford 8 May 1771. [*Signed with a mark.*] ITBK The King v William and Ann Archer.

That the deponent lived three years as a servant to William. Elizabeth was never beaten except when William hit Elizabeth on the head with his hand, but she was never hit hard enough to leave a mark. Ann never struck her, and William never struck Elizabeth without provocation. Once Elizabeth showed the deponent a welt on her arm which she said was made by William with a horsewhip, when he struck her for not moving her chest of clothes out of the deponent's lodging room.

---

[83] Clement Kynnersley of Loxley was named by William Archer as one of two trustees in his will: see note to affd [88].

[7] Affdt of Frances Elizabeth Proctor wife of Metcalf Proctor esquire of Thorpe (Yorks), sworn before Thomas Oakes at Wakefield (Yorks) 20 May 1771. ITKB The King v William and Ann Archer.

That the deponent is the sister of Ann Archer. [*She swears to the good character of William and Ann.*] The Archers took Elizabeth into their home as an infant when her parents died, rearing her and several other children in low circumstances; they brought her up in a manner superior to her circumstances. During lengthy visits to the Archers' home the deponent saw Elizabeth behave in an indecent and unbecoming manner deserving correction. If she was ever chastised, it was done in no violent manner and with the view of promoting her welfare.

[8] Affdt of Richard Archer tanner, brother of William Archer, of Shrewley in Hatton parish (Warws), sworn before John Parry at Warwick (Warws) 5 June 1771. ITBK The King v William Archer.

That at the age of four on the death of her mother Elizabeth went to live with William, and continued there after her father's death nine years ago. When she left William's house she was 19. William provided all her necessaries without recompense, except for some of her school fees, which were paid by this deponent as her guardian and receiver of her rents from old buildings; the income is about £9 a year. William gave, lent and lost very large sums of money to Elizabeth's father and brother and tried to save her and them from ruin. In William's various wills he bequeathed a handsome legacy to Elizabeth; the latest left her an annuity of £8 a year for life. William treats her tenderly and uses only parental correction to bring her up in the fear of God and as a useful member of society. The deponent asked Elizabeth if she liked living with William and she never made the least complaint. If he thought Elizabeth was ill used he would have removed her.

[9] Affdt of Mary Edkins, wife of Thomas Edkins of the parish of Coleshill (Warws), sworn before John Parry at Warwick (Warws) 5 June 1771. ITKB The King v Ann Archer.

That the deponent stayed at William's house for several days last August. Elizabeth told her that her aunt had boxed her ears and once turned her out, but was a good-natured woman. Elizabeth also said that Ann told her she was at liberty to leave if she wished, but would always be taken back. Ann would never mistreat Elizabeth.

[10] Affdt of Elizabeth Foden, wife of Thomas Foden maltster of Stafford, sworn before John James Stevens at Forebridge 3 June 1771. [*Signed with a mark.*] ITKB The King v William Archer.

That she never saw William beat Elizabeth except for a slap or two on the face which swelled her nose for less than an hour. [*Otherwise as affdt [5]*.]

Further affidavits for defence, to dispense with personal appearance:

Trin 11 Geo III 1771[84]

[11] Affdt of Ann Archer defendant and wife of William Archer esquire of Castle Church, sworn before John James Stevens at Forebridge 3 May 1771. [*Verso*]: 'Mrs. Archer's affdt. In the King v Ann Archer.' ITKB The King v Ann Archer.

That Elizabeth has lived with the deponent since she married William nine years ago. For the first seven years she never slapped Elizabeth once, despite Elizabeth's proud, perverse, idle, disobedient and sometimes indecent behaviour. In the last two years she gently boxed Elizabeth's ears and slapped her face because Elizabeth had beaten and abused the deponent's own children. Otherwise she has been kind to Elizabeth, and particularly requested her husband to give Elizabeth a large sum of money as provision in case he parted with her. He declined to do so,[85] fearing Elizabeth's disposition would bring her misfortune.

[12] Affdt of Margaret Collins spinster of Oxley in the parish of Bushbury, sworn before W. Perks at Wolverhampton 14 May 1771. [*Signed with a mark.*] ITBK The King v William and Ann Archer.

That in Oct 1767 the deponent went to live with the defendant at Tettenhall as his servant for eight or nine months. Elizabeth frequently dressed and undressed in the bed chamber of Richard Thrustans. She continued to do so in spite of threats of a beating from William. Elizabeth told her that William then beat her with a horsewhip, but the deponent saw only a small mark upon her arm.

---

[84]   The defence affidavits in this term are found in bundles 6, 14, 18, 19, 64, 65, and 67. They are presented here in date order. The placement of the first four is: bundle 6 (affidavit [13]), 14 ([22]), 18 ([[23]]), 19 ([24]). The remaining defence affidavits in Trinity were filed in bundles 64, 65 and 67; prosecution affidavits were filed in bundles 29 and 66. It is not clear whether the bundles were always created in the order in which affidavits were filed with the court; the dates suggest otherwise.

[85]   The original wording is equally ambiguous.

[13] Affdt of William Archer esquire of Castle Church, sworn before Lord Mansfield at Guildhall (London) 29 May 1771. [*Verso*]: '6. Staffordshire. The King agt William Archer and his wife. Affdt for Defts. Nisi to dispense with defts' appearance. Barlow.' ITKB The King v William and Ann Archer.

That the deponent has business of great importance to conduct on his estate in Carnarvonshire which requires his personal appearance. It would be very injurious to him to have to make a personal appearance in court. It would also be highly inconvenient if his wife were required to appear. She has many young children, some of whom are ill, who require her attention.

[14] [*An identical affdt in the King v Ann Archer alone.*]

[15] Affdt of William Boyce yeoman of Stafford, sworn before John James Stevens at Forebridge 3 June 1771. [*Verso*]: 'The King agt. William. Archer. William.Boyce's Affdt. 5 fo. 6.' ITKB The King v William Archer.

That the deponent has been a servant to William since 1769. He never saw William strike Ann with a stick or weapon; he slapped Elizabeth once or twice with an open hand, which never left a mark nor caused illness. William never hit her without provocation: she was of a very stubborn, idle and disobedient temper. When she left at five o'clock in the morning (unknown to this deponent) she appeared free of bruises and infirmities and in very great spirits.

[16] Affdt of Katharine Yeomans spinster of Rodsley (Derbs), sworn before John James Stevens at Forebridge 3 June 1771. [*Verso*]: 'Catherine Yeomans's Affidt. The King agt. William Archer Esqr. 10 fo. 6.' ITKB The King v William Archer.

That the deponent lived eleven months with William Archer as his servant. [*Similar evidence to that of affdt [15].*]

[17] Affdt of Mary Collins spinster of Streetway [*sic*], sworn before John James Stevens at Forebridge 3 June 1771. [*Signed with a mark.*] [*Verso*]: 'The King agt. William Archer Esq. Mary Collins's Affdt. 6 fo. 6.' ITKB The King v William Archer.

That during the three years of her service with William Archer, he gave Elizabeth slaps with an open hand which she deserved. Once to prevent her ruin he gave her a few strokes with a slender whip on her stays for keeping her clothes and undressing in Richard Thrustan's room notwithstanding warnings from William Archer. She was never ill and frequently behaved in a very indecent unbecoming manner so as to deserve correction.

[18] Affdt of Mary Collins spinster of Streetway against Ann, sworn before John James Stevens at Forebridge 3 June 1771. [*Signed with a mark*.][*Verso*]: 'The King agt Ann Archer. Mary Collins's Affdt 7 fo.3.' ITKB The King v Ann Archer.

That the deponent left the service of William Archer two years ago. During her service, Ann Archer never beat, struck, or assaulted Elizabeth but behaved with great tenderness toward her.

[19] Affdt of William Archer esquire of Castle Church, sworn before John James Stevens at Forebridge 3 June 1771. ITKB The King v William Archer.

That Elizabeth has lived with the deponent, her uncle and guardian, since she was four years old, when she had no mother and at the request of her father. She has been educated at an eminent boarding school. On 17 Dec last, being 19 years old, Elizabeth was secretly enticed away by John Barker. She was maintained at an expense to the deponent of between £200 and £300, was never sick, was never corrected with violence, yet was of slender capacity and of a very remarkable idle, stubborn, disobedient temper and from her infancy perversely disposed, causing him far more trouble than his own six children. He has corrected her only to prevent her utter ruin. He was advised to remove the indictments into King's Bench because the most eminent counsel were retained against him at Stafford sessions. He pleaded guilty to the indictment on the advice of counsel and friends to save the expense of trying it. John Barker has commenced the prosecution against the deponent and his wife out of private resentment.

[20] Affdt of William Boyce yeoman of Stafford, sworn before John James Stevens at Forebridge 3 June 1771. [*Verso*]: 'The King agt Ann Archer. William Boyce's Affdt. 4 fo. 4.' ITKB The King v Ann Archer.

That the deponent, a servant with the defendant, never saw Ann assault, beat or strike Elizabeth.

[21] Affdt of Katharine Yeomans spinster of Rodsley (Derbs), sworn before John James Stevens at Forebridge 3 June 1771. [*Verso*]: 'The King agt Ann Archer. Catherine Yeoman's Affdt. 9 fo. 4.' ITKB The King v Ann Archer.

That the deponent, a servant of the defendant, never saw Ann beat or strike Elizabeth during the time of her service.

[22] Affdt of Richard Tolley gentleman of Dudley (Worcs), sworn before George Cookes at Stafford 4 June 1771. [*Verso*]: 'Staffordshire. 14. King's Bench. Affidt of Serv of Rule to dispense with deft's personal appearance. The King agt William Archer Instrs. To move to make rule absolute. Johnston.' ITKB The King v William Archer.

Affdt of service of the annexed rule to Barker, Elizabeth and James Tompkinson, principal attorney.

[*Annexed*]: the rule of 31 May 1771 for dispensing with personal appearance of the accused.

[23] Affdt of Francis Brookes gentleman of Stafford, sworn before Thomas Harvey at Lichfield 5 June 1771. [*Verso*]: '18 Staffordshire Affidt of Service of Notice of Confessing Indt. & for Small Fine. The King agt. Wm. Archer. Mr. Brooks' affidt. Johnston.' ITKB The King v William Archer.

Affdt of service to John Barker and Elizabeth Archer on 1 June of the annexed notices.

[*Annexed*]: notice by William Archer to John Barker 1 June 1771 that King's Bench will be moved 11 June that William Archer may submit and take judgment, pleading guilty to the indictment. Witnessed by Francis Brookes.

[*And a similar notice to Elizabeth Archer.*]

[24] Affdt of Francis Brookes gentleman of Stafford, sworn before Thomas Harvey at Lichfield 5 June 1771. [*Verso*]: '19 Staffordshire. Affdt of Service of Notice of confessing indt. & for small fine. The King agt. Ann Archer. W. Brooks Affdt. Johnston.' ITKB The King v Ann Archer.

[*A copy of the preceding affdt and notices, but on behalf of Ann Archer.*]

[25] Affdt of John Archer druggist of Snow Hill (London), sworn before E. Willes at his house in Lincoln's Inn 20 June 1771. ITKB The King v William and Ann Archer.

That the deponent is brother to Elizabeth and nephew to the defendant William Archer. He has been several times to William's home, at one time for six months. Elizabeth was there for part of that time, and he and his wife have always treated Elizabeth with great propriety, tenderness and care. They are incapable of cruel or ill behaviour. Elizabeth is a person of weak capacity, liable to be influenced, and could not herself have framed such a charge. The defendants are incapable of cruel or immoderate correction other than was necessary and proper, moderate and in such manner as to promote her welfare. He has been informed that William Archer made a will, still extant, in which he left Elizabeth, the deponent, and another brother and sister each a handsome legacy, and he really thinks it great ingratitude and cruelty to join in the prosecution. She has been reared, maintained, clothed and educated at William's expense. He has been her best and truest friend. Having read Elizabeth's affidavits, he is much shocked and doubts that she understands the meaning and consequence of them.

[26] Affdt of Mary Collins spinster of Streetway, sworn before Francis Brookes at Forebridge 25 June 1771. [*Signed with a mark.*] ITKB The King v Ann Archer.

That Elizabeth used to dine in the parlour with William and Ann until she refused to do so. She was well clothed but had the practice of selling her clothes. She could have asked for more clothes at any time, but she was so proud that no one could compel her to speak except when William threatened to beat her. Elizabeth was so silent and sullen that the neighbours said she was dumb mad. She had a habit of dressing and undressing in Richard Thrustans's room, though she had a room of her own. Elizabeth left her room unkempt for months at a time until it was overrun with vermin. She was filthy, wretched and given to drink. She was addicted to lying. Ann never struck her.

[27] Affdt of Katharine Yeomans spinster of Rodsley (Derbs), sworn before John Hayne at Doveridge (Derbs) 12 July 1771. [*Verso is the wrapper for bdl 65*]: '65 Staffordshire The King agt Archer and wife. Afft on behalf of defendt. for defts additional 12 affts fo. 132. Yet Trin.: Term 1771.[86] Johnston fo. 11.' ITKB The King v William Archer.

That the deponent worked as a servant for William from March to December 1770. She never saw William beat Elizabeth except once, when he gave her a slap with his open hand on her shoulder which left no marks. Nor did she see or hear William beat Elizabeth in May 1770 after receiving the sacrament. Elizabeth told the deponent she had been struck across the face for refusing to eat a child's breakfast she had spoiled. She complained that her nose was swelled, but the deponent did not think so. She never saw William strike Elizabeth with a whip. In the summer of 1770 she never saw William beat Elizabeth on the head with his first for not carrying coals which was normally done by the deponent or William Boyce. In September or October 1770, she never saw William strike Elizabeth's head against the wall for being sloppy with her needlework. Nor did he strike her for not being ready for church, nor because the children were not ready for school. These assertions are false and Elizabeth is addicted to lying. She did not do the work of a servant; the work she did in a week could have been done by any other woman in a day.

[28] Affdt of Elizabeth Lees, wife of Thomas Lees labourer of Tettenhall, sworn before W. Perks at Tettenhall 15 July 1771. [*Signed with a mark.*] ITKB The King v William and Ann Archer.

---

[86]   The date was originally written 1772, corrected to 1771.

That in 1767 the deponent lived with William as a servant under her maiden name Elizabeth Cook. That William and Ann treated Elizabeth with all the affection they do their children and the deponent never saw them strike her.

[29] Affdt of Mary Collins spinster of Streetway, sworn before John James Stevens at Stafford 16 July 1771. [*Signed with a mark.*] ITKB The King v William Archer.

That the deponent worked for William Archer several different times as a servant. Elizabeth was not a servant. The work she did in a week could have been done by a good woman in 12 hours. She dined with the family until she refused to do so, sold her clothes, and was too sullen and proud to accept William's offer to buy her more. Though William struck Elizabeth a few strokes on her stays with a slender whip, no marks were left and not one drop of blood fell from any horsewhipping, nor did he knock her down. [*Repeats her account in affdt [26] of Elizabeth's dressing in Thrustan's bedchamber, saying it occasioned the whipping.*] Elizabeth was given to lying and drinking strong liquor. She was treated better than she deserved. Elizabeth was so sullen and obstinate that the neighbours called her dumb mad.

[30] Affdt of Richard Thrustans cutler of Forebridge, sworn before Francis Brookes at Forebridge 22 July 1771. [*Signed with a mark.*] ITKB The King v Ann Archer.

That the deponent lived with William Archer as his servant from Christmas 1766 for three years. He never saw Ann assault, strike or beat Elizabeth in the summer of 1769 or at any other time for cutting the box hedge in the garden; William had no garden that summer. The deponent never saw William or Ann beat Elizabeth for not bringing tea nor was she beaten for not sweeping the cobwebs from the ceiling of the bedchamber. The deponent never saw William or Ann take Elizabeth by the hair and knock her head against the wall for not going into the parlour when called. During the whole time the deponent lived there as a servant he never saw nor heard William or Ann beat Elizabeth. At Epiphany sessions 1771, when Elizabeth first prosecuted Ann for the assaults, Elizabeth told him of being cut in the arm by a knife thrown by Ann but never mentioned being cut in the face.

[31] Affdt of Elizabeth Burton,[87] wife of William Burton labourer of Pattingham, sworn before W. Perks at Wolverhampton 22 July 1771. ITKB The King v William Archer.

---

[87] She signs 'eliz: burten'.

That the deponent worked for William from 1764 to 1767 and was then known by her maiden name Elizabeth Rhodes. Elizabeth Archer had come from Mrs Croft's of Stourbridge to live with William as his niece, not as his servant. She was never beaten nor put to servile tasks. She was entrusted with the keys of the cellar and employed to work with her needle and to take care of the children. She was ill trusted, as she often drank and fell asleep. William often got angry and sometimes gave her a slight box on the ear which she well deserved. William and Ann behaved with great tenderness to her, and did all in their power to make her good and preserve her virtue.

[32] Affdt of Elizabeth Foden wife of Thomas Foden maltster of Stafford, sworn before Francis Brookes at Forebridge on 22 July 1771. [*Signed with a mark.*] ITKB The King v Ann Archer.

That the deponent worked as a servant in William Archer's house from June 1767 to October 1769. She never saw nor heard of William beating Elizabeth for not getting the tea ready, nor for not dusting the bed chamber. She never saw her beaten for cutting the box hedge in 1769; the Archers did not have a garden that year. She never saw or heard of the Archers taking Elizabeth by the hair and knocking her head against the wall for not going into the parlour. The only blow she saw was a slap by Ann with her open hand against Elizabeth's head in May or June 1770, when she told her to leave the house and go where she could amend herself. When Ann spilled some water from a basin on Elizabeth's clothes in summer 1770 she did not throw it, and Elizabeth was not indisposed. She did not see Ann hit her with tongs, nor ever strike Elizabeth so as to leave black marks. About August 1770 Ann did order her to starch and wash some clothes, and when Elizabeth refused, told her she should have no tea for breakfast, but bread, cheese, cold meat and other provisions were always open at the pantry to her and all the family. All the washing Elizabeth did in all the years she and this deponent lived in the house might be done by a good washing woman in one day, scarcely sufficient to instruct her how to wash her own necessaries. She saw no knife thrown in October 1770 nor any wound on Elizabeth. The accusations are false, malicious and groundless. Elizabeth was given to lying and to strong liquor; her sullen and obstinate behaviour was so extraordinary that the neighbours reported her to be dumb mad.

[33] Affdt of Elizabeth Foden wife of Thomas Foden maltster of Stafford, sworn before Francis Brookes at Forebridge 21 Oct 1771. [*Verso*]: '9 fo. 6.' [*Signed with a mark.*] ITKB The King v William Archer.

That the deponent never saw William strike Elizabeth with his clenched first or in any other manner in June 1770 for not cleaning the chicken trough; nor with a walking stick between Michaelmas and Christmas 1767 for not fetching linen drying on a hedge. Nor did he beat her with a horse whip in Christmas 1768, but was informed that William did beat Elizabeth with a hand whip for not removing her clothes from Richard Thrustans's room, after repeated strict orders to do so. She saw no blood and believes such beating was of trifling consequence. The deponent did not see William beat Elizabeth in June 1769; in August he gave her a slap or two with his hand in her face that caused her nose to swell for no more than an hour. There were no other assaults.

[34] Affdt of Eleanor Leek servant of Ann Archer, sworn before Francis Brookes at Forebridge 22 Oct 1771. [*Signed with a mark.*] ITKB The King v Ann Archer.

That the deponent has lived with Ann since 4 Dec 1770, never saw any marks of violence on Elizabeth nor saw her beaten. Elizabeth never made any complaints, was in good health; she went away from the defendant's house remarkably merry, talking about her sweethearts the evening before she left. Deponent never saw either of the Archers beat or mistreat her.

[35] Affdt of William Boyce yeoman of Stafford, sworn before Francis Brookes at Forebridge 23 Oct 1771. [*Verso*]: '11 fo.8.' ITKB The King v Ann Archer.

That he has been in service with the defendant's husband since 14 Dec 1769, and never saw Ann strike Elizabeth with tongs on the arm, or with a dusting brush on the head. He never saw William or Ann take Elizabeth by the hair and knock her head against the wall, or tear her cap to pieces, or throw a cold basin of water at her bosom, or throw a knife at her face and cut her forehead. These charges he believes to be a wicked detestable and malicious falsity, for the deponent spent many hours in Elizabeth's company. Nor did he see or hear of a beating with a handwhip, nor heard of her arms bleeding, nor ever saw Ann beat Elizabeth in any manner whatsoever.

[36] Affdt of Ann Archer defendant [*no residence given*], sworn before Francis Brookes at Forebridge 28 Oct 1771. ITKB The King v Ann Archer.

That Elizabeth's affidavit contains most dreadful false and wicked accusations. In the summer of 1769 she did not order Elizabeth to cut the box hedge. The deponent did give Elizabeth a slap or two with an open hand in 1769 or 1770 because she obstinately refused to pull a few slips of box with which to decorate a fireplace; she never hit her with her clenched fist. The deponent never beat Elizabeth because the tea was not ready, nor strike her with tongs (as she hopes for mercy before God who knows her heart). She does not remember striking Elizabeth in connection with a kitchen fire, nor does she recall hitting Elizabeth with a dusting brush. She did not take Elizabeth by the hair in 1769 and bang her head against the wall or tear Elizabeth's cap or bruise her head with any beating. In May or June 1770 she slapped Elizabeth with an open hand and turned her out of the house because Elizabeth had beaten and abused her children, particularly William whom she had used so cruelly that this deponent had reason to believe she caused a rupture. In the summer of 1770 deponent never threw a basin of cold water at Elizabeth. In August of September last she ordered that Elizabeth have no tea to her breakfast, but the pantry was open and full of provisions. She did not that evening beat her or even slap her with her open hand, nor take a clothes stick into her hand. The deponent did not fling a knife at Elizabeth in Oct 1770 or any other time. In October or November 1770 she called Elizabeth into the parlour several times before she came in. For that and for telling a lie, she rather thinks she gave Elizabeth a slap or two in the face or head, but denies whipping her. Elizabeth had not the least mark of violence upon her when she left. In December 1770 William told the deponent to slap Elizabeth for disobeying her, which she did, but she did not clench her fist to do this. When Elizabeth's younger brother Thomas came a week or ten days after she had left, he asked defendant's husband to overlook her bad behaviour and allow her to come again. Elizabeth was a notorious lying stubborn idle disobedient girl, much given to drinking when opportunity offered. The deponent once found Elizabeth asleep on her bed with a candle burning, endangering her and the house. Another time Elizabeth was found asleep on Thrustans's bed in the afternoon.

[37] Affdt of William Archer defendant [*no residence given*], sworn before Francis Brookes at Forebridge 28 Oct 1771. [*Verso*]: '13 fo. 20.' ITKB The King v William Archer.

That Elizabeth did not reside with Mrs Croft but visited only a few weeks before returning to reside with him, as she had since the age of four years. Elizabeth has been tenderly and affectionately reared as his own child, kept chiefly to service, and dined with them until she would not observe orders. Her needlework was of very little consequence whether she worked or played. She had been asked to do different sorts of business for two or three years past, his wife desiring if possible to find something Elizabeth might find pleasure in to get her bread and be preserved from the ill effects of such detestable idleness as was rarely seen in any young person whatever. She was not employed in any manner unsuitable to her very small fortune. It would have been extremely inconsistent on the defendant's part not to have brought her up to some kind of employ as this defendant hath but a small fortune considering what he has done for her and her family. Having an increasing family at this time of six children, he must bring them up possibly to much closer business than Elizabeth engaged in.[88] It is untrue that she has not been compensated for her service other than by maintenance and wearing apparel; she has cost a great deal of money in education and had plenty of pocket money. She never wanted for clothes, she had only to ask, but he has been told on good authority that she frequently sold them. She has most basely falsely and wickedly sworn to charges against the deponent, who never expected to be called to account for his conduct respecting the fatherless, one of the best and most charitable actions he ever did in his life. Not being conscious of using her ill, he never made any minutes of his behaviour toward her, and cannot speak to time and circumstances positively and precisely. But when she makes nine charges against him of beating, beating with his fist with violence, he can with the greatest certainty recollect and affirm that he never once in all the years from the age of four when she came to reside with him, strike her with his fist to the best of his knowledge, remembrance and belief. He never once beat her head against the wall, nor strike her knocking her down, but recollects on some occasion several years since giving her a slap with his open hand when she, being a clumpsey[89] girl and in a hurry, stumbled and either fell or was falling. The charge of twice kicking her several times is false; he never kicked her more than once and that was only one kick upon her backside. He also recalls giving her one slight stroke with a stick which he happened accidentally to have in his hand. He only beat her once with a hand whip and that was over her petticoats and stays, but accidentally at that time gave her one stroke on her arm which never broke the least particle of skin, but might leave one small mark or weal. He did so because she kept her clothes in Richard Thrustans's bedchamber for several weeks or months, and dressed and undressed herself there contrary to many orders to cease doing so. This mode of correction had been long threatened, to terrify her from the practice and to prevent her entire ruin, without success. Elizabeth showed a bad disposition early in life, stealing money from a box he kept for the poor, which was the

---

[88] See note 102.

[89] *Oxford English Dictionary* Clumse, clumpse: 'stupid, dull, stolid of mind; inept of hands, unhandy, unready, idle, lazy; in mod. dial., also, gruff, surly.'

first time he corrected her. He has slapped her with an open hand several times since to correct her many stubborn, lying, filthy, idle, disobedient bad actions and drinking to excess, but never with violence to do her any injury. She had no mark of violence on her when she left his house; he never used a poker or other unlawful weapon on her, nor desire his wife to pull her nose much less wring it. Elizabeth enjoyed excellent health for many years and never required the least assistance from any surgeon or apothecary. The charges are wicked and malicious; he should have been ashamed to trouble the court with the removal of the indictment from sessions had not the only two eminent counsel that attended there been retained against him, and also on account of this defendant's opposing the interest of a certain noble lord at a public turnpike meeting who generally presides at the general quarter sessions held for this county.[90]

Affidavits for prosecution, to show cause against the rule to dispense with personal appearance of the defendants:

Trin 11 Geo III 1771[91]

[38] Affdt of Elizabeth Archer spinster of Lichfield, aged 20 years and about one month, sworn before Richard Hinckley at Lichfield 8 June 1771. [*Verso is the wrapper of the bundle*]: '29 Staffordshire. (3). The King agt. William Archer and Ann Archer. Eliz. Archer's affdt. on behalf of prosectx. to s.c. agt Rule Nisi to dispense with defts. personal appces. 3 affdts—fo:46. Trin 11th Geo 3d for prosr. Manley. fo. 15.' ITKB The King v Ann Archer.

That the deponent lived as a common servant with her uncle William at Forbridge from May 1769 to 17 Dec 1770. Ann made several assaults on her. In summer 1769 Ann struck her on the head with clenched fists in the garden because she did not cut the box edging on the borders as directed. Soon after, Ann beat her in the kitchen because the tea was not ready. In October 1769 Ann became furious at the deponent's stirring the kitchen fire and struck her twice with tongs on the arm with so much force that it was difficult to use her arm for some time; that month Ann also hit her on the head with a dusting brush for not dusting the cobwebs from the bed chamber. Late in 1769 Ann pulled her by the hair and knocked her head against the wall several times with great vio-

---

[90] John Lord Viscount Dudley and Ward presided at Epiphany and Translation sessions 1771. SRO Q/SO.

[91] Bdls 29 (affdts [38–40]) and 66.

lence, tearing her cap into shreds and leaving her head very sore because she did not go into the parlour when called; this deponent, who is rather hard of hearing, had gone at the first call she heard. In early 1770 Ann struck her with her fist on the head and turned her out of doors because the deponent and William, Ann's son, had disagreed about the boy's supper. In summer 1770 Ann threw a basin of cold water onto her bosom, giving her a violent cold, because she had not folded some clothes. In Aug or Sept 1770 Ann forbade her to have breakfast because the washing water was not ready. She had nothing to eat until 7pm and Ann beat her on the head with her fists until she almost fell to the ground. Ann took the clothes stick and threatened to beat her because she had not done the washing as quickly as Ann had expected. In Oct 1770 Ann threw a knife in her face, cutting her forehead, because she had been too long fetching parsley in the garden. In Nov 1770 Ann called her into the parlour and she went inside after changing her cap. When she went in Ann rose from the chair in a great passion, slapping her face and head. She took from one of the children a handwhip and whipped her, leaving blood and marks which lasted a month after she left the Archers. On 15 Dec she was mending stockings at night and appeared sleepy. The defendant William Archer ordered Ann to beat her and wring her nose off. Ann beat her and when William put his hands on the poker, the deponent ran out of the room.

The deponent gave evidence of these assaults upon a bill of indictment preferred by her uncle John Barker at last Epiphany sessions against Ann Archer, who has given notice that she will plead guilty in this court.

[39] Affdt of Elizabeth Archer spinster of Lichfield, sworn before Richard Hinckley at Lichfield 8 June 1771. [*Verso*]: 'No 1. Eliz. Archer affidt. fo 28.' ITKB The King v William Archer.

That in 1765 the deponent left the employ of Mr Croft of Stourbridge, a distant relation who treated her with affection, on William's order. She moved with the family from his house at Tettenhall to Forbridge. She was poorly treated and received no wages; at Tettenhall in late 1766 she complained to Ann about not being paid, and William called her into the parlour, shut the door and hit her head with his fists. Her head and neck were so swelled and bruised that she could not work for several days. In June 1767 William struck her on the head while she was feeding the chickens because he thought she had not cleaned the trough. Late that year he beat her on the back with a large walking stick for not bringing in some washing. About Christmas 1768 he beat her with a handwhip until blood flowed on her arms, for not taking a chest of her clothes out of a manservant's room, and for falling asleep while

William read a sermon the previous evening. About June 1769 William beat and kicked her and she showed the bruises to Mrs Price, a neighbour. About August 1769 he beat her for smoking the milk she was boiling for the children's breakfast, first with his fist, then with a whip. She again showed the bruises to Mrs Price. She was beaten for cutting a slice of bread and meat, which William Archer's son gave to a beggar at the door, and for not addressing William and his wife as 'sir' and 'madam'. He beat her several times on Sundays after receiving the sacrament. During one beating William Archer remarked that it was impertinent of Mrs Sherwyn to advise him how to act. Mrs Sherwyn, Elizabeth's cousin, gave a letter to William Archer relating to a service she had procured for Elizabeth. There were several other beatings: over not being ready for church, carrying the warming pan too near the floor, not having the children dressed in time for school, and similarly trifling matters.

On 17 Dec the deponent escaped the house before the family awoke. She gave evidence upon a bill of indictment preferred by her uncle John Barker at last Epiphany sessions at Stafford. She has received notice that William Archer intends to plead guilty in King's Bench.

[40] Affdt of John Barker gentleman of Lichfield, sworn before Richard Hinckley at Lichfield 8 June 1771. [*Verso*]: 'No 4. Affidt of Mr. Barker for prosx. fo: 3 Barlow.' ITKB The King v William and Ann Archer.

That at the last Epiphany Sessions he preferred and the jury found and returned true bills of indictment against William and Ann. The deponent understands from notices served on him that the defendants have or will plead guilty to the indictments. The deponent needs more time to obtain testimony of material witnesses living at a distance.

[41] Affdt of Thomas Archer brother of Elizabeth and gunfinisher of Birmingham (Warw), sworn before Edward Hickman at Stourbridge (Worcs) 15 June 1771. [*Verso*]: 'In the Kings Bench Staffordshire. 66 The King agt Archer & an. Affdt of Thos. Archer for the protrix. Sworn 15 June 1771. No 5. Trin: Term 1771. 21 additional Affts of this Term. fo. 221 for prosx.[92] fo : 8 Manley.' ITKB The King v William Archer.

That in 1769 on a visit to Elizabeth she asked the deponent to find her a new family with whom to live. Mrs Sherwin, Elizabeth's cousin, agreed to take her but William refused to let her go. The deponent warned his uncle that a prosecution would be commenced if matters were not accommodated; William told him never to return to his house. Elizabeth is much changed and unable to make that figure in life that

---

[92]   This is the wrapper for bdl 66.

might have been expected. William is a man of fortune, Elizabeth a poor orphan who only has the fourth share in some leasehold property in Birmingham in poor repair, and what she may recover from William her uncle under a bequest in the will of her late grandmother, a will secreted eleven years by her uncle, the whole of which fortune [*illegible*] to maintain her.

[42] Affdt of Mary Croft widow of Stourbridge (Worcs), sworn before Edward Hickman at Stourbridge (Worcs) 15 June 1771. [*Verso*]: 'In the King's Bench. The King agt Archer & an. Affidt of Mary Croft Wo for the Protrix. Sworn 15 June 1771 No.6 fo:10.' ITKB The King v William Archer.

That the deponent has known Elizabeth since childhood as she is a relative of her late husband. In 1763 the deponent visited Mrs Mason, Elizabeth's great aunt. Mason said that Elizabeth was leaving school at Yardley to live with William. Elizabeth was concerned because her elder sister was ill used by William. The deponent therefore offered to take Elizabeth to her house, provided she behaved herself, where she would endeavour to qualify her for a housekeeper's place or a lady's waiting woman so that she could earn wages. The deponent communicated this to Richard Archer tanner, brother of William Archer, and Elizabeth was permitted to stay with the deponent. She did so because Elizabeth appeared to be a sensible and well disposed young person and her grandparents had shown kindness to the deponent's husband during his minority. After some weeks, William Archer sent for Elizabeth. When Elizabeth expressed concern, the deponent had Gill, an apothecary of Stourbridge, write a letter for her to William requesting that Elizabeth return to her house to work for wages when she was capable and deserving of them so that she would be no expense to her friends. After Elizabeth had been with William she visited the deponent twice. She appeared stupid, awkward, senseless and in a ragged, poor condition. She complained of the ill usage she received from William and Ann. The deponent advised her to bear it as well as she could until she reached the age of 21.

[43] Affdt of Hannah Wells wife of Joseph Wells gardener of Ilmington (Warws), sworn before John Gill the younger at Ilmington (Warws) 15 June 1771. [*Signed with a mark.*] [*Verso*]: 'In the King's Bench. The King agt Archer & an. Affidt of Hannah Wells wife of Josh Wells. Sworn 15 June 1771. No (9). fo. 5.' ITKB The King v William Archer.

That the deponent knows Elizabeth and William, a man of considerable fortune. Four years ago she worked as a servant to William for six months. Elizabeth always behaved in a very obedient, obliging and respectful manner and was never intoxicated with liquor. The deponent has often heard William reprimand and abuse Elizabeth without cause and for the most minute offence; she was made to do the most slaving part of the work of the house. The defendant allowed the nurse-maid tea and bread and butter for breakfast, giving Elizabeth only bread and wallspring[93] cheese that stunk, or skimmed milk.

[44] Affdt of Sarah Steward spinster of Bilston, sworn before Stephen Falknor at Bilston 15 June 1771. [*Signed with a mark.*] [*Verso*]: 'In the King's Bench. The King agt Archer & an. Affdt of Sarah Stewart Spr. for prstrix. Sworn 15 June 1771. No 7. fo. 6.' ITKB The King v William Archer.
    That the deponent was a servant of William. About Michaelmas 1766 Elizabeth asked her aunt to be paid wages for her work. She came crying to the deponent and told her she had been beaten by her uncle for asking and was beaten often. The deponent saw William strike Elizabeth on the side of the head, and kick her unmercifully. Elizabeth always behaved in a dutiful manner. The beatings greatly impaired Elizabeth's capacity. In 1766 Elizabeth was indisposed and the deponent approached Ann and told her Elizabeth's usual diet of milk, bread and cheese was not proper, and suggested a little tea, which Ann refused to give her.

[45] Affdt of Richard Thrustans cutler of Forebridge Castle Church, sworn before S. Fernyhough at Stafford 16 June 1771. ITKB The King v William Archer.
    That the deponent lived as William Archer's servant from Christmas 1766 to Christmas 1769. Elizabeth was treated as a common servant. William beat Elizabeth very hard on the head with his hands and fists, on the most trifling occasions. Elizabeth often complained to the deponent of the beatings. At Tettenhall William once knocked her down for not carrying some water to the chickens. Elizabeth Foden (maiden name Brookes), also a servant, told the deponent that she had seen Elizabeth struck down by William. Foden now denies it. [*See affdts [32] and [33].*] After Christmas 1768 Elizabeth told the deponent that William had beat her with a whip; she showed him the marks on her arms. On 15 Jan last, the deponent gave evidence to the grand jury against William Archer for the assaults on Elizabeth. After the grand jury indictment Archer sent for the deponent and told him that he had whipped Elizabeth, but to prevent her from becoming a whore. Elizabeth gave no reason for suspicions so injurious. The deponent had

[93] Perhaps for 'wellspring'.

advised Elizabeth to quit, for it would be better for her to beg bread than to stay with Willam, whose violent passion greatly terrified her. Since the prosecution was begun, Ann has brought the deponent's wife presents of wine and cloth. Ann and the deponent's wife had no acquaintance or connection before the prosecution.

[46] Affdt of Mary Scott, wife of John Scott farmer of Bridgeford, parish of Seighford, sworn before S. Fernyhough at Stafford 6 July 1771. ITKB The King v William Archer.

That Elizabeth, who is a distant relation, asked the deponent if she could arrange with William for her to leave for her uncle Barker's house as she was being ill treated. The deponent asked William if Elizabeth could visit Barker. In a great passion, William said no one would take her away from him until she was of age.

[47] Affdt of Ellen Dikes, wife of Peter Dikes miller of Gom's Mill parish of Stoke upon Trent, sworn before Ralph Wotton at Trentham 24 July 1771. [*Signed with a mark.*] [*Verso*]: '14 The King v Archer Ellen Dikes affid fo 6'. ITKB The King v William Archer.

That Elizabeth, who lived in a mean and servile capacity at William Archer's house, frequently cried and complained to the deponent that William beat and abused her cruelly. Elizabeth expressed her desire to leave William's house provided she could go to her friends, but the deponent dissuaded her from doing so until she turned of age. Elizabeth told her that William had beaten her violently with his walking stick on returning from church. She was a sober, diligent and industrious young woman.

[48] Affdt of Ellen Dikes, wife of Peter Dikes miller of Gom's Mill parish of Stoke upon Trent, sworn before Ralph Wotton at Trentham 24 July 1771. [*Signed with a mark.*] ITKB The King v Ann Archer.

That in 1769 the deponent was employed by William to do washing on several occasions and knew Elizabeth. She did see Ann Archer compel Elizabeth to do the most servile offices. Elizabeth complained of being beaten several times by Ann, declaring she would quit if she had friends to fly to. The deponent counselled Elizabeth not to leave William until she was 21 years old. Elizabeth complained of being beaten over the head by Ann about cutting the edge of the box border in the garden at Forbridge. In 1769 Ann ordered tea for 6pm and went into a violent passion when it was not ready at 5pm; the deponent assisted Elizabeth, who told her that Ann beat her while the deponent was out of the kitchen. The deponent knew Elizabeth as a very sober, diligent and industrious young woman who did not deserve ill usage.

[49] Affdt of John Green maltster of Yardley parish (Worcs), sworn before George Hollington Barker at Birmingham (Warws) 26 Sept 1771. ITKB The King v William Archer.

That in 1762 Elizabeth was put under the care of the deponent's wife Mary, who then kept a boarding school, for two years. Elizabeth was a smart, sprightly, sensible, capable girl with a good temper and disposition. He was paid by Elizabeth's late father, Thomas Archer, during his life and then by Richard Archer of Shrewley, one of her uncles.

[50] Affdt of Thomas Archer gunsmith, brother of Elizabeth, of Birmingham (Warws), sworn before George Hollington Barker at Birmingham 9 Oct 1771. ITKB The King v William Archer.

That the deponent visited William in 1769. Elizabeth complained to him then and in letters and in person at other times of the ill treatment she received from William and Ann Archer. The deponent had William agree to move Elizabeth. Mrs Sherwin, a relative, found a place for her but William then refused to let her go. Last December the deponent went to the house of John Barker of Lichfield, Elizabeth's uncle, where she was staying. She complained of her treatment, and referred him to Elizabeth Brookes (now Foden) of Little Wyrley, a former servant of William Archer. Foden confirmed that Elizabeth had been beaten and called an idiot, and that when she told Ann that the neighbours talked of the abuse, William was very angry. Elizabeth waited on table and was treated as a servant. The deponent confronted William with Foden's statements and William said that if she was an evidence against him he would prosecute her for theft and charge Elizabeth for her board.

The deponent went at Barker's request to tell William that a prosecution would be begun if matters were not accommodated; William set him at defiance. Since the time of her going to William's house, Elizabeth is much altered in appearance and capacity, incapable of making that figure in life that might have been expected. William is of very ample fortune; Elizabeth is of very small fortune arising from her fourth share in some old leasehold houses in Birmingham and what she may hope to recover from William Archer under a bequest in the will of her late grandmother. This will had been kept secret for eleven years by William Archer. This whole fortune will be insufficient to maintain her.

[51] Affdt of Mary Sherwin, wife of Robert Sherwin joiner and carpenter of Prestwood, sworn before Thomas Gretteth the younger at Prestwood 12 Oct 1771 [*and enclosed letters*]. [*Verso*]: 'Mrs. Mary Sherwin Affidt 12 Oct 1771. The King agst. Archer & Wife. The Affidt of Mrs.

Sherwin with several Ltres. annexed. No (20 21) 6. fo. 26.' ITKB The King v William Archer.

That she has known Elizabeth, her second cousin, from infancy, her mother having on her deathbed recommended the care of her children to this deponent. Three years ago on a visit to see her, Elizabeth complained of abuse. She advised Elizabeth to please William and Ann in hopes that he would behave better to her in the future. The deponent received letter (A) from Elizabeth and forwarded it to John Barker, Elizabeth's uncle and a person of character and fortune. She wrote Elizabeth saying she could recommend her to wait on a lady if she wished to leave. She received letter (B) from Elizabeth, and letter (C) from Barker. She wrote Elizabeth that her uncle John Barker offered an asylum in his house. The deponent received letters (D) and (E). Before receiving letter (E) the deponent wrote William informing him she had a place for Elizabeth to stay but received no reply. The deponent knows Elizabeth's handwriting well and believes she wrote the letters. Before she went to live with William she was a very sprightly, sensible girl of good morals.

[*Annexed Letters*]:

[*Verso*]: 'To Mrs Shaurvin at Prestwood.' '(A) This letter is mentioned and referred to by the affidavit of Mrs Mary Sherwin hereunto annexed and sworn before me. Thos Gretteth Jun.'

[*John Barker's hand*]: 'Eli. Archer. June 1770. To Mrs. Sherwin with complaints of his cruel usage and design of leaving her uncle, wch letter Mrs Sherwin sent J. Barker in a letter on 31 Aug. 1770.'

'June the 27. Dear Mrs. Sherwin I have taken this oppertunty of riteing thees few lines to you hopeing you will send me a few as sown as you can me. <u>Aunt youses me extrnmly hill makes me stand the big noses with I ant able to do.</u> I have ad a letter from my Dear Sister shee as been very bad of a favour and thought shee should a died shee dus not stay at Coventry. <u>I sent our wourd wat a life I ad</u> shee ses shee whould take a house at Lutterworth and theach [*damaged; illegible*] Clearstarch fin linen and I should live [*damaged*]th our and we should gone in bisness to gather & we should have a home have our hone &tc that is the most comfortabilst. I beg you will give me your a pinnoun of it <u>for I cant possible stay for shee sets the sourvans to almost peck my hyes out</u> for sence I came to Stafford <u>the are 10 times wors shee</u> came in to the browhous & bids the souravants box me hers. Mrs. Pourshous as left me five ginnes but I have lost a very great frea[*damaged*] but I must be contented what pleasis god but hope for better I <u>ham</u> [*illeg.*] <u>in such a manner as you whould earse think</u> pray excuse bad pen shee lies in have our 6 Chield we luck for a very day & so cant buck much & is as likely to have as many mor. I should be very glad if you could talk to me Uncle Ruchard I should be very glad a bought it but plese to send me a fue lines as scoon for I shall received theam with great pleasur direct to me at Stafford Green to be leaft at Mr Priceis or healce it will be opend the nusmaid dus not tuch a rage to wash not so much as our hown clos & I am not able to do it I have wated a long mile to part in frandship but feer I cant at last me sister ses I must teal me Uncle William if I should like it to live with our but whould have me leave im in anney ungeanteel mannar [*illegible*] to see own stree tournd me out a door twise sence we came to heare whean hee was out wich dus not shoe such hears when be fore in a very boddy bleam me for staying with them pray give my compliments to Mrs Hogshcagetts and Mr faschall your loving Cuse[*torn*] Eliz Archer'.

[*Verso*]: 'To Mrs Shaurvin to be left at Mr Collis oppisite the [*illeg.*] in Stourbridge' '(B) This letter is mentioned and referred to by the affidavit of Mrs Mary Sherwin hereunto annexed and sworn before me. Thos Gretteth'.

[*John Barker's hand*]: 'Bessy Archer to Mrs Sherwin 2d Sepr 1770 To desire she will write to her Uncle to let her go & complain of the cruel usage & the servants insulting her'.

'September 2 1770. Dear Mrs. Sherwin. I am very sorry that I did not annsar yours sooner but that the reason was that I did not no where to direct to you but I did not recaive yours till the 02 of larst mounth. I am much oblid[*damaged*] for sending me word of the place [*damaged*] to send me word [*damaged*] is not too late i should be very glad of it. I do the Uutmost of my power to in struct my sealf & doant feer but what I could do to wait of a lady if it is not too late. I should be very glad if you whould write to him but not mension anithink a bought you seing me so hill for it will but make him but the worse hoe its me of the [*illegible*] of my poor farther wich makes me very [*illegible*] & keeps me very bear of clouse & the let the sourvants all be misses hover me & make me such a slave of me but please to say nothink a bout him when you write to me & direct to me Mr Archer at Stafford green Mrs Hedkins advises me to stay with them til I am at age but it gose very hard with me. I am [*illegible*] may shee as hordered me to get a place but yet ses hee whould not let me go but i think you are the likeest pourson to prevail of him my sister sent me word of a milliner that whould have taken me for 13 ginnes but me Uncle Richard whould not advance us a farthing me Aunt [*illegible*] me the other day that the [*illegible*] brook wickad me farthers things we are very unfortninest. I received yours it gave me great pleasur pray excuse these few lines for I am asheam of them but am oblidge to have so mayny tourns at tham pray give my compliments to Mrs Fakall & I am much oblidge to you for all favours. I am yr afftly E Archer'

[*Verso*]: 'To Mrs Sherwin at John Hodgetts Esqr at Prestwood'. '(C) This letter is mentioned and referred to by the affidavit of Mrs Mary Sherwin hereunto annexed and sworn before me. Thomas Gretteth Jun.'

'Mrs Sherwin. Madm. I have your obliging letter which I should have answered sooner but my wife has been exceeding ill. I should be glad to know if Mr Richard Archer did pay the 40 pounds to your Brthr on 6 Aug 1762 as you mention in your letter as by the former part you seem doubtfull if it was paid.

'I am concerned to hear that Bessey Archer is so disagreeably situated. If the usage she recieves is too bad to bare and she approves better of coming to Lichfield my house is at her service till a proper place offers & my wife will endeavour to instruct her all in her power till that offers, her scheme of living with her sister is a bad one & what I hope you advise her against. I am Madam your mo hble servt John Barker Lichfield 22 Sepr 1770.'

[*Verso*]: 'To Mrs Sherwin at John Hodgetts Esquyer at Prestwood to be left att the Talbot Inn in Storbridge.' '(D) This letter mentioned and referred to by the affidavit of Mrs Mary Sherwin hereunto annexed and sworn before me Thos Gretteth Jun.'

[*John Barker's hand*]: 'Bessy Archer to Mrs Sherwin 28 Sepr 1770 think her self obligd to J.B for his offer but thinks her uncle will not let her leave & desires Mrs Sherwin to write to him, mentions her ill usage as the servants insult her & keeps her bare of cloths & says her uncle tells her she is a scandle to him.'

'Sep the 28 1770. Dear Mrs Sherwin. I am much obligde to you for all favours and take it very kind of me Uncle Barcear ofering me is hous to be at but I think it will tuch him very much and am sad afread hee will not let me come away. I think hee cant in der me But shall be very glad if you whould rite to him for hee youses me very [*illegible*] more then you or aneboddy wold believe with out the seed it. I have noboddy to tell my mind to but you & My sister shee made hers Edkins belive fine things and told our that shee intended parteing with our mis maid but in sted of that shee in courags our in being mises hover and shall be very glad if you whould oblidge him to let me come away for i lets this oppertunty by I shall puraps never meet with such a nother hee ses I am a candle to him but I dont know no in what shape with out it is one go so shabby in clous with shee lets our nus maid whear white a [*illegible*] if I was from them I should be very glad me dear sister is rauther a fraunted at me that I doant go to live with her. I must conclude Dr Mrs Sherwin and I sincerly wish you your health. I am your affct. cousin Elizabeth Archer.'

[*Verso*]: 'To Mrs Sherwin at Mr Hadgost at Prestwood to be left at the Talbot Inn in Sturbridge' '(E) This letter is mentioned and referred to by the affidavit of Mrs Mary Sherwin hereunto annexted and sworn before me. Thomas Gretteth Jun.'

[*John Barker's hand*]: 'Bessy Archer to Mrs Sherwin 13 Oct 1770 desires her to acquaint JB of her cruel usage & mentions her aunt opening her box.'

'Oct. 13 1770. Dear Mrs Sherwin. I received yours with great pleasur but could not get time to rite sooner. I am resoulved not to stay & should be very much oblidge to y if y please to send me Uncle Barker word that I am much oblidge to him for is kind invitation but me Uncle as not tuck anny notis to me abought yr riting to him but intend spakeing to him. Shee as opend my box & as seen your letters but little thinks I no anny think abought it & I have not hard any think more abought the man pray excuse this for in such heast time will not permit lunger is from yr Afft. &c Eliz Archer.'

[52] Affdt of William Keen gentleman of Stafford, sworn before T. Fernyhough at Stafford 21 Oct 1771. ITKB The King v William Archer.

That the deponent showed Elizabeth Foden (maiden name Brookes) the paper annexed and asked her if the mark on it was hers. She answered yes. He asked if her assertions on the page were true and she answered yes. She refused to take an oath, saying she had made an affidavit before and would not swear again unless forced to.

[*Annexed*]: Declaration of Elizabeth Brookes spinster of Little Wyrley, signed before Thomas Hinckley 31 Jan 1771. [*Verso*]: 'Eliz Brooks's Evidence taken by Mr. Thos. Hinckley. 31 Jan 1771 and on x day 1770 by T. Archer & S. Palmer.' [*Signed with a mark.*]

That she lived as a servant with William Archer for three years, until three months ago, first at Tatenhill [*sic*] and then at Stafford. Elizabeth Archer, niece to William, lived there the whole time. Elizabeth did the work of a common servant and was treated as such. Sometimes William beat Elizabeth and once he caused her nose to swell after having struck her on the head or face for smoking some milk. She frequently heard Elizabeth cry out, who then said she had been beaten by her uncle. The declarant has seen Ann beat Elizabeth and on one occasion turn her out of the house at night; soon after she called her back. The declarant told Ann that the neighbours talked of the ill treatment Elizabeth received. Ann told her husband, who threatened 'to give her as much' if she did not hold her tongue. Ann gave her orders to beat Elizabeth, but she never did. Elizabeth was sometimes in fault, particularly towards the children, but that on the whole William and Ann Archer were to blame. Elizabeth once told her that 'Mr. Archer had better kill her out of her misery.'

[53] Affdt of William Keen gentleman of Stafford, sworn before T. Fernyhough at Stafford 21 Oct 1771. [*Verso*]: 'No. 18. The King agt. William Archer. Affidts of William Keen for the prosecutrix. The former sworn 21 Oct. 1771. fo. 18. fo. 9.' ITKB The King v William Archer.

That last June the deponent, who had acted in part as solicitor for Elizabeth Archer, heard that Mary Watwood[94] was a material witness. His examination convinced him that she could fully prove an assault by William Archer and in July he requested that she give her testimony on oath. She gave her consent to his drawing her affidavit, which is annexed; he read her the affidavit and she agreed to its truth. As she was about to swear it, Ann Archer entered her house; the deponent asked Mary to repeat her account of William striking Elizabeth with a stick. Ann expostulated that her account was impossible: the other washerwoman, Nanny James, saw no blows. Mary claimed she could not have as she was breaking the coals at the time. Since then Mary still says the affidavit is true but refuses to swear anything against William unless compelled to do so.

[*Annexed*]: Unsigned, undated draft affdt of Mary Watwood, wife of Benjamin Watwood labourer of Rising Brook, in the parish of Castle Church.

That the deponent had been employed as a washerwoman by William and heard frequent complaints by Elizabeth. She asked Elizabeth why she did not go to her friends; Elizabeth said she did not know how to reach her friends. In November last the deponent saw William in a great passion strike Elizabeth two violent blows on her back and shoulders with a thick walking stick, saying Elizabeth did not come when called. Mary Collins, a material witness, has been living at William Archer's house for five weeks. Collins has declared that she quit a good service in order to come to William's house to give her testimony in his favour, that she intended to continue there until he was quit of the prosecution, and that she would insist upon having a year's wages for her loss of time.

[54] Affdt of Mary Archer spinster (and sister of Elizabeth Archer, the prosecutrix) of Coventry (Warws), sworn before John Stanton at Coventry 24 Oct 1771. ITKB The King v Ann Archer.

---

[94] Given as Wetwood in this affdt and draft, and in affdt [98].

That the deponent received several letters from Elizabeth while she was living with William. In one letter Elizabeth complained of much ill treatment, in particular an occasion on which Ann ordered a servant to beat her. On another occasion Ann turned her out of doors. The deponent does not have the letter in her custody. Elizabeth mentions in one letter that a lady, who was first cousin to her uncle Mr Barker, and whose name Mary Archer believes is Scott, told Elizabeth that if her mother were alive and saw her used in such a manner it would break her heart.

[55] Affdt of John Minors shoemaker of Eccleshall, sworn before T. Fernyhough at Stafford 29 Oct 1771. [*Verso*]: 'No (25). The King agt William. Archer. Affdt of John Minors for the prosecutrix. Sworn 29 Oct 1771. fo 5.' ITKB The King v William Archer.

That the deponent is an intimate acquaintance of Katharine Yeomans and often visited her at the Archers where she worked. From her declarations to him he believes she is a material witness for Elizabeth. In Dec 1770 she told him that William treated Elizabeth with uncommon cruelty, worse than a dog. Katherine said she had seen William strike Elizabeth across her breast with a poker because she had not dusted the furniture.

[56] Affdt of Jane Price, wife of William Price carpenter of Wolverhampton, sworn before Stephen Falknor at Wolverhampton 30 Oct 1771. [*Signed with a mark.*] ITKB The King v William Archer.

That the deponent was a neighbour to William. Elizabeth often came to her house, complaining of mistreatment. On one occasion her nose was swollen and she said William had struck her twice on the face for smoking the milk she was preparing for the children. On another occasion Elizabeth complained that William had kicked her thigh until it turned black. She could not show the deponent because someone came into the house. She said that Ann threw a knife at her and beat her arm black with a pair of tongs. She also said that Ann once threw a basin of cold water down her back when she did not sprinkle the linen satisfactorily. Elizabeth was ill clothed, wore shoes that made her feet wet, and was not even fed as well as the servants, seldom getting tea and usually having only cold meat or bread and cheese for breakfast. The Archers made their niece carry heavy loads of meat from market, and she stopped at the deponent's house, seeming ready to faint. Elizabeth's capacity has been much injured by the ill treatment.

[57] Affdt of James Tomkinson gentleman of Dorfold (Ches), sworn before Henry Tomkinson at Dorfold (Ches) 1 Nov 1771. ITKB The King v William and Ann Archer.

That on 24 Dec at the request of John Barker he asked Mary Collins, then a servant to Mr Tomkins, a Birmingham mercer, if she knew anything about ill treatment of Elizabeth. Mary said Elizabeth had been treated with much severity and cruelty and was frequently beaten. She did not suggest that Elizabeth had given any cause. She also said Elizabeth Brookes knew of and had complained of Elizabeth Archer's mistreatment. The next day the deponent wrote a letter concerning this to Barker, but did not reduce Collins's examination into writing, as he had no doubt or suspicion but that she would testify to the same effect.

[58] Affdt of Elizabeth Archer spinster of Lichfield, sworn before Richard Hinckley at Lichfield 2 Nov 1771. [*Verso*]: 'The King agt. Wm. Archer. Affidt. of Eliz. Archer the prosecutrix. Sworn 2d Nov. 1771. No 29. fo 10.' ITKB The King v William Archer.

That the deponent, who is 20 years old, swore an affidavit last June of William Archer's assaults; it was prepared quickly because the defendant had pleaded guilty in King's Bench. It omitted certain assaults which she perfectly recollects. In winter 1767 William beat her with his fist on her head and other parts of her body because she spilled some water from a basin. Soon after he beat her on the head for breaking a jug, for which she was made to pay 6d. In summer 1768 he beat her violently with his fist on her head and shoulders because foul linen was left in the maid servant's room, although placed there on the orders of Ann. In 1768 William beat her head and shoulders because there was a small hole in a stocking he put on; another time he beat her for crying when she was ill, dragging her into the kitchen where he beat her so hard she nearly fell into the fire. Elizabeth Brookes, who was present, ran away. After Michaelmas 1768 William beat her violently on the back with a walking stick because she took longer to pick turnips than he thought necessary. That winter he hit her with his fist because she had not removed a fork out of the barn; he also beat her head against the barn doors. On Easter Monday 1769 he beat her violently on the head and shoulders with a walking stick, leaving her in pain for a considerable time, after one of the children reported her behaviour with a visitor who joked with the servants, and he beat her for not attending when his children called, although she had not heard them. In Oct or Nov 1769 Ann ordered her to move a stone from a sough; when she could not do so William beat her severely with a stick. Another time he beat her on the head for not calling him 'sir'. In summer 1770 William beat her for bringing a smoking coal to the nursery fire. Later that year he beat her head against a wall for hanging a pair of bellows in the wrong place.

The deponent has suffered considerably, has been beaten repeatedly and treated worse than a common servant. She was not allowed to sit at table, although her uncle promised her dying mother he would take care of her. She scarcely ever saw him but with terror; his correction was generally so violent that her body was frequently discoloured and sore. She has never given him cause for such cruelty. She has a very small provision, nor knows how to earn her livelihood. William Archer is well able to make her compensation, as he has a large estate and is in wealthy circumstances.

[59] Affdt of John Barker merchant of Lichfield, sworn before Richard Hinckley at Lichfield 2 Nov 1771. ITKB The King v William and Ann Archer.

That the prosecution was begun in full expectation of a conviction in order to obtain a suitable recompense for Elizabeth, who had only a small provision, and from no malice toward the defendants. He learned of the abuse from Elizabeth and from Mary Sherwin, a near relation of William. The abuse was confirmed by Elizabeth's brother Thomas. He told Thomas she should stay with the Archers if they would treat her with kindness, but invited her to his house in December when he heard other reports of their many severities. Elizabeth's accounts of abuse are consistent, supported by the evidence of servants questioned by persons of credit at his request. The deponent sent Thomas Archer to tell the defendants of his intention to prosecute unless they made recompense; they refused and the indictments were preferred. On 6 May William came to the deponent's house in Lichfield with an attorney to propose a compromise; the deponent told them he had employed Mr Tomkinson as his attorney in the prosecutions and referred them to him. William acknowledged he had beaten Elizabeth, and then with seeming warmth admitted having beaten her with a horse whip which he then had in his hand, and struck with violence upon a table in the room. He admitted also that Ann had beaten Elizabeth in the year before she left their house.

[60] Affdt of Catherine Barker, wife of John Barker merchant and prosecutor in the cases, and Catherine Collins spinster, both of Lichfield, sworn before Richard Hinckley at Lichfield 2 Nov 1771. ITKB The King v William and Ann Archer.

[*Both*]: They have both known Elizabeth, now 20, for seven years. Six years ago, when staying with the Barkers for six weeks, Elizabeth behaved with propriety, care and prudence, and was entrusted with the keys of the stores. She could read, write and sew tolerably well.

[*Catherine Barker*]: That when Elizabeth came to her house after six years with the defendants, she was destitute of proper clothing.

[*Both*]: That Elizabeth's education was much neglected while she stayed with the Archers. Six years before she was a lively apprehensive girl, very capable of learning. On her return in December she could scarcely read, nor sew as well as she had six years before, and was ignorant of housewifery.

[*Catherine Barker*]: That upon leaving the defendants Elizabeth was unacquainted in religious duties.

[*Both*]: That since Elizabeth has been with the Barkers she has been depressed, intellectually impaired, and her hearing damaged and her spirits broken due to the severe and ill usage she has received. She is now not capable of earning a livelihood.

[*Catherine Barker*]: That when Elizabeth arrived from the Archers she had a large weal on one of her arms which did not go away for over two months. When William Archer came to compromise matters he admitted to having whipped Elizabeth with the horsewhip he then held in his hand. Elizabeth has remained in the deponent's family since leaving the defendant and has in all respects behaved with decency and prudence.

[61] Affdt of George Hollington Barker gentleman of Birmingham (Warws), sworn before Amb. Mainwaring at Birmingham 2 Nov 1771. ITKB The King v William and Ann Archer.

That last January the deponent interviewed Mary Collins, servant to Mr Tomkins mercer in Birmingham, in connection with the prosecution of William Archer. She told him that William had often boxed Elizabeth's ears, beaten her with a stick and kicked her thighs until they were black and bruised. He took her evidence in writing at another interview in February, when she said she was prepared to testify but declined to sign the examination, saying that she feared losing her present place, as a nephew of William Archer was apprenticed to them.

By submitting to the indictments after they had removed them into King's Bench, the defendants have prevented Mary Collins and several other material witnesses, who were intended to have been subpoened and examined, from making their discoveries.

[62] Affdt of Samuel Palmer the younger, apprentice of John Barker merchant and prosecutor in these cases, of Lichfield, sworn before Richard Hinckley at Lichfield on 2 Nov 1771. ITKB The King v William and Ann Archer.

That the deponent was ordered by John Barker, his master, to enquire if the abuse could be confirmed before the prosecution began. On 8 Jan he took an account of Elizabeth's abuse from Katharine Yeomans who signed his written account, which is annexed. On 23 Oct he asked her to give her evidence by affidavit. She refused, although she affirmed that the deponent's written account of her earlier evidence was true. She gave no reasons for refusing to swear.

[*Annexed*]: Statement 8 Jan 1771 of Katharine Yeomans taken by Samuel Palmer.

That she heard them beat Elizabeth in the parlour. Ann offered her 6*d* to take a towel out of the wash and beat Elizabeth with it. She has seen her face swollen from beating and has seen both her aunt and her uncle beat her; they often beat her without cause. Elizabeth had to rise about 3am to do the wash until 8am or later and Ann ordered that she not have breakfast while doing the washing.

Affidavits for defence, in mitigation:

Mich 12 Geo III 1771[95]

[63] Affdt of Elizabeth Collins spinster of Castle Church, sworn before Francis Brookes at Forebridge 16 Dec 1771. [*Signed with a mark*.] [*Verso*]: '2 fo. 7.' ITKB The King v William Archer.

That Elizabeth walked with Mary Collins, the deponent's sister, to her father's house at Streetway, where she drank ale in a very plentiful manner, then went on to the deponent's uncle's house, where she drank ale and wine in such large quantities that she staggered and stumbled and had to be helped home. Elizabeth sold her clothes to a number of people, was of a bad disposition, and a great liar. She once was given 9*d* by Ann to pay the milk woman but instead spent it on sweet meats. She lied and then confessed to having done so. She was always a very fat robust healthy girl of a weak capacity but of a strong constitution, with a rosy complexion and the pampered appearance of too much indulgence.

[64] Affdt of Frances Elizabeth Proctor wife of Metcalf Proctor esquire of Thorpe Rathwell (Yorks), sworn before George Beavers at Wakefield (Yorks) 28 Dec 1771. [*The verso is the wrapper for this bundle of affidavits*]: '67. Staffordshire. The King agt. Wm. Archer and Wife for deft. Afft. 3 affdt fo. 17. Mich Term 1771. fo. 5 Johnston.' ITKB The King v William Archer.

That the deponent, who is William Archer's sister in law, often visited his house and found Elizabeth always in so very rude, insolent, and indecent a manner that she well deserved correction. She was frequently quite intoxicated, and appeared from conversation to be weak, ignorant, and addicted to lying. The deponent well remembers an occasion some years ago when some money William kept for the

---

[95] Bdl 67.

poor was missing; she and Ann searched and found the money in Elizabeth's pockets, and the girl confessed that she had stolen money from the box several times before.

[65] Affdt of William Cotton butler to Mrs Kirby of Doveridge (Derbs), sworn before John Hayne at Uttoxeter 2 Jan 1772. [*Verso*]: '3 fo.5.' ITKB The King v Ann Archer.

That the deponent has known Elizabeth for nine or ten years; she was always a stupid girl, addicted to very bad customs and practices, often stupefied with drink. He has seen her in her bed with her clothes on all night and once with her petticoats turned up to expose her private parts. Mary Collins also told him she frequently went to bed with her clothes on. Elizabeth was a very fat robust healthy girl, much given to indulgence both in eating and drinking. The deponent has worked for Mrs Kirby, Ann's mother, for 30 or 40 years, and Ann always had the most amiable and best of characters, was never guilty of any bad action, and is a woman of the greatest merit; William is truly a sober honest man of good morals.

Hil 12 Geo III 1772[96]

[66] Letters of Penelope Kynnersley and William Archer to James Burrow, master of the crown office, 19 Nov 1771.

[*Verso*]: 'James Burrow Esq Master in the King's Bench. Inner Temple. fo 5.'

'Sir,

I last post received a letter from Mrs Archer of Stafford, who has a disagreeable law suit in your court, and imagining (as she is unknown to you) you may be prejudiced in your opinion against her, she wished me to call of you before term time, to speak my sentiments of her, but as I am also unknown to you, I thought it more eligible to write to you. I am mother to Mr Kynnersley of Loxley[97] in Staffordshire who Mrs Archer informs me has given his affidavit in her favour, and have a house in Orchard Street Portman Square, where I now reside; but when my husband was living, Loxley was my place of residence, near which Mrs Archer's mother and family lived, and I have known them [*illegible*] and twenty years, during which time her mother has born the character of a religious, just person, and brought up her <u>five</u> daughters in the same good principles, and I have never heard or seen anything to

---

[96] Bdl 75. The letters to Burrow are filed separately.
[97] See affdts [4] and [88] note 102.

the contrary of any of them, tho I have known [*illegible*] from children, and Mrs Archer I've always esteemed a sensible good humoured, worthy woman, and from my good opinion of her, left my children for some months in her care. She has been a good wife and tender mother, nor during my acquaintance with Mr Archer have I known any ill of him, tho' 'tis impossible to live without slander in this world. If you have any particular questions to ask me, should be greatly obliged if you would either send or come here, as I'm at present too ill to [*illegible*] out, this will inform you where to find me. I am Sir your humble servant, Penelope Kynnersley.'

[*Verso*]: 'Letter from Mr Wm Archer of Stafford Green near Stafford 19th Nov 1771.'
   'Sir,
   I this day received a letter from Mr Johnson informing me that the affair between John Barker and Elizabeth Archer, plaintiffs, and myself and wife defendants, was at present deferred.
   'I much hope you'll excuse this particular freedom and think myself happy (tho I have not the pleasure of the least personal acquaintance) to find myself under the judgment of a gentleman whose unexceptionable good character emboldens me most humbly to request the matters in dispute may be ended this term; my wife being at this time with child, and the more sensible of distress as her reputation through life never was before impeached, and I can with the greatest truth affirm her conduct to be totally in my sentiments as irreproachable as any womans in the county, and perhaps in the whole kingdom. I shall say nothing for myself but leave the affidavits of friends and servants to point out the grossness and falsity of the charges against me, as well as the nature, and difficulty of such an affair will well admit. I hope you have been informed by Mr Johnson, if you have not already seen them, that he has thirty three affidavits in our defence. All of which (two only excepted) were sent up on or before the 24th of last month and the two last on the 28th being anxious for their perusal before the term began, and which I could multiply to twice that number if necessary, but was afraid of intruding on your patience, as well as desirous of avoiding all further trouble and expence of that sort.
   'Johnson acquaints me that Mr Manley seemed desirous of making the affair up, and I have been applied to before on that head, and it was also signified I might do it for a trifle, but not being in the least conscious of any injury, but the contrary, could not by any means consent to give the girl money as that method appeared to me not only to carry with it severe reproach, but so much to countenance and encourage future practices of this sort otherwise I should have disdained a little

money, and been much ashamed to trouble any court on so scandalous an occasion.

'Could I flatter myself I should receive the favour of a single line, I should ever esteem it a singular favour conferred on your much obliged and very humble servant, William Archer

'Stafford Green near Stafford, Nov the 19th 1771'

[67] Affdt of Ann Eykin spinster of Boningale (Salop), sworn before Francis Brookes at Boningale 30 Jan 1772. [*Verso*]: '3 fo.3.' ITKB The King v William Archer.

That the deponent was a governess at a boarding school in Wolverhampton from 1757 to 1761. She had great trouble teaching Elizabeth to read, being a very dull scholar and not endowed with a talent for learning.

[68] Affdt of Mary Watwood wife of William Watwood labourer of Rising Brook parish of Castle Church, sworn before Francis Brookes at Forebridge 1 Feb 1772. [*Verso*]: '4 fo.4.' [*Signed with a mark.*] ITKB The King v Ann Archer.

That Ann never gave or promised her money or clothes, before or after the prosecution began, to testify on her behalf, as reported by Elizabeth Watwood alias Hubball of Castle Church. The allegation is malicous and false. Elizabeth told the deponent in November 1770 that Ann Archer always behaved extremely well to her.

[69] Affdt of Anne Paget spinster, age 30 and upwards, of the Hill, Cheswardine parish (Salop), sworn before W. C. Norcop[98] at the Hill Cheswardine 1 Feb 1772. ITKB The King v William Archer.

That Elizabeth was under the instruction of Mrs Brett a governess in Wolverhampton for several years and under the care of the deponent for nine months in 1765. Elizabeth had not become as proficient in learning to write as deponent might reasonably have expected. William paid for Elizabeth's schooling and seemed very fond of her when she was young. She never heard any complaints about William or Elizabeth's treatment of Elizabeth; they bore a general good character.

[70] Affdt of Richard Archer tanner of Hatton (Warws), sworn before Richard Wright at Warwick (Warws) 3 Feb 1772. [*Verso*]: '75. 1. Staffordshire. The King agt Wm Archer Esq. Afft: for Deft. 4 Affts filed

[98] William Church Norcop appears in *Browne's General Law List* for 1782 and 1787, at Drayton (Salop).

7 Feb 1772 fo.18 Hilary Term 1772 Johnston fo:8'. ITKB The King v William Archer.

That the will and testament of Elizabeth's grandmother mentioned in her brother Thomas Archer's affidavit was never secreted by William Archer but lay in the hands of this deponent, one of the executors, until Elizabeth and her brother and sister came of age, and the deponent produced it immediately after it was asked for. The grandmother was only tenant for life of the properties and could not dispose of them by will or charge with debt. Elizabeth's small fortune arises from her fourth share of houses part leashold and part freehold secured by her father's marriage settlement; the deponent has always received the rents and is very willing to pay them to her when she comes of age, her share of the grandmother's personalty not amounting to £20.

William Archer never received one shilling of Elizabeth's money or any effects from the deponent nor he believes from anyone else. He took her into his house at four years of age at his own expense, and paid for her education, except for two and one-quarter years, paid by this deponent, of the nine or ten she spent at boarding schools. The appearance she makes in life mentioned in Thomas Archer's affidavit is not due to bad treatment or any want of instruction, but entirely owing to a natural weakness of capacity and bad conduct in herself. William is an honest, moral and just man; he and his wife are of unexceptionable good character.

Further affidavits for prosecution, in aggravation:

Hil 12 Geo III 1772[99]

[71] Affdt of Mary Bird widow of the Reverend Samuel Bird, and Ann Trahern, spinster, both of Hereford (Herefs), sworn before E. Bramston at Hereford 30 Dec 1771. [*The verso is the wrapper for this bundle of affidavits*]: '76 Staffordshire the King agt Archer & Wife. Affdt on behalf of Prosectx. 28 Affts fo. 281 Hilary Term 1772. Manley. fo 6.' 'The King & Archer. Mrs Bird and anr affid. Manley.' ITKB The King v William and Ann Archer.

[Both]: That they were at John Barker's house for seven weeks while Elizabeth was there. They discussed her injuries at length with her. Her accounts were uniform and consistent. They were present when she was sworn to an affidavit against the Archers. She was interrogated on every point and warned to depose the truth; she appeared thoroughly to understand the contents and declared it contained the truth only.

---

[99] Bdl 76.

During their stay Elizabeth conducted herself with decency in all respects, was always clean and neat, and did not appear to have any inclination to drink immoderately. Nor so far as they could observe was she addicted to theft, lying or any other vice. Judging from what they observed during their visit, they believe her to be a virtuous and well disposed person of a mild good temper.

[72] Affdt of Richard Thruston cutler of Forebridge Castle Church, sworn before W. Keen at Stafford 2 Jan 1772. [*Verso*]: 'Mr. Richard Thrustans Affidavit. 8 fo. 15.' [*Signed with a mark.*] ITKB The King v William and Ann Archer.

That during the three years the deponent lived as a servant to William Archer, Elizabeth was sober, modest, virtuous, diligent, honest, dutiful and obedient. He never saw her drink nor tell a lie. The defendants' assertions about Elizabeth are utterly false. All Elizabeth's affidavits are true except that one assault – the one concerning the box hedge – occurred in 1770, not in 1769 as Elizabeth deposed. Mary Collins who made affidavits on behalf of the defendants is a vile abandoned and perjured prostitute and her oath ought not to be regarded. Mary Collins accused the deponent of being the father of her child, which is untrue; at the time William Archer himself testified to the justices that Mary Collins was a woman of bad and loose character and that he believed the father was not the deponent. Collins has perjured herself in the affidavits, having several times informed this deponent of acts of cruelty by William Archer.

Elizabeth's clothes and chest of drawers were kept in Richard's room but she never dressed or undressed there, nor did anything indecent. She did once sell a cloak that was too small for her, and a worn-out gown when she had the itch, but her clothes were ragged and dirty because she had so few changes, particularly of shoes and stockings. William Archer has a large fortune and has served as sheriff of Carnarvonshire, but a penurious man who would not have tolerated drinking. Of morose and sour temper, he often frightened Elizabeth till she trembled when she had not done the least thing to provoke his anger. His neighbours at Tettenhall often declared that he never missed an opportunity to indulge his pride or to get his revenge, and that at these times he would lay aside his religion of which he is very fond of making a show. The deponent would not have testified before the sessions grand jury if he had not been well satisfied that Elizabeth was used with great cruelty.

[73] Affdt of Martha Jones wife of William Jones yeoman of Horton, sworn before Stephen Falknor at Horton 3 Jan 1772. [*Signed with a mark.*] [*Verso*]: '19'. ITKB The King v William Archer.

That the deponent was a servant for William. Although Elizabeth used to draw drink for the family the deponent never saw her disguised in liquor. She was a sober, honest, modest and virtuous girl of a mild disposition. The deponent lay in the same bed with Elizabeth, who was a decent cleanly person. She used to mend the children's clothes and do such work she was set to do in the best manner she could. She had no more clothes than were absolutely needful and it is improbable she should sell any of them.

[74] Affdt of Elizabeth Hubball widow aged 48 of Forebridge, sworn before W. Keen at Stafford 5 Jan 1772. [*Signed with a mark.*] ITKB The King v William and Ann Archer.

That the deponent is William Archer's neighbour. Elizabeth, a person of strict veracity, frequently complained to her that she had been beaten by William and Ann. Elizabeth did a great deal of slavery and hard work, supplied the place of a common servant, and appeared to this deponent to be diligent, dutiful, careful of the children, and a person of chastity, sobriety, honesty, truth, and honor.

In the summer of 1771 the deponent met Mary Collins in the fields going to Forbridge, who told her she was going to Archer's house, who had sent her father for her [*sic*] from Birmingham with orders to fetch and bring her dead or alive. The deponent said to Collins 'I hope you are not going to forswear yourself against that poor fatherless and motherless creature Bessy Archer'. Collins replied only that she had lost her place and a month's wages by coming over and that she would make William Archer not only pay her wages but also maintain her until she got another place. When Collins had been lying in of a bastard the deponent often heard her say that Elizabeth was a very good girl, whom she had seen beaten and abused to a shameful degree by the Archers. Collins bears a very bad character and her testimony should be given no credit.

[75] Affdt of Jane Price wife of William Price carpenter of Wolverhampton, and Sarah Steward spinster of Bilston, sworn before Stephen Falknor at Wolverhampton 8 Jan 1772. [*Jane Price signed with a mark.*] [*Verso*]: '18 Jane Price and Sarah Steward sworn 8 Jan 1772.' ITKB The King v William Archer.

[Jane Price]: That she was intimately acquainted with Elizabeth almost two years, that she is a very honest and inoffensive young woman, neither a liar nor a drinker, who would not forswear herself for the world. Several of the servants wrote letters to Elizabeth in the name of William Smith and persuaded her to answer them, to decoy her into his company. He was a young man of indifferent character. Elizabeth kept herself as clean as she could, and worked like a slave for the defendants.[100] Elizabeth told the deponent that Mrs Archer took the clothes that had been left to Elizabeth by William's late wife, and wore them herself. Mary Collins is poor, ignorant, illiterate woman of very bad character. Mary Collins was at one time with child, but swore to the deponent that she was not. She was delivered of a child soon afterwards.

[Sarah Steward]: That she was a servant for William for about half a year. She new saw Elizabeth drink ale or strong liquor. Ann Archer had Elizabeth tell false tales of other servants to William, on one occasion falsely accusing the deponent of carelessness with a hot iron near the children; she told the deponent that her aunt forced her to do so. Elizabeth was a very modest, inoffensive girl and never took any notice of the men unless obliged to do so. Her work left her insufficient time to mend her own clothes, but she kept herself as clean as she could, and swept her room twice a week when she had time. Her aunt took a fancy to a red silk gown that had been left her by the late Mrs Archer, and Elizabeth dared not refuse to give it to her on a promise of a new one or money for it. Mary Collins is a poor ignorant illiterate woman of bad character, who tells palpable lies and swears to them; she is ignorant of the nature of an oath. When she asked Collins why she told so many lies, she replied that 'she would always hold with the hare and run with the hounds for that was the only way to live.'

[76] Affdt of Hannah Earp age 37 wife of Isaac Earp fishmonger of Stafford, sworn before W. Keen at Stafford 8 Jan 1772. [*Signed with a mark.*] [*Verso*]: 'Hannh Earp fo: 6.' ITKB The King v William and Ann Archer.

That Elizabeth frequently bought fish from the deponent's husband. Elizabeth often complained of being beaten and of being treated like a slave. Once in 1770 she told the deponent that after washing all night she was compelled by Ann Archer to wash all the dirty stockings, and showed the deponent that some of her skin was rubbed off by the hard washing. She said she wished her uncle Barker knew how she was used, for he would not suffer her to stay. Elizabeth is not addicted to lying, and when she lived with the Archers was a sober, decent, modest, and well behaved young woman esteemed by all her neighbours, and bore an unblemished character.

[77] Affdt of the Reverend John Ravenhill clerk of Tettenhall, sworn before Stephen Falknor at Tettenhall 10 Jan 1772. [*Verso*]: '12. Rex v.

[100] The clerk wrote in error, 'for the said prosecutrix and her wife.'

Archer Esq. Revd Mr Ravenhill aft fo:12'. ITKB The King v William Archer.

That he thought Elizabeth a sober, virtuous and modest girl, honest and inoffensive, not addicted to lying and that she would not be guilty of perjury.

[78] Affdt of Francis Stokes esq of Tettenhall, sworn before Stephen Falknor at Tettenhall 10 Jan 1772. [*Verso*]: '13. Rex v. Archer Esq. Mr Stokes's Affidt'. ITKB The King v William Archer.

That the deponent lived near the Archers. He never saw her in the least fond of strong liquor or to tell an untruth, and found her to be very reserved in the company of gentlemen. She was modest, decent, inoffensive, and believes her very honest and would not be guilty of perjury. She was always kept bare of clothes and the Archers always used her in a very cruel manner.

[79] Affdt of Hannah Wells wife of Joseph Wells gardener of Erdington, Aston parish (Warws), sworn before George Hollington Barker at Birmingham (Warws) 10 Jan 1772. [*Signed with a mark.*] [*Verso*]: '14. Hanh Welles Affdt 10 Jany 1772 fo:11'. ITKB The King v William Archer.

That the deponent was a servant of William's for six months four and a half years ago. She shared a bed with Elizabeth, and never saw any lewdness or immodesty in conversation or behaviour. Elizabeth never spoke to any of the men servants or any other men, unless the business of William Archer required it. She was sober, and commonly refused to taste drink when invited to do so by the deponent, who believes her to be a chaste, sober, virtuous and honest girl.

[80] Affdt of Katherine Edwards widow and relict of Nathaniel Edwards; Elizabeth Walton, wife of Thomas Walton; and Hester Bayley spinster, all of Lichfield, sworn before Charles Howard at Lichfield 11 Jan 1772. [*Verso*]: '16. Mrs Edwards, Mrs Walton and Miss Bayly Affidav 11 Jan 1772'. ITKB The King v William and Ann Archer.

[Katherine Edwards]: That she is Elizabeth's aunt.

[All]: That Elizabeth is a good young person of good character not addicted to any theft, drunkeness, lying or any other vice. For over a year she has lived in the family of John Barker, and the deponents have found her prudent, modest, and decent in every respect, clean and neat in dress and person. The believe she would not knowingly swear an untruth or be guilty of wilful perjury.

[Elizabeth Walton]: That respectable friends and acquaintances who lived near the defendants told her of the cruel and improper manner in which William and Ann treated Elizabeth. The deponent also received letters from her sister to that effect; she communicated the information to Mrs Catherine Barker wife of John Barker, a person of great tenderness and humanity, in hopes that he would interpose. He made inquiries and offered to receive Elizabeth into his family to screen her from the Archers' cruelty, and began prosecutions from motives of compassion and not from any malicious design. The clothes Elizabeth brought with her to Barker's house were very bad and old, not fit to be worn, particularly the linen which consisted only of three shifts, two of which appeared to be very old, and were of a very large size or make, and improper for the said Elizabeth Archer.

[81] Affdt of Ann Battey age 48 wife of William Battey maltster of Stafford, sworn before W. Keen at Stafford 12 Jan 1772. [*Verso*]: 'Ann Batty 7'. ITKB The King v William and Ann Archer.

That the deponent washed and ironed linen for William Archer and his family. Elizabeth sometimes brought it to her house, sometimes the deponent brought it back to Archer's house at Forebridge. Late in 1770 William's servant Katherine Yeomans quit service and spent several days with the deponent, sleeping with her servant Margaret Malpass. Yeomans said that William Archer accused her of stealing his raisin wine, and insisted on stopping a guinea of her wages. She said that Ann Archer had accused Elizabeth Brookes (who lived in her service and has since married Thomas Fodens) with theft, searched her box, and found many lost things in it.

In the summer of 1771 Katherine Yeomans called at the deponent's house, surprising her by bringing with her two of William Archer's children. She did not expect Yeomans to have any connection with the Archers after having quitted his service in the way described. Yeomans said 'You seem surprised Mrs Batty at seeing me here'. 'Indeed I am', answered this deponent, 'for before I would have come there again I would have begged my bread. I hope Kitty you are not come to Mr Archers to forswear yourself about Miss Archer, for it is a very wicked thing to take a false oath.' To which Yeomans answered that she had declared all she knew, but that she had not nor would not take any oath about the matter. Elizabeth was always a modest, decent, industrious and well behaved young person; the deponent never heard or saw nor believes that she was addicted to telling lies, to drinking, to idleness, or any other bad habits.

[82] Affdt of John Minors cordwainer of Eccleshall age 22 years, sworn before W. Keen at Eccleshall 12 Jan 1772. [*Verso*]: '8 fo:' ITKB The King v William and Ann Archer.

That the deponent often went to see his sister Elizabeth Minors and Katharine Yeomans at the house of William Archer, where they lived as servants. Between Michaelmas and Christmas 1770 he heard Archer declare in the kitchen and in the presence of Elizabeth Archer that Elizabeth Brookes, lately a servant, had stolen from him three sheets, two cheeses, and many children's clothes. He said he had 'a great inclination to trounce the jade for it.' After she left Archer's service Yeomans told him that he had accused her of stealing raisin wine from him, and had stopped her wages, although the wine was sealed up with his coat of arms. This deponent never heard nor believes that Elizabeth was addicted to idleness, to lying, or to drinking; she bore a good character amongst the neighbours.

Affdt[101] of Elizabeth Minors spinster of Eccleshall age 27 years, sworn before W. Keen at Eccelshall 12 Jan 1772.

That at the beginning of 1770 she went to live as a servant with William Archer. In November Elizabeth Archer, who lived in the family as a servant, came crying out of the chamber, saying her uncle had been beating her. The deponent believes this to be true, as Elizabeth frequently made similar complaints. Ann Archer told the deponent soon after she went to live with her that Elizabeth Brookes, who had lately left her service and is now named Elizabeth Foden, had stolen cheese and sheets and a great many other things belonging to the children, some of which Ann Archer said Elizabeth Brookes offered to pay for, which she said made it evident to her [*affidavit incomplete*].

[83] Affdt of Thomas Archer gunfinisher and brother of Elizabeth Archer of Birmingham (Warws), sworn before George Hollington Barker at Birmingham (Warws) 13 Jan 72. [*Verso*]: 'Thos Archer's Affidav 13 Jan 1772 fo: 21'. ITKB The King v William and Ann Archer.

That soon after Elizabeth left her uncle on 17 Dec 1770 the deponent went to William Archer, at the request of another uncle, John Barker, with the intention of informing William of the prosecution to be begun for his cruelty and ill usage. However he had only slight conversation with him, in part because William expressed himself sorry for such behaviour, in part because of the deponent's unwillingness to have his relations at variance. After speaking to Elizabeth he was however further convinced of William's cruelty, visited him again and remonstrated with him for his cruel behaviour as in the deponent's former

---

[101] Elizabeth Minors's affidavit is sworn below that of John Minors, on the same page, but with a separate caption, and is incomplete; it was apparently resworn and filed again, as affdt [93].

affidavit. Neither time did he request William to give Elizabeth leave to return to live with him. If William had wanted her to do so the deponent would have strongly opposed it. Elizabeth is a sober, virtuous and honest girl, incapable of the crimes of theft, drunkeness, lying and loose behaviour, and the charges are totally false, malicious and groundless. On the first visit, William told the deponent that Elizabeth had faults but he believed her to be a very virtuous girl.

The deponent has repeatedly heard from Elizabeth's own mouth uniform and consistent accounts of the cruel treatment she received from her uncle, never contradicting herself, and he has also heard John Barker her uncle caution her to speak nothing but what was perfectly true. Elizabeth left William solely because of his cruel treatment and because he refused to let her go to the place arranged for her by Mrs. Sherwin. Elizabeth was not enticed away from William Archer by John Barker for any motives of malice; the prosecution is solely to obtain a suitable redress and satisfaction for the injury done her.

The deponent believes that after removing the indictments [into King's Bench] the defendants submitted thereto, and that as a consequence some material witnesses who were to have been subpoened have been prevented from testifying.

On 24 Nov last the deponent informed his brother John that William Archer had sworn an affidavit that he had lent money to John or the deponent. John replied that William had not lent him money, nor did William lend money to the deponent. When he first set up in trade, William promised to lend him £50, but subsequently refused to do so.

The letter marked 'B' is in the handwriting of his brother John Archer.

[*Annexed letter 'B' of John Archer to Thomas Archer 12 Jan 1771.*] [*Marked*]: '(B) This letter was produced and shown to Thomas Archer and is the same mentioned and referred to in the affidavit this day sworn to be him before me. George Hollington Barker.' [*Verso*]: 'John Archer to Tom Archer 12 Jany 1771 he is glad that his sister has left Staff thinks it high time but must be mute at present here all & say nothing has many things in his mind Thanks JB for his kindness Intends to sell the Buildgs.' 'To Mr Thos Archer Gunsmith To be left at No 20 St. John Street Birmingham.' [*The envelope has been used for several sums and inventories of guns and parts.*]

'London 12 Jany 71. Dear brother, On Thursday last I recd yours & according to your request have sent you two barrells of oysters per Timmins this morning being Saturday who comes to the Coach & Horses in Dale End carriage paid and directed them to be left at Mr Guest's in Digbeth which I wish safe to hand and hope this will prove good, but since I have sent them have rec'd your other letter to countermand the order which I think very strange as a gentleman of your capacity can't tell his mind for four and forty hours together but without you give me a very particular account in your next (as you say in your last you will) I shall believe something very particular has happened in Digbeth, if you have not a mind for the oysters to go to Mr Guest's the only remedy I know is to go to the Warehouse in Dale End and desire Mr Adkins who is Bookkeeper not to send the oysters there but that you will call or send for them, they will be there on Wednesday next or Thursday morning without fail, would have you have them eat as soon as you can as frosty weather is very hurtful to them, you see very plainly I am not in fault as you desired to have them sent by the first waggon.

'I am very glad Bessy has left Stafford as I think it high time tho as I before have told you we must be mute at present, hear all & say nothing tho have a many things in my mind. I am rather supprised [*sic*] you should think I should be so neglectful not to return Mr Barker thanks for his kind offer tho I don't at this time except of it, I have no objection in regard to selling the building pervised [*sic*] I have a more particular acct for your reason no I am supprised you as a brother should write so short, as I allway told you the content of my mind & whether uncle's are consulted about it, Dear brother you never had no reasons for me being an impeacher of your secrets nor never shall so believe me to be for ever your sincere and Loving Brother John Archer. P.S. I shall be glad to hear from you soon & know how the oysters proved likewise must beg you to give best respects to all friends & particular my love to Miss Sanders & tell her I shall expect to hear from she [*sic*] by every post & would be obliged to her to let me know whether Miss West Niece to Mr Thos Wight the Grocer is married yet to Mr Budd. Adieu.'

[84] Affdt of Mary Sherwin of Prestwood, wife of Robert Sherwin joiner and carpenter, late of the county of Chester, sworn before Edward Hickman at Prestwood 14 Jan 1772. [*Verso*]: '5 [2 *is erased*] Mrs Sherwin's affid. fo.8'. ITKB The King v William Archer.

That two or three years ago Elizabeth came from William Archer's to the house of John Hodgett esquire, where the deponent then and now lives. Elizabeth, then about 17, appeared in a very mean dress. She stayed about a fortnight, did not show any tendency to immoderate drinking, nor any propensity to a gay or light behaviour that might indicate she was lewdly disposed. She is a sober well-disposed young person whose oath is to be credited.

Some time in 1771 Sarah Scott of Wolverhampton visited the deponent to request that she accompany her to John Barker at Lichfield to try to accomodate the dispute between Elizabeth and the Archers, which the deponent declined to do. Scott confirmed that Elizabeth had often complained to her of the ill usage, and that she had offered Elizabeth accommodation until she could get a place, if she was not able to bear the ill usage of her uncle. Scott told deponent of Ann throwing water in Elizabeth's face, and striking her. Elizabeth, and Thomas and Mary, her brother and sister, have written the deponent of the ill usage, and she had procured a place for her, informing William Archer by letter. She received no reply. William once visited her at Prestwood, when he declared that he believed Elizabeth was entirely virtuous.

[85] Affdt of Thomas Langford esquire of Trowell (Notts), sworn before Robert Evans at Nottingham (Notts) 14 Jan 1772. [*Verso*]: '6 Mr Langford's affid. Fo.7'. ITKB The King v William and Ann Archer.

That the deponent is a friend of John Barker of Lichfield, merchant, and stayed at his house for a month last July and August, when Elizabeth Archer was living there. She had care of the stores of the house, and kept the keys to his tea, wine and liquors. Barker and his wife were away from home, but Elizabeth never showed the least inclination to drink to excess or any other vice. She appeared a person of veracity, sobriety, chastity and honesty. Barker, whom the deponent has known from infancy, is a person of great humanity and integrity and before he began the prosecution, and now, is fully convinced that Elizabeth was greatly abused. The deponent also believes Elizabeth's frequent declarations of cruelty and abuse by the Archers.

[86] Affdt of Mary Croft widow of Stourbridge (Worcs), sworn before Edward Hickman at Stourbridge 16 Jan 1772. [*Verso*]: '23 Mrs Crofts Affdt fo: 3.' ITKB The King v William Archer.

That since Elizabeth left this deponent's house, as mentioned in her former affidavit, Elizabeth visited twice, most recently about two or three years ago, when she stayed a fortnight. She was about 17, behaved in a remarkably decent manner, did not drink to excess nor show any inclination to a gay or light behaviour that would suggest she was lewdly inclined. The deponent does not believe she is a liar, a drunkard or disposed to incontinence, but looks on her as a sober, virtuous well disposed young person.

[87] Affdt of Elizabeth Archer spinster of Lichfield, sworn before Charles Howard at Lichfield 18 Jan 1772. [*Verso*]: '22 Miss Eliz Archer the prosecutrix affidt. fo. 27'. ITKB The King v William and Ann Archer.

That notwithstanding the assertions and insinuations in the defendants' affidavits, and in answer to the several crimes and vices with which the deponent stands accused by them, the deponent admits to selling old clothes to their servants and a pair of old shoes to another person. The clothes were old and unfit to wear, worth only 5s, only in part given to her by William, and all sold with the privity of Ann Archer except for a few the night the deponent left. Under Ann's direction she sold gold earrings to a Stafford silversmith for only 1s. She sold these things to buy necessary articles and postage for letters, as William provided no pocket money except once when he gave her a few half pence; other relations and friends gave her small sums which she used to purchase some necessary articles of wearing apparel. Ann gave her 10s 6d, part of the vales at the christenings of two of her children. Deponent also received a legacy of 5 guineas which she brought to Lichfield, with a further sum of 6s 3d; £4 10s 6d remains. She sometimes asked for proper clothes and was refused, although she was in such terror of William that she declined speaking to him when she could avoid it.

The deponent denies drinking to excess and does not recollect drinking any spirits or wine while she resided with the defendants, except once when Ann gave her a glass of wine after she had a tooth drawn. She never stole anything except some drippings from a roast which she ate with bread. The deponent has been told that when she was four years old she took some half pence from a window, although she does not remember doing so.

The deponent did not behave indecently or with impropriety to Richard Thrustans or any other person. Although her clothes were at one time stored in Thrustans's room, which had been her bedroom until it was given to Thrustans when Ann Archer was lying-in, she never dressed nor undressed in his presence.

She does not recall that her brother John Archer, who has sworn that she was well used by the Archers when he stayed with them for six months, was ever at the house when they lived at Stafford; and in recent years spent only a night or two when the defendants lived at Tettenhall.

Katharine Yeomans and William Boyce, who have deposed for the defendants, advised and assisted her to leave the defendants; Boyce carried her box and lit the deponent from the house when she took chaise to Lichfield.

The deponent gave no just cause for her cruel usage, and she had no opportunity to inform her guardian, Richard Archer, of the abuses when he was last at the house. She did complain to Mrs Atkins, daughter of Richard Archer. Last April the deponent received the letter marked P which is in the hand of Sarah Scott wife of Benjamin Scott of Wolverhampton brass founder.

[*Annexed letter*]: [*Verso*]: 'S. Scott to Eli. Archer 31 March 1771.' 'To Miss Archer at Mr. Barker's Banker in Lichfield.' 'P' 'S. Scott was at Lichfd 24 Feb 1771.'

'Dear Miss Archer. I have made bold at last to write to you wich I thought to have done longe before now. I returned back by Stafford endeavouring to moderate the matter in the beast manner I knew how Mr Archar was at first <u>very hot</u> and said he would <u>try it in all the coaurts in the kingdom before he would give anything to make it up</u>. I then said all that was in my powar in your behalf I told him that Mr Barker spoke as fair as anyone could and that he would leave the referrance to any proper person. I told them Mr Barker decleard he did not wish them the least ill and had he not been calld upon by their own relations and a gentleman from Staford he could not have believed it he then said If Mr Barker had a mind to drop it & leave it to his honnar they should see whether he intended doing anything for you or not. Miss Kerby was their and she & I had deal of talke about it. Shee promised if it was in her power shee would do all ye sirvis shee could and shud & let me know when shee went home. But shee has let me know thay will <u>do nothing towards making it up</u> but are all for having it <u>tryde</u> which I am very sorry for. I mensiond ye <u>knife</u> and they said they had heard of such a repoert but both decleared they knew nothing of any such thing and Mr Archar said who [woe] be to them that swore to that or any such <u>falsity</u> for he would prosscute them to the utmost of ye law. There is so much difarance betwean what you say and what they say at Staford that <u>ameases me to think </u>what will be <u>the event of it</u>; for my part when I am calld I will spake the truth on all sides to the best of my knowledge and beg for <u>gods sake</u> you that you <u>will do the same</u>; I hope you will not take it ill at me for spaking so free to you but I hear such vearirous stories is the reason why I caution you <u>pray miss recallect</u> what <u>ye Dovarege [Doveridge] sarvant is to say of you if it comes into courte</u> I know nothing of it; your uncle said the reasson why you went so bare with shoes and othar things you would not ask him for them you was so stubburn and that he was abligd to scold you and thratten you before he could <u>make you ask for what you wanted</u>. I then recollected an instance at Hampton tho I said nothing of it to them: If you remember when you was at Mrs Parshouses you askd your aunt for money shee asked you what it was for and you told hur more then that it was I think for shoes and for that affair you was turned over to ask your uncle for money. I shud say much more to you but cannot spear time but to conclude beg for the sake of your future welfeaire you <u>will endeavour to put an end to it if you can</u>. as by the whole I see it if it is carried on theare will be much more troble then you are awear of: so that it may end to the welfare & saterfaction of you & your relations general is the sincear wish of your humble servant. Sarah Scott. Wolverhampton 27 March 1771.

PS If agreable should be glad of a line from you.'

[*Subscribed*]: 'This is the paper writing or letter mentioned and referred to in the affidavit of Miss Elizabeth Archer sworn the 18th day of January 1772 before me Cha: Howard.'

[88] Affdt of John Barker merchant of Lichfield, prosecutor in these cases; his wife Catharine Barker; Samuel Palmer the younger, apprentice of John Barker, sworn before Charles Howard at Lichfield 18 Jan 1772. [*Verso*]: 'Mr. John Barker & other affidavits. 20 fo. 27.' ITKB The King v William and Ann Archer.

[All]: That Elizabeth has resided with them for over a year and is not addicted to lying, drunkenness, lewdness, or theft. The allegations made by the defendants are false and malicious, calculated to blast her reputation and destroy her credit, to allow them to escape with impunity. Elizabeth has had access to wine and liquors, and John Barker has left the key in the cabinet where he keeps cash and bills, often many thousands of pounds, but the deponents have never seen Elizabeth in the least disordered with drinking nor ever suspected her of drinking or of stealing cash or any goods whatsoever.

[John and Catharine Barker]: That the deponents entrusted Elizabeth with the keys to the stores of their house as well as the liquor cabinet when they have been away from home. They never heard that she was suspected of any crimes until after she left the defendants' house, and that while living with the deponents, and, so far from being negligent and filthy in person and dress, has been clean and neat and shown more attention to dress than the deponent Catharine has always approved. Elizabeth has been clear, uniform and consistent in her accounts of abuse, despite close examination by them. They saw a weal on Elizabeth's arm soon after she left the Archers, which Elizabeth told them was caused by a blow from a whip by Ann Archer.

[John Barker and Samuel Palmer]: That they heard Richard Thrustans say at Stafford quarter sessions when the indictments were preferred, that Elizabeth was beaten for not removing her clothing from his room, although it was not her fault; he never saw her in his room, although she made his bed, and he declared that she had never behaved indecently or improperly in his presence.

[John and Catharine Barker]: That Elizabeth has been prudent in her expenditures since living with them, her expenses not exceeding one guinea, having been provided with clothes and other necessaries by John Barker. The deponent John did not refuse to let the defendant William Archer see or ask Elizabeth questions last May, but seeing that she suffered great agitation of mind from seeing him pass by the window, and expressing great terror, the deponent Catharine informed William that she feared an interview would terrify Elizabeth, William desisted seeking an interview on the advice of his attorney and seemed perfectly satisfied.

[Samuel Palmer the younger]: That when he took an account in Jan 1771 from Katharine Yeomans of the defendants' ill usage, as mentioned in his former affidavit, Yeomans showed him a letter from William Archer charging her with stealing a barrel of raisin wine.

[John Barker]: That he did not commence these prosecutions out of malice, or in consequence of an old quarrel, as William Archer has asserted. He did so after having fully inquired, on the advice of his friends, and in the sincere conviction that the defendants grossly abused Elizabeth. He believes that the defendants removed the indictment into King's Bench and pleaded guilty in order to deprive him of several material witnesses and to prevent cross examinations of his witnesses. Letter R is a copy of a letter sent by him to William Archer; letters S and T are in the hand of William Archer.

[*Annexed letters all attested by Charles Howard 18 Jan 1772*]:

[*Letter R*]: '(A copy of a letter to Mr William Archer at Stafford).

Sir,

As you may be under some bad apprehensions for Bessy Archer, this serves to inform you that she came to my house yesterday morning. I am, Sir, etc,

John Barker

Lichfield 18 Dec 1770.'

[*Letter S*]: [*Verso*]: 'To Mr John Barker Mercer in Lichfield.' 'Wm Archer 21 Decr 1770 12 o''

'Mr John Barker,

'I received your very obliging letter to inform me of Bessy's situation, which after the various methods used to seduce her from me, was very unnecessary.

'If ever she could be of the least service to my family it is now. However, I give you joy of your valuable acquisition, and sincerely wish she may find a much better friend in you, than she ever did in me, as she has now effectually excluded herself from my favour, after caring and providing for her (at my own expense) so many years, from infancy (a few years excepted) to this present time. She has well recompensed me for my care, and strict attention to her welfare and I must tell you my sentiments frankly, that I verily believe it is more a malicious pride in you to draw her from me, than any real design of doing the girl service, and thus far I shall again say, when you find out her inability to serve you and her incapacity of getting her own bread, and taking a proper care of herself. If you either turn her out of doors, and thereby expose her to those snares she has hitherto by my diligence escaped or make any money demand upon my brother for clothes or necessaries for her use, I shall always say, you are as arrant a scrub as need to exist and that your conduct in this affair is similar to that upon another occasion, very infamous, respecting my brother, the creditors, and myself.

'I am with all that esteem towards you, that every wretched mean spirited fellow deserves.

Yours, Wm Archer
Green Hall by Stafford
Dec 21 1770'

[*Letter T*]: [*Verso*]: 'Mr Thos Archer at Mr Edmd Tompkins's Mercer in Birmingham.'

'Dear Nephew

'In answer to yours must inform you that Mary Collins has some months since been dismissed my service, and since then has brought forth a bastard, and taken her trial at the sessions here for fathering her child upon my servant man, whom I have also dismissed, tho I have some reason to believe she swore falsely on that occasion. In short she is a very bad servant, very ignorant, very wicked, and I cannot answer either for her honesty, or sobriety. I suppose her only reason for going to Birmingham is, that nobody in this neighbourhood will have any thing to do with her, pray give my compliments to your master and Mrs and let them see the just character I give her, as I should take it very ill of any one that would deceive me on the like occasion. Am glad to hear all your friends are well. Pray give my compliments to Mr and Mrs Guest and tell them if he finds Sarah Toft in distress shall be glad if he will give her half a guinea or a guinea and must desire you to apply to your father to repay Mr Guest and place it to my account. Some days ago I saw in the newspapers William Archer esquire of Llechan appointed High Sheriff[102] for the county of Carnarvon, and have since received certain information that by that Welch name I am the person

---

[102] PRO, Lists and indexes no.9, *List of Sheriffs for England and Wales* (Kraus reprint, 1963), 250 gives William Archer of Llechan, esquire, as sheriff of the county of Caernarfon (Carnarvan) 9 Feb 1770 (to 5 Feb 71). Llechan is a property in Gyffin parish. Archer is identified as 'of Conway' in a manuscript list of high sheriffs of the county held in the archives of University of Wales Bangor (information from Elen Wyn Hughes, assistant archivist). He had interests in Conway, but by 1774 his residence was Dearnford (Salop). The trustees appointed in his will were Clement Kynnersley of Loxley (Staffs) and Charles Boyer Adderley of Hams Hall (Warws). They were charged with raising on the lands he left in trust £2000 for each of his five sons, and £1500 for each of his three daughters, with remainder to the eldest son, and £50 to the New Church in Wolverhampton 'towards purchasing a handsome new altar piece.' In 1779 he agreed to convey lands to Owen

intended shall I fear be obliged to have two or three very disagreeable journeys there on that account his summer.

'I am with best respects to your brother and all friends, your affectionate uncle

Wm Archer.

Green Hall by Stafford

Feb 19 1770'

[89] Affdt of Mary Archer, spinster and sister of Elizabeth Archer, of Coventry, sworn before John Stanton at Coventry 18 Jan 1772. [*Verso*]: '24 Miss Mary Archer's Affidavit fo: 17'. ITKB The King v William and Ann Archer.

That the defence affidavits have falsely charged Elizabeth with want of virtue, sobriety, and integrity to mitigate the offences of which the defendants stand convicted or the satisfaction they ought to make in respect thereof. Elizabeth was not addicted to drinking, as William has charged since these prosecutions were begun, nor indecent, immoderate, or deserving of censure. She did not drink, although she may have had the opportunity to do so on several occasions. The deponent visited John Barker last May and Elizabeth did not drink there although she had keys to the cabinet, and free access to the room where he kept large sums of money. The deponent lay with her sister during the visit, who showed no inclination to drink, or to commit any immoral, dishonest or disreputable act or thing.

Elizabeth told the deponent of abuse at the hands of the Archers, both before and after the prosecutions were begun, in terms consistent with the truth. She is satisfied that Elizabeth understands the import of an oath and would not swear falsely, and has never been known to do so. John Barker received her out of compassion and tenderness. Elizabeth while at the Archers had insufficient and unsuitable clothing, and had to sell a pair of gold earrings to pay the postage on a letter she had received from this deponent.

[90] Affdt of Fettiplace Nott esquire of Lichfield, John Levett esquire formerly of Wychnor now of Lichfield, William Inge esquire of Thorpe Constantine, James Falconer clerk master of arts of Lichfield, George Hand the younger gentleman of Cathedral Close Lichfield, sworn before Charles Howard at Lichfield 18 Jan 1772. ITKB The King v William and Ann Archer.

Holland for £13,800, but died within a year and before the transaction was completed. Archifdy Caernarfon, XM/849/1–25, XM/1818/1–11.

[All]: That they have been intimately acquainted for many years with John Barker, merchant and banker, who has ever acted toward them with probity and fidelity. Nott, Inge, Levett and Falconer have deposited with him many thousands of pounds; they have purchased clothes and liveries for their servants from him. He is a man not only of strict integrity, but of great decency, humanity and morality. They believe he commenced these prosecutions not in consequence of an old quarrel as suggested by William Archer, but from laudable motives of compassion for the sufferings he believed to have been sustained by his niece.

[John Levett]: That he has conversed with Elizabeth in Barker's counting room where sums of money lie about; she would not have been allowed to do so if there were the least suspicion of dishonesty.

[William Inge and James Falconer]: That John and Catherine Barker in late 1770 told them of the reports of mistreatment, asked for advice, requested them to enquire into the truth of the matter, and to get word to Elizabeth that Barker would receive her in his house and screen and protect her. Persons of fortune and good repute confirmed that it was generally reported and believed that the Archers used Elizabeth with great severity and cruelty, and that she was often seen in the streets of Stafford in very wretched and improper apparel. The deponents gave directions to inform Elizabeth of Barker's offer, in consequence of which she came to his house. She was not secretly enticed away.

[James Falconer]: That on the many occasions on which he did business with Barker in the past year, Elizabeth has always appeared clean and neat, and has several times seen her sitting alone in the room where he keeps his bills and cash. Last week at the request of Barker he examined Elizabeth as to her idea of the nature and belief of the obligation of an oath, of which she has very proper sentiments. As a clergyman he warned her of the dreadful consequences of forswearing herself, but she declared to him that she had deposed nothing but the truth.

[George Hand]: That when William called on Elizabeth at the Barkers last May she was so terrified of him she could not see him. William behaved with great impropriety and violence of passion, confessed he had beaten Elizabeth with a horsewhip which he produced and struck on the table. He said he would beat her again if she was in his power. Barker behaved with great propriety and moderation, and did not appear averse to a compromise of these prosecutions on suitable terms, referring William Archer to Mr Tomkinson, Barker's attorney. William Archer's attorney, then present, said that he was perfectly satisfied.

[91] Affdt of John Boot farmer and maltster of Forebridge in Castle Church age 33, sworn before W. Keen at Forebridge 19 Jan 1772. [*Verso*]: '26 – etc'. ITKB The King v William and Ann Archer.

That in 1769 he was overseer of the poor of the parish, and that in October Mary Collins was removed from Tettenhall, where she had lately lived as a servant of William Archer's house, to Castle Church as her place of settlement. She gave birth to a child before Christmas, and charged Richard Thrustans on oath as the father. At the trial of the filiation at January sessions William Archer, although an inhabitant of the parish, testified in defence of Thrustans, saying he believed Collins to be a wicked lying and abandoned woman whose testimony was not to be credited. He proved that she had told him many lies, including denying with horrid oaths that she was with child. He testified that he had requested her to pull off some of her clothes and that he had privately examined and inspected those parts of her body the most capable of affording him the necessary information and a discovery of her pregnancy. He found she was big with child, and had ever since considered her a vile wicked woman.

Collins frequently applied to the deponent for relief and told him that she had seen Archer horsewhip Miss Bessy Archer his niece, and had by kicking and abusing her made her flesh upon one of her thighs black. Elizabeth Archer was well known to the deponent, who was a near neighbour, and was a very sober diligent modest and well behaved young woman. It was reported and generally believed in the neighbourhood that the Archers mistreated her.[103]

[92] Affdt of William Smith cabinet maker age 23 and Robert Atkins grocer age 20 both of Stafford, sworn before W. Keen at Stafford 20 Jan 1772. [*Verso*]: '21 Affid of Wm Smith and Robt Atkins. fo:3'. ITKB The King v William Archer.

That near the end of 1770 William Boyce, then a servant to William Archer, told them in the course of a conversation about the then much talked of abuse of Elizabeth, that he had seen Archer in a great passion strike Elizabeth a violent blow with a pair of tongs over her breast.

[*Annexed*]: [*Verso*]: 'To Mr. John Manley in the Middle Temple A Single Sheet. London.'

'Sir,

'The King agt Archer Esqr.

'Imagining the master will make his report this term I should be obliged to you for a line to inform me whether you are allowed any and what further time to answer the defendts affidts.

'I am sir, your most obedient servant,

W. Keen

Stafford 22 January, 1772.'

---

[103] A signed but slightly different version of affdt [97], crossed out, appears at the end of affdt [91].

[93] Affdt of Elizabeth Minors spinster of Eccleshall, sworn before W. Keen at Eccleshall 24 Jan 1772. [*Verso*]: '9 Eliz. Minors for prosx fo: 5'. ITKB The King v William and Ann Archer.

[*The first part of the affdt is identical to Elizabeth Minor's evidence in affdt [82].*] ... made it evident to her the said Anne Archer that Elizabeth Brookes had stolen them. While this deponent lived in the family Elizabeth was employed doing the business of a common servant and a great deal of the worst work and dirtiest business in the house. She was sober, diligent and very modest and virtuous and a person of veracity. This was her character among all her neighbours and acquaintances, many of whom the deponent has heard pity her as uncommonly ill used by William and Anne Archer.

[94] Affdt of Margaret Malpass spinster of Offley Hay Eccleshall parish, sworn before W. Keen at Offley Hay 24 Jan 1772. [*Verso*]: '10 Marg. Malpass. fo. 7.' [*Signed with a mark.*] ITKB The King v William and Ann Archer.

That the deponent was a servant of William Battey of Stafford in 1770. Katharine Yeomans left William Archers service and came to stay at Battey's house, where she shared a bed with the deponent, and told her that Archer accused Yeomans of stealing wine had and had turned her away and stopped her wages. The Archers called at the house after church and told Battey that Yeomans had stolen a great deal of raisin wine.

Elizabeth often came to the house to drop off linen to be washed. Yeomans told the deponent that Elizabeth had been beaten on many occasions, and that she had seen William Archer beat her with tongs until her flesh was black. Yeomans also told the deponent that the Archers had charged Elizabeth Brookes (now Foden), who had also left their service, with stealing cheese and cloth.

[95] Affdt of Anne Marston age 60 and upwards, wife of William Marston joiner and carpenter of Stafford, sworn before W. Keen at Stafford 24 Jan 1772. [*Verso*]: 'Ann Marston 4 fo.10'. ITKB The King v William and Ann Archer.

That in Dec 1770 Elizabeth told her that she was so much beat and abused by the Archers that she could live with them no longer, and was determined to leave their house in as private a manner as possible at the first opportunity. She asked and it was agreed to send her box to the deponent's house, and the deponent promised to assist Elizabeth, a very decent well behaved person, to escape William Archer. She was very afraid Archer would discover her intentions. A horse was procured which waited many hours to carry Elizabeth to Lichfield, but she was unable to quit the house undiscovered. A few days later Elizabeth told the deponent that it was impossible to bear such ill treatment and that she was determined to go to Mrs. Scott's, a relation at Worston, four miles from Stafford. The deponent dissuaded her on the grounds that William might discover her there and fetch her back, and instead the deponent procured her a place on an empty post chaise that was going to Lichfield next morning, and instructed her to leave the house before the family was up. William Boyce brought Elizabeth's box to the deponent's house. William also helped Elizabeth make the escape; he was very friendly and sorry for her sufferings. Elizabeth was chaste, sober, honest and diligent and a passion for veracity and all depositions to the contrary by persons of any rank or fortune whatsoever are scandalously false and unjust.

[96] Affdt of Ellen Dikes agd 39, wife of Peter Dikes miller of Gom's, Stoke upon Trent, sworn before Ralph Wotton at Gom's Mill 24 Jan 1772. [*Verso*]: '17 Ellen Dikes fo:3'. [*Signed with a mark.*] ITKB The King v William and Ann Archer.

That when living with the Archers Elizabeth supplied the place of a common servant, making the beds, cleaning the rooms, and any other business. Ann Archer ordered the deponent on several occasions to tell Elizabeth to wash the dishes. Elizabeth was not addicted to idleness, telling lies, drinking, or any other bad habits or any immodest or indecent action, but was a person of diligence, veracity, sobriety and chastity and always bore a very good character. Her conduct while living with the defendants was unblameable.

[97] Affdt of Elizabeth Harvey wife of Joseph Harvey of Forebridge Castle Church, sworn before W. Keen at Forebridge 26 Jan 1772. [*Versos*]: 'Sir, on the other side is Eliz Harvey's Affidt resworn.[104] From yr most obed. servt, W Keen. Staff. 26 Jan'. '27 Affidit of Eliz Harvey'. ITKB The King v William and Ann Archer.

That she is a neighbour of the Archers for whom she sometimes did needlework. Elizabeth was treated as a common servant, and did the worst and dirty work in the house, being kept as an underling to most of the servants. The deponent always believed her to be a sober, modest and inoffensive young person, and she never saw or heard that she was addicted to drinking, lies, idleness, or any indecent or improper behaviour.

[104] On 19 Jan she had sworn another affidavit, written on the same folio as the affidavit of John Boot [91], but struck through and used as the wrapper for that affidavit.

In Dec 1771 Katharine Yeomans informed the deponent she had seen William strike Elizabeth with a poker, and order his wife to strip her of her clothes and to turn her out of doors the next morning. After she left the service of William Archer, Yeomans told the deponent that he had charged her with stealing their raisin wine and stopped a guinea of her wages.

When Mary Collins was big with a bastard child she lived next door to the deponent, and told her that when she lived with the Archers she had seen William horsewhip Elizabeth, and that he frequently pinched her ears until they were black and sometimes until they bled, and that Elizabeth was seldom without black flesh from the abuse.

[98] Affdt of Elizabeth Hubball widow of Forebridge Castle Church, sworn before W. Keen at Forebridge 27 Jan 1772. [*Verso*]: '28 Anr Affdt of Eliz. Hubball fo:5.' [*Signed with a mark.*] ITKB The King v William and Ann Archer.

That the deponent is a relative of Mary Watwood wife of Benjamin Watwood of Rising Brook Castle Church, and has read Mary Watwood's unsigned affidavit.[105] Mary, whom she believes is a material witness, told her 25 Jan that Ann had offered her a new hat if she agreed not to testify against them, and in expectation of this or some other gratuity Mary Watwood is prevented from testifying on behalf of Elizabeth.

When Mary Collins was lying in with a bastard child, the deponent asked Ann Archer, at Mary Collins's request, for a small present. Ann Archer refused, declaring in an angry way that she knew Collins to be a vile base wicked woman, who had forsworn herself.

[*Annexed letter*]: [*Verso*]: 'To Mr. Manley in the Middle Temple London. A Single Sheet.'

'Sir,

'Inclosed I send you another affidavit from Mrs Hubball, which I believe is the last you'll receive from this quarter. I am wishing you success.

Sir, your most obedient servant,
W. Keen
Stafford 27 January 72'

---

[105] See affdt [53].

Affidavit for defence:

Hil 18 Geo III 1778

[99] Affdt of William Johnston gentleman and agent for the defendants, of the Inner Temple London, sworn before [Mr Justice] E. Willes at Serjeants Inn 28 Jan 1778. [*Verso*]: '28 Staffordshire. The King a Archer & his Wife Hilary T: 1778. Please to move that the Defts Recognizance may be *respited until the Court shall otherwise order*[106] discharged. Mr Cowper. Johnston.' ITKB The King v William and Ann Archer.

That since Hilary term 1772 there have been no proceedings other than respiting the defendants' recognizance every issuable term, at great expense to them. The prosecutrix has not taken any step in the cause since that term.

Sources: KB 1/18 Ea 11 Geo III bdl 67, Trin 11 Geo III bdls 6, 13, 14, 18, 19, 29, 64-67 , Mich 12 Geo III no.2 bdl 67, Hil 12 Geo III no.1 bdl 75 and bdl 76. KB 1/21 Hil 18 Geo III no.2 bdl 28. KB 11/47 Ea 11 Geo III 1771 #9, #10. KB 21/40 Trin 11 Geo III. KB 29/430 Ea 11 Geo III #9,10. KB 39/6 Ea, Trin 11 Geo III.

F.12 Certiorari on an indictment from quarter sessions, by defendants (19 June 1771)

Defendants: Thomas Gould*, butcher of Manchester (Lancs);[107] Thomas Buxton*, butcher of Manchester; William Brownson*, yeoman of Parwich (Derbs); William Gould*, yeoman of Parwich ; William Spencer*, blacksmith of Kniveton (Derbs); Samuel Hodgkinson the younger*, labourer of Kniveton ; Anthony Wain, butcher of Kniveton; John Redfern*, labourer of Bradbourne (Derbs) ; William Taylor*, yeoman of Bradbourne; George Fern*, labourer of Brassington (Derbs) ; William Harrison, labourer of Hurdlow (Derbs); Isaac Smith and Samuel Dutton, labourers of Ashbourne (Derbs); and several others unknown.[108]

Writ and return:
Mich 12 Geo III 1771

---

[106] The italicized words are struck out.
[107] The residence of Thomas Gould and Thomas Buxton is given as Manchester, apparently in error for Mayfield: see the next case.
[108] See also the following three cases.

Writ 19 June [1771][LDT], to be returned [4 Nov 1771, FDT Mich]; returned by John Eld.[109]

Schedule that the indictment was presented at Staffs Ea quarter sessions, 9 April 1771.

Indictment for riotously rescuing, with sticks and stones, at Mayfield[110] on 13 Feb [1771], 5 horses value £47 distrained by Charles Ensor of Throwley gentleman on 11 Feb on a debt of £84 6s 8d rent for a farm in Bradbourne (Derbs), owed by Sarah Buxton, widow, and John Buxton. The horses had been conveyed to Mayfield in an attempt to prevent distrainer. [*Bottom left*]: 'Rescuing goods distrained for Rent.' [*Verso*]: Thomas Blurton, Jonathan Dean, William Corden, William Hitchcock, William Lees. A true bill.

Rules and process:
Hil [24 Jan 1772]: rule to compel defdts to plead or recognizance estreated (side bar). Trin 1772: defdts* appear and plead not guilty; rule for a special jury, instance of prosr. Trin Vac 16 July 1772: notice of trial for defdt (Wace). Staffs summer assizes 1772: not guilty; without day.[111] Mich [6 Nov 1772]: rule nisi for judgment (side bar).

Sources: ASSI 4/5 Staffs summer 12 Geo III. IND 1/6661 Trin 12 Geo III. KB 11/47 Mich 12 Geo III 1771 #25. KB 15/15 Trin Vac 1772. KB 21/40 Hil, Trin 12 Geo III, Mich 13 Geo III. KB 28/282 Trin 12 Geo III, roll 18. KB 29/431 Mich, Trin 12 Geo III.

F.13 Certiorari on an indictment from quarter sessions, by defendant (19 June 1771)

Defendant: Thomas Gould, butcher of Mayfield.

Writ and return:
Mich 12 Geo III 1771

[109] See SRO, Q/SB Mich 1771 for a note that in this and the following three cases John Darys Browne acknowledged receipt 27 Nov 1771 from Mr Fernyhough, clerk of the peace, Stafford of the writs of certiorari with returns, records, recognizances and indictments annexed for the use of Mr Goodwyn, attorney for the defdts.
[110] Given as Mathfield in this and the other cases.
[111] In cases F.12 to F.15, the prosecution was represented by Dean, the defence by Goodwin; the postea for each was received by Robert Want as agent of the defendants, 28 Nov 1772, except for F.14, which was received by Michael Barbor 14 Nov 1772.

Writ 19 June [1771][LDT], to be returned [4 Nov 1771, FDT Mich]; returned by John Eld.[112]

Schedule that the indictment was presented at Staffs Ea quarter sessions, 9 April 1771.

Indictment for assault on Jonathan Dean 13 Feb [1771] at Mayfield. [*Bottom left*]: 'assault'. [*Verso*]: Jonathan Dean. A true bill.

Rules and process:
Hil [24 Jan 1772]: rule to compel defdt to plead or recognizance estreated (side bar). Trin 1772: appears and pleads not guilty; rule for a special jury, instance of prosr. Trin Vac 16 July 1772: notice of trial for defdt (Wace). Staffs summer assizes 1772: not guilty; without day. Mich [6 Nov 1772]: rule nisi for judgment (side bar).

Sources: ASSI 4/5 Staffs summer 12 Geo III. IND 1/6661 Trin 12 Geo III. KB 11/47 Mich 12 Geo III #28. KB 15/15 Trin Vac 1772. KB 21/40 Hil, Trin 12 Geo III, Mich 13 Geo III. KB 28/282 Trin 12Geo III, roll 17. KB 29/431 Mich, Trin 12 Geo III.

F.14 Certiorari on an indictment from quarter sessions, by defendant (19 June 1771)

Defendant: William Taylor, farmer[113] of Mayfield.

Writ and return:
Mich 12 Geo III 1771

Writ 19 June [1771][LDT], to be returned [4 Nov 1771, FDT Mich]; returned by John Eld.[114]

Schedule that the indictment was presented at Staffs Ea quarter sessions, 9 April 1771.

Indictment for assault on William Corden 13 Feb [1771] at Mayfield. [*Verso*]: William Corden, William Hitchcock. A true bill.

Rules and process:
Hil [24 Jan 1772]: rule to compel defdt to plead or recognizances estreated (side bar). Trin [1772]: appears and pleads not guilty. Trin Vac

---

[112] See previous case.

[113] So identified in the indictment, although best practice suggested that a farmer should be described as 'husbandman': William Hawkins, *Pleas of the Crown* (1721), ii, ch. 23, s.115; ch. 25, s.72.

[114] See previous case.

16 July 1772: notice of trial for defdt (Wace). Staffs summer assizes 1772: guilty. Mich [6 Nov 1772]: rule nisi for judgment (side bar). ST [1772]: postea and judgment against; conviction. ST [26 Nov 1772]: with consent of attorneys, referred to Burrow, master of the crown office, for determination of all differences (side bar). Hil [3 Feb 1773]: recognizances respited.

Sources: ASSI 4/5 Staffs summer 12 Geo III. IND 1/6661 Trin 12 Geo III, Mich 13 Geo III. KB 11/47 Mich 12 Geo III 1771 #27. KB 15/15 Trin Vac 16 July 1772. KB 21/40 Hil 12 Geo III, Mich 13 Geo III, Hil 13 Geo III. KB 28/282 Trin 12 Geo III, roll 19. KB 29/431 Mich, Trin 12 Geo III.

F.15 Certiorari on an indictment from quarter sessions, by defendant (19 June 1771)

Defendant: William Critchlow[115] labourer of Bradbourne (Derbs) and others unknown.

Writ and return:
Mich 12 Geo III 1771

Writ 19 June [1771][LDT], to be returned [4 Nov 1771, FDT Mich]; returned by John Eld.[116]
   Schedule that the indictment was presented at Staffs Ea quarter sessions, 9 April 1771.
   Indictment [*for the same offence charged against Thomas Gould et al, above*]. [*Verso*]: Thomas Blurton, William Lees, Thomas Beck. A true bill.

Rules and process:
Hil [24 Jan 1772]: rule to compel defdt to plead or recognizances estreated (side bar). Trin [1772]: appears and pleads not guilty. Trin Vac 16 July 1772: notice of trial for defdt (Wace). Staffs summer assizes 1772: not guilty; without day. Mich [6 Nov 1772]: rule nisi for judgment (side bar).

Sources: ASSI 4/5 Staffs. Summer 12 Geo III. IND 1/6661 Trin 12 Geo III. KB 11/47 Mich 12 Geo III 1771 #26. KB 15/15 Trin Vac 16 July 1772. KB 21/40 Hil 12 Geo III, Mich 13 Geo III. KB 28/282 Mich 12 Geo III, roll 20. KB 29/431 Mich, Trin 12 Geo III.

---

[115] Cricklow in some of the sources.
[116] See previous case.

F.16 Certiorari on an indictment from assizes, by prosecutor (29 Nov 1776)

Defendants: John Child, gentleman of Cheadle; Thomas Harvey, gentleman of Cauldon.[117]

Writ and return:
Hil 17 Geo III 1777

Writ 29 Nov [1776][LDT] [*for two indictments, filed as #22 and #23*] to be returned by [20 Jan 1777, FDT Hil]; returned by Sir George Nares.[118]
    Schedule by Price[119] that the two indictments were presented at Staffs summer assizes, 17 Aug [1775] and found true bills.
    Indictment for conspiring 17 Aug [1775] to suborn a witness, John Wigley, to swear falsely at the trial of Thomas Fallows [*in #23 the name is given as Lawrence Fallows*], yeoman of Cauldon, at summer assizes [1775] for stealing two sheep value 5s, on 15 June [1775], the property of John Wigley, in order to acquit Fallows; at which trial Fallows pleaded not guilty and was acquitted. [*Verso*]: William Fallows, George Smith, James Simpson. True bill for Child and Harvey, no true bill for Keen.[120]

Rules and process:
Hil 1777: summons, leave to imparl. Ea 1777: plead not guilty. Trin [17 June 1777]: rule for a special jury, instance of defdts (Howorth). Trin Vac 24 June 1777: notice of trial for the king on both indictments (Barlow).[121]

---

[117] The indictments also name William Keen gentleman of the borough of Stafford, but the charges are not found true bills.

[118] Puisne justice of the court of common pleas, 1771–1786.

[119] No given name; probably Meredith Price, clerk of assize.

[120] In the assize records for Staffs summer 1776 is filed a record that at summer assizes 1775, it was presented that Lawrence Fallows, late of the parish of Cauldon, yeoman, on 15 June [1775] stole two sheep the property of John Wigley; he pleaded not guilty and was discharged, to go without day. At the trial, Wigley, a miner, who was a witness, swore that the sheep were not his, nor stolen, in order to acquit Fallows. Subsequently, on 25 July [1776] (summer assizes 1776) he confessed to the perjury and was sentenced to prison for six months. ASSI 5/96 Staffs summer 1776.

[121] A similar entry for 19 June is struck out.

Sources: IND 1/6662 Ea 17 Geo III. KB 11/50 Hil 17 Geo III #22, #23. KB 15/4 Hil 1777. KB 15/15 Trin Vac 17 Geo III 1777. KB 21/41 Trin 17 Geo III. KB 29/436 17 Geo III. KB 36/238 Trin 17 Geo III.

F.17 Certiorari on an indictment from assizes, by defendants (10 June 1777)

Defendants: John Stockton, carpenter of the borough of Stafford ; Richard Hill, labourer of Farley; Joseph Bagot, yeoman of Stone ; Joseph Hunt, labourer of Stone ; Charles Daniel, labourer of Stone ; Edmund Rowley, labourer of Stafford.

Writ and return:
Trin 17 Geo III 1777

Writ 10 June [1777], to be returned immediately; returned by James Eyre.[122]

Schedule that the indictment was presented at Staffs summer assizes, 25 July [1776].

Indictment with threats, noise and approbrious language, [1] entered the dwelling of James Adams of Stone, 9 Aug [1775], remained ten hours and terrified the family, making threats, pulling down a stucco ceiling; [2] 6 Sept [1775] riotously began to destroy the house; [3] 13 Feb [1776] stayed two hours, made clamour, and riotously demolished two windows; [4] 19 Feb [1776] stayed six hours and riotously demolished the stairs and rails. Also [5] forceable entry and detainer. [*Verso*]: James Adams, prosecutor and witness; Ellin Howitt witness. A true bill.

Rules and process:
Ea [6 May 1777]: on reading the affdt of Richard Hill, FDT to prosr to show why a certiorari should not issue to the justices of oyer and ter-miner. Trin [10 June 1777]: on reading the affdt of Thomas Weston Powell and the annexed rule, order for certiorari at the instance of the defdt (Cowper); summons. ST: appear; leave to imparl; plead not guilty. ST [17 June 1777] rule for a special jury, instance of defdts (Cowper). ST 8 July 1777: notice of trial for defdts (Midgley). Trin [1778]: postea and judgment for: acquitted. ST [19 June 1778]: rule nisi for judgment for defdts. ST [6 July 1778]: recognizance discharged (side bar).

---

[122] Baron of the court of exchequer 1772–87, chief baron 1787–93, chief justice of common pleas 1793–99.

Affidavits for defence:

Ea 17 Geo III 1777

[1] Affdt of Richard Hill gentleman[123] of Farley, sworn before Thomas Weston Powell at Burston in the parish of Stone on 2 May 1777. ITKB 'The King against Richard Hill and others. On the prosecution of James Adams.' [*Verso*]: '48 Staffordshire x The King on the prosecution of Adams agt Hill & oth. Affids. Mr Cowper, Please to move for a certiorari on the behalf of the defts on the within affidt. 1 Gna Allen & Atkinson Barlow fo: 4.'

That the indictment found against him and the other defendants at the last Stafford summer assizes is for a supposed forceable entry into some rooms which the prosecutor had for some time used as a domestic of Edward Weld esquire; he occupied them in no other right. This deponent received orders from Weld to discharge the prosecutor from his employment and to stop his salary; he informed the prosecutor and requested him to quit the rooms, which the prosecutor did not do. Weld decided to pull down the house and rebuild, and the prosecutor was obliged to quit. These are the sole grounds of this vexatious and groundless prosecution; it will be necessary to have a view and a special jury to try the cause.

Trin 17 Geo III 1777

[2] Affdt of Thomas Weston Powell gentleman of Rugeley, sworn before Charles Weston at Rugeley 21 May 1777. ITKB 'The King against Richard Hill and others. On the prosecution of James Adams.' [*Verso*]: '3. Staffordshire. The King ag Hill & oth. Affidt of Service of Rule Nisi. Pd for Copy. Allen & Atkinson. fo [*illegible*].'

That the deponent 17 May 1777 served John Platt, attorney for the prosecutor, with a copy of the [*annexed*] rule nisi, at the same time showing him the original.

[*Annexed*]: [*Verso*]: ' 5.0 rule. 2.0 affds. Allen & Atkinson.' Rule nisi of [6 May 1777], granted on reading the affdt of Richard Hill gentleman, that the first day next term be given to the prosecutor to show cause why a writ of certiorari not be issued to the justices of oyer and terminer. On the motion of Cowper; by the court.

Sources: IND 1/6662 Trin 17 Geo III, Trin 18 Geo III. KB 1/20 Ea 17 Geo III no. 2 #48, Trin 17 Geo III no. 1 #3. KB 11/50 Trin 17 Geo III 1777 #11.

---

[123] The indictment gives the addition 'labourer late of the parish of Farley.'

KB 15/4 Trin 1777. KB 15/15 Trin Vac 1777. KB 21/41 Trin 17 Geo III. KB 21/42 Trin 18 Geo III. KB 29/436 Trin 17 Geo III. KB 36/238 Trin 17 Geo III.

F.18 Certiorari on an indictment from quarter sessions, by prosecutor (4 July 1781)

Defendants: Thomas Bache the younger and Francis Haywood, both yeoman of Over Arley.

Writ and return:
Hil 22 Geo III 1782

Writ 4 July [1781][LDT] to be returned by [3 Nov 1781, FDT Mich].
Schedule by T. Fernyhough, clerk of the peace, 12 July [1781] that the indictment was presented at Staffs Trans quarter sessions 1781.
Indictment [1] assault on Arthur Annesley Viscount Valentia JP in the execution of his office 2 July 1781 at Over Arley; [2] common assault. [*Verso*]: Arthur Annesley Viscount Valentia, Edmund Case, esquire, William Farmer, William Bateman, William Briscoe. A true bill.

Rules and process:
Hil 1782: summons; leave to imparl; plead not guilty.[124]

Sources: KB 11/52 Hil 22 Geo III 1782 #15. KB 15/4 Hil 22 Geo III 1782. KB 29/441 Hil 22 Geo III.

F.19 Certiorari on an indictment from assizes, by defendant (12 Feb 1782)

Defendant: Henry Tomkinson, gentleman and attorney of Nantwich (Ches).[125]

---

[124] This entry in the Appearance Book, KB 15/4, is struck out, with the annotation 'entered by mistake.' A note of the removal of the indictment by writ of certiorari is entered in SRO, Q/SO 18 for Trans 1781.

[125] Probably Henry Tomkinson of Dorfold, near Nantwich, gentleman, who moved to Nantwich sometime between 1768 and 1776. A Henry Tompkinson is listed among the gentry there in the 1790s. Cheshire RO, DDX 104/15 and DDX 112/6,7; *The Universal British Directory* (5 vols., London, [1790–98], repr. King's Lynn , 1993), iv, 91. Samuel Pipe-Wolferstan noted in his diary for 15 March 1782, 'To court at 8 – morning mostly taken up with the King on prosecution of Salt against Tomkinson junior for an

Writ and return:
Hil 22 Geo III 1782

Writ 12 Feb [1782][LDT] to justices of assize, for return immediately; returned by Sir George Nares.[126]

Schedule that the indictment was presented at Staffs summer assizes, 16 Aug [1781].[127]

Indictment [1] assault on John Salt, wounding and ill treating him, at the parish of Eccleshall 28 March [1780], and violently and unlawfully taking two parchment writings, his property; [2] common assault. [*Top of indictment*]: po se.[128] [*Verso*]: John Salt, Thomas Smallwood, Thomas Hart. A true bill.

Rules and process:
Hil [12 Feb 1782]: venire facias juratores; rule for a special jury at instance of the defdt (Davenport). ST: leave to imparl, pleads not guilty. ST 26 Feb 1782: notice of trial for defdt (Midgley). Staffs Lent assizes

assault from King's Bench on certiorari...' SRO D1527. Tomkinson is identified as an attorney in the original depositions at Stafford summer assizes 1781. Lloyd Kenyon, chief justice of King's Bench 1788–1802, was reported to have articled in the 1740s with an attorney Tomkinson of Nantwich, probably the father: *ODNB*, 'Lloyd Kenyon'.

[126] Sir George Nares, justice of common pleas 1771–86.

[127] Henry Tomkinson of Nantwich gentleman entered into a recognizance to appear to answer the indictment at the assizes, with sureties Thomas Wilenhall and the Reverend Lancaster Wilenhall, before James Tomkinson and E. Tomkinson, 11 April 1781. Thomas Smallwood of Berkswich, yeoman, was bound to give evidence, and John Salt butcher of Houghton to prosecute, by T. Broughton, 17 and 15 April 1781. In his 5 April deposition before the magistrate, Sir Thomas Broughton bart., Salt swore that he met Tomkinson, an attorney, to receive £500 for Salt's interest in a lease under John Crewe; Tomkinson was Crewe's agent, and Salt also gave Tomkinson £100 for a tenement he had bought from Crewe. He paid Tomkinson £10 for his trouble. An hour later in conversation Salt told one Major Dean that there were no incumbrances on the lease sold by Salt, as Dean suggested. Tomkinson flew into a passion, pulled Salt into a chair, and after a struggle seized the documents back from the weak and infirm Salt. Smallwood's deposition of 11 April added that Tomkinson had damned Salt as a rogue and swore he would take the documents back, seized them from his pocket, and swore he would never have them again, although Salt begged him to return them. ASSI 5/101/7 Staffs Summer 1781.

[128] *ponit se* ... ('puts himself on the country'), a plea of not guilty.

1782: guilty.[129] Ea [17 April 1782]: rule nisi for judgment. ST: postea and judgment against Tompkinson, for the King; dismission of record, convicted. ST [25 April 1782]: rule nisi for dispensing with the personal appearance of the defdt on understanding that his clerk in court pay such fine as might be imposed for the assault of which he is convicted; one of the KB justices to wait on Nares for his report (Cowper). ST [2 May 1782]: personal appearance of defdt dispensed with; fined 6s 8d and to pay costs of prosn (Howorth for prosr, Bearcroft for defdt). Trin [19 June 1782]: recognizances respited. Hil [6 Feb 1783]: recognizances respited (side bar).[130] Hil [9 Feb 1784]: recognizances respited.

Affidavit for prosecution, to increase costs:

Ea 24 Geo III 1783

[1] Affdt of John Salt butcher of Haughton, Charles Simpson of Lichfield, attorney for John Salt, and Richard Bell, writing clerk to Charles Simpson of Lichfield, sworn before William Cooper at Lichfield 2 Aug 1782. [*Verso*]: '36. The King v. Tomkinson. Affidt to incr. costs. Babor & Browne.'

[John Salt]: That he has undergone considerable expense in this prosecution. He paid 2s for the original information and warrant, 1s to a justice's clerk for endorsing the information and two guineas to Phillip Seckerson for two journeys from Lichfield to Nantwich (Ches). He went to Stafford with two other witnesses to prefer an indictment at the assizes against the defendant for the assault, paying the clerk 6s 8d for preparing the indictment. He paid 1s 6d to the cryer for swearing three witnesses, 1s 6d to the bailiff, and two guineas for himself and his witnesses Thomas Smallwood and Thomas Smart.

[Charles Simpson]: That he attended the Staffordshire assizes 16 miles from Lichfield and paid house expenses of 12s. He made preparations for trial and several times travelled to see the prosecutor and his witnesses and to draw the indictment and direct the prosecution, which

---

[129] The KB 28/320 Hil roll 20 entry names the jurors as John Marsh esq of Lower Penn, Thomas Fowler esq of Penford, Sir Edensor Heathcote esq of Longton, William Pigott esq of Bolton, Josiah Flavell esq of Harlaston, William Inge esq of Thorpe, Egerton Alcock gentleman of Abbot's Bromley, all of whom were on the panel. The rest of those called did not appear, forcing the sheriff to make up the jury with talesmen, bystanders in the court, at the request of James Wallace, the attorney general. The talesmen were John Wetton, Edward Dilkes, John Turner, Brian Ward, and William Preston.

[130] There is a pencilled ms addition, '200' next to this and the following rule.

was removed by the defendant into King's Bench for trial at assizes before a special jury. He went three miles to Armitage to see an award to be introduced into the defence as instruction for drawing a brief for the prosecutor. He drew the brief and made two copies containing nine brief sheets. He caused notice to be drawn, and served a subpoena on four witnesses to compel them to give evidence. He attended the assizes on behalf of the prosecution and gave to counsellor Howorth, with his brief for the prosecutor, five guineas and a retainer of one guinea, and to his clerk 2s 5d. To counsellor Lane, with his brief, he gave three guineas as well as 2s 6d to his clerk. After the defendant was found guilty, he paid £2 9s 6d to the associate, £1 16s to the marshal, £1 19s to the cryer and 4s to the bailiff. The deponent was at the assizes for three days and while there he paid £1 7s 3d to Silvester at the Swan in Stafford for house expenses.

[Richard Bell]: That by order of Simpson and before the assizes, he served Thomas Smallwood of Baswich near Stafford, Isaac Hammersley of Haughton, and Francis Lees of Stafford, giving each 1s with a ticket of subpoena. He went over 40 miles to Nantwich (Ches) to deliver a notice to the defendant to produce the deeds and writings mentioned in the trial. The trip took two days and cost 8s for horsehire and 10s for traveling expenses.

[John Salt]: That Thomas Smallwood, Isaac Hammersley, Francis Lees, Thomas Hammersley, Thomas Hart, Mary Hubbald, John Lees of Haughton, Joseph Hodson and Ann Hodson attended the assizes as witnesses for the deponent. He paid William Cooper innholder at Stafford 36s for entertaining these deponents and the witnesses. He paid three guineas to Thomas Smallwood and other witnesses for their attendance and loss of time.

Sources: ASSI 4/6 Staffs Lent 1782. IND 1/6662 Hil 22 Geo III. KB 1/23 Ea 24 Geo III no.1. KB 11/52 Hil 22 Geo III 1782 #24. KB 15/4 Hil 22 Geo III. KB 15/16 Hil 22 Geo III. KB 21/43 Hil, Ea, Trin 22 Geo III, Hil 23 Geo III, Hil 24 Geo III. KB 28/320 roll 20. KB 29/441 Hil 22 Geo III. SRO, D1527/7, 15 March 1782.

F.20 Certiorari on an indictment from quarter sessions, by prosecutor (28 Nov 1782)

Defendants: Benjamin Bratt alias Brett, maltster; William Smart, baker; Isaac Collins, tailor; all of West Bromwich.

Writ and return:
Hil 23 Geo III 1783

Writ 28 Nov [1782][LDT] to be returned by [23 Jan 1783, FDT Hil]; returned by J. Dickenson.

Schedule 10 Oct 1782: record of process until plea, at Staffs Mich quarter sessions [1782].

Indictment [1] for violent assault (with sticks, fists and feet) at West Bromwich 20 Sept [1782] on William Stringer who was beaten on the ground, lost £5 10s 8d from his pocket, and made incapable of work; [2] common assault. [*Verso*]: Stringer, Isaac Pugh, Charles Danks. A true bill.

Rules and process:
Hil [1783]: summons, appear, pray a day to answer, given leave to imparl. Ea [1783]: plead not guilty; venire facias juratores. Trin 23 July 1783: notice of trial for the King (Barlow). Summer 1783 Staffs assizes: by consent, defdts found guilty, prosr agreeing not to call upon them to receive judgment and to discontinue the action at law brought against the defdts, without costs.

Sources: ASSI 4/6 Summer 1783. IND 1/6662 Hil, Ea 23 Geo III.[131] KB 11/52 Hil 23 Geo III 1783 #10. KB 15/4 Hil, Ea 23 Geo III. KB 15/16 Trin 23 Geo III. KB 29/442, Hil, Ea 23 Geo III.

F.21 Certiorari on an indictment from quarter sessions, by defendants (12 Feb 1784)

Defendants: John Smith and Thomas Blore, both labourers of Blore; Thomas Harrison, James Wardle, and Thomas Allcock, all labourers of Waterfall.

Writ and return:
Ea 24 Geo III 1784

Writ 12 Feb [1784][LDT], for return by [26 April 1784, FDT Ea]; returned by John Williamson.

Schedule by T. Fernyhough 15 Jan [1784] that the indictment was presented at Staffs Ep quarter sessions.

Indictment for conspiracy to charge the parish of Ipstones with the maintenance of the pauper Hardy family, 1 Nov 1783, who were moved and left in Ipstones. [*Verso*]: George Lees, James Hardy. A true bill.

---

[131] Reference given to 'Ro: 22.'

Rules and process:
Ea [1784]: leave to imparl. Trin [1784]: plead not guilty; venire facias juratores. ST 23 June 1784: notice of trial for defdts (Midgley). Hil [29 Jan 1785]: recognizances respited (side bar). Ea [7 May 1785]: recognizances discharged (side bar).

Sources: IND 1/6662 Trin 24 Geo III.[132] KB 11/53 Ea 24 Geo III #9. KB 15/4 Ea 24 Geo III. KB 15/16 Trin 24 Geo III. KB 21/43 Hil, Ea 25 Geo III. KB 28/330 Trin 24 Geo III ro. 28. KB 29/443 Ea, Trin 24 Geo III.

F.22 Certiorari for outlawry on an indictment from assizes, by prosecutor (16 June 1789)

Defendants: Edward Merry, labourer of Tatenhill. [*Also indicted, but not removed on certiorari*: Michael Woolley and William Hollis, labourers; Joseph Geary, baker; all of Tatenhill, *all tried and acquitted at Lent assizes*.[133]]

Writ and return:
Trin 29 Geo III 1789

Writ 16 June [1789] to justices of oyer and terminer and general gaol delivery, for return immediately; returned by John Heath.[134]
  Schedule that the indictment was presented at Staffs Lent assizes 26 March [1789].
  Indictment [1] for assault and affray in Barton Ward after 10 June 1776,[135] that is on 10 Jan [1789] on John Kent, of Sherrolt Lodge, while in the execution of his office as assistant to George Venables Lord Vernon, keeper of Barton Ward, an extraparochial place in Needwood Forest, while armed with guns and staffs with intent to kill the fallow deer; [2] [*'Chase' instead of 'Forest'*]; [3] armed assault while in execution of his

---

[132] 'Ro: 28', a reference to membrane 28 of the Crown Roll (KB 28), which records the process only to the plea of not guilty.

[133] Although the first controllment roll entry names all four : KB 29/448 Trin 29 Geo III, entry #13.

[134] Justice of common pleas 1780–1816. Although both KB 11 and KB 21 give 16 June, an entry in the assize process book states 'certiorari into KB allowed 6 July 1789'. ASSI 4/22 p. 289.

[135] 16 Geo III, c.30 s.9 (1776) made attacks on keepers and their servants a felony punishable by transportation to America for seven years. Compare an earlier case, F.10, for details of the procedure in outlawry. Sherrolt Lodge appears as Shirrall Lodge on Yates's 1775 map.

office in the extraparochial Chase with intent to kill the fallow deer; [4] armed assault and affray and assault on Philip Turner, keeper of Barton Ward in Needwood Forest; [5] [*'Chase' instead of 'Forest'*]; [6] armed assault on Philip Turner [*etc*] in Needwood Chase, an extraparochial place.[136] [*Verso*]: John Kent, William Morris, Philip Turner, Benjamin Lynn. A true bill.

Rules and process:
Trin [16 June 1789]: rule for a certiorari for the purpose of proceeding to outlawry (Abbot); entry of a capias. Hil 23 Jan [1790]: capias cum proclamatione and exigent, both returnable [3 Nov 1790]. Mich [1790]: entry of outlawry.

Sources: IND 1/6663 Trin 29 Geo III. KB 11/55 Trin 29 Geo III 1789 #13. KB 21/45 Trin 29 Geo III p. 103. KB 29/448 Trin 29 Geo III. KB 29/449 Hil 30 Geo III; KB 29/450 Mich 31 Geo III.

F.23 Certiorari on an indictment from assizes, by defendant (12 Feb 1790)[137]

Defendant: John Gough, esquire of Handsworth.

Writ and return:
Ea 30 Geo III 1790

Writ 12 Feb [1790][LDT] to the justices of oyer and terminer and assize, for return by [19 April 1790, FDT Ea]; [*verso*]: returned by Sir Richard Perryn, knight.[138]
    Schedule that the indictment was presented and found a true bill at Staffs summer assizes 13 Aug [1789].
    Indictment [1] erected a wall near his house, 400 yards long, and thereby narrowing and obstructing the highway, between Walsall and Birmingham, from 1 Jan [1779] until the assizes; [2] stopped up and enclosed a common footpath from the Hamsted Bridge to Perry Bridge highway towards the parish church of Handsworth; [3] on a lane from Walsall through Perry Barr to Birmingham, erected on this King's highway a wall 30 yards long. [*Verso*]: A true bill. Sworn: Benjamin Dawes, Thomas Simcox, Solomon Smith.

---

[136] The indictment measures approximately two feet by three feet.
[137] IND 1/6663 Ea 30 Geo III 1790 incorrectly describes this case as an information quo warranto.
[138] A baron of exchequer, 1776–1799.

Rules and process:
Ea [1790]: summons; appears; prays a day to answer; leave to imparl. Trin [1790]: pleads not guilty. ST [11 June 1790]: motion for a special jury at the instance of defdt (Caldecott); venire facias juratores. ST [23 June 1790]: that six or more jurors be mutually consented; or by default of such consent, by the sheriff. Premises to be viewed by them at noon on 16 July. Expenses to be borne mutually. John Partridge farmer of Oxolt [Oncott] in the parish of Handsworth (for the King) and John Bennett carpenter of Great Barr (for the defdt) to attend to direct jurors; no evidence on either side to be given to jurors at the view. Jurors to meet 11am 16 July at the Sun Dial, Great Barr, the house of William Wright (Caldecott). ST 24 June 1790: notice of trial for defdt (Dealtry and Barlow). Summer assizes 1790: not guilty on counts one and two, guilty of the last. Hil [11 Feb 1791]: recognizances respited. Ea [24 May 1791]: personal appearance of convicted defdt dispensed with as Barlow undertakes to pay fine (Bower). Trin [1 July 1791]: defdt having been convicted, on reading the rule made [24 May] and affdts [1 to 5] and on hearing counsel on both sides, defdt fined 6s 8d, paid (Lane for prosr, Bower for defdt). ST [12 July 1791] recognizance discharged. ST: dismission of record for John Gough.

Affidavits for defence, for a view:[139]

Trin 31 Geo III 1790

[1] Affdt of John Gough esquire, and defendant, of Perry Barr Handsworth, sworn before Thomas Butler at Perry Barr 16 Nov 1790. ITKB 'Between the King on the prosecution of Thomas Lane Clerk against John Gough Esquire For pretended incroachments and nuisances.'

That at the summer assizes 1789 held at Stafford a bill of indictment was preferred and found against the deponent by the prosecutor Thomas Lane charging him with continuing his park wall in Perry Barr for the length of 400 yards, built by a person unknown to the jurors. It was alleged to have narrowed the roads and diverted a footway. He was also charged with erecting a wall of 30 yards by a lane near his dwelling house, thereby narrowing the same lane. To have a view of the wall and lane and to try the matter by special jury, the deponent

---

[139] All the affidavits are captioned, 'In the King's Bench. Between the King on the prosecution of Thomas Lane Clerk against John Gough Esquire For pretended incroachments and nuisances.' See also case A.24 affdt [1].

removed the indictment by certiorari into this court and the matter was tried at the last Staffordshire assizes. The jury acquitted him of the first two charges, but found against him on the last charge of erecting the 30-yard wall, on the evidence of Solomon Smith, the prosecutor's clerk. The wall which the jury found against the deponent is in fact part of a wall of 220 yards erected by him. The wall is a half mile from the deponent's house, not near it as the jury found. The deponent, having erected a wall of 30 yards by the side of the road near his dwelling house, thought this was the wall to which the prosecution referred. The deponent instructed his attorney to conduct the defence with respect to the 30-yard wall, which was not the wall charged in the indictment. The deponent improved the road, making it wider. William Bennett and other neighbours confirm this. They cannot tell the deponent where it has encroached, or where to take down any part of it or he would have removed it. He does not know of the 20-yard wall for which he stands convicted. He will take the wall down if he is shown where it is and has sent his attorney to Thomas Lane for this purpose.

[2] Affdt of Richard Gildart esquire of Norton and John Bracebridge Hawkesford esquire of Aldridge, sworn before Thomas Butler at Perry Barr 15 Nov 1790. ITKB 'Between the King on the prosecution of Thomas Lane Clerk against John Gough Esquire For pretended nuisances and encroachments.'

[Both]: That they were summoned by the sheriff of Staffordshire as special jurymen and viewers in this cause. They were shown two parts of Gough's park wall and a foot lane at Perry Barr. The first viewing, relating to the first indictment, was a wall of 400 yards which led from the public road along the private road to the defendant's house and mill. At trial it was shown to have been erected 38 years ago. The second place relating to the second charge was a foot road on Gough's private land. The last place shown related to the third charge and was a 30-yard wall extending from the park gates to his garden wall. The deponents believe these three places were the only matters on the indictment. There was evidence led at trial regarding the first charge and Gough was acquitted. Evidence was led on the second charge that the wall in question was built by Gough's father 40 years ago. The evidence was contradicted by the prosecutor's witness and the defendant was acquitted. On the third charge, the only evidence given was by Solomon Smith who said Gough had completely enclosed part of a lane 20 yards long. Since the evidence was uncontradicted, the jury found against John Gough. This wall was not one of the three places shown to the deponents.

[3] Affdt of Thomas Butler gentleman of Sutton Coldfield (Warws), sworn before George Hollington Barker at Sutton Coldfield (Warws) 16 Nov 1790. ITKB 'Between the King on the prosecution of Thomas Lane Clerk against John Gough Esquire For pretended incroachments and nuisances.'

That the deponent is the attorney for John Gough and knows Perry Barr. At the last Staffordshire assizes, prior to the trial, the deponent obtained a rule for a view and a special jury for trial. John Bracebridge Hawkesford esquire and Richard Gildart esquire who later served as two jurymen viewed the wall before the trial. As the showers appeared ignorant and illiterate the two attorneys present volunteered to be the showers. For the first charge on the indictment, the new showers showed the viewers three places. [*Substantiates account in affdt [2] of the places that were the subject of the three charges on the indictment.*] The deponent was unprepared to deal with any but those three walls or roads during the trial. He was surprised therefore when Solomon Smith brought evidence of a road built by the defendant in 1787 a half mile from his house. He told the court that the viewers had not seen this wall or road. The judge, after conferring with counsel, concluded that there had been a view and perhaps some of the jury had seen it, although no jurors were asked. As the deponent could not contest Solomon Smith's evidence, this pretended substituted charge was found against the defendant. [*Substantiates affdt [1] to the effect that Bennett and neighbours believe the new road is an improvement for the public.*] The deponent informed Lane that there was no encroachment of the wall and if such encroachment could be found, the defendant would take it down. Lane said the defendant had to obey the law. The prosecution arose from mere resentment.

[4] Affdt of William Bennett carpenter and builder, and John Reeves workman, both of Great Barr near Perry Barr, sworn before Edward Sadler at Birmingham (Warws) 4 Nov 1790. ITKB 'Between the King on the prosecution of Thomas Lane Clerk against John Gough Esquire by an indictment for pretended nuisances.' [*John Reeves signed with a mark.*]

[William Bennett]: That he erected the wall and road in question for Gough in the summer of 1787. [*Substantiates account in affdt [2] as to the length of the road and the narrowness of the old road.*] When he built the wall, the deponent left some of Gough's land exposed to be used to widen the road. In one section, to make the wall straight, he made the wall enclose four feet of ditch; the wall did not interfere with the road. In late 1787 these four feet were knocked down at night, letting Gough's deer out of the park. Lane later demolished these houses. He later rebuilt the wall, narrowing the wall by two feet from what Gough had built. At the last Staffordshire assizes the deponent was requested by Gough to view the wall to see if it encroached on the road; Gough told him he would tear it down if it did. The deponent concluded the road was wider after the wall was built. The prosecution is brought with malice only.

[John Reeves]: That he was a workman for William Bennett in constructing the wall in question. The wall stands no further than two feet from the middle of the hedge in any place. [*Supports the assertion of Bennett, above, that the road was improved and that the action is brought with malice*].

[5] Affdt of Charles Lebon miller, William Standley wiredrawer, and Thomas Wildig wiredrawer, all of Perry Barr Handsworth, sworn before Thomas Butler at Perry Barr 5 Dec 1790. ITKB 'Between the King on the prosecution of Thomas Lane Clerk against John Gough Esquire For pretended incroachments and nuisances.' [*Standley and Wildig signed with their marks.*]

[All]: That they have lived for over 30 years near the park wall and road in Perry Barr. In 1787 Gough cut down his hedge fence and built a brick wall of 220 yards by the side of the lane or road and that is all the wall he built. Before the wall was built the hedge was very crooked and the lane near it was so narrow that wagons and carts sometimes traveled on the bank of the hedge. Now the lane is much wider and is a benefit to all people in the community. The prosecution of Gough was prompted by malice alone.

Sources: ASSI 4/7 summer 1790. IND 1/6663 Ea, Trin 30 Geo III, Trin 31 Geo III. KB 1/27 Trin 31 Geo III. KB 11/56 Ea 30 Geo III 1790 #3. KB 15/5 Ea, Trin 30 Geo III. KB 15/16 Trin 30 Geo III. KB 21/45 Trin 30 Geo III, pp. 303, 321, 401, 434, 470, 487. KB 29/449 Ea, Trin 30 Geo III.

F.24 Certiorari on an indictment from quarter sessions, by prosecutor (12 Feb 1796)

Defendant: Joseph Goodwin, surgeon of Cheadle.

Writ and return:
Ea 36 Geo III 1796

Writ 12 Feb [1796][LDT] to be returned [11 April 1796, FDT Ea]; returned by John Sparrow.
   Schedule by Hinckley[140] that the indictment was presented and found a true bill at Staffs Ep quarter sessions, 14 Jan [1796].

[140] No given name. Thomas Hinckley was clerk of the peace 1792–1804: Sir Edgar Stephens, *The Clerks of the Counties 1360–1960* (1961).

Indictment for assault 4 Jan [1796] on Daniel Davis. [*Verso*]: A true bill. Daniel Davis, Robert Hakin.

Rules and process:
Trin [1796]: appears; leave to imparl; pleads not guilty.

Sources: IND 1/6664 Trin 36 Geo III. KB 11/59 Ea 36 Geo III #23. KB 15/5 Trin 36 Geo III. KB 29/455 Ea, Trin 36 Geo III.

Section G

Like certiorari, habeas corpus was one of the so-called 'prerogative' writs, issued on extraordinary occasions rather than as part of the routine administration of the law. A prisoner could not directly obtain certiorari,[1] but by using the writ of habeas corpus could raise in King's Bench the legality of his or her detention and be discharged or bailed if the court agreed. He or she was brought from the place of detention (in most cases Stafford gaol) up to London and into Westminster Hall, where the court sat, or to the judge's chambers, if the writ had issued between law terms (see below). When the writ issued, the court might order certiorari as well, to bring before it the warrants and other documents that had been used to commit the prisoner to gaol in the first instance (case G.7).[2]

For centuries habeas corpus was used by the state to compel defendants to appear in its courts, and it continued to be used to move prisoners in one gaol to that of another county when they became crown witnesses there. But by the eighteenth century habeas corpus had evolved into the celebrated shield of civil liberties at common law.[3] Its fame was not diminished by the fact that parliament frequently suspended its operation in the face of revolutionary or democratic agitation, allowing the arrest and detention of suspects without trial. Blackstone's praise was much quoted:

> the great and efficacious writ, in all manner of illegal confinement, is that of *habeas corpus ad subjudiciendum*: directed to the person detaining another, and commanding him to produce the body of the prisoner, with the day and cause of his caption and detention, *ad faciendum, subjudiciendum, et recipiendum*, to do, submit to, and receive

---

[1]   Chitty, i, 118–9.

[2]   See below, text at n.18. A prosecutor could similarly use habeas corpus with certiorari: Gude, i, 143.

[3]   William F. Duker, *A Constitutional History of Habeas Corpus* (Westport, CT and London, 1980), ch.1; R. J. Sharpe, *The Law of Habeas Corpus* (2nd ed., Oxford, 1989); Paul D. Halliday, *Habeas Corpus: From England to Empire* (Cambridge, MA and London, 2010).

whatsoever the judge or court awarding such writ shall consider in that behalf.'[4]

By the eighteenth century, of the several varieties of the writ described by Blackstone, three were important in criminal procedure.[5] By far the most important was the writ *habeas corpus subjudiciendum et recipiendum*, and all the eight cases in this section originated with this version of the writ. Exchequer and common pleas had a limited power to issue habeas corpus, but after 16 Charles I, c.10 (1640) common pleas had equal power with King's Bench with respect to the common law writ.[6]

The Habeas Corpus Act of 1679 (31 Charles II, c.2) remedied a variety of shortcomings in the writ, among them making it possible in criminal cases to obtain the writ between the terms in which the courts were sitting by applying to a judge in chambers; prohibiting the transferring of those in custody out of the kingdom in order to evade the writ; and providing that the person to whom the writ was directed had to bring the prisoner before the court by a near date. The limits were within three days if the distance was 20 miles or less; ten days if more than 20 and up to 100 miles; and 20 days if more than 100 miles. (All the prisoners in Staffordshire were brought before the judges in less than ten days, with apparently one complicated exception, case G.4). The Act also provided that payment to the gaoler should be 12 pence a mile, to be paid by the prisoner's representative, if the prisoner was remanded (as in case G.3). The practice was to pay the gaoler his fee for bringing the

---

[4] Blackstone, iii , 131. Of the quoted words, *ad faciendum* ('to do') do not appear in the form of the writ found in the original records for the cases in this volume, which agree with the seventeenth- and eighteenth-century versions given in Holdsworth, i, 660, and those in Chitty, iv, 123–4; Hands, 520; and Gude, ii, 225–35. Blackstone appears to be summarizing the main clauses of all the main forms of the writ, or perhaps the form used in civil cases that included the *ad faciendum* clause, but was commonly called *habeas corpus cum causâ*, as his main discussion of the writ (130–38) occurs in the third volume of the *Commentaries*, which deals with civil rather than criminal law. See William Henry Watson, *A Practical Treatise on the Office of Sheriff* (2nd ed., 1848), 235–6, and the next note.

[5] *Habeas corpus subjiciendum et recipiendum, habeas corpus ad deliberandum et recipiendum,* and *habeas corpus cum causa*. Of the latter two, the first lay 'to remove a prisoner to take his trial in the county where the offence was committed' and the second could be 'issued by the bail of a prisoner who has been taken upon a criminal accusation, in order to render him in their own discharge': Chitty, i, 132.

[6] Chitty, i, 125.

prisoner, and give a bond to pay the charge of taking him back, if he was remanded.[7] For misdemeanour charges, the judges were to remand, discharge, or bail the prisoner, if bailable, within three days of the return made to the writ; if the charge in the warrant of commitment was treason or felony, the Act provided that the prisoner had to be indicted the first day of the next term of King's Bench, or at the next assizes in the county where he or she was held.[8] However, it was said that the court could remand the prisoner, and bring him or her up from time to time, until they had determined whether to discharge or detain in prison. Once the writ was returned, counsel ordered it filed, and then argued the prisoner's case, alleging illegality in the commitment, and the prisoner's right to discharge or bail.[9]

The eight cases of habeas corpus in this volume illustrate two main uses of the writ. Seven applications were brought by prisoners being held for trial who sought bail: five at Stafford (G.3, G.4 twice, G.5, G.7), one at Lichfield (G.6), and two Leicester prisoners (G.2) , a case presented here because of its close connections with several others in this volume. The court usually required bail from the prisoner and from four sureties in felony cases, two sureties in misdemeanours. All but one of the applicants (G.3) were successful, and at least two (possibly four) of the bailed prisoners did not appear for trial and presumably escaped, although their recognizances and those of their sureties were forfeit (G.4, G.6, and possibly G.2 and G.7). In one case, that of Isaac Jones (G.4), two writs of habeas corpus resulting in two sets of recognizances to appear for trial led in the end to two defaults on failure to appear, an expensive course that nonetheless appears to have allowed the accused to escape his trial for uttering counterfeit coin. That crime was highly organized, and it is clear that Jones had London connections, and the resources to exploit legal process. Two other defendants (case G.2) also had important criminal connections in both Staffordshire and London. The crimes of which all eight men stood accused were stealing a quantity of woodscrews, receiving stolen lead, uttering counterfeit coin (two cases), maliciously killing a horse, and horsetheft.

[7] Gude, i, 278.
[8] In my copy of Hands (see General Introduction, note 98), a manuscript addition at p.71 adds, 'The provisions of this act apply chiefly to the cases of commitments for crimes *under* felony. But at common law, the judges of *this* court award writs of Ha. Cor. where Treason or felony is expressed in the warrant and where parties are improperly detained with any commitment at all.' Emphasis in original.
[9] Chitty, i, 128; Gude, i, 279.

Two other cases in this section illustrate the uses of the writ in domestic relations (see also case A.17). The writ (although not the Act[10]) applied to all persons unlawfully detained, not only prisoners in gaols, and it was used to test the detention of wives by husbands, young girls by presumed seducers, children by parents in separation cases. The last two uses are illustrated by cases G.1 and G.8. The first was an unsuccessful attempt by a prominent Lichfield musician to find a daughter whom he believed had been seduced by her uncle in London. The latter was a successful habeas corpus brought by Lord Valentia against his estranged wife for the return of their son to his custody, part of the entangled litigation that ended their marriage, in which the Viscountess attempted to keep her son by accusing his father of homosexual acts with the servants.

Obtaining habeas corpus
The procedure for obtaining the writ (and a few details of its form) differed according to whether the prisoner sought it in term time (when the court was sitting), or out of term time, from a judge in chambers. The court would order the writ in open court; the single judge issued a fiat for it. Six of the Staffordshire writs in this volume began with an order in court (cases G.1, G.4 (first writ), G.5, G.6, G.7, G.8). Two (G.3 and G.4 (second writ)) originated with a judge's fiat between terms.[11] Writs issued on a fiat are tested (dated) the last day of the preceding term. The judicial fiats appear to have been destroyed.[12] In the case of writs ordered by the court, the return (that is, the answer of the person to whom it was addressed, with or without the prisoner) was to Westminster Hall; if by a judicial fiat, the return was usually to the chief justice if in town, or 'if he be in the country at a place to which it is convenient to bring the prisoner.'[13] By the Act, if a prisoner had neglected

---

[10] Remedied by legislation in 1816, 56 Geo III, c.100. On this change, see Halliday, 246, and Hay, *The Judges and the People*.
[11] Case G.2 was an habeas corpus sent into Leicestershire, included here because of its connection with several other Staffordshire cases. See also the use of habeas corpus in cases B.13, C.6 to remove prisoners from Buckingham and London.
[12] *Reprint of Statutes, Rules and Schedules Governing the Disposal of Public Records by Destruction or Otherwise 1877–1913* (HMSO, 1914), 109. For the form of the fiat see Gude, ii, 219–22. For the differences in the form of the ensuing writ see Gude, ii, 225–35.
[13] Hands, 72, manuscript addition. However all the writs in this volume are for return immediately 'before us at Westminster'.

to ask for habeas corpus for two whole terms after being imprisoned, the application had to be made to the court in term time.

Probable cause had to be shown for the issue of the writ, and this was done by counsel on affidavit of the circumstances.[14] The two writs obtained between terms (G.3, and the second writ in G.4) lack affidavits, perhaps because they were destroyed with the fiats. Once probable cause was shown, the writ was a writ of right, and the court or the judge made the order or fiat for it to issue. The clerk in court then made out the habeas corpus, which the solicitor for the prisoner then delivered to the party to whom it was addressed, who had to make answer (the 'return') within the time specified by the Habeas Corpus Act, or face an attachment for contempt.[15] Once the prisoner appeared, he or she was remanded to prison, bailed, or discharged.[16] In applications for bail, it was necessary to give notice of the day when the prisoner was to appear, and the names of the persons proposed for bail given to the prosecutor and committing magistrate a reasonable time ahead, to allow them to contest the adequacy of bail.[17] An instance is case G.4.

In some cases a return could be made without the prisoner: if the charge was treason or felony in the warrant of commitment, or when the prisoner was being held for a civil cause or action. A return might also state that the supposed prisoner was not in fact being held (see case G.1). When the prisoner was brought to King's Bench by a gaoler, the return he made had to specify the date and cause of the original detention, and at the same time the committing magistrate usually returned

---

[14] Blackstone, iii, 132; Hands, 73; Gude, i, 274–5; Chitty, i, 123–4, 129. See also Chitty, i, 113 to the effect that on bail applications on a habeas corpus, the court required the depositions to see if there was just cause to discharge or bail, whether the commitment was properly drawn or not. They stated this as a general rule in a 'recent case': *R v Horner* (1783), Cald 295 and 1 Leach 270, 168 ER 270, in which it was stated, 'The practice of this Court is, and upon reference to the Officers of the Crown Office we find it to have been long established, that even where the commitment is regular, the Court will look into the depositions to see if there be a sufficient ground laid to detain the party in custody; and if there be not, they will bail him. So also, where the commitment is irregular, if it appear that a serious offence has been committed, they will not discharge or bail the prisoner without first looking into the depositions, to see whether there is sufficient evidence to detain him in custody.'

[15] Gude, i, 280. Examples of attachments for contempt in other matters appear in section H.

[16] Hands, 73–74; Chitty, i, 125.

[17] Hands, manuscript addition to 74; Gude, i, 277–8.

the original depositions on which he gaoled the prisoner, in response to a certiorari usually issued by the Crown Office with the habeas corpus.[18]

Orders and fiats for habeas corpus are not noted on the controlment rolls, KB 29. The orders are recorded in KB 21, but headed 'England' rather than 'Staffordshire'. The affidavits in KB 1 are similarly endorsed 'England', although often the county name is added also.[19] The writs with the returns attached are filed in KB 16.

CASES

G.1 Habeas corpus (24 April 1779)

Prisoner: Sarah Alcock,[20] spinster.

Writ and return:
Habeas corpus 26 April [1779] to Giles Panchen to bring the body of Sarah Alcock, spinster, said to be detained in his custody, before this court immediately on receipt of the writ, together with the day and cause of her taking and detainer by whatever name the said Sarah Alcock is called. By the court. Burrow. [*Verso*]: 'By rule of court.' [*Another hand*]: 'The within named Sarah Alcock spinster was not in my custody or power at the time of my receiving the within writ nor has she been in my custody or power at any time since nor do I know where the said Sarah Alcock was at the time of my receiving the said writ nor at any time since nor do I know where she now is the answer of [*signed*] Giles Panchen.' [*Another hand*]: 'Recd 29 April.'

Rules and process:
Ea [26 April 1779]: order for a writ of habeas corpus to Giles Panchen for the body of Sarah Alcock (Bearcroft).

Affidavits for applicant:

Ea 19 Geo III 1779

---

[18]   Chitty, i, 127; Gude, i, 275. See case G.7.
[19]   See for example the versos of the affidavits in cases G.4, G.5, G.7.
[20]   One of three daughters of John Alcock (1715-1806): 'John Alcock' in *ODNB* and *The New Grove Dictionary of Music and Musicians*, ed. Stanley Sadie (2nd ed, 29 vols, 2001).

[1] Affdt of John Alcock doctor of music of Lichfield, sworn before W. H. Ashhurst at his chambers in Serjeants' Inn 24 April 1779. [*Verso*]: '20 England. Dr John Alcock's Affidt in support of motion for an Ha Co agt Giles Panchen for Ha Co ad. subjc. for Sarah Alcock. Spr. Marshall. Grey's Inn.'

That in March 1779 he heard that his daughter, Sarah Alcock, had quitted the service of Miss Pocock, one of the sisters of Admiral Pocock, with whom Alcock lived as a companion or servant,[21] and was suspected to have been enticed or spirited away by Giles Panchen of Little Carter Lane, in the parish of St Mary Magdalen, Old Fish Street, City of London, Sarah's uncle. Knowing the infamous and abandoned character of Panchen the deponent came immediately to London, where he has searched unsuccessfully more than a fortnight for his daughter. He was informed and believes that his daughter is secreted and kept out of the way by Panchen contrary to her will. She cannot stir outside except in his company, and is often in want of the common necessities of life. Panchen refuses to tell the deponent anything of his daughter.

[2] Affdt of Sarah Stroud piece broker of Hollywell Street in St Clement Danes parish (Middx), sworn before W. H. Ashhurst at his chambers in Serjeants' Inn 24 April 1779. [*Verso*]: '20. Mrs Sarah Stroud's Affdt in support of motion for an Ha Co agt Giles Panchen. Marshall. Grey's Inn'.

That Sarah Alcock was a lodger in the deponent's house for four months in 1777, and that Panchen frequently visited Alcock there. The deponent has seen nothing of her since last October. In early April 1779 Panchen came to her house wanting lodgings for Sarah. She knew Panchen's infamous and abandoned character and that he was married. She refused, suspecting something bad was going forward between Panchen and Alcock. Panchen instructed the deponent to hold for him all letters addressed to Alcock. She believes Sarah Alcock is in the power and custody of Panchen.

Sources: KB 1/21 Ea 19 Geo III no. 2 bdl 20. KB 16/18/3 19 Geo III 1778/9. KB 21/42 Ea 19 Geo III [26 April 1779].

---

[21] Sir George Pocock (1706–92): *ODNB*.

G.2 Habeas corpus and bail (4 May 1782)

Prisoners and defendants: Charles Cox and John Sincox[22] alias Simcox.

Writ and return:
Habeas corpus 3 June [1782] to keeper of Leicester gaol, for return immediately. [*Verso*]: By rule of court. The execution of this writ appears in
the schedule hereto annexed. William Jordan.
  Schedule by William Jordan that Cox and Sincox were committed by
the Reverend William Clayton, clerk and JP for Leicestershire, 5 May
1782 on the sworn information of John Tongue of Gatacre, parish of
Claverley (Salop), on suspicion of stealing from the stable a black gelding, property of Samuel Tongue father of John, on Friday night or
Saturday morning 3–4 May. The horse was found by John in possession
of Cox and Sincox at the house of Richard Pooter, the Queen's Head
Inn, on Coleorton Moor, parish of Coleorton (Leics), at 9 pm on 4 May.

Rules and process:
Trin [13 June 1782]: Cox being brought into court in custody of the
keeper of Leicester gaol on habeas corpus, order that the writ and
return be filed, and the defdt having given a recognizance for his
appearance at the next assizes and gaol delivery for Leicestershire,
order that he be discharged out of custody (Mingay).[23] Like rule for
Sincox.

Affidavits for prisoners:

Trin 22 Geo II 1782

[1] Affdt of Thomas Wild maltster and farmer of Bilston Hall, sworn
before W. West[24] at Bilston 23 May 1782. ITKB 'The King agt Charles

---

[22] 'Sincocks' in some of the affidavits. Although the habeas corpus is to
     Leicester gaol, the case is included here because it involves Staffordshire
     men, who are parties in subsequent proceedings: see cases A.21, H.1, H.2.
[23] [*In margin*]: 'England. Leicestershire. The King agt Charles Cox. 100 50 50 50
     50.' These are the sums, pounds sterling, for the recognizance and sureties
     for each defendant: see affidavit [3].
[24] In affidavit [1] of the ensuing contempt case H.1 he is identified as 'J. West
     or W. West'; the signature here could be either. He is identified as William
     West solicitor of Wolverhampton in the writ of attachment and affidavit [1]
     in that case.

Cox and John Sincocks on the prosecution of Samuel Tongue for felony'. [*Verso*]: '23 In the King's Bench. The King agt. Samuel Cox and John Sincocks on the prosecution of Samuel Tongue for felony. Wilds affidavit. Bail'd on ha cor 100, 50, 50, 50, 50 each West Solicr fo: 8'.

That the deponent met Charles Cox and John Sincox[25] 2 May at the Welch Harp Inn, Stonnall, where they discussed business; he is intimately acquainted with them. They saw two men who later called themselves William and John Jones who said they were taking their string of seven or eight horses bought in Yorkshire to sell in Birmingham. Cox agreed with William Jones to buy a black gelding for £12 and half a crown, and paid the money in the deponent's presence. Cox and Sincox agreed to accompany the deponent to Stafford on condition he agreed to go with them into Leicestershire to purchase a lot of sheep, the deponent to have what part of them he chose. They stopped at the Queen's Head Inn in Coleorton Moor (Leics) where the gelding was seized by the prosecutor's son who said the horse was stolen from Gatacre (Salop) near Wolverhampton, and that it was the property of his father. Cox and Sincox were carried before the Reverend Mr Clayton, a JP of Leicestershire, where the deponent gave evidence of the horse being bought. Clayton said he would release them go if they gave the horse to the prosecutor's son, which Cox and Sincox refused to do unless their money was returned. The justice then threatened to deliver the horse to Tongue's son, and to commit them to prison on suspicion until they could find bail, unless they agreed, which they again refused to do. He immediately committed them solely on the evidence of Tongue's son, and ordered the horse delivered to him.

[2] Affdt of James Mason hostler of the Welch Harp Inn, Stonnall, sworn before W. West at Walsall 24 May 1782. ITKB 'The King agt Charles [sic] Cox and John Sincocks on the prosecution of Samuel Tongue for felony'. [*Verso*]: 'In the King's Bench. The King agt Samuel Cox & John Sincocks on the prosecution of Samuel Tongue for felony. Mason's affidavit. West Solicr fo:4'.

That two men who said they were William and John Jones stopped at the Inn 2 May 1782 on their way to Birmingham with a string of horses, to refresh themselves and the horses. Several persons at the Inn, including Charles Cox and John Sincox, whom the deponent knew perfectly well by their frequently calling at the inn, looked at the horses which were for sale. [*Similar evidence to that in affdt [1] of sale of gelding to Cox.*] Jones gave the deponent half a crown for cleaning and taking care of the

---

[25] 'Sincocks' in the original.

horses. The defendants and a friend left an hour and a half after the two Joneses.

[3] Affdt of William Mason yeoman of Bilston, sworn before W. West at Wolverhampton 8 June 1782. ITKB 'The King agt Charles Cox and John Sincocks on the prosecution of Samuel Tongue for felony'.

That on 5 June the deponent served a copy of the [*annexed*] notice on Samuel Tongue, prosecutor at Gatacre near Wolverhampton in the parish of Claverley Home [*sic*] and 6 June he served a copy of the notice on the Reverend William Clayton, JP for Leicestershire, delivering it at his house.

[*Annexed*]: Notice 5 June 1782 by W. West, Wolverhampton, defendants' solicitor, that William Harding of Bilston farmer, Thomas Smith of Sedgley farmer, William King of Ettingshall[26] Lane in the parish of Wolverhampton farmer, and Charles Stone of No.1 Castleyard, parish of St Andrew Holborn (London) painter, will become bail 12 June 1782 in King's Bench in a writ of habeas corpus in this prosecution for the personal appearance of Cox and Sincocks at the next general gaol delivery for Leicestershire. 'To the Rev Mr Clayton and also to Samuel Tongue.'

Sources: KB 1/23/1 Trin 22 Geo III, bdl 23. KB 16/19/3 23 Geo III 1782/3. KB 21/43 Thurs next after the quindene of Holy Trin 22 Geo III [13 June 1782].

G.3 Habeas corpus, bail refused (28 Nov 1787)

Prisoner and defendant: William Jordan, labourer of Walsall.

Writ and return:
Habeas corpus Mich 28 Nov [1787][LDT] to the sheriff of Staffordshire and keeper of the county gaol, to be returned immediately on receipt. Templer. [*Verso*]: Return of Thomas Whieldon esquire, sheriff, that before receipt of the writ William Jordan, whose body he has ready as commanded, was taken and detained in prison 14 Oct [1787] on a warrant of Willis Kempson esquire, JP for Staffordshire.

Warrant of committal: by Willis Kempson 9 Oct 1787 at Bilston to the constables of Bilston and the keeper of the county gaol, for William Jordan, labourer of Wolverhampton, brought before him on a warrant of Sir Alexander Thompson, baron of exchequer and judge of assize at

---

26   Given here as 'Ettensal'.

the last Staffordshire assizes, dated 11 Aug 1787, reciting that it was certified to him by Meredith Price esquire, clerk of assize for the Oxford circuit, that a bill of indictment was presented and found a true bill against Joseph Savage for theft from a building of 200 pounds weight of lead value £1 14s, property of Richard Wilkes, and against William Jordan for receiving 100 pounds weight value 17s, and William Jordan not appearing, the said warrant therefore requiring Jordan to be arrested and brought before him at the assizes or before a justice near where he was taken.

Rules and process:
Hil [10 Feb 1788]: defdt being brought into court in custody of the sheriff of Staffordshire and the keeper of Stafford gaol on habeas corpus, order that the writ and return be filed; defdt appears by the said return to be charged with a warrant from Willis Kempson JP of Staffordshire [*recites the terms of the warrant*]. On hearing counsel on both sides, ordered that the defdt be remanded to the custody of the said sheriff and keeper until discharged by course of law (Mingay for prosr, Manley for defdt).[27]

Affidavit for prosecution:

Hil 28 Geo III 1788

[1] Affdt of Richard Wilkes gentleman of Bescott Hall parish of Walsall, prosecutor, Samuel Hanson japanner and late constable of Bilston, and

---

[27] William Jordan labourer of Wolverhampton was charged on two indictments for receiving 200 pounds of lead value £1 14s and 400 pounds value £3 8s stolen by James Westwood, a collier, and Edward Westwood, William Westwood, Joseph Savage and Richard Clark, all indicted as labourers of Walsall, from Richard Wilkes, ironmonger. At summer assizes 1787 James and Edward Westwood were found guilty and sentenced to seven years transportation; Clark was acquitted; William Westwood, Joseph Savage and William Jordan were at large. William Jordan and William Westwood were both tried at Lent assizes 1788 and convicted. Jordan was sentenced to transportation for 14 years, Westwood for seven years. A petition on Jordan's behalf resulted in a report from Adair, the recorder of London, in July 1788, that the judge considered the verdict proved satisfactorily, and said that Jordan had been captured only with difficulty, and that he tried both to pay a witness to lie and to pay for his own bail through one of his defence witnesses in order to escape. But because there was some doubt about the construction of the statutes, he recommended transportation for seven years.

Jonathon Hartshorn victualler and late headborough of Bilston, sworn before John Willim at Bilston 5 Feb 1788. ITKB 'The King against William Jordan: On the prosecution of Richard Wilkes for feloniously buying and receiving goods knowing them to be stolen.'

[Richard Wilkes]: That last April a large quantity of lead was cut and stolen from the roof of the deponent's house at Bescott. He obtained a warrant from Willis Kempson esquire JP against James Westwood, Edward Westwood and others and against William Jordan for receiving some of the lead. The Westwoods were arrested, committed to gaol and convicted at the last Staffordshire summer assizes. William Jordan fled; he was indicted at the same assizes, but did not appear for trial. This deponent has not had notice of the persons proposed as bail for Jordan's appearance at the next assizes.

[All]: That they are informed and believe that Jordan has considerable real and personal estates at Bilston; if he is admitted to bail they believe he will dispose of them and quit the kingdom and not take his trial.

[Jonathan Hartshorn]: That he arrested Jordan at Hagley (Worcs) 3 Oct 1787. With the assistance of one Walker, Jordan escaped from custody.

[Samuel Hanson and Jonathan Hartshorn]: That they afterwards pursued Jordan and retook him; he was committed for trial by Willis Kempson.

Sources: ASSI 2/25 Staffs summer 1787, Lent 1788. ASSI 5/107 Staffs summer 1787, ASSI 5/108 Staffs Lent 1788. HO 47/7/83, 12 July 1788. KB 1/25 Hil 28 Geo III no. 1 bdl 69. KB 16/20/2. KB 21/44 p. 507.

G.4 Habeas corpus and bail (28 April 1790)

Prisoner and defendant: Isaac Jones.

Writs and returns:
[*First writ*[28]]: 1 May [1790] [LDT], for return immediately, to the keeper of Stafford gaol or his deputy. [*Verso*]: return by Littleton Scott, keeper, no date: 'I do herby certify that before the coming of this writ to me to wit on ... [17 May 1790], Isaac Jones was taken and detained in my custody by virtue of a warrant under the hand and seal of John Daniell esquire one of his majesty's justices of the peace for the said county

---

[28]   This writ with returns, issued the last day of Trinity term, and returned at the beginning of Michaelmas term, was filed with the Easter term affidavits in KB 1, rather than with writs in KB 16.

which warrant is herunto annexed. And that the same is the day and excuse of the within named Isaac Jones being taken and detained in my custody, whose body I have ready at the place within written as I am within commanded.' [*Second verso*]: by Littleton Scott, 7 May 1790: 'And I do further certifie that since the coming to me of this writ I have also received another warrant of detainer against the said Isaac Jones under the hand and seal of the said justice dated the 1st day of May instant, a true copy whereof is also hereunto annexed.'

[*Annexed*]:

Copy by L. Scott, keeper, of warrant of J. Daniell 1 May 1790 to the keeper of Stafford gaol. [*Verso*]: '48 East 90 England Staff Ha Cor for Isaac Jones & Return. Bennett'.

To detain Isaac Jones, further charged by Elizabeth Orton with uttering to her a counterfeit half crown, and by Richard Wright for having in his possession at that time other counterfeit half crowns, until discharged by due course of law .

[*Annexed*]: L. Scott's copy of Daniell's warrant of 15 March 1790.

[*Second writ*]: 13 July [1791] [LTD], for return immediately, to the keeper of the common gaol or deputy. [*Verso*]: 'For the defendant. W. H. Ashhurst.' [*Another hand*]: 'The execution of this writ appears in the schedule hereunto annexed. The answer of Littleton Scott, Keeper of his Majesty's Gaol in and for the county of Stafford.' [*Another hand*]: 'To the gaol keeper of Stafford gaol. Please to observe that notice of bail is given for Wednesday the 23d day of Nov instant at eleven o'clock in the forenoon to justify in open court and you must then and there have the prisoner. Richard Polhill No. 10 Old North Street Red Lyon Square 16 Nov 1791.'

Schedule by Littleton Scott, that before he received the writ, Jones was in his custody under an order of court made at Stafford assizes 24 Aug [1791], that he was to remain in gaol until next assizes to take his trial on two indictments for uttering, unless he gave a recognizance and sureties of £40, £20, and £20 to appear at the next assizes and prosecute his traverses; recognizance only to be taken on proof of 14 days previous notice to the mint solicitor of the names and addresses of the sureties, it appearing to the court that Isaac Jones at the last assizes forfeited two recognizances by him and his sureties, which have been estreated into exchequer. The prisoner is therefore still in his custody.

Rules and process:

15 March 1790: arrested and committed to Stafford gaol. 15–16 April 1790: bill preferred at Staffordshire quarter sessions, which refuse bail. Ea [28 April 1790]: on reading affdt [1], order for writ of habeas corpus

to keeper of the common gaol, Stafford (Leycester).[29] ST 1 May 1790: writ issues. ST [7 May 1790]: Isaac Jones brought into court; writ to be filed; peremptory rule that prosr (the mint solicitor) show cause by [12 May] why the defdt should not be bailed for his personal appearance at next Stafford assizes, on notice of names of bail given to prosr; Jones remanded in custody of the keeper of Stafford gaol, to be brought up again 12 May (Silvester for prosr, Leycester for defdt). ST 8 May 1790: notice of the rule for bail is served on the prosr. ST [12 May 1790]: prosr files affdt to oppose bailsmen, but court grants bail on recognizances for Isaac Jones's appearance next Stafford assizes, Frederick English and William Welchman (bailsmen) to pay the keeper of Stafford gaol £1 11s 6d and Jones to be discharged; [*in margin*]: 80 40 40.[30] Stafford summer assizes 1790: Jones appears and is bailed further to appear at Lent assizes 1791. Lent assizes 1791: does not appear, recognizances estreated. [*Date unknown, but before or at summer assizes 1791, 24 Aug 1791*]: surrenders. Trin [13 July 1791, LDT]: second writ of habeas corpus tested.[31] Summer assizes 24 Aug 1791: bailed at assizes, but failed to give notice to the prosr and therefore committed again to the gaol until he gives bail at Lent assizes 1792, with proper notice to the prosr. Mich 9 Nov 1791: notice given to prosr of new bailsmen. ST [24 Nov 1791]: Isaac Jones is brought into court by keeper of Stafford gaol on the second habeas corpus; writ and return filed. On affdts [5] to [8], defdt ordered to give recognizance for his appearance next Stafford assizes and discharged from custody (Marryat); [*in margin*]: 80 40 40.[32]

Affidavits for prisoner:

Ea 30 Geo III 1790

[1] Affdt of William Jones, brother of the defendant, of Union Place Westminster (Middx), sworn before the court in court at Westminster Hall 1 May 1790. ITKB [*Verso*]: '28 East 90 England Staffords. In the Kings Bench. Afft for Ha Cor for Isaac Jones. The King agt Isaac Jones. On the prosecution of Elizabeth Orton for a Misdemeanour. Please to move that the Deft may be Allowed a Habeas Corpus to bring him into

[29] Although the affidavit is dated later.
[30] Recognizance of £80 with two sureties of £40 each.
[31] Because the second writ of habeas corpus was issued by judicial fiat, the return was not due until Michaelmas term, which began 7 Nov 1791.
[32] For this complicated case, the summary of King's Bench rules and process has been supplemented by the evidence in the affidavits and in other records cited in the source note.

court to be discharged and to put in Bail for his appearance to take his Trial at the next Assizes to be held at Staffs. Mr. Leicester. 1/2 Gn. H. Leycester. 1 May Ha Cor Houldston (by J. Williams) Attorney for the Defendant'.

That 15 March 1790 Isaac Jones, the defendant, was taken into custody and committed by J. Daniell JP to Stafford gaol as appears in the copy of commitment [*annexed*]. It is not specified in the commitment whether defendant is to take his trial for misdemeanours at the quarter sessions or at the assizes. On 16 April 1790 at Stafford quarter sessions, two propertied inhabitants of Stafford offered to become bail in a recognizance. The justices presiding, of whom the committing magistrate was one, refused to take bail, saying they had no power to do so. The deponent remains a close prisoner, his health impaired. No other proceedings have been launched. The deponent asked why no bail could be posted and the gaoler said he supposed it was because the defendant was to be tried at the next assizes, many months away, and advised the deponent to apply to have defendant moved up and bailed.

[*Annexed*]:

[*Verso*]: 'A Coppy of Joneses Warrant'.

Copy of warrant of committment 15 March 1790 by J. Daniel[33] to the constables of Longdon, especially to Henry Wright and John Hodson, and to the keeper of Stafford gaol. Wright and Hodson to deliver into custody Isaac Jones, charged this day by Elizabeth Orton of the parish of Longdon for tendering to her 14 March 1790 an imitation half crown, and also Isaac Jones charged with having concealed in the lining of his hat and about his person other counterfeit pieces to the amount of 5 guineas and 39 shillings, each separately wrapped in paper. To be kept in custody until delivered in due course.

[2] Affdt of John Penny gentleman of Rosoman's Street Clerkenwell (Middx), at No 10 Lincoln's Inn New Square (Middx), sworn before W. H. Ashhurst at Serjeants' Inn 11 May 1790. 'The King on the Prosecution of Elizabeth Orton against Isaac Jones.' [*Verso*]: '49 East 90 England Staff. Afft to admit Isaac Jones to Bail. The King agt Isaac Jones. Affidt of Service of Notice of Bail &c. 12 May. Bail'd to app at Ass. 80 – 40 – 40. Bennett'.

That 8 May 1790 he served Mr Vernon mint solicitor at 10 Lincoln's Inn New Square (Middx) the [*annexed*] rule and notice.

[*Annexed*]: Copy of rule of [7 May 1790], and notice 8 May 1790 by W. Bennet, solicitor for defdt Bull Head Court Newgate Street to Vernon, solicitor for prosr, that Frederick English weaver of No 5 Hand Court

---

[33] Spelled 'Daniell' in other depositions and copies of warrants.

New Street Bishopgate Street (London) and William Welchman
Staffordshirewarehouseman of No 10 Rose Street Covent Garden
Market (Middx) will appear as bail for defdt on the writ of habeas
corpus.

Affidavit for prosecution:

Ea 30 Geo III 1790

[3] Affdt of William Deavey clerk to Mr Vernon junior solicitor to the
mint, sworn before F. Buller at Serjeants' Inn Hall 12 May 1790. ITKB
'The King on the Prosecution of Elizabeth Orton Agt Isaac Jones.'
[*Verso*]: '50 East 90 England Staff Afft to oppose bailing Isaac Jones 12
May Bailed to app at Ass 80-40-40 Vernon Junr.' [*A second verso*]:
'Staffordshire The King vs Isaac Jones Affidavit to oppose Bail. Mr
Silvester to oppose Bail on the within Affidavit. Mr Silvester – Vernon
Junr Solr to the Mint.'
    That the deponent went to Covent Garden Market 11 May to inquire
about the character of William Welchman, one of the persons mentioned in the notice of bail. A person there told him that Welchman was
a job constable, lately in difficulties, and that he was unfit to be bail in
any cause. The deponent also went to Hand Court Bishopgate to
inquire into Frederick English's character. A poor looking woman said
English was living from hand to mouth like herself. Both men appear to
be very insufficient bail for the defendant in this cause.

Affidavits for prisoner:

Mich 32 Geo III 1791

[4] Affdt of service of Daniel Bishop of Dean Street, Holborne (Middx),
sworn before the court by the court at Westminster Hall[34] 23 Nov 1791.
'King's Bench'. [*Verso*]: 'Mic 91 England Staff In the Kings Bench Affts to
bail Isaac Jones The King agst Isaac Jones on the prosecution of Mary
Mokes for uttering counterfeit money Mr [*struck out*: Knowles?] Mayrott
[*sic*] ½ Gn Saml Marryat. To move to justify bail upon the affidavit and
notice herewith and please to observe that the defendt was bail'd in
this court for his appearance at the last assize at Stafford and he rendered in discharge of that bail but neglecting to give the proper notice to
the pros of such render he was committed till he gave bail again for his

---

[34] The words 'in Serjeants Inn Hall' are erased; 'in open court at Westminster
    Hall' is inserted.

appearance at the next assize and he is now in court for that purpose. 24 Nov. Bail'd to appr at next assize for Staff in 80-40-40 Polhill'.

That the deponent served Mr Vernon solicitor to the mint 9 Nov 1791 a true copy of the annexed notice by delivering the same to his clerk at his chambers in Lincoln's Inn.

[*Annexed*]:

'Staffordshire: The King agst Isaac Jones: On the prosecution of Mary Mokes for uttering counterfeit money.' Notice from Isaac Jones 1 Nov 1791 to Vernon, mint solicitor, that John Jaaffe of the Admiral Kepple, Rope Makers Fields, Limehouse (Middx) victualer, and William Cook of No 223 Bermondsey Street in the parish of St Mary Magdalen[35] (Surrey) working goldsmith will on Wednesday 23 Nov at 11am in open court in Westminster Hall become bail for his personal appearance at the next Staffordshire assizes to try his traverse upon the indictment prefered by Mary Mokes and found against him for uttering counterfeit money.

[*Annexed*]:

'A copy of the Kalendar at the last assizes for Staffordshire as far as relates to the undermentioned prisoner. Isaac Jones. To remain in gaol till the next assizes to take his trial on two indictments against him for uttering counterfeit money unless he with two good and sufficient sureties enter into two recognizances himself in forty pounds and his sureties in twenty pounds apiece in each recognizance on condition that he shall be and personally appear at the next assizes and general session of oyer and terminer and general gaol delivery to be holden for the said county of Stafford and then there prosecute his traverses with effect to the said several indictments and shall not depart the court without leave but the said recognizances shall not be taken but on proof of 14 days previous notice having been served on the solicitor of his majesty's mint of the names and places of abode of the persons to be by him proposed for such sureties it appearing to this court that the said Isaac Jones did at the last assizes and general session of oyer and terminer holden for the said county forfeit two recognizances by him and his sureties theretofore entered into which said former recognizances have been estreated into his majesty's court of exchequer.'

[5] [*An identical affdt and notice, but without the extract from the assize calendar, for the King against Jones on the prosecution of Elizabeth Horton.*[36] *The*

---

[35] 'Maudlin' in original.

[36] So spelled in affdts [5] and [7].

verso does not include the words following 'purpose' on the verso of the affidavit and notice [4] in the prosecution brought by Mokes.]

[6] Affidavit of Thomas Bayliss gentleman of Prince's Street Drury Lane (Middx), sworn by the court in court at Westminster Hall 24 Nov 1791. ITKB [*Verso*]: 'England Staff In the Kings Bench The King agst Isaac Jones on the prosecution of Mary Mokes for uttering counterfeit money Saml Marryat To move to Justify Bail upon the within notice and affidt Polhill.'
    That this deponent served Mr. Vernon solicitor with a true copy of the annexed notice 23 Nov 1791 by giving that notice to Mr. Vernon's clerk at his chambers no. 10 Lincoln's Inn.
    [*Annexed*]:
    'Staffordshire: The King agst Isaac Jones: on the prosecution of Mary Mokes for uttering counterfeit money.' Notice from Isaac Jones to Vernon, mint solicitor, that Jaaffe and Cook [*see notice in affdt [5]*], the same bail of which he has before had notice, will tomorrow 24 Nov 1791 become bail [*as in affdt [5].*]

[7] [*An identical affdt and notice, for the King against Jones on the prosecution of Elizabeth Horton.*]

Sources: ASSI 4/22 summer 1790 Staffordshire process notes. KB 1/26 Ea 30 Geo III nos.1, 2 (bdls 28, 48, 49, 50); KB 1/27/3 Mich 32 Geo III bdl 91, Mich 32 Geo III no.1 (bdl 2). KB 16/21/1. KB 21/45 pp.269, 274, 279, 529.

G.5 Habeas corpus and bail (19 Jan 1792)

Prisoner and defendant: John Darlastone.

Writ and return:
Habeas corpus 4 Feb [1792] to the sheriff of Staffordshire and keeper of the county gaol, to be returned immediately on receipt. [*Verso*]: By rule of court. [*No schedule or return.*][37]

Rules and process:
Hil [3 Feb 1792]: On reading affdt [1] and [2] and a copy of the commitment of the said John Darlastone annexed, order for a writ of habeas

---

[37] Another document was once pinned to this, doubtless the schedule and return.

corpus to the keeper of Stafford gaol to bring Darlastone before this court immediately (Baldwin; by the court). ST [11 Feb 1792]: Darlastone brought into court under habeas corpus in custody of the keeper of Stafford gaol; writ and return filed; defdt gives recognizance for his personal appearance at next assizes for Staffordshire, and is discharged out of custody (Baldwin).[38]

Affidavits for defence:

Hil 32 Geo III 1792

[*Wrapper*]: '44 Hil 92 England. In the King's Bench Staff 2 Affdts for Ha Cor for John Darlastone. The King agst Darlastone: copy commitment not charged feloniously[39] 3 Feb Ha Cor Punton[40] fo:6.'

[1] Affdt of John Darlastone, farmer and prisoner in the gaol at Stafford, and Ann Wade widow, both of Longdon, sworn before John Heeley at Stafford 30 Jan 1792. ITKB 'The King against John Darlastone: On the Prosecution of Richard Pace for wounding a Bay Gelding his property.' [*Verso*]: 'The King v Darlastone: Affidavit of Deft & another. Punton fo:10.' [*2nd Verso*]: 'Gaoler's cert & affidt Darlastone.' [*Ann Wade signed with a mark.*]

[John Darlastone]: That for six months before his commitment he resided at Longdon. On the night of 9 Jan 1792 the deponent and

---

[38] A marginal note gives the recognizance and sureties: one of £80 and four of £40. For process, see Gude, ii, 632 #14.

[39] A commitment on a felony charge would have been 'on the statute' 22 & 23 Charles II c.7 (1670), which made malicious killing of a horse at night a felony for which the punishment was transportation for seven years. Although committed for 'unlawfully wounding and killing', Darlastone, a butcher of the parish of Elford, and William Marshall, a yeoman of Longdon, were indicted on the statute at Lent assizes 1792 for maiming a horse belonging to Lord Uxbridge by shooting it through a stable window. The prosecutor was Richard Pace yeoman and the witness before the grand jury was William Walbank labourer. The prosecution hoped to use the testimony of a former groom, Richard Amies, whose evidence was expected to be crucial. The recognizance at assizes was for £80; the sureties were Charles Marshall, farmer of Longdon, William Webb, farmer of Haselour, and Samuel Heath, butcher of Stafford, in £40 each. Darlastone and Marshall were both acquitted at trial.

[40] The *Law List 1805*, 82, records attorneys James Punton of Hind Court, Fleet Street, and Christopher Punton of Furnival's Inn.

William Marshall of Longdon, farmer, were taken before John Sparrow
JP on a charge of maliciously and unlawfully wounding and killing in
the night time a bay gelding, the property of Richard Pace, 14 Oct last,
and committed to the gaol. His remaining in prison will be materially
injurious and detrimental to his affairs. He seeks a writ of habeas corpus in order to offer sureties that he will appear at next general gaol
delivery. The only material witness for Pace, William Wallbank
labourer, did so for gaining reward from the deponent, or was instigated by someone aiming to ruin the deponent. The deponent is innocent and was at his lodgings at the home of Mary Marshall widow of
Longdon the whole evening, and in bed from 10pm to 6am.

[Ann Wade]: The deponent is the daughter of Mary Marshall;
Darlastone was at home all evening and in bed before 10pm until 6am.

[*Annexed*]: From John Sparrow esquire JP to the constable at Longdon:
'You are commanded forthwith to convey into the custody of the
Keeper of the goal of Stafford, John Darlastone and William Marshall
who are charged with killing a bay gelding belonging to Richard Pace,
so that they may be discharged by due course of law.' Certified by
Littleton Scott, keeper of Stafford gaol, where Darlastone is a prisoner,
20 Jan 1792.

[2] Affdt of James Bostock painter of Stafford, sworn before John Heeley
at Stafford 20 Jan 1792. 'King's Bench.' [*Verso*]: 'Gaoler's cert. & Affidt.
Darlastone.'

That the deponent witnessed Littleton Scott keeper of Stafford gaol
write and witness the certificate annexed.

[*Annexed*]: Copy of the warrant of John Sparrow 9 Jan 1792 to the constable of Longdon and the keeper of the county gaol, committing
Darlastone and Marshall for unlawfully and maliciously wounding a
bay gelding, now dead of its wound, of Richard Pace. Certificate
of Littleton Scott, keeper, Stafford gaol, 20 Jan 1792, that Darlastone is
detained under the warrant of which this is a true copy, and not for any
other cause.

[3] Affdt of Benjamin Heath shoemaker of Stafford, sworn before John
Heeley at Stafford 8 Feb 1792. ITKB 'Staffordshire. The King agt John
Darlastone.' [*Verso*]: '74 Hil 92 England Staff. In the King's Bench Afft
of service Notice of Bail for John Darlastone. The King v Darlastone.
Affidavit of Service of Notice on the Prosecutor & Magistrate. 11 Feb
Bail'd to app at next Ass in – 80 – 40 – 40 – 40 – 40. Punton. fo: 5.'

That the deponent delivered a copy of the [*annexed*] notice 6 Feb to a
servant of John Sparrow magistrate of Bishton and to the wife of
Richard Pace at Longdon.

[*Annexed*]: Notice 4 Feb 1792 by J. Punton solicitor for the defendant to Richard Pace, prosecutor and John Sparrow esquire, a magistrate of Staffordshire. That the defendant will be brought up to King's Bench 11 Feb 1792 by virtue of a writ of habeas corpus, to be bailed until the next assizes at Stafford. The persons proposed as bail are John Darlastone butcher of Elford, Charles Marshall farmer of Longdon, William Webb farmer of Haselour, and Samuel Heath victualler of Stafford.

Sources: ASSI 5/112 Staffs Lent. KB 1/27/4 Hil 32 Geo III no.2, bdls 44, 74. KB 16/21/1. KB 21/45 pp. 558, 573. SRO, D603, Jos. Perks to Lord Uxbridge 11 March 1792.

G.6 Habeas corpus and bail (16 June 1792)

Prisoner and defendant: John Zachariah, yeoman.

Writ and return:
Habeas corpus 18 June [1792] to the keeper of the common gaol, city of Lichfield, for return immediately. [*Verso*]: 'By rule of court.' Return by John Smith, keeper.
    Schedule that John Zachariah was detained in custody 26 May 1792 by a warrant of Samuel Palmer JP of Lichfield on the oaths of the Reverend Richard Buckeridge and John Profitt on suspicion of having unlawfully uttered to Buckeridge 24 May a counterfeit silver half crown, and possessing other false money; to be detained until the next general gaol delivery, Lichfield.

Rules and process:
Trin [16 June 1792]: on reading the affdt of William Cooper and a copy of the commitment annexed, order for a writ of habeas corpus to the gaoler of Lichfield (Marryat). ST [22 June 1792]: John Zachariah appears in court in custody of the keeper of Lichfield gaol; order that the writ and return be filed, and on reading the affdts of William Cooper and two paper writings annexed, and of John Smith, and John Zachariah giving a recognizance for his personal appearance at next Lichfield gaol delivery, discharged from custody.[41] By the court (Marryat).

---

[41] In margin: '40 20 20 20 20', the recognizance and sureties, amounting to £120. John Zachariah yeoman was indicted at Lichfield gaol delivery 2 July 1792. He was said to have been given two half crowns by Buckeridge for three pairs of slippers, and to have switched one for a counterfeit, which he gave back to Buckeridge as a fake. 'John Zachariah was called but did not appear pursuant to his recognizance.'

Affidavits for defence:

Trin 32 Geo III 1792

[1] Affdt of William Cooper, an attorney of the court of common pleas, of Lichfield, sworn before William Gill the younger at Lichfield 13 June 1792. ITKB

That John Smith, keeper of the common gaol, signed his name to the annexed paper 13 June 1792. The annexed copy of the warrant of commitment mentioned in the certificate is a true copy of the original.

[*Annexed*]: 'City and county of Lichfield. To the keeper of the common gaol in the said city and county.

'These are in his majesty's name to charge and command you to receive into your custody the body of John Zachariah apprehended in the parish of St Mary in the city and county of Lichfield and charged before me Samuel Palmer gentleman one of his majesty's justices of the peace for the said city and county upon the several oaths of the Reverend Richard Buckeridge and John Proffitt upon suspicion of having on the twenty-fourth day of May instant at the parish of St Mary in the city and county aforesaid unlawfully uttered to the said Richard Buckeridge a certain piece of false or counterfeit money purporting to be a silver half crown of the current coin of this realm but which was in fact counterfeit, knowing the same to be false and counterfeit having at the time of such utterance other false money in his possession. And also upon suspicion of obtaining from the said Richard Buckeridge by false pretences a silver half crown the property of the said Richard Buckeridge, that is to say, by fraudulently exchanging a certain silver half crown of the current coin of this realm delivered to him by the said Richard Buckeridge and returning to the said Richard Buckeridge a certain counterfeit half crown pretending that the said last mentioned counterfeit half crown had been delivered to him by the said Richard Buckeridge with intent to defraud the said Richard Buckeridge of the said real half crown and by the said false pretences obtaining from the said Richard Buckeridge another half crown of the current silver coin of this realm at the parish of St Mary in the city and county aforesaid. And you are safely to keep the said John Zachariah in your custody in the said common gaol until the next general gaol delivery to be held in an for the said city and county then and there to take his trial for the said several offences and until he shall be discharged by the due course of law. Given under my hand and seal this twenty-sixth day of May in the year of our Lord 1792. [*signed*] Samuel Palmer.

'The above is a true copy of the original commitment being examined with the same this thirteenth day of June 1792 by us [*signed*] William Cooper, Stephen Simpson.

'I John Smith keeper of his majesty's common gaol in the city of Lichfield hereby certify that John Zachariah hereinbefore named is a prisoner in my custody by virtue of the warrant of commitment a copy of which is hereinbefore written, and that the said copy is a true copy of the said original commitment. As witness my hand this thirteenth day of June in the year of our Lord 1792. [*signed*] John Smith, gaoler.

'13th June 1792 annexed at the time of swearing the affidavit. William Gill junior.'

[2] Affdt of William Cooper gentleman of Lichfield, sworn before Stephen Simpson at Lichfield 21 June 1792. ITKB 'The King against John Zachariah on the prosecution of the Reverend Richard Buckridge and John Profitt for a Misdemeanour.' [*Verso*]: 'The King agt John Zachariah. On the Prosecution of Rd Buckridge and John Proffits for a Misdeamnr. Affdt. Mr Marryat – ½ Ga. Saml Marryat. Please to move that the Deft, who is brot up by Virtue of Writ of Hab Corp from the City of Lichfield may be admitted to Bail pursuant to notice for that purpose given. B. John Lloyd solicr for deft. Belt. Att in Court.'

That the deponent delivered the [*annexed*] notice to Samuel Palmer esquire and JP of Lichfield the committing magistrate [*marked as version A*] and John Proffit hatter of Lichfield [*marked as version B*], and to Richard Buckeridge by his servant Jane Mosedale of Lichfield [*marked as version B*], Buckeridge being out of town; Mosedale agreed to deliver it to him as soon as possible. 20 June 1792.

[*Annexed*]: Notice by John Lloyd solicitor for the defendant of No 22 New Bishopsgate Street (London), to Samuel Palmer 20 June 1792.

That the defendant John Zachariah will be brought into King's Bench 22 June 1792 at 10am in accordance with a writ of habeas corpus. The court will be moved that he may be admitted to bail and the persons listed will become bail for him: Joseph Mendes hardwareman of No 10 Plumber's Row near Whitechapel Church (Middx), Thomas Pixley surveyor of No 24 Chapel Street Curtain Road parish of St Leonard Shoreditch (Middx), Robert Ward worsted manufacturer of No 15 Hare Street Brick Lane parish of St Mathew Bethnall Green (Middx) and William Strangeway tailor of No 44 Clerkenwell Close in the parish of St James Clerkenwell (Middx).

[*An identical notice to Buckeridge.*]

Affidavit for prosecution:

Trin 32 Geo III 1792

[3] Affdt of John Smith, keeper of Lichfield gaol, sworn in court by the court 22 June 1792. ITKB 'The King on the prosecution of Richard Buckeridge, clerk against John Zachariah.' [*Verso*]: '39 King 2 England Litchfield. Afft to oppose bailing John Zachariah. 22 June. Bailed to appear at Gaol Delivery. 40 – 20 – 20 – 20 – 20. Willington'.

That a general gaol delivery will be held for the city and county of Lichfield on 2 July 1792, at which time the prisoners will take their respective trials.

Sources: KB 1/27 Trin 32 Geo III. KB 16/21/1 32 Geo III 1791/2. KB 21/45 pp. 629, 636. Lichfield Record Office, D25/1/1, fols. 183v, 184, 2 July 1792.

G.7 Habeas corpus and certiorari on committal proceedings, by defendant (3 June 1793)[42]

Prisoner and defendant: Joseph Tysoe of Birmingham, victualler and bucklemaker.

Writ and return:
Habeas corpus 13 June [1793] to the keeper of Stafford gaol, to be returned immediately. [*Verso*]: By rule of court. 'The execution of this writ appears in the schedule hereto annexed. George Molineux Esq Sheriff.'[43]

Schedule by Molineux: that on 29 April [1793] Joseph Tysoe was detained on the inclosed

Committal [*paper copy*] by J. Carles and B. Spencer 25 April 1793 on oaths of Benjamin Hughes, William Nicholls, Richard Wooldridge and Thomas Wooldridge on violent suspicion of stealing 15 March at Wolverhampton 162 gross and a half of iron blanks for woodscrews and 30 gross of iron woodscrews the property of Benjamin Hughes.

Rules and process:

Trin [13 June 1793]: on reading affdts [1] to [7] and annexed papers, order for a writ of habeas corpus issue to the keeper of Stafford gaol to have the body of the said Joseph Tysoe before this court immediately (Bayley; by the court). Also order for a writ of certiorari to Carles and

---

[42] This case is an instance of the use of certiorari to remove depositions on an application for bail (*Halsbury's Laws of England*, ed. Viscount Hailsham, 2nd ed., 1937, vii, 840), and habeas corpus. See also Chitty, i, 127.

[43] In a different hand.

Spencer to remove all informations and depositions concerning the commitment of Tysoe to Stafford gaol (Bayley).[44] ST [19 June 1793]: Joseph Tysoe being brought here into court in custody of the sheriff of Staffs on writ of habeas corpus, order for the writ and return to be filed. On reading affidavit [8] and two rules of this court and three other annexed paper writings, and Joseph Tysoe having given in court a recognizance for his personal appearance to answer at the next Stafford assizes, and not to depart that court without leave, order for the discharge of Tysoe from the custody of the sheriff of Staffs. It is further ordered that the said Joseph Tysoe be now discharged out of the custody of the said sheriff (Bayley). [*In margin*]: 80 50 50 50[45]

Affidavits for defence:

Trin 33 Geo III 1793

[1] Affdt of Joseph Tysoe victualler and bucklemaker late of Birmingham (Warws) and now a prisoner in Staffs, sworn before J. Dickenson at Stafford 3 June 1793 [*signed with a mark*]. ITKB 'The King agt Joseph Tysoe: On the prosecution of Benjamin Hughes on a Suspicion of his having Stolen a quantity of Wood Screws and Iron blanks for Wood Screws.' [*Verso*]: 'England Staff In the King's Bench. The King agt Joseph Tysoe: On the Prosecution of Benjn Hughes. Please to Move for an Habeas Corpus to [*struck out*: directed to the Keeper of Stafford Gaol] bring up the Deft to be bailed on the within Affidavits. June 7th 1793 Mr Bayley 1 Ga. J. Smart No. 86 Hatton Gardens Agent. fo:13.'

That the deponent is presently in custody in Stafford gaol on a commitment by Joseph Carles JP, charged by Benjamin Hughes of Wolverhampton with stealing 162 gross and a half of iron blanks for wood screws and 30 gross of wood screws 15 March 1793. The deponent carried on an extensive trade as grocer at Hoxton (Middx) from 1781 to 1790, when he moved to Birmingham where he continued in this trade for two years. Having an opportunity of entering a beneficial business in the plated buckle trade and of keeping the Turk's Head

---

[44]   The writ of certiorari is not filed in KB 11/57/2 Trin 33 Geo III, nor noted in KB 29. It issued 13 June: see [8][a] below.

[45]   The sums of his recognizance and sureties. The recognizances and examinations of Tysoe's prosecutor and his witnesses, Benjamin Hughes, William Nicholls, Thomas Woodridge and Richard Woodridge, were filed at Stafford summer assizes. There is no record of Tysoe's appearance or trial.

public house in Birmingham, he left the grocery business for the plated buckle trade, which is now carried on by his wife. He supplies hawkers and other travellers with buckles and other goods, and barters and exchanges buckles and other goods made in Birmingham for goods the manufactury of other counties.

A person calling himself William Hope came into the public house 16 March 1793 asking the deponent to buy iron blanks and wood screws. He replied that money was scarce, but liking the screws and blanks he agreed to take them for seven dozen plated buckles; Hope sent a man to the Wolverhampton carrier's inn for the blanks and screws. The agreement was made in the presence of William Davis bucklemaker, William Haywood spur and buckleplater, and Thomas Hodgetts buckleplater, all citizens of Birmingham; deponent has been informed that the seven dozen buckles were a full, fair and valuable consideration for the screws and blanks. These he kept at his house, selling them openly until 19 April 1793. On that day, as William Nicholls was examining the deponent's wares, Hughes observed the screws and said they had been stolen from him 15 March, and had the deponent committed to Stafford county gaol as a suspected thief. Hughes has visited him in gaol on several occasions since then to say that he is convinced of the deponent's innocence, believing the culprit to be another person, since absconded. He advised the deponent to apply to this court to get bail, voluntarily offering to give his consent if the deponent could procure friends to become sureties.

[2] Affdt of Joseph Tysoe prisoner in Stafford county gaol, late of Birmingham (Warws), sworn before Owen Lloyd the younger at Stafford 11 June 1793 [*signed with a mark*]. ITKB 'The King v Joseph Tysoe: On the Prosecution of Benjn Hughes.' [*Verso*]: 'England Staff. In the King's Bench. The King agt Joseph Tysoe. Affidavit of the Prisoner. J. Smart No 86. Hatten Gardens Agent fo: 3.'

That the deponent has worked for a long time as a chapman and factor at Birmingham (Warws), buying goods from manufacturers in and about Birmingham and Wolverhampton, and selling and exchanging them with tradesmen coming to Birmingham to buy them. In the course of his business he purchased some wood screws and blanks from William Hope for fair, just and full consideration and did not know they were unjustly obtained, as those and such articles are frequently brought to Birmingham to be disposed of.

[3] Affdt of John Maddox gentleman of Birmingham (Warws), solicitor for Tysoe, sworn before John Parrott at Wolverhampton 3 June 1793. ITKB 'The King agt Joseph Tysoe: On the prosecution of Benjamin

Hughes on a suspicion of his having stolen a quantity of Wood Screws and Wood Screw Blanks.' [*Verso*]: 'England. Staff. In the Kings Bench. The King agt Joseph Tysoe: Notice of Bail and affidt service notice of bail. Smart for Maddox. fo: 9.'

That the deponent personally served the prosecutor Benjamin Hughes 2 June instant with a true copy of the annexed notice. He was present that day and saw Hughes sign his consent that John Blame, Thomas Pixley, William Strangeway and John Moore should be admitted sureties for the appearance of Tysoe at next Stafford assizes. He verifies the signatures of Hughes and himself on the said consent.

[*Annexed*]: ITKB 'The King agt Joseph Tysoe: On the prosecution of Benjamin Hughes on a suspicion of his having stolen a quantity of Wood Screws and Wood Screw Blanks.' Notice to Hughes that the court would be moved 8 June for a habeas corpus to the sheriff of Stafford to have Tysoe before the court so enter into sureties for his appearance at next Stafford assizes to answer your charge of a violent suspicion of stealing your goods. The names of the bail or manucaptors are John Blame no.11 Bell Yard Temple Bar London, carver and gilder; Thomas Pixley no.70 Fetter Lane London, scale beam maker; William Strangeways no.12 High Street Islington (Midd) tailor; and John Moore no.21 Islington Road (Midd), tobacconist. 1 June 1793. John Maddox solicitor for Joseph Tysoe.

[*Subscribed*]: Benjamin Hughes consents that the above named John Blame, Thomas Pixley, William Strangeways and John Moore will be admitted to the court as sureties for the appearance of Joseph Tysoe at the next assizes. 2 June 1793. Witness John Maddox B. Hughes

[4] Affdt of John Maddox gentleman of Birmingham (Warws), sworn before George Treen at Birmingham on 10 June 1793. [*Verso*]: '39 Trin 93 England Staff. Affts for Ha Cor for Joseph Tysoe. In the King's Bench. The King agt Joseph Tysoe. Affidavit of service of notice on the committing magistrate. 13 June Ha Cor & Certior for depositions. G Smart. No 86 Hatton Gardens Agent fo: 7.'

That the deponent personally served Joseph Carles JP 9 June with a true copy of the annexed notice.

[*Annexed*]: ITKB 'The King agt Joseph Tysoe: On the prosecution of Benjamin Hughes on a suspicion of his the said Joseph Tysoe having on the fifteenth day of March last at Wolverhampton in the County of Stafford feloniously stolen taken and carried away one hundred and sixty two Gross and half of Iron Blanks for Wood Screws and Thirty Gross of Iron Wood Screws the property of the said Benjamin Hughes.'

[*Notice identical to that in [3] above, except that the motion is to be made 16 June and Hughes's consent to bail not included.*]

[5] Affdt of William Davies buckleplater of Digbeth, Thomas Hodgetts buckleplater of Dean Street, William Haywood spurplater of Dudley Street, all of Birmingham (Warws), sworn before Thomas Barnhurst at Birmingham 4 June 1793. [*Verso*]: 'England. Staff. In the King's Bench. The King agt Joseph Tysoe: on the prosecn of Benjamin Hughes. Affidts of Thomas Hodgetts, William Davis and William Haywood. Smart fo: 4.'

[All]: That they are all well acquainted with Joseph Tysoe, bucklemaker and victualer but now a prisoner in Stafford gaol. They were at Tysoe's house 16 March and saw him exchange with a person from Wolverhampton who said his name was Hope seven dozen plated buckles for some wood screws and iron blanks. They have always had the highest opinion of Tysoe's honesty and integrity; the common repute of the neighbourhood is that he was an honest and industrious tradesman.

[6] Affdt of William Wills grocer and William Barlow ironmonger of Birmingham (Warws), sworn before Thomas Barnhurst at Birmingham 4 June 1793. ITKB 'The King agt Joseph Tysoe: On the prosecution of Benjamin Hughes on a Suspicion of his having Stolen a Quantity of Wood Screws and Iron Blanks for Wood Screws.' [*Verso*]: 'England Staff. In the King's Bench. The King agt Joseph Tysoe: On the prosecution of Benjamin Hughes. Affidts of William Wills and William Barlow. Smart. fo: 3'.

[Both]: That they have had considerable dealings with Joseph Tysoe for three years and have always found him strictly fair and honest in all his dealings.

[7] Affdt of Littleton Scott keeper of Stafford gaol, sworn before Owen Lloyd the younger at Stafford 11 June 1793. [*Verso*]: 'In the King's Bench. The King agt Joseph Tysoe. Copy warrant of commitment and affidavit verifying the same. G Smart No 86 Hatton Gardens agent fo 5.'

That Joseph Tysoe was committed 29 April to the custody of the deponent by a warrant (copy annexed) under the hands and seals of J. Carles esq and the Reverend B. Spencer clerk, two justices for Staffordshire. Joseph Tysoe remains a prisoner in his custody under only that charge.

[*Annexed*]: Warrant of Carles and Spencer to the constable of Wolverhampton and the keeper of Stafford gaol, the constable to deliver Tysoe into custody, being charged on the oaths of Benjamin Hughes, William Nicholls, Richard Wooldridge and Thomas Wooldridge [*describes charge*] and the keeper to receive and keep Tysoe until delivered by due order of law. 25 April 1793. Assizes.

[8] Affdt of Thomas Hodgetts buckleplater of Dean Street Birmingham (Warws), sworn before Thomas Barnhurst of Birmingham (Warws) 17 June 1793. ITKB 'The King agt Joseph Tysoe: On the prosecution of Benjamin Huges [*sic*] on a suspicion of his having stolen a quantity of Wood Screws and Iron Blanks for Wood Screws the property of the said Benjamin Hughes.' [*Verso*]: '67 Trin 93 England Staff Afft to bail Joseph Tysoe Original Rules 19 June Baild to appear at next Assize for Staffordshire in 80 – 50 – 50 – 50 Smart. fo: 24.'

'Affts fo: 44 & Dw 1. 9. 16

> R –. 2. –
> D –. 3. –
> ———————
> 1. 14. 10'

That the deponent delivered to Joseph Carles 15 June 1793 the writ of certiorari [a]. He served Carles 15 June and Spencer 17 June with the notice [b] of Tysoe's appearance for bail. The deponent served Hughes 15 June with notice [c]. He served Spencer 17 June and Carles and B. Heath 15 June with true copies of the rules [d, e]. He tried to serve Spencer 15 June but his wife, who said Spencer was away until 17 June, refuse to receive the notice and copies of rules.

[*Annexed*]:

[a] [*Copy*] Writ of certiorari to J. Carles[46] and B. Spencer clerk, JPs to return all informations and depositions in the commitment of Tysoe immediately together with this writ. Witness Lloyd Lord Kenyon 13 June [1793].

[b] Notice 15 June 1793 by G. Maddox to Joseph Carles esq and B. Spencer that Tysoe will be brought into court 19 June 1793, last day of Trinity term, on habeas corpus to enter into sureties for his appearance at next Stafford assizes to answer [*repeats the charge*]. [*Bail named as in the notice in [3].*]

[c] [*identical notice to Benjamin Hughes*].

[d] [*the rule of 13 June for habeas corpus*].

[e] [*the rule of 13 June for certiorari*].

Sources: ASSI 2/26 and ASSI 4/22, Staffs. summer assizes 1793. KB 1/28 Trin 33 Geo III. KB 16/21/2, 33 Geo III 1792/3. KB 21/46 pp.135, 136, 149.

---

[46] Spelled here and elsewhere 'Carless'.

G.8 Habeas corpus applied for, and granted (26 April 1796)

Prisoner: George Arthur Annesley, an infant.

Writ and return:
Habeas corpus 26 April [1796] to Anne Lady Viscountess Valentia of Ireland to bring the body of George Arthur Annesley, said to be detained in her custody, with the day and cause of his taking and detainer, before this court immediately on receipt of this writ. Witness Lloyd Lord Kenyon. By the court. Templar. [*Verso*]: 'By rule of court.' 'In pursuance of this writ I have the body of the within named George Arthur Annesley before our sovereign Lord the King as I am within commanded. The answer of Ann [*illeg.*] Valentia.'

Rules and process: Ea [26 April 1796] On reading affdt [1] of Lord Valentia, order for the writ (Erskine). ST [1 May 1796]: On reading affdt [2], order that Viscountess Valentia have two days' time to return the writ (Gibbs). ST [7 May 1796]: George Arthur Annesley being brought into court by Anne Lady Viscountess Valentia, on reading affdts [3] to [12], and on hearing counsel on both sides, ordered that the writ and return be filed and that George Arthur Annesley be delivered to Viscount Valentia (Erskine for Lord Valentia, Gibbs for Lady Valentia).[47]

---

[47] After affdt [2] was read in court, Gibbs moved that the child should not be taken from his mother. 'Lord Kenyon said that it was a very unfortunate affair, and that he wished some person could be found, to whom they could both consent to surrender the custody of the child.' Erskine refused on the grounds that Lord Valentia would be able to disprove every charge in the affidavit. On 7 May, after argument and the reading of affdts [3] to [12], Garrow said they showed that Lord Valentia was innocent and by his marriage 'one of the most unfortunate of men.' He argued it was a foul conspiracy to destroy his honour. Gibbs for Lady Valentia said he had allowed opposing counsel to go as far as they had only because they needed to vindicate the honour of Lord Valentia. He admitted they had 'certainly completely answered Lady Valentia's affidavits [*sic*].' This seemed to be a conspiracy, but it was premature to draw that conclusion as the whole case would not be heard that day. Kenyon congratulated Gibbs, admitted that he too had been inclined to hear the case 'up to the same extent, and drawn arguments for so doing from my own feelings as a man.—The day of reckoning will come.' He felt bound to say the attack on Lord Valentia appeared unwarrantable. 'I cannot forbear saying (perhaps it may be extrajudicial), though I only know Lord Valentia as a public character, when I went the

Affidavit for applicant:

Ea 36 Geo III 1796

[1] Affdt of the Rt Hon George Annesley, commonly called Viscount Valentia of Ireland,[48] of Baker Street Portman Square (Middx), sworn in court, by the court, 26 April 1796. 'Ex parte The Rt Honble George Annesley commonly called Viscount Valentia of the Kingdom of Ireland.' ITKB

That he married the Honorable Anne Courtenay daughter of the late William Viscount Courtenay Sept 1790, of which marriage one son George Arthur Annesley is issue, now or lately with her in Sloane Street. Anne having lately been detected in acts of adultery, the deponent has commenced an action against John Bellenden Gawler esquire for criminal conversation.[49] As their son, if he survives, will inherit the deponent's titles and estates in England and Ireland, the deponent is very desirous of having him under his own care and protection. He is informed that Anne now cohabits with Gawler and that she has lately been brought to bed of a son of which this deponent is not the father.

Affidavit for respondent:

Ea 36 Geo III 1796

> Oxford Circuit, I have more than once seen him in the most honorable of all situations in which a country gentleman, as a member of society, can be placed—I have seen him at the head of the counties of Worcester and Stafford, as foreman of the grand jury, inserted in the society of the most honorable men there, and I protest I thought he very much became that situation.—The child must be delivered over to his father.' *Proceedings in the Court of King's Bench, ex parte George Viscount Valentia 1796* (Kidderminster, 1799), 10–11, 32–34.
>
> [48] Born 4 Dec 1770, Earl of Mountnorris from 1816.
> [49] At least three different accounts of the criminal conversation trial were published between 1795 and 1799. Lord Valentia won £2000 damages against J. B. Gawler; he also fought a duel with Henry Gawler, who shot him in the breastbone, while Valentia's shot went through Gawler's hat. J. B. Gawler (later Ker) claimed unsuccessfully the Barony of Bellenden of Broughton, and had two illegitimate sons by Lady Valentia, born in 1801 and 1804. Lady Valentia died in 1835. Lord Valentia rebuilt Arley Hall in Norman style, and was buried at Upper Arley at his death in 1844. George Arthur Annesley, styled Viscount Valentia from 1816, died in 1841. George Edward Cokayne, *Complete Peerage* (London, 1959), xii, 210–11.

[2] Affdt of Ann Viscountess Valentia of Sloane Street in the parish of St Luke Chelsea and Jane Smith spinster of the same, sworn in court, by the court, 2 May 1796. ITKB

[Anne Viscountess Valentia]: That in 1790 at the age of 15 she married Viscount Valentia and that the child the subject of the writ is about two and a half years of age. Soon after their marriage they went to live at Petersham (Surrey), when he appeared to take a great aversion to the deponent and gave her reason to suspect he did not have his esteem or love, although she tried all means in her power to conciliate his affections. Near the end of 1791 they went to live at Arley (Worcs)[50] where his aversion increased: he appeared anxious to avoid the deponent and sought every pretence to treat her with harshness and severity. She observed a great intimacy between the Viscount and a livery servant named George, with whom he spent most of his time. They were frequently playing and toying with each other; she saw Valentia pinch George and make use of the most indecent familiarities with him, and they frequently retired to Valentia's bedroom in the early evening, remaining for several hours. When this deponent went up stairs to bed she found George in the room without his shoes; the bed had been laid upon.

[Both]: That Viscount Valentia frequently quit his bed early in the morning and went in his shirt and bed gown into the garrets where the servants including George slept. The deponents heard them making a great noise and at play with each other, and have been informed that Valentia pulled the clothes off the beds of the servants before they were up, and behaved in the most indecent manner.

Viscount Valentia frequently quitted the room he shared with the deponent Anne, and went to a separate bed, when George would lie or pretend to lie on a small mattress in the bedroom.

[Jane Smith]: That as the housemaid who made the beds she had frequent opportunities of observing this conduct.

[Anne Viscountess Valentia]: That about the same time Viscount Valentia became extremely intimate with his coachman, and frequently left the deponent's bed early in the morning and went in his shirt and bedgown to the coachman's apartment before he was up, and spent several hours there with him. Valentia encouraged him and George to behave with the greatest insolence to this deponent; uneasy, she

---

[50]   An error corrected in the printed *Proceedings*: the viscount's seat was in the parish of Upper Arley, then in Staffordshire. The parish was transferred to Worcestershire in 1895 by 58 & 59 Vict., c.86.

complained to her friends, who represented to Valentia the infamy of his behaviour and advised him in her presence to part with the said servants. Valentia, much alarmed, accordingly sent George away, but being uneasy at his absence took him back again. He and Valentia afterwards travelled abroad together.

The deponent believes that the intimacy of Valentia with his servants was attended with circumstances of the most criminal nature. Often in her presence he made use of the most licentious and indecent conversation and always encouraged such discourse in her company. This deponent humbly submits to the judgment of the court whether the Viscount is a proper person to have the care of and to superintend the education of George Arthur Annesley their son.

This deponent does not cohabit with nor has any adulterous connection with John Bellenden Gawler, and she is frequently visited by her relations.

Affidavits for applicant:

[3] Affdt of the Rt Honorable George Annesley commonly called Viscount Valentia of Ireland, sworn in court by the court 7 May 1796. ITKB

That he married Viscountess Valentia 6 Sept 1790 entirely from affection. George Kingsbury lived with the deponent as his valet and was of course much about his person. During all the time the said servant was in attendance on him [*Interpolated*: 'either when this deponent was indisposed or otherwise'] he never was guilty of the detestable vice insinuated against him nor of any unnatural or indecent familiarity nor was the attendance of George Kingsbury on this deponent [*Interpolated*: 'when indisposed'] with a view to such unnatural practice or criminal partiality for him. During such attendance Kingsbury slept on a bed or mattress for that purpose, to the knowledge of Lady Valentia. The deponent was sometimes ill and obliged to sleep in a separate room from her, and on retiring from his bedside she used to send Kingsbury to attend him. He slept with his wife except in cases of real illness, absence from home, or her indisposition. The dress described in affdt [2] is his ordinary morning dress, in which he has walked considerable distances from his house, and he used commonly to remain in that dress till the middle of the day, and has often walked miles and inspected improvements and works in which he was engaged in that dress.

Four, five or six men slept in the garrets, and when he was up before the servants he has frequently gone to call them. About the time alleged in affdt [2] he had a coachman named Henry Edmonds (now in the service of Thomas Clarke Jervoise esq) who used to sleep in the same building with the stables a considerable distance from the house with the rest of the stablemen. This deponent has frequently gone to the stable to call the coachman in the manner he called the other servants, but positively denies that he ever spent much time with the coachman other than when looking over the stables or at his carriages and horses. In the most solemn manner in the presence of God, the deponent denies that he ever went to the coachman or to the room where he and the other servants slept for the horrid purpose imputed by the false affidavit of his wife, or that he ever thought of committing such an horrible and detestable crime. He positively denies that in consequence of any complaint she made of the infamy falsely and wickedly imputed to him, he ever turned away George Kingsbury or any servant, nor did the deponent ever hear such a horrible crime being imputed to him until after he had discovered the adultery of his wife.

In the beginning of 1793 finding his circumstances extremely embarrassed partly owing to his never having spared any expense to gratify the wishes of his wife, and partly from his own imprudence, deponent on the advice of his friends broke up his establishment and Henry Edmonds and the rest of the stable servants were dismissed. Kingsbury and many other house servants were dismissed in February. The sole reason was economy. In May 1793 the deponent went to London with John Maxwell his brother in law on business, when George Kingsbury happened to be out of place, and the deponent having no servant with him, Kingsbury offered to attend him while in town, which offer deponent accepted. John Maxwell urged him to take Kingsbury back, but having promised his friends never to increase his establishment until freed from his embarrassments without the consent of Wilson Aylesbury Roberts esq, and Henry Gawler esq, his trustees on his settlement with his creditors, he applied to them for liberty to rehire Kingsbury, which they readily and cheerfully gave. This application was made in the presence of Maxwell.

In the beginning of 1794, his affairs, which were managed by Mr John Gawler (father to John Bellenden Gawler), grew so desperate and his creditors so urgent that he was obliged to quit England. George Kingsbury attended him to Germany and Flanders. The deponent denies in the most solemn manner in the presence of God and as he hopes for eternal salvation that he ever had any criminal unmanly improper or indecent intercourse or familiarity of any nature of kind whatsoever with Kingsbury, Edmonds, or any other person. The deponent ever had and still has the utmost abhorrence of all abominable unnatural and unmanly practices or propensities. Before the seduction of Lady Valentia by John Bellenden Gawler they lived in mutual affection and that no charge or suggestion of the unmanly propensities imputed in affdt [2] were ever made or insinuated by Lady Valentia. He believes they were made to destroy the honor of the deponent and to protect Gawler against the action for criminal conversation.

Since the matter has been depending in court, he has obtained strong evidence that the attack on his character has originated from the combination and criminal connection between Lady Valentia and Gawler, inasmuch as the affidavit of Jane Smith was prepared after an examination of Smith for that purpose in the presence of Lady Valentia and Henry Gawler the brother of John Bellenden Gawler against whom the action for seduction is now pending.

[4] Affdt of John Maxwell esq of Portman Square (Middx), sworn in court, by the court, 7 May 1796. ITKB

That he is married to Lady Lucy Maxwell sister of Lord Valentia, and has been and is on terms of strictest intimacy with Lord Valentia, from a few weeks' after his marriage. Lord and Lady Valentia have visited this deponent and his father, the bishop of Meath, in Ireland and he has frequently visited them at Arley. They lived in the greatest harmony when in Ireland, and since then Lord Valentia has treated Lady Valentia with kindness and indulgence.

By the advice of this deponent and the consent and approbation of Mr Henry Gawler trustee for Lord Valentia in a deed between him and his creditors, Lord Valentia took back into his service George Kingsbury, who had been dismissed on the reduction of Lord Valentia's establishment. The deponent never heard any imputation of any unnatural propensity until it was publicly known that Lord Valentia intended to bring an action against John Bellenden Gawler for criminal conversation with Lady Valentia, and he heard it from Gawler's brother, Henry, who stated it as a threat to deter Lord Valentia from proceeding against his brother. Henry frequently urged this deponent to use his influence with Lord Valentia to give up the action. If he had been suspected of any unmanly or unnatural practices this deponent could not fail to have known.

The said George Kingsbury is now in Ireland, and as soon as this deponent heard of the affidavit made by Lady Valentia he wrote to procure the immediate attendance of George to obtain his testimony. The deponent is convinced from his most intimate knowledge that Lord Valentia abhors and detests all abominable and unnatural propensities and believes him incapable of harbouring an inclination of the kind.

[5] Affdt of Benjamin Dugard esq of Arley, sworn in court by the court 7 May 1796.[51]

That he lives within a very short distance of Arley Hall and was on terms of the greatest intimacy with Lord and Lady Valentia. His lordship's conduct was always kind and indulgent towards Lady Valentia, and from his intimate knowledge of Lord Valentia as well as from his general character the deponent believes him incapable of entertaining any unnatural propensity whatever. He never heard of such insinuation before Lady Valentia's affidavit.

[6] Affdt of Henry Edmonds coachman to Thomas Clarke Jervoise esq, sworn in court by the court 7 May 1796. ITKB

That he lived with Lord Valentia from his first settlement at Arley until the end of Jan 1793 when he was discharged with the other stable servants on the reduction of his lordship's establishment. That his lordship used frequently to call up his table servants early in the morning to dress and exercise his horses, but never stayed several hours in the deponent's apartments before the deponent was up, nor any longer time than was necessary for calling him to his duty or to give him directions [*Interpolated*: 'concerning his business'] Nor does the deponent believe such a circumstance could have taken place without the knowledge of Joseph Buggs and Richard Wood who for the greatest part of the time he lived with said lord slept in the room with the deponent, and afterwards in a room immediately adjoining separated only by a thin partition. Nor did his lordship ever encourage him to behave with insolence to Lady Valentia. He does most solemnly call God to witness that Lord Valentia never took any indecent liberty with him. He has no reason to believe or suspect that Viscount Valentia had any unnatural propensity or inclination nor ever heard such an insinuation until within this day or two. He never observed Lord Valentia to take such liberties with George Kingsbury or any other person, nor does he think such proceedings could have gone forward without being known to or suspected by the servants of the family. He solemnly believes Lord Valentia to be incapable of any unmanly or unnatural practice.

[7] Affdt of James Fryer surgeon and apothecary of Bewdley (Worcs), sworn in court by the court 7 May 1796. ITKB[52]

---

[51] This affidavit is headed not 'In the King's Bench', but '2/Affids 2 Expar'.

[52] The following words are struck out at the beginning of this and affdts [8] and [12]: 'Ex parte the Right Honourable George Annesley commonly called Viscount Valentia of the Kingdom of Ireland.' The affidavit was possibly copied from one to be used in the criminal conversation proceedings.

That from Lord Valentia's first settling at Arley until the establishment was broken up this deponent frequently visited the family in his professional line. During this time Lord Valentia was several times so much indisposed as to render it eligible that he should sleep in a separate apartment from his wife, and he took medicines that were to be repeated occasionally, making it necessary that someone attend him to administer the same in the night as required. From many years intimate knowledge of his lordship's general character the deponent firmly believes that Lord Valentia is incapable of any disposition or propensity to the abominable crime insinuated in Lady Valentia's affidavit.

[8] Affdt of Thomas Platt groom to Mr Tongwire in Grosvenor Street, sworn in court by the court 7 May 1796. ITKB

That he lived with Lord Valentia for near a year in 1793, about seven months of which George Kingsbury was there as Lord Valentia's valet. During that whole time he and Kingsbury slept in the same room. Lord Valentia used occasionally to rouse them but he solemnly swears that he never saw the least indecent familiarity between his lordship and George or any other person, never heard any suspicion in the family on the subject, and is positively certain that Lord Valentia did not make a great noise in the room, nor play with the servants, nor ever pull the clothes off the men servants beds or behave in any indecent manner whatever. Nor did he hear any such insinuation until this day, and believes it altogether false.

[9] Affdt of Mary Kininmore[53] waiting maid to the Rt Honourable ladies Sophia and Amelia Grey, sworn in court by the court 7 May 1796. ITKB

That she lived as a waiting maid with Anne Viscountess Valentia from the time of her marriage until Jan 1795, during which time Lord Valentia was indulgent and affectionate towards Lady Valentia. She placed great confidence in the deponent, and often communicated with her on subjects not immediately related to her service. Lady Valentia never mentioned any suspicion of Lord Valentia's having any unnatural propensity or criminal familiarity with his men servants, which the deponent is inclined to believe she would have communicated to her. The deponent never heard any such imputation until she saw a copy of Lady Valentia's affidavit, and she is firmly persuaded that any such insinuation is false and without foundation.

[10] Affdt of William Goodwin valet to the Earl of Pomfret, sworn in court by the court 7 May 1796. ITKB

---

[53] 'Kennimore' in the pamphlet of 1796.

That he lived as butler with Lord Valentia for about six months in 1793 and 1794, when George Kingsbury lived there as valet. The deponent never saw the least indecent familiarity between Lord Valentia and George or any other person. He never heard such insinuations until the last few days. Lord Valentia was tender and affectionate to Anne Viscountess Valentia, and he in his conscience believes that any insinuations against the honour of the Viscount imputing and propensities of any unnatural kind are utterly false unfounded and groundless.

[11] Affdt of Elizabeth Beaver of Down Street Piccadilly, and Margaret Elliott, cook to the lord bishop of London, sworn in court by the court 7 May 1796. ITKB
[Both]: That they lived with Lord and Lady Valentia as housekeeper and cook from their first settlement at Arley until the breaking up of the establishment in 1793 when they were discharged the same day as George Kingsbury and other servants. They never observed, nor heard until the swearing of Lady Valentia's affidavit, of any insinuation of any indecent conduct of Lord Valentia toward George or any other person, nor any suspicion of his having any propensity to any unnatural intercourse or crime; they firmly believe any such insinuation is grossly false. His conduct to his wife was tender and affectionate.

[12] Affdt of Charles Hambling servant to Thomas Green esq of Bedford Square (Middx), sworn in court by the court 7 May 1796. ITKB
That having heard that Jane Smith had joined in an affidavit with Lady Valentia, the deponent called on Smith Tuesday last and asked her if she had made an affidavit in which she had reflected on Lord Valentia in the most shocking manner. She replied that she was convinced that what she had sworn would not injure Lord Valentia. The deponent asked who she had seen and what had been said to her, and Smith said that [*Words struck out*: 'He Mr Gawler meaning as this deponent believes Mr John Bellenden Gawler and'] Mr Henry Gawler was [*Stuck out*: 'were'] with Lady Valentia Saturday last, that Jane Smith was called into the room and examined by Mr Henry Gawler, who asked her whether she recollected Lord Valentia going to call the men servants, and she told him she did recollect it, Mr Henry Gawler then asked her if she recollected his proceeding from thence to the stables to call the coachman, she said she believed so, that Mr Henry Gawler asked her if she did not observe him to go out without anything on but his morning gown, she said she did not examine whether he had or not. Jane also informed this deponent that she had not sworn that she heard or believed Lord Valentia pulled the clothes off the servants bed and had been at play wit the men servants and if that was in the affidavit it

was put in without her knowledge. She said Mr Henry Gawler asked her if she did not recollect Lord Valentia sleeping in a room from Lady Valentia and she replied that she did, when he was ill; Gawler asked if George slept with him and she replied no, she was sure of that as she and another servant carried a bed down for George to sleep on when he slept in the room with Lord Valentia. Gawler then asked if George's bed was not placed by the side of Lord Valentia's and she said no, it was at the other side of the room. Jane Smith told the deponent that she never had any suspicion of Lord Valentia being guilty of any crimes with men, and did not mean in her affidavit to insinuate anything of the kind.

This deponent lived as footman with Lord Valentia from Oct 1791 to Nov 1793, and during all that time never heard of Lord Valentia being suspected of the crime insinuated in Lady Valentia's affidavit, nor heard of it before the affidavit.

Sources: KB 1/29/1 Ea 36 Geo III. KB 16/21/5. KB 21/46 pp.511, 518, 523.

Section H

Like the judges of all higher courts, those of King's Bench had the right
to punish contempt of their orders through an attachment for contempt.
As the highest court of criminal law, the justices of King's Bench also
defined the boundaries of the offence of contempt at common law
through their decisions in individual cases. The punishment at common law was imprisonment at the discretion of the judges. The writ of
attachment for contempt was used against magistrates and officers of
the court (sheriffs, bailiffs, gaolers) for disobedience to the king's writ,
or failure to make adequate returns to writs; for acts of oppression,
extortion, neglect of duty in proceedings of the court; against recalci-
trant witnesses and jurymen; against non-appearing defendants; but
chiefly for non-payment of money such as fines, awards, costs.[1]

One of the two cases in this section (H.2) was an attachment for contempt of a judgment in a civil case in Common Pleas, which the defendant failed to pay, but it is included here because it is part of a complex
of litigation arising out of a criminal charge of horsetheft, including a
habeas corpus application (G.2), an attachment for contempt in those
proceedings by using false bailsmen (H.1), and a criminal information
against the gaoler of Stafford (A.21). The whole group of cases shows the
usefulness of the high courts for what was probably a criminal gang, and
the involvement of corrupt attorneys, one of whom went to gaol himself
for conspiracy in another case; he was also struck off the roll of attorneys.
The contempt in H.1 was purged simply by a negative answer to all the
allegations in the interrogatories (see below). Many of the affidavits in
H.1 arose out of a dispute three years later between two brothers (one
of whom was the defendant in the attachment for contempt, the other of
whom had given surety for his appearance) and their attorneys about
who had the right to the return of £100 paid for a discharged recognizance. Each of the attorneys was attempting to claim it for his fees. The
case illuminates some of the practices of the attorneys, who were officers
of the court and who controlled what litigation came before it. One of the
brothers also worked for one of the lawyers, appearing regularly as a

---

[1] Hands, 60–62; Gude, i, 250–51. For an attempt to get an attachment for contempt of an award see case F.1, and case F.5 for contempt of an order of
King's Bench.

bailsman for his clients at Westminster. The other attorney also ended up under arrest, for debt, and a third, based in Rowley Regis, was a close associate of the London attorney who was struck off.

Attachment and interrogatories

Most attachments were granted on a motion by counsel, as a rule to show cause (a rule nisi), by a rule of court on the motion of counsel, on the basis of an affidavit. Notice of the rule had to be served on the defendant. If (as in case H.1) the contempt arose in a civil court, these steps took place there, only moving to the crown side of King's Bench once the attachment issued. Once the rule was made absolute, the clerk in court made out the writ, had it sealed at the seal office in Inner Temple Lane, and the solicitor then obtained a warrant on it from the sheriff's office. The writ had to be returned in four days, if within 40 miles, or six days, if farther. Once in custody or bailed, the defendant had to answer interrogatories, unless that was waived by the prosecutor.

Interrogatories were detailed questions about the contempt, which the defendant could not refuse to answer; they were taken ex parte, not in the presence of the prosecutor. Interrogatories, which could lead to self-incrimination, entered political controversy at mid-century as an egregious relic of the court of Star Chamber, when chief justice Lord Mansfield tried to use them against critics of the government, and of himself, in a case involving the particular contempt of scandalizing the court.[2] Those in this volume arose out of ordinary criminal and civil cases. In case H.1 one set of interrogatories and answers to them have been reproduced in full.

Interrogatories were drawn up and signed by counsel, engrossed, and filed with the examiner, one of the clerks in the crown office, who made an office copy for the defendant. If he or she was in custody, the prosecutor's solicitor got a side bar rule (for prisoners in King's Bench prison) or a habeas corpus (if held elsewhere) for the defendant to be brought up and examined; if bailed, an appointment was made. A poor prosecutor unable to pay for interrogatories of a defendant held in a county gaol could get an order for examination by a commissioner of the court living near the gaol. After full answers to clear the defendant of the contempt were taken down, they were referred by a motion of either party to the master of the crown office. The solicitors and clerks in court on both sides (and sometimes counsel) then attended the master with the papers; once he was ready to report, the prosecutor gave notice of motion for the report and a brief to counsel to move for the

---

[2]   D. Hay, 'Scandalizing the Court: A Political History of the First Hundred Years, 1721–1821' *Osgoode Hall Law Journal*, xxv (1987), 431–84.

master's report. The master then informed the court whether the contempt had been cleared; the defendant had to be present. Discharge, or punishment, followed.[3]

Punishment
Neither of the cases in this section resulted in punishment, but the penalties at common law were fine and/or imprisonment, or corporal punishment, and the court usually ordered payment of the prosecutor's costs. However, a defendant who purged the contempt on interrogatories did not usually get costs, unless the judges believed the prosecution to be groundless.

CASES

H.1 Attachment for contempt for false bail; dispute between attorneys and clients on costs (22 Nov 1782)

Defendant: James Mason, butcher of Rowley Regis.

Writ and return:
Writ of attachment to the sheriff of Staffordshire to have Charles Cox, John Sincox alias Simcox, William West and James Mason in court on [7 May 1783] to answer for contempt. [*Lower left corner*: into Worcester and Stafford]. [*Verso*]: Return by Richard Gildart, sheriff, that none of them are found in his bailiwick. [*Another hand*]: 'Samuel Midgely Clerk in Court, 27 Jan 1783. 6 10.'[4]

Rules and process:
Mich [27 Nov 1782]: on reading the affdts of William Dudley,[5] William Mason, James Mason, Thomas Wild and of Samuel Tongue and two

---

[3]   The preceding account is from Hands, 62–67, who gives examples of the writ, recognizances, and interrogatories and answers at 507–18, and Gude, i, 250–59.

[4]   The figures are probably 6s 10d, likely the fee in the crown office for an attachment; Gude, i, 253 cites a slightly higher fee in 1828. Although the writ issued against four defendants, instructions were given to prosecute only West and Mason (see affidavit [1], *verso*); no further proceedings appear against West. See also cases A.21, G.2, H.2 for related proceedings.

[5]   Dudley's affidavit has not been found; his role is mentioned in affidavit [1], and the entry in KB 21/43 may be a clerical error. For the affidavits of Wild, James Mason, and William Mason see case G.2.

others [1], rule nisi to FDT for a writ of attachment for contempt against Cox, Sincox, West, and James Mason (Howorth).[6] 27 Jan 1783: writ issues; returned 7 May 1783 'not found.' Mich [25 Nov 1783]: defdt having now here in court put in bail by consent of the attorney for the prosn for his personal appearance to answer first day of next term on an attachment of contempt, ordered that a writ of supersedeas issue (Sir Thos Davenport). [*In margin*]: '100 100'.[7] Trin [22 June 1784]: defdt having been thrice publicly called and not appearing, ordered that his default be recorded and the recognizance estreated (Bower). ST [25 June 1784]: on reading affdt [3] of John Stuart and an annexed rule of this court, ordered that an alias attachment issue against the defdt for his contempt (Bower). Ea [21 April 1785]: order that [25 April] be given to prosr to show cause why defdt should not be at liberty now to enter into a recognizance to answer interrogatories, on notice of the rule to be given to prosr (Garrow). ST [3 May 1785]: defdt being present here in court and is sworn to make true answer to all such interrogatories as shall be exhibited against him touching a contempt supposed to be committed against this court (Garrow). Mich [22 Nov 1785]: ordered that it be referred to James Templer [master of the crown office] to examine the interrogatories [5] filed against the defdt in this cause and also the answers [6] and to report same to the court (Lowes). ST [26 Nov 1785]: defdt being present here in court, and on hearing the master's report defdt is adjudged not to be in contempt; ordered that the recognizance of the defdt be discharged (Sheridan). Hil [6 Feb 1786]: recognizances of defdt to be discharged (side bar).[8] Hil [10 Feb 1787]: on reading affdt [7] of Thomas Mason ordered that Edward Gosnell gentleman answer by [12 Feb 1787] the matters contained in the said

---

6   This rule appears annexed to affidavit [1]; Gude, i, 250 notes that attachments were issued by a clerk in court in the crown office on production of the original rule, which was copied into a rule book and then returned to the solicitor, but that 'all rules for attachments for not obeying writs issued out of the Crown Office are entered and drawn up in that Office in the first instance.'

7   The recognizances in £100 each of Thomas and Joseph Mason (see affidavits). Two bail only were required in attachments: Gude, i, 256.

8   In the margin, '250', the sum of the recognizances in pounds sterling. In affidavit [7], Thomas Mason swears that he entered into a second recognizance of £100 after the first was estreated; he gives Mich 1786 as the term in which James Mason was found not in contempt and the second recognizance discharged. This appears to be an error in dating; however, there may have been a third recognizance in the course of the proceedings in this and the subsequent litigation.

affdt (Mingay). ST [12 Feb 1787]: first day of next term further given to Gosnell to answer (Mingay). Ea [21 May 1787]: ordered that third day of next term be further given to answer the matters in the affdt of Thomas Mason, already filed, and affdt [8] of William Morris gentleman now filed (Mingay). Trin [12 June 1787]: on reading affdt [12] of Edward Gosnell gentleman, ordered that the prosr of the rule made last term (an order that Gosnell should answer matters in the affdts of Mason and Morris) be given to [15 June] to show cause why the said rule should not be set aside for irregularity, and why Mr Priddle the attorney for the said prosr should not pay to Gosnell the costs of this application, on notice of this rule to be given to Priddle in the meantime (Garrow). ST [14 June 1787]: on reading the several affdts [12], [13] of Edward Gosnell gentleman and of Gosnell and another [10] now filed in this cause, ordered that the prosr of the rule made last term whereby [*as before*] be further given to [16 June] to show cause why the said rule should not be set aside for irregularity, and why Mr Priddle the attorney for the prosr should not pay to Gosnell the costs of this application, on notice of this rule to be given to Priddle in the meantime (Garrow). ST [27 June 1787]: on hearing counsel both sides, ordered that it be referred to James Templer [master of the crown office] to determine whether Mr Edward Gosnell mentioned in the rule of [14 June] is entitled to retain the whole or any part of the sum of £100 mentioned in the affdts filed in this cause, upon the undertaking of Gosnell to pay over what the said [master] shall order or to deliver up the constat of an estreat and also a letter from the surveyor of the green wax[9] mentioned in the said affdts if the [master] shall so order (Garrow for Gosnell, Mingay for Mason).[10]

Affidavit for a rule for an attachment for contempt:

Mich 23 Geo III 1782

[1] Affdt of Samuel Tongue farmer of Claverley (Salop), sworn before William Chrees at Wolverhampton 22 Nov 1782; William Field collier

---

[9] The surveyor of green wax was the official in charge of estreats delivered to sheriffs out of the exchequer, under the seal of that court, to be levied in the counties. A constat was 'a certificate which the clerk of the pipe and auditors of the exchequer chamber made, at the request of any person who intended to plead or move in that court, for the discharge of anything.' Giles Jacob, *A New Law-Dictionary* (2nd edn, London, 1733).

[10] Affdts [16] to [20] were filed in connection with this reference to the master, but no further process or rules have been found.

of Tipton, sworn before William Chrees at Birmingham (Warws) 23 Nov 1782; and William Johnston gentleman of the Inner Temple (London), sworn before E. Willes at his chambers at Sergeants' Inn 26 Nov 1782. [*William Field signed with a mark.*] ITKB 'The King against Sincocks otherwise Sincox.' [*Verso*]: '10 Kings Bench Wolverhampton The King agst Sincox: H. Howorth. Mr Howorth, Please to move for an attachmt agst West and Mason shew cause 29+14=43 Johnston.'

[Samuel Tongue]: That on or about 4 May last his black gelding was stolen out of his stable at Claverley and Charles Cox and John Sincox were apprehended on suspicion of the felony and committed to Leicester gaol for trial by the Reverend William Clayton JP of Leicestershire.

[William Field]: That some time after Cox and Sincox were committed Sincox was informed that J. West or W. West of Wolverhampton was employed as solicitor for the prisoners and had engaged to get them removed from Leicester gaol to London. Thomas Worsey of Wednesbury asked the deponent to go to London to give Sincox a character, telling him they were to be tried there and not at Leicester, and he would pay his expenses. The next day the deponent and James Mason of Rowley Regis, William Dudley of Dudley (Worcs) screwfiler and Jonathan Taylor of Rowley Regis went to Leicester where they were informed that Cox, Sincox and West had gone to London. The deponent, Mason, Dudley and Taylor were met by West in London two days later. The next day the deponent, West, Mason, Dudley and Taylor and a person who called himself Charles Stone met in a public house in Clare Market. West informed them that Cox and Sincocks were not to be tried in London but would be admitted to bail and that the deponent, Dudley, Taylor and Stone must become bail under assumed names for the prisoner's appearance at the next assizes in Leicester. When the deponent expressed his fear of doing wrong, West told all four of them that it was no sin or harm, if any person lay in the lash it must be him and if any person must be hanged for it he must be the person. The deponent was a stranger in London, some 120 miles from home, no friend to advise with, only a few shillings in his pocket and not knowing how to return to his family. At the instigation of West and Mason and for the two guineas promised him by Mason, he agreed to become bail for the prisoners in a fictitious name and Dudley and Taylor, whom he believes to be friends of Mason, did also; Mason appeared to be the friend and agent of the prisoners. Charles Stone is an utter stranger to him and the name may have been assumed. The deponent heard West agree to give Charles Stone three guineas for becoming bail, two in hand and one after the bail had passed. West and Mason also promised Dudley and Taylor that they should be paid. West and Mason told

Dudley, Taylor and Stone what names to assume for the bail. The deponent was to assume the name of William Harding farmer of Bilston, Dudley was to assume the name of William King farmer of Ettingshall Lane parish of Wolverhampton, Taylor was to assume the name of Thomas Smith farmer of Sedgley, and Charles Stone was to assume the name of Charles Stone painter of Castleyard, parish of Saint Andrew Holborn (London). The next morning these instructions were repeated to them, and before the court of King's Bench in Westminster Hall they acknowledged recognizances of bail in the fictitious names. Cox and Sincox were set at liberty. West told them they must either make it up with the prosecutor Tongue or leave the country.

[William Johnston]: That on examining and inspecting the bails taken in the crown side of the court, bail appears to have been put in for Sincox in the several names, additions and descriptions deposed to by Field. West acted as attorney for Cox and Sincox on the acknowledging of bail. On enquiring at the crown office the habeas corpus on which Cox and Sincox were bailed appears to have been obtained upon the several annexed affidavits sworn before West.

[Samuel Tongue]: That he was never served with the notice of bail mentioned in James Mason's affidavit[11] and believes that no such notice was ever served on Clayton, the JP who committed Cox and Sincocks. Mason and the persons making such affidavits did so under fictitious descriptions to evade prosecution. He has made enquiries after the persons who became bail for Cox and Sincocks and he believes the bail was made under fictitious names and that no such persons exist.

[William Johnston]: That he has compared the several copies of the affidavits with the originals in the crown office.

[*Annexed*]: Copies of 8 June 1782 affdt of William Mason of service of notice and annexed 5 June 1782 notice by William West [*affdt [3] of case G.2*] and a copy of the 27 Nov 1782 rule for writ of attachment for contempt.

Affidavit for defence:

Mich 24 Geo III 1783

[2] Affdt of Samuel Lea yeoman of Stafford, sworn before J. Dickenson at Stafford 11 Nov 1783. ITKB [*Verso*]: '40 The King v Mason [*Following words lightly crossed out*]: 'To Mr Lowes ½ Ga. R. Paull To move to put in bail for the defdt upon an attachment of contempt in Stafford gaol. Priddle.'

---

[11] This is an error; the annexed affidavit is by William Mason.

That the deponent saw Littleton Scott sign and subscribe the [*annexed*] certificate.

[*Annexed*]: 'To the right honourable William Earl of Mansfield Lord Chief Justice of his majesty's court of King's Bench and the rest of the justices of that honourable court. I Littleton Scott keeper of his majesty's gaol for the county of Stafford do hereby certify unto your lordships that James Mason now a prisoner in the said gaol was delivered into my custody on the nineteenth day of June last by virtue of a warrant under the seal of office of Richard Gildart esquire sheriff of the said county of Stafford of which the following is a true copy.

'Staffordshire. Richard Gildart esquire sheriff of the county aforesaid to the keeper of the gaol of the said county and also to John Holmes and Brian Silvester my bailiffs and also to William Randle a special bailiff at the request and peril of the plaintiff hereinafter mentioned, greeting.

[*In margin*: 'No bail By rule of court (L: S.)'] 'By virtue of the writ of our sovereign lord the king to me the said sheriff directed I hereby command you and every of you jointly and severally that you some or one of you do not forbear by reason of any liberty in my bailewick but that you attach James Mason so that I may have him before our said lord the king at Westminster on [20 June 1783]... to answer to our said lord the king for certain trespasses and contempts brought against him in our lord the king's court before the king himself. Hereof fail not at your peril. Given under my seal of office the twenty fourth day of May in the year of our Lord one thousand seven hundred and eighty three.

'Wace and Midgley clerks in court. By the same sheriff

'And I the said Littleton Scott do further certify that the said James Mason now remains in my custody by virtue of the said warrant and not for any other cause. Witness my hand the eleventh day of November one thousand seven hundred and eighty three. [*Signed*]: L: Scott'

[*Annexed*]:

Acknowledgement of William Johnston dated 24 Nov 1783. 'In the Kings Bench. The King v James Mason on an attachment of contempt'.

That Johnston consents and agrees on behalf of the prosecutor that Thomas Mason and Joseph Mason may be taken in a recognizance as bail for the appearance of the defendant in the court for the first day of Hilary Term next to be sworn to answer such interrogatories as shall be exhibited against him.

Affidavits for prosecution for interrogatories and a second attachment:

Trin 24 Geo III 1784

[3] Affdt of John Stuart clerk to William Johnston gentleman of the Inner Temple (London), sworn before E[dward] Willes[12] at his chambers in Sergeant's Inn 21 June 1784. 'The King agt James Mason'. [*Verso*]: '35. The King agst James Mason: Affidt. That deft & his Bail may appear and enter into [*struck out:* Interrogatories] Recogce to answer Interrogatories [*struck out:* and that *illegible* Recogs may be estreated]. Jos. Bower. Johnston Inner Temple.'

That on Saturday 19 June instant the deponent served the [*annexed*] notice to Mr. Midgeley clerk in court for the defendant at his seat in the Crown office.

[A*nnexed*]: [*Verso*]: 'The King agt Jas Mason: Copy Notice served on a Mr Midgeley. Served Mr Midgeley the 19th June 1784—JS. Johnston Inner Temple.' 'England The King agst James Mason [Mr Priddle *struck out*] Mr Midgeley: Take notice that I have filed the interrogatories for the examination of the defendant in the crown office in the Temple and take further notice that the court of King's Bench will be moved on [*struck out:* the last day of the present Easter term that] Tuesday next 22 June instant or so soon after as counsel can be heard that the said defendant and his bail may appear and enter into a recognizance to answer such interrogatories and in case the said defendant shall not appear the court will be moved to estreat the former recognizance. Dated the 19th [18th *struck out*] day of June [May *struck out*] 1784. Yours, W. Johnston agent for the prosecution.'

[4] Affdt of John Stuart, clerk to William Johnston gentleman, of the Inner Temple (London), sworn by the court in court 25 June 1784. ITKB 'The King agst James Mason.' [*Verso*]: '40 The King agst Mason: The deft having suffered his recognizance to be estreated after having been thrice publicly called. Please move for an Al[ia]s attachment against the deft. Fos. Bower. Johnston for the prosecution.'

That on 19 June the deponent personally served William Midgeley, clerk in court for the defendant, with a notice that the interrogatories had been filed for the examination of the defendant in the crown office in the Temple and that King's Bench would be moved [22 June] that Mason and his bail appear and enter into a recognizance to answer such interrogatories, and that unless they appeared the court would be moved to estreat the former recognizance. This court was accordingly moved and a rule obtained [22 June] that not having appeared after being thrice called, the defendant's recognizance should be estreated.

---

[12] A puisne justice of King's Bench 1768–87.

Interrogatories and answers by James Mason:

Mich 26 Geo III 1785

[5] 'England Ss. Interrogatories Exhibited in the Court of our Lord the King before the King himself against James Mason for a Contempt of the said Court.' [*Verso*]: 'Easter Term 24th G. 3d 1784. England. The King agt James Mason for procuring persons to become bail in false names. Filed May 18th 1784. RB fo:24.'[13]

'First – Were you or were you not in or about the month of June last or at any and what other time in the year one thousand seven hundred and eighty three present and in company with one William West, one William Dudley one Jonathan Taylor a Person calling himself Charles Stone and one William Field or any or either and which of them at a public or some and what other house in Clare Market in the parish of Saint Clement Danes in the county of Middlesex and was or was not the bailing of one Charles Cox and one John Sincox otherwise Simcox who had just then been or were then about to be brought up by virtue of a writ of habeas corpus from Leicester gaol for trial to which they stood committed at the then next assizes and general gaol delivery at Leicester for horse stealing the subject of conversation at such meeting, and was it or was it not thereupon proposed that the said William Field William Dudley and Jonathan Taylor the said person calling himself Charles Stone or any or either and which of them should become bail in the court of our lord the now king before the king himself here for the said Cox and Sincox otherwise Simcox on the said writ of habeas corpus in false and fictitious names different from their own. And did you or did you not as well as the said William West thereupon request the said William Field to become one of such Bail and did you not thereupon promise the said William Field the sum of two guineas or any and what other sum of money or reward if he would be one of such bail and become bail for the said Cox and Sincox otherwise Simcox in a fictitious name. And did or did not the said William Field thereupon agree to become one of such bail for the said Cox and Sincox otherwise Simcox?

'Secondly – Did or did you not together with the said William West or either and which of you separately at the said meeting in Clare Market in the first interrogatory mentioned or at any and what other

---

[13] The interrogatories are on parchment, the answers [6] on paper. They are both fully transcribed here, with abbreviations in the text expanded. The interrogatories were prepared in Easter 1784 but not answered until Michaelmas 1785: see '*Rules and process*', above.

time or place make any and what promise offer or agreement to or with the said William Dudley Jonathan Taylor and the said person calling himself Charles Stone or to one or either and which of them to induce them and each of them or any or either and which of them to enter into a like recognizance or the aforesaid writ of habeas corpus and to become bail in fictitious and false names and descriptions in the said court of our said lord the king before the king himself for the said Charles Cox and John Sincox otherwise Simcox or either and which of them at the then next assizes and general gaol delivery at Leicester. And did or did not the said William Dudley and Jonathan Taylor and the said person calling himself Charles Stone or any or either and which of them thereupon and in consequence of such promise or reward as aforesaid then and there agree to enter into such recognizances and to become bail for the said Charles Cox and John Sincox otherwise Simcox or either and which of them in false and fictitious names. And did you or did you not and did or did not the said William West thereupon or at any and what other time proceed to instruct inform and direct and actually instruct and direct the said William Field, William Dudley and Jonathan Field and the said person calling himself Charles Stone or any or either and which of them what name and description or names and descriptions they or any or either of them should assume and answer to as bail for the appearance of the said Charles Cox and John Sincox otherwise Simcox at the said assizes at Leicester. And did you or did you not and did or did not the said William West or either and which of them instruct and direct the said William Field William Dudley, Jonathan Taylor and the said person calling himself Charles Stone to assume and answer to and become bail on the aforesaid writ of habeas corpus in and by the several names and descriptions following (that is to say) the said William Field by the name and description of William Harding of Bilstone in the county of Stafford farmer, the said William Dudley by the name or description of William King of Ettingsall Lane Tanner [*sic*] in the parish of Wolverhampton in the said county of Stafford farmer the said Jonathan Taylor by the name or description of Thomas Smith of Sedgley in the said county farmer and the said person calling himself Charles Stone by the name or description of Charles Stone of Castle Yard or by any and what other name or names description or descriptions set forth the truth herein fully and at large declare.

'Thirdly – Did you or did you not on the thirteenth day of June in the year one thousand and seven hundred and eighty two or at any and at what that other time attend the said William Field, William Dudley and Jonathan Taylor and the said person calling himself Charles Stone or any or either and which of them to the court of our said lord the king before the king himself here and repeat unto them or to any or either and which of them the false and fictitious names and descriptions they were respectively to assume and answer to and desire them not to make any mistake but to take care and answer to such respective names and descriptions as they should be severally called over. And did or did not the said William Field, the said William Dudley, the said Jonathan Taylor and the said person calling himself Charles Stone and each and every of them or any or either and which of them thereupon become bail for the said Charles Cox and John Sincox otherwise Simcox in the said court upon the aforesaid writ of habeas corpus and severally enter into recognizance of bail in the said court for the appearance of the said Charles Cox and John Sincox otherwise Simcox at the then next assizes, and general gaol delivery at Leicester in and by the said several names and description in the second interrogatory mentioned (that is to say) the said William Field by the name and description of William Harding of Bilstone in the county of Stafford farmer the said William Dudley by the name and description of William King of Ettingsall Lane in the parish of Wolverhampton in the said county of Stafford farmer, the said Jonathan Taylor by the name and description of Thomas Smith of Sedgley in the said county farmer and the said person calling himself Charles Stone by the name and description of Charles Stone of Castle Yard or by any and what other name or names description or descriptions and were or were not such names and descriptions or any or either and which of them merely assumed and not the real names and descriptions of the said William Field, William Dudley, Jonathan Taylor and the said person calling himself Charles Stone but false and fictitious. And did you or did you not know as well at the time of its being so proposed as aforesaid that they the said William Field, William Dudley, Jonathan Taylor and the said person calling himself Charles Stone should become such bail as at the time of their becoming such bail and entering into such recognizances as aforesaid that the said several and respective names and additions by which they so became bail were not or that some or one and which of them in particular were or was not their true names and descriptions but merely assumed and false and fictitious in themselves. Set forth and declare the truth herein fully and at large.

'Lastly – Did you or did you not by the ways and means in the foregoing interrogatories mentioned or by any what other means persuade entice or procure the said William Field, William Dudley, Jonathan Taylor and the said person calling himself Charles Stone or any or either and which of them to become such bail as aforesaid for the said Charles Cox and John Sincox otherwise Simcox in this court here upon the aforesaid writ of habeas corpus and to enter into such recognizance

as aforesaid in by and under such false and fictitious names and
descriptions as aforesaid or any or either and which of them and did or
did not the said William Field, William Dudley, Jonathan Taylor and
the said person calling himself Charles Stone as aforesaid or any or
either and which of them by and through the means and by reason and
in consequence of such your enticement persuasion and procurement
become such bail and enter into such recognizance as aforesaid. And
were or were not the said Charles Cox and John Sincox otherwise
Simcox discharged from Leicester gaol in consequence of such bail
being put in for them in the said court upon the said writ of habeas corpus as aforesaid. And being so at liberty, did they not abscond and was
not Cox again apprehended for horsestealing and tried at Leicester.
And did not Sincox otherwise Simcox abscond and omit to appear or
surrender himself for trial pursuant to the aforesaid recognizance and
hath he not been since tried at Worcester for horsestealing and com-
mited [*sic*]. Set forth and declare the truth herein fully and at large.

Thos. Lowes'

[6] 'In the Kings Bench – of Michas Term in the 26th year of King George
the 3d

'The examination and answers of James Mason to certain interrogatories exhibited against him in his majesty's court of Kings Bench at
Westminster touching a contempt supposed to be by him committed
against the said court. [*Verso*]: 'Michas 26 Geo. 3. England The King agt
James Mason. Defts Answers to Interries.'

'To the first interrogatory this examinant answereth and saith that in
or about the month of June in the year 1783 he was present and in company with one William West but not with William Dudley Jonathan
Taylor or a person calling himself Charles Stone or William Field or any
of them at a public house called the Peacock in Claremarket. And that
the bailing of Charles Cox [*Struck out: and John Sincox otherwise
Simcox*] was the subject of conversation between the said West and this
examinant, the said West asking this examinant if he would be bail for
the said Cox which this examinant refused but nothing passed between
the said West and this Examinant concerning the said John Sincox otherwise Simcox. That it was not thereupon proposed in the presence or
hearing of this examinant that the said William Field William Dudley
and Jonathan Taylor the said Person calling himself Charles Stone or
any of them should become bail in the court of our lord the now king
before the king himself[14] here for the said Cox and Sincox otherwise
Simcox on the said writ of habeas corpus in false and fictitious names

---

[14]   i.e., King's Bench.

different from their own. That this examinant did not request the said William Field to become one of such bail nor did he thereupon promise the said William Field the sum of two guineas or any other sum of money or reward if he would become one such bail and become bail for the said Cox and Sincox otherwise Simcox in a fictitious name. That the said William Field did not thereupon agree to become one such bail for the said Cox and Sincox otherwise Simcox nor was the said William Field present or in company with the examinant and the said West.[15]

'To the second interrogatory this examinant answereth and saith that he did not together with the said William West or separately at the said meeting in Claremarket in [*Struck out:* this examinant's answer to] the first interrogatory mentioned but at which William Dudley Jonathan Taylor a Person calling himself Charles Stone and William Field in the same interrogatory mentioned were not nor was any of them present or at any other time or place make any promise offer or agreement to or with the said William Dudley Jonathan Taylor and the said Person calling himself Charles Stone or to any of them to induce them and each or any of them to enter into a like or any recognizance on any writ of habeas corpus or to become bail in fictitious and false names and descriptions in the said court of our said lord the king before the king himself for the said Charles Cox and John Sincox otherwise Simcox or either of them at the then next assizes and general gaol delivery at Leicester. That the said William Dudley and Jonathan Taylor and the said person calling himself Charles Stone or any of them did not thereupon or in consequence of any such promise or reward then and there agree to enter into such recognizances or to become bail for the said Charles Cox and John Sincox otherwise Simcox or either of them in false and fictitious names. That this examinant did not nor did the said William West in the presence or hearing of this examinant thereupon or at any other time proceed to instruct inform or direct or actually instruct or direct the said William Field William Dudley Jonathan Taylor and the said person calling himself Charles Stone or any of them what name and description or names and descriptions they or any of them should assume and answer to as bail for the appearances the said Charles Cox and John Sincox otherwise Simcox at the said assizes at Leicester. That this examinant did not nor did the said William West in the presence or hearing of this examinant instruct or direct the said William Field William Dudley Jonathan Taylor and the said person calling himself Charles Stone to assume and answer to or become bail on any writ of habeas corpus in only the several names and descriptions

---

[15]   Each answer is initialled 'J.M.'

following (that is to say) the said William Field by the name or description of William Harding of Bilstone in the county of Stafford farmer the
said William Dudley by the name and description of William King of
Ettingsall Lane farmer in the parish of Wolverhampton in the said
county of Stafford farmer [*sic*] the said Jonathan Taylor by the name
and description of Thomas Smith of Sedgley in the said county farmer
and the said person calling himself Charles Stone by the name and
description of Charles Stone of Castle Yard or by any other name or
names description or descriptions whatsoever.

'To the third interrogatory this examinant answereth and saith that
he did not on the 13th day of June in the year 1782 or at any other time
attend the said William Field William Dudley and Jonathan Taylor and
the said person calling himself Charles Stone or any of them to the court
of our said lord the king before the king himself and repeat unto them
or to any of them the false and fictitious names and descriptions they
were respectively to assume and answer to or desire them not to make
any mistake but to take care and answer to such respective names and
descriptions as they should be severally called over. That this examinant does not know nor can set forth whether the said William Field the
said William Dudley the said Jonathan Taylor and the said person calling himself Charles Stone and each and every of them or any or either
of which of them did or did not thereupon become bail for the said
Charles Cox and John Sincox otherswise Simcox in the said court upon
any writ of habeas corpus and severally enter into a recognizance of bail
in the said court for the appearance of the said Charles and John Sincox
otherwise Simcox at the then next assizes and general gaol delivery at
Leicester in and by the said several names and descriptions in the second interrogatory mentioned (that is to say) the said William Field by
the name and description of William Harding of Bilstone in the county
of Stafford farmer the said William Dudley by the name and description of William King of Ettingsall Lane in the parish of Wolverhampton
in the said county of Stafford farmer the said Jonathan Taylor by the
name and description of Thomas Smith of Sedgley in the said county
farmer and the said person calling himself Charles Stone by the name
and description of Charles Stone of Castle Yard and or by any other
name or names description or descriptions but this [*Struck out*: depon-
ent] examinant has since been informed and believes such names
and descriptions might be merely assumed and not the real names and
description of the said William Field William Dudley Jonathan Taylor
and the said person calling himself Charles Stone but false and fictitious. That this Examinant did not know at the time of its being so proposed as by the interrogatories is supposed that they the said William
Field William Dudley Jonathan Taylor and the said person calling

himself Charles Stones should become such bail or at the time of their becoming such bail and entering into such recognizances as aforesaid that the said several and respective names and additions by which they so became bail was not or that some or one or any of them in the particular were or was not their true names and descriptions or name and description but merely assumed and false and fictitious is themselves.

'To the last interrogatory this examinant answereth and saith that he did not by the ways and means in the foregoing interrogatories mentioned or by any other means persuade entice or procure the said William Field William Dudley Jonathan Taylor and the said person calling himself Charles Stone or any or either of them to become such bail as aforesaid for the said Charles Cox and John Sincox otherwise Simcox in this court here upon any writ of habeas corpus or to enter into such recognizance as aforesaid in by and under such false and fictitious names and descriptions as aforesaid or any of them and the said William Field William Dudley Jonathan Taylor and the said person calling himself Charles Stone as aforesaid or any or either of them did not by or through the means or by reason or in consequence of any enticement persuasion or procurement of this examinant became such bail or enter into such recognizance as aforesaid. This examinant has been informed and believes the said Charles Cox and John Sincox otherwise Simcox were discharged from Leicester gaol in consequence of bail being put in for them in the said court upon a writ of habeas corpus but whether the same was put in in the manner by the interrogatories supposed this examinant cannot set forth. This examinant has heard and believes but does not know that they did abscond and that Cox was again apprehended for horsestealing and tried at Leicester and that Sincox otherwise Simcox did abscond and omit to appeal or surrender himself for trial pursuant to any recognizance and that he hath been since tried at Worcester for horsestealing and convicted.

James Mason
November the 21 1784'

Hil 27 Geo III 1787

Affidavit to require answers from Edward Gosnell:

[7] Affdt of Thomas Mason farmer of Wednesbury Hall, sworn before R. Bayley at Wednesbury 2 Feb 1787 [*signed with a mark*]. 'King's Bench. The King agst James Mason upon an Attachment for a supposed contempt.' [*Verso*]: '52 Hil 87. England. King's Bench. Afft for Edwd Gosnell to answer the M[atte]rs: of Aff't. The King and James Mason J:M Mr Mingay 1 Ga To Move for Edwd Gosnell To Ansr the M[atte]rs.

It's but a single question to ansr he may shew cause Monday 10 Feb R to answer. Priddle fo.10.'

That in Michaelmas term 1783 the deponent entered into a recognizance in this court for £100 for the personal appearance of James Mason on first day Hilary term 1784. James Mason did not appear and the deponent forfeited his recognizance, which estreated to the court of exchequer and process was issued against the deponent. He paid the sheriff of Staffordshire £100 and believes it was paid into the treasury. Since James Mason's failure to appear was not the result of wilful neglect, the deponent entered into another recognizance. In Michaelmas 1786, James Mason was judged by the court not to be in contempt and the second recognizance was ordered discharged. The deponent authorized his attorney, William Priddle, to apply to the lords of the treasury for their order to return the £100. Priddle has since told the deponent that he was informed by the clerk of the pipe that Edward Gosnell, acting under the pretence that James Mason had employed him as his attorney to get the £100, had already obtained the constat.[16] The lords had received a letter requesting the money which they referred to William Chamberlain esq for consideration. Chamberlain said the money should be returned. Gosnell is an entire stranger to the deponent and he never authorized him to act for the deponent.

[8] Affdt of William Morris gentleman of Northhampton Street Clerkenwell (Middx) and James Mason, defendant and butcher of Rowley Regis, sworn before the court in court 19 May 1787. 'King's Bench. The King agst James Mason.' [*Verso*]: '61 East. 87 England. 113 King's Bench. Afft of Edward Gosnell Gent to ans M[att]res . The King v James Mason. Afft of Morris and anor. Mr Mingay. 21 May. Enlarged till the 3d [*struck out*: first] day of next term with liberty for [*struck out*: the Deft to file an] this additional afft to be filed. fo 14. Priddelle L S.'

[William Morris]: That 12 Feb 1787 at Westminster Hall he met Gosnell, who took him into one of the boxes in the court of exchequer where Gosnell wrote a letter to Thomas Mason at Wednesbury Hall near Bilston,[17] which he antedated 3 Feb. Gosnell said he would post the letter himself as he must swear to it; deponent believes he posted the letter before he made the said [*sic*] affidavit. Gosnell then filled up the affidavit which he had been preparing for his defence to the rule that had been made, to which he intended to show cause later that day. While Gosnell was writing the affidavit, he lay the letter on one side of

[16] See notes to '*Rules and process*', above.
[17] Written in error as 'Bilson'.

the table. One Mr Law approached and, waiting to see Gosnell on business, began reading the letter but the deponent turned it over and Law immediately withdrew from the box. Gosnell said 'I hope he did not see the letter.' The deponent replied that Law did not have time to see much of it. Gosnell then went to court and swore the affidavit, intending immediately to show cause. During the last two elections for Middlesex coroner, for which Gosnell was a candidate, he often heard Gosnell say that he was out of money and had £100 due to him from the treasury, apparently referring to Thomas Mason's money.

[James Mason]: That the original rule having been enlarged on 12 Feb to the present term and it being suspected that Gosnell might raise money on green wax's letter[18] to Rose in the meantime, it was thought advisable to summon Gosnell before a judge of King's Bench in order to impound the letter until the court had decided the rule. Priddle got William Geast an attorney to attend the summons for him and immediately after the attendance, Thomas Mason, Geast and Gosnell came to the deponent at Temple bar where Gosnell produced his affidavit of 12 Feb, which he said he had produced before Justice Grose on showing cause. The deponent asked how he could possibly lay claim to the £100. Gosnell replied that Thomas Mason employed him and had a bill for £18 and had applied for the £100 to satisfy the £18 owing, claims which he had made in the affidavit. The deponent told Gosnell that Thomas Mason neither knew nor hired him and that his affidavit was false, and that he should take care. Gosnell eventually confessed this to be true in the presence of Geast. Gosnell has since thought proper to sink the false affidavit and is attempting to frame another ground of defence to the rule by another affidavit.

Trin 27 Geo III 1787

[9] Affdt of Robert James gentleman of Whitefriar's (London), sworn before N. Grose at his chambers 5 May 1787. 'King's Bench. The King v James Mason.' [*Verso*]: '64 Trin 87 England. May 1787. Afft of Service of R on Edwd Gosnell. The King v James Mason. Mr James's Affidt of service of Rule. L.S. Priddle.'

That the court ordered on the last day of Hilary term [12 Feb 1787] that the first day of the current term be given to Edward Gosnell to answer Thomas Mason's affidavit. The deponent served Gosnell 5 March by leaving a copy of the rule on his seat in the exchequer office in Lincoln's Inn. Gosnell later acknowledged that he received it and would show cause.

---

[18] See note to '*Rules and process.*'

Answers of Edward Gosnell:

[10] Affdt of Edward Gosnell gentleman of the exchequer office Lincoln's Inn (Middx) and Thomas Gosnell, gentleman and clerk to Edward Gosnell, of Shakespears Walk in St Paul's parish Shadwell (Middx), sworn in court by the court 21 May 1787. ITKB 'Between The King agt James Mason on an attachment for a supposed contempt.' [*Verso*]: 'King & Mason' [*Struck out*]: 'To move that the Affidt of service of the enlarged Rule be filed that the Rule for the Attachmt be discharged for irregularity & all Proceeds stayed & that Robt James answer the matters in the Affidt & that he be ordered personally to attend the Court the 1st day of next Term.' 'Gosnell'

[Edward Gosnell]: That he was not served with notice of the enlarged rule and believes that Robert James did not leave such notice on deponent's desk or at his seat in the exchequer office as sworn, because all notices and papers left there always came to his hand. He has asked the clerks if James had been seen since last term, and one who scarcely ever leaves the office while it is open did not recollect seeing him. He denies telling Robert James that he received the notice, or having any conversation with him on the subject, except once when James delivered a message from William Priddle, that Priddle would give him half the money if he would deliver up the order; he avoided going near Priddle. Robert James is well known throughout the courts and has been tried for perjury, and the deponent believes that he is under the influence of Priddle. The affidavit of the service of the enlarged rule was not delivered to the counsel who moved for it till very lately owing to the deponent having informed some of Priddle's friends that he had neglected to serve him with the rule.

[Thomas Gosnell]: That Edward Gosnell's business is carried on in the exchequer office of pleas, and that this deponent sits as his clerk in a seat opposite to him. He never received notice of the enlarged rule, nor did he see Robert James in the exchequer office since the last term.

Further affidavit against Gosnell:

[11] Affdt of William Geast gentleman and attorney of this honourable court, of Rowley Regis, sworn before Thomas Southale at Birmingham (Warws) 7 June 1787. 'Kings Bench. The King v James Mason.' [*Verso*]: '7 June 1787. The King v James Mason. Mr Geast's Affdt. L. S. Priddle fo. 10.'

That an order for the £100 levied on Thomas Mason on a forfeited recognizance as a manucaptor of James Mason was obtained by Edward Gosnell in the name of Thomas Mason from the Lords of the

Treasury. The deponent believes that by impersonating Mason he obtained from the surveyor of the green wax his letter to Mr Rose to pay the £100 to him the supposed Thomas Mason. The impersonation was detected by Priddle, Thomas Mason's attorney, before the money was received, and Mason complained to the court last Hilary term and obtained a rule against Gosnell to answer matters on the last day of term. Gosnell, having been served with the rule, prepared and swore his affidavit to show cause. Gosnell declared to the deponent that he would have shown cause had the rule not been enlarged to next Easter immediately after he had sworn the affidavit. In Hilary vacation last, Priddle summoned Gosnell before a judge to show cause why he should not bring the letter into court, fearing he would otherwise encumber the letter. The deponent attended at Priddle's request before Mr Justice Grose, who ordered Gosnell to file the affidavit so that Priddle might take an office copy for his client Thomas Mason, but said he would make no order respecting the letter as the matter was before the court. Grose admonished Gosnell not to make any use of the letter, nor to receive the £100 from the Treasury on any pretence whatsoever. The deponent later went to the Cock at Temple Bar where Gosnell followed. Knowing that every material part of the affidavit was false, he asked Gosnell how he could swear a false affidavit and told him he would most surely be indicted for perjury, to which Gosnell replied he had removed his affidavit from the judge's chambers rather than file it as the judge directed, and proceeded to pull it out of his pocket. The deponent has heard that Gosnell made an affidavit that he had not been served with the enlarged rule. In the last Hilary vacation Gosnell acknowledged to the deponent that he was served with a copy of the enlarged rule by Robert James, that James was indebted to him in upwards of £100, and that he was determined to send James to gaol for the debt because he had so served him with the rule.

Further answers of Gosnell:

[12] Affdt of Edward Gosnell gentleman of the exchequer office Lincoln's Inn (Middx), sworn in court by the court 12 June 1787. ITKB 'The King agt James Mason on an attachment for a supposed contempt.' [*Verso*]: '13 Trin 87 England. K.B. King agt Mason. To move for Rule to shew cause why the Rule made last Term for Mr Gosnell to answer etc shd not be dischd for irregularity no affidt of the service of the enlarged Rule of Hil [this?] Term having been filed and why Mr Priddle the atty for Prosn shd not pay the costs of the applnt. Mr. Garrow. ½ Gn W Garrow. 12 June. R Nisi. Gosnell. fo 11.'

That he was with William Priddle the attorney for Thomas Mason at 8pm on the evening of Saturday 10 February, the last day but one of Hilary term, and the day that the motion was made requiring the deponent to answer matters in Mason's affidavit. Priddle said nothing to him about the motion, although he caused him to be served with a copy two hours later. The deponent believes Priddle designed to prevent him obtaining an office copy of Mason's affidavit in time to answer it. Finding the deponent prepared to answer, counsel for Mason successfully moved for the rule to be enlarged to the first day of last Easter Term. The deponent believes the enlarged rule was never drawn up because he was not served with a copy, nor has an affidavit of service been filed. He was advised by counsel not to move for discharge of the enlarged rule, but to wait to see whether Mason's counsel would proceed. He believes Priddle heard of his comments on Priddle's neglect in not serving the enlarged rule, and then prevailed on Robert James of Abberley to make an affidavit of having served it by leaving a copy on this deponent's desk in the office of pleas of the court of exchequer. If James had done so the deponent would have received it; he believes no such copy was left on his desk. He is more confirmed in that belief by the fact that Priddle has not filed nor made any use of James's affidavit. But Priddle by some means not only got the rule enlarged to the third day of the present term, but got affidavit [8] of William Morris and another received, and this deponent ordered to answer the matters contained in it and in affidavit [7], notwithstanding the fact that no affidavit of service of the first enlarged rule has ever been filed.

[13] Affdt of Edward Gosnell gentleman of the exchequer office Lincoln's Inn (Middx), sworn in court by the court 14 June 1787. 'England. The King agt James Mason.' [*Verso*]: '19 Trin 87 England. King v Mason. Be pleased to move for leave to file this affdt also another affdt of this deponent and another [*remainder of text struck out*: and that the rule be enlarged to Saturday and that the rule be enlarged to Saturday next]. W Garrow. ½ Gn. W Garrow. Gosnell.'

That in a recent conversation with William Geast at Birmingham, the deponent informed Geast that Robert James had made a false affidavit of service, swearing he served the deponent with the enlarged rule. Geast replied that there was no guarding against such people for they were an infamous lot, and expressed his abhorrence. The deponent was rather surprised, as he knew the intimate connection between Geast and Priddle, for whom Geast worked as an agent while Priddle was confined in the King's Bench; Geast also lately lived in Priddle's house in Scotland Yard. Geast said he had seen James Mason, who he said had arrived the night before at Dudley or Rowley from London, and who had a long affidavit which he wanted Geast to swear to. Geast said he had refused because he did not approve of the business. He then offered deponent £30 to settle, saying he had authority from Thomas Mason to do so. On this deponent refusing, he offered to go with him to Mason's house at Wednesbury Hall to settle, saying this deponent was owed a large sum, and the labourer was worthy of his hire. The deponent met Robert James this day and asked him how he could make such an affidavit swearing service which was never made, and asked him did he not remember the message he had delivered from Priddle to this deponent asking to settle. James said he recollected the message but that the deponent had acknowledged receipt of notice of the rule; the deponent positively denies having done so. He asked James to recollect the time of the conversation. James said it was the Friday or Saturday before he was taken at this deponent's suit and that he, Robert James, was detained in prison two days. Robert James executed a warrant of attorney for securing this deponent's debt on 9 March; James was arrested 7 March and the conversation therefore was supposed to have occurred on 2 or 3 March, when this deponent was confined to bed for a week with a violent inflammation of the bowels, as he was when he heard of James's arrest and of the execution of the warrant of attorney.

Further affidavits against Gosnell:

[14] Affdt of William Priddle attorney and prisoner[19] at Newgate (London), sworn before George Newland at Newgate (London) 18 June 1787. 'Kings Bench. The King agst James Mason on an attachment for a supposed contempt.' [*Verso*]: 'The King agst Mason. William Priddle's Afft L.S. Priddle fo 34.'

That the deponent, named in the affidavit of Gosnell mentioned in the rule of [12 June], was employed by Thomas Mason as his attorney to apply for the £100 from the treasury, having been found not to be in contempt. The deponent had often employed Gosnell as a clerk in court on the plea side of the court of exchequer; Gosnell often called at the deponent's home in Scotland Yard, and was generally shown into his private office, where he occasionally sat down to assist the deponent. He believes the first time Gosnell learned of the £100 transaction was from perusing the papers in the deponent's office.

---

[19] Priddle had been convicted in April of conspiracy to charge George Crossley with perjury, and sentenced to two years in Newgate: *Old Bailey Proceedings*, 18 April 1787, no. 448 (and www.oldbaileyonline.org, case t17870418-118). He was also struck off the roll of attorneys. See Hay, *Crime, War and Justice*.

The deponent sent to the clerk of the pipe for a constat of the recognizance for that purpose of claiming the money, when he was informed that Gosnell had already petitioned as Thomas Mason's solicitor and that the order had been made for payment. He immediately wrote to Thomas Mason about Gosnell's interference; Mason replied from Wednesbury 2 Feb 1787 that he did not even know Gosnell, did not authorize him to petition, and instructed the deponent to obtain the £100 for James Mason, from which he (Priddle) could deduct his fees.

The deponent immediately showed the letter to Gosnell and expostulated with him several times last Hilary term on the impropriety of his conduct and asked him to deliver up the letter he had obtained from the surveyor of the green wax for payment; Gosnell several times promised in the presence of James Mason to do so. The deponent, suspecting Gosnell had raised money on the letter or otherwise encumbered it, importuned him to answer, and offered to lay money down to redeem it if it was not encumbered too deep. He warned Gosnell that the court would be moved against him and advised him not to suffer it (not wishing to trouble the court).

On 10 Feb 1787 the deponent caused the court to be moved against Gosnell on affdt [7] and left John Stanley, the deponent's clerk, to serve him. The deponent then met Gosnell at the Sussex and Surrey coffee house in Fleet Street, where he met Gosnell; he tried to delay him until Stanley could serve him, but Gosnell left after three or four minutes. Gosnell was otherwise with the deponent that evening only when he arrived where the deponent was with a client and a clerk at his office; Gosnell hesitated then left, the deponent believes to avoid being served. Gosnell usually drank with the deponent during the preceding fortnight, but he could not be persuaded to sit down, nor drink a glass. The deponent therefore sent a person to follow him, to serve him once Stanley brought the rule. He did not mention the rule to Gosnell at this time, and had no other opportunity to talk to him that evening. If he had stayed, he would have told him, and served him.

Stanley returned and left to serve Gosnell. The deponent was very diligent to serve Gosnell as soon as possible after it had been granted, and did not delay with the design of taking him by surprise. Nor did the deponent use means to get the rule enlarged on finding that Gosnell was prepared to answer. Rather, it was his wish to get the matter settled as soon as possible to give Mason his £100 and the deponent his costs. The deponent believes that notwithstanding Gosnell's affdt [12] saying he was ready to show cause on last day Hilary term, he does not intend to produce the affidavit of 12 Feb he made for that purpose. After producing it before Mr Justice Grose he was admonished by Geast for going too far in the affidavit, and therefore struck out several lines and engrossed a fresh one, and said that if the deponent moved the court to have him file that affidavit, he would swear that his wife had burned it.

The deponent swears that because the rule of Hilary term was enlarged to Easter, and suspecting Gosnell of having encumbered the letter, soon after Hilary term he had him summoned before a judge to have the letter brought into court. The judge ordered Gosnell to file his 12 Feb affidavit; instead he took it away and obliterated it, in the manner described. The deponent attempted to serve the enlarged rule on Gosnell without success. He then prevailed on Robert James, a client of Gosnell's, to serve him, giving James a copy of the rule on 3 or 4 March. The deponent is satisfied by affdts [8], [9], and [11] that Gosnell was served. Gosnell denied service in his affidavits [10], [13] of Easter[20] and Trinity terms to keep Thomas Mason from receiving the money in the long vacation.

He does not believe that James told Gosnell that the deponent would split the £100 evenly with Gosnell if he would deliver it to him, nor did he ever propose it. Gosnell arrested James for his fees and disbursements merely because he had served Gosnell.

James's affidavit of service [9] was taken 5 May and sent immediately to Thomas Mason's counsel, not at the end of Easter term about 21 May as Gosnell alleges; the deponent made every effort on behalf of Mason to make the rule absolute. The deponent never heard that Gosnell said he had not been served; Geast and Mason before they left London said that after he was served with the enlarged rule Gosnell asked them to intercede on his behalf and make matters up. The deponent wrote to them to get affidavits about what they knew of the affair. They replied that Gosnell told them James served him with the rule and was arrested for it. Geast was never this deponent's agent but Geast did live with him at Scotland Yard, when the deponent let him an apartment for a month when he was in town.

[15] Affdt of James Mason defendant of Rowley Regis, sworn before W. H. Ashhurst at Serjeants' Inn 18 June 1787. 'King's Bench. The King agt James Mason on an attachment for a supposed contempt'. [*Verso*]: '70 Trin 87 England. Affts on Reference agt Edw Gosnell. The King & James Mason. Defts Affidts. L. S. Priddle fo: 15.'

That his brother Thomas Mason having paid £100 for a forfeited recognizance, he employed Priddle, his attorney in this and earlier matters, to apply to the lords of the treasury for the money, Priddle to deduct his fees and pay the balance to the deponent for the use of Thomas Mason. Thomas Mason asked the deponent to go to London to

[20] Now found with Trinity term affidavits.

retrieve the money. He made three expensive journeys to do so and discovered that Gosnell was attempting fraudulently to get the money. When he went to the treasury to stop the payment, a clerk said that the person who obtained the letter for the money claimed to be Thomas Mason; by the description the deponent believes it was Gosnell. In Hilary term 1787 before the original application against Gosnell, the deponent and Priddle went eight or ten times to obtain the money and letter from him. Priddle wanted to settle the matter out of court. The deponent believes Gosnell denied service of the rule by Robert James in order to settle the matter privately with Thomas Mason. The deponent was summoned by him 3 June; Thomas told him he had refused an offer from Gosnell at Wednesbury Hall the day before to give him a bond and judgement for £100 if he would discharge the rule. Mason refused because he did not know the value of Gosnell's security. Geast told the deponent that Gosnell then tried to get him to convince Mason to accept the offer but he refused, telling Gosnell his behaviour was heinous and that he would make an affidavit on behalf of Mason.

Gosnell's affidavit of 14 June 1787 [13] is false in every particular. Gosnell designedly smothered the fact of his trip of 120 miles to Wednesbury last vacation and his dealings with Mason and Geast because discovery would militate against getting his business over this term. At a meeting between the deponent and Gosnell, Gosnell dropped a letter which the deponent took up and preserved. The letter, in Gosnell's hand, read, 'The King against Thomas Mason on a Forfeited Recognizance. Received of George Rose esquire surveyor of the Green Wax the sum of £100 being the sum directed by the Lords of the Treasury to be repaid me on the above account by virtue of a letter from the Lords signed by Mr Steel and directed to me for that purpose.' This receipt Gosnell obtained from a clerk of the treasury to be given to George Rose on receipt of the money, and deponent believes Gosnell would have entered Thomas Mason's name if he had not been detected in time. Gosnell is now in custody for money he borrowed upon the credit of the letter.

Further answers of Gosnell:

[16] Affdt of Edward Gosnell gentleman of the exchequer office Lincoln's Inn (Middx), sworn in court by the court 21 June 1787. ITKB 'The King agt James Mason'. [*Verso*]: '63. Trin 87. England. Afft of Edward Gosnell agt Rule to ansr m[atter]s in Rex v James Mason. 27 June Referred to the Masr. Gosnell.'

[*Describes the recognizance and its estreat into exchequer.*] Process issued and the sum was paid to the sheriff of Staffordshire or perhaps to

Burgh, a clerk of the pipe. Thomas Mason may have entered into a further recognizance in Michaelmas term 1786 which was ordered discharged when James Mason was judged not to be in contempt. The deponent does not know whether Priddle was Thomas Mason's attorney from the beginning or not. James Mason informed the deponent that Priddle advised him to petition the lords of the treasury for a return of the money, but for certain reasons which James mentioned to the deponent, he rather chose to employ this deponent.

That James Mason told the deponent he had authority from his brother to employ whom he pleased, and asked the deponent to recover the £100; he said he could get an authority from his brother at any time to do so, and on this assurance the deponent proceeded. The deponent and James Mason went to his clerk in court in the crown office who informed him of the state of the proceedings, as represented by James Mason and set forth in Thomas Mason's affidavit. The deponent then prepared a petition to the lords of the treasury, preferred the same and got their order of reference to their solicitor as stated in the affidavit of Thomas Mason.

That James Mason went several times to the crown office and the pipe office for the constat and certificate to enable the deponent to go on with the business. Relying on the promises and assurances of the said James[21] Mason that he would obtain Thomas's authority to proceed, the deponent was prevailed upon by James Mason to prosecute several actions in the court of exchequer against some 30 persons. Some of these went to trial and costs were issued, amounting to over £100. He would not have been employed by James Mason as his attorney but on his assurances of procuring the said Thomas[22] Mason's authority ['and' *struck out*]on the credit of receiving the said £100 [*illegible word struck out*] [*another illegible word inserted then struck out*] pay himself the costs in case the actions miscarried this deponent knowing James Mason to be in mean circumstances with no place of residence and has been informed that he has been discharged from King's Bench prison at the suit of one of his creditors.

That diverse applications have been made to the deponent on behalf of Thomas Mason to settle this business. Thomas Mason employed William Geast to offer the deponent £30 to give up the treasury order. He refused. Geast said Thomas Mason had given up hope of receiving anything (having given it to his brother) and that Geast could and would settle it with Thomas Mason on the deponent's own terms. Geast said the deponent acted on the credit of receiving Thomas Mason's

[21] 'James' is written over 'Thomas'.
[22] 'Thomas' is written over 'James'.

authority, that a large sum was due the deponent, and that the labourer was worthy of his hire.

That the deponent received an offer from a friend of Priddle of £18 to give up the order. He refused it as well as an offer brought by Robert James to visit Priddle, to settle the business on dividing the money. He refused to go near Priddle.

That in answer to William Morris's affidavit [8], he did write a letter to Thomas Mason informing him that he had received an order from the treasury for receiving the £100, asking for his authority to do so, telling Mason that he had acted of the assurance of James. He does not recall the date on the letter but admits it was written 12 Feb, as stated in affdt [8].

That in answer to James Mason's affidavit, a summons was taken out before Mr Justice Grose to show cause why the order should not be delivered up. Geast having attended on behalf of Priddle, Grose refused to so order. The deponent does not recall telling James Mason that he had Thomas Mason's authority or had been employed by him as attorney or that he had a bill on Thomas for £18 or that he had applied to recover the said £100 as attorney of Thomas Mason to pay himself the bill of £18. He denies that the affidavit shown to Grose was to that effect; on the contrary, the deponent never pretended that he was employed by Thomas Mason or ever applied to the treasury for payment. He had kept the order in his possession until he could get Thomas Mason's authority, writing to him not in the least doubting but he would send his authority to the deponent. He has paid several sums incurred in obtaining the order and has a lien of his costs.

[17] Affdt of Harriet Gosnell wife of Edward Gosnell gentleman of Lincoln's Inn (Middx), sworn before T. Ll. Anwyl[23] at Shrewsbury (Salop) 7 July 1787. 'The King agt James Mason on an attachment for contempt.' ITKB [*Verso*]: '5 The K & Mason. Affdt of Harriet Gosnell. fo 5'.

That when the petition to the lords of the treasury was in prosecution, James Mason came frequently to Gosnell's house in George Street Black Friar's Road to speak to Gosnell about the petition and express his anxiety for speedy recovery of the money. He pledged Thomas Mason's authority to hire Gosnell and begged him to go on with the business. The deponent has often heard James Mason say that Priddle advised him to prefer a petition to the lords of the treasury and wanted James Mason to employ Priddle to do so. James Mason said if he employed

---

[23] Thomas Lloyd Anwyl was an attorney of Shrewsbury in 1775: Shropshire Archives, More Collection, 1037/21/67 28 Oct 1775.

Priddle, Priddle would have kept it, and he would not have had a far-thing of it.

[18] Affdt of Edward Gosnell gentleman of the exchequer office Lincoln's Inn (Middx), sworn before W. H. Ashhurst[24] at his house in Spring Gardens 13 July 1787.[25] ITKB 'The King agst James Mason'.

That in spring 1786 the deponent advised James Mason that the £100 could be recovered by petition to the lords of the treasury, but that the money belonged to his brother Thomas Mason. James replied that Thomas had given the money up for lost, would spend no more on the case, and had told him that the money was his if he wished to try to recover it, saying he would give him an authority to whomever he employed to recover it. During the deponent's conversation with James Mason, the latter told him that William Priddle was very desirous that Mason should employ him, and had several times solicited an author-ity from him to do so. Mason said he had put Priddle off with excuses, and that if he hired him, Priddle would keep the money and never let him have a shilling.

That the deponent, relying on James Mason's assurance that he would procure his brother's authority, went to the crown office with Mason to see how the matter stood and was told by the clerk in court who had been employed by Mason to defend the interrogatories that matters were in the state represented to this deponent by Mason. The deponent then procured a constat of the recognizance from the clerk of the pipe and a certificate from the clerk of the crown that Mason had been examined on interrogatories and acquitted. He afterwards pre-ferred the petition to the lords of the treasury and got their order of ref-erence to their solicitor, who in consequence of this report gave the deponent the letter to the secretary of green wax for payment of £100, which the deponent humbly hopes he has a right to retain, having done business for James Mason to a larger amount on Mason's assurance that his brother had given up claim to it and would give an authority. He would never have been employed by James Mason to anything near the amount otherwise. James Mason was in mean circumstances without a place of residence and wholly incapable of paying this deponent's bill, having been discharged out of custody under the Lord's Act. If the deponent is ordered to deliver up the treasury order he will wholly lose his costs.

[24] Puisne justice of King's Bench 1770–1799.
[25] In the left margin: 'Resworn the 16th July 1787 at the House of Thomas Burton in Houghton Street Clare Market the Depon't being detained there a Prisoner before me Thos Linley a Commissioner.'

The deponent denies that he ever saw any papers in Priddle's office relating to his business, as Priddle falsely swears. Priddle never stirred a step in the business until the deponent received the letter for repayment, because the deponent was asked by Mason not to mention a word of it to Priddle because Priddle would be much displeased with him for not employing him. Priddle was not employed until the business was all over, as can be seen from his affidavit, where he first swears that his knowledge of the business came from perusal of the papers in his (Priddle's) office; immediately after he swears that when he sent to the clerk of the pipe for a constat he was told the deponent had preferred a petition to the lords of the treasury. The deponent believes that the letter Priddle swears came from Thomas Mason was fabricated by Priddle, as Thomas Mason cannot write.[26] Priddle never showed the deponent the letter, nor does he remember any conversation with him on the subject of the £100 before the application to the court for this deponent to answer the matters in Thomas Mason's affidavit.

William Geast (who has thought proper to swear to the affidavit [11] which the deponent supposes is the one James Mason brought to him ready prepared, which Geast informed the deponent of, as in the deponent's former affidavit [13]) in last Hilary vacation applied to the deponent on Thomas Mason's behalf to settle the business. Geast said he had a letter of attorney executed by Thomas Mason, and proposed on behalf of Thomas Mason that the master of the exchequer office should tax the deponent's bill on James Mason and also the bill of James Mason on this deponent, and that after allowing to James Mason what the master should find due that he William Geast would pay the deponent the difference.

Geast and James Mason attended at the exchequer office when this deponent's bill was taxed by the master. A bill of James Mason's was produced which was so extravagant and exorbitant that the deponent could not possibly submit to the payment and terms. In further conversation at the door of the exchequer chamber the three of them agreed to refer the matter to some gentlemen of credit in the profession of the law. This deponent therefore wrote a receipt intending the same should be sent to[27] Thomas Mason to sign that as soon as the report was made on the reference the money might be received[28] which is the very receipt James Mason swears this deponent dropped, which he took up and preserved.[29] Geast afterward produced a letter of attorney from Thomas

[26] See affdt [7], where Thomas Mason signs with a mark.
[27] The preceding seven words replace an illegible passage struck out.
[28] A longer illegible passage of one line is struck out here.
[29] Another two and a half lines are struck out here.

Mason to demand of this deponent the letter to the surveyor of the green wax; the deponent told Geast he had acted a very deceitful part and expostulated with him on the impropriety of his conduct, at which Geast seemed ashamed. He told this deponent that he would proceed on the reference, or give this deponent £30; deponent replied he would rather the matter was referred. Geast appointed 6 March to call on the deponent to choose a referee, but the day following he received a letter from Geast suggesting a meeting and that deponent had better accept his proposal. That evening Geast came to the deponent's house in Black Friar's Road. In the presence of Henry Hugh Ferguson esq and others he acknowledged that he had full power from Thomas Mason to settle James Mason's bill of costs and that he would go with the deponent the following day to an attorney of credit for the purpose. But Geast went out of town without calling on the deponent, and he did not see him afterwards till he met him in the road near Rowley Regis when the conversation passed that is described in the deponent's former affidavit.

The deponent went to Worcester on other business, not for the purpose of settling the matter with Thomas Mason (as untruly sworn by James Mason). Returning through Birmingham, the deponent happened on the road near Rowley to meet Geast, who made a voluntary offer to go with this deponent to Wednesbury Hall to settle the business with Thomas Mason. Geast said that as Mason had given him a letter of attorney for the purpose, that he did not doubt but he could procure a settlement of the business on the deponent's own terms (as in the deponent's former affidavit). Geast arranged to meet the deponent at Birmingham the following day at 11am to go to see Mason. Geast did not set out until 7pm, on horseback, the deponent on foot until he came to the coach that was setting off for Wolverhampton, which went through Wednesbury near Thomas Mason's residence. Geast, seeing the horses were not yet put to the carriage, said he would go on shortly and that the coach would soon overtake him. It did not overtake him. Reaching Wednesbury, the deponent alighted and went to Mason's house but Geast was not there. On telling Mason that Geast was to meet them there to attempt a compromise, Mason said he had nothing to do with it, but that he would meet the deponent the following week in London. No proposals of accommodation were made by the deponent, nor anything said other than that Geast had promised a settlement at the meeting. The deponent would not have gone to Thomas Mason but for Geast's proposal.

By Geast's deception the deponent was detained two days on the road longer than he proposed to stay, and Thomas Mason could not have told James Mason that this deponent offered to give Thomas a bond and judgement for £100 if Thomas would sign a discharge to the rule. It is a story contrived by James Mason and Priddle to strengthen their case, and though they intended that Geast should corroborate the fact by joining in the same tale, yet they so far mistook the matter that the deponent has not seen Geast since being with Thomas Mason. He neither saw him nor had conversation with him at Dudley, as James Mason has falsely sworn; no such conversation of anything like it passed between Geast and the deponent.

The deponent never applied to the treasury or anywhere else for payment of the order, and never intended to apply without Thomas Mason's authority notwithstanding the opinion James Mason has formed of the deponent.

That James Mason has been many years in the habit of swearing under the direction of William Priddle for whose clients he has become bail in many actions in sums to large amounts by which and other practices he is become notorious in the courts of law at Westminster. Although Priddle swore that he never employed Geast as his agent in any cause, Geast swears he attended the judge for him, at Priddle's request; the deponent can prove as occasion requires that Geast was employed by Priddle on many occasions and took long journeys for him. The deponent recollects Geast telling him when he attended the judge on the summons, that Priddle had sent one of his clerks to be a spy on his conduct for he was only agent in the business.

That Geast is made to swear that he believes deponent personated Thomas Mason and in that character to obtain the said letter to the surveyor of green wax, as the supposed Thomas Mason, with a view to hurt this deponent's character, as deponent never made use of such or any unfair means in the business never pretending that he was employed by the said Thomas Mason as his attorney.[30]

Mich 28 Geo III 1787

Further affidavits against Gosnell:

[19] Affdt of Thomas Mason yeoman of Wednesbury Hall, sworn before William Geast the younger at Wednesbury 4 Oct 1787 [*signed with a mark*]. 'Kings Bench. The King Against James Mason'.

That as a result of sickness James Mason had been unable to appear to the deponent's recognizance, which was forfeit; the £100 was levied

---

[30] This last sentence (given here verbatim) appears compressed in a few lines at the bottom of the page.

on the deponent 10 Oct 1784. He was obliged to sell his goods and stock at Wednesbury, and greatly distressed and hurt in his credit. When James Mason was out of contempt the deponent heard that he could have the sum restored to him, and he hired Priddle to make the application. He never employed Gosnell or any other person, nor did desire James Mason or anyone else to employ Gosnell. Gosnell was an entire stranger to him until some time in March last, when Gosnell applied to him at Wednesbury, offering to deliver up the green wax letter if the deponent would forgive him the costs of the application, which the deponent refused to do and referred him to Priddle.

The deponent denies that James Mason ever asked or requested the deponent to give him the money, or that the deponent ever promised or consented to let James Mason have the money or any part of it. Nor was the deponent ever in circumstances or situation to give away any sum of money whatsoever; he was greatly distressed in raising the sum and the stock on his farm has been ever since short.

[20] Affdt of James Mason butcher of Rowley Regis, and David Finlay gentleman of Gray's Inn (Middx), sworn before W. H. Ashhurst at his house in Spring Gardens 9 Nov 1787. 'King's Bench. The King agt Mason'. [*Verso*]: '103 Mich 87 England. Kings Bench 9 Nov 1787. Afft on Reference to the Master in the King agt James Mason agt Edward Gosnell. Mason and Finlay's Affdt. L. S. Priddle.' [*Another verso*]: '103 Mich 1787 England Afft on Reference in Rex v James Mason agt Edwd Gosnell. L.S. Priddle'.

[James Mason]: Denies that he advised with Gosnell concerning the forfeited recognizance of Thomas Mason, or that Gosnell told him it might be recovered by petition. Denies that he ever told Gosnell that Thomas Mason had given up the £100 as lost and that he, James, could seek it if he wished. Nor did Thomas ever tell the deponent that he might employ whom he wished, or that he would give an authority to him to do so. The deponent never had any such conversation as is set forth in Gosnell's affidavit.

Gosnell never told him the method of recovery was by petition, nor did he tell Gosnell that Priddle had solicited the deponent for the business, or say that if Priddle had it he would keep the money and never let the deponent have a shilling. He most solemnly denies that he ever had an authority from Thomas Mason to employ Gosnell or any other person to recover the money; he never said anything to Gosnell that could induce him to think so. He positively denies that he ever went to the crown office with Gosnell or any other place to see how the matter stood. He never employed Gosnell as his attorney in any cause or business whatsoever.

That he employed William Geast of Rowley to prosecute an action against Parker[31] and another against Barnett. And the said Edward Gosnell acting for the said William Geast as his agent the said Edward Gosnell transacted the business of the said actions by the employment of the said William Geast as such agent.[32] The deponent is informed by Geast that Gosnell's bills for his fees as such agent amounted to £30 and not more. As for Gosnell's claim that he did business worth more than £100 for the deponent on assurances that Thomas Mason had given up claim to the recognizance, Gosnell had transacted the business of the causes before the deponent ever heard that he had applied for the money on the recognizance. At the time Gosnell applied for it the deponent had a house at Rowley and was in trade there, and the misfortune of his imprisonment was owing to Gosnell misconducting the action against Parker as agent for Geast, by which means the deponent was subjected to costs and taken in execution for the same. He most positively denies that he owes Gosnell any money whatever.

That the first intimation he had of Gosnell attempting to receive the said sum of £100 was upon this deponent's accompanying Priddle to the office of the clerk of the pipe in Gray's Inn in Hilary term last when Mr Burgh informed Priddle that a constat had already been given to Gosnell. Deponent denies that he ever mentioned anything about the petition to the lords of the treasury in the presence or hearing of Harriet Gosnell, or that he ever went to Gosnell's house or any other place, nor did he ever express his anxiety to recover the money to Gosnell or desire him to proceed with all possible expedition. Denies that he ever mentioned in the hearing or presence of Harriet Gosnell anything about Priddle's desire to be employed in the case, or that Priddle would keep the money and never give the deponent a farthing, or anything to that effect. He believes Thomas Mason never employed or planned to employ any other person than Priddle, who had been his attorney several years, to apply for the £100, nor gave any letter of attorney or other authority to Geast to do so.

That although Gosnell alleges in his letter to Thomas Mason which he collusively dated 3 Feb last that there was a bill of costs of about £18 due from Thomas Mason to Gosnell, Gosnell never had the pretence or colour of a demand on Thomas Mason of the amount of a single shilling for any matter, cause or thing whatsoever. All and every one of the slanderous insinuations against this deponent in Gosnell's affidavit are false and groundless.

---

[31] See case H.2.
[32] This sentence is reproduced here verbatim.

[David Finlay]: That upon it being discovered that Gosnell had applied to the treasury for the £100, he and Priddle placed a wager. In order to determine the wager, he and Isaac Gillatt went to Gosnell's house where Gosnell said repeatedly that he had Thomas Mason's authority for what he had done in the business. Never once did he attempt to defend himself on the grounds that he was employed by James Mason.

Sources: KB 1/23/2 Mich 23 Geo III no. 2, #10; KB 1/23/6 Trin 24 Geo III no.1 # 35, 40. KB 1/25 Hil 27 Geo III # 52; KB 1/25/2 Ea 27 Geo III # 61; KB 1/25 Trin 27 Geo III no.1, # 63, 64, 70, 71 and no.2, # 13, 19; KB 1/25 Mich 28 Geo III no.1 # 2, and no.2, # 103. KB 16/19/3 23 Geo III 1782/3. KB 21/43 Mich 1783, Trin 1784, Ea 1785; KB 21/44 Mich 1785, Hil 1786.[33] KB 32/20/1.

H.2 Attachment for contempt for unpaid costs and damages in a civil suit (2 Jan 1789)[34]

Defendant: James Mason butcher of Rowley Regis.

Writ and return:
[*None found.*]

---

[33]   KB 21/43 and part of KB 21/44 are not paginated.
[34]   Other contempts on civil suits are not included in this volume, but this case arises out of several criminal cases included here. James Mason, following his acquittal for an earlier contempt in 1785 (see case H.1), sued the then sheriff of Staffordshire, Thomas Parker, on a writ of trespass on the case for a false return; he lost, and Parker recovered from Mason in the court of exchequer £42 4s 1d : see affidavit [3] below by Benjamin Price, Parker's London solicitor, and affidavit [3] of case A.21. In the latter case, Price took the first step toward obtaining a criminal information against the gaoler of Stafford, Littleton Scott, for altering another writ of habeas corpus sent to remove Mason from Stafford gaol into King's Bench, apparently to prevent Mason's removal at that time. The grounds Scott gave for not returning Mason into King's Bench were that he was also held under another capias to satisfy a different debt, one to a John Stanley. John Stanley was the name of a clerk of Edward Gosnell, who claimed to be acting for Thomas Mason, the brother of James; William Priddle also claimed to be acting for Thomas Mason (see case H.1 affidavit [10]). By April 1787 Priddle was himself in prison (see case H.1 affidavit [14]), which accounts for Lewis Shirley Priddle, presumably a relation, acting for James Mason in this contempt case.

Rules and process:
Hil [27 Jan 1789]: ordered that the marshal of the Marshalsea[35] or his deputy bring into court the body of defdt James Mason on [29 Jan] to undergo etc (side bar). ST [29 Jan 1789]: defdt being brought into court in custody is sworn to make true answers to all such interrogatories as shall be exhibited against him in this court touching a contempt supposed to be by him committed against the court; remanded to the marshal to be kept in safe custody until discharged by due course of law (by the court). ST [11 Feb 1789]: ordered that the marshal bring the defdt before the examiner of this court to be by him examined on certain interrogatories exhibited against him in this court touching a contempt supposed to be by him committed against this court (side bar). Ea [18 May 1789]: ordered that the interrogatories exhibited to the defdt and his answers be referred to James Templer [master of the crown office] to examine and afterwards to report his opinion to the court (Leycester).[36] Trin [1 July 1789]: on hearing the report of James Templer [master of the crown office] and on hearing counsel on both sides, adjudged by the court that the defdt is not in contempt, thereupon ordered that defdt be discharged of the attachment against him in this cause without costs; further ordered that he be detained in the custody of the marshal of the Marshalsea in execution for the sum of £42 (Leycester for prosr, Baldwin for defdt). Mich [20 Nov 1789]: on reading affdt [1], ordered that the prosr be given to [21 Nov] to show cause why defdt should not be discharged out of custody of the marshal as to the execution at suit of the prosr (Baldwin). ST [27 Nov 1789]: on hearing counsel both sides order that the rule made this term that the prosr should show cause why defdt should not be discharged, be now discharged. (Baldwin for defdt; Leycester for prosr).

Affidavits for defence:

Mich 30 Geo III 1789

[1] Affdt of Lewis Shirley Priddle, defendant's late attorney, of Kerry (Montgomery), sworn before W. H. Ashhurst[37] at his chambers at

---

[35] Prisoners brought to King's Bench on habeas corpus could be remanded to the Marshalsea prison, then brought into court, and remanded again, as necessary. See introduction to section G. No record of an attachment in Staffordshire was found.

[36] The interrogatories, which should have been filed (as in case H.1) have not been found for this case, nor has the writ and return.

[37] Puisne justice of King's Bench 1770–1799.

Serjeants' Inn 16 Nov 1789. 'Kings Bench. The King agst James Mason on the prosecution of Thomas Parker on an attachment of contempt'.

That the prosecutor, not having filed interrogatories for the examination of the defendant in the usual time, applied to the court 3 Feb 1789 and was given 10 days further. The 10 days elapsed and none were filed. The deponent procured the certificate of Robert Belt the examiner, certifying to the lord chief justice and other judges of the court that no interrogatories had been filed. On that basis he obtained a summons to show cause, served on Benjamin Price, attorney for the prosecutor, for the discharge of the defendant out of custody on the attachment. The deponent attended the return of the summons but Lord Kenyon being absent, he and Price argued the issue in the presence of Mr Platt. Price agreed to waive the execution upon the judgment on condition that the deponent allowed Price to be at liberty to file interrogatories. The deponent agreed. Price filed interrogatories and the defendant was examined and reported out of contempt. Contrary to his agreement, on the last day of term, on the defendant moving for the master's report, Price moved that the defendant be detained on the execution. Had he not believed Price bound by the agreement, the deponent should not have agreed to the interrogatories being filed, but should have insisted on the defendant being discharged because interrogatories had not been filed in time.

[2] Affdt of Stephen Hunt yeoman of White Cross Street, Moorfields (London), sworn before Fr[ancis] Buller[38] at his chambers at Serjeants' Inn 26 Nov 1789. ITKB 'The King on the Prosecution of Thomas Parker against James Mason'. [*Verso*]: '74 Mich. 89 England. In the Kings Bench Afft to make R[ule] abs[olute] for dischg James Mason ex Cus[tody] Mars[all] 28 Nov. [*struck out*: Abs. N.C.] Dischd. Priddle.'

That the deponent on 21 Nov 1789 served Benjamin Price with a copy of the [*annexed*] rule.

[*Annexed*]: Rule of 20 Nov 1789.

Affidavit for prosecution:

Mich 30 Geo III 1789

[3] Affdt of Benjamin Price, gentlemen and agent for the prosecutor, of Chancery Lane (Midd), sworn before N[ash] Grose[39] in court at

---

[38]   A puisne justice of King's Bench 1778–94, and of Common Pleas 1794–1800.
[39]   Puisne justice of King's Bench 1787–1813.

Serjeant's Inn Hall 28 Nov 1789. ITKB 'The King agt James Mason on the Prosecution of Thomas Parker Esquire'. [*Verso*]: '75 Mich 89 England. King's Bench. Affts to sh[ow] C[ause] agt dischg James Mason ex cus[tody] mar[shall] The King agt Jas Mason on the Prosecution of Thos Parker Esquire: Affidavit 28 Nov. R[ule] dischd Price Chancery Lane.'

That the defendant brought an action in the court of exchequer against Parker, the prosecutor, as sheriff of Staffordshire, for a false return, and at trial a verdict was found for Parker on the merits. Parker's costs being taxed at £42 4s 1d, a ca. sa.[40] issued out of the court of exchequer to the sheriff of Staffordshire against James Mason. Mason was committed to Stafford gaol, but got himself removed into the custody of the marshal of King's Bench in another action but charged with the execution in Parker's suit. James Mason had not been in the marshal's custody long before he appeared publicly in the country, to Parker's great surprise. It was discovered that he obtained his discharge under the *Insolvent Act* through fraud, perjury, and imposition on the court.

Parker and his attorney in the country have denied by affidavit notice of the petition and rule for bringing up James Mason. Application was made to the court against Mason and others for his fraudulent liberation and on 25 April 1788, the court ruled that Parker could sue out a fresh execution for his costs and that writs of attachment should issue against James Mason and his attorney Geast. Several writs were issued against both. In Hilary Term last the deponent was directed to exhibit interrogatories for the examination of Mason concerning his contempt. Not being able to get the interrogatories drawn and settled by his counsel and approved by his clients who live in Staffordshire by the last day allowed by the rule, he was summoned by Priddle to show cause why the defendant should not be discharged from the attachment. The deponent attended the summons at the chambers of the chief justice with the draft of the interrogatories completely prepared and in hand. Without entering into the question of whether James Mason was dischargeable, the deponent said he would file the interrogatories that afternoon, and give Priddle a copy of them gratis, and said that if the defendant was reported out of contempt he would recommend to his clients not to recharge him with the original debt. Priddle seemed satisfied; no order was made, and he gave Priddle a copy of the interrogatories. The deponent never agreed to waive the execution of the original judgment because he had no authority to do so. He believes he did say

[40] A writ of capias ad satisfaciendum: a writ for the arrest of the defendant in a civil action when judgment has been recovered for a sum of money, and has not been satisfied.

that if the defendant got rid of the matter of the attachment the deponent would not without special directions issue a fresh ca. sa.

The deponent acted as he did because of the great trouble he had had with James Mason and his associates and the heavy costs that had attended and would attend the motions and proceedings had to be had against them, and also because of Mason's poverty. The deponent did not and does not believe James Mason could be set at liberty without the interrogatories being answered. The deponent did his best with his clients to get a discharge for Mason but they refused. He did not charge the defendant with a fresh execution or instruct counsel to make a fresh motion for the detention of Mason for the original debt. The deponent instructed counsel to apply to have him detained until he paid the prosecutor's very heavy costs incurred by the attachment. The court ruled that James Mason should be discharged of the attachment without costs and that he should be detained in the custody of the marshal in execution of the £42 4s 1d recovered against him by judgment of the court of exchequer by Parker.

In July 1789 James Mason took out another summons before the chief justice to show cause why the part of the last rule relating to his detention on Parker's suit should not be expunged. The chief justice discharged the summons and dismissed the application.

Sources: KB 1/26 Mich 30 Geo III no.2 bdls 74, 75; KB 21/45 pp.12, 15, 44, 80, 134, 175, 194.

Glossary of Legal Terms

Page or case references are to explanations or discussions found in the notes or text. The wording used for rules and process in each case in the text is a short form current at the time or adopted for this book; where the full form used by the clerks is given in Gude, Hands, or Chitty, the reference is given below. For fuller definitions see Earl Jowitt, *The Dictionary of English Law* (London, 1959). See also the Table of Statutes and Table of Cases.

absolute, rule
  See rule nisi

affidavit
  A sworn statement made by a witness before a commissioner of the court, the court itself, or a judge in chambers. They were made ex parte (that is, not in the presence of the opposing party, and therefore not subject to cross-examination). The heading was called the caption, and the statement at the end of its being sworn before a commissioner was termed the jurat. See the General Introduction, 'The uses of affidavits'.

allocatur
  See exigent

appearance
  An entry of an appearance was made on behalf of litigant by his solicitor or clerk in court; an appearance in person was not necessary, except on conviction, to receive judgement, and a motion could be made to dispense with that appearance also. See Gude, i, 107, 147; ii, 657.

arbitration
  See reference to master of the crown office

arrest of judgment
  Any time between conviction and sentence the defendant could move the court in arrest of judgment, but solely for objections 'on the face of the record', that is, technical errors in wording. The judges themselves could arrest judgment if they thought on a review of the whole case that the defendant was not guilty. See Gude, ii, 657.

assizes

The circuit courts conducted by the twelve judges of Westminster Hall, who went throughout the country on six defined circuits twice a year, visiting most counties, including Staffordshire, twice a year for Lent and summer assizes. Lent assizes took place in the vacation between the central courts' Hilary and Easter terms, summer assizes between Trinity and Michaelmas. In each county the judges tried criminal cases on indictments found by the grand jury in the crown court, and civil cases in the nisi prius court. All criminal cases begun or brought into King's Bench by information or certiorari, if they went to trial, were heard in the nisi prius court, not the crown court.

attachment

The step by which process was begun on an information qui tam; also the first stage in proceedings for contempt. It directed the sheriff to arrest the defendant.

bill (of indictment)

A parchment document, in formal language, brought by a prosecutor with his or her witnesses to the grand jury (*qv*) at assizes or quarter sessions, in a hearing behind closed doors. If the prosecution evidence convinced the grand jury there was a case to answer, they endorsed the parchment 'A true bill', transforming the bill into an indictment, the formal charge against the accused.

capias

The writ for an arrest. The capias ad satisfaciendum was for the arrest of a judgment debtor (Gude, ii, 157); the capias utlagatum was used in the process leading to outlawry (Gude, ii, 162). A capias ad respondendum issued against a person indicted for a misdemeanour, to be arraigned.

caption

See affidavit, schedule

certiorari, writ of

The common law writ that removed proceedings from a lower court into King's Bench. *See* Sections E, F, and Gude, ii, 186-8, 216.

cessat proces (cesset processus)

A stay of proceedings on the record. *See* noli prosequi.

commissioner
A lawyer qualified to take affidavits on oath for use in litigation in the central courts.

committal proceedings
When a charge was brought before a magistrate (justice of the peace, or borough magistrate), he either dealt with it as a summary proceeding, and summary conviction (*qv*), or, if it could only be prosecuted on indictment, he heard the parties, and dismissed the charge, or bailed the accused until the sessions or assizes at which the prosecution intended to proceed, or committed the accused to prison until trial.

commitment
The warrant by which a magistrate committed an accused or convicted person to custody.

comparentia
An appearance by the defendant to a conviction returned by certiorari into the crown office.

concilium, consilium
The formal argument conducted by counsel when a demurrer was filed to the charge; there had to be an order for a concilium. *See* the introduction to Section E.

contempt
The courts had an inherent power to punish as contempt any abuse of their process, or disobedience by officials to their orders. *See* the introduction to Section H, and Gude, i, 252-4; ii, 151ff.

conviction
See summary conviction

criminal information
See information

day in court
For many purposes a law term was considered to be one day in court.

demurrer
One of the stages in pleading: a defendant might demur to an indictment removed on certiorari on the grounds that the facts did not

support the prosecutor's case. The opposing party might then reply by joinder. *See* case F.1n5 and the introduction to Section F.

deposition
Informally, affidavits (*qv*) were sometimes termed depositions. *See* the General Introduction.

distringas, alias, pluries
Writs to enforce appearance to an information, indictment or inquisition.

enlarged rule nisi
Allowed the party further time to show why a rule absolute should not be made. *See* rule nisi.

estreat
When a recognizance was forfeited for failure to carry out its condition, it was estreated into the exchequer.

exigent
In outlawry, the writ to the sheriff to call the defendant to five successive county courts until taken or outlawed. An allocatur exigent commanded the sheriff to proceed if he had called the defendant at least twice, but there were fewer than five county courts before the return date of the exigent. *See* introduction to Section F, and case F.10 and notes.

ex officio information
See information ex officio

felony
See misdemeanour

fiat
Order of a judge in chambers, in the vacation between terms (for a writ of certiorari or habeas corpus). See Gude, ii, 216, and introductions to sections E, F, G.

four-day rule
See plead, rules to

grand jury
A jury, of at least 12 and usually of 23, which sat at quarter sessions and assizes to hear the prosecution evidence only, behind closed

doors. In trials on indictment, the formal charge set out on the 'bill of indictment' had to be found a 'true bill' by a majority, and at least twelve, of the grand jurors in order to go forward to trial. At assizes grand jurors were gentlemen; at quarter sessions often farmers or tradesmen. *See also* jury, special jury, bill (of indictment)

habeas corpus, writ of
See the introduction to Section G

imparl, imparlance, leave to imparl, asks leave to imparl, prays a day to answer
The right of a defendant not in custody to defer pleading: *see* the introduction to Section A, at note 22. Abolished for most cases in 1819.

in forma pauperis
See pauper

indictment
See bill (of indictment). Felonies and treasons had to be tried on indictment; misdemeanours could be prosecuted by indictment or by criminal information (*qv*). All these cases were tried by juries.

information
See the introductions to Sections A,B,C, and the General Introduction, note 72.

information ex officio
An information brought by the attorney general; *see* the introduction to Section C.

information in the nature of a quo warranto
An information to try the right of an incumbent to hold office; *see* the General Introduction.

information qui tam
An information brought by a common informer, who shared the penalty, under certain statutes. *See* the introduction to Section D.

interrogatories
Formal questions put to a defendant in contempt proceedings; failure to answer resulted in imprisonment. *See* the introduction to Section H.

joinder
> *See* demurrer

judgment
> The formal statement of the outcome of a case, after trial, and after any motions in arrest of judgment or motions for a new trial. *See also* postea

jurat
> *See* affidavit

jury
> The 'common' or 'petty' jury which heard trials and found verdicts in trials on indictment at quarter sessions and assizes also sat in King's Bench, but usually only for ordinary cases arising in Middlesex; trials resulting from certioraris or informations almost invariably involved special juries (*qv*). *See also* grand jury

King's attorney and coroner.
> *See* master of the crown office

mandamus
> One of the prerogative writs (*qv*) issuing from King's Bench; it compelled the performance of a duty. *See* the General Introduction and case B.4.

master of the crown office
> Formally called the 'King's coroner and attorney', the official who directed the bureaucracy of King's Bench; he also heard arbitrations agreed to by the parties, among other duties (*see* reference). *See also* the General Introduction.

misdemeanour
> An indictable offence less than felony, it could also be prosecuted by information (*qv*) as well as indictment (*qv*). Whether an offence was a felony, misdemeanour, or treason was defined by statute and the common law; there were differences in the prosecution and defence of each. *See* the General Introduction.

motion
> Most stages of a proceeding in King's Bench required that the prosecutor or defendant's counsel obtain rules from the court by making a motion. *See* 'Rules and process' for each case, where the name of the lawyer is given in parentheses.

nisi
    See nisi prius, rule nisi

noli prosequi (nolle prosequi)
    A stay of proceedings entered by the attorney general (often at the
    request of a private litigant) at any time before judgment; it did not
    preclude later prosecution.

outlawry
    See the introduction to section F.

pauper
    Under statutes of 1495 and 1523 a litigant swearing he was worth no
    more than £5 and his clothes could bring an action without paying
    court fees, and have assigned to him an attorney and barrister who
    acted without payment; termed *in forma pauperis*. *See* the introduction
    to Section C.

peremptory rule
    A rule requiring an immediate answer. *See* plead, rules to

plead, rules to
    A party was made to answer the accusation by the sequence of a first,
    second, and peremptory rule to plead. The first two were side bar
    rules, the last was not. Also called four-day rules. See the General
    Introduction, and Gude i, 144—147; ii, 649 no.19.

postea
    The formal record of the outcome of trial. The solicitor for the suc-
    cessful prosecutor applied to the clerk of assize (for the Oxford
    circuit, in the case of Staffordshire) for this document, which was
    used to get a rule nisi for judgment. See the General Introduction, and
    Gude, i, 102; see also Gude, i, 152, 305; ii, 657.

prays a day to answer
    See imparl

prerogative writ
    Processes issued upon extraordinary occasions (i.e., in distinction to
    the ordinary writs by which juries and litigants were summoned,
    arrested, etc) on proper cause shown, at the discretion of the court.
    There were six of these: certiorari (*qv*), habeas corpus (*qv*), mandamus
    (*qv*), quo warranto (*qv*) , procedendo (*qv*) and prohibition (a writ

issuing out of any the courts of Westminster Hall, which restrained an inferior court within the limits of its jurisdiction).

procedendo
A prerogative writ commanding judges in an inferior court to proceed to judgment; it also was used where proceedings had been removed from an inferior court by habeas corpus, certiorari or a similar writ, on what to the superior court appeared insufficient grounds. In the latter case, it remanded the case to the inferior court, from which it could not again be removed. *See* the introduction to Section F.

process
The proceedings in any criminal or civil case, from beginning to end; narrowly, the summons by which the defendant is called into court.

prohibition
See prerogative writ

quarter sessions
The four meetings each year at which county justices of the peace tried less serious criminal offences at Stafford, and conducted much of the business of local government. The four general sessions of the peace, as they were formally termed, were Epiphany, Easter, Translation and Michaelmas.

quash
Render void: convictions and indictments removed by certiorari into King's Bench from a lower court might be quashed, or affirmed. Hands, 30, 41.

quo warranto
See information in the nature of a quo warranto

recognizance
A bond entered into as a requirement for the carrying out of a procedural obligation, expressed as the condition of the bond; recognizances to appear, to give evidence, and to prosecute were among the most common. If the time to carry out the obligation was extended, the recognizance was respited; once the obligation had been carried out or was no longer required, it was discharged. See also estreat, sureties

reference to master of the crown office
A proceeding by which the parties agreed to have the master decide the case, and to drop further proceedings in court. Often used to reach a settlement.

replevin
Restitution of goods wrongfully distrained, a remedy given by a sheriff on receipt of a bond with two sureties to twice the value of the goods within five days, on which the goods were to be immediately returned, until the outcome of the suit in replevin.

respite
See recognizance

retraxit
Withdrawal of a plea.

rule absolute
See rule nisi

rule nisi
Many rules of the court required that the opposed party first be allowed opportunity to show cause against the motion for the rule, who was therefore first served with a rule nisi; if no satisfactory answer was made, the rule nisi was followed by a rule absolute. Also called a rule to show cause. *See also* enlarged rule nisi; plead, rules to

rules of court, general
Procedural requirements promulgated by the judges from time to time. *See* the General Introduction, and Gude, i, 367-93.

rules to plead
See plead, rules to

schedule
Statement of the proceedings in the lower court returned with a writ of certiorari and the indictment; the formal statement extracted from it, entered on the rolls of the court, was termed the caption. *See* case F.1, n41.

side bar rule
Many less important rules in court could be obtained without a motion, by simply requesting them from the clerks at the 'side bar',

which was originally a bar at the side of the court: *see* the General Introduction, 'An outline of criminal procedure'. They included rules to estreat recognizances, to enter a retraxit, to tax costs, to change a name in an information, and first and second rules to plead. *See also* Hands, 39-40.

special jury
A trial jury of higher social class than the 'common' or 'petty' jury. A special jury could be requested and paid for by either party in misdemeanours removed into King's Bench. *See* the General Introduction, 'An outline of criminal procedure'.

stay
See cesset processus, noli prosequi

summary conviction
A conviction before an inferior magistrate (justice of the peace or borough magistrate), without a jury; in the eighteenth century many poaching, excise, and other minor offences could be so prosecuted, by statute, but almost no thefts, which almost always had to be tried on indictment (*qv*).

summons
The writ calling a defendant to answer an information or an indictment for misdemeanour removed on certiorari was a venire facias ad respondendum, of which the English form began 'cause to come'; summons is the word used in this volume. *See also* attachment

supersedeas
A writ which stayed or put an end to a proceeding, such as certiorari: if the writ had been wrongly granted, and returned, the court granted a supersedeas. *See also* the introduction to section F, note 58.

sureties
The persons who served as guarantors (two, three, or four, depending on the process) for the obligation of the person who entered into a recognizance; usually their obligations were each half that amount.

taxation of costs
A hearing before the master of the crown office to approve costs claimed by parties and their lawyers. See the introduction to Section A, note 48.

terms
The four terms of the royal courts were Hilary, Easter, Trinity and Michaelmas: see Editorial Notes. *See also* vacation

teste
The date on a writ and other documents; hence 'tested' means dated.

traverse
The not guilty plea of a defendant, not in custody, to an indictment for misdemeanour; its effect was to postpone the trial until the next session or term of the court. Abolished in 1851.

treason
By the 1696 Treason Act, the accused had many more protections than in the case of felony. Treason, felony, and misdemeanour (*qv*) process differed significantly.

true bill
See bill (of indictment)

vacation
The intervals between the law terms, when the court did not sit.

venire facias ad respondendum
See summons

venire facias juratores
The writ commanding a sheriff to summon a common jury; it was abolished in 1852.

warrant
'An authority; a precept under hand and seal to some officer to arrest an offender, to be dealt with according to due course of law; also a writ conferring some some right or authority, a citation or summons.' (Jowitt). *See* commitment

writ
A document under the seal of the crown, a court, or officer of the crown. It commanded the person addressed to do or forbear from doing something. Original writs began every action at common law until 1832; judicial writs issue out of a court under its own seal. *See also* prerogative writ

Table of Statutes

Table of Reported Cases

Index of Cases

Index of Persons

Names in square brackets and dates of appointments have been supplied from J. C. Sainty, *Treasury Officials 1660–1870* (London, 1972); Sainty, *A List of English Law Officers, King's Counsel and Holders of Patents of Precedence* (London, 1987); Sainty, *The Judges of England 1272–1990* (London, 1992); David Lemmings, *Professors of the Law: Barristers and English Legal Culture in the Eighteenth Century* (Oxford, 2000); the *Law List*; *Oxford Dictionary of National Biography*; and other sources.

Abbreviations: AG attorney general; BEx baron of Exchequer; CBEx chief baron Exchequer; CJCP chief justice Common Pleas; CJKB chief justice King's Bench; co official in the crown office; cr created; DD doctor of divinity; JCP justice of Common Pleas; JKB justice of King's Bench; KC king's counsel; KPS king's prime serjeant; KS king's serjeant; ktd knighted; PP patent of precedence; SG solicitor general.

Index of Places

Newborough, in Hanbury, 129
Newcastle under Lyme, 267–274,
    290n21, 301–302, 317,
    320–321, 342, 357
Newport (Salop), 139, 144
New Zealand, 277n2
Northwood, 180–181
Norton (Derbs), 364–367, 369
Norton (Salop), 133
Norton in the Moors, 321
Nottingham (Notts), 419

Offley Hay, in Eccleshall, 428
Old Fallings, 245, 248
Oldswinford (Worcs), 311, 316–317
Oncott, in Handsworth, 445
Over Arley *see* Arley, Upper
Oxley, in Bushbury, 380
Oxolt *see* Oncott

Packington, in Weeford, 330n8
Parwich (Derbs), 431
Pattingham, 385
Penn, 257, 259–260
    The Lloyd, 257
Perry Barr, in Handsworth, 4, 68,
    186, 190, 252, 444–448
    Boar's Head Inn, 249, 254–257
    Perry Bridge, 444
    Perry Hall, 186, 193, 244, 248, 251
    Perry Warren, 187
Petersham (Surrey), 482
Prestwood, 396–397, 399–400,
    418–419
Public houses *see* Alehouses

Ramshorn, in Ellastone, 180
Red Hall (land in Wootton), 179
Repton (Derbs), 171
Reynolds Hall, 68, 218
Ridware. *See* Hill R., Mavesyn R.
Rising Brook *see under* Castle
    Church
River Trent, 265
Rodsley (Derbs), 381–382, 384
Romsey and Romsey Extra (Hants),
    198–201
Rowley Regis, 6, 314–315, 492–493,
    496, 507, 509, 514, 520, 522,
    523, 524
Rugeley, 71–74, 84, 113, 345, 437

Rushall, 217
Ruthin (Denbighs), 132

Salisbury (Wilts), 199
    Church of St Martins, 199
Scotland, 83, 115, 176
Seckington (Warws), 149, 151, 165,
    170–171
Sedgley, 57, 59, 69, 310–311, 460,
    501–502, 505
Seighford, 105. *See also under*
    Bridgford.
Sheen, 364, 366–367
Sheepy (Leics), 185
Shelfield, in Walsall, 215, 219
Shenstone, 68, 286. *See also under*
    Stonnall.
    Shenstone Park, 359n51
Shirrall (Sherrall, Sherholt) Lodge
    see Needwood
Shifnal (Salop), 285
Shrewley, in Hatton (Warws), 379,
    396
Shrewsbury (Salop), 517
Shropshire, ixn8, 49–50, 89, 91,
    132–133, 138, 140–141, 144,
    177n127, 221–222, 285, 321,
    409, 424, 458–460, 495, 517.
    *Also indexed under place
    names.*
Shugborough Hall, 119, 122
Smestal Stream, 342
Smisby (Derbs), 171n125
    Daniel Hay Farm, 171n125
Stafford, 3, 17, 19, 38, 83, 92, 98,
    100–104, 106, 108, 110, 114,
    116–117, 120–121, 123–124,
    130–133, 139–140, 143,
    176–177, 180, 182–183, 187,
    198–199, 206–208, 212–213,
    217, 219, 226, 231, 243, 247,
    251, 257, 259, 268, 271, 280,
    282n11, 283–284, 293n31, 294,
    298, 333, 341, 358n50, 359n51,
    376, 378, 381–383, 385, 387,
    392, 394–395, 400–402, 407,
    408–409, 411–413, 415, 418,
    420–421, 425, 427–430,
    432n109, 436, 440–441, 445,
    459, 463–467, 469–471,
    475–478, 481n47, 491, 493,